D1542008

F
853
M4

8322

AUTHOR

Meinig, Donald William

TITLE

The Great Columbia Plain

F
853
M4

8322

in

The GREAT COLUMBIA PLAIN

A HISTORICAL GEOGRAPHY, 1805-1910

By D. W. Meinig

SEATTLE AND LONDON

University of Washington Press

08322

F
853
97 M4
M477g

Copyright © 1968 by the University of Washington Press
Library of Congress Catalog Card Number 68-11044
Printed in the United States of America

The Emil and Kathleen Sick Lecture-Book Series in Western History and Biography

UNDER the provisions of a Fund established by the children of Mr. and Mrs. Emil Sick, whose deep interest in the history and culture of the American West was inspired by their own experience in the region, distinguished scholars are brought to the University of Washington to deliver public lectures based on original research in the fields of Western history and biography. The terms of the gift also provide for the publication by the University of Washington Press of the books resulting from the research upon which the lectures are based. This book is the first volume in the series.

For my Mother and Father who made
a fine home on a high Palouse hill

"... from the top of a high part of the mountains ... I had a view of an emence Plain and *leavel* country to the SW. & West."

William Clark, September 18, 1805

"... the plains smoked with dust and dearth ... , so unlike my native land, in all its features."

Thomas Farnham, emigrant, 1839

"East of the Cascades the great rolling plain of the grain belt greets the eye of the traveler. ... The 'desert' so called is a desert no longer."

Davis' New Commercial Encyclopedia,
The Pacific Northwest, 1909

Preface

THIS is a study in historical regional geography which attempts to show how a large and important part of the Pacific Northwest has been explored, evaluated, organized, and developed over the span of a century or so.

Some prefatory comments on both the region and the manner of its treatment seem warranted, for the Great Columbia Plain is about as little known to the American public as the field of historical geography is to American scholars.

For most Americans the whole Pacific Northwest no doubt seems the most distant and least familiar of the four corners of the nation, and despite its size and its position at the very center of that Northwest, the Great Columbia Plain (by that or any other name) is given no place at all in the common image of the whole. The sand and sage, barren coulees and canyons, grain-covered hills and irrigated valleys of that part of the interior are not only overshadowed but seem completely contradicted by impressions gained from the rain-soaked, forest-clothed, mountain-girded, water wonderland of the more famous coast. Spread over parts of three states, the Great Columbia Plain has failed to stamp any one of them with its own character in the public mind. To anyone really familiar with the Pacific Northwest, of course, the sharp contrasts between coast and interior are taken for granted, and the importance of the country east of the Cascades to the region as a whole and especially to its ports and cities is readily appreciated.

The Great Columbia Plain is only one part of that interior, and a part no longer readily recognized under that name, for reasons made clear in the text. That the name and concept have faded from use and been replaced by others of different roots and bounds puts an appropriate stress on the dynamic character of human geography, while the fact that it was once commonly used and recognized as a distinct region makes it an appropriate framework for a historical study. In general I have kept this work consistently focused within that frame and have reached beyond only where it has seemed necessary, which is to say that I have treated the Great Columbia Plain primarily as a whole rather than as a part—a discrete region rather than as a hinterland.

The principal emphases of this study may be succinctly referred to as ecology and strategy. The first focuses upon man's relationship with his physical environment, the second upon man's organization of area. Tracing these interdependent themes through time in a specific area results in a work which can best be called historical geography. Such a term does not imply any attempt at a complete fusion of the usual content of history and geography, but only some combination of the basic dimensions of those fields. As this work methodically traces developments over a span of time, it obviously exhibits an essential characteristic of history. Yet it remains basically and thoroughly geographical, for the consistent focus is upon a single area; the principal subject is how men have dealt with that portion of the earth; an essential method has been field study of the face of that land; and a special product is the maps which depict the areal patterns formed within that region.

Or, to stress a different contrast, one might say that the distinguishing mark of historical geography is its emphasis upon places rather than persons. Now, people are obviously an important part of most places, but the focus here is not upon them directly but upon how they have affected or given character to places. Many persons famous in regional history appear in this study, but they are here not primarily as personalities who were important as traders, missionaries, soldiers, or politicians but as ecologists and strategists who in an important way judged or tested, selected sites or established routes upon, the land.

To put it more briefly in rather pedantic terms, the regional geographer is typically more concerned with patterns than processes, and to seek some synthesis of a whole rather than just an analysis of parts. Such an approach is only a matter of emphasis, not of exclusion, for these terms merely denote different aspects of the same thing. But the difference is critical to methods and results. This book is structured around an alternation of geographical descriptions and historical narrations, in which a series of verbal and cartographic depictions of the region at particular times is linked by descriptions of developments between those times. That it opens with a regional overview of about 1800 and closes with one as of about 1910 exhibits the primacy given to areal patterns over temporal trends in a work of geography.

I hope that these remarks will save at least some readers from trying to get out of the book what the author has had no intention of putting in. For if any try to read it as regional history they will be bewildered by the complete absence of most of the personalities and events they would naturally expect to find; if they should read it as economic history they will be distressed at so few measures of production, so little on trade, and no attempt at all to deal with such things as capital investment and labor; even if the last half is read as agricultural history, it will seem imbalanced, with no direct description of agrarian society and little indication of how the typical farmer fared during those years. But if it is read as what the author intended it to be, I hope that it will be accepted as a useful complement to these other historical approaches, and that even those who already know the region well will find not only considerable new information but a fresh and interesting way of looking at old.

I would be especially pleased if this book could foster in residents of the region, even to a small degree, some sharper appreciation of their surroundings, a deeper consciousness of their antecedents, and a clearer recognition of the dynamic character of so many regional patterns. I dare to hope that it might, because it has done just that for me. The project began with a lively curiosity but not much knowledge about my homeland, and it was extended in time and area to provide answers that satisfied me. The fact that it has been so much a personal as well as professional project has left its mark in the considerable unevenness of coverage and in the decision to carry the work forward only to 1910. It will probably be apparent that I know the Palouse better than the Yakima, the small towns better than the cities, and more about wheat farming than horticulture. I have tried to balance this bias in my background chiefly by field reconnaissance, and I have visited every district and almost every hamlet and locality mentioned in the text. In the last chapter I have offered reasons why the years on the eve of World War I marked a significant transition and thus a defensible termination. The half century since is worthy of another book, but someone else will have to write it for I must confess that my interest wanes as developments merge into that which I have directly experienced. Furthermore, such a book should be set within a different framework, for those years mark the emergence of the concept of the Columbia Basin and of the role of irrigation and water power into a dominant position.

Acknowledgments

BECAUSE of various interruptions this book has been far longer in the making than originally planned and thus in some cases this public thanks for help received seems distressingly belated. I wish first to acknowledge the help of my father, William A. Meinig, whose personal experiences with and keen memories of Palouse country farming in the early years of this century enlarged my understanding of many things. He never tired of reminiscing, and I never tired of listening. Similarly, Evner A. Malsed taught me a good deal, and I have much appreciated his interest and friendship. The late Howard H. Martin gave me much help and encouragement at the critical earliest stages of the project. I am grateful to Herman J. Deutsch for his most generous support at the last stages and for his detailed critique of the entire manuscript.

I thank Ronald Todd for help in getting started in the Pacific Northwest Collection at the University of Washington; and H. Dean Guie for a delightful field trip to Fort Simcoe and for checking over the chapter on the military. One of my most pleasant memories is the week I spent at the headquarters of the Northern Pacific Railway Company in St. Paul. Most especially I want to express my thanks to William P. Jensen, then Assistant Manager of the Advertising and Publicity Department, who gave extraordinary help to a young scholar seeking all sorts of old, odd, and elusive information. I was in a dozen different offices of the company and never failed to receive courtesy and help. I also thank W. Grant Burden, assistant to the General Director of Public Relations of the Union Pacific Railroad Company, for his kind assistance during my much shorter stop in Omaha.

I thank James E. Sheridan, then Executive Vice-President of the American Title Association, and other officers of that organization for their willingness to support my requests for access to the private records of local title companies, and I am indebted to the Whitman Title Company, Colfax, the Latah Title Company, Moscow, and the Citizen's Abstract Company, Pasco, for allowing me use of their plat books showing early land sales. I also appreciate the assistance of officials of the Bureau of Land Management in Portland and Spokane for help in use of the Federal Land Office records.

I have been helped by many kind librarians: those at the University of Washington, Washington State University, University of Wisconsin, the Bancroft Library, Syracuse University, the Oregon Historical Society, the Dalles Public Library, and of the Library Association of Portland, to list only those of whom I asked the most. I also thank officials of the *Wenatchee World*, the *Spokesman Review*, and the *Lewiston Tribune* for access to their back files.

A generous grant from the American Philosophical Society first allowed me to tap libraries and archives beyond the Northwest, and another from the University of Utah supported further library and field research. Syracuse University has underwritten the entire costs of typing and the preparation of the maps. I also thank my departmental chairmen over these years, H. Bowman Hawkes at the University of Utah, and Preston E. James at Syracuse University, who in each case not only provided a congenial and stimulating atmosphere but many practical aids in support for this work.

I am indebted to Erwin Raisz for permission to use portions of his "Landforms of the Northwestern States." John Fonda has either drawn or supervised the drawing of the other maps, and I am pleased to have his skilled work so prominently featured in the book.

And, finally, my thanks to Lee for everything, through all these years.

D. W. MEINIG

Syracuse, New York

Contents

Illustrations

PHOTOGRAPHS

MAPS

The Great Columbia Plain

A HISTORICAL GEOGRAPHY, 1805-1910

> ...that broad topographic province known as the Great Plains of the Columbia...[wherein] the inequalities of the surface, while relieving the monotony of the landscape, do not determine its character, nor make its designation as a great plain seem inappropriate to one familiar with the region.
>
> FRANK C. CALKINS

Setting: Landscapes, Seasons, and People, ca. 1800

LANDSCAPES

General

IN THE far Northwest of the United States lies an unusual land. So sharply is it set apart from its surroundings that it can be recognized immediately, at a mere glance. Approached from any direction the visible change at its borders is striking: the forest thins then abruptly ends, the mountains lower then merge into a much smoother surface, and a different kind of country, open and undulating, rolls out before the viewer like a great interior sea.

As long as men knew this land in its primitive state it must have always been understood in some manner as a distinct realm. Those who first recorded their impressions left no doubt about it. Viewing it freshly as a part of the face of nature unscarred by the works of man, they described it in vivid terms, defined it by its obvious aspects, saw it as a single broad region, and gave it a name: the *Great Plain of the Columbia*.

Curiously, this remarkable area has lost its name; no modern map gives it clear identity. For regions exist in the minds of men, and maps mirror their times, and such regional bounds and terms as appear today reflect the views of minds that have quite a different image of order and arrangement in that part of the nation. Even though the gross patterns of nature are still discernible, other patterns within and without, subdividing and overlapping, now suggest a different sense of regional identities. Those general labels, such as *Columbia Plateau, Columbia Basin, Inland Empire,* which today loosely include or apply to much of the area, express more specialized views of more recent significance. And so the simple, superficial, visual unity of the area, serving no practical purpose, no longer delineating what was once an obvious setting to traveler and resident, has become so obscured as to warrant no common designation.

But for more than half a century "Great Plain of the Columbia" or a close variant of that title held a firm and honored place on the maps and in the descriptions of the far Northwest. It was simple, convenient, and commonly understood. It was a good title because it conveyed an impression of the scale, character, and location of the region. If small in comparison with the vast plains of interior America, it was nevertheless "great" when compared with the numerous lowlands and valleys scattered throughout the generally mountainous Northwest. "Plain" marked it off from its rugged borderlands, and in those days the term often implied an open treeless country as well. "Columbia" tied the region to one of its outstanding features, the great river system which has cut deeply into its surface for hundreds of miles.

On the map the area appears as a rather fat, somewhat tilted and deformed triangle measuring about 250 air miles along each side, with its apex at the mouth of the Okanogan River in north central Washington, its southern corners in the Deschutes country of eastern Oregon and the Camas Prairie of northern Idaho (Map 1).[1]

The distinguishing general marks of the area are its broadly undulating or rolling surface and its lack of native forests. That relatively even surface is primarily the product of the relatively stable, thick lava platform upon which it rests. The later further uplift of the surrounding mountains warped that foundation so that it is now

[1] The relative location and general character of the region are well described and illustrated in various chapters of Otis W. Freeman and Howard H. Martin (ed.), *The Pacific Northwest, an Overall Appreciation* (2nd ed.; New York, 1954). The colored plates in O. E. Baker (ed.), *Atlas of American Agriculture* (Washington, 1936) vividly display the integrity of the Columbia Plain as a physical region within the mountainous framework of the Pacific Northwest. See especially "Soils," plate 2, plate 4, and plate 5 of Section 4, and "Natural Vegetation."

saucer shaped with the center of the basin lying less than four hundred feet above sea level while the rim varies from fifteen hundred to more than three thousand feet. This concavity of surface and the girdling highlands have given a special character to the two great rivers, the Columbia and the Snake, which join near the center of the Plain. Both reach its margins through long stretches of mountainous country, first skirting the edges of and then cutting into that elevated rim of the Plain through deep canyons. As each river flows toward the center, the concave surface of the Plain reduces the depths of their entrenchment, and within a few miles of their confluence the river banks merge into nearly level country. Almost immediately beyond, however, the surface is abruptly elevated, and the Columbia trunk crosses the southwest rim in another trench which changes at the western border of the Plains into a gorge through the high Cascade Range toward the sea. These are large and powerful streams and generally no more than minor rapids disturb their swift but superficially placid flow across the Plain, but at low-water stages at Celilo and The Dalles a sharp fall and a constricted, rock-braided channel changed the broad steady pace into a plunging, churning maelstrom of fearful velocity, causing the Columbia to make a thunderous, spectacular departure from the Great Plain.

This land lies open and barren because the Cascade Range bars the importation of large amounts of moisture from the Pacific. Even in the short distance between ocean coast and mountain crest the cooler land induces a heavy fall from the winter westerlies, especially on the high windward slopes, while on the lee side the air, warming as it flows downslope, becomes drier. In few areas of the world is there so sharp a change from humid to arid: from almost one hundred inches annually at the low Snoqualmie summit to less than ten inches eighty miles beyond in the Kittitas Valley, and a further reduction to an average of less than six inches in the center of the region. The higher plains to the north and south receive double that minimum, and as the storms move eastward the rising surface induces a gradual increase to twenty inches or slightly more along the base of the eastern mountainous border.

Although in its mountain-girded setting it is a "great plain," and so appears to be in a panoramic view from any high point along its border, it is so far from being one great flatland that the traveler who enters the region, leaves the narrow bank of a stream, and cuts out across the grain of the country will find its intricate texture such an endless succession of ups and downs as to seem a mockery of a "plain." And local textures vary a good deal from one part of the region to another—some are coarse and angular, full of abrupt canyons and narrow ridges, some are fine and smooth, a dense pattern of steeply rolling hills and hollows, while others have other peculiarities, the whole variety reflecting differing ages and agents of formation: the persistent infinitesimal daily work of the same winds and waters of today, the gigantic corrosive forces of anomalous glacial floods of the recent geological past, or the slow warping and buckling by the underlying compressions of an older time. This variety may be generalized into a set of four major local landscapes lying west, south, east, and north of the junction of the Columbia and Snake (Map 1).[2]

Local

To the west of the Columbia the dry country in the lee of the Cascades looks as if it were starved as well as desiccated, with the bare ribs of the earth exposed and only thinly fleshed with soil. Those ribs are a succession of long narrow ridge folds, great wrinkles on the surface from the compression of the foundations below. The Wenatchee Range-Frenchman Hills are the northernmost, the Horse Heaven Hills the southern, and a half dozen major and several lesser parallel folds in between, with their complementary long narrow valleys, complete the full pattern of corrugation. For the most part the crests of these ridges are unbroken, but the Columbia has bisected the northernmost two, and to the west the Yakima has cut a succession of narrow gorges through most of the series (Map 2A). Some of the lowlands are mere troughs, but in the south the main Yakima Valley broadens out into an extensive basin ten to fifteen miles wide and fifty miles long. A characteristic view of this country would encompass a narrow, sage-covered flat with a thin line of willows, low bushes, and tall grasses tracing a creek course; sparsely grassed, smooth slopes rising to the north and south, culminating in

---

[2] These local terrain regions are described and briefly explained in Nevin M. Fenneman, *Physiography of Western United States* (New York and London, 1931), and, in a somewhat different pattern, in Otis W. Freeman, J. D. Forrester, and R. L. Lupher, "Physiographic Divisions of the Columbia Intermontane Province," *Annals of the Association of American Geographers,* 35 (June, 1945), 53-75, and William D. Thornbury, *Regional Geomorphology of the United States* (New York, 1965), pp. 442-59. Because the Great Columbia Plain was defined historically in terms of vegetation as well as terrain, its boundaries do not coincide exactly with those of these physiographic treatments.

a bare basaltic ridge top; a glimpse of open pine forest on the higher ridges and foothills toward the Cascade Range, and narrow, almost vertical walled, water gaps where the river has cut through the basaltic barrier ridges; a country at once open and rugged, very dry in general, but curiously trellised with perennial streams.

South of the Horse Heaven these ridge and valley corrugations give way to a high plains surface which has been broken not by upheaval from below but by sharp and deep incision from above. The Columbia bends into the region through the picturesque columnar towers of Wallula Gap and bisects the whole of it through a broad barren trench. Creeks and rivers from the north and south make their way to that west-flowing trunk stream, carving the countryside into high narrow peninsulas and in places into a veritable archipelago of small, flat-topped highland remnants separated by narrow canyons and basaltic badlands (Map 2B). This section, between The Dalles and the Walla Walla, lies athwart what was long the main line of traffic and gave most travelers their first and many their only view of the Great Columbia Plain. It was rarely a favorable one. Any route near the Columbia led along a rocky, sandy, difficult trail through a country barren of grass and with only the thinnest cover of stunted sage, hot in summer, miserable in spring or fall from violent gusts of dust and sand, devoid of anything but driftwood for a winter fire. Back farther from the river, the slopes and tops carried a light cover of bunch grass, but there the trail led across a succession of canyons and creeks and high narrow divides; and while the grass became progressively thicker and better on the higher country to the south, the streams here were so deeply, sharply, and intricately entrenched as to make any traverse other than on foot almost impossible. Some parts were better than others; the eastern portion between the Walla Walla and Umatilla rivers, is much less dissected, the few streams flow through round-shouldered valleys and make only shallow incisions upon the undulating surface; the Klickitat country to the north of the Columbia was a more gently rolling grassland less eroded; and between the Deschutes and John Day rivers an uncut upland rises back from the Columbia in a series of broad smooth steps until it abuts against the margins of the mountains.

Northeast from the Walla Walla Valley the country again assumes a different texture. Here the basalt foundation is mantled by a fine-grained, fertile soil. Reworked by the prevailing southwesterly winds, that deep layer has been piled and shaped into a dune-like

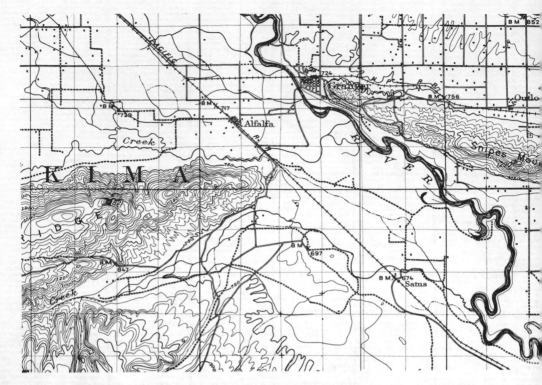

Map 2A

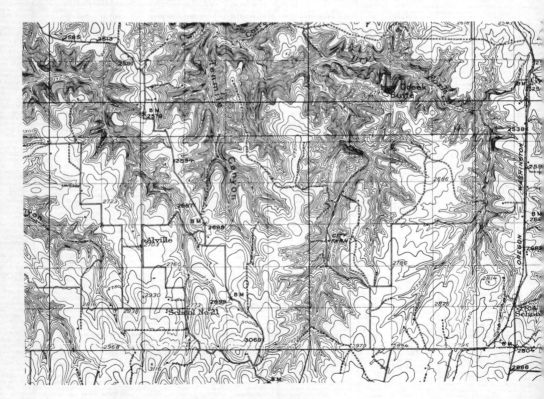

Map 2B

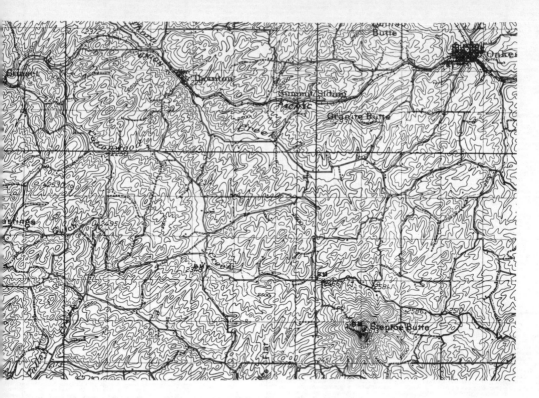

Map 2C

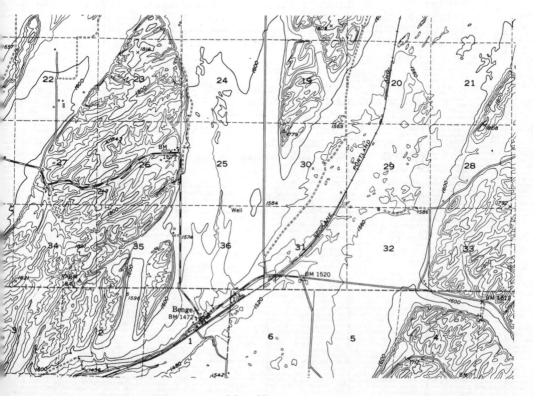

Map 2D

Map 2

A. The Yakima Ridge and Valley Terrain. The Yakima flows through a water gap in the ridge folds of Toppenish Ridge to the west and Snipes Mountain to the east, with the flat-floored valley broadening out to the northwest and the southeast. Creeks flowing along the bases of the ridges are part of the original trellis drainage pattern; most of the others shown are irrigation distributive or drainage ditches. (Portion of U.S. Geological Survey Zillah Quadrangle, January, 1910, edition. Scale: 1:125,000. Contour interval: 50 feet.)

B. The Frayed High Plateau in Oregon. The almost level surface has been deeply cut by streams into a series of raggedly serrated peninsulas separated by deep rugged canyons in which small creeks flow northwesterly to the John Day River, and ultimately to the Columbia. (Portion of U.S. Geological Survey Condon Quadrangle, 1916 edition. Scale: 1:125,000. Contour interval: 50 feet.)

C. The Smooth and Intricate Texture of the Palouse. The very technique of contour mapping falls short of representing adequately this steeply yet smoothly rolling terrain. The dense dendritic network of shallow creeks is well revealed, as is the anomalous symmetrical quartzitic pinnacle of Steptoe Butte, a relict feature of an older landscape buried under these Palouse hills. (Portion of U.S. Geological Survey Oakesdale Quadrangle, 1905 edition. Scale: 1:125,000. Contour interval: 50 feet.)

D. Massive Sculpture in the Scablands. Several of the most characteristic features of this unique terrain are well represented in this small sample (note the difference in scale from the others): from west to east, a large "island," a "peninsula," and the "eastern shore" of Palouse-type hill country separated by broad intervening swaths of nearly level rock-strewn channels worn into the basaltic platform by rushing waters. The steepness and straightness of the channel walls are clearly shown. Just beyond this area to the northeast are several small lakes and swamps lying in depressions within these channels, and just to the southwest these spillways focus into a narrower "coulee." (Portion of U.S. Geological Survey Benge Quadrangle, 1952 edition. Scale: 1:62,500. Contour interval: 40 feet.)

terrain. Viewed from some high bordering point, the whole landscape, clothed with waving bunch grass, could with little imagina-
tion appear to be in motion—a heavy sea swelling into high crests,
breaking into concave slopes, piling up against the forested mountainous "shore." Although this country is cut in half by the deep,
curving canyon of the Snake, streams have not carved it as elsewhere.
Even the Palouse River, which drains most of the country north of
the Snake, is only slightly entrenched into the underlying rock, and
although the surrounding countryside has a dense network of creeks
and rivulets, these mostly flow upon the deep soil mantle, sluggishly
winding through alluvial "flats" or bottomlands, broadening and
smoothing rather than breaking the rolling surface (Map 2C). The
Tucannon and the short streams tributary to the Snake are the only
significant exceptions.

A few strips of pine fringe the larger streams some distance into
the plains, but the main eastern boundary of the Columbia Plain is
here formed by a succession of embayments of deep, grass-covered
soils piled eastward into the valleys and up on the south slopes of the
bordering mountains, separated by narrow, westward-projecting
ridges whose steep and rocky northern faces are clothed with pine.
That this margin marks the high tide of what has been, through tens
of thousands of years, a steady encroachment of these wind-shaped
hills upon the adjacent mountains is revealed by a few isolated gran-
itic summits projecting above the hill surface, the high peaks of an
older landscape now buried under lava and soil.

Tucked away in the far southeastern corner is a variation of this
eastern section. The Clearwater Canyon separates it from the Palouse Hills to the north, that of the Snake severs it from lands to the
west, and it is bordered elsewhere by rugged, pine-covered mountains. The terrain of this Camas Prairie is more similar to that of
Oregon—a high, undulating surface frayed at its edges and in places
sectioned by entrenched streams—but differing in its deep soil, lux-
urious cover of bunch grass, and the pine forests in its canyons, a
land reflecting the heavier rainfall along this mountainous border
zone.

There remains still another landscape in the north, bounded on
two sides by the "Big Bend" of the Columbia River, merging on the
southeast with the Palouse Hills. It is an elevated, rolling, grassy
plain, similar to, though much less steeply contoured than, the country to the southeast, but distinguished everywhere by the scars of

glacial ice and melt water.[3] The direct impress of glaciation was limited in extent. A long tongue of ice ground down the Okanogan Valley, blocked the Columbia channel, and pushed up over what is now the apex of the triangular Great Plain. There it stagnated long enough to leave a short moraine, a ridge of unsorted rock and soil laid down along its melting edge. Receding it left the once buried plain strewn with "haystacks" of enormous boulders which it had ripped and transported from the Okanogan country to the north. The stream of melting water issuing from the stationary edge of that ice lobe flowed southward and etched a canyon into the plains surface, which today, as Moses Coulee, is a great trench carrying an incongruously tiny creek draining the local countryside.

Blocked by this ice projection, the Columbia, swollen by the melt water from the Northern glaciers, filled its canyon until it overflowed at the lowest point along the southern rim, gouged out a thirty-mile channel across the plains, tumbled off a broad basaltic ledge in a thunderous falls, continued southward through a lesser canyon, and then spread out into the central depression. When the ice barrier withdrew, the Columbia returned to its old channel, leaving its gigantic scars upon the high plains surface: the Grand Coulee, Dry Falls, an intricate pattern of minor features mirroring the arteries and eddies of lesser flows, and a series of brackish, marshy lakes.

Farther east the countryside was even more generally imprinted with the marks of this glacial era. Water poured across this land also, but it appears that instead of a single-channeled main stream, a tremendous flood, probably unleashed by the collapse of an ice dam in a mountain trench to the east, flowed through the Spokane Valley and swept southwesterly across the plains. Shaped by the rolling surface but easily cutting through the soil mantle, the running water carved a network of channels in the underlying rock, fanning out as it moved downslope into a series of distributaries flowing into the central depression. Then as the glaciers receded to their remnants on the peaks of the Canadian Rockies, the mountain streams dwindled into narrow channels, reformed the network feeding into the Columbia, and ceased to flow across the plains, leaving behind an

[3] The classic interpretation of this area is that put forth by J. Harlan Bretz in a whole series of papers and monographs, beginning with "The Channeled Scablands of the Columbia Plateau," *Journal of Geology,* 31 (1923), 617-49. A summary of the present status of interpretations is given in Thornbury, *Regional Geomorphology.*

A view of the canyon of the Snake River, looking upriver from near Almota, at the apex of its long arc through the southeastern corner of the Great Columbia Plain. The river surface here is only about six hundred feet above sea level, twelve hundred feet below the canyon rim visible in this photograph, and about eighteen hundred feet below the general hill surface on either side. *(Photo by author)*

A view across a characteristically smooth but heavy rolling surface of the Palouse country, looking directly north toward Steptoe Butte in the center distance. The line of trees follows the shallow canyon of Union Flat Creek. *(Photo by author)*

In the middle distance is a portion of the terminal moraine of an ice lobe, disrupting the neat rectilinear fields on this high undulating surface of the Great Plain near Waterville. The view is to the west, with the Wenatchee Mountains, beyond the Columbia, on the horizon. *(Photo courtesy of John S. Shelton)*

Between the smooth deep-soiled hills of the foreground and those in the middle distance lies a typical scabland channel, a narrow strip of virtually bare basalt, its once-deep soil mantle swept away and its surface complexly scoured and gouged by the swirling waters. Rock Lake occupies a deepened section on the middle left, and beyond lies the "choppy" surface of the Palouse Hills, reaching eastward to the mountainous fringe along the Idaho border at the horizon. *(Photo courtesy of John S. Shelton)*

incongruous landscape of stream-sculptured patterns starkly incised upon a dry, barren land. Where that flood had first entered the region it was stripped of soil, and in time colonizing pines spread a tongue of forest well out into the grasslands to the southwest. Along the margins, and farther downslope, the broadening waters left a complex of braided basaltic channels enclosing isolated remnants of the original hills, a mosaic of scoured rock and deep soils which, in the vivid language of the pioneers, became known as the "scablands," and has so remained for scientist and settler alike (Map 2D). Still farther out, the more definite distributary channels left a series of "coulees," steep-walled, usually dry, rocky trenches radiating across the otherwise undulating plains. In detail the legacy of this remarkable era is far more complex: deep, rockbound lakes, ponds and swampy meadows, potholes, basaltic mesas and pinnacles, extensive gravel bars. Much of the sand and gravel which characterize the barren basins near the center of the Great Plains is derived from the deposits of this gigantic erosion, while the deep soils of the eastern hills are in some degree a reworking of the silts of glacial waters.

Together these landscapes make up the regional scenery of the Great Columbia Plain. Each area has its own character, but each is merely a variation of the same theme, a reworking by different agents of the same basic materials, interrelated in general structure and harmonious in over-all appearance, the whole clearly set apart from its surroundings. Those limits are marked by forests as well as mountains on the west and east, but more by mountains alone on the north and south. The forest edge is a sinuous and in places deeply serrated border, but almost always a sharp demarcation, rarely a thinning gradation into open country. On the south the rolling surface gives way to high mountains which become forested only in the higher, more rugged country beyond. A similar change is evident in the extreme North, although only minor segments of open plains country lie beyond the Columbia, and that canyon may therefore be taken as the general boundary. In two places there are nonforested corridors connecting the Great Plain with regions beyond its margins. At the apex the Okanogan trough provides an avenue northward toward the Fraser River country. Almost opposite, in the extreme southwestern corner, the Deschutes Canyon leads southward to the high lava plains which stretch far into the Great Basin. However, tongues of juniper forest projecting eastward from the

Cascades to the canyon rim mark the general limit of the Great Columbia Plain.

Cover

The Great Columbia Plain was therefore open country, rolling prairie or sagebrush flats, with trees nowhere more than straggling invaders: a thin strip of willow or cottonwood clinging to the moisture of a creek; narrow tongues of yellow pine projecting in from the forested borders along the thin soils of a ridge line, a canyon wall, or a coulee; a copse of thornbush tucked in the northern slopes of the Palouse Hills. The whole was dominated by the bunch wheat grass,[4] with its varied cover—from the scattered tufts of the desert margins to the luxuriant carpet of the eastern hills—which reflected all the regional variations of sun and rain, slope and elevation. Whether this broad, treeless tract was fully an expression of nature or in part the result of man and his fires through a long primitive past is not certain; but when first seen by those who recorded their impressions, it had been as it was for a long time.

SEASONS

The character of these countrysides was as much the product of the atmosphere as of the visible surface. The chief characteristic of the climate is its relatively low precipitation; the seasonal cycle is one of cool, moderately rainy and snowy winters, wet springs, hot dry summers, and warm, predominantly dry autumns. But such gross generalizations only set a framework; the actual conditions are varied among localities, the seasons, and the years.

Cycle and Variations

Midsummer has the most stable weather, characterized by heat and drought, occasionally modified in degree but rarely broken in kind from early July to early September. This can be a hot land. Clear skies, a blazing sun, and little breeze build temperatures to ninety degrees and more day after day over much of the region; in the low central basins and in the canyons and coulees days of one hundred degrees and more are not uncommon, though the higher

[4] *Agropyron spicatum;* detailed descriptions of the native flora are given in Charles V. Piper, *Flora of the State of Washington* (Washington, D.C., 1906), and R. F. Daubenmire, "An Ecological Study of the Vegetation of Southeastern Washington and Adjacent Idaho," *Ecological Monographs,* 12 (1942), 53-79.

eastern margins rarely experience these extremes. Even before the onset of this simmering heat the bunch grass has yellowed, and now it withers to a dusty tan, the great streams narrow in their channels, local creeks dwindle to stagnant, intermittent pools, the moist draws in the eastern hills dry out, and the soils of the sagebrush and sparsely grassed plains crumble into a fine dust to be sifted by sudden sporadic breezes and whirled into momentary "dust devils"; out over the central flats heat waves blur the distant view. Such heat cannot persist. Some moisture is always drifting in aloft; after a few days high clouds form, building up until on a late afternoon huge cumulus thunderheads unleash a heavy downpour, freshening the air, wetting the soil, reviving the creeks. At times these summer storms may be widespread over the region; on occasion they are remarkably localized into "cloudbursts" of extreme intensity, the waters ripping down slopes, canyons, and coulees with tremendous force; and then again such atmospheric turbulence may bring only local dust storms with little or no rain. The season is punctuated not only by these caprices but by more general importations of cooler air, drifting across the Cascades or down from the northern highlands, moderating daytime temperatures as much as twenty degrees, lowering those of night even more. Then, as the inflow weakens, the air stabilizes, the breezes slacken, and the gradual build-up of heat begins again.

This weather may continue well past the equinox—late September can be as hot as August—but almost imperceptibly the seasonal change develops. Daytime temperatures taper off, but the nights soon become distinctly cool. Frost in the bottomlands among the high eastern hills is likely by mid-September, common in October, and moves diurnally in upon the lower lands of the center. Early autumn is a time of warm days, crisp nights, dry, hazy skies, which are often a smoky blue gray from lightning-set fires in the brittle-dry pine forests around the borders. The dew lies upon the grass each morning; streams are at their lowest ebb, even the Columbia recedes to mid-channel between widening gravelly margins. Weak storms pass over the region, marked at first by scattered clouds; then, usually in early October, these fronts bring the first general rain. For a month or two the weather alternates between periods of clear mild days and cool, cloudy, rainy conditions. Through November the westerly storms increase in frequency, bringing longer periods of overcast skies, more frequent light rains; night frosts affect the whole region.

Soon, perhaps in late November, almost surely by mid-December, the mark of winter appears upon the higher plains. That first snow may come in any of several ways: a cold rain turning to sleet, a light filtering of dry flakes, an abrupt, sustained fall blanketing the countryside. Early winter may have pulsations of snow; clear, crisp days; cloudy rainy spells; then more snow. By mid-January the entire region has experienced the full grip of winter—intermittently in the central basin, more persistently elsewhere. On the higher plains the snow cover begins to accumulate, though shifted and piled by the winds; in the rolling hill country, large drifts form in the northerly concave faces, while the gentle southerly slopes may be swept bare. Even midday temperatures may hang below freezing for many days, at night they may edge toward zero or even below. Ponds and small streams become icebound. Invariably, winter is punctuated by clear, dry days, sometimes cold and crisp, now and then warm enough to produce surface melting, which night then seals into a firm crust.

Winter produces the most regional variation. The canyon floors, low central plains, and Yakima country may lie open throughout the entire season; at the same time the higher lands may have a persistent cover. A light drizzle in the west may turn into a sustained snowstorm in the eastern hills. The high prairie south of the Clearwater may lie under a blanket of drifts while the adjacent canyon floors are bare and even without frost. Such regional contrasts and local patchiness are characteristic.

Late winter and early spring is the most inconstant season. Even in February the low country may warm enough to start the new grass. More generally, conditions remain cool and stormy. The westerly storms now move in rapid succession across the region, bringing heavy, wet snows, sleet, or cold rains. The first mark of the season ahead may be a peculiar, region-wide "chinook" (foehn) wind, a strong, westerly, downslope surge of warm air which may melt all but the deeper drifts in a day or two, turn every rill and gully into a stream, and bring a sharp rise in the creeks and rivers. Snows and cold days may return, but their persistence is broken. Winds blowing up from the Columbia gorge, not uncommon at any season, become notable in spring, at times whipping the river sands into a stinging gale. Through April and into May, rains are common and at times heavy. The landscape takes on a green, fresh appearance, prairie flowers and riverine bushes blossom, the soils darken with dampness, the rivers edge up toward their highest terraces.

In May the lower country becomes warmer, even hot, and dry, but the north and east portions experience light showers and protracted drizzles well into June. Local night frosts may persist almost as late. By late June the onset of summer is well marked over the whole region, though moisture-laden soils may sustain the growth and greenness of the grass and sage. But soon the sky clears, the air stills, the heat builds up—and the annual cycle is completed.

In any year this average weather pattern may be disrupted by extreme conditions. Summer heat can broil the lower country in temperatures of more than 110 degrees, several localities have recorded as high as 115 degrees, and the recorded maximum is 119 degrees.[5] The extremes of winter are a more radical departure from the average. Although westerly storms and local high pressure systems usually govern the season, there is the occasional shock of bitterly cold, dry, northeasterly winds that marks the invasion of an arctic front. Temperatures plummet to twenty-five or thirty degrees below zero, or lower, sealing ground birds under the snow in an icy shroud, chilling and starving small animals, and freezing solid the surface of the Columbia. A full frontal assault of such air is rare; a shallower, marginal inflow over the eastern mountains is not uncommon but less protracted and severe.

There are other variations: in the amount of rain and snow; in the length of the frost season and the drought; in the timing of the autumn rains and the spring chinooks. But any one year will differ in no more than one or two main features, and over time these variations blend into a climatic history which depicts a rhythmic, predictable weather pattern; despite local differences caused by positions, elevations, and exposures, the general climate responds to broader controls, and thus wet years, dry years, unusual heat or cold, are shared by all sections of the Columbia Plain proportionate to their local situations.

Wildlife

The barren monotony of the early historic landscape of the Great Columbia Plain was accentuated by its dearth of prominent wildlife. No vast numbers of bison roamed its grassy expanses as in the mid-

[5] A good general view of the climate as well as of certain local patterns, averages, and extremes can be obtained from the relevant state sections in *Climate and Man, Yearbook of Agriculture, 1941,* 77th Cong., 1st sess., H. Ex. Doc. 27 (1941).

continent plains, no large antelope herds graced its arid shrub lands as in the high deserts to the south. Archaeological evidences of both have been found, but the isolated position must have precluded the entry and survival of sustaining herds.[6] The only large grazing animals were marginal and seasonal, the elk and deer forced by the snows down below the forest edge. The Great Plain was home only to a meager variety of small life, such as the ground squirrel, badger, coyote, white-tailed jack rabbit, the sage grouse of the arid plains, and the sharp-tailed grouse of the prairies. Rattlesnakes were numerous in the rocky canyons and coulees. Doves, sparrows, blackbirds, and meadowlarks were common birds; the streams, and especially the ponds and marshes of the scablands, provided spring nesting and autumn resting grounds for migratory fowl, such as mallards and Canada geese.

Although the land appeared poorly stocked, the rivers teemed with life. From January into November the salmon were thick in the Columbia, Snake, and some of the larger tributaries. Several varieties—chinook, sockeye, silver, chum—each in its particular season, made annual runs upriver, combining into a peak period of prodigious richness in late spring and early summer. These great streams, which shaped the visible character of the region, were also corridors of important living resources.

PEOPLE

Ecology

All of these patterns of life and landscape have shaped the geography of man through a long period of settlement. This was not a bountiful land for a people who could only glean directly from nature. The Columbia Plain had no good animal staple, few usable plants, and little material for fire and shelter. But it did have one plentiful resource, and the salmon bound all the Indian groups of the Plain to the river system; it was either an anchor or a magnet: holding some permanently along the banks, drawing others seasonally to replenish their supplies.

[6] See Helmut K. Buechner, "Some Biotic Changes in the State of Washington, Particularly During the Century 1853-1953," *Research Studies of the State College of Washington*, 21 (June, 1953), 162-64, and Douglas Osborne, "Archaeological Occurrence of Pronghorn Antelope, Bison, and Horse in the Columbia Plateau," *Scientific Monthly*, 77 (November, 1953), 260-69.

Salmon was the staple, but there were other important materials, few of which could be obtained from the Plain region itself: deer, elk, and bear; berries, bulbs, and nuts; pine and cedar timbers; flints, agates, and obsidians. Thus the Indian settlement pattern was predominantly peripheral. Even those groups most oriented to the streams were concentrated along the regional borders near the forested mountains: at The Dalles and lower Deschutes, and along the Columbia above the Wenatchee. Those whose river ties were more seasonal also lived around the fringes, wintering in the low country and canyons, congregating at favorable fishing sites for short periods, but spending much of the year hunting and gathering in and along the forested highlands.

Thus a large portion of the Great Columbia Plain remained virtually empty. Along the lower Snake and middle Columbia a few villages were at scattered wide intervals, but the arid countryside was hardly used at all, and the higher grassy plains to the north and east were entered only to hunt for rabbits and grouse and gather the eggs of waterfowl.

Viewed more broadly, the Columbia Plain throughout most of its prehistory stands out as a rather empty zone within a larger culture region.[7] That region encompassed the whole of the interior country between the Cascades and the Continental Divide, and from the Blue–Salmon River mountain country far into the upper Fraser drainage in the north (Map 3). Although more than two dozen distinct groups lived within that area, all shared certain cultural fundamentals. All were riverine fishing economies, supplemented by hunting and gathering; all used similar materials, tools, and techniques; in dress and decoration, social customs and organization, religion and ritual, political order and attitudes, there was sufficient identity to indicate a common heritage. Furthermore, within this region neighboring groups had lived in peace over a long period of time.

[7] The broader patterns of Indian culture areas are well displayed in Robert F. Spencer, Jesse D. Jennings *et al., The Native Americans* (New York, Evanston, and London, 1965); for the interior I have relied upon Verne F. Ray, "Cultural Relations in the Plateau of Northwestern America," *Publications of the Frederick Webb Hodge Anniversary Publication Fund,* 3 (Los Angeles, 1939), which describes culture areas, traits, and intertribal relationships. Alvin M. Josephy, Jr., *The Nez Perce Indians and the Opening of the Northwest* (New Haven, Conn., and London, 1965), chap. i., is a masterly synthesis and presentation of historical and ethnological materials on one of the most important tribes.

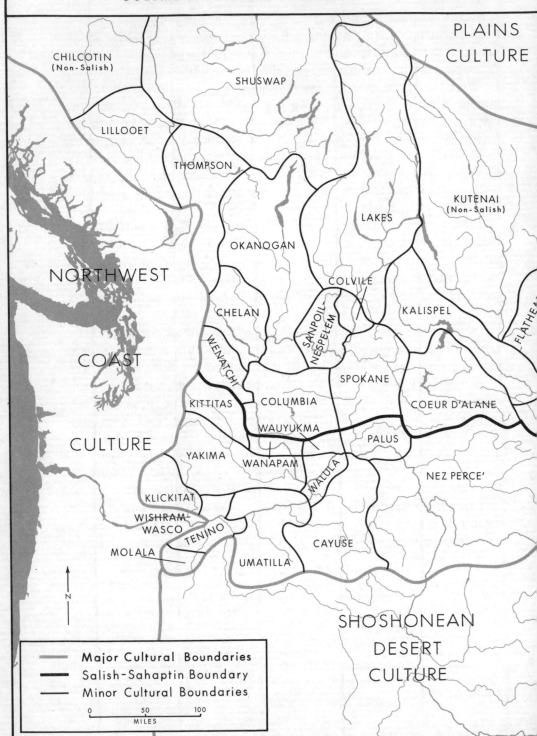

INDIAN GROUPS OF THE
COLUMBIA—FRASER INTERIOR C. 1800

PLAINS
CULTURE

CHILCOTIN
(Non-Salish)

SHUSWAP

LILLOOET

THOMPSON

KUTENAI
(Non-Salish)

LAKES

OKANOGAN

COLVILE

NORTHWEST

KALISPEL

CHELAN

SANPOIL-
NESPELEM

FLATHEA

WENATCHI

COAST

SPOKANE

KITTITAS

COLUMBIA

COEUR D'ALANE

CULTURE

WAUYUKMA

PALUS

YAKIMA

WANAPAM

WALULA

NEZ PERCE'

KLICKITAT

WISHRAM-
WASCO

TENINO

MOLALA

CAYUSE

UMATILLA

N

SHOSHONEAN
DESERT
CULTURE

Major Cultural Boundaries
Salish-Sahaptin Boundary
Minor Cultural Boundaries

0   50   100
MILES

Map 3

Contacts and Changes

These features suggest a high degree of isolation and stability. In general that was true, but neither characteristic was absolute. The borderlands limited and channeled contact with outside groups. West of the Cascades lived the vigorous, aggressive, northwest coastal peoples whose highly developed social systems differed from the interior. But the physical barriers confined sustained contact to two narrow river corridors: the Fraser and the lower Columbia. By historic time coastal influences had penetrated up the Fraser, but on the Columbia, The Dalles had long persisted as a point of cleavage. Here the Wishram and Wasco of coastal culture (Lower Chinook) dwelt almost side by side with the Tenino of the interior.[8] They occupied carefully delimited sites at this richest fishing area, and they served as intermediaries in the flourishing trade between coastal and interior peoples. Relations with alien cultures along the other border zones were more sporadic and of a different character. Intermittent warfare was carried on with the Shoshonean peoples to the south,[9] and with several tribes east of the Rockies, especially the Blackfeet. Yet, just prior to historic time, a major cultural change was introduced into the Great Columbia Plain from these contacts.

Even prior to that change, however, the internal patterns of this interior zone were not completely stable. Despite the basic similarities in culture, these peoples were separated into two distinct language groups. Each group included several different spoken tongues. The linguistic boundary cut across the Columbia Plain, dividing the Salish languages on the north from the Sahaptin on the south and indicating that two distinct peoples entered the region at some remote time. Further evidences suggest that Sahaptin peoples had long been shifting to the north and west, infiltrating and absorbing Salish groups. However, this encroachment was peaceful and gradual, and the peoples were so similar that it produced no real disruption.[10]

The Horse

Far more significant was the acquisition of the horse. Through trades and raids Spanish horses were spread northward from one In-

[8] Leslie Spier and Edward Sapir, "Wishram Ethnography," *University of Washington Publications in Anthropology,* 3, No. 3 (1930), 151-300.

[9] Verne F. Ray *et al.,* "Tribal Distribution in Eastern Oregon and Adjacent Regions," *American Anthropologist,* n.s., 40 (July-September, 1938), 384-415.

[10] Melville Jacobs, "Historic Perspectives in Indian Languages of Oregon and Washington," *Pacific Northwest Quarterly,* 28 (January, 1937), 55-74.

dian culture to another. About the end of the seventeenth century, Shoshonean tribes in the upper Snake River plain acquired a few horses, and within two or three decades parties of Flatheads, Nez Perces, and Cayuses had obtained their first animals. Brought into the mountain valleys and the richly grassed plains, these animals thrived, multiplied, and soon became an integral part of Indian life.[11]

The impact of the horse upon these societies was immense. This new mobility improved hunting efficiency, enlarged the economic area, extended trading contacts, and intensified warfare with traditional enemies to the south and east. Expeditions to the buffalo range far to the southeast now became annual affairs, often marked by intermittent fighting with Plains culture tribes. Increased contacts with these alien peoples brought further changes. The Indians of the Columbia took over many of the Plains "horse culture" characteristics, especially the techniques and rituals associated with warfare. Wealth and prestige became bound up with horses and war. Access to the buffalo and increased range and efficiency of hunting enhanced economic security, and this in turn allowed larger groups to live together. Numerous autonomous fishing villages tended to amalgamate into organized bands, necessitating political and social change, and over-all populations probably began to increase.

At the opening of historic time these changes had been under way for little more than half a century. They were still in progress and unevenly spread over the region, and the peoples of the Great Columbia Plain mirrored the full gradation of differences which had appeared. Along the southeast, the Nez Perces and Cayuse, who had obtained horses first and who occupied areas where a combination of low protected valleys and high, thickly grassed plains provided superb year-around grazing, were the most deeply altered. Each was a linguistic unit composed of several large bands; each band owned hundreds of horses, fishing was less important, buffalo expeditions were major annual events, and trading contacts within and beyond the Plain were extended.

Beyond this southeastern corner, the intensity of change decreased, the number of horses held were fewer, and the veneer of new, imported cultural characteristics became shallower. The Uma-

[11] Francis D. Haines, "The Northward Spread of Horses Among the Plains Indians," *American Anthropologist*, 40 (July, 1938), 429-37; and Josephy, *The Nez Perce Indians*, pp. 27-29.

tilla and Yakima on the west, and the Palus, Spokane, and Coeur
d'Alene to the northeast were in the process of change, but their
herds were smaller and the fishing and gathering economy was still
important. The Tenino, Molala, and Klickitat in the southwest and
Kittitas, Wenatchi, Okanogan, and Columbia owned few horses and
were only slightly affected. A few villages in the arid center, and the
San Poil and Nespelem along the northern branch, remained as
riverine fishing communities almost untouched by the new influences.

Introduction of this valuable animal resulted in more mobile relationships which heightened trade, trespass, thievery, and petty
quarrels. Yet peace prevailed and the geographic pattern of these
groups remained stable. However, the higher grassy plains took on a
new value, and tribal limits, formerly vague zones in the empty interior, now became more sharply defined.

By the beginning of the nineteenth century perhaps twenty-five
to thirty thousand Indians lived in and around the Great Columbia
Plain. The horse was opening a new way of life, transforming social
relations within and without, extending the perimeters of contact,
enlarging available resources, and promising a new period of social
enrichment and progress.

But at this very time a different kind of influence was becoming
vaguely known. Rumors began to spread over the interior of a new
kind of people—of foreign tongue, curious customs, odd clothing
and adornments—who came in huge boats to the ocean shore and
even up the great river for some distance. At The Dalles the Chinook traders displayed a few objects—beads, bracelets, knives—unlike anything known before. And then one early autumn, to the delighted interest of the local Indians, a party of these strange men
appeared at the opposite corner of the region.

CHAPTER TWO

By whatever course may be taken from the Atlantic, the Columbia is the line of communication from the Pacific Ocean, pointed out by nature....

ALEXANDER MACKENZIE

Entry: By East and by North

LEWIS AND CLARK, 1805-6

Journey West

"WE TO our inexpressable joy discovered a large tract of Prairie country lying to the S.W. and widening as it appeared to extend to the W. Through that plain the Indian informed us that Columbia river, (in which we were in surch) run."[1]

That "inexpressable joy" of Meriwether Lewis and his party at their first glimpse through the autumn haze of the high margin of the Columbia Plain was a compound of many things. The spirits of the party were in need of revival. The exhilaration upon reaching the Pacific slope had waned. For more than three weeks after attaining "that long wished for point" they had searched for a feasible route west. They had finally negotiated a difficult crossing at Lolo Pass and for three days had struggled along the ridge tops (Map 4). Now, on a chilly September 19, 1805, that distant high plain "greatly revived the spirits of the party," for it promised relief from the afflictions of previous days: open country, navigable streams, game, friendly Indians, and a quickened pace to their goal.[2]

Three days later, when the party broke out of the mountains and

---

[1] Reuben Gold Thwaites (ed.), *Original Journals of the Lewis and Clark Expedition, 1804-1806* (New York, 1905), III, 73. Except where otherwise indicated, all material on the Lewis and Clark expedition is based upon this edition. As most of such material in this chapter is organized in chronological sequence and is readily followed in the journals, citations are made only for extended quotations or those of special significance.

[2] William Clark and six men had gone ahead as a hunting party and had sighted the plains from the same point on the previous day, *ibid.*, III, 72; see epigraphs preceding Chapter 1.

EARLY EXPLORATIONS

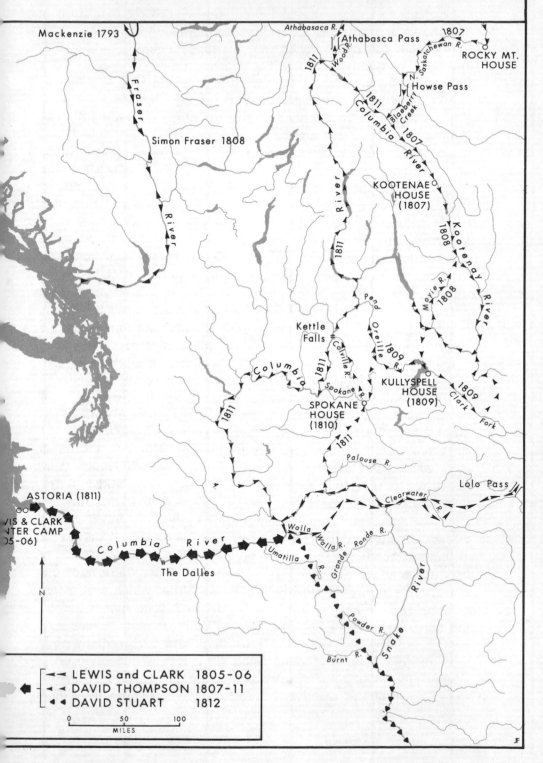

Mackenzie 1793

Simon Fraser 1808

Fraser River

Athabasaca R.

1811

Athabasca Pass

Wood R.

1807

ROCKY MT. HOUSE

Saskatchewan R.

Howse Pass

1811

Columbia River

Bloeberry Creek

1807

KOOTENAE HOUSE (1807)

1808

Kootenay River

1811

Moyie R.

1808

Pend Oreille

Kettle Falls

1811

Colville R.

Spokane R.

1809

KULLYSPELL HOUSE (1809)

1809

Clark Fork

Columbia

1811

SPOKANE HOUSE (1810)

1811

Palouse R.

ASTORIA (1811)

WIS & CLARK
NTER CAMP
05-06)

Columbia River

The Dalles

Walla

Walla R.

Umatilla R.

Clearwater R.

Lolo Pass

Grande Ronde R.

Snake River

N

Powder R.

Burnt R.

LEWIS and CLARK 1805-06
DAVID THOMPSON 1807-11
DAVID STUART 1812

0   50   100
MILES

JF

Map 4

reached the Clearwater River, Lewis could record their pleasure at "having tryumphed over the rockey Mountains." In the main their hopes about this plains region were satisfied. Game was still scarce, and they suffered from a new diet of dried salmon and camas, but the threat of hunger was gone, the climate was milder, and the Indians gave every assistance. Most important, the Clearwater was navigable and, they were informed by the Indians, soon joined the Columbia to form a thoroughfare to the sea. The Columbia Plain, where they spent a month in camp and travel, received only intermittent attention in their westward journals, for canoe travel in the canyons of the Clearwater, Snake, and Columbia kept them walled in a basaltic corridor below the surface of the country. Only near the confluence of the Snake and Columbia did the canyon walls lower and the plains merge into the river margins; here as the prospect enlarged the unattractiveness of the country increased, and the most vivid impression left upon the explorers was the "one continued plain" covered with "great quantities of a kind of prickley pares, much worst than any I have before seen" (Lewis). Elsewhere, brief glimpses by hunting parties resulted only in concise, nearly identical journal entries: a "wavering" plain, no trees, little game.

On October 21 they made out the Cascade foothills, the western margin of the open country: " . . . a fiew scattering trees . . . on high and rugid hills." But the transition in landscape was overshadowed by the spectacular change in the river itself. Reaching Celilo Falls on October 22, the party spent a disagreeable week getting past the succession of falls, rapids, and narrows through which the Columbia churned its way, "swelling and boiling in a most tremendous manner" (Lewis). The Indians were an unfriendly, filthy, and pilfering lot; the fleas, rattlesnakes, and polecats were an irritating menace. Immediate tasks and troubles monopolized attention, and the sharp change in countryside received only slight mention. Nevertheless, as they reached the vicinity of the falls there were numerous clues of very different country ahead. In a camp just above Celilo they saw acorns and clothing of squirrel and racoon skins, which were noted as "signs of a timbered country not far distant." Immediately beyond the falls they came upon two large, skillfully decorated cedar dugouts: " . . . butifull canoes of different Shape and Size to what we had seen above." Then they came upon "the first wooden houses . . . since we left those in the vicinity of the Illinois"; there were quantities of sea otters in the river beyond The Dalles. Moreover, their

Indian guides refused to accompany them farther, pleading that "they could no longer understand the language of those below the falls," that their peoples had been at war and to proceed would mean certain death. The party had encountered a point of decisive transition, the contact zone of plains and mountains, of grassland and forest environments, of interior and maritime realms, of plains and coastal cultures: an abrupt change in both man and land.

Two weeks of voyaging downriver brought them to their Pacific goal, where they made preparations for a winter camp on the Columbia estuary. These first white explorers of the Columbia Plain, covering 350 miles across the region in 36 days, had little opportunity to accumulate a detailed, continuous report on the region. Nevertheless, they noted many facts, obtained general impressions, and recognized the Columbia Plain as a distinct physical and biotic area.[3]

Return East

On May 23, 1806, the party headed for home. They reached The Dalles in mid-April, struggled around the stupendous barriers in the Columbia, negotiated with the "poor, dirty, proud, haughty, inhospitable, parsimonious and faithless" Indians for horses, food, and fuel, and they moved once more into the interior country.[4]

Again, their initial contact with the interior plains provided a needed lift to their spirit, and again the exhilaration sprang in part from the unpleasantness of the country behind:

> . . . even at this place which is merely on the border of the plains of Columbia the climate seems to have changed, the air feels dryer and more pure. The earth is dry and seems as if there had been no rain for a week or ten days. The plain is covered with a rich virdure of grass and herbs from four to nine inches high and exhibits a beautiful seen,

[3] Raymond Darwin Burroughs, *The Natural History of the Lewis and Clark Expedition* (East Lansing, Mich., 1961), is a convenient summation of the fauna described.

[4] This was Lewis' description of a small group of "Skillute" Indians encamped on the north bank at The Dalles. His journal entries of previous days suggest it to be an exasperated outpouring of his opinion of all the Indians in the immediate vicinity, an opinion which was to be amply corroborated by many subsequent travelers. Lest the explorers be misjudged on the basis of this reference with regard to their over-all relations with and opinions of the various Indian cultures encountered, attention is called to the following critical evaluation: Verne F. Ray and Nancy Oestreich Lurie, "The Contributions of Lewis and Clark to Ethnology," *Journal of the Washington Academy of Sciences*, 44, No. 1 (November, 1954), 358-70.

particularly pleasing after having been so long imprisoned in mountains and those almost impenetrably thick forests of the seacoast.[5]

Such exhilaration soon waned. For most of the way to the Walla Walla, they traveled along the sandy and rocky terraces between the river and the high escarpment of the plains. Food was far from ample and fuel seriously scarce. Weed and sagebrush fires were used to boil the dog, dried meat, or salmon and to soften the chill of the April evenings. But despite their discomfort and the appearance of infertile soil, parched from weeks of drought, they were struck by the quality of the short brown grass. As Lewis reported: "It astonished me to see the order of their horses at this season of the year when I knew that they had wintered on the drygrass of the plains and at the same time road with a greater severity than is common among ourselves. I did not see a single horse which could be deemed poor and many of them were as fat as seals."[6]

On April 26 the expedition reached the great bend of the river, and following the Indians' recommendations, they took an easy trail leading eastward to the Clearwater Valley. This departure from the course of their westward travels proved to be advantageous, giving them direct contact with one of the most important subregions of the Columbia Plain. The plains of the lower Walla Walla Valley appeared poor and sandy, but the country soon improved. Cottonwood, birch, haw, and willows lined the stream ("a good store of timber"), and there was a plentiful supply of game birds ("curloos, crains, ducks, prairie cocks"); viewing it on a fine day, they were prompted to pronounce it "a pleasant looking country" (IV, 341-47). Farther on, near the Tucannon, the high plains seemed fertile, the soil a dark, rich loam: ". . . lands of a high quality." On May 10 they set up camp on the upper Clearwater to wait until the Lolo route was passable. En route up the Clearwater the party climbed out of the deep canyon and traversed a sector of the Camas Prairie. It was an impressive landscape: ". . . the face of the country when you once have ascended the river hills is perfectly level and partially

[5] From Lewis' journal, April 17, 1806. The party left camp at the mouth of Mill Creek, the present site of the city of The Dalles, and proceeded along the south bank to the lower end of The Dalles River narrows. On the following day they crossed to the north bank and proceeded eastward. Thwaites (ed.) *Journals of Lewis and Clark,* IV, 290.

[6] *Ibid.,* IV, 323. Comment made on April 25, 1806, while in southern Benton County. Text references are to volume and page of the *Journals of Lewis and Clark.*

covered with the long-leafed pine. The soil is a dark rich loam thickly covered with grass and herbatious plants which afford a delightful pasture for horses. In short it is a beautifull fertile and picturesque country" (IV, 368).

Such contacts prompted Lewis to revise his earlier view of the trans-Rocky country. Previously he had suggested the Willamette Valley "as the only desirable situation for a settlement which I have seen on the West side of the Rocky mountains." After a good look at the high prairies along the timbered margins of the Walla Walla and Camas Prairie, however, he suggested that

> ... the country along the rocky mountains for several hundred miles in length and about 50 in width is level extreemly fertile and in many parts covered with a tall and open growth of the longleafed pine, near the watercourses the hills are steep and lofty tho' [they] are covered with a good soil not remarkably stony and possess more timber than the level country. the bottom lands on the watercou[r]ses are reather narrow and confined tho' fertile & seldom inundated. this country would form an extensive settlement; the climate appears quite as mild as that of similar latitude on the Atlantic coast if not more so and it cannot be otherwise than healthy; it possesses a fine dry pure air. the grass and many plants are now upwards of knee high. I have no doubt but this tract of country if cultivated would produce in great abundance every article essentially necessary to the comfort and subsistence of civillized man [V, 11].

This opinion, recorded on May 9, 1806, is the expedition's final extended notation on the nature of the Columbia interior. It was a prophetic comment, but many years were to pass and many men were to see the same area before there would be any positive response to such attractions.

After a restless month in camp, the expedition resumed its journey homeward, arriving in St. Louis on September 23, 1806.

Strategy

The party had brought back a rich store of information about the far Northwest in journals, field books, maps, sketches, specimens, and their memories of scenes and events. But no prearrangements for publication had been made, nor was the complete official report ever issued by the sponsoring government.[7] Not until 1814 did an accurate, approved edition appear. Delayed, condensed, and scarce (evidently only 1,417 copies were distributed), it was to become a

[7] For a concise history of the problems of publication and a chronology of eventual printings, see *ibid.*, I, xxxiii-xciii.

basic source of information on the Columbia country for almost half a century.

Despite its abridged nature, it was a mass of information, though by the nature of its organization any particular topic was fragmented across many pages. Nevertheless, "Columbia Valley" was printed across the accompanying map in the area between the parallel north-south margins of the Rockies and Cascades (Map 5), and the "Grait Plains of Columbia" emerges from the daily notations as a region set apart from lands to the east and west: a broad, treeless, grass-covered, semiarid, level to rolling country, cut by large, swift-flowing streams; a land, according to the explorers, with at least some attractive, fertile localities.[8] Through these journals the Columbia Plain was introduced to the American and European public and began to take on vague shape and character, but in the first years of the century there was little direct interest. Settlers were still probing the Ohio tributaries, and the whole of Louisiana intervened. It was difficult to have a continental vision when three thousand miles of wilderness lay beyond the margins of home.

The expedition itself, however, evidenced the breadth of Thomas Jefferson's perspective. In his detailed instructions to Lewis, the President stated specifically: "The object of your mission is to explore the Missouri river, & such principal stream of it, as, by it's course & communication with the waters of the Pacific Ocean, may offer the most direct & practicable water communication across this continent, for the purposes of commerce."[9] The final phrase was important. This was not to be merely a scientific adventure: "What a route for the commerce of Europe, Asia & America."[10] The furs of the Pacific coastal waters had already lured American and English

[8] As an 1814 edition was not readily available, I have relied upon *Travels to the Source of the Missouri River and across the American Continent to the Pacific Ocean. By Captains Lewis and Clarke* (London, 1815), 3 vols. This is an exact reprint of the 1814 edition except for the omission of an appendix on Indian tribes.

[9] Thwaites (ed.), *Journals of Lewis and Clark,* III, 247-52. In a letter to Lewis, dated Nov. 16, 1803, Jefferson re-emphasized, despite the variety of information it was hoped that the expedition would procure, that nothing must interfere with this main objective: "The object of your mission is single, the direct water communication from sea to sea formed by the bed of the Missouri & perhaps the Oregon." *Ibid.,* III, 281-82.

[10] The quotation is an excerpt from a letter of a distinguished French scientist, reporting upon Lieutenant W. R. Broughton's exploration up the Columbia in 1792, which Jefferson extracted and forwarded to Lewis. *Ibid.,* III, 258.

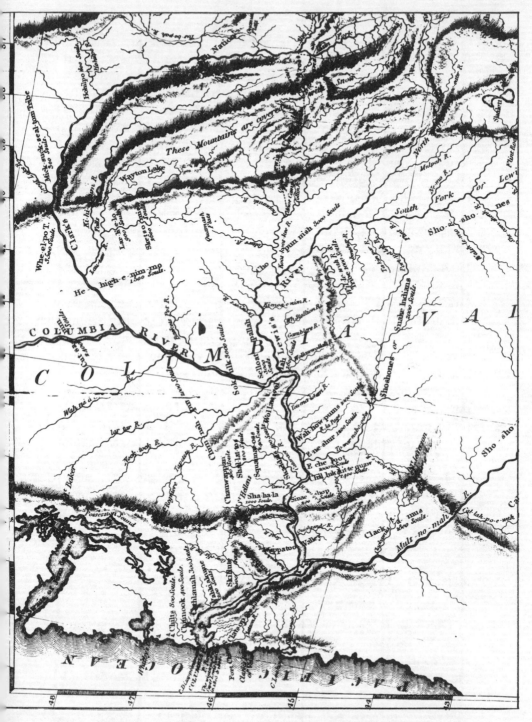

Map 5. William Clark's Map of Lewis and Clark's Track
Across the Western Portion of North America

merchant captains. Jefferson hoped for a profitable diversion of this traffic across the continent (III, 251). Contemporary maps prompted him to suggest an "interlocking" of the headwaters of the Missouri and Columbia. When Lewis returned, he had to report the Rocky Mountains as "a most formidable barrier" which necessitated an overland portage estimated at 340 miles between the navigable portions of the Missouri and Clearwater rivers. Nevertheless, he was confident that he had discovered the most practicable transcontinental route in this latitude, and one which provided a feasible summer passage. The difficulties of the portage were offset by the availability of horses " in immence numbers and for the most trivial considerations" from the Indians of the plains country of either side of the divide. But whereas Jefferson had envisioned a reorientation of the Pacific fur trade eastward across the continent, Lewis suggested the opposite. The furs of the upper Missouri ("richer in beaver and Otter than any country on earth") and even of the upper Assiniboine and Red rivers could be sent westward to the Columbia mouth and thence forwarded to Canton, a principal market. In return, the goods of the East Indies could be brought to the Columbia and thence forwarded to the Missouri and St. Louis. He suggested a main post somewhere on the Clearwater to serve as the point of exchange for Missouri furs and Oriental goods. The Columbia country, while not as rich in furs as the Missouri, was "by no means dispicable in this respect" and would profitably augment such a trade.[11]

Here then, in the first report of the returned leader was a practical design for the commercial organization of the Columbia country. The Columbia Plain as a particular region was not of central concern. But by lying astride the great Pacific waterway, it was caught up into the schemes arising from this initial contact.

THE NORTH WEST COMPANY, 1793-1811

Alexander Mackenzie

There were others who were interested in the Columbia country. The North West Fur Company, headquartered in Montreal, had reached the Pacific shores a decade before Jefferson could put his ideas into action. On June 12, 1793, Alexander Mackenzie and his party had crossed the Continental Divide at the watershed of the

[11] This discussion is based upon Lewis' letter to Jefferson of September 23, 1806, *ibid.*, III, 334-37.

Arctic-flowing Peace River and Pacific-bound streams. Six weeks later, after a devious and difficult journey, the Scot explorer heard the roar of the Pacific surf as it pounded up Bentinck Inlet. But this triumph of exploration was a disappointment to the company. Mackenzie had reached the Pacific, but not by way of a practical thoroughfare. Because of the condition of his party, he had been unable to explore the only apparent possibility, a south-flowing river which he assumed to be the Columbia. The Indians' contradictions notwithstanding, he alleged to the Montreal headquarters that this was the avenue to the sea, which presented grandiose strategic possibilities:[12]

> But whatever course may be taken from the Atlantic [Saskatchewan, Athabasca, or Peace], the Columbia is the line of communication from the Pacific Ocean, pointed out by nature, as it is the only navigable river in the whole extent of Vancouver's minute survey of that coast: its banks also form the first level country . . . and, consequently, the most Northern situation fit for colonization, and suitable to the residence of a civilized people. By opening this intercourse between the Atlantic and Pacific Oceans, and forming regular establishments through the interior, and at both extremes, as well as along the coasts and islands, the entire command of the fur trade of North America might be obtained, from latitude 48. North to the pole, except that portion of it which the Russians have in the Pacific. To this may be added the fishing in both seas, and the markets of the four quarters of the globe.[12]

Mackenzie had forged ahead of the actual operational frontier of the fur company, however, and not until 1808, after several posts had been established on either side of the Continental Divide, did Simon Fraser and his party launch their bark canoes upon the large stream which Mackenzie had discovered and head for the open sea. They soon learned that this incredibly difficult and dangerous waterway was not the Columbia at all, nor even a tributary, but a distinct river (to be known thereafter as the Fraser).[13]

Mackenzie's journey had suggested that the Peace River route

[12] Alexander Mackenzie, *Voyages from Montreal, on the River St. Lawrence, Through the Continent of North America, to the Frozen and Pacific Oceans; In the Years 1789 and 1793* (London, 1801), p. 411.

[13] The posts were Fort McLeod, 1805, Fort St. James and Fraser Fort, 1806, and Fort George, 1807; Hubert Howe Bancroft, *History of the Northwest Coast* (San Francisco, 1884), II, 87-88, 109-13; Gordon Charles Davidson, *The North West Company* (Berkeley, Calif., 1918), pp. 113-18; Lawrence J. Burpee, *The Search for the Western Sea: The Story of the Exploration of Northwestern America* (London, 1908), pp. 506-28.

could not be extended westward, and Fraser had shown that it could not be turned southward to connect with the Columbia. At this very time information from the Lewis and Clark expedition was becoming available and furnished the British traders with further clues as to the probable nature of the Columbia system. Thus the North West Company shifted the focus of its attention southward where David Thompson was exploring.

David Thompson

In 1807 Thompson had ascended the North Saskatchewan and discovered a pass (later to be known as Howse Pass) through the heart of the Canadian Rockies (Map 4). On June 22 he contacted a small stream "whose current descends to the Pacific Ocean—may God in his mercy give me to see where its waters flow into the ocean and return in safety." Following this creek (Blaeberry) he soon reached a larger river. He was on the upper Columbia, but he had no reason to suspect so, for the river flowed to the northwest. In fact Thompson would spend a good part of the next four years amidst the labyrinth of ranges and trenches trying to sort out the remarkable trellised patterns of the upper Columbia system. During those years Thompson or other members of the North West Company established four fur posts—Kootenae House (1807), Kullyspell House (1809), Saleesh House (1809), and Spokane House (1810), and the need for a Pacific outlet became ever greater. Not until 1811, however, did Thompson come upon what appeared to be the indisputable, navigable main trunk of the Columbia.[14]

On July 3, 1811, together with seven companions and two Indian guides, he set out in a large cedar canoe "to explore this river in

[14] Evidently one of the Montreal partners had solicited information from Lewis shortly after the latter's return. Also the journal of Patrick Gass, one of the members of the party, was published in 1807, and copies were known to be in the possession of the British traders. See M. Catherine White (ed.), *David Thompson's Journals Relating to Montana and Adjacent Regions, 1808-1812* (Missoula, Mont., 1950), p. 206, note 94. Elliott Coues (ed.), *New Light on the Early History of the Greater Northwest: The Manuscript Journals of Alexander Henry and David Thompson, 1799-1814* (New York, 1897), II, 692. This work contains some valuable extracts from Thompson's manuscripts. The complete journals of Thompson have never been published; however, most of his trans-Rocky explorations have been printed in separate sections. The most useful source on Thompson is White (ed.), *Thompson's Journals*, which contains not only his Montana journals, but an excellent biographical sketch and analysis of his work, brief biographies of other fur traders related to Thompson's work and

order to open out a passage for the interior trade with the Pacific Ocean." As they approached the northern edge of the Great Plain, Thompson noted changes in the countryside:

> The first part [of the day] the land always fine though high and many fine prospects. Latterly this country, though still meadows, showed much rock. . . .There are no woods but a chance tree, and then a straggling fir. The whole may be said to be a vast low mountain of meadow showing much rock, irrigated into valleys that come down to the river. . . .

There could be little of interest to fur traders in this kind of country: "Of course there can be no beaver, they [the Indians] have bears and rats with a few sheep and black tailed deer. Horses they have many and the country appears good for them." Reaching the junction with the Snake River, Thompson erected a small pole and marked on a half sheet of paper a claim for his country and company:

> Know hereby that this country is claimed by Great Britain as part of its territories, and that the N. W. Company of Merchants from Canada, finding the factory for this people inconvenient for them, do hereby intend to erect a factory in this place for the commerce of the country around. Thompson. Junction of the Shawpatin River with the Columbia. July 9, 1811.[15]

As the party rounded the next bend and headed westward, the

---

area, an extensive bibliography, and a complete chronology of his trans-Rocky travels together with citations to each published section. T. C. Elliott edited the journals relating to travel in Idaho and Washington, which appeared in various issues of the *Oregon Historical Quarterly* and the *Washington Historical Quarterly*. A third outstanding authority on Thompson is J. B. Tyrrell, who edited Thompson's narrative summary of his work written after his retirement: *David Thompson's Narrative of His Explorations in Western America 1784-1812* (Toronto, 1916). All of the published journals as well as the later work have been consulted for this study and are listed in the bibliography. As any reader seriously interested in Thompson would be well advised to consult White, detailed documentation of sources for this general summary is hardly essential.

[15] T. C. Elliott (ed.), "Journal of David Thompson," *Oregon Historical Quarterly*, 15 (March, 1914), 43, 48, 49, 57. The second quotation refers to the voyage from the San Poil River to Nespelem Canyon; the comment about fur traders was made while encamped near the mouth of the Okanogan. His encounter with Yellepit, chief of the Walla Wallas, a few miles downstream must have underscored whatever understanding Thompson may have had of the incipient political and economic competition over this region, for the chief carried the medal and small American flag given him by Lewis and Clark five years previously. Thompson talked at length with Yellepit and gained his approval for the contemplated trading post at the junction.

wind blew at gale force and the plains appeared to be increasingly poor and sandy, "covered with short grass, now faded for want of rain . . . it may do for sheep, but what we see is not fit for any other animal." Passing the Columbia barriers at The Dalles with much less difficulty than their American predecessors, as the high water obscured Celilo Falls and many of the rapids, the party now entered the forested mountains, "a most agreeable change from bare banks and monotonous plains." On July 14, twelve days after Kettle Falls, the party paddled its way through the fog and a strong head wind to the landing of the partially constructed Pacific Fur Company post near the Columbia mouth: ". . . thank God for our save arrival, we came to the House of Mr. Astor's Company, Messrs. McDougal, Stuart & Stuart, who received me in the most polite manner, and here we hope to stay a few days to refresh ourselves.[16]

This voyage had added a new northward dimension to the Columbia system, but Thompson's work was not finished for there was still no effective connection between the Rocky Mountain summits and Kettle Falls. A week later he departed from Astoria. Above The Dalles he erected a mast and sail to take advantage of the otherwise annoying, sand-filled winds and voyaged rapidly upstream, the August sun and desolate landscape reinforcing his earlier opinions of the Columbia Plain. Upon reaching the Snake River, Thompson cut northeastward to Spokane House to avoid the long upstream voyage around the Big Bend of the Columbia. Moving up the Snake to the mouth of the Palouse, he obtained some horses from the Indians encamped at that point and started overland. A midsummer journey through the "scablands" in no way improved his impression of this treeless interior: "The land very rocky and full of rocky hills cut Perpend. wherever the rocks show themselves, . . . with much fragments in splinters, etc. Very bad for the horses and the soil a sandy fine impassable powder which suffocated us with dust and no water to drink where we camped." As he approached the timbered margins of the Spokane country, the grass and soil were better, but "parched for wanting rain, which rarely or never falls during the summer months." Reaching Spokane House on August 13, Thompson had marked out another link in the developing network of routes, an overland short cut potentially useful for eastbound

[16] Tyrrell (ed.), *Thompson's Narrative,* pp. 495, 498. This is Thompson's narrative summary, based upon his notes and recollections, of the country below Umatilla to The Dalles. T. C. Elliott (ed.) "Journal of Thompson," p. 63.

parties. Beyond this point he took the easy, previously traveled trail via the Colville Valley back to Kettle Falls and from there began to ascend a long, unexplored portion of the Columbia. Just beyond its upper bend he reached Wood Creek, the western entry to Athabasca Pass, a new crossing of the Rockies which Thompson had discovered the previous January. After a quick trip east of the mountains for a cargo of trading goods, Thompson returned across Athabasca Pass, descended the Columbia to Kettle Falls, and then headed for the Flathead country where he spent the winter. Having tested the Columbia route on both upward and downward voyages, David Thompson had completed his mission. A feasible transcontinental route had at last been opened.[17]

The practical importance of Thompson's efforts was immense. When he retired to Quebec in 1812, the North West partners voted him three years of full pay while he set about preparing his map of northwestern America (Map 6). Unpublished and relatively unknown during his lifetime, this great map was to hang for many years upon the walls of the North West Company's inland headquarters at Fort William, a remarkably accurate depiction of all those intricate patterns of nature upon which a transcontinental empire might be built.

THE ASTORIANS, 1811-1813

Westward Failure

Two routes had now been opened across the continent to the great river portal on the Northwest coast: the Saskatchewan-Athabasca-Columbia by the Canadians, and the Missouri-Clearwater-Snake-Columbia by the Americans. But the latter had been discovered by a government expedition; it awaited a commercial enterprise to follow and give it operational meaning. An attempt to do so was well under way concurrent with the Canadian explorations in the North. The American establishment which Thompson en-

[17] T. C. Elliott (ed.), "Journal of Thompson," p. 122; Coues (ed.), *Journals of Henry and Thompson,* II, 661, 668-69. Thompson had been blocked from using the usual North Saskatchewan–Howse Pass route by embittered Piegán Indians, who were smarting from a defeat by the Flatheads, who had obtained guns from the traders. The lower course of the Athabasca was an important trade artery, and, lying between the Peace and the Saskatchewan, it was an obvious possibility. Some half-breed "free trappers" had crossed previously but Thompson is appropriately credited with its effective discovery.

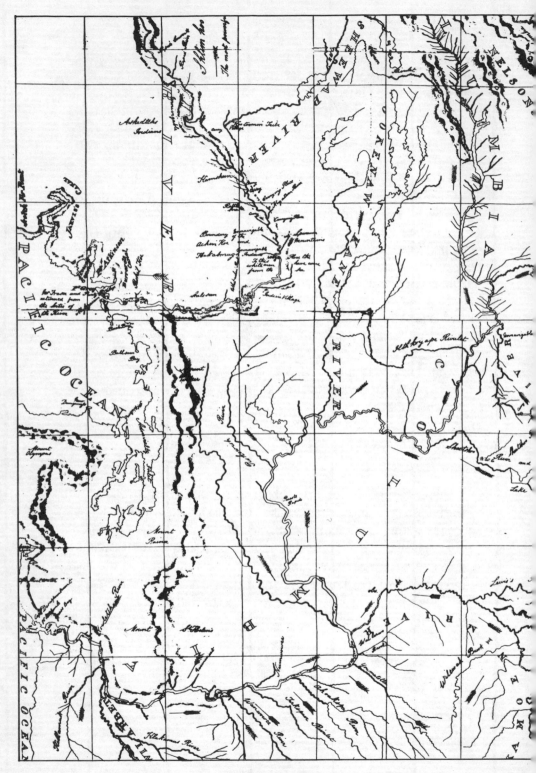

Map 6. David Thompson's Map of the Northern Portion of the Columbia River System

countered near the mouth of the Columbia had been erected by the sea expedition of John Jacob Astor's Pacific Fur Company, which had arrived at that site on March 24, 1811. But an overland party under Wilson Prince Hunt had been sent out to reconnoiter a route and sites for a string of posts from the Missouri to the Columbia. When Thompson arrived at Astoria on July 14, 1811, Hunt was encamped at the Aricara village on the Missouri, near the present boundary between the Dakotas, trading for horses and supplies and trying to hold his party together in preparation for the journey ahead.[18]

Hunt had intended to follow the route of Lewis and Clark at least as far as the Rockies, but traders returning from the upper Missouri country warned of the hostility of the powerful Blackfeet tribe, and upon their advice he decided to head directly westward. The result was disastrous to the purpose of the expedition. Most of the members made it to Astoria, but only after extreme privation and six months of struggling through an awesome wilderness: skirting the Black Hills and the Big Horns, crossing the Wind River Range, the Tetons, and the Snake River Plain, finally disintegrating into small parties, each seeking a way to the Columbia. The arrival of the last group in mid-February prompted a joyful celebration at Astoria, with cannonry, feasts, and dancing, but a practical route between the Missouri and the Columbia remained to be found.

Eastward Discovery

Distance, time, and risks of the ocean voyage made such an overland path a strategic essential to the whole Pacific Fur Company scheme, and the search was renewed in the following summer. On June 29, 1812, Robert Stuart with six companions sailed upriver from Astoria to deliver reports on the company's operations to John Jacob Astor in New York, who as yet knew nothing of the fate of

[18] The basic source of Hunt's expedition is "Journey of Mr. Hunt and His Companions from Saint Louis to the Mouth of the Columbia by a New Route Across the Rocky Mountains," in Philip Ashton Rollins (ed.), *The Discovery of the Oregon Trail* (New York and London, 1935), pp. 281-328, which is a translation of Hunt's diary from *Nouvelles Annales des Voyages* (Paris, 1821). A colorful but essentially accurate account is found in Washington Irving, *Astoria or, Anecdotes of an Enterprise Beyond the Rocky Mountains* (rev. ed.; New York, 1850), chaps. xiii-xxxvii. Useful supplementary accounts are in Bancroft, *Northwest Coast*, II, chap. viii, and Hiram M. Chittenden, *The American Fur Trade of the Far West* (New York, 1935), I, chap. x.

the expeditions he had sent out nearly two years before. Reaching The Dalles on July 14, the party passed this dangerous area without serious incident (although they maintained a careful guard against "the abominable miscreants" in residence there) and entered the upriver plains country. Stuart recorded in his journal the sharp change in the landscape: whereas the region around Astoria was "a impenetrable wilderness," the interior country "is without a stick of wood, and the soil is an entire desert of sand, even on top of the bluffs." These observations from the river were reinforced when the party disembarked at the mouth of the Walla Walla and started overland (Map 4). They journeyed forty-five miles under a blistering midsummer sun, "almost suffocating" with the dust and thirst, before reaching the Umatilla near the foot of the Blue Mountains. From there they began the passage through the mountains and the Grande Ronde, and down the Burnt River to the Snake. On this Columbia-Snake cutoff they followed the track of one of the Hunt parties, but under circumstances so different as to produce an opposite reaction. Whereas in midwinter Hunt had found the area extremely difficult and greeted the plains with relief, the midsummer Stuart party suffered on the drought-ridden Columbia Plain and thought the mountain country, with its plenty of grass and game, a delightful respite. Reaching the Snake River on August 12, Stuart followed the south bank through the plains, a country which he likened to the Columbia Plain: in both "the sages, Worm wood, & salt wood cover a parched soil, of sand, dust and gravel." Although it was not a pleasant journey, they crossed the area without serious hardship, further extending the feasibility of this route.[19]

Leaving the Snake at the mouth of the Portneuf, Stuart moved southeastward almost to the Green River, but then, on the advice of one of the trappers who had been detached from the Hunt party

[19] This account is based upon Rollins (ed.), *Oregon Trail*, pp. 1-263; the same journal is available in *On the Oregon Trail: Robert Stuart's Journey of Discovery, 1812-1813*, edited and with an introduction by Kenneth A. Spaulding (Norman, Okla., 1953). Chaps. xliii-l of *Astoria* contain Washington Irving's retelling of Stuart's journey. Irving has been accused with some justification of overembellishing his account with dramatic and colorful language, but his description of the region between the lower Walla Walla and the Umatilla as "a tract that might rival the deserts of Africa for aridity" was hardly a literary exaggeration when in the Stuart manuscript before him he could read that the party was so desperate from thirst that one member drank his own urine. Irving, *Astoria*, p. 368; cf. Rollins (ed.), *Oregon Trail*, pp. 75-76.

to winter in the Snake country,[20] he turned north into Star Valley only to find himself upon the upper Snake River. Having lost his intended trail, he picked up Hunt's trail through the mountains and followed it to the Green River. From this point, however, Stuart departed once more from the previous route. Instead of crossing the Wind River Range, he followed its southerly slope until the mountains lowered and nearly merged into the plain and thus, on October 22, 1812, crossed the Continental Divide at or very near South Pass.

Stuart's party soon reached the "Great River Platte," where they wintered, resuming the journey in late March. They followed the Platte to the Missouri, and on April 30, 1813, "a little before sun set we reached the Town of Saint Louis all in the most perfect health after a voyage of ten months from Astoria."[21]

Stuart's arrival was sensational news, as it brought the first reports of the Astor expeditions; less dramatic but of far greater significance was the geographical information acquired by his journey. Within two weeks the St. Louis paper published a brief description of Stuart's journey, and concluded:

> By information received from these gentlemen, it appears that a journey across the continent of N. America, might be performed with a waggon, there being no obstruction in the whole route that any person would dare to call a mountain in addition to its being much the most direct and short one to go from this place to the mouth of the Columbia river.

That item was soon widely reprinted in newspapers on the eastern seaboard and ultimately appeared in books published in Paris and London.[22] Not only the path, but the concept of an "Oregon Trail" had been opened.

THE EMERGENCE OF A REGION

Within eight years of the first contact with the Columbia interior, three transcontinental routes had been laid out (Map 7). In terms of functional importance the first was largely a failure. Despite Lewis' belief that he had found the most practical route through the mountains in that latitude, which was at least partially correct, it

---

[20] Stuart had encountered three of these men, utterly destitute, along the river on August 20, and they had joined his eastbound party.

[21] Rollins (ed.), *Oregon Trail*, pp. 197, 239.

[22] *Ibid.*, p. lxvii, quoting the *Missouri Gazette,* May 15, 1813. Also p. lxviii.

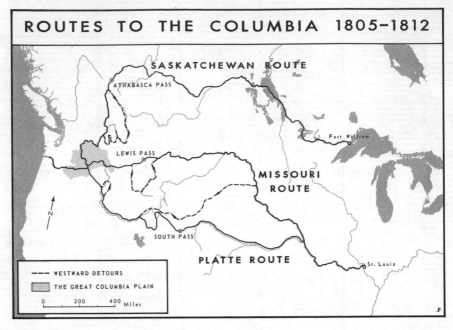

ROUTES TO THE COLUMBIA 1805–1812

SASKATCHEWAN ROUTE

ATHABASCA PASS

Fort William

LEWIS PASS

MISSOURI ROUTE

N

SOUTH PASS

PLATTE ROUTE

St. Louis

- - - - WESTWARD DETOURS

▨ THE GREAT COLUMBIA PLAIN

0   200   400 Miles

Map 7

never became a thoroughfare. For half a century the labyrinth of mountains and valleys, reinforced by the human barrier of Blackfeet and Sioux, blocked its use; and not until the 1960's was a road built across Lolo Pass to the Clearwater. The practical discovery of that first expedition was the "Columbia Pass" through the Cascade Range, a navigable waterway with only short interruptions between the interior and the Pacific. Confirmation of this passageway focused the attention of Americans and British entrepreneurs upon the Columbia country and intensified the need for feasible links from the east.

The years 1811-12 marked the turning point. Almost simultaneously Thompson and the Astorians laid out the key lines of strategy for Britain and the United States. The one was anchored in Fort William (later to be shifted to York Factory), the other in St. Louis; each followed the rivers across the plains (the Saskatchewan-Athabasca, and the Missouri-Platte), each threaded a strategic corridor across the summit of the continent (Athabasca Pass and South Pass), then curved to contact the outspread sources of the upper Columbia and the Snake, and finally merged into the trunk route through the Cascade Range to the sea. For forty years these were the overland arteries through which the commercial and political interests of the nations were maintained.

The Great Plain of the Columbia became bound into this international, transcontinental strategic network. Neither mountain passes nor Columbia portal were more important than the zone of convergence, the Columbia interior. The area between the mouths of the Snake and Umatilla rivers became the nexus of all the paths to the Pacific revealed by these initial explorations: the upper Columbia, the overland Spokane cutoff, the lower Snake, the Walla Walla-Clearwater route, and the trail across the Blue Mountains to the upper Snake and South Pass. Though of unequal significance, each path was to have lengthy historical importance, and in these beginning years they confirmed the strategic importance of the area.

The Great Columbia Plain was noted in all the reports and journals of these explorers. On their maps its identity, nature, and bounds are less clear. Although Lewis and Clark consistently employed some variation of "Columbia Plain" in their journals to refer to this area, their published map displays "Columbia Valley" printed across a much broader zone between the Cascades and Rockies (Map 6). Thompson, whose interests were more narrowly hydrographic, avoided any regional designation in journal or map (Map 7). But if the region itself received no clear cartographic label, lesser features within it were identified in considerable detail. Both of the maps relied heavily upon what were assumed to be Indian names for local streams. *Ki-moo-e-nim, Tho-qual-a-tough,* and *To-wan-ow-hi-ooks* suggest how valiant were the attempts of Lewis and Clark at accurate anglicization, but even more melodious examples had a bewildering instability in their reports: *Wallah Wallah, Wallow Wallow, Wollow Wollah, Waller Waller.* Interspersed among indigenous terms was the toponymic imprint of the expedition itself: *Lewis's River* (lower Snake), *Drewyer's River* (Palouse), *Lapage's River* (John Day), each named after a member of the party.[23]

---

[23] *Map of Lewis and Clark's Track Across the Western Portion of North America from the Mississippi to the Pacific Ocean.* "Compiled by Samuel Lewis from the Original Drawing of William Clark." London: Longman, Hurst, Rees, Orme and Brown, April 28, 1814. *Map of the North West Territory of the Province of Canada from actual survey during the years 1792 to 1812* ... "by David Thompson, Astronomer & Surveyor."

Stuart referred to the region as the "Columbia Plains." Rollins (ed.), *Oregon Trail,* p. 61. There is much inconsistency in the use of these names.

Inevitably there was much confusion and contradiction between the maps of two separate explorations. The interpretations of local Indian names had little in common. Of the lesser streams in the interior which both parties had contacted, only the Umatilla is recognizable in name as clearly the same: *You-ma-tol-am* (Lewis and Clark) and *Youmatilla* (Thompson). There was contradiction even in regard to portions of the great trunk streams, because neither party was personally familiar with both the upper Columbia and the Snake. Nevertheless, a base map had been established, which began its long evolution toward accuracy. The Lewis and Clark map was a rude sketch compared to the skilled cartography of Thompson, the professional surveyor.[24] Yet it represented more of a real geographic synthesis, for it attempted to exhibit human as well as physical geography. Each Indian tribe was identified in its approximate location, together with a notation of tribal population. Some idea of both pattern and density were thus revealed, and the journals contained much detail on local cultures.[25] Despite the unsystematized mass of information, any careful reader could recognize the Columbia Plains with its unique combination horse and salmon culture as a distinctive ethnographic region.

Equally important, with these initial contacts began the accumulation of information, impressions, and ideas about the nature of the land. Each traveler who wrote of his experiences noted something of the characteristics of this region, so different from its bordering lands, and most expressed conscious or implicit opinions about its value. Although the general public had access only to the account of Lewis and Clark, those of the British and Astorians were soon well known by interested parties and began to infiltrate the ideas of a broader audience. Varied by a host of circumstances, such mix-

---

Ki-moo-e-nim is clearly the middle Snake on one of their sketch maps, but becomes what is apparently the Tucannon on their published map. *Tho-qual-a-tough* is the Tucannon on one sketch map, *To-wan-ow-hi-ooks* is the Deschutes.

[24] Lewis and Clark, dependent wholly upon Indian sketches, oversimplified and distorted the stream patterns to the north, and show the upper Columbia more nearly in the position of the Okanogan. Thompson relied upon the earlier expedition for his knowledge of the Snake above the Palouse, but he shifted *Lewis's River* from the main Snake to the lower Clearwater, replacing it with *Kamoenim*.

[25] There is considerable discrepancy in both name and number between the map and list compiled by Lewis. See "Estimate of the Western Indians," Thwaites (ed), *Journals of Lewis and Clark*, VI, 113-20.

tures of observation and evaluation laid the bases for and materially shaped subsequent ideas and actions. That first glimpse on September 19, 1805, of the high eastern margin of the Columbia Plain set in motion the study of the land: a gradual, uneven, often conflicting, cumulative growth of knowledge which proceeds with quickened pace, enlarged scope, and sharpened perception yet today—and it is an unending pursuit. These first years, then, mark discovery, exploration, the beginnings of knowledge, and the foundation of a skeletal strategic frame of operations. The Great Columbia Plain had been firmly annexed into history.

CHAPTER THREE

It is the peculiar nature of the Fur
Trade to require a continual extension
of its limits, into new Countries; because the number of Animals dimin-
ishes in those Countries where the
trade has been for any considerable
time, established. . . .

PETITION OF THE NORTH WEST
COMPANY FOR A CHARTER, 1812[1]

Competition: By Land and by Sea

THE PACIFIC FUR COMPANY

John Jacob Astor's Pacific Fur Company was an intercontinental
scheme grand in scope and daring in execution (Map 8). Firm
knowledge of the Columbia as the trunk of an immense river system
prompted selection of its estuary as the logical point for the main
depot. Astoria was to collect the furs from subsidiary posts in the interior, from vessels to be sent north and south along the coast, and
from the share of the rich maritime fur operations of the Russians
to be obtained in trade for essential subsistence supplies. A ship
would be sent annually from New York around Cape Horn to Astoria with reinforcements, supplies, and trading goods. This same
ship would then cross the Pacific to dispose of the furs in the Canton
market, and carry Chinese goods on around to Europe and America.
An overland route, with protective forts and trading posts, was to be
established primarily as a line of rapid communication between Astoria and New York.[2]

Probing the Interior

The construction of Astoria was a solid beginning, but it was the
portal to a wilderness only indirectly and imperfectly known. The
arrival of David Thompson, who with his sextant, chronometer, and

[1] Davidson, *North West Company,* p. 287.
[2] Paul Chrisler Phillips, *The Fur Trade* (Norman, Okla., 1961), Vol. II,
provides a good perspective on the characteristics and strategies of the several
companies involved in the Pacific Northwest. Irving, *Astoria,* pp. 37-39.

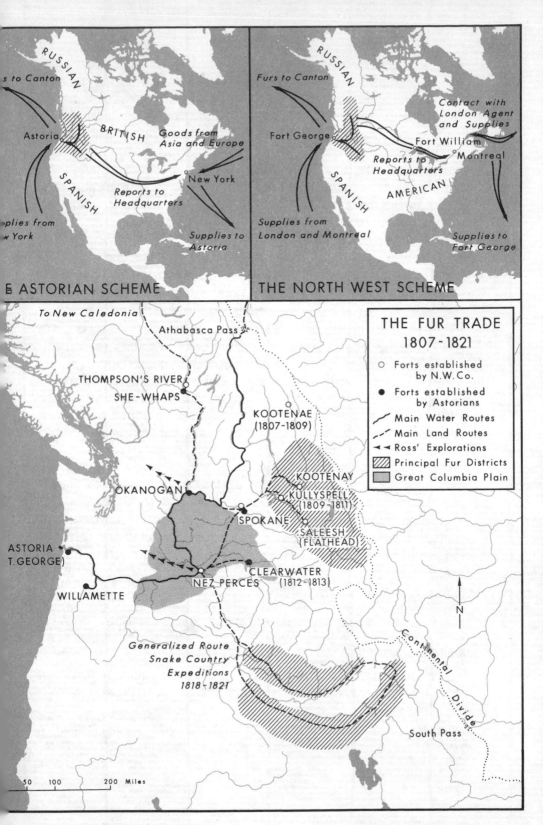

THE ASTORIAN SCHEME

Furs to Canton

Astoria

BRITISH

Goods from Asia and Europe

SPANISH

Reports to Headquarters

New York

Supplies from New York

Supplies to Astoria

THE NORTH WEST SCHEME

RUSSIAN

Furs to Canton

Fort George

Reports to Headquarters

SPANISH

AMERICAN

Contact with London Agent and Supplies

Fort William

Montreal

Supplies from London and Montreal

Supplies to Fort George

THE FUR TRADE 1807-1821

○ Forts established by N.W.Co.
● Forts established by Astorians
—— Main Water Routes
– – – Main Land Routes
◄◄ Ross' Explorations
▨ Principal Fur Districts
▓ Great Columbia Plain

To New Caledonia

Athabasca Pass

THOMPSON'S RIVER
SHE-WHAPS

KOOTENAE
(1807-1809)

KOOTENAY

KULLYSPELL
(1809-1811)

OKANOGAN

SPOKANE

SALEESH
(FLATHEAD)

ASTORIA
(F.GEORGE)

CLEARWATER
(1812-1813)

NEZ PERCES

WILLAMETTE

Generalized Route
Snake Country
Expeditions
1818-1821

Continental Divide

South Pass

N

50 100 200 Miles

Map 8, upper left; Map 9, upper right; Map 10, below

barometer impressed the Astorians as "more like a geographer than a fur trader," enlarged their knowledge but not their prospects.[3] But the descriptions of a rival trader were suspect, preparations for an upriver reconnaissance had already been made, and a party, led by David Stuart and accompanied by Thompson, set out in three canoes on July 22, 1811. The objective was to look over the country, make contacts with the natives, and establish a permanent post somewhere in the interior. Impatient with the slow progress, Thompson soon left and hurried back to his own outpost at Spokane.

As a site for a permanent post the traders were seeking a combination of three features: a location strategic in its position on navigable streams, a hinterland of rich beaver country, and a numerous and friendly Indian population who would gather furs. Thompson recorded that the Astorians planned "to build a Factory somewhere below the falls of the Columbia [Kettle Falls], at the Lower Tribe of the Shawpatin Nation," which would indicate the Walla Walla, lower Snake, or Yakima. But when they came upon Thompson's flag and note at the mouth of the Snake, in which he claimed the area for Britain and announced his intention to build a post, and when the Indians inferred that the North West Company hoped to keep the Americans south of that point, reserving the entire upper Columbia for itself, they determined to frustrate their rivals and to establish a post deep in the interior.[4] And so they continued up the barren canyon of the Columbia. On August 31 they came to the Okanogan, and the prospects seemed favorable. The tributary valley appeared to offer an easy avenue into an extensive area to the north, and although Alexander Ross thought "the general aspect of the surrounding country . . . barren and dreary," the thick woods on the mountain

[3] The brief journal of Patrick Gass had been published, and Astor had doubtless been able to obtain much additional information about the Lewis and Clark expedition. As most of his personnel were recruited from the North West Company, some specific information about the upper Columbia country was also known. According to one Astorian, ". . .the description which [Thompson] gave us of the interior of the country was not calculated to give us a very favorable idea of it." Gabriel Franchère, *Narrative of a Voyage to the Northwest Coast of America . . .*, ed. and trans. by J. V. Huntington (New York, 1854), reprinted in Reuben Gold Thwaites (ed.), *Early Western Travels, 1748-1846* (Cleveland, 1904), VI, 254.

[4] Elliott (ed.), "Journal of Thompson," p. 106; Alexander Ross, *Adventures of the First Settlers on the Oregon or Columbia River* (London, 1849), reprinted in Reuben Gold Thwaites (ed.), *Early Western Travels, 1748-1846* (Cleveland, 1904), VII, 138-39.

slopes to the west suggested a potential fur district. Moreover, they were met by "a great concourse of Indians" who were anxious for them to establish a post, and after some negotiations the Astorians agreed. They selected a site near the point of the peninsula at the confluence of the Okanogan and Columbia, and gathered driftwood to construct a small dwelling.

The principal objective of this first reconnaissance was thus achieved. The party now split: Alexander Ross remained in charge at Okanogan, one group was sent to explore the upper Okanogan and to winter with the Shuswaps Indians on the Thompson River, while the remainder returned to Astoria to report that the prospects were "highly satisfactory," the climate of the interior "salubrious," and that they had been "well received" by the Indians.[5]

Competition and Conclusion

Buoyed by new supplies, personnel, and good returns from their first winter of trading, the Astorians moved energetically in 1812 to develop their full system. While Robert Stuart headed east to open the overland connection with New York, several other parties set out to establish posts at strategic points deeper in the interior. Their strategy was a direct challenge to the North West Company. Two years earlier the British firm had built Spokane House on a peninsula at the junction of the Spokane and Little Spokane rivers. It was their farthest outpost in the Columbia country, marking out a claim to a broad rich region between that point and the Rockies. Undaunted by this, the Astorians set up camp immediately adjacent, called an assembly of Indians to declare their readiness to compete for furs, and dispatched wintering parties to the Coeur d'Alene, Kootenay, and Flathead districts. The British soon retaliated in identical style. Another Astorian party was at the same time erecting She-whaps post on the south bank of the South Thompson River, a locale which had yielded well for them the past winter. The North West Company built a rival post across the river (which became known as Kamloops).[6]

Another Astorian group headed for the Clearwater country, an area as yet well south of British penetrations. A camp was established

[5] Franchère, *Narrative of a Voyage,* p. 260.
[6] Ross, *First Settlers,* pp. 158-59, 194-95, 205, 208ff.; and F. Henry Johnson, "Fur-Trading Days at Kamloops," *British Columbia Historical Quarterly,* 1 (July, 1937), 171.

on the lower Clearwater, but they soon found that the Nez Perces were different Indians from those to the north. This proud and wealthy tribe "spurned the idea of crawling about in search of furs" as a life "only fit for women and slaves."[7] They did have large herds of horses, however, and so the Astorians settled in to barter.

The returns from these operations (as well as from a post in the Willamette and trade with the Russians at Sitka in the spring of 1813) were less than anticipated but still represented a substantial income for the first year of the complete program. However, the belated news of the outbreak of war between Britain and the United States clouded their prospects. Commercial rivalry might now be transformed into a military encounter, and circumstances placed the American company in a weak and difficult position. Tentative arrangements were made for the 1813-14 season, but when they received news of the impending arrival of a British warship on the Columbia, and when a large party of North West personnel voyaged down the Columbia and encamped adjacent to Astoria in a sort of passive, disorganized siege, the Astorians decided to salvage what they could by selling the entire Pacific Fur Company operation to their British rival. In December, the British sloop arrived, the official British claim to the Oregon country was reaffirmed, and Astoria became "Fort George."[8]

Thus ended the first attempt at a comprehensive program for the exploitation of the Columbia country. Though speculative in initial plan and brief in duration, had the Astorian venture remained im-

[7] Ross, *First Settlers*, pp. 215-16, 221. On the location of Mackenzie's camp, see Jean C. Nielsen, "Donald Mackenzie in the Snake Country Fur Trade, 1816-1821," *Pacific Northwest Quarterly,* 31 (April, 1940), 163, and Francis D. Haines, "Mackenzie's Winter Camp, 1812-13," *Oregon Historical Quarterly,* 37 (December, 1936), 333. It was apparently somewhere near or below Lapwai Creek.

[8] Irving, *Astoria,* p. 484, lists what was probably the total mainland catch for that season: 17,705 pounds of prime beaver and a miscellany of other furs. Various information in the journals of Ross and Franchère allow one to make a rough estimate that about 50 per cent of this was obtained from Okanogan and She-whaps, 40 per cent from Spokane and tributary posts, and 10 per cent from the Willamette. Ross, *First Settlers,* pp. 239-50. The decision to sell out to the British involved a complex of circumstances, hinged crucially upon certain personalities, and its interpretation has been a controversial matter among historians. Irving gives a detailed account in *Astoria,* and sets forth a sharp indictment of the capitulation. Any standard history of the Pacific Northwest will likewise deal extensively with these events.

mune to the larger international contest it might have been a successful operation, for it was based upon an impressive geographic strategy (Map 10). Astoria, on a sheltered, deep-water harbor which could be fortified against naval assault, at the ocean terminus of the trunk stream, was well situated as a headquarters and central depot. Inland, the Walla Walla Valley was the junction of routes fanning out north and east to the forested zones and for the overland path to the United States. The fact that the Indians were friendly and large numbers of pack horses could be pastured and watered here made it a convenient and adequate rendezvous and might in time have led to the establishment of a permanent depot. Use of the Columbia, the Spokane "cutoff" across the plains, and the lower Snake gave the most direct access to the peripheral forested mountain realm. Okanogan was near the first point of upriver contact with the forested highlands, and the terminus of the overland trail along the valley leading north toward the Thompson River post, which gathered from an extensive hinterland. Spokane had convenient lowland access upriver to the Coeur d'Alene country, and also to the Pend Oreille and Kootenay-Flathead region. Though a failure as a fur post, Donald Mackenzie's location on the Clearwater was on the grassland-forest margin central to the Nez Perces' wintering grounds, and thus was ideal, given amicable relations, as a horse procurement station. Finally, Stuart's success in marking out a relatively easy and direct route to St. Louis made the idea of an overland administrative contact quite feasible. Add to these arrangements Hunt's success in obtaining eighty thousand seal skins through trade with the Russians at Sitka (though not without difficulty and the necessity of voyaging clear to the Pribilof Islands to take on the cargo), and the general soundness of Astor's visionary scheme and the faithfulness and vigor of its implementation become apparent.

THE NORTH WEST FUR COMPANY

The Necessity of the Columbia

It is ironic that Astor's strategy for exploiting the Columbia country was far superior to that of his rivals. The British were operating at the terminus of a tenuous continental axis which allowed import of supplies and export of furs only at exorbitant cost. Spokane was poorly located either as a fur post or a depot within the British scheme, and they were at a serious disadvantage in the Thompson River district, where the most practical orientation was southward to Okanogan. Indeed, so disadvantageous was the British position that their anxious desire to acquire the American company was governed less by the removal of competition than by the need to extend, reorient, and rationalize their whole trans-Rocky operation.[9]

Even before their fortuitous acquisition of the American posts, the British company had decided to try to use the Columbia to serve their Pacific slope establishments. Thompson had proved it a feasible outlet in 1811, and at the annual meeting in 1812 it was decided to send a ship to the Columbia with supplies for the interior.[10] Meanwhile plans were laid to reorient the pattern of operations in that vast area.

The company's establishments beyond the Rockies were in two widely separated regions as the result of separate westward expansions: up the Peace River into New Caledonia in the far North, and up the Saskatchewan and Athabasca into the Columbia. The former had resulted in the founding of Fort St. James, Fraser Fort, and Fort George in the mountain and lake country near the upper bend of the Fraser River, a realm known as New Caledonia. To the south,

[9] Davidson, *North West Company,* p. 288. In their petition to London for a monopoly charter for trans-Rocky operations, the North West Company leaders stated: "...traders going over Land from Canada, cannot possibly carry on the Trade of that Country, upon an equal footing with those who get their Supplies of Goods by Sea to the North West Coast, and from thence through the Columbia and other Rivers, into the immediate scene of competition." It should be pointed out that the American establishment at Astoria did not represent any exclusive legal political control. The British could have built a rival port adjacent as they did at Kamloops, for both countries had a basis for claim to the area, a fact which was later to result in legal agreement for temporary joint occupation. Nevertheless, the prior position of the Americans upon the lower Columbia was a strategic victory and complicated any British designs upon use of that route. In fact, Astoria was restored to American title in 1818; the North West Company did build alongside and remained in firm control of the fur trade.

[10] One of the great academic controversies over the history of the fur trade relates to the action of the North West Company, and David Thompson in particular, with reference to control of the Columbia River. Much has been written of the "race" to secure the mouth of the Columbia. That Thompson did not "race" to beat the Astorians is clear from his journal which relates his leisurely journey downstream; whether he was negligent in not striving to beat the Americans remains in dispute. For an excellent evaluation of the controversy, see White (ed.), *Thompson's Journals,* Appendix B, "David Thompson and the 'Columbian Enterprise,'" pp. 247-55. Davidson, *North West Company,* p. 135.

on Columbia waters, Thompson and his associates had by 1810 established Kootenae House (near the source of the Columbia), Kootenay Fort (near Libby, Montana), Kullyspell (near Hope, Idaho), Saleesh House (near Eddy, Montana), and Spokane (Map 10). The post on the Thompson River at Kamloops in 1812, constructed to meet the Astorian challenge, was midway between their two fields of operation, suggesting the possibility of focusing the Fraser posts southward in the direction of the Columbia drainage. Accordingly, in May, 1813, a party left Fort St. James with the idea that if they should find a practicable trail to Kamloops, "we shall, for the future, obtain our yearly supply of goods by that route, and send our returns out that way, to be shipped directly for China. . . ."[11] By these actions the North West Company was admitting that the Astorian scheme, with its Pacific orientation, Columbia artery, and Canton market, was the most efficient plan for exploiting the trans-Rocky country. The war and forced sale of the American company therefore merely cut short the incipient extension into the lower Columbia and Astoria of British and American strategic competition, previously confined to the local fur districts.

Difficulties

Yet when the entire Columbia system unexpectedly fell into its lap, the North West Company soon found it a vexatious blessing. Inland, its situation in and on the periphery of the Great Plain of the Columbia was serious. At the junction of interior routes, the Walla Walla Valley, the natives, smoldering from harsh treatment by

[11] Fort McLeod, on McLeod's Lake, also functioned as part of the same group, though it was just east of the divide on one of the headwaters of the Peace River. These posts are shown on the Thompson map of 1815. For the approximate location with reference to modern places, see J. Neilson Barry, "Early Oregon Country Forts: A Chronological List," *Oregon Historical Quarterly*, 46 (June, 1945), 101-11. For additional information on Kootenae House, see T. C. Elliott, "The Discovery of the Source of the Columbia River," *Oregon Historical Society Quarterly*, 26 (March, 1925), 23-49; for Kullyspell House, see T. C. Elliott (ed.), "David Thompson's Journeys in Idaho," *Washington Historical Quarterly*, 11 (April, 1920), 99, and T. C. Elliott, "David Thompson and Beginnings in Idaho," *Oregon Historical Society Quarterly*, 21 (June, 1920), 54 (this post was abandoned in 1811); for Saleesh House, see Tyrrell (ed.), *Thompson's Narrative*, pp. 411-12, and M. Catherine White, "Saleesh House: The First Trading Post Among the Flathead," *Pacific Northwest Quarterly*, 33 (July, 1942), 251-63. Daniel Williams Harmon, *A Journal of Voyages and Travels in the Interior of North America* (Toronto, 1904), pp. 191-92.

the Astorians, had become hostile. Both the annual overland express in the autumn of 1814 and the spring brigade in 1815 were temporarily halted by Indian opposition, and the spring expedition got through only after a brief battle.[12] Such actions at this vital communications point were a critical threat to the entire Columbia enterprise.

At the established posts, conditions were unpromising. At Okanogan, Ross had hopes of extending the trade into the Cascades to the west, and he set out with an Indian guide upon a reconnaissance in July, 1814. But after a fruitless month in a rugged tangle of mountains and forests, vainly trying to discern the Indian trail his guide insisted they were following, he found neither furs nor Indians, and no feasible short cut to the coast. The promising initial fur returns obtained by the Astorians at Okanogan had seemingly exhausted either the beaver population or the energies of the natives. The Factor in charge during the winter of 1814, complained to Ross Cox that it was "a horribly dull place. . . . The Indians here are incontestably the most indolent rascals I ever met." Cox was soon to find out for himself, for he was transferred there in 1816, and later described the situation at Okanogan. Though upon reflection he saw many attractions to the locale—a climate "highly salubrious," fertile soil, fish in the rivers, plentiful game (grouse, ducks, geese, and deer), and horses upon the plains—and he suggested that the strategic location would make it an ideal spot for a trading town when the country became settled, his recorded experiences were a contradiction. On hot days "dreadful whirlwinds" drove sand and dust into everything, the mosquitoes necessitated smudge pots to make life bearable for men and horses, large packs of coyotes attacked the horses in the winter, and the chief immediate advantage of the specific site was the absence of rattlesnakes on the point of the peninsula. Nevertheless, as the junction of the New Caledonia trail, the post was necessary, and in the summer of 1816 the establishment was rebuilt about a mile from the original site. Three dwellings, a storehouse, and a trading shop were constructed and enclosed with a stockade of palisades fifteen feet high flanked by two bastions with mounted cannons. This transformation of Okanogan from a trading post into a

---

[12] Alexander Ross, *The Fur Hunters of the Far West* . . . (London, 1855), I, 52, 57-58. Ross, like several of the Astorians, joined the North West Company after the Astorian sale. In this second book he recounts his experiences with the British company.

fort was evidence of the growing insecurity of fur-trade relations with the tribes of the Columbia Plain.[13]

There were problems at Spokane also, but they were the reverse of Okanogan: a pleasant location but of little strategic value. The exact context of its founding is unknown. The post was established by an associate of Thompson in 1810 and represented the outermost salient of the probe southwestward through the forested valleys of the upper Columbia tributaries. At that time the exact location of the main Columbia was unknown, and the fur traders probably did not realize how close they were to the edge of the forested zone. In time Spokane House proved to have little functional value. The immediate area was not rich in furs, and the local Indians showed little interest in trapping. Though it became the headquarters and central depot for the interior Columbia posts, it had no water connections with any, and was, according to Ross, "six weeks' travel out of the direct line of some, and more or less inconvenient to all." It was therefore necessary to dispatch large pack trains, yet few horses were available locally, for the Spokane Indians depended upon the Nez Perces for their supply. "Spokane House, of all the posts in the interior, was," Ross insisted, "the most unsuitable place for concentrating the different branches of the trade." Strategic needs suggested removal to the mouth of the Walla Walla or the Snake, but an outcry of opposition protested the dangers of those locations. Ross acrimoniously suggested that other reasons were more compelling:

> Spokane House was a retired spot; no hostile natives were there to disquiet a great man. There the Bourgeois who presided over the Company's affairs resided, and that made Spokane House the center of attraction. There all the wintering parties, with the exception of the northern district, met. There they were all fitted out: it was the great starting point. . . .
> At Spokane House, too, there were handsome buildings: there was a ball-room even; and no females in the land so fair to look upon as the nymphs of Spokane; no damsel could dance so gracefully as they; none

[13] *Ibid.*, pp. 43-52. Ross stated that the Okanogan Indians traded wild hemp to the coastal Indians, who used it for fishing nets, in return for sea shells and trinkets. The condition of the trail, however, pointed to infrequent contact. Ross never states whether he was seeking a new outlet to the sea, but it would seem an object of logical interest, and he later speculated on the possibilities of such an alternate route via the Yakima and Chehalis. Ross Cox, *The Columbia River* (3rd ed.; London, 1832), I, 69, 70-75, 84, 86-89, 238. On the location of the two Okanogan posts, see William C. Brown, "Old Fort Okanogan and the Okanogan Trail," *Oregon Historical Quarterly,* 15 (March, 1914), 1-38.

were so attractive. But Spokane House was not celebrated for fine women only; there were fine horses also. The race-ground was admired, and the pleasures of the chace often yielded to the pleasures of the race. Altogether Spokane House was a delightful place....[14]

Though Ross's sarcasm may have been prompted by his relegation to the dismal monotony of first Okanogan and then Kamloops, his analysis was probably sound, for the proposed removal was quelled.

Roots of the Problem

Such difficulties and attitudes were transforming the Columbia region from a triumphant conquest into an exasperating, costly burden. In large part the trouble was rooted in fundamental differences between the nature of this country and that east of the Rockies, differences which were accentuated by a persistence of established modes of conduct and operations ill suited to the new domain. East of the divide, the fur trade had spread out over a magnificent extent of uninterrupted forested plain interconnected in all parts by a maze of streams and lakes. Such a country allowed a mobility and efficiency of operations basic to the economics of the trade. The Pacific slope was a different kind of land: rugged mountains, impenetrable in winter; unnavigable streams, often so narrowly entrenched in deep canyons as to make it impossible even to follow along the banks; rivers and valley pathways winding among successive ranges; and in the middle of the Columbia country, athwart the main line of travel, a barren plain of simmering heat and dust in summer, a land alien to the north-woods man. Here large pack trains became primary, waterways supplemental, to the movement of men and goods, with a consequent increase in cost, personnel, and trouble, a decrease in speed, flexibility, and simplicity. Even east of the Rockies, the fur trade consumed half its costs in transportation;[15] west of the mountains the outlay threatened the feasibility of the entire business. Moreover, there were important differences other than terrain. The winters, except in the high mountains, were warmer and shorter, which reduced the quality of the furs, while the forest vegetation was more heavily coniferous with but scattered birch, aspen, and willow, which reduced the quantity of beaver.

The large number of personnel necessitated by the extent and

[14] Cox, Columbia River, pp. 180, 182; Ross, Fur Hunters, pp. 137-38.
[15] Harold A. Innis, The Fur Trade in Canada: An Introduction to Canadian Economic History (New Haven, Conn., and London, 1930), p. 246.

mode of operations and the overhead of a Pacific terminal and interior depot placed a heavy burden on subsistence supplies. Here, too, the unique conditions of the area complicated the problem. East of the Rockies the staple food was pemmican, easily prepared, efficiently packed for shipment, with superior preservation qualities and food value. The bison of the northern plains provided the main source, and posts were maintained on the middle Saskatchewan primarily for that purpose. But west of the mountains there was neither buffalo nor an adequate substitute. Venison was used wherever available but could not supply the needs. Moreover, west of the Cascades experience in the Willamette proved that the winters were too damp to dry the meat and too mild to allow its shipment fresh for any distance.[16] The Indian staple in the Columbia region was salmon; dried roots of several kinds, especially the camas, were an important supplement. But the fur men never acquired a taste for roots and except in dire necessity would never consider grubbing about for them in the moist bottomlands. Even salmon was not an obvious alternative. To obtain a supply by trading with the Indians was unsatisfactory; one could never count on a proper quantity or quality, the negotiations were often difficult, and it was poor strategy to become dependent upon the natives for any vital need. Yet to provide their own supply would aggravate the already heavy overhead costs. Moreover, few of the fur personnel were happy about a steady diet of fish. In particular, the Canadian *voyageurs*, who were accustomed to northern whitefish as a supplement, were only content on their prodigious normal daily ration of eight pounds of meat.

A change was not at all a simple matter, for it involved an integrated complex of diet, techniques, and incentives. Pemmican was not only preferred (and buffalo tongue was the standard delicacy), but its preparation was part of a familiar pattern of life, while fishing for and preparing salmon required special skills, and it was drudgery compared with the thrill of the buffalo hunt on the plains. Thus while of necessity making use of fish, and supplementing whenever they could with deer and elk, grouse and geese, the staple for the north men in the Columbia country was horses. And they

[16] There were apparently variations in the recipe, but common pemmican was a mixture of about thirty-five pounds of melted grease and fifty-five pounds of shredded dried meat, blended and packed in leather bags; *ibid.*, p. 303. Franchère, *Narrative of a Voyage*, p. 314.

ate hundreds of them every year, many thousands during their three decades or so of activity in that region. The pack trains of summer became the meals of winter, and a new supply for each post had to be obtained each year. There was a serious flaw in the practice, for not only were they forced to use a large share of their trading goods for horses instead of furs, they became dependent upon the very Indian tribes whose horses provided the self-sufficiency, mobility, and war complex which made them the most dangerous adversaries of the fur network.

And, as the Astorians had found, the Indians west of the Rockies were more a drawback than an aid to the objectives of the trade. Not only did the horse-culture tribes of the southern Columbia Plain sneer at trapping furs to obtain the white man's goods, those with no horses to trade had no pressing incentives. Unlike the Indians of the Canadian north woods, who lived on a bare margin of subsistence in a land of meager resources and long winters remote from richer tribes, the Indians even in the distant interior of the Pacific slope enjoyed a more ample and reliable food supply of fish, game, berries, and roots, had a shorter, less severe winter starvation season, and had long-standing trade relations with both the neighboring horse-culture tribes and the wealthy coastal Indians. Even though some districts were moderately rich in furs, the traders' goods never brought the persistent response achieved in older territories. Moreover, the Columbia traders were dependent upon the Indians rather than the reverse, yet they attempted the same high-handed tactics used east of the Rockies and were always getting into dangerous difficulties through policies of threat and defiance, which rarely worked.

And if old ways persisted in matters of diet and dealings with the Indians, so they did in equipment, though new conditions suggested a change here also. The Astorians had adopted the cedar canoes of the coastal Indians. Strong and durable, such craft could carry three thousand pounds, yet could be portaged and were much safer in rough water. But the North West Company brought in the customary birch-bark "North" canoes, used over all the waterways east of the mountains, with half the capacity and less stability in mountain streams and the swift currents of the Columbia. Moreover, birch was scarce on the Pacific slope. Ross, the former Astorian, was highly critical of the policy and wrote that the Columbia country "was ransacked for prime birch bark more frequently than for prime furs," and the company even had a stock of bark sent from Montreal via London and Cape Horn to Fort George in 1814.[17]

Revisions

The partners of the North West Company were aware of many of these problems. The languishing trade of the Columbia was soon a matter of concern at Fort George and suggestions were made to Fort William. In the autumn of 1815 the annual express from headquarters brought a plan for improvement of the trade. It was decided that New Caledonia would be oriented to the Columbia for both supplies and export of furs.[18] The Columbia country would be divided into two administrative regions, coastal and interior, and the trade was to be extended south toward California and southeast into the Snake country. To overcome the lack of Indian interest in trapping, and to make unnecessary the establishment of numerous permanent posts in new districts, trapping parties of company personnel were to be sent out each year. All furs west of the Rockies were to be brought to Fort George for shipment to Canton. To halt the waste of manpower, only one annual express was to convey documents and personnel across the continent.

A major impact of this new program was to be felt in the interior, and especially in operations related to the Great Plain. Donald Mackenzie, a former Astorian who had led the Clearwater party in 1812, was placed in charge, and after another reconnaissance of the Nez Perces' country in 1816 he set forth a new scheme of operations for the region. His major suggestion was the abandonment of Spokane as "a useless and expensive drawback upon the trade of the interior,"

[17] "North canoes" were used on all routes west of Lake Superior. They consisted of a frame of cedar ribs and longitudinal lath covered with birch bark; a typical example was thirty-two and a half feet long, four feet, ten inches wide in the center but quickly tapered toward each end, and weighed about three hundred pounds; see Davidson, *North West Company*, pp. 216-18. Ross, *Fur Hunters*, p. 72. Some of the preceding contrasts in conditions and difficulties of the North West Company in the area are based upon this section of Ross. The bark shipment was confirmed in Henry's journal—Coues (ed.), *Journals of Henry and Thompson*, p. 903.

[18] Ross, *Fur Hunters*, p. 73. In addition to cost, a compelling reason for this reorientation was the matter of distance related to travel climate: "From New Caledonia it was necessary for the canoes to start from McLeod Lake immediately on the breaking up of the ice and in spite of constant traveling they were caught in the ice on Peace River on their return"—Innis, *Fur Trade in Canada*, p. 234, relating the experience of Harmon conveying furs to Fort William in 1808.

and the erection of a new post in the Walla Walla region. An outcry against this drastic upsetting of old patterns forced a delay. Undaunted, Mackenzie returned to the Nez Perces Indians to arrange further for extension of the trade. He presented his plan again the following spring, and he won his main objective, the establishment of a new post, although Spokane was to be retained.[19]

On July 11, 1818, the building party arrived at the chosen location at the mouth of the Walla Walla River. It would have been difficult to find a more bleak and unattractive site: a barren gravel terrace overlooking the Columbia, but a view blocked on the south and west by basaltic walls, and to the east extending over the drab sandy sagebrush plain of the lower Walla Walla Valley. The almost constant wind, channeled violently up between the black ramparts of the river corridor, drove sand and dust into everything and, as attested by many a journal account, was to imbed itself upon the memories of a host of travelers in subsequent decades. Little wonder that few wished to forego the pleasant valley of the Spokane for such a spot. But Mackenzie was governed by strategy, not beauty, and from that standpoint Fort Nez Perces was superb. Under the Astorians the lower Walla Walla Valley had been the main rendezvous for parties departing for and arriving from the several peripheral districts. The North West Company not only inherited this traffic pattern but had now enlarged its significance by focusing the whole of New Caledonia southward to the Columbia; the intentions of opening up the Snake River country to the southeast would provide added emphasis. Increasing trouble with the Indians necessitated transforming it from an informal rendezvous into a permanent post. It was "the most hostile spot on the whole line of communications," wrote Ross, and it was also the most vital, for all routes converged into the trunk line to the sea. Furthermore, it was a location significant to the Indians themselves as a major meeting and trading ground, and as the site of their first encounter with the whites where Lewis and Clark made an informal treaty of friendship. This was not just another post, therefore, but the key strategic position west of the Rockies.

An uncommonly important and difficult situation called for an uncommon design and structure. The dwellings and storehouse were enclosed inside a twelve-foot wall of sawed timbers; all trade with

<hr />

[19] Ross, *Fur Hunters*, pp. 94ff., 139. For this and the following material on the founding of Fort Nez Perces, see pp. 172-83.

the Indians was to be conducted through a small aperture in this wall. Surrounding this inner cluster was a formidable outer palisade of planks twenty feet high topped by a range of balustrades four feet high, which was served by an encircling gallery. At each corner was a wooden fortified tower and two-hundred-gallon water reservoirs to combat fire. The whole was designed to be defended with cannons, muskets, and pikes. The double wall, an arrangement by which the Indians were admitted only through the outer wall and never into the inner post, was a plan unique among the company's posts at that time. As Ross summarized, Fort Nez Perces was "the strongest and most complete fort west of the Rocky Mountains, and might be called the Gibralter of the Columbia."[20]

He also noted that "to effect the intended footing on this sterile and precarious spot was certainly a task replete with excessive labor and anxiety," the latter rising from the opposition of the natives, which gradually gave way as the traders persisted in carrying out their mission. Meanwhile protracted negotiations were held with the Cayuse Indians for right of passage through their tribal grounds of the Umatilla and Blue Mountains. Once these were secured, preparations were made for the Snake country expedition, a grand departure from common practice. In September, 1818, Mackenzie left his new base at the head of a party of 55 men, with 195 horses and 300 beaver traps, and started across the Plain to the Blue Mountains, picking up the trail of Hunt and Stuart for the upper Snake country. They spent the winter trapping the southern tributaries of the Snake River. They would establish a main camp, and the men would disperse in small parties among the several streams; as the beaver were depleted the main camp would be shifted onward and the parties would follow to another promising area. There was virtually no trade with the Indians. The return in July of the following year was triumphant, for the expedition "made up for all deficiencies elsewhere and gave a handsome surplus besides." Such profits won Mackenzie his point and the praise of the Fort George council; it was agreed that the founding of Nez Perces, the opening of this distant new fur country, and the change in the method of operations were solid accomplishments and that the Snake country expedition should become an annual affair.

Meanwhile, Ross had been placed in charge at Fort Nez Perces and sought to extend the company's operations in the opposite direc-

[20] *Ibid.*, p. 217. The foregoing description is drawn from pp. 214-17.

tion by sending a trapping party across the Yakima country and into the Cascades north of the lower Columbia. The expedition was turned back by hostile Indians before reaching the Cowlitz, and the experiment was not repeated. Nevertheless, Ross suggested that it did provide a good alternative route via the Yakima and Chehalis rivers to Puget Sound should the company for any reason become blocked from the lower Columbia.[21]

The System and Its Legacy

The North West Company monopolized the trans-Rocky country from 1813 to 1821, when it was absorbed by the Hudson's Bay Company. Combining its own positions on the Fraser and upper Columbia with those of the Pacific Fur Company, and orienting the whole to the Pacific, it had actually put into practice the Astorian design (Map 9). Each spring a ship arrived at Fort George with trading supplies, provisions, and miscellaneous needs. These provisions were distributed upon the return of annual interior brigades, which converged on Fort George in the spring with the season's catch. The furs were loaded on the supply ships and sent across to the Canton market. There tea and other Oriental goods were purchased and taken to Britain, completing the global circuit. To convey local reports, letters, and personnel, an overland express made a round trip each year, following the transcontinental thoroughfare up the Columbia across Athabasca Pass, down the Athabasca River to Fort Assiniboine where a long portage (with horses) was made to the North Saskatchewan at Edmonton, thence down that stream into Lake Winnipeg, Lake of the Woods, Rainey Lake, and across to Fort William on Lake Superior.[22] Fort William served as the main

[21] *Ibid.*, pp. 176, 184, 198-99, 211-14.

[22] Typical of the goods used in the Indian trade were the following items included in an initial shipment inland from Fort George in 1814: axes, gun flints, balls, shot, powder, knife blades, metal buttons, needles, thimbles, awls, thread, blankets, flannel shirts, combs, rings, copper and brass kettles, tobacco; as listed in the Henry journal, Coues (ed.), *Journals of Henry and Thompson,* pp. 822-23. Among the goods shipped to the Columbia for use at the posts, some as necessities, some to ease the harsh conditions of life, were such items as: butter, cheese, pickles, sauces, vinegar, sugar, pepper, tobacco, brandy, rum, wine, tea, bar iron, glass, saddlery, fishing gear, soap, firearms and associated equipment, and a great variety of textile and apparel goods; for specific lists of exports from London to the Columbia as listed in customs reports for the years 1814-15, 1817-19, see Davidson, *North West Company,* pp. 221-23.

From 1816 to 1820 the British company worked through American shippers in order to avoid restrictions which the East India Company placed upon other

interior administrative base and depot, and was in direct communication via the Great Lakes and Ottawa River with Montreal, the company headquarters. The Columbia country was thus an integral part of a prodigious network. In this initial commercial development it became oriented to distant and foreign markets, a type of economic dependence which was to persist for much of the area, for a succession of products, through much of its subsequent history.

Because detailed reports of fur returns under North West Company operations are unavailable, any analysis of regional patterns or over-all contributions of the area is impossible. Nevertheless, fragmentary evidence suggests that the Pacific slope, and particularly the Columbia Department, did not yield as expected. Complaints of "indolent" Indians are numerous. Okanogan and Spokane evidently produced very few furs; at Kamloops there were serious problems with the Indians and therefore, no doubt, few furs. It appears that the Kootenay and the Snake country were the only consistently profitable domains, and they, together with the New Caledonia returns, made up the largest share of the total exports from Fort George.

The main legacies of the North West Company's operations were the functional orientation of the Pacific slope to the Columbia estuary, the construction of a key post at the mouth of the Walla Walla, and the inauguration of the Snake country trapping expeditions. Fort Nez Perces was the symbol of the coalescence of key functions at this mid-point of the Great Columbia Plain. Guarding the junction of radial routes with the trunk line, a position of strength at the contact point with dangerous Indians, a convenient center for the procurement of horses, and an advance base for the exploitation of a realm stretching far to the southeast, the erection of this little "Gibralter of the Columbia" was the outstanding move of the North West Company during its tenure on the Pacific slope. Overlaying nature's patterns of streams, scabland channels, and mountain passes with a functional network of operations, the company gave the first visible human imprint to this inhospitable, disagreeable site which was to persist through decades of differing activities. If eight years of experience had proved most of the Columbia country poor in furs, they had also confirmed its importance as a zone of communications.

British ships trading into their chartered monopoly area. Davidson, *North West Company,* p. 165.

The normal schedule for the annual overland trip was as follows: leave Fort George April 1, arrive Fort William July 1; leave Fort William July 20, arrive Fort George October 20. Ross, *Fur Hunters,* p. 304.

> .. for years past I had flattered myself
> with the idea that the loss of the Co-
> lumbia would in reality be of very little
> consequence to the Honble. Coys. in-
> terests . . . but . . . I now, with much
> concern find, it would be ruinous. . . .
>
> GEORGE SIMPSON

Monopoly:
London Rules the Columbia

RATIONALIZING THE SYSTEM

A Questionable Acquisition

WHEN the North West Company was merged into the Hudson's Bay Company in 1821, the fur trade of British America became a monopoly of prodigious proportions: a single operation encompassing hundreds of establishments, thousands of men, and millions of square miles, sprawling from the Atlantic to the Pacific and north to Artic shores.[1] But among its newly acquired territorial assets the venerable "Company of Adventurers of England Trading into Hudson's Bay" viewed the Columbia country with a singular lack of enthusiasm, at best a useful shield to protect New Caledonia, at worst unworthy of retention at all.

"We understand that hitherto the trade of the Columbia has not been profitable," the Governor and Committee wrote their chief American subordinate in early 1822, "and from all that we have learnt on the Subject we are not sanguine in our expectation of being able to make it so in the future." George Simpson, the governor of the Northern Department of Rupert Land, was instructed to

---

[1] The general background, character, and strategies of the companies leading up to the amalgamation are effectively presented in E. E. Rich, *The History of the Hudson's Bay Company 1670-1870. Vol. II, 1763-1870* (London, 1959). The reference map facing p. 248 in that volume, however, has several glaring errors in the Columbia region.

"collect all the information which you can obtain from individuals acquainted with the Country." They suggested that if the losses could be reduced sufficiently, it might be worth retaining, but "should the result of all . . . enquiries be unfavourable to the plan of continuing the trade of Columbia," Simpson should advise as to the most practicable means of disbanding operations.[2] This attitude, so different from that of the North West Company, was based upon two main factors. One was ignorance. The Columbia was a vague and distant realm far beyond the intense struggle over the Red River, Saskatchewan, and Athabasca regions which had absorbed Hudson's Bay Company energies for a decade. When the area fell into company control, there was little more than ledger accounts and rumors upon which to base an evaluation of its significance. Secondly, the North West Company had reoriented its trans-Rocky operations to the Pacific because of the impossible distance from Montreal, its Atlantic export outlet. But the Hudson's Bay Company operated out of York Factory on Hudson's Bay, a thousand miles closer to the fur realms of the interior. The advantage of sending New Caledonia returns to the Columbia port was therefore by no means certain, and it was more logical to try to handle trade along established eastward lines than to plunge into an unfamiliar Pacific operation.

During the year of merger the North West Company established Fort Alexandria on the middle Fraser as an important way station between Okanogan and New Caledonia, designed to improve the Pacific orientation. Despite that fact, the Hudson's Bay Company laid plans to service New Caledonia by way of York Factory, a policy initiated in 1822 to be effective the following year.[3]

The first detailed report on Columbia operations, however, did much to forestall ideas of abandonment. In the spring of 1822, the

[2] R. Harvey Fleming (ed.), *Minutes of Council Northern Department of Rupert Land, 1821-31* (London, 1940), Appendix A, Letter 6, pp. 302-3. Rupert Land referred to all lands draining into Hudson Bay, which was the monopoly of the company according to their charter. Upon amalgamation, North American operations were divided into two large departments. The Southern included in general lands south and east of Lake Winnipeg, the Northern all north and west.

[3] Alexandria was constructed before news of the coalition reached the Pacific slope; E. E. Rich (ed.), *Part of a Dispatch from George Simpson Esqr., Governor of Ruperts Land, to the Governor & Committee of the Hudson's Bay Company, London, March 1, 1829. Continued and Completed March 24 and June 5, 1829* (London, 1947) (hereafter cited as *Simpson Dispatch, 1829*), p. 21, note 2. Fleming (ed.), *Minutes,* pp. 17, 302.

chief trader outlined to Simpson an encouraging prospect: the returns were surprisingly large, the Indians seemed anxious for trade goods, expenses could be lowered by reducing surplus personnel under the new regime, and huge tracts of potential fur country lay yet untapped. Simpson therefore advised his London superiors that "it might be premature to relinquish that Trade. . . ." The next few years confirmed the value of the region. The season of 1822-23 yielded nearly twenty thousand beaver and otter, and in the following year the Columbia became the greatest fur producer among the company's many districts.[4]

Inspection and Reform

The Hudson's Bay Company had fallen heir to a country of unsuspected wealth, yet the costs of operations in that distant realm remained exorbitant, and political tensions and commercial competition of the Oregon country were a vexatious concern which threatened to undermine the entire trans-Rocky system. In 1824, after three full years of control, Simpson observed that "our Council know little about that Country" and had not taken "an enlarged view of its affairs either in regard to political or commercial prospects. . . ."[5] In remedy, he embarked upon a whirlwind inspection tour of the district for purposes of rationalizing the trade. He thereby not only left a profound impact upon every phase of activity, but also a detailed journal account of his actions and impressions, revealing a succession of strategic designs, modified as his understanding of peculiar local conditions increased.

Departing from York Factory (Map 11) on August 17, 1824, Simpson subjected every man, post, portage, and route to piercing scrutiny. Exactly two months later, he struggled across Athabasca Pass through rain, sleet, and snow, and even the indomitable Governor was fully impressed by this, his first contact with mountain country of the far West. The difficulties of scaling such a formidable

[4] Frederick Merk (ed.), *Fur Trade and Empire: George Simpson's Journal, 1824-1825* (Cambridge, Mass., 1931), Appendix A, pp. 176, 184-85, 195, 210-11; Fleming (ed.), *Minutes*, pp. 343-44. He also suggested that a supply ship be sent direct from London rather than working through American shipping as had the North West Company. The 1823-24 results show Columbia returns valued at over £11,000 or nearly 20 per cent of the total. It should be observed, however, that the district was enormous in extent and that Athabasca and New Caledonia were richer producers per size of area.

[5] Merk (ed.), *Simpson's Journal*, pp. 243-44.

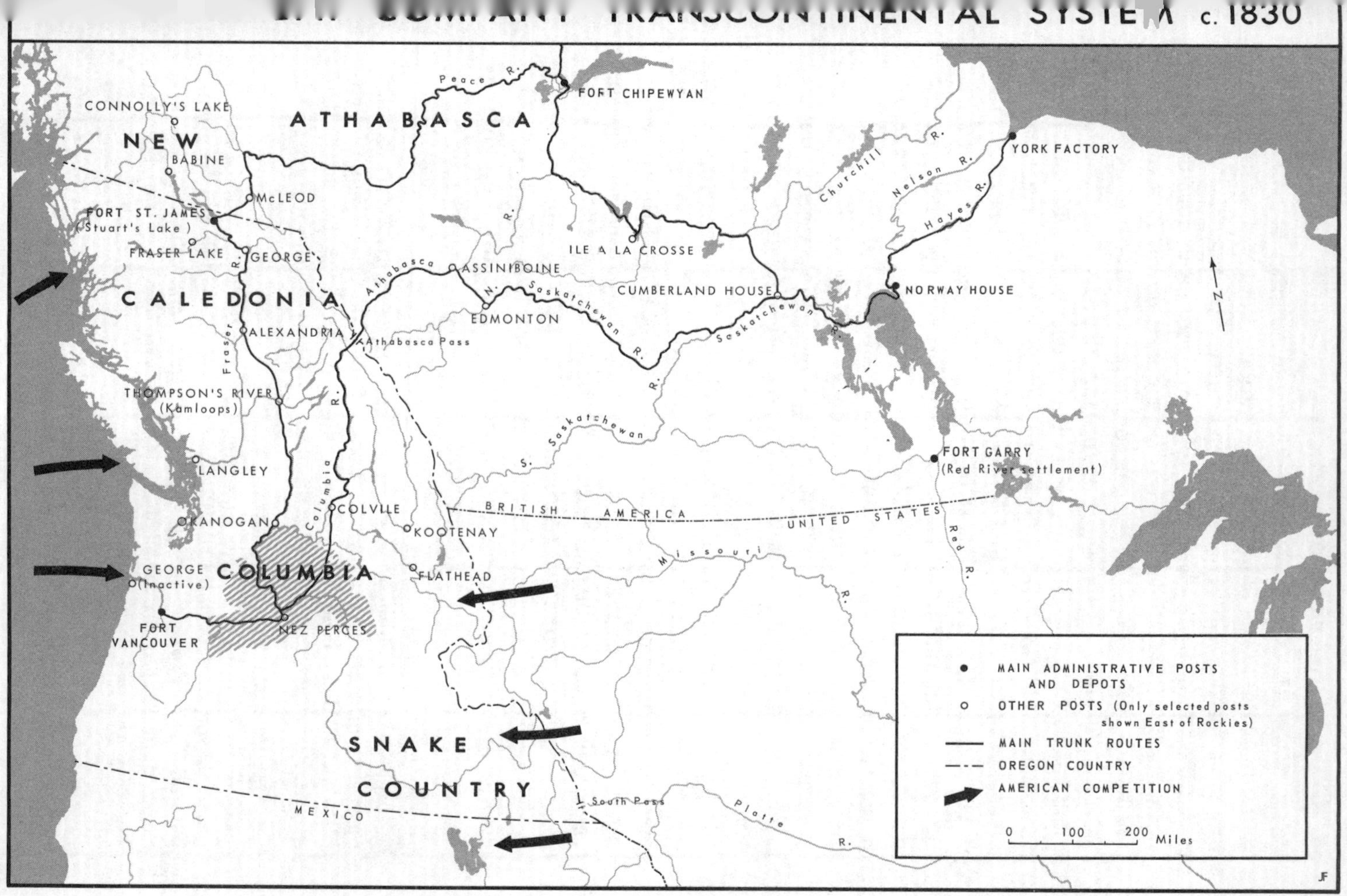
c. 1830
ATHABASCA
NEW CALEDONIA
COLUMBIA
SNAKE COUNTRY
FORT CHIPEWYAN
CONNOLLY'S LAKE
BABINE
McLEOD
FORT ST. JAMES
(Stuart's Lake)
FRASER LAKE
GEORGE
ALEXANDRIA
THOMPSON'S RIVER
(Kamloops)
LANGLEY
KANOGAN
GEORGE
(Inactive)
FORT VANCOUVER
NEZ PERCES
COLVILE
KOOTENAY
FLATHEAD
ASSINIBOINE
EDMONTON
Athabasca Pass
ILE A LA CROSSE
CUMBERLAND HOUSE
NORWAY HOUSE
YORK FACTORY
FORT GARRY
(Red River settlement)
Peace R.
Athabasca R.
Fraser R.
Columbia R.
N. Saskatchewan R.
S. Saskatchewan
Saskatchewan R.
Churchill R.
Nelson R.
Hayes R.
Red R.
Missouri R.
Platte R.
South Pass
BRITISH AMERICA
UNITED STATES
MEXICO
N
MAIN ADMINISTRATIVE POSTS AND DEPOTS
OTHER POSTS (Only selected posts shown East of Rockies)
MAIN TRUNK ROUTES
OREGON COUNTRY
AMERICAN COMPETITION
0 100 200 Miles
JF

Map 11

barrier must have given pause to his paper schemes of reorienting the trade of the Pacific slope toward Hudson's Bay. And once across, Simpson sensed a different kind of country. He noted an "almost incredible" immediate change to towering coniferous forests and a warm, rainy winter climate, and as he voyaged down the Columbia past village after village he began to realize that the mild climate and available resources made the Indians in many cases "perfectly independent of us for any necessary." But he also found some less permanent conditions which "grated like a rasp on his Scotch soul." Every station was overstaffed and overstocked with luxury provisions. With each successive post his indignation mounted at the extravagance, culminating in his arrival at Fort George where, rather than being impressed with the bastions, cannons, and stockades of his Pacific headquarters, he deprecatingly observed that its "air or appearance of Grandeur and consequence . . . does not become and is not at all suitable to an Indian trading post. . . . Everything appears to me on the Columbia on too extended a scale *except the Trade. . . .*"[6]

It was not so much the original cost of the European imports as the expense of transporting them to the posts which was burdensome. In the interior Columbia three or four boats and thirty-five to forty men were kept for the sole purpose of distributing once a year the "Eatables Drinkables and other Domestic Comforts." Such prodigality seemed especially reprehensible in view of the local resources and agricultural possibilities. At post after post Simpson was shocked at the neglect of local subsistence and curtly ordered a change:

At Spokane:
. . . they have an abundance of the finest Salmon in the World besides a variety of other Fish within 100 yds. of their door. . . , Game if they like it, in short everything that is good or necessary for an Indian trader; why therefore squander thousands uselessly in this manner?

At Okanogan:
In regard to Provisions and Luxuries not one oz. is required for this place beyond the established allowance as excellent fish can be got in abundance with little cost or trouble, and at merely the expense of a little ammunition the table of the Gentleman in charge can be occasionally supplied with game.

[6] *Ibid.,* pp. 33, 34, 40, 42, 47, 65. The phrase "grated like a rasp . . ." is from Merk's introduction, p. xix.

At Nez Perces:

As an example of the Waste and extravagance of Provisions some time ago no less than Seven Hundred Horses were slaughtered for the use of this Establishment in three years besides Imported Provisions and it has been left for me to discover that neither Horse Flesh nor Imported Provisions are at all required as the River with a Potatoe Garden will abundantly maintain the Post.[7]

Among the most important of Simpson's reforms was his insistence upon agricultural development in the Columbia. Not only was it prompted by the need to reduce expenses, but also by the favorable reports and impressions he received of the natural conditions. He described the climate of the Spokane area as "delightful scarcely a Cloud to be seen for Months together, little Frost or Snow Some Winters not exceeding a few Days but the Rains Spring and Fall are constant when they set in for about a Fortnight or three weeks at a time; there are occassional refreshing Showers in the course of Summer." The soil at Okanogan impressed him as excellent, producing the finest potatoes and capable of producing plenty of grain if planted. But he found that little had been accomplished anywhere. There was little interest in farming, and it was viewed as a menial task ill suited to the dignity of the fur trader. Simpson had little patience with these attitudes: "It has been said that Farming is no branch of the Fur Trade but I consider that every pursuit tending to leighten the Expence of the Trade is a branch thereof. . . ." He promoted it not only by a virtual embargo on imported provisions, but through an active interest in the conditions and potentials of each post. Thus, on his outward voyage, he determined to "send some Garden and Field seed across next Season to be tried at Spokane House and I feel confident that they will thrive, *Indian Corn cannot fail.*" And on his return upriver he brought—"in order that there maybe no excuse for neglecting the Gardens hereafter"—ten bushels of seed potatoes to Fort Nez Perces, which were delivered to the Factor "with a long lecture on the advantages to be derived from attention to the Horticultural Department of the Post."[8]

Strategic needs prompted the building of two new posts in 1824-25, and in each case the site was chosen with an eye toward agricultural development. Thus, whereas Fort George was judged to have a poor soil and a ground so rough that there were not over fifteen to

[7] *Ibid.,* pp. 47, 50, 52, 128.
[8] *Ibid.,* pp. 49, 50, 128-29.

twenty acres where a plough might be used, its replacement, Fort Vancouver, was located where "a Farm to any extent may be made . . . , the pasture is good and innumerable herds of Swine can fatten so as to be fit for the Knife merely on nutricious Roots that are found here in any quantity and the Climate so fine that Indian Corn and other Grain cannot fail of thriving." Likewise, Fort Colvile at Kettle Falls was selected as a promising farming area which, Simpson noted with obvious exaggeration, could raise enough grain and potatoes to "feed all the Natives of the Columbia and a sufficient number of Cattle and Hogs to supply his Majesty's Navy with Beef and Pork."[9]

Politics and Strategy

With far-ranging perspective and detailed knowledge, harsh admonition and patient advice, Simpson laid the foundations for a remarkable change in the local Columbia fur-trade economy. But despite the importance of such mundane matters, there were larger questions of over-all strategy which demanded his attention. According to the treaty of 1818 Great Britain and the United States were to enjoy equal rights in the Oregon country for ten years. By the time of Simpson's inspection only four years remained, and the question of an ultimate division of this vast portion of the Pacific slope loomed large in the thinking of the Hudson's Bay Company. At the moment the British assumed that the lower Columbia would become the probable international boundary. This inference suggested certain shifts in the company's position in that sector. Thus, even prior to Simpson's departure it had been determined to remove from Fort George to a location north of the river. And, as Simpson recognized upon his visit, the same plan seemed advisable for Fort Nez Perces. The position of Spokane and its tributary posts appeared less vulnerable, for it was thought that the British claim of prior

[9] *Ibid.*, pp. 87, 105, 139. Simpson did report that potatoes, cabbages, and turnips produced excellently at Fort George and that they had accidentally discovered from some sweepings that oats would grow. In a letter to John McLoughlin written upon his return to York Factory, Simpson noted: "Fort Colvile is well adapted for a Farming Establishment. . . . Indian Corn, Pease, Wheat and Barley I am satisfied would thrive there, Potatoes in any quantity may be raised and the country is so well adapted for the rearing of Hogs that I expect he (the factor) will very soon be able to furnish any quantity of Pork we may require." This statement is found in a collection of extracts from original sources labeled "Information Concerning Fort Colville, Washington," on file in the Archives, Library of Washington State University.

occupation was there firm enough to obtain a boundary following the Snake and Clearwater rather than the upper Columbia.[10]

"Our present uncertain tenure of the Columbia" was thus uppermost in Simpson's mind and forced him to develop contingent strategies. If the Americans became established at the mouth of the Columbia, he recommended a shift northward to the Fraser, orienting the interior Columbia to that point via Okanogan and Kamloops. If the coast were relinquished in exchange for British control of the interior, he thought that operations could be maintained as far west as the northern Cascades, with perhaps a shift of Fort Nez Perces to the Yakima country. But such a plan was not Simpson's real hope; his reconnaissance had led him to believe that "the Trade of this Coast and its interior Country is unquestionably worth contending for." He therefore recommended that New Caledonia be reoriented to the Pacific. Because of expense and probable American competition, however, he came out strongly for shifting the main Pacific depot to the mouth of the Fraser River. Dismissing earlier reports of the impossibility of this route as superficial and unreliable, he concluded that "Frazers River appears to be formed by nature as the grand communication with all our Establishments on this side of the Mountain." Supplies direct from England and the Canton market rounded out his design, which, with reductions in personnel and provisions and an energetic expansion of the trade, would bring about a doubling or even trebling of returns and a handsome profit.[11]

Under Simpson's supervision a new site was also selected on the north bank one hundred miles upriver from Fort George, and on

[10] See letter of the "Governor & Committee" dated July 22, 1824, in Merk (ed.), *Simpson's Journal*, pp. 240-42. The claims of the two nations rested upon analogous contacts. Vessels of both countries had entered the river in 1792. Each could claim an early transcontinental traverse—Mackenzie in the north and Lewis and Clark in the south. And each had been represented by fur company establishments: those of the North West Company on the Fraser and upper Columbia, and those of the Astorians on the Columbia and Thompson. The treaty of 1818 recognized the American establishment of Astoria and gave the United States the right to reassert its claim over that site, thus making it doubly urgent for the British to relocate. Merk (ed.), *Simpson's Journals*, p. 59. Curiously, the letters of the London headquarters at this time indicate that they understood Fort Nez Perces to be on the north side, which again suggests how little specfically was known of their trans-Rocky operations. Cf. pp. 240, 242, which speak of the "Establishment at Walla Walla and any other Post of the North Bank of the Columbia."

[11] Merk (ed.), *Simpson's Journals*, pp. 67-69, 71-83, 244.

March 19, 1825, he "Baptised it by breaking a Bottle of Rum on the Flag Staff and repeating the following words in a loud voice, 'In behalf of the Honble. Hudsons Bay Coy. I hereby name this Establishment *Fort Vancouver* God Save King George the 4th' with three cheers." It was a beautiful location of great agricultural promise; its only drawback, the long distance upriver, was dismissed as being of little importance as it was to be a subsidiary post within the contemplated Fraser orientation.[12]

In the interior, the disadvantages of comfortable Spokane—Simpson himself thought it "delightfully situated"—condemned it in the eyes of the economy-minded Governor. A post at Kettle Falls would not only save the cost of the delivering furs and goods over the sixty miles between Spokane and the Columbia, but would also be in a more attractive farming area. On his return east, he personally negotiated with the Indians and selected the site for the new establishment, Fort Colvile, on the south bank just above the portage. An important corollary of the new strategy was the emphasis given to the annual Snake expedition. Initiated by the North West Company as the most practicable means of exploiting a distant fur region, these expeditions, for all their hardship and danger, had brought a major increment to the Columbia fur returns. Economics was now reinforced by politics. Foreseeing the possibility of losing the whole region to the Americans, the company directed that "it will be very desirable that hunters should get as much out of the Snake Country as possible for the next few years." The purpose was not only to reap a maximum profit before relinquishing, but to exhaust the fur resources, thereby creating a buffer zone to shield the British operations on the Columbia. Characteristically, Simpson suggested new strategies. If the expeditions could reach the Snake country by way of the Willamette, Umpqua, and Great Basin, instead of operating out of Flathead Post or Fort Nez Perces, it would not only reduce the overhead at these posts but reduce overland traffic on the Columbia Plain. He hoped to send the Kootenay returns by water to Colvile, rather than overland to Nez Perces, for the same reason: to

---

[12] *Ibid.*, pp. 86-87, 123-24. "The object of naming it after that distinguished navigator is to identify our claim to the Soil and Trade with his discovery of the River and Coast on behalf of Great Britain." John A. Hussey, *The History of Fort Vancouver and Its Physical Structure* (Portland, Ore., 1957), is a beautiful volume with a detailed history and description, illustrated by plans, sketches, and photos, of every aspect of this post.

reduce dependence upon and contacts with what he judged to be the most dangerous Indians on the Pacific slope. "The less intercourse we have with the Nez Perces beyond what is absolutely necessary the better."[13]

In April, 1825, Simpson once more struggled over Athabasca Pass. In six months' time he had instigated changes affecting every aspect of activity in the far Northwest. Though some of his plans were to prove unsuitable—chiefly because he lacked personal knowledge of certain important streams and areas—in total he had worked a revolution and given shape to the Hudson's Bay Company operations in the Columbia country for the next two decades. "We consider that you have acquired a more perfect knowledge of the Indian Trade than perhaps was ever possessed by any one Individual or even by any body of men . . . ," the Governor and Committee congratulated Simpson in 1826, and in recognition increased both his responsibilities and salary.[14]

Their respect was well merited, yet even his "more perfect knowledge" was not free of error. His biggest mistake was selecting the Fraser River as the key to his alternative strategy for the Pacific slope. Fortunately that strategy was not needed, as the position of the company was eased by the breakdown of Anglo-American negotiations and the renewal in 1828 of joint occupancy for an indefinite period. This arrangement favored the British, for they were so well entrenched as to be confident of withstanding competition. Any Americans who encroached upon British-occupied territory were to be undersold, a policy calculated to "damp their sanguine expectations of profit. . . ." The Snake country program was likewise to be pushed with greater vigor to discourage American penetration into that strategic sector as an avenue toward the main Columbia.[15]

In this same year, 1828, Simpson made a second journey to the

[13] Merk (ed.), *Simpson's Journals,* pp. 43-47, 54-57, 134-35, 139, 242; and "Information Concerning Fort Colville," p. 1. For details on the removal of Spokane to Colville, see the several sections of T. C. Elliott (ed.), "Journal of John Work," *Washington Historical Quarterly,* 5 (April, July, October, 1914), 83-115, 163-91, 258, 287; 6 (January, 1915), 26-49. "Colvile" as a place, river, and valley becomes "Colville" after the Americans take control following the boundary settlement of 1846.

[14] Merk (ed.), *Simpson's Journals,* pp. 285-86. Simpson was given charge of the Southern Department and Montreal in addition to the Northern Department, making him Governor of all American operations.

[15] *Ibid.,* pp. 294-95.

Pacific, this time taking pains to examine the Fraser personally. Although his party ran the river in a light canoe, he thought such passage would mean "certain Death, in Nine attempts out of Ten," and he admitted that the Fraser "can no longer be thought of as a practicable communication with the interior" and that "the loss of the Columbia would be ruinous." The finality of that conclusion stabilized the operation on the Pacific. Fort Langley, established near the mouth of the Fraser in 1827, was relegated to a minor coastal post rather than the potential Pacific depot, and Fort Vancouver, now prosperous in agriculture as well as furs, was established as headquarters for all trans-Rocky operations.[16]

Simpson's strategy for the interior likewise failed in some degree. His proposal of sending the Snake expeditions by way of the Willamette, Umpqua, and Great Basin was based upon an inadequate knowledge of streams, distances, and the inhospitable nature of the country, and his hopes for bringing the Kootenay returns to Colvile by water foundered upon the rapids and shoals of the Kootenay River.[17] Thus Fort Nez Perces and the Columbia Plain remained as central as ever to the whole pattern of operations.

THE PATTERN OF OPERATIONS

In general, after 1825 the Columbia Department (Map 12) settled into a stable pattern of activities; a routine adapted to various local conditions which had evolved out of nearly two decades of fur exploitation and now tightened and rationalized by the reforms of the Governor.

The Seasonal Cycle

A marked seasonality was evident in all operations. Winter was the prime season for trapping and trading. In good beaver country, such as at Flathead and Kootenay, it was a busy time; Indians came

[16] *Simpson Dispatch, 1829,* pp. 38-39, 41. New Caledonia, now wholly oriented to the Pacific, became a district within the Columbia Department in 1828. See Fleming (ed.), *Minutes,* p. 187. Simpson, ever the strategist, took the long-range view and began to direct attention to an examination of streams far to the north as a possible outlet for New Caledonia should the Columbia be lost to British control, but the urgency of previous years is lacking; see Merk (ed.), *Simpson's Journals,* p. 300.

[17] E. E. Rich (ed.), *Peter Skene Ogden's Snake Country Journals 1824-25 and 1825-26* (London, 1950), Appendix A, pp. 252-53; also editor's note, p. 60; Elliott (ed.), "Journal of John Work," pp. 186-87.

HUDSON'S BAY COMPANY

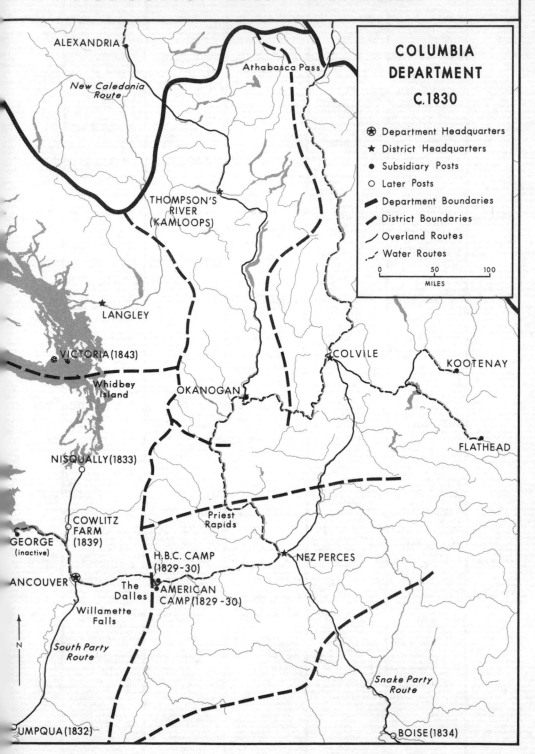

COLUMBIA DEPARTMENT C.1830

⊛ Department Headquarters
★ District Headquarters
● Subsidiary Posts
○ Later Posts
▬ ▬ Department Boundaries
▬ ▬ District Boundaries
╱ Overland Routes
╱· Water Routes

0   50   100
MILES

ALEXANDRIA

Athabasca Pass

New Caledonia Route

THOMPSON'S RIVER (KAMLOOPS)

LANGLEY

VICTORIA (1843)

Whidbey Island

OKANOGAN

COLVILE

KOOTENAY

FLATHEAD

NISQUALLY (1833)

COWLITZ FARM (1839)

Priest Rapids

GEORGE (inactive)

H.B.C. CAMP (1829-30)

NEZ PERCES

ANCOUVER

The Dalles

AMERICAN CAMP (1829-30)

Willamette Falls

South Party Route

N

Snake Party Route

UMPQUA (1832)

BOISE (1834)

Map 12

in to trade, and brief excursions were made into the countryside to contact more distant tribes and to stimulate hunting. Far to the south, the Snake expedition made its slow circuit of the Snake River plains trapping the peripheral streams. In the "route posts," such as Nez Perces and Okanogan, it was a dull period, enlivened only by intermittent quarrels with local Indians, who neither hunted furs nor had any pressing need of the company's goods, but who pestered and pilfered and made a general nuisance of themselves.

In the spring, activity quickened throughout the region. The Snake party, laden with furs and short of provisions, gravitated back toward the Columbia. In the distant outposts of New Caledonia and Kootenay the furs were packed for shipment, ready to move as soon as the ice broke on the rivers or the snow melted on the trails. Sometime in April the winter proceeds of Kootenay would be brought downriver as far as the broad glacial trench (near the present Bonners Ferry, Idaho). From there they were taken overland to the Pend Oreille, where the Flathead returns from the upper Clark Fork were joined, taken a short distance downriver, and then brought over the mountains to Fort Colvile on the Columbia.[18] At Colvile the preceding weeks had been devoted to preparing for the downriver brigade. In May the outbound party departed in a fleet of several bateaux—long, sturdy, cedar-plank boats manned by a crew of eight, capable of carrying over four thousand pounds of furs and provisions. Meanwhile, far to the north similar collections and arrangements had been made, with an energy and timing spurred by the later season and longer distances. Fort St. James (Stuarts Lake) was the entrepôt for New Caledonia. From here furs were sent down the Fraser River in canoes to Fort Alexandria. Then began the overland pack-horse journey of ten to fourteen days to Kamloops and an equal time on to Okanogan. Arriving on the Columbia usually in late May, the New Caledonia party was joined with that of Colvile. As quickly as possible the combined brigade shoved off for the voyage downriver. About a week later the boats reached Fort Nez Perces, collected the local returns, and went quickly on their way, hopefully with sufficient numbers and bravado to defy any

[18] The trail from the Pend Oreille to Colvile was opened by John Work in 1826 to provide a more direct route, made desirable with the shift of Spokane to Colvile. See Elliott (ed.), "Journal of Work," pp. 38-39. Operations in the Flathead and Kootenay outposts varied from year to year and did not necessarily accord with this description as to season and route.

troublesome Indians, in particular at the difficult portage at The Dalles. During the first week or two of June the party arrived at Fort Vancouver, where the Chief Factor received the reports and returns from the interior traders, while the crews and laborers laid siege upon the provisions and amenities of this outpost of civilization. The annual returns of the interior were completed with the arrival of those of the Snake expedition, which was too unpredictable as to route and timing to allow a scheduled junction with the main brigade. These furs usually arrived at Fort Nez Perces in midsummer and were dispatched to Vancouver. Often the brigade brought down extra boats from Colvile and let them at Nez Perces to facilitate prompt shipment of the Snake proceeds.

Spring at Vancouver was a busy season. The annual ship from London usually arrived in March. Its cargo of trading goods, special provisions, and needed equipment was apportioned and packed for distribution to the inland posts. With the arrival of the brigade, the furs were inspected, repacked, invoiced, and loaded on the vessel as quickly as possible for shipment to London. The inland brigade was readied for departure in early July, two or three weeks after its arrival. John Work's description is a useful example of composition, schedule, and experiences. In 1826 the brigade left Fort Vancouver on July 5. Nine boats, each with a crew of six and with five company officers and wives and nine children distributed among them, made up the flotilla. The inbound cargo of trading goods was apportioned as follows:

    60 pieces for Fort Nez Perces
    52 pieces for Thompson's River
    106 pieces for New Caledonia
    72 pieces for Fort Colvile
    1 piece for York Factory (including orders and reports)

In addition, provisions for the brigade itself—corn, peas, grease, and meal—amounted to fifty-seven pieces, and personal baggage, four cases of muskets, and a "trading chest" completed the cargo. After a voyage of nine days the party arrived at Fort Nez Perces. Here they had expected to obtain the sixty or seventy horses necessary for the distribution of goods to the several remote districts. However, as was often the case, none were available, and the Nez Perces Indians refused to trade on the spot, insisting that it be done only on their home grounds to the east. There was no alternative, and while the brigade toiled up the Columbia through the desert, Work and his party headed up the Snake to trade for horses. From the Palouse River on, Nez Perces and Palouses joined the party. They had many horses and made a great game of negotiations, but the price was held high, and they were not anxious to trade; but thirty-two horses were obtained on the upriver journey. Arriving at the Snake-Clearwater junction, the party found two hundred Nez Perces encamped, and in five days they obtained forty-seven more, at considerable cost in trading goods. On July 31 the party drove the seventy-nine horses up out of the deep canyon and headed north across the rolling prairie of the Palouse country. At the site of abandoned Spokane House the animals were apportioned: twenty were taken on to Colvile, fifty-nine were driven west to Okanogan.[19]

At Okanogan, the Thompson River and New Caledonia pieces were transferred from the boats onto the horses and dispatched inland to Alexandria. Some impression of that leg of the journey and of the disadvantages of horses as compared with bateaux may be obtained from a letter written by Father Demers, the first Catholic priest in that area. Although his journey up the Okanogan trail was made several years later (1842), the routine was the same, and he left a vivid description of all the daily "tedium and vexations" of an inland brigade:

This type of caravan is composed of a numerous troup of men and/or horses loaded with baggage and merchandize destined for the different posts of the north. All this grouping of men, horses and baggage natur-

[19] *Ibid.*, pp. 26-49. A "piece" of goods or provisions was analogous to a "pack" of furs: a compactly packed unit of about eighty to ninety pounds. Thus this brigade carried a load of some thirteen to fourteen tons on this upriver voyage.

The previous year Work had gone to the Nez Perces country (to the site of Lewiston, Idaho) and traded for 112 horses which were driven to Spokane and Okanogan to implement the New Caledonia brigade, now once more to be oriented to the Columbia. See Elliott (ed.), "Journal of Work," pp. 83-115.

From Vancouver to the mouth of the Snake, sails greatly reduced the labor of the upriver journey; beyond, however, the change in direction, lessening strength and persistence of the westerly breeze, and depth of the canyon made sails useless and "near the Snake river the masts were hidden in the wormwood to be picked up again the following year." Alexander Caulfield Anderson, "History of the Northwest Coast" (1878 MS, Bancroft Library, Berkeley, Calif.), p. 96.

The price for a horse was generally nineteen to twenty "beaver," meaning that blankets, cloth, beads, and so forth which would purchase that many skins were given for each animal.

ally renders the march slow and wearisome. Each morning's preparations are not finished until nine or ten o'clock. Horses let out haphaz-
ard during the night and scattered in every direction must be hunted
up. After long delays you at last find everything ready, and the neigh-
ing of horses, the shouts of the engagés, the oaths jerked out by impa-
tience, the disputes, the orders of the leaders form a hullabaloo by
which scrupulous ears are not always flattered. At last, after having
eaten on the grass a repast of dried salmon, the horses are loaded, and
at ten o'clock you are on your way. The march is extremely slow and
filled with incidents more or less disagreeable. There is a feverish atmosphere, an oppressive sun, a choking dust, a hill to climb, a rivine
to cross. . . . Good luck indeed if some untoward wind does not force us
to breathe a thick dust which prevents us from seeing two rods ahead
of us. A low buzz of conversation is heard with a monotony only
broken when passing through a creek of a river. Then we draw closer
together, horses hesitate, men shout, get angry, jostle each other, tum-
ble; and often wrecks follow, exciting general hilarity and reviving
conversations for the rest of the day. Halts are made only for camping,
that is to say in the idiom of the country, one only hitches up once;
and the day's travel ends in three or four hours. Then arrangements
are made for camping; the horses are turned loose and sent to pasture
as they can; the baggage is arranged in an orderly manner; men gather
in groups to pass the night; they eat their meal of dried salmon, and
the sun has vanished from the horizon"[20]

This portage to Alexandria usually took about two weeks. From
that point the pieces were sent up the Fraser to Fort St. James by
canoes and then distributed to the outposts by a variety of con-
veyances: ". . . large and small canoes, Horses, Dog Sleds and Men's
backs." The incoming brigade usually did not reach the upper Fraser country until middle or late September, only a short time before
the onset of winter.

In 1826, the remainder of the party reached Colvile on August 7,
twenty days out of Fort Nez Perces. Work was waiting with the
horses, and nine days later departed with a pack train on a quick
trading foray into the Flathead and Kootenay country. On September 10, a single boat continued on for Boat Encampment at the
western terminus of Athabasca Pass. Here eastbound letters and departmental reports would be exchanged for the mail and orders sent
out from York Factory and a quick return made down the Columbia
to Fort Vancouver.

[20] *Notices and Voyages of the Famed Quebec Mission to the Pacific Northwest* (Portland, Ore., 1956), pp. 152-53.

The Snake Country

The Snake country expedition, whether operating out of Flathead, Nez Perces, or Vancouver, was an autonomous operation led by a company officer responsible to Columbia headquarters at Vancouver.[21] Ranging over a vast country, running risks of encounters with American competitors and the dreaded Blackfeet Indians, it was organized as a self-sufficient and flexible venture which varied with the peculiar circumstances of each year. As furs taken in winter were of better quality, the expedition departed in late summer or fall.

From Fort Nez Perces the most direct route to the main trapping grounds was southeastward along the trail opened by Hunt and Stuart of Astorian days. With 250 to 300 horses loaded with supplies, the expedition would move ponderously along, reaching the Snake at the mouth of Burnt River in about ten to fifteen days. From here the broad, sagebrush-covered lava plains stretched out far to the south and east, monotonous, harsh, and dangerous—"a more gloomy Barren looking Country I never yet seen" (Ogden). The Snake River itself, entrenched in a narrow, barren canyon cutting through the middle of the plain from east to west, had no beaver, but around the borders a succession of smaller streams running down from the higher ranges carried strips of birch, willow, and cottonwood out onto the plains margins. These tributary valleys were the rich trapping grounds. As the expedition reached the first of these areas, small trapping parties would be detached into the back country, while the main expedition settled into a fixed camp. As the beaver were exhausted the small parties ranged on ahead, and the central camp shifted to another convenient base. In such manner a circuit around the margin of the Snake River plain was made, tapping the Weiser, Payette, Boise, Big Wood, and Lost rivers, Henry's Fork, upper Snake, Blackfoot, Portneuf, Raft, Bruneau, Owyhee, and Malheur, to name only the larger streams. The expedition was planned to take nearly a year, with the main Snake circuit to be made in winter and early spring. But no real schedule was possible. The beaver returns of any locality were unpredictable, and births, deaths, sickness, lost parties, provision shortages, and a host of other un-

---

[21] Between 1824 and 1831 the Snake expeditions were headed successively by Alexander Ross, Peter Skene Ogden, and John Work; the latter two held the rank of chief trader at the time.

predictable events did much to govern the pace of any particular season.

The dangerous area was the eastern sector, where they might encounter war parties of Blackfeet or American trapping parties, with at times serious dissension and conflict. Yet there were good reasons for venturing that far. Not only was it rich fur country, it was important to exhaust that district in order to destroy its attraction for the Americans. Moreover, despite the heavy load of provisions, it was impossible to support such huge parties for so long a time on imports alone. Buffalo provided an essential supplement, and by this date they were rarely encountered west of the Raft River Valley. Without a successful buffalo hunt, the expedition would experience serious deprivation before the long journey home was complete. Only in extreme situations was it permissible to eat horses, for they were necessary to bring out the furs and the party: ". . . you cannot be too careful *all* depends on them," Ogden cautioned Work in his letter of advice in 1830. Moreover, horses provided no succulent fare, for rough as these expeditions were on men, the horses suffered far more. Work's tally for the 1831-32 party is illustrative:

Started with	289 horses
Traded enroute for	40
Total available	329
Lost and died	75
Stolen by Blackfeet	16
Sold or killed for meat	16
Not accounted for	7
	114
Total on Return	215

The Snake country was thus approached with trepidation by even the most experienced and hardened leaders: ". . . it will alone depend on the success of our hunters and the resources of the Country if any, if we escape starvation and from the poverty of the Country so far as we can judge from appearances we cannot entertain great hopes of escaping may God preserve us." Add to these problems the caprices of nature—heavy squalls, driving sleet, deep snows, bitterly cold east winds, sudden freshets, and quick freezes—and the total rests in full support of Ogden's summation: "What cursed Country is this."[22]

Every expedition tapped the margins of the Snake River plain, but none repeated the exact routes of other years. During the period 1823-32 a huge area was reconnoitered in search of both furs and knowledge of the country. Ogden ranged the farthest: to the Great Salt Lake, to the Humboldt, the Klamath, and Shasta regions, and, in 1827-28, far south through the Great Basin to California. More local areas in the Northwest were also examined with care. In 1825 Ogden took his party downriver from Nez Perces to the Deschutes and worked south and then east up the Crooked River and upper John Day, descending the Burnt River to the Snake; the trapping results were disappointing. In 1831 Work followed the old Lewis and Clark trail east across the Bitterroots and then moved south and recrossed that range into the upper Salmon River region. Here he detached four men in a small canoe to travel down the Salmon. "It is expected they will make a good hunt as this part of the river is not known to have ever been hunted by whites," he noted hopefully; but upon his arrival at Fort Nez Perces four months later he found the treacherous country had taken its toll: the canoe was lost, two men had drowned, the other two had struggled out destitute; no beaver.[23]

Fort Nez Perces

Each post likewise had its own peculiar functions and problems. Fort Nez Perces continued as one of the key establishments, whose general role and features Simpson summarized in 1828:

> This Post has never been very productive, as the country in its neighbourhood is not rich, and the Natives who are a bold Warlike race do little else than rove about in search of Scalps, plunder and amusement. It is necessary however, on many accounts to keep on good terms with them, and to maintain a Post for their accomodation whither it pays or not, as in the first place, they from their numbers and daring character command the main communication; in the next place, our Snake Ex-

---

[22] Burt Brown Barker (ed.), *Letters of Dr. John McLoughlin Written at Fort Vancouver 1829-1832* (Portland, Ore., 1948), p. 128; Lewis and Phillips (ed.), *Journal of Wo,* p. 176. Relatively few horses were killed for meat, but the fact that any were needed in view of the 309 buffalo killed illustrates the tremendous pressure for provisions. In the previous year Work started with 272 horses and returned with 190. Rich (ed.), *Ogden's Snake Country Journals,* p. 108. Ogden's comment was made while headed east from the Crooked River country of central Oregon in the early winter of 1825-26.

[23] Lewis and Phillips (ed.), *Journal of Work,* pp. 140, 176.

pedition usually passes through their Country to its hunting grounds, which they could not do if we were not on good terms with them; in the third place, we depend on them principally for an annual supply of about 250 Horses, and finally, the Trade in Furs altho' falling off pays tolerably well. . . .

This little "Gibralter of the Columbia" persisted as "one of the most troublesome posts (if not the most troublesome) in the Country," yet as McLoughlin also observed, it was necessary to "be Extremely cautious in our proceedings as . . . any trouble at Walla Walla will interfere with the Whole Interior of the Department."[24]

Characteristic of the company's administrative orderliness, each post had a specific tributary area, usually defined in streams and watersheds, the most familiar and convenient landmarks at the time. That of Fort Nez Perces was described by its factor as "From Priests Rapids to the Chutes along the Chutes River to its sources and along the Sources of John Days River to Grand Round from thence to Nez Perces & Louis River." It thus drew upon the entire southern portion of the Great Columbia Plain, plus the Blue Mountains and Wallowa region. It was not much of a fur country, and it is surprising that it paid even "tolerably well," inhabited as it was by Indians who, in the Factor's estimation, were "inconcevbly laizie" in hunting and indifferent about the Company's goods ("except their Necessaries Ammunition Guns Kettles Axes &c."). Beaver were always of primary significance, but like all posts, Nez Perces' complete fur

---

[24] *Simpson Dispatch, 1829,* p. 51; E. E. Rich (ed.), *The Letters of John McLoughlin: First Series, 1825-38* (London, 1941), p. 196, and Barker (ed.), *Letters of McLoughlin,* p. 254. (Unless otherwise indicated, references to Rich's edition of the McLoughlin letters are to the First Series.) Such caution and accommodation of the Indians were well illustrated in the attempt to move the post across the river to the north bank. The London Committee had suggested this action as politically desirable, and Simpson gave the order. McLoughlin sent a party upriver in 1825 to prepare for removal, and when he passed through that autumn, he personally secured the approval of the local Indians. Yet, when the local trader attempted to carry out the plan the following spring, he found that the Indians had decided it would be inconvenient for them, and they were solidly opposed. As he judged that to defy their wishes "would expose it to Great Danger and also the Communication Up and Down the River and Greatly Injure the Whole of the Columbia Trade of the Interior," he deferred action; see Rich (ed.), *McLoughlin Letters,* p. 26. The Committee in London was not happy about this failure and suggested that it would have been wiser to build on the north bank and maintain two posts temporarily. However, as the prospect of a boundary settlement diminished they did not press for such action. See Merk (ed.), *Simpson's Journals,* p. 287.

returns showed a wide variety of skins and considerable fluctuation from year to year as to species:[25]

Fort Nez Perces Returns	1830	1831	Fort Nez Perces Returns	1830	1831
Badger	—	39	Lynxes	68	75
Bears, black	4	15	Martens	5	—
brown	26	40	Minks	41	9
grizzly	1	7	Muskrats	717	808
Beaver, large	531	541	Otters, land	85	80
small	243	227	Raccoons	8	80
Fishers	35	32	Wolverines	11	3
Foxes, red	44	28	Wolves	18	229
cross	4	8			

Such furs were almost entirely the product of the Indian trade, as no local expeditions or detached winter outposts were maintained. A chief factor or clerk and five or six men were therefore a normal staff throughout the year. Their main duties were to keep the peace with the Indians, give local assistance to the passing brigades, help organize equipment and supplies for the annual Snake expedition, and to trade for and look after the horses. Fort Nez Perces was the only post west of the Rockies in direct contact with the main "horse-culture" Indians, and therefore procurement of horses was its main economic function. Orders perennially came upriver to "please trade all the Horses you can," and there was reiterated concern that not enough were available.[26] To provide the 100 to 250 head a year needed to reconstitute the several interior parties was a major responsibility, and a difficult one. Ever since Astorian days the Indians had capitalized on the importance of their herds, and this cut deeply into the fur returns, as the Indians obtained most of the trading goods they needed in exchange for horses rather than beaver.

Despite Simpson's admonitions and lecture on horticulture in 1825, little was accomplished toward building a local food supply at Nez Perces. Five years later McLoughlin noted that a harvest of

[25] "Report of Nez Perces District (1827)," Appendix A, *Simpson Dispatch, 1829,* pp. 221-22; "Fur Trade Returns—Columbia District & New Caledonia, 1825-57" (MSS in the Archives of British Columbia, Victoria). These beaver totals are only about half of those for 1827 and 1829, suggesting that Simpson's comment on the profitability of this district might not apply to the 1830 and 1831 catch.

[26] Merk (ed.), *Simpson's Journal,* p. 270; Barker (ed.), *Letters of Mc-Loughlin,* pp. 52, 95, 173, 189, 193, 195, 206, 279.

twenty-five bushels of corn at least proved that it could be grown there. In 1830 a request for seed potatoes and a plough indicate continued interest, but even McLoughlin, as ready as his superiors to promote any kind of activity contributing to reduction of expenses, held but meager hopes and suggested that a hoe would suffice and that "corn Pumpkins and Potatoes is all I would advise you to cultivate at Walla Wala." Curiously, the Cayuse Indians were anxious for cattle, and four calves were sent up from Vancouver in 1831 with the hope that they "will be gratifying to your Indians to see on their lands." An inquiry as to whether some ought to be sent for the post itself brought no immediate response; later "two heifers and a bull, and a few goats" were offered, apparently in answer to a request from the fort. But it is clear that such limited efforts did little to meet provision needs even of the local staff, and contributed nothing to the requirements of major expeditions and passing brigades. At such a traffic point the "comers and goers" cut heavily into stocks, and bags of flour, peas, corn, and meat were often ordered down from Colvile to replenish the supply. In return, Fort Nez Perces served as a minor depot for equipment and trading goods which could be forwarded to other inland posts when necessary. Such an establishment was a burden, but clearly a necessary one, "whither it pays or not."[27]

Posts Upriver

Upriver, the old pioneer Astorian fort at Okanogan now functioned as an outpost of the Thompson River district, subsidiary to Kamloops (formerly She-Whaps). The district limits embraced a huge tract extending from the Wenatchee River nearly to Athabasca Pass and west to the Fraser River, but, as the Kamloops Factor lamented, "alas he [the beaver] is but rare enough considering the extent of country." In 1824 Simpson had considered abandoning the entire district, but he held out hope that a drastic pruning of personnel and wages together with better management might put it on a profitable footing. His 1828 visitation, however, proved how ill-founded were these anticipations, and Simpson was forced to dismiss Kamloops as a "very unprofitable Establishment," the country being poor in furs and the natives "exceedingly indolent"; Okanogan was even worse: "...the few skins it yields are not worth naming." There had been a rapid decline in the fur returns since his last

[27] Barker (ed.), *Letters of McLoughlin*, pp. 3, 130, 173, 179, 189-90, 201, 236.

TABLE 1

HUDSON'S BAY COMPANY BEAVER RETURNS*

	1826-30	av.	1831-35	av.	1836-40	av.	1841-45	av.	1846-50	av.
Fort Nez Perces	5,913	1,183	7,136	1,427	3,669	743	1,995	399	1,222	244
Fort Colvile	15,638	3,128	14,492	2,898	10,181	2,036	5,362	1,072	3,735	747
Thompson's River	4,867	973	5,321	1,064	3,513	703	1,462	292	421	84
Total Columbia Interior	26,418	5,283	26,949	5,389	17,363	3,472	8,819	1,763	5,378	1,075
Fort Vancouver	17,646	3,529	13,178‡	3,294‡	12,178	2,436	8,896	1,779	4,421	884
Snake Party	7,649†	2,550†	2,662§	665§	9,573	1,915	8,852	1,770	3,271	654
New Caledonia	34,537	6,907	35,630	7,126	24,863	4,973	17,680	3,536	17,629	3,526
TOTAL	86,250	18,269	78,419	16,474	63,977	12,796	44,247	8,848	30,699	6,139

* These figures refer to the number of large and small beaver only, compiled from the detailed statistics in "Fur Trade Returns—Columbia District & New Caledonia, 1825-1867" (MSS in the Archives of British Columbia, Victoria).

† Snake party returns for 1827 and 1829 not given.
‡ Fort Vancouver returns for 1835 not available.
§ Snake party returns for 1833 not available.

contact, for which the local Factor had "no other pheasable way of accounting, than the Beaver run on the verge of extermination." Yet, again, it was necessary to maintain the establishments. Okanogan, with few Indians and very few furs, continued as the terminal of the New Caledonia trail and was the abode of two or three men for the purpose of "Watching Boats, Horses, Provisions &c. left here from time to time" at this route junction. The "compact and well palisaded Fort" at Kamloops was a more sizable affair, occupying the mid-point on the overland trail connecting Columbia to Fraser navigation. Although the Indians were peaceful at this time, past experience suggested the importance of keeping a considerable staff in order not to "appear too contemptable before them," as the Factor put it. About a dozen men were therefore attached, with duties geared to the annual overland brigades and the responsibility for 250 to 300 pack horses. Again, maintenance expenses were high, as little local produce was available. Whether gardens were cultivated at this time is not clear, but the Kamloops Factor's observations about "the intense heat and constant drought of the interior of the Columbia" and that "very little can be said in favour of the Soil," suggest that little was attempted.[28]

Fort Colvile was the one place in the interior where Simpson's plans and hopes were largely fulfilled. Its location on the Columbia facilitated shipments and reduced costs by a large measure over the old Spokane system. Although Colvile itself was not too productive in furs, the Flathead and Kootenay countries continued to yield well, often accounting for half or more of the total interior Columbia returns, including the Snake country (Table 1). The Americans at times intruded into the Flathead region, but the Governor was confident that the combination of stiff competition plus severe clashes with the Blackfeet would soon end such encroachment. Best of all was the success of the Colvile farm. The first sowings of wheat and corn in 1826 yielded poorly, but other crops did well, and in following years the farm flourished with grain, vegetables, and livestock.[29]

---

[28] "Thompson River District Report, 1827," Appendix A, *Simpson Dispatch, 1829*, pp. 224-26, 230, 232; *Simpson Dispatch, 1829*, pp. xxx, 30-31, 50; Merk (ed.), *Simpson's Journals*, pp. 30, 52, 131, 247; "Fur Trade Returns." Okanogan usually accounted for only one-fifth of the annual total for Thompson's River shown in Table 1.

[29] *Simpson Dispatch, 1829*, pp. 47-50; "Information Concerning Fort Colville," p. 3.

This agricultural productivity was important to the entire Pacific operation; from 1828 on it supplied all the provisions for the interior posts, allowing a reduction of thirty men formerly employed in transportation from Fort George or Vancouver, and giving a much-needed increase and reliability to the subsistence. Thus the records of routine activities in the Columbia Department are replete with requests that Colvile "please furnish Thompsons River with Seven Bags flour"; "please forward to Walla Wala ten Bags Indian Corn"; "please forward all the provisions you can to Okanogan." Such orders related not only to local needs but to the major annual demands of the New Caledonia brigade and the Snake expedition. The value of this farming station was underscored in the spring of 1832 when the failure of the salmon runs the previous year left all New Caledonia desperately short of food. Upon receipt of the news, McLoughlin was able to provide relief simply by ordering twenty horses with provisions from Colvile. With its outposts, farm, and transport functions, Colvile was a busy and important post. The usual complement of a dozen or more men included several skilled in boat making, as the post also furnished the interior with the new boats needed for the brigades and express.[30]

These were the permanent posts related directly to the Columbia interior. In the winter of 1829-30 a temporary post was established at The Dalles solely to counter American competition, and it was withdrawn immediately upon the removal of that challenge. McLoughlin found his Columbia Department involved in a two-front commercial war with the Americans, though the two attacks were sporadic and completely uncoordinated. On the one hand there were the encroachments of American trapping parties beyond the Rockies into the Snake and Flathead regions, on the other were the American ships which cruised the Pacific coast and its waterways.

The most disturbing intrusion—for this the Hudson's Bay people felt it to be, though politically the Americans had a right to move freely about the whole Oregon country—was on the lower Columbia, where New England captains sailed up the river, even to limits of navigation at the Cascades, anchoring here and there en route to

[30] *Simpson Dispatch, 1829,* p. 49; Barker (ed.), *Letters of McLoughlin,* pp. 88, 108, 122-23, 132, 199, 263-64, 271. "It is necessary that twenty-four Bags Corn be sent to Okanogan for New Caledonia and a sufficient quantity to take Back the Brigade from Walla Walla to the Interior and Sixty Bags to remain at Walla Walla for the use of that post and of Mr. Ogden and party (Snake party)." Barker (ed.), *Letters of McLoughlin,* p. 8.

trade with the Indians. Alarm was warranted not only over the loss of skins, but, even more important, over the complete upsetting of the terms of trade. Whereas under monopoly conditions the British held to a standard of five beaver for one blanket, American competition reduced this to one beaver per blanket. If confined to one sector this scale might not prove especially destructive of the company's profits, but if applied to the whole Pacific slope the result would be disastrous. Thus McLoughlin insisted that the interior posts, especially Fort Nez Perces (the nearest to the coast and therefore most vulnerable), hold to the old terms, even if some Indians came downriver to seek a better deal. In September, 1829, when an American and two helpers were detached from a ship and sent to The Dalles to set up a trading camp, the British countered by establishing a party opposite on the north bank and began trading on the same cut-rate terms. The move was successful, for the following spring the Americans withdrew; the British then did likewise and the Columbia interior was once more insulated from commercial attack.[31]

Operating the System

Aside from such major but temporary disturbances, the Hudson's Bay Company operations in general followed these routines of movement and function during the years 1826 to 1832. A view in greater detail would disclose many additions and variations to each activity from season to season, year to year. The letters of McLoughlin give an idea of the daily details of administering this vast department. From his comfortable Vancouver headquarters he directed the strategy, evaluated the problems, and transferred materials from post to post with the changing needs of the moment. Men were ordered from one duty to another through the courteous, formal letters of the Chief Trader: "... please ... furnish men to complete the crews of three Boats ..." [Kamloops]; "I send you two Owhyees and a Canadian ..." [Colvile]; "you may keep an additional man to enable you to Collect all the wood necessary to build up your Fort ..." [Nez Perces]. Horses, too, were almost constantly being shifted about to meet special circumstances: "... if you have any Horses to spare you will send them ... to Walla Wala ..." [Colvile]; "I wish they bring ... two saddle Horses from Okinagan to Colvile where they are to remain till further orders ..." [Colvile]; "the horses we

[31] Barker (ed.), *Letters of McLoughlin,* pp. 57, 60, 71, 92, 103.

have here will not be able to thrash our grain so that if you find you can dispense with any it will be well to send them . . . [Nez Perces]. All sorts of trading goods, equipment, and supplies were likewise apportioned: "Mr. Ross will leave the two cases of Beads and Bag of Ball at Walla Walla . . .;" "Take . . . to Colville 1 Case Guns, 1 Bag Nails and plow share, Junk, 1 Bale, Iron Works for the Mill"; "Please deliver . . . four Bags Ball, two Bags Shot and one Keg powder (for Colvile District) out of the Depot at Your place" [Nez Perces]; "If you can not use your Bolting Cloth will you please send it to us by the Express Boat this Fall . . ." [Colvile]. And when occasionally the interior demands could not be fulfilled from the Vancouver supplies, McLoughlin would pen a courteous apology: "I am sorry to say our stores will not admit our fulfilling your requisition . . ." [Kamloops]; "I am sorry we have no Green beads . . ." [Nez Perces].[32]

A Summary View, ca. 1830

These transactions, selected to illustrate operations in the Columbia interior, are representative of the Hudson's Bay Company system over the entire Columbia Department, an imperial domain of impressive dimensions reaching from the waters of the Peace River to and beyond those of the Humboldt deep into the Great Basin, and from the Continental Divide to the islands, bays, and estuaries of the Pacific coast. Physically it was a varied holding: north-woods country of dense bush laced with streams and lakes; the interior plateau and valley region of long, narrowly entrenched lakes and open pine forests; the dense woods and high meadows of the rugged Kootenay and Flathead area; the rain forests of the fog-bound coastal fringe; the deserts of sand and rock, dry lake beds and foul-tasting streams, sparsely clothed with sage and dry grasses; and central to all, the broad, treeless, undulating Columbia Plain with its great rivers coursing through the lava platform. A country varied in animal life: from north-woods wolverines to coastal sea otter and desert coyotes; moose and buffalo, elk and antelope; rich fur country and poor fur country, but everywhere, in some quantity, the beaver, the mainspring of all endeavor.

Mainland operations secured over eighteen thousand beaver pelts in 1830 and made the once disparaged Columbia equal the catch of all the remaining Northern Department. In that year, fifteen posts

[32] *Ibid.,* pp. 2, 3, 14, 99, 113, 115, 122, 125, 196, 213, 235, 270.

and one major annual expedition were maintained, operated by twenty-seven commissioned gentlemen and several hundred men— interpreters, mechanics, guides, *voyageurs,* laborers, and trappers. Operations were divided into six districts, each with a headquarters post, some with subsidiary establishments; in addition, the Snake expedition and the coastal shipping activities were under separate management and carried under special accounts. Staff complements for winter arrangements 1830-31 were as follows.[33]

District and Posts	Commissioned and Special Staff	Total Men
Fort Vancouver	1 chief factor 1 chief trader 3 clerks 1 surgeon 1 postmaster	89
Fort Colvile Flat Heads	1 chief trader 1 clerk	28
Containais (Kootenay)	1 interpreter (in charge)	
Thompsons River (Kamloops) Okanogan	1 clerk 1 laborer (in charge)	17
Fort Nez Perces	1 chief trader	6
Fort Langley	1 chief trader 1 clerk	15
Snake Expedition	1 chief trader	30
Shipping	4 ship captains	?

[33] "Fur Trade Returns." The Northern Department was, however, considerably richer in small furs; e.g., 234,000 muskrats compared with 18,000 from the Columbia. See Table 1 for summary statistics. Barker (ed.), *Letters of McLoughlin,* pp. 344-45, has an excellent summary description of the several ranks within the Hudson's Bay Company hierarchy. Posts and commissioned and special staffs are from Fleming (ed.), *Minutes,* pp. 262-63. The number of men for each district is from Barker (ed.), *Letters of McLoughlin,* p. 95, which gives no figures for New Caledonia or Shipping. Colvile's complement was unusually large because of extra men sent to build a stockade.

District and Posts	Commissioned and Special Staff	Total Men
New Caledonia		?
Stuarts Lake	1 chief factor 1 clerk	
Frasers Lake	1 chief factor 1 clerk	
McLeods Lake	1 clerk	
Alexandria	1 chief trader	
Babines	1 clerk	
Connolly's Lake	1 clerk	
Fort George	1 clerk	
"Disposable" (surplus)	2 chief traders 4 clerks	

Through the strenuous reforms and innovations of Simpson, the department was largely self-sufficient. The prosperous farms of Vancouver and Colvile supplied provisions to supplement the local produce of gardens, streams, and the hunt. Sawmills, blacksmith forges, and carpenter shops provided materials for repairs and expansion of buildings and equipment. Nez Perces recruited the horses; Vancouver, Colvile, and New Caledonia built and repaired the boats and canoes. Pack saddles, bags, cord, and lodges were shaped from the hides of buffalo, elk, deer, and horses. The only essential imports were the arms, ammunition, and trading goods—cloth, beads, kettles, knives, and trinkets.[34] The "Company of Adventurers" had fashioned an impressive, efficient, and profitable empire on the Pacific slope.

Lying near the center of this vast department, the Great Columbia Plain was caught up into its activities. Along its arteries of river and trail, the life of this intricate system throbbed with the movement of men and horses, provisions, supplies, and documents—an

[34] Because of its location and the shortage of buffalo west of the Rockies, New Caledonia did import some goods—moose skins, pack cords, pemmican, and so forth—from the Saskatchewan-Athabasca region. These supplies were annually assembled at Dunvegan for transport westward; Fleming (ed.), *Minutes,* p. 264.

erratic pulsation, varied by season and circumstance. The entire interior was bound up with this region. Far-off New Caledonia drew upon and through it, posts of the near periphery were in constant contact with it, the Snake expedition was based within it, and at its barren center Fort Nez Perces represented in form and function the importance of the Plain to the over-all system.

The Hudson's Bay Company of 1830 represented the culmination of two decades of efforts to organize the Columbia country. It was more than just an economic system to be measured by profits and losses, it was a strategic system—with forts, garrisons, and logistic lines, and contested, unstable frontiers—a system to be evaluated also in terms of success and failures in the control of area. And, momentarily, it was a way of life, of daily, seasonal, and annual routines, adapted to the special circumstances of each specific locality. Yet upon the Great Plain, it was all temporary, its roots were shallow, for the human occupation of the land was dependent wholly upon circumstances extraneous to the region itself: upon the furs of distant districts, the ports of the coastal fringe, and the political temper of remote governments. People were here, in posts and camps, moving upstream and down along the old Indian trails and the scabland channels, yet they were here only on assignment, put here, not attracted. In short, in all these twenty years, no one had built a home in this land; no one had settled down to deal with the Great Columbia Plain on its own terms for its own resources.

CHAPTER FIVE

> The remote region of Oregon, appears
> at present as if on another planet.
>
> WILLIAM DARBY

Matrix:

American Visions and Ventures

VISIONS

Plans for Oregon

MR. EDWARD BATES of Missouri had the floor: "As yet, we know little of the geography of that extensive country," he argued, "and almost nothing of its topography and geological peculiarities." And thereby at least one accurate statement was placed in the long record of debate that December day in 1828, as the second session of the Twentieth Congress considered the question of Oregon. The bill at hand, proposing the establishment of an American military post at the mouth of the Columbia, unleashed a torrent of verbal conflicts. Pro and con the orations waxed with equal argument and eloquence; there was little middle ground. Bates was strongly opposed, but, more candid than most, admitted to a paucity of reliable information. A colleague, Mr. John Taylor of New York, formalized his suggestion into an amendment which would direct the President to

> Cause an exploring expedition to be organized and executed, to consist of not more than eighty persons, including a corps of geographers and topographers, for the purpose of collecting information in regard to the climate, soil, natural productions, civil and political conditions, harbors, and inhabitants, of the territory of the United States west of the Rocky Mountains.

It was the most reasonable proposal of the day, but when the roll was called neither the amendment nor the original bill was passed.[1]

[1] *Register of Debates in Congress,* 20th Cong., 2nd sess. (1828-29). The Oregon debate covers pp. 125-53, 168-75, 187-92; Bates's statement, p. 151; Taylor's amendment, p. 153.

The Columbia country thus remained unoccupied and largely unknown by the Americans, despite the fact that legally they held equal rights with the British. But while Congress might block official action, it could not legislate against interest and agitation. Indeed, the issue of 1828 was far from new; for a decade there had been recurrent schemes for American action toward that distant Pacific frontier. While the Hudson's Bay Company rationalized its Columbia system and settled down into a complacent monopoly, a current of American interest throbbed sporadically among a vociferous minority of varied aspirations and designs. There were, of course, strong reasons for continued interest. The journeys of Lewis and Clark were a proud achievement and still fresh in mind. The Astorian venture, though its full story was untold to the public, remained a smarting memory of defeat. The negotiations with the British in 1818 and 1828 had both momentarily necessitated direct political concern and had resulted in a protracted compromise, which must eventually be resolved. And all the while, New England ship captains and Rocky Mountain trappers covetously probed the seaward and landward margins of a domain which was as rightfully American as British.

There were reasons, also, which had no direct relation to Oregon conditions and events. The debate over schemes for the occupation of the Columbia was befogged in the first flush of "manifest destiny," of expansion as the inevitable, God-given destiny of the United States. An interlocking, overlapping, and at times contradictory set of arguments, buttressed by historical and statistical evidence, was marshaled in support of the central theme, which found perhaps its most succinct expression in a retort of Congressman Francis Baylies: "Gentlemen are talking of natural boundaries. Sir, our natural boundary is the Pacific Ocean." The opposition relied heavily upon matters of distance, physical barriers, and antithetical commercial orientations. To point out that everything east of the Rockies was "Atlantic country" and could not possibly be tied by effective bonds of commerce and mutual interest with "Pacific country" was a telling argument for many. Others emphasized the awesome inhospitality of western lands—"mountains almost inaccessible . . . skirted with irreclaimable deserts of sand"—which nature had "kindly interposed as our Western barrier."[2] Such arguments rever-

---

[2] *Annals of Congress,* 17th Cong., 2nd sess. (1822-23), cols. 682-83. An excellent reference for such conflicting views is the collection of reprints with ac-

berated, and indeed thrived, in a near vacuum of facts about the actual nature of Oregon itself. But ignorance was no deterrent to those who wanted to establish an American hold upon that distant corner.

The first comprehensive program was that offered by Congressman John Floyd of Virginia, who was chairman of a committee "to inquire into the situation of the settlements upon the Pacific Ocean, and the expediency of occupying the Columbia River." The first Floyd Report of January, 1821, was optimistic about both the value to be derived from and the practicability of a transcontinental fur operation for the gathering of Oregon profits. A Missouri-Columbia route was proposed, with principal forts to be established near the upper bend of the Missouri (Mandan area) and at the mouth of the Columbia. A single "portage of only two hundred miles" connected the Great Falls of the Missouri to the Clark Fork of the Columbia, and the labor of ten men for twenty days would be sufficient "to enable a wagon with its usual freight to pass with great facility," for the Rocky Mountains were in many places "smooth and open." Floyd proposed the occupation of an area near the mouth of the Columbia by agricultural colonists and the establishment of a port, customs house, civil administration, and Indian agents; and he drew up a program for the careful regulation of the fur trade.[3]

For all its sincerity, the Floyd Report and Bill set a pattern of fantasy which proponents of American action perpetrated for years.

companying commentary by Archer Butler Hulbert, *Where Rolls the Oregon: Prophet and Pessimist Look Northwest, 1825-1830* (Colorado Springs and Denver, 1933). The foregoing paragraph was drawn specifically from the reprinted speeches in Congress of Mr. George Tucker, pp. 54-58, and Mr. Albert Tracy, pp. 58-71.

[3] Floyd's interest in such remote matters was derived from a close friendship with William Clark and perhaps sustained by the memory of his cousin's grave in distant Dakota, where Sergeant Charles Floyd had died as a member of the outbound Lewis and Clark party. *Ibid.*, pp. 41-47. 16th Cong., 2nd sess., H. Rept. 45 (1821), p. 11. *Annals of Congress*, 16th Cong., 2nd sess. (1821), cols. 958-59; also reprinted in Hulbert, *Where Rolls the Oregon*, pp. 45-49. The debate over the Floyd Bill carried on into the next Congress and the attractiveness of the lower Columbia was further supported by the publication of another report, written in 1818 and based upon Astorian information, which spoke favorably of the ingress and anchorages of the estuary and of two navigable streams "which disembogue opposite to each other within twenty-five leagues of the port" (Willamette and Cowlitz); 17th Cong., 2nd sess., H. Ex. Doc. 45 (1823).

Floyd's Missouri-Columbia route was derived from Lewis and Clark, but its easy practicability could not have been established by even the most careless reader. The "smooth and open" Rocky Mountains may well have been based upon a shred of Astorian experience, but what of the country beyond South Pass? Floyd's horizon lay on the Pacific, but if his mind's eye could see that distant shore, all intervening was a mirage, which obliterated mountains and deserts, distances and difficulties. The unreality of his program for the fur trade begins with its restriction to those of "approved moral character" and culminates in the scheme to legislate into being an orderly, agricultural Indian population served by government-constructed grist mills. Floyd's bill, with modifications, after a stormy career through several congressional sessions, was defeated on March 1, 1825.

Ironically, the debate had so stimulated interest that, despite an adverse decision, it insured a continued and heightened concern over Oregon. In the next year the Baylies committee, whose chairman had supported Floyd, examined in detail the nature of the far Northwest region and further argued for the necessity of American occupation. Although imbedded in a mixture of motives—embracing Pacific commerce, whaling, and the need to grab this last great ocean arena from the ever extending tentacles of the British—the Columbia fur trade continued to be a major objective. A more comprehensive strategic occupation than that of the earlier report was proposed. Mr. Baylies recommended that small military posts be established at the mouth of the Columbia, the Multnomah (Willamette) junction, the Great Falls (The Dalles), on Lewis's River (exact location unclear, probably at confluence with the Columbia), and on Clarke's River "somewhere on the elevated plain bordering on the Rocky Mountains." Such a system, he confidently assumed, would "overawe all the Indians on the waters of the Columbia, and secure a monopoly of trade." It was a fine scheme, but it overlooked one matter: not a word in the report suggested that the Hudson's Bay Company had established posts at or near several of these locations, held a rather firm monopoly, and might not be so easily overawed. The omission was hardly excusable, for two years earlier a Senate document had given at least some indication of the British system, relating that the company had four posts: " . . . one at the mouth of that river, one near its junction with Lewis's River, one near the mountains convenient to the *Flathead* Indians, and one

other higher up." But such reliable information was as readily ignored as unreliable information was accepted in order to buttress
the argument.[4]

Congressional interest persisted, and new compilations of information on the fur trade continued to appear. But a gradual change
in tone begins to suggest that the experiences of American traders
in the zones of contact with the British had undermined the confidence of earlier years. The British success (and tantalizing figures
of Hudson's Bay Company profits were often cited) was seen to rest
upon some rather solid advantages, which the Americans were unable to duplicate. The problem of trading goods recevied greatest
attention, for a few years of experience had shown that the Indians
preferred British goods and refused American substitutes. Furthermore, American free enterprise had proved decidedly inferior to the
British monopoly. The Americans at times created a chaos of competition among themselves, which resulted in an alarming instability
of prices and profits and ugly unregulated relationships with the Indians. As the Superintendent of Indian Affairs pointed out, the
Hudson's Bay Company was quick to take action against any trader,
British or foreign, who showed improper conduct, and they won the
allegiance of the Indians through the stability and orderliness of
their "rather despotic yet salutary sway." Yet, as one report emphasized, geography was the real key, for despite all the matters of
tariffs and organization, "the most important advantage enjoyed by
the Hudson's Bay Company, is the admirable harbor at the mouth
of the Columbia. . . ." Characteristically, the meagerness of specific
information about the situation in Oregon prompted the committee
to append in chief support of this view the published statement
(1793) of Alexander Mackenzie, who had never seen the Columbia
and was quite mistaken about its interior course.[5]

While the Americans argued, investigated, and compiled volumes

[4] 19th Cong., 1st sess., H. Rept. 35 (1826), p. 16. 18th Cong., 1st sess., S. Ex.
Doc. 56 (1824), p. 18. This information about the Hudson's Bay Company was
given to Senator Thomas Hart Benton by Joshua Pilcher, an American active in
the Rocky Mountain fur trade who was well acquainted with the Missouri
country. Cf. a supplementary report of the Baylies Committee, 19th Cong., 1st
sess., H. Rept. 213 (1826); reprinted in Hulbert, *Where Rolls the Oregon*, pp.
12-22, which presents some of the misinformation of Samuel Adams Ruddock,
who described the Willamette as rising in the Utah lakes.

[5] 20th Cong., 2nd sess., S. Rept. 67 (1829), pp. 10, 15; this report also contains John Jacob Astor's reaction to the English monopoly. 22nd Cong., 1st
sess., S. Ex. Doc. 90 (1832), p. 6.

of fragmentary information, the Hudson's Bay Company "damped the sanguine expectations of profits" of those few Americans who crossed the thresholds of Oregon on the lower Columbia, the Flathead, and the upper Snake.[6] More than a decade of American agitation failed to advance American fur trade interests.

But furs and sheer expansionism were not the only issues. The essential difference between the British and American views of Oregon lay not in the degrees of knowledge but in the kind of thinking. The British interest was commercial, the concern of a company (not of a government) whose success was measured by profits, and for whom the fur trade was paramount; farming, in Simpson's incisive comment, was "a branch thereof" because it served "to leighten the Expence of the Trade." But the American vision, though it tended to focus upon furs as the known exploitable resources of immediate value, was not one of *voyageurs* roaming the wilderness but of settlers, farmer-traders, whose tools were to be wagons and plows as well as traps and rifles. The evidence shows in nearly every debate and report published. The proposals of Floyd, despite their aura of unreality, were important not only for sparking American thinking about Oregon, but for the kind of thinking they revealed. Every aspect of the scheme—the colonization at the Columbia estuary, the requirement of fixed habitation and cultivation on the part of licensed traders, and the assumed necessity of converting the Indians to agricultural pursuits—exhibited a very different view from that of the British. American reports are filled with arguments over the practicability of wagon routes to Oregon.[7] But wagons were not an essential of the fur trade; the British did not use them, and, though used, they were not essential to the Americans in the Plains and Rockies. To Americans the Oregon fur trade was seen as the initial and transitory stage of progressive settlement. The Columbia country was a distant extension of the American frontier, to be occupied as Kentucky and Tennessee had been and Illinois and Missouri were being occupied. And so it was that nearly every debate and report displayed more concern about the land of Oregon than about its furs.

[6] The preceding chapter has noted the successful campaign of the Hudson's Bay Company against encroachment up the Columbia; pertinent sections of Rich (ed.), *Hudson's Bay Company,* succinctly treat competition in the Rockies.

[7] Recall that Robert Stuart's arrival in St. Louis in 1813 prompted the local newspaper to speak of the feasibility of taking wagons to the Columbia; see above, p. 43.

Views of Oregon

What kind of country was Oregon? Seemingly it was whatever kind a speaker or writer wished it to be. Reliable information was scarce. The one great source was the published journals of Lewis and Clark, and judging from a decade of congressional debates those few copies available must have become well-worn and marked in the service of the nation.[8] As a source these journals had their defects, chiefly because of limited seasonal contact with each area and the lack of local reconnaissances beyond the main line of travel. Yet few explorations produced such a wealth of honestly reported facts so uncolored by personal whims. All the daily irritations are there—the dust, the dampness, the snow, the sun, the "prickly pears," and the dripping rainforest—yet there is an unusual restraint in pronouncing sweeping judgments as to good and bad country. Ironically, this very objectivity allowed these explorers unwittingly to provide persuasive testimony for both sides of the bitter Oregon debates. The facts were there, all that was needed was a careful selection and Oregon could become readily a western "Eden" or a "most appalling" country.

The journals provided sufficient fuel to enflame the controversy on every point. Proponents who spoke of the Columbia entrance way and its commodious harbors were countered by descriptions of an "iron-bound coast," a dangerous bar, unfavorable winds, and a harbor "at all seasons, bad, and, during the winter months, almost, if not altogether, impracticable." A climate "exceedingly mild, pleasant, and salubrious," was to others bleak and inhospitable, with almost unremitting drenching rains. The "rich Valley of the Columbia" with its enormous fir trees as "sufficient proofs of the strength and exuberance of the soil, and of a climate most friendly to vegetation" was likewise an area of impenetrable forests, barren of game, where even the "occassional tracts" of better ground were subjected to summer floodings. There was equal dissension over the nature of the Columbia interior. The favorable view was grounded upon the "pure and dry" air, those features "peculiarly genial to horses," and the extended comment of Lewis about the settlement prospects of the eastern grassland-forest margins. Those opposed could dismiss

[8] E.g., Mr. Baylies once noted in debate that he was unable to get hold of the Lewis and Clark report because it had been constantly checked out of the library during that session. *Annals of Congress*, 17th Cong., 2nd sess. (1823), col. 684.

it with simple condemnation: ". . . forest trees totally disappear, and nothing larger than the common willow is to be seen. This whole intervening tract is one of gravel and sand, with just soil enough to sustain a scanty covering of grass."

Though the first American explorers provided the bulk of the ammunition for both sides, interspersed through the reports and debates are comments obtained from the Astorians. In general, these were put to better use by the opposition than by the promoters. A letter from Wilson Price Hunt referred, not unexpectedly, to "frightfull difficulties," and to a few radishes and turnips as the full measure of agricultural prospects. Another shred of "authentic" information reported the failure of maize trials, presumably at Astoria, and concluded that the expectations for other grains were "miserable indeed." One of the few attempts to suggest that Oregon might well be neither a country of extraordinary attractions nor yet totally sterile and inhospitable was the only published account of Astorian experiences, that of Gabriel Franchère (French edition published in Montreal in 1820); significantly, the remarks were confined to the area west of the Cascades, for a weary midsummer journey from The Dalles to Okanogan had prompted him to label the whole Plain as the "Great Columbia Desert."[9]

All the debates and many of the published arguments marshaled the evidence in bits and pieces, a fragment selected here on climate, there on soils, another on vegetation. Many did follow the general division, so obvious in the Lewis and Clark reports, separating the lands east and west of the Cascade Range, but often items were cited without clear reference as to which part of Oregon was being described. This vagueness as to regional variations was to persist for decades. Not until 1831 was anything like a balanced regional picture presented, when the extended views of Joshua Pilcher, an American trader who knew the Rockies well and had ventured into the Columbia country (exactly how far is not clear), were given in a letter to the Secretary of War and published by the government. In his opening remarks, under the heading "Face of the Country," he stressed the need to see the whole in terms of its parts:

[9] The material for the foregoing section has been drawn entirely from the reports and debates previously cited; the specific references to Hunt and Franchère are from *Register of Debates in Congress*, 20th Cong., 2nd sess. (1928-29), pp. 126, 171-72. On the "Great Columbia Desert," see Franchère, *Narrative of a Voyage*, p. 336.

The country must be viewed under three distinct regions—

1st. The mountain region, drained by the upper waters of the Mult-nomah [Willamette] Lewis's river [Snake] Clark's river, and McGil-bray's river [Kootenay] all of which fall into the Columbia on its south side.

2nd. The Plains which lay between the foot of the mountains and the head of tide water.

3rd. The tide water region, which extends from the foot of the plains to the sea.

The mountain country was described as having numerous fine valleys with an abundance of excellent grasses and mild winters. The "middle region," or plains, was depicted as "sandy, destitute of timber, quite unfit, in general, for cultivation, and famous only for the fine horses that are found among the Indians." Climatically it was a mild and attractive area "remarkable for a clear sky, a serene atmosphere, and a soft and brilliant sunshine." The tidewater region was quite distinct: ice or snow were seldom seen, summers were mild, the heavy rains and mists along the coast lessened toward the interior, and the Fort Vancouver area had an attractive and "altogether healthy" climate; though heavily timbered, there were "considerable tracts of fertile soil." Compared to lands east of the Alleghenies, the climate was everywhere much milder, the prospects for agriculture probably "inferior," for stock raising "superior," for fishing "the very finest in the world." This, at least, had the ring of an honest evaluation by a man who had seen some parts of Oregon.[10]

Thus, if in the decade from Floyd to Pilcher (1821-31) American fur interests had not been advanced, American interest in and knowledge of the Columbia country had been expanded. If that knowledge was still sparse, imprecise, and inaccurate, it only reflected the limited contact of Americans. It was no simple task to build a picture of a land thousands of miles away and quite unlike that known by the congressmen and publicists of the time. There was even some uncertainty as to its name. The British had established "Columbia" as a regional term and given it stability as an administrative area. "Oregon," the distinctly American term, re-

[10] 21st Cong., 2nd sess., S. Doc. 39, reprinted in Hulbert, *Where Rolls the Oregon,* pp. 149-67. Another section of this same Senate report offered further specific information by relating the brief observations of the famous American trapper and explorer Jedediah Smith, who had visited Fort Vancouver via California in 1828. Smith gave a good description of the post and its flourishing agricultural activities, which could serve as some proof of Oregon fertility, at least in that locality. See *ibid.,* pp. 168-75.

ceived its first prominence in the amended Floyd Bill of 1822, which proposed recognition of a "Territory of Origon." Popular gazeteers of the day mirror the evolution of terms, from the loosely descriptive "Country watered by Columbia River and its Tributary Streams" in 1819, to the synonymic "Basin of Columbia, or Territory of Oregon" in 1828, to simply "Oregon Territory" in 1833.[11]

Despite the extravagances of the arguments, a few moderate ideas of the qualities of Oregon gradually emerged. There was evidence that at least some attractive localities existed west of the Cascades, assumptions based in part upon the fact that descriptions of a humid, wooded land of temperate climate sounded like familiar country capable of producing the staples of home. The Great Plain of the Columbia, however, was anything but familiar, it was a new type of country related in kind only to those broad, still somewhat mysterious expanses stretching across the vast center of the continent. How could it be described? What common terms could be applied to an uncommon land? The popular books of the time reveal the difficulty: "The Rocky Mountains . . . are succeeded by an elevated plain of great extent . . . the country seems to descend by large plates, or steppes, to the Pacific Ocean"; "beyond the mountains [Rockies] the country descends by regular belts, in the form of immense terraces, or descending plains, disposed regularly the one below the other."[12]

The pitfalls in trying to visualize a landscape from an armchair while leafing through travelers' accounts is shown in the description of a "high chain of mountains" just beyond the confluence of the Snake and Columbia where the river takes a sharp turn to the west. How could one describe a land of great rivers coursing through deep, perpendicular, basaltic-walled canyons below the undulating surface of a vast treeless plain if one had never seen any land remotely like it? And how does one evaluate the unknown? Was this "middle region" good country or worthless country? All the accounts

---

[11] Hulbert, *Where Rolls the Oregon;* Edmund Dana, *Geographical Sketches on the Western Country* . . . (Cincinnati, 1819), p. 303; William Darby, *View of the United States, Historical, Geographical, and Statistical* (Philadelphia, 1828), p. 326; Timothy Flint, *The History and Geography of the Mississippi Valley* . . . (Cincinnati and Boston, 1833), I, 462; and Bishop Davenport, *A New Gazetteer, or Geographical Dictionary, of North America and the West Indies* (Baltimore, 1833), p. 157.

[12] John Melish, *A Geographical Description of the United States* (Philadelphia, 1822), p. 417; Flint, *History and Geography,* I, 462.

show that there was no firm basis for judgment. Those who sought a favorable view might read of "prairies . . . covered with grass, and a profusion of the most beautiful flowers," or of a country "extremely broken and hilly, but occasionally interspersed with beautiful rich valleys; . . . Here are many fine streams of water, and much of the country is well adapted to the raising of cattle and sheep." Yet all accounts admitted that it was "destitute" or "barren" or "naked" of trees.[13] In some accounts this absence of trees obviously implied little fertility of soil; others pointed to attractive "valleys," despite a "light" soil, while still others sought to reassure with accounts of "luxuriant" grass, flowers, and sagebrush. Such phrasings are hesitant and rationalized, for whatever the opinion of the writer, he could not describe a familiar kind of country which the reader in New England, Pennsylvania, Ohio, or Tennessee might relate to his own surroundings. Thus, one may infer from the literature of 1820's what was to be confirmed in the actions of the 1840's: that those who migrated to Oregon farms would not be bound for the Great Columbia Plain.

Such was the American view of Oregon, dimly, distantly pieced together during a decade of spasmodic but heightening interest. As for the British, two decades of contact with all its localities through all the seasons certainly gave them a greater understanding. They knew that the land west of the Cascades was not all mist, rain, floods, and impenetrable forests. The Willamette invariably excited praise, and the farms at Vancouver offered proof of agricultural productivity; Colvile, too, demonstrated the richness of a mountain valley. But the plains country east of the Cascades was another matter. Although superb for horses, it had little else to prompt visions of civilized settlement. Barren of furs, it lay as a barrier of heat and dust, rock and sage, nearly devoid of game or fuel. Despite occasional comments on the attractions of certain localities, Franchère's "Great Columbia Desert" expressed the common opinion. Despite Simpson's interest in developing agriculture to serve the company's local needs and optimism about the possibilities at Spokane and Colvile, he never found much to praise about the Columbia Plain. His personal experiences led him to make such journal notations as "Clouds of Dust & Sand," "a Sandy Desert," "Withered Grass," a

[13] Melish, *Geographical Description*, p. 417; Flint, *History and Geography*, p. 462; Dana, *Geographical Sketches*, p. 304.

country "dismally barren," and a final summation: "The most Sterile tract Country perhaps in North America." Even a scientist with an eye for country sang the same refrain. In 1826 David Douglas, the eminent British botanist, spent four months traveling about the plains and periphery in the company of Hudson's Bay parties, journeys which took him across the richest prairie sections of the Palouse and Big Bend areas. But it was a hot, dry summer; day after day the thermometer registered from 97 to 106 degrees in the shade, with little shade to be found in these plains "destitute of timber" and mantled by a "light, dry, gravelly soil, with a scant sward of grass." Douglas, by his own description "parched like a cinder with heat and thirst," found nothing about this region (excepting only the water available from the rivers) to render it "superior to the deserts of Arabia." To whatever degree British ideas may have seeped into American considerations, they could serve only to reinforce the common view of the Cascades as the dividing range between good country and poor.[14]

VENTURES

If the decade preceding was one of intemperate argument, visionary speculation, and ineffective agitation, the five years of 1832-36 was a time of direct action, feeble and fumbling though it was, which marked the beginnings of an American occupation of Oregon. Many of the events of these years are related to the activities of a Massachusetts ice merchant, Nathaniel J. Wyeth, and his actions

[14] Cf. the remarks of Donald Mackenzie: "The west of the mountains [Rockies] have every where been chequered by my steps & really in all my travels even to the borders of New Mexico I found no spot which I judged calculated for agriculture excepting only the river Walamitt." T. C. Elliott (ed.), "Letter of Donald Mackenzie to Wilson Price Hunt, July 30, 1822," *Oregon Historical Quarterly*, 43 (1942), 196. Merk (ed.), *Simpson's Journal*, pp. 126, 130. Simpson's contact was confined to the Columbia route, which of course did lead through the most barren, unattractive areas. David Douglas, *Journal Kept by David Douglas During His Travels in North America, 1823-1827* (London, 1914), pp. 159-61, 200-209. A portion of this journal was published, with some alterations, as "Sketch of a Journey to Northwestern Parts of the Continent of North America During the Years 1824-'25-'26-'27," in *Companion to the Botanical Magazine*, 2 (London, 1836), and reprinted in the *Oregon Historical Quarterly*, 5 (1904), 230-71, 325-69; 6 (1905), 76-97, 206-27. Like so many of the early botanists, Douglas showed surprisingly little interest in grasses, in contrast to trees, shrubs, flowers, and herbs. Though the Columbia Plain was a new botanical province to him, it obviously had little to excite his curiosity.

were, in part at least, prompted by the obsessed, shrilly argumentative schoolmaster, Hall J. Kelley. Unraveling the skein further, Kelley's interest issued from a reading of the Lewis and Clark journals and became strengthened by and entwined in all the congressional agitations of the 1820's.[15] Through such tenuous ties was the American initiative of the 1800's connected to the American actions of the 1830's.

Kelley, Wyeth, and Bonneville

Kelley took his first formal initiative in 1828, when he instigated a memorial in Congress pleading support for American colonization. In 1829 he formed the "American Society for Encouraging the Settlement of the Oregon Territory," and in the following year published the first and most important of his pamphlets, *A Geographical Sketch of that Part of North America called Oregon*.[16] It was in several ways a remarkable work. Based largely upon Lewis and Clark, plus information gathered from New England merchantmen familiar with the North Pacific coast, it was compact, detailed, and well organized. Between an introductory section outlining American rights to the area, and a concluding argument listing the national advantages to be gained by colonization, was the main geographical report, organized both regionally and topically. Kelley recognized four main "natural divisions": (1) a mountainous section bordering the coast, (2) the Willamette Valley–Puget Sound lowlands, (3) the treeless interior hill and plains country, and (4) the mountain and valley region east to the Continental Divide.

His detailed commentary reflected his extreme bias, and he lavished praise upon nearly every aspect. Interestingly enough, rather than ignoring many seemingly disadvantageous features, as so many

[15] Fred Wilbur Powell, *Hall J. Kelley on Oregon* (Princeton, N.J., 1932), pp. ix-xi.

[16] 20th Cong., 1st sess., H. Doc. 139 (1828), reprinted in Archer Butler Hulbert, *The Call of the Columbia: Iron Men and Saints Take the Oregon Trail, 1830-1835* (Colorado Springs and Denver, 1934), pp. 3-6. In this same year Simpson reported to London of American settler interest, knowledge of which he derived from the visit of Jedediah Smith. He ridiculed the whole idea as being based upon an utterly unrealistic conception of the ease of the transcontinental crossing, and concluded confidently that "we have little to apprehend from Settlers in this quarter, and from Indian traders nothing." *Simpson Dispatch, 1829*, pp. 66-67. Kelley's pamphlet is reprinted in Powell, *Kelley on Oregon*, pp. 1-67; four other lengthy Kelley pamphlets are also reprinted in this volume. A number of Kelley's other publications of the next few years are reprinted in Hulbert, *Call of the Columbia*, pp. 11-66.

of his contemporaries had done, Kelley attempted to rationalize some advantage from them. At times the result was inadequate, as when he admits the sterility of the area around the Snake-Columbia junction but states: "If, in this district, the eye, sometimes, glances upon a bed of naked rocks, or barren sand; it is, on all quarters, attracted to delightful landscapes of hills, and dales and verdure." The most interesting example refers to the Columbia Plain as a whole. Having already pointed to the tremendous trees and dense growth west of the Cascades as proof of the "great fecundity" of the soil, Kelley, unable to deny the goodness of any section, is faced with the apparent contradiction of a *fertile but treeless* region. His explanation was ingenious: "How the trees should have been exterminated, root, branch and seed, from places of great fertility; is not certainly known. There are, however, many strong reasons to believe it, the peculiar and habitual practice of the Indians, from time immemorial, in burning over the plains." Knowledge of this Indian practice was derived from Lewis and Clark and was well known by fur traders in the area; however, it is doubtful if many readers were convinced by this argument.[17]

But Kelley's importance rested not upon the details of his writings, but upon his role as propagandist, and if his personality and his extravagant statements produced as much ridicule as admiration, they at least stirred a storm of interest.[18] Kelley's trip to Oregon in 1833-36 via Mexico and California was a failure and of little impor-

[17] While Kelley's comment may perhaps best be dismissed as a rather desperate rationalization, it is still of great interest. In recent years anthropologists, geographers, and botanists have given much greater attention to the role of primitive man in modifying the natural environment. The role of burning in the creation of grasslands has aroused great interest and controversy, and many scientists are now prepared to accept the theory that at least some large grassland areas are primarily culturally induced; indeed doubt has been cast upon the idea of the prairie as a "climax vegetation." For early references to Indian burnings in the Columbia grasslands, see Ross Cox, *The Columbia River*, I, 41, 147; II, 124; Lewis and Phillips (ed.), *Journal of Work*, p. 80; John K. Townsend, *Narrative of a Journey Across the Columbia River*...(Philadelphia, 1839), reprinted in Thwaites (ed.), *Early Western Travels*, XXI, 107-369, reference on p. 356.

[18] Both Powell and Hulbert amply document the controversy which swirled around Kelley. Hulbert reprints two lengthy refutations of Kelley's views on Oregon by W. J. Snelling, with the pithy introductory comment: "... it was an epoch in the history of American humor (if not historical criticism) when a pompous ignoramus like Snelling set out to correct the equally ignorant Kelley's innumerable mistakes! ... the resulting jumble exactly represents public opinion on Oregon in 1832!" Hulbert, *Call of the Columbia*, p. xiv.

tance, but his influence upon Nathaniel Wyeth was of direct significance.

Wyeth's interest was evidently aroused or at least whetted by a visit with Kelley in 1829. He borrowed pamphlets and enrolled as an emigrant in the proposed colonizing expedition. For various reasons, however, Wyeth soon withdrew and organized his own party to carry out a scheme reminiscent of Astor's plan: a small overland party, a supply ship dispatched around Cape Horn, and the establishment of an operations base in the lower Columbia area. Wyeth and his party of twelve departed in the spring of 1832; on October 14 they reached Fort Nez Perces, where the evidences of civilization —"a bull and a cow & calf, hen & cock, punkins, potatoes, corn"— looked "strange and unnatural and like a dream" after the first westward tracing of the "Oregon Trail" all the way from the Missouri to the Columbia.[19] Arriving at Fort Vancouver two weeks later, Wyeth was dismayed to find that his ship had been lost at sea. Without essential supplies his scheme of trade and settlement was doomed, and Wyeth dismissed his party and spent the winter at Vancouver as a guest of the Hudson's Bay Company. In the spring of 1833, he journeyed to Flathead Post with the interior brigade, reached the upper Snake via the Clark Fork and Salmon, and with two companions made his way back to New England.

Undaunted by the disaster and evidently encouraged by his contact with the British company, Wyeth immediately laid plans for a second expedition in the next year, similar in scheme to that of his first. The overland party of 1834, as prearranged, brought supplies across the plains to the American rendezvous on the Green River, but the Rocky Mountain Fur Company broke its contract and refused the goods. Wyeth therefore proceeded to the Snake plains, and near the mouth of the Portneuf he erected Fort Hall, where he set himself up as an independent trader to the Indians and trapping parties. On August 5, 1834, this first American post in the Oregon country since Astorian days was properly dedicated: "I have made the establishment . . . and raised the Stars and Stripes amid explosions of gun powder and whiskey according to custom, and they now wave to the wind in the naked wastes of central America."[20]

[19] F. G. Young (ed.), "The Correspondence and Journals of Captain Nathaniel J. Wyeth, 1831-6," *Sources of the History of Oregon,* 1 (1899), 173.
[20] *Ibid.,* p. 146. For an account of this event by an American trapper who accompanied Wyeth, see Osborne Russell, *Journal of a Trapper* (Portland,

Leaving his fort in charge of a subordinate, he pushed on to Fort Vancouver; and his supply ship arrived the following day. Wyeth candidly stated his purpose to McLoughlin: ". . . to salt salmon for the Boston market . . . to equip some American trappers in the mountains and to farm in the Willamette." As for the fur trade, Wyeth worked out an arrangement with McLoughlin whereby he would obtain horses from Fort Nez Perces, trap the area south of the Columbia and lower Snake, would not interfere with the British north of that region, and would purchase supplies from and sell his furs to the Hudson's Bay Company.[21]

Though this was an intrusion, McLoughlin justified his action to his disturbed superiors by explaining that he could not legally stop Wyeth, but he could use him as a dependent tool to compete with other Americans in the Snake country where the company had no monopoly anyway. Moreover, the boundary issue was a factor, and Wyeth would be another instrument, along with its own Snake expedition, by which the company could "make all they can out of it [the area south of the Columbia] while it is in our power." As it turned out, and as McLoughlin had also predicted, there was little to fear from Wyeth's fur activities. Wyeth's journal of his winter trapping expedition of 1834-35 was well described as "a perfect Book of Lamentations"; sickness, desertions, accidents to horses and boats, and, to compound it all, practically no beaver left in the area, made the venture a disappointment to the Americans. Neither the trading at Fort Hall nor the salmon-packing enterprise fared any better, and by the autumn of 1835 Wyeth gave up the effort. In 1836 he abandoned Fort William, his Columbia headquarters on Sauvies Island at the mouth of the Willamette, and headed back to New England and the security of the ice business.[22]

Wyeth's was not the only American failure in the Oregon fur trade of the time. A less complicated but equally luckless and in some ways more naïve venture was that of Captain Benjamin L. E. Bonneville. In 1832 Bonneville obtained leave from the United States Army for

Ore., 1955), p. 5. A useful summary history of this post is Richard G. Beidleman, "Nathaniel Wyeth's Fort Hall," *Oregon Historical Quarterly,* 58 (September, 1957), 197-250.

[21] Rich (ed.), *McLoughlin Letters,* p. 128; Young, *Correspondence and Journal of Wyeth,* p. 78.

[22] Rich (ed.), *McLoughlin Letters,* pp. xcvi-xcvii, cvii-cxiii, 149, 150, 165-71; F. W. Howay, W. N. Sage, and W. F. Angus, *British Columbia and the United States* (Toronto, 1942), pp. 83-84.

the purpose of "exploring the country to the Rocky Mountains and beyond" and gathering information on the natives and the area. In the phrase of his famous literary publicist, Washington Irving, it was "a rambling kind of enterprise" in which the commercial side far outweighed the scientific or strategic.[23]

In 1832-33 Bonneville wintered along the upper Salmon River among the eastern Nez Perces. After a year of indecisive and unproductive operations to the east and south, Bonneville headed for the main Nez Perces country. Attempting to follow the Snake downstream, he encountered an impossibly difficult region (Hells Canyon) and only extricated himself by an arduous detour up over the west wall of the Snake River gorge into the Imnaha and Grande Ronde valleys. Following down almost to the Clearwater mouth, he turned westward, skirted the northern margin of the Blue Mountains, and arrived at Fort Nez Perces on March 4, 1834. Though hospitably received by the local Factor, he sooon found, in Irving's words, "the difference between being treated as a guest, or as a rival trader."[24] Unable to obtain supplies, Bonneville left, determined to return to the lower Columbia with a fully equipped party.

After retiring to his main camp on the Portneuf, he reappeared in September, this time crossing the Blue Mountains and reaching the Columbia via the Umatilla. But the Indians along the Columbia refused to trade even fish and provisions and by their actions made it quite clear that they wished to have nothing to do with the American intruders. The Captain now saw that his plan of erecting a post near Fort Vancouver and grabbing a share of the trade was hopeless, and he departed from the Columbia before winter marooned him into dependence upon the British rivals whom he had challenged so feebly. He turned southward up the John Day and, after a difficult journey through a country which he, as Wyeth, had erroneously thought rich in furs, reached the Snake River plains and headed for home.

These two unprecedented attempts to compete directly with the Hudson's Bay Company in the Columbia interior, far beyond the peripheral zones of chronic rivalry, were complete commercial failures, yet they demonstrated a new American boldness and a tentative westward thrust of the American sphere of operations. Most im-

[23] Washington Irving, *The Adventures of Captain Bonneville* (New York, 1843), pp. 3-5, 291-92.
[24] *Ibid.,* pp. 205, 207.

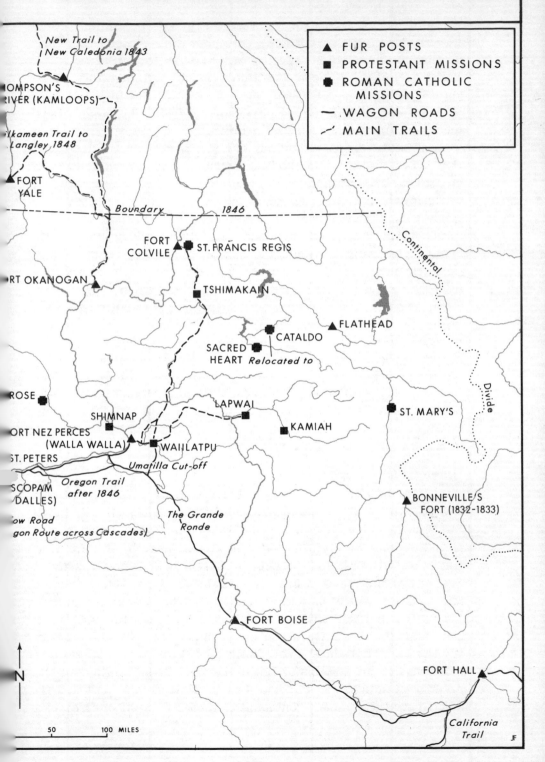

New Trail to
New Caledonia 1843

▲ FUR POSTS
■ PROTESTANT MISSIONS
✚ ROMAN CATHOLIC
  MISSIONS
— WAGON ROADS
⌇ MAIN TRAILS

▲ THOMPSON'S
RIVER (KAMLOOPS)

Similkameen Trail to
Langley 1848

▲ FORT
YALE

Boundary — 1846

Continental

FORT
COLVILE ▲ ■ ST. FRANCIS REGIS

FORT OKANOGAN ▲

■ TSHIMAKAIN

✚ CATALDO

▲ FLATHEAD

SACRED ■
HEART *Relocated to*

Divide

ROSE ■

■ LAPWAI

✚ ST. MARY'S

SHIMNAP ■

FORT NEZ PERCES
(WALLA WALLA) ▲

■ KAMIAH

ST. PETERS

■ WAIILATPU

Umatilla Cut-off

WASCOPAM
(DALLES)

*Oregon Trail
after 1846*

*The Grande
Ronde*

Barlow Road
(Wagon Route across Cascades)

BONNEVILLE'S ▲
FORT (1832-1833)

N

▲ FORT BOISE

FORT HALL ▲

*California
Trail*

50   100 MILES

Map 13

portantly, failure in the fur trade did not lessen interest and action. Indeed, the Wyeth expedition represented a blend of many American interests in Oregon: Wyeth's own plans included the fur trade, Pacific commerce (salmon and lumber), and farming; the accompanying naturalists—Thomas Nuttall, a Harvard Botanist, and John K. Townsend, a Philadelphia physician and ornithologist—expressed the strong American scientific curiosity about these still mysterious western lands; the Reverend Jason Lee, his nephew the Reverend Daniel Lee, and three Methodist laymen marked the sudden implementation of American missionary interest, which had been building up during the preceding decade.

Thus the Wyeth expedition combined several frontiering instruments of America into a small but bold intrusion deep into British-held Oregon. Although trading and commerce failed, farms and missions remained; and the expedition brought back firsthand information, which was soon disseminated to an interested public. Several members had joined the party with the principal intention of establishing Oregon farms, and more turned to that as other activities proved unsuccessful. The missionary scheme also was to found permanent, agriculturally supported stations as centers for proselytizing the Indians. Thus, a nucleus of American farmer colonists became rooted in the fertile soils of the lower Willamette Valley and thereby posed a new and indirect challenge to the British, which could not be countered by the efficiency, experience, and resources of an entrenched trading system.

Hudson's Bay Company

Though these years were, in retrospect, to mark a turning point in Oregon history, the Hudson's Bay Company continued to flourish and, insofar as trade was concerned, showed an alert adaptability to new situations. Fur returns for Vancouver, the Columbia interior, and New Caledonia for the period 1831-35 held almost exactly at the level of the previous five years (Table 1, p. 88). However, the Snake country catch showed a marked decline, reaching a low of 378 beaver in 1835, which revealed the heavy depletion of the region and the extensive American competition. In response to Wyeth's Fort Hall, the company built Fort Boise, near the mouth of that river, in an attempt to blunt the westward extension of the American trading zone. Purchase of Fort Hall from Wyeth in 1837 finally gave the company command of the very portal of Oregon, a position of little commercial but significant strategic value. Insofar as over-all Pacific slope operations were concerned, the decline of the Snake country was more than offset by a vigorous development of the coastal trade. The principal change in that sector was the establishment of several permanent posts, which reduced the number of vessels (thus reducing manpower requirements), maintained continuing contacts with the Indians, and allowed the company to gain competitive advantage over American vessels. Fort Nisqually was constructed near the head of Puget Sound, and Forts McLoughlin and Simpson were spaced along the coast north of Fort Langley.[25]

In addition, the company, prompted at least in part by the example of American enterprise, gave serious attention to diversifying its activities. A sawmill was erected at the Willamette Falls in 1831, and lumber shipments were begun; proposals and investigations for agricultural development and cattle raising were also underway. Farming at Vancouver continued to expand and in good years produced beyond company needs.[26] Retired company servants and free trappers already had established a nucleus of British farms in the lower Willamette. But if such developments might suggest that the alert company was beating the Americans at their own schemes, one difference remained and was to prove decisive: All these British actions were company controlled and existed as mere adjuncts of the fur trade. Although, for the moment, their agricultural development surpassed that of the Americans, it was neither initiated by farmer colonists nor could it draw upon a vast reservoir of land-seeking immigrants. In short, the Columbia country was a "company frontier" for the British, a "national frontier" for the Americans.

Interest in the Interior

That initial American commercial, agricultural, and missionary interests concentrated upon the Willamette and lower Columbia

[25] See "Fort Boise: From Imperial Outpost to Historic Site," *Idaho Yesterdays,* 6 (Spring, 1962), 15-16, 33-39, for a useful historical survey and a fine aerial view of the exact site. Rich (ed.), *McLoughlin Letters,* pp. 154-55. So important was the coastal region, with a consequent shift in the geographical balance of operations, that London proposed the removal of Columbia Department headquarters from Vancouver to a point strategic to the coastal waterways, such as Whidbey Island; McLoughlin returned a negative report on Whidbey Island and recommended Fort Simpson for this purpose, but no further action was taken at this time.

[26] *Ibid.,* pp. 137-38, 143-44, 228. In 1836 McLoughlin requested that two reapers be sent to facilitate the grain harvest.

was not surprising, in view of prevailing American ideas of Oregon regional qualities. The British farming success at Vancouver and vicinity substantiated distant speculations, and in every way—quality of the land, climate, timber, inland water communication, access to the sea—the Willamette was a country of superior attraction. Thus, although the Wyeth party made extensive reconnaissance of the interior, the knowledge did not alter their colonization plans. Their views of the Columbia Plain are of interest, however, for they stem from the first American contact since Lewis and Clark by persons whose over-all plans specifically included agricultural settlement. In February, 1833, Wyeth rode out for a look at the country around Fort Nez Perces. He examined the small garden of vegetables and corn (150 bushels) three miles upstream from the fort and concluded that the lower valley of the Walla Walla appeared to have good soil, but of very limited extent, and it had no wood. A ride up the Touchet and across to the Snake afforded a good glimpse of the western edge of the rolling, bunch-grass-covered hills: "... light sandy land with little sage grass good and in tufts," the terrain "very level except some trifling roundly swelling hills these make one think of gently swelling breasts of the ladies." John Ball, a member of the expedition trained in geology and a careful observer, offered a summary view in a letter to friends at home:

> ...one immense prairie extends from the mountains ... to the Falls of the Columbia. Along the streams are willows, and often rank grass; but as you recede from them, a thin crop of grass and shrubbery succeeds, and the soil generally becomes barren.... In the prairie regions there is but little water.... In travelling from the forks of the Platte river to the Falls of the Columbia, I did not witness more rain than I have known fall in other places in one day. The sky is usually serene by day and always by night. Indeed there is but little rain or dew about this region.[27]

This letter and others were published by eastern newspapers, and the returning members soon brought further firsthand accounts, all of which must have added weight to pessimistic views of the potentialities of the Columbia Plain. If "prairie" and "grass" might suggest something other than desert, "barren" and "little rain" must suggest little else. But the question was of little immediate practical significance, for the praise and proof of Willamette attractions laid

---

[27] Young, *Correspondence and Journal of Wyeth*, pp. 184-85; Hulbert, *Call of the Columbia*, pp. 176-77.

open an ample farming frontier, and the American colonization of Oregon was to proceed independent of any ideas about the interior.

Yet settlement in the interior was begun at this time, though more restricted in scale and objective than that in the Willamette. The mounting attention toward Oregon coincided with a general upsurge in American missionary interest, and it was inevitable that the two became intertwined. Propaganda for the occupation of Oregon almost invariably enlisted the cause of Christianity in its support, and as published accounts offered a clearer picture of Indian life and numbers, the challenge to mission societies seemed increasingly exciting and imperative. The Methodist church began to consider an Oregon mission 1832. In that same year a report from the frontier claimed that the previous autumn an Indian delegation had come all the way from the far Northwest to St. Louis to plead for gospel teachers, and the call was irresistible. The mission party which accompanied Wyeth to the Willamette was sent in direct response. Concurrently, the American Board of Commissioners for Foreign Missions—a joint agency of the Congregational, Presbyterian, and Dutch Reformed churches in New England and New York—after a longer but somewhat desultory interest in Oregon, was spurred to commence work among the Flathead and Nez Perces. These were the tribes that had sent the delegation, but they had lost out to the greater attractions of the Willamette, which had lured the Methodist mission away from its original intent.[28]

Thus, the initiation of settlement in the Columbia interior was

[28] E.g., Hall J. Kelley, "Letters to a Member of Congress" (1832), reprinted in Archer Butler Hulbert and Dorothy Printup Hulbert, *Marcus Whitman, Crusader: 1802 to 1839* (Colorado Springs and Denver, 1936), I, 9-10, 11; also the review in the *Methodist Magazine,* 14 (July, 1832), of Ross Cox's recently published experiences in the Columbia (reprinted in part in Hulbert, *The Call of the Columbia,* p. 54, note 31), in which the reviewer called for an establishment at Astoria from which the Christian cause could be carried eastward to the Rockies. The famous "call from Macedonia" quickly became imbedded in a morass of fanciful interpretations. A valuable attempt to discover the actual historical details is that of Clifford M. Drury, *Henry Harmon Spalding* (Caldwell, Ida., 1936), pp. 72-90.

The importance of New England commercial activities in the Pacific to the patterns of New England missionary work is well illustrated by the activities of this board: in 1820 a Hawaii mission was established, and in 1828 Jonathan Green was sent to that post with special instructions to reconnoiter the Oregon coast for possible mission work. However, because of bad weather the American trading vessel which he joined was unable to enter the Columbia and his report was of limited value. See Hulbert and Hulbert, *Marcus Whitman,* I, 2-7.

predetermined in distant New England on the assumption that the Indians of the region offered a fruitful Christian harvest, with little real knowledge of or immediate concern over the nature of the country. Still, Yankee prudence demanded more specific information before a major program was endorsed, and the Reverend Samuel Parker was sent west to make a reconnaissance. In the spring of 1835, Parker and the Reverend Dr. Marcus Whitman traveled with the American Fur party to the rendezvous on the upper Green River. Here they contacted parties of Flathead and Nez Perces, and their reception, together with the information garnered from the trappers and traders (including Nathaniel Wyeth), convinced them that their scheme was entirely favorable. To expedite matters, Whitman returned to the East to recruit workers and arrange for supplies, while Parker, in the company of the Nez Perces, started toward their home grounds to search for advantageous mission locations.

Parker's Reconnaissance

Just thirty years, almost to the day, after the first American explorers caught their initial glimpse of the Great Columbia Plain, Samuel Parker, the first American to enter the region with specific plans for its settlement, struggled along the same Nez Perces trail, rejoiced to find himself through the most difficult mountains he could imagine, and reached the edge of the prairies along the Clearwater. Despite the differences in interests and aims, this New England clergyman was a worthy successor of Lewis and Clark: an alert, intelligent observer with an eye for the wonders of God's earth. His journal is packed with careful notations of minerals, geology, hydrology, vegetation, and animal life. If, in keeping with his time and training, he had a ready teleological explanation for the unusual and often breath-taking peaks, canyons, and lava fields encountered, he was at least free of many common prejudices against these unfamiliar western lands. Entering the luxuriant prairies beyond the Missouri, he predicted a dense population in a few years, despite the lack of timber; and, as he proceeded westward along the Platte into the "Great American Desert," he recognized that "the country begins to diminish in its fertility, but still is very good."[29]

[29] Samuel Parker, *An Exploring Tour Beyond the Rocky Mountains in North America . . .* (Dublin, 1840), pp. 26-27, 31, 75. From the Green River rendezvous, the Nez Perces returned via the upper Salmon, the Bitterroot Valley, and thence west across Lolo Pass.

That his predetermined scene of operations was found to be a barren, treeless country was therefore not in itself an occasion for despair.

> This country differs very much from what I had expected; for while the soil is generally good, and furnishes a supply for grazing, yet there is such want of summer-rains, that some kinds of grain cannot flourish, especially Indian corn. The crops sown in the fall of the year, or very early in the Spring, would probably be so far advanced before the severity of the drought should be felt, that they would do well. In general there is great want of wood for building, fencing, and fuel; but at the confluence of these rivers [Snake and Clearwater], a supply may be brought down the Cooscootske. This place combines many advantages for a Missionary station.

Following this guardedly optimistic introduction, Parker proceeded overland along the Indian trail westward from the Clearwater to Fort Nez Perces (duplicating Lewis and Clark's eastward journey), from where he embarked in a canoe with three Indians for a nerve-wracking voyage down the Columbia. Cordially received by McLoughlin at Vancouver, as he was at all Hudson's Bay posts he was to visit, Parker spent the winter there as a guest of the company. He made numerous reconnaissances—to Astoria, the Willamette Valley, and other localities—and gathered information about the country, the Indians, and general prospects for missionary work in the Northwest.[30] Wishing, however, to learn more about the interior, he returned to the Clearwater in April, 1836, and visited the Spokane country, Fort Colvile, and Fort Okanogan, then returned by canoe to Nez Perces and Vancouver. In this manner he had contacted much of the country and most of the tribes with whom work was contemplated.

That Parker was blazing a trail for a limited colonization already set in motion makes his views of the interior unusually important; the fact that, with characteristic integrity, he confined his remarks

---

[30] *Ibid.*, pp. 76-77. Parker's astonishment at the meager, primitive character of Astoria (now Fort George)—two rude log huts, two acres of cleared ground, and two white residents—was an excellent testimony of the exaggerated impression created by a decade of propaganda about this famous American emporium:

> ... we passed Tongue Point, ... Soon after this Astoria was announced. My curiosity was excited. I looked, but could not discover what to all on board, was so plainly seen—I blamed my powers of vision—and reluctantly asked the captain, where is Astoria?" I said within myself, is that the 'far famed New York of the West?' Sic transit gloria mundi!" *Ibid.*, pp. 97-98.

"to those things which have been corroborated by, or came under, my own observations" further enhances their value. Some of the most remarkable of Parker's comments relate to the open prairie plains, which he saw not only in the freshness of late spring but also, in his first encounter, near the end of the summer drought. He noticed the surprising fact that the upper prairies were as fertile as the lower, narrow, riverine strips, and that his horses, "contrary to my expectations, preferred the dried grass to the green." The quality of this "natural hay" was confirmed by his own experience. On his outbound journey, Parker had left his horses and mule with the Nez Perces while he proceeded by canoe; in May the animals were returned to him at Fort Nez Perces, with astonishing results:

> I was surprised to find them in fine order, with their coats shed and in high spirits. They had run out on the prairies without any shelter from the storms, and nothing more to eat than what the remains of the previous summer's growth afforded. Who would have supposed, considering their worn down condition, when I left them in October, and with no other fare, they would have fattened during the winter. This fact shows the superior mildness of the climate, and nutritive quality of the prairie grass, even after being dried up with the summer drought.[31]

The cattle at the fort, some of which were "actually fat, and in as good condition for market as oxen driven from the stalls of New England," were further evidence in support of the observation he had made the previous autumn, while voyaging down the Columbia toward The Dalles: "This section of the country is well supplied with grass, which during the summer-drought is converted into hay. Who can calculate the multitudes of cattle and sheep, which might be kept here summer and winter, with no other labour than the care of a few herdsmen and shepherds."[32] And that remark was applied to a section of the Great Plain which, especially when viewed from the river during the summer, had been labeled "barren," "sterile," "sandy," or "desert."

In the course of his reconnaissance, Parker nominated four localities as attractive mission sites: the confluence of the Snake and Clearwater; the upper Walla Walla Valley; the Colville Valley; and The Dalles. The first three combined fertile soil, availability of timber, and a local Indian tribe amenable toward mission work. Parker was especially impressed with the Walla Walla region be-

[31] *Ibid.*, pp. 75-76, 97-98, 123, 157.
[32] *Ibid.*, p. 83.

tween the lower Snake and the Blue Mountains. He described it as
an area "uncommonly pleasant, diversified with hills and valleys,
and covered with a self-provided carpet of lovely green"—again,
remarks akin to those applied to the same locality by Lewis and
Clark thirty years before. Though the upper Walla Walla Valley
was "not so central for either the Nez Perces, Cayuses, or Walla
Wallas as could be desired," the land was sufficiently attractive to
make it a "delightful situation" for a missionary station: "...how
easily might the plough go through these vallies, and what rich and
abundant harvest might be gathered by the hand of industry." The
"remarkable" fertility of the lower Colville Valley was confirmed by
the achievements at Fort Colvile, where the lessening of the summer
drought allowed both winter and summer crops to thrive. And the
mild climate, forests, and proximity to several Indian tribes made
it a fine prospective mission location. Nothing was said of agricultural promise at The Dalles; salmon, evidently, was to be the principal basis of the "comfortable subsistence" foreseen. The asset here
was the large Indian population; although, in Parker's delicate
phrase, there was "great want of neatness" among them, their sheer
numbers suggested a bountiful missionary harvest.[33]

Parker's keen eye for country led him to describe in detail and
speculate upon many interesting features: the peculiar restrictions
of the stream bed at The Dalles, the Grand Coulee ("undoubtedly
the former channel of the river"), the enigma of the channeled
scablands, the fascinating pinnacles of columnar basalt, and nearly
everywhere the magnitude of the river channels entrenched in this
great "volcanic" surface. If such incomparable features of this uncommon land strained his eastern terminology—he consistently referred to the deep, steep-walled canyons of the Columbia interior as
"gulphs"—his encounters with those longer resident in the West
gave a hint that new terms for new landscapes were creeping into

[33] *Ibid.*, pp. 83, 85, 155. Parker's phrase about the Walla Walla recalls the
observations of two of Captain Bonneville's party, one a native of Kentucky and
the other of Ohio, who in passing through the same locality in March, 1834,
were excited by its agricultural promise. In Irving's words, "they declared that
it surpassed any land they had ever seen, and often exclaimed what a delight it
would be just to run a plough through such a rich and teeming soil, and see it
open its bountiful promise before the share." *Bonneville*, p. 204. And, in turn,
this quotation is excellent testimony of the contrasting character of the American and British fur-trading ventures; it is difficult to imagine a British trader,
and almost impossible to imagine a French-Canadian *voyageur*, becoming en-
raptured over putting a hand to the plough.

the general vocabulary. He recorded his entry into the Rockies, in the company of an American fur party, by way of "a very deep and narrow defile . . . , called by the hunters, Kenyon."[34]

People, after all, were the critical concern, and they were subjected to the same close and honest scrutiny. Whole sections of his journal are devoted to lively descriptions of Indian character, habits, dress, and ways of living, and additional facts and opinions are interspersed wherever daily events called attention to interesting and curious features. If the whole is colored by concern over the veil of darkness which everywhere enshrouded the heathen mind, here also he attempted to cut through common prejudices. Parker repeatedly insisted that "as a part of the human family, they have the same natural propensities and the same social affections" as other peoples, and properly labeled much of that which was base and deplorable as being the result of the "influence of bad examples, and unrestrained licentiousness" of the whites with whom they were in contact.[35]

He was as alert to variations among Indian tribes. The basic division between those of the Columbia interior and those of the coast is recognized and accurately described. Extended experience with both confirmed the original program of work, for he thought those of the interior were in every way the more attractive in habits, intelligence, and receptivity to Christian instruction. In part it was a matter of basic cultural differences, in part the result of the degradation of coastal tribes through long contact with the whites. Then, too, the Methodists had already commenced work in the Willamette, and recent malaria epidemics had devastated the population, reducing it perhaps to a tenth of that before 1829. Within the interior, Parker's principal contact was with those tribes inhabiting the eastern margins of the Columbia Plain: the Cayuse, Walla Walla, Nez Perces, "Paloose," and "Spokein." He noted that the first four were similar in every way and spoke languages of only dialectical differences, while the Spokanes were a distinct language group. In a summary section he listed the separate tribes, noting their numbers, locality, and principal characteristics. The population estimates for those related to the Columbia Plain are of interest:

[34] *Ibid.*, p. 51; presumably "canyon" was gradually being spread northward from Taos by traders and trappers.
[35] *Ibid.*, pp. 125, 135, 186.

Nez Perces	2,500	Coeur d'Alene	700
Cayuse	2,000	Kettle Falls	560
Walla Walla	500	Sinpauelish (San Poil)	1,000
Paloose	300	Okanogan	1,050
Spokein	800	Yookooman (Yakima)	700

The total of more than ten thousand did not include the few along the Columbia between the Okanogan and the Snake, nor the many around The Dalles.[36]

That the Willamette Valley was a magnificent land, Parker had no doubts ("for richness of soil, and other local advantages, I should not know where to find a spot in the valley of the Mississippi superior to this") but for Indians—the prime attraction for the missionary—the Great Plain of the Columbia was superior in quantity and quality. If the land itself was not the object, however, it was nonetheless fundamental, for not only must the missionary himself live from the soil, he must teach the Indians those rewards which were assumed to be the natural result of husbandry: stability, sobriety, industriousness, and thrift. As Parker's successor Henry Spalding so aptly phrased it, "No savage people, to my knowledge, have ever become Christianized upon the wing."[37]

Having satisfied himself as to the practicability and promise of the Oregon mission program, Samuel Parker boarded ship in June, 1836, for the voyage home. But this was a curious thing to do, for at that time Marcus Whitman and his new associates were toiling

[36] *Ibid.*, pp. 121-22, 124-42. The one-tenth figure was McLoughlin's estimate; Parker suggested that probably seven-eights had died. An excellent study of the epidemic which establishes its nature and extent is S. F. Cook, "The Epidemic of 1830-1833 in California and Oregon," *University of California Publications in American Archaeology and Ethnology*, 43, No. 3 (1955), 303-26. Interestingly, McLoughlin thought the "fever" was related to the breaking of the sod, as it coincided with the initiation of Willamette cultivation. Parker, however, pointed out that the same fever was prevalent in the United States at the time.

The true Cayuse language was significantly different, but later missionary reports make clear that the Cayuse had largely shifted over to the Nez Perces language.

Population figures are from pp. 176-79. However, some of these figures are greatly different from those in Parker's "Report" to the American Board made soon upon his return. There the Nez Perces are listed with 1,600 members, the Cayuse with but 400, and the total of these tribes was only 7,200. See Hulbert and Hulbert, *Marcus Whitman*, I, 122.

[37] Parker, *Exploring Tour*, p. 112; *The Missionary Herald*, 36 (1840), 231.

across the continent eager to confer with Parker and begin the great work. Disappointed in not encountering him somewhere en route, they were astonished to find upon their arrival that he had left Vancouver, and perplexed that he had left behind no report for their guidance.[38] This remarkable clergyman-explorer, with a keen eye for man and the land, had blocked out a logical geographic framework for the incipient mission frontier; he then carried it back to New England, where it was of no direct value. Perhaps his enigmatic behavior was a fitting symbol, at the outset, of the misunderstandings and discordant human actions which were to characterize this next stage in the settlement history of the Great Columbia Plain.

[38] Hulbert and Hulbert, *Marcus Whitman,* I, 57-58, 69, 229-31.

CHAPTER SIX

> We must use the plough as well as the
> Bible, if we would do anything to
> benefit the Indians. They must be set-
> tled before they can be enlightened.
>
> THE REVEREND ELKANAH WALKER

Missions: Protestants and Priests

THE PROTESTANT SYSTEM

Arrival and Selection

"As WE were decending the last Mountain I was almost awed into
Adoration while looking at the scenery around me [;] before lay
the Plains of Columbia in full view . . . made sublimely Grand by
the Sun which was just settin in fire beyond the Paciffic Ocean."[1] A
first glimpse of this sun-browned, treeless plain which was so abruptly spread before the early westward traveler must always have
made a profound impression, but it had a special emotional impact
upon this little band of Protestant missionaries in the late summer
of 1836. For the first time, men and women were looking upon this
country as their new home, and though its remoteness and strange-
ness might have prompted a sense of exile and faintheartedness, such
candid journal entries as that of William Gray suggest that timing
and emotions more nearly produced a momentary vision of a glitter-
ing, awesome "promised land."

"Our eyes have actually seen the long, long, long-wished-for Walla
Walla, the end of our journey of 4100 miles," Henry Spalding reported to friends in the East. This journey, so remarkable an experience for the missionaries, was routine for the fur parties which
they accompanied, although it was made memorable by the presence
of the missionaries' wives, the nagging delays caused by their cattle,
and Whitman's dogged perseverance in trying to take a wagon
through to Oregon. The wagon, reduced to a mere set of wheels, was
finally left at Fort Boise. On September 1 the Whitmans and Gray,

[1] Letter of William H. Gray, Sept. 9, 1836, in Hulbert and Hulbert, *Marcus
Whitman*, I, 226-27.

the lay worker, arrived with the vanguard at Walla Walla; the Spaldings came two days later with the remaining group, which brought along the travel-weary cattle and pack horses at a slower pace. Although Fort Nez Perces was their destination, for several reasons it was decided to go on for a brief visit to Fort Vancouver. For one thing, they expected to find Parker there, for another they needed to find out from McLoughlin what supplies and equipment might be made available to them, and, moreover, they did not wish to choose a mission location until the Indians had returned from their hunting expeditions in the mountains.[2]

The selection of a suitable location had been a matter of interest from the moment the project had been conceived. A site east of the Cascades was clearly in mind, a decision guided by the specific tribes with which work was contemplated. A great amount of information was gathered en route, especially at the rendezvous from fur traders and Indians who knew the country. Such information was encouraging:

> From all we can learn we are satisfied it will not be difficult to fix on a location which will in every way accomodate us and the Indians. All agree that our cattle and horses can winter well in the part we design to locate without being fed. Some valleys are said to be free from snow & in others only a few inches from two to 4. They say we may locate where the climate is mild grass soil & timber good. The valleys free from timber. Plenty Elk, Deer & fish & about three days ride from Walla Walla.

The attractiveness of the valleys along the southern margin of the plain was enhanced by what they saw and learned at Fort Nez Perces. As Gray wrote home:

> On the W.W.R. many fertile places are to be found and we are told that at or near the Mountains it is verry fertile. Mr. Pambran raises the best Potatoes, pumpkins Onions Cucumbers Mellens etc. On the W.W.R. about 2 miles from the Fort. Better Mellons I have never eaten in the states. Mr. P. has also thirty head of the fattest cattle I

[2] "Letters of Rev. H. H. Spalding and Mrs. Spalding, Written Shortly After Completing Their Trip Across the Continent," *Oregon Historical Quarterly,* 13 (December, 1912), 371. The missionary party consisted of Spalding and his wife, the Reverend and Mrs. Marcus Whitman, and William Gray, a lay worker. Traveling with an American fur party from the Missouri to the rendezvous on the upper Green River, in mid-July they had joined the Hudson's Bay Company's Snake Expedition camp nearby and started for the Columbia. T. C. Elliott, "The Coming of the White Women, 1836," Part 3, *Oregon Historical Quarterly,* 37 (December, 1936), 276-77; Hulbert and Hulbert, *Marcus Whitman,* I, 174, 204ff.

ever saw the best of beef not excepted his hogs seame as if they could scarcely moove from fatness.

The suitability of the Walla Walla vicinity was made complete by the expressed desire of the Cayuse Indians for missionaries.[3]

After conferring with McLoughlin at Vancouver, they assessed the possibilities more specifically. The Grande Ronde, which they had considered before leaving the East, was dismissed as being "too much exposed to the Snake Indian Country." They were aware, presumably through McLoughlin, that Parker had recommended a location along the Clearwater. They had more or less committed themselves to work among the Nez Perces, and they therefore decided upon this general location. A decision to split their party and begin work simultaneously in two localities posed a further choice, which was narrowed to either the Walla Walla area or near The Dalles ("say back from two to four miles; where they say the land is good").[4]

On the first day of autumn, the three men left Vancouver with a Hudson's Bay Company party for the voyage upriver to Fort Nez Perces. By October 2, Spalding reported that Whitman had selected "an excellent strip of land" in the Walla Walla Valley. None of the letters and journals mentioned further examination of The Dalles en route nor any reason for its rejection. Two weeks later the men returned from the Nez Perces country and announced their second location, on Lapwai Creek two miles upstream from the Clearwater. The Lapwai locale had been chosen by the Indians themselves but did not make a favorable first impression upon Spalding. The "soil was dry as an ash heap," and, as he recalled a few years later, the narrow canyon and steep, barren hills seemed so inferior to the Walla Walla Valley that he trembled with despair upon first sight. But the presence of a spring, clay, stone, timber on the higher slopes, and a few acres of irrigable land made the prospect at least tentatively feasible.[5] During the next few weeks the women came inland

---

[3] Whitman letter from Green River, July 16, 1836, in Hulbert and Hulbert, *Marcus Whitman*, I, 209, 228. "Mr. Pambran" was Pierre Pambrun, chief trader in charge at the post.

[4] *Ibid.*, I, 231; Mrs. Whitman noted another disadvantage of the Grand Ronde, which must have been discussed: the distance and difficulty of access over the Blue Mountains from the Columbia; see Elliott, "White Women," Part 2, p. 184.

[5] Hulbert and Hulbert, *Marcus Whitman*, I, 233-35; "Letters of Spalding," pp. 375-77; Elliott, "White Women," p. 186. Spalding Letters, Spalding to Rev.

to join their husbands, supplies were packed in, and the construction of a house at each location was completed. By late autumn, 1836, the mission era in the Columbia interior was solidly underway.

This handful of workers began their task with the confident expectation that they were the vanguard of a program which would steadily expand in scope and numbers. Such hope sustained an interest in other localities as promising mission sites, and through the next decade numerous areas were considered and several new establishments were undertaken. Actually, however, the next post to be founded within the region was established in March, 1838, by two Methodist missionaries from the Willamette who selected a site on high ground on the south side of the Columbia overlooking The Dalles. Although both Parker and Whitman had looked favorably upon this location, the Methodist Mission was not regarded as an improper invasion.[6] For the moment, at least, the number of workers was so small and the task so great that any expansion of Protestant activity was regarded with sympathy by the other group.

In that same year the American Board also initiated work in the Spokane country. Two newly arrived missionaries, the Reverend Elkanah Walker and the Reverend Myron Eells, were assigned to that task. After conferring with the Chief Trader at Colvile, who consulted the Spokane Indians, they chose a site on a small prairie along the main trial a few miles north of the Spokane River. They started construction of two log cabins that autumn, but did not take up residence and begin work until the following March. Thus "Tshimakain" on the northern periphery of the Plain among a separate Indian group was added to the Protestant system.[7]

The third new missionary who had come as part of the 1838 reinforcement, the Reverend Asa Smith, spent the winter at Waiilatpu, but soon he, too, wanted a separate station. The Nez Perces had

---

David Greene, Sept. 22, 1840 (MSS in the Washington State University Archives, Pullman), p. 147; and Drury, *Spalding*, p. 159.

[6] Marcella M. Hillgen, "The Wascopam Mission," *Oregon Historical Quarterly*, 39 (September, 1938), 222-23; after selecting Waiilatpu, Whitman mentioned The Dalles as a good location for the next missionary who might be sent, and just prior to the Methodists' move he again called attention to the importance of the site and recommended an establishment "if it not first be occupied by our Methodist Brethren"; Hulbert and Hulbert, *Marcus Whitman*, I, 233, 300.

[7] Clifford M. Drury, *Elkanah and Mary Walker, Pioneers Among the Spokanes* (Caldwell, Ida., 1940), pp. 58-59, 63, 85, 88, 99, 101, 106.

The Wacopam Mission at The Dalles, as sketched by a member of the Pacific Railroad Survey party in the 1850's. *(Photo courtesy of Washington State University Library)*

"Old Fort Walla Walla," sketched by a member of the Pacific Railroad Survey party in the 1850's. The view is to the south toward the "Wallula Gap" of the Columbia. *(Photo courtesy of Washington State University Library)*

shown him a favorable site at Kamiah, east of Lapwai where the Lolo Trail crossed the Clearwater. Smith camped there with the Indians during the summer of 1839 in order to learn the language, and in September obtained the approval of the other missionaries to establish a station. He built a house on the west bank of the river, and laid plans to fence the small open plain and to extend his cultivation beyond the garden he had planted that year.[8]

At the same meeting in which Kamiah was approved, Gray received permission "to explore the Yaukoomoo [Yakima], Auhi, Cootenae & Couer de Lion countries with a view to select a suitable place for a station." A month later he announced that he had selected a site near the mouth of the Yakima. However, Spalding opposed Gray's plan, and Gray left in disgust for the Willamette. Later he returned, and in July, 1840, was granted permission to establish a mission at "Shimnap" as he had wished.[9]

Geography of the System

These half dozen posts represented a fresh phase in the human geography of the Columbia interior. Although it was a program new in nationality, motives, and personnel, it was intimately related to all that had preceded it. Oregon was not merely a field of missionary endeavor that had grown out of the general publicity about peoples and places stemming from the explorers and fur traders; the entire, detailed effort showed a close dependence upon and a geographical continuity with the existing fur-trade system. Without that established framework, the Oregon missions could have been neither inaugurated nor maintained.

Passage to the Columbia was made possible by the American and British trade routes, which were connected each year at a rendezvous near the Continental Divide. Once the missions were established in the area, the very strands that bound them to their source of administration, finance, and supply in New England were those forged and maintained by the fur traders. Letters and light parcels were forwarded along the St. Louis-Rendezvous–Snake country route or through British America by Hudson's Bay Company express.

---

[8] Drury, *Spalding*, pp. 217, 221, 225, 228. For details of the Kamiah mission, see Clifford M. Drury (ed.), *The Diaries and Letters of Henry H. Spalding and Asa Bowen Smith Relating to the Nez Perces Mission 1838-1842* (Glendale, Calif., 1958), pp. 99-212.

[9] Drury, *Spalding*, pp. 229, 232, 250. The exact location of this post is not clear.

Shipments of goods usually arrived on New England ships trading in the Pacific, which linked these Oregon missions not only with home but with their sister mission in Hawaii.[10]

Regionally, the shaping influence of the Hudson's Bay Company was evident in numerous ways. The factors' advice as to locations was eagerly sought and strongly considered. The missions remained at least partially dependent upon the company for several years. Moreover, though directly adjacent locations would not have been favorable to the interests of either group, the importance of communications, protection, and companionship were never underrated by the missionaries. Hence, they themselves favored sites which would be within reasonable distance along established trails to the fur posts. Waiilatpu and Tshimakain maintained close contacts with Forts Nez Perces and Colvile, respectively, and Spalding made numerous trips to each from his more remote Lapwai. Although some writers have suggested that the British company sought to control the location of mission activity, the Hudson's Bay "influence" was much more a product of the missionaries' recognition of their own interests than something craftily imposed upon them.[11]

Mission geography was also influenced by other factors. Indians, after all, were the prime objective, and the patterns of tribal areas

[10] "Missionary barrels" of donated clothing, personal articles, and books usually came in this way, as did various kinds of heavier equipment. For example, in 1845 Spalding took sixteen horses to The Dalles to pick up a shipment of ploughs that had been sent by boat to that point. Contact with the Sandwich Island Mission was of some practical value; the famous mission printing press was obtained from there, and on another occasion eight sheep were sent. *Ibid.,* pp. 185-86, 198, 317.

[11] This same kind of superimposition of geographic patterns was evident west of the Cascades. There each of the Methodist missions was near a fur post; two in the lower Willamette (near Fort Vancouver), one at Clatsop (near Fort George), and another at Fort Nisqually. The Reverend Myron Eells, in his biography *Marcus Whitman, Pathfinder and Patriot* (Seattle, Wash., 1909), pp. 50-51, claimed that the Hudson's Bay Company carefully steered Whitman away from the Cowlitz and The Dalles in order to protect their strategic grasp upon the Oregon country. I have found nothing in missionary letters and journals or in the McLoughlin letters which would substantiate such a view. In fact, Whitman continued to consider the Cowlitz as an excellent possibility, and Spalding reported that McLoughlin recommended it as a mission location; see Spalding Letters, p. 70. Insofar as the Columbia interior is concerned, any portrayal of opposition and hostility to missionaries by local company personnel is directly contradictory to testimony of the missionaries themselves. Some of the company's officers did in time become suspicious of American missionary motives, but this grew out of the quite different Willamette context.

The mission to the Spokanes at Tshimakain, from an original sketch by Karl Geyer, a German botanist who visited the Walkers in the winter of 1843-44. *(Photo courtesy of Washington State University Library)*

were significant. Lapwai, Tshimakain, and probably The Dalles were selected as points of contact with particular tribes, and Kamiah was also prompted in part by the request of the local Indians. Yet the Waiilatpu site was apparently chosen for other reasons than a desire to work particularly with the Cayuse; and as the program of mission activities evolved, it is clear that at times the missionaries either made or contemplated important moves which appear curiously unrelated to any rational plan of work with the Indians. Certainly Shimnap, near the mouth of the Yakima, was not central to any significant Indian group, and the briefly contemplated relocation of Whitman to a site somewhere along the Palouse River was prompted by other considerations and would have been a poor choice for a teaching mission. Any further geographic analysis of these missions would have to take into account the complications arising from the individual personalities involved.[12]

[12] On the Palouse project see Drury, *Spalding*, p. 251. Several years after the event Spalding stated that the initial decision to establish two missions, a hundred miles apart, stemmed from personal animosity (*ibid*, p. 251). Kamiah and Shimnap were grudgingly authorized out of similar feelings; both were abandoned in 1841 (*ibid.*, pp. 257, 263, 266, 282). Such incessant bickering led the governing Board in Boston to order in 1842 the closing of Waiilatpu and Lapwai and the retention of Tshimakain, an action completely contradictory to the relative accomplishments (*ibid.*, pp. 275-90, and Hulbert and Hulbert, *Marcus Whitman*, II, 253-57). Whitman made a famous ride to the East that winter and got that order rescinded. The fact that during the course of his return the next summer he served as guide to a Willamette-bound emigrant train, would

The American Board missions functioned only as a fitful and limited network (the Methodist station at The Dalles was under separate control). Contact among the several posts was maintained by visits and letters, and general meetings were convened at least annually, and more often if needed. Waiilatpu was the center for the school intermittently maintained for the missionaries' own children; and because Whitman was a trained physician, it became the medical center as well, though more often he made hurried trips to the other posts when needed. As local facilities were elaborated, a degree of competition developed and posed a basic question of policy. Whitman urged that the main productive facilities—such as grist mill, blacksmith ship, and printing press—ought to be concentrated at Waiilatpu to serve the needs of all, but Spalding stoutly opposed any such centralization.[13]

Agriculture

Basically, of course, each station had to be self-sufficient. The American Board could sit in Boston and write admonitions suggesting greater emphasis upon teaching and less upon agriculture, but on the Oregon frontier the mind and the body were not so conveniently separated. Walker felt it necessary to retort with a rather obvious truism: "So long as he [the missionary] is in the flesh he must be fed & clothed as other men. He cannot stay the cravings of nature."[14] The only way he could satisfy such cravings was to raise his own food, or shed his heritage and live with the Indians as an Indian, or buy from a dependable supply. To live as the heathens did would contradict their whole purpose, and although they were very much dependent upon the Hudson's Bay Company's farms and facilities in the first years of work, they felt it necessary to lessen that dependency as quickly as possible.

---

give rise to one of the most famous controversies in American historiography: did Whitman "save" Oregon for the Americans against the British? Both Drury and the Hulberts carefully examine this question.

[13] Hulbert and Hulbert, *Marcus Whitman*, II, 219; also p. 200 for a similar statement. Hulbert notes (p. 48) that this program was not a matter of self-aggrandizement, for Whitman recommended that he be relieved at Waiilaptu. Drury, *Spalding*, pp. 199, 220-21, 240-41, 315. Grist mills were built at Waiilaptu and Lapwai; the printing press was sent to Lapwai; a sawmill was also constructed there, but later the irons were sent to Whitman, who built a considerable mill at the foot of the Blue Mountains.

[14] Elkanah Walker Letter (MSS in the Washington State University Archives, Pullman), Walker to Greene, Oct. 15, 1838.

These reasons for mission agricultural enterprise were but half the story. If the mind and the body were inseparable for the missionaries, so they were for the Indians, and, furthermore, so were Christianity and a settled, "civilized" mode of life. The Indians must be brought to the teachers and anchored to the soil within the unbroken daily influence of school and church and missionary example; in short, "they must be settled before they can be much enlightened." Furthermore, a different but very compelling reason was soon added to the argument: it was the only hope of saving the Indians from eventual extinction. Spalding was the first to grasp what had happened and was happening to Indian subsistence as a result of changes produced by the white invasion:

> Once game was plenty & furnished a great amount of their food..., but the introduction of fire arms frightened the game to a distance which called in the use of the horse, an animal of recent date in this country from the Spanish—& the consequence was a great havoc among all kinds of game.... The Beaver vanished in a day on the arrival of the trapper. The absence of game in their food has been partially supplied, though at great expense of labor by an increased proportion of roots & fish. Hence disease & decrease of population....

It was true that the salmon still came in plenty on their annual upriver migration, but the Willamette Valley was certain to become densely settled, and the salmon wealth of the lower Columbia would no doubt prompt local exploitation.

> The Salmon will be arrested in their upward course by some measure which the untiring invention of man will find out & which is not necessary here to conjecture. That day will be the date of universal starvation of nearly all the tribes of this vast country, if they be not timely settled upon their lands & furnished with means of a substantial subsistence.

Such a stark view was reason enough for insistence upon an agricultural policy. Thus, if Boston and Oregon held different views of the missionary task, it was a divergence between theory and practice, between a distant idealization and a proximate reality. Defense of their dual role of salvation—soul and body—was a recurrent theme in the letters of all the missionaries. Walker's statement that they "must use the plough as well as the Bible" was even more vividly echoed by Whitman:

> ... while we point them with one hand to the Lamb of God which taketh away the sins of the world, we believe it to be equally our duty to point with the other to the hoe, as the means of saving their famish-

ing bodies from an untimely grave & furnishing the means of subsistence to future generations.[15]

As might be expected, the actual results of agriculture, both that initiated by the missionaries for their own use and that of the Indians, varied greatly among the stations. Shimnap and Kamiah were of such short duration as to have been inconsequential. At The Dalles, wheat and potatoes thrived under irrigation and, supplemented by a few other garden vegetables and salmon, gave an adequate subsistence for the missionary families, but the Indian program was hopeless. With an abundance of salmon and sturgeon available through half the year and other resources from game and gathering, there was not the slightest chance of interesting them in "such arts of civilization as shall enable them to improve their condition." In command of "the great emporium . . . of the Columbia, and the general theatre of gambling and roguery," they were quite content with the arts they had long since mastered. A visitor in 1841 concluded that "it is not to be expected that the missionaries could be able to make much progress with such a set," which would have been considered an understatement by anyone better acquainted with the situation.[16]

[15] *Ibid.* Smith of Kamiah was the only one who came to believe that the Indians ought to be allowed to live in their usual manner. "I cannot say send ploughs and cattle for this people," he wrote, "I have no hope of converting them in this way." It is significant that Smith was the best linguist and during his brief sojourn with the Nez Perces, initially at least, probably established the best rapport. However, none of the others agreed with his idea. Spalding was "passionately" opposed and, as both men were working with the same tribe, this was merely one more example of how individual differences undercut the effectiveness of the program. On Smith's views, see Drury, *Spalding*, pp. 228-29. Spalding Letters, Spalding to Greene, Oct. 2, 1839, p. 108. Walker Letters, Walker to Greene, Oct. 15, 1838; Hulbert and Hulbert, *Marcus Whitman*, I, 306.

[16] Thomas Farnham reported five acres of wheat, potatoes, and vegetables successful without irrigation in 1839; later accounts usually mentioned irrigation. See Thomas J. Farnham, *Travels in the Great Western Prairies, The Anahuac and Rocky Mountains, and in the Oregon Territory* (New York, 1843), reprinted as Vol. XXVIII of Reuben Gold Thwaites (ed.), *Early Western Travels* (Cleveland, 1906). The description of the Indians at The Dalles is that of Alexander Ross, *First Settlers*, p. 129. The 1841 visitor was Mr. Drayton of the Wilkes expedition; see Charles Wilkes, *Narrative of the United States Exploring Expedition* (Philadelphia, 1845), IV, 382-87. Numerous brief descriptions of The Dalles mission are found in the journals of travelers and emigrants, e.g., Farnham, *Travels in the Western Prairies*, pp. 357-60; George Simpson, *Narrative of a Journey Round the World* (London, 1847), I, 170; Joseph Williams, *Narrative of a Tour from the State of Indiana to the Oregon Territory in the Years 1841-2* (Cincinnati, 1843), p. 62.

The circumstances at Tshimakain were so different from those at The Dalles that the comparable lack of success is remarkable. Not only had the Spokanes requested and welcomed the establishment, but at least a few of them were already cultivating small patches of potatoes. Eighty pupils, young and old, attended the opening of the school in the autumn of 1839, but it was soon obvious that they were for the most part merely curious. The missionaries had little talent for the difficult language problem, and the Indians soon became indifferent and even opposed to their presence. Eells reported that during the first year some cultivation was attempted "by the Indians near us" (whether prompted by the missionaries or not is unclear), but the season was particularly unfavorable. Frosts on May 15 and August 20 and a severe summer drought caused a failure of the potato crop, which may have destroyed whatever slight interest in agriculture the Indians might have had. Certainly no evidence of success and but few expressions of hope emanated thereafter from Tshimakain. Father Pierre DeSmet, the itinerant Jesuit priest, reported upon his visit in 1841 as follows:

> They cultivate a small farm, large enough, however, for their own maintenance and the support of their animals and fowls. It appears that they are fearful that, should they cultivate more, they might have too frequent visits from the savages. They even try to prevent their encampment in their immediate neighborhood, and therefore they see and converse but seldom with the heathens, whom they have come so far to seek.

This seemingly paradoxical attitude is confirmed by the missionaries themselves.[17] It is clear from their journals and letters that as the Indians refused to accept the severe puritanical restrictions demanded at Tshimakain, the mission families increasingly found it

[17] Cultivation had evidently been fostered by Garry, a prominent tribal member who had spent some time at the Hudson's Bay Company's Red River settlement; see Drury, *Elkanah and Mary Walker*, p. 108. Spalding obtained some seed potatoes from Garry in the spring of 1837; Drury, *Spalding*, pp. 168-69. *The Missionary Herald*, 36 (November, 1840), 439. Walker reported in the following year that "if these Indians are urged to cultivate they reply that it is so cold, that it is of no use." Paul C. Phillips and W. S. Lewis (ed.), "The Oregon Missions as Shown in the Walker Letters, 1839-1851," *Sources of Northwest History*, No. 13 (Missoula, Mont., 1930), p. 9. P. J. DeSmet, *Letters and Sketches with a Narrative of a Year's Residence Among the Indian Tribes of the Rocky Mountains* (Philadelphia, 1843), reprinted as Vol. XXVII of Reuben Gold Thwaites (ed.), *Early Western Travels* (Cleveland, 1906), quotation p. 368. See also Paul Kane, *Wanderings of an Artist Among the Indians of North America* . . . (Toronto, 1925), p. 215.

almost unbearable to have the Indians around. This lack of rapport doomed them to nine years of cultivating alone, praying among themselves, and baptizing none but their own children.

The undoubted truth of Walker's observation that "it is as hard & unnatural for them to lead a settled life as it would be for a New England farmer to change & lead a wandering life," makes even the limited and temporary achievements at Lapwai and Waiilatpu all the more remarkable. Certainly the beginnings at Lapwai were auspicious. The Nez Perces assured their new teachers that they would "go no more to Buffalo, but stay with them, grow corn and potatoes, and live as the white man does." The first spring some Indians joined with Spalding to plant fifteen acres for their own use, while he sowed a small garden and set out a few apple trees. The following year Spalding decided to move his station to the mouth of Lapwai Creek on the Clearwater, hoping that it would be cooler and less troubled with mosquitoes. Having obtained a yoke of oxen from Colvile, he was able to plough new fields more efficiently; sixty or seventy Indian families "cultivated more or less" with hoes, and the total crop and the increase in livestock in 1838 was very hopeful. The drought of 1839, which so handicapped the initial trials at Tshimakain, affected Lapwai also, but rather than discourage the Nez Perces it stimulated them to prepare to irrigate their crops. A hundred families were reported cultivating in 1840, hoes were in great demand, and more ploughs were urgently desired.[18]

During the next three of four years progress continued. About 140 Indians cultivated up to four or five acres each, some had fenced their plots, eight had ploughs, and several had been allotted a few head of cattle, sheep, or hogs. Perhaps the best indication of success was the fact that about half of the Indians had begun to cultivate in scattered localities beyond the valley, including at and around the vacant station at Kamiah. By 1843 Lapwai was essentially self-supporting, with sufficient crops and livestock, its own grist mill and a sawmill. The school had 234 at peak attendance.[19] At the moment, the achievement here was impressive.

Whitman's agricultural endeavors at Waiilatpu were also success-

---

[18] Drury, *Elkanah and Mary Walker*, p. 167; Hulbert and Hulbert, *Marcus Whitman*, I, 295; Drury, *Spalding*, pp. 170, 183, 185. Spalding reported 251 bushels of grains, 800 of potatoes, and 50 of various garden produce. Livestock numbers were 20 cattle, 9 hogs, 11 sheep, 25 horses, 40 hens.

[19] *Ibid.*, pp. 301-2, 326.

ful. He soon had a flourishing garden and farm, with a wide range of vegetables and a considerable acreage of the three staples—wheat, corn, and potatoes. All were raised either under irrigation or on sub-irrigated land bordering the streams.[20] The luxuriance of the crops at Waiilatpu never failed to impress the immigrants and travelers who came through in increasing numbers in the 1840's. Usually arriving just as the crops were maturing in late summer, after a wearisome trip across a thousand miles of unsettled country, they quickly spread the fame of Waiilatpu as an oasis in the midst of a sunburned wasteland.

As at Lapwai, the number of Indians who took up cultivation increased during the first five or six years, and Whitman was encouraged to believe that they were doing so more out of self-interest and less merely to please him. In 1843 a visitor found about sixty Cayuse cultivating small plots of a quarter to three acres each, and he thought they seemed proud of their new labors. But the Cayuse blended their agricultural tasks into their old migratory routine to a greater extent than did the Nez Perces at Lapwai. In February, March, and early April they made desultory preparations for planting; in April they moved to the upland streams and meadows to dig camas; in mid-May they shifted to the Columbia for the annual salmon run, perhaps pausing to weed their crops on the way. July was the time for the trading rendezvous with the Shoshones in the Grande Ronde. Returning near the end of that month they could begin to harvest their wheat, corn, and (about October first) potatoes. Autumn was the season for expeditions to the buffalo country, from which they returned to winter quarters scattered widely over their tribal area. Such movements precluded sustained missionary instruction and showed at the most a marginal partaking of "the arts of civilization."[21]

Transformation

Aside from the fact that the Cayuse were a less amenable tribe, the major difference between Waiilatpu and Lapwai was the increasing volume of emigrants who passed through en route to the Wil-

---

[20] Farnham, *Travels in the Western Prairies*, p. 80.

[21] *The Missionary Herald*, 36 (1840), 439. "They are very fond of ploughing," Whitman reported in another letter, and described how amusing it was "to see them break their horses to work generally one man or woman leading in front and one on each side with sticks and one holding the plough." Hulbert and Hulbert, *Marcus Whitman*, I, 313; II, 294-97. Gustavus Hines, *Oregon: Its*

lamette. Many required assistance—medicine, food, fresh cattle or horses, wagon repairs—and Waiilatpu became more and more oriented to their needs. The demands for food were an incentive to expand production; for various reasons there were nearly always several men and families encamped with the Whitmans for weeks or months, and the extra labor was therefore often available to enlarge the farming output. The warning from Boston headquarters that Whitman must take "special pains that your station does not assume the appearance of a farming & trading establishment,"[22] was a natural consequence; but the doctor pleaded with equal logic that it was his Christian duty to help and comfort any traveler in need.

Though Whitman was a man of prodigious energy, any greater attention to his countrymen meant less toward the Indians. Not that the latter felt neglected, for they, too, shifted their attentions to the emigrants. Where Whitman saw the Christian necessity of succor, the Cayuse saw the "civilized" opportunity for trade. Joel Palmer passed through in 1845 along the Umatilla, by then a popular short cut bypassing Waiilatpu, and found that the Indians had a scattering of fields all along the valley and were well prepared for business: "They brought us the different products of their farms for traffic. As they expressed great eagerness to obtain clothes, and we had a like desire to obtain vegetables, a brisk traffic was continued until dark." When he reported also that the crops were cultivated by squaws and slaves, it becomes apparent that whatever "success" might be inferred from numbers, acres, or bushels, the missionary agricultural program had gone somewhat awry. Whitman was far from blind to the fact. A year earlier he had lamented that "the Indians want settlers among them in hopes to get property from them."[23] And indeed it was clear that just such hopes had largely prompted their welcome of the missionaries themselves.

As the growing volume of emigrants began to warp the program at

History, Condition and Prospects (Buffalo, 1851), p. 167. *The Missionary Herald*, 39 (1843), 356-58; Wilkes, *Exploring Expedition*, IV, 394-97.

[22] Hulbert and Hulbert, *Marcus Whitman*, III, 206; see also pp. 162, 165-66.

[23] Joel Palmer, *Journal of Travels over the Rocky Mountains to the Mouth of the Columbia River; Made During the Years 1845 and 1846*, reprinted as Vol. XI of Reuben Gold Thwaites (ed.), *Early Western Travels* (Cleveland, 1906), p. 111. Whitman admitted in that same year that the "upward tendency to industry and enterprise" on the part of the Indians was "owing partly to better markets, occasioned by the annual immigrations," Eells, *Whitman*, p. 135. Hulbert and Hulbert, *Marcus Whitman*, III, 101.

Waiilatpu, Whitman sought to anticipate and adapt to the changes. Even in spiritual matters there were divergent pressures; and the pressing material needs of the emigrants soon caused him to reason that, if Waiilatpu could not serve them adequately, enterprising squatters would soon set up in business to do just that. Thus Whitman's zeal to expand his farm, sawmill, and repair shop was heightened by a protective motive: "I was anxious to so manage as to cause the Indians & the Mission to so far supply the wants of the Immigration in transit as not to force the early occupancy of this part." But the "Oregon fever" was raging, and Whitman had no delusions about the inevitable result. The Indians had acquired some skills in the art of husbandry but "still it cannot be hoped that a settlement will be so delayed as to give time for the advance to be made so that they can stand before white settlement." If this meant that the missionary task was largely hopeless, then the Indians themselves must share the blame: "For the Command is multiply & replenish the earth neither of which the Indians obey. Their indolence, violence & bloodshed prevent the first & indolence & improvidence the second. How then can they stand in the way of others who will do both."[24]

Whitman came to see himself in the path of "one of the onward movements of the world," and therefore redirected his energies toward channeling the flow and softening the impact of change. His pleas to Boston and to eastern friends increasingly emphasized the need for good Christian settlers: "What we very much want is good men to settle two three or four in a place & secure a good location & hold a good influence over the Indians & sustain religious institutions as a nucleus for society. . . ."[25] Here the Yankee heritage showed through: the hope of shaping the colonization process by the orderly selection of sites and colonists to insure Christian social cohesion on the frontier.

With such a mutation of purpose, mission geography was likewise transformed. Chosen for ease of communication and access to the fur posts and Indians, the mission sites now were clothed with an unforeseen strategic significance. Walker summarized this new perspective:

> As the stations are now no influence can get in to the best part of the country without coming in contact with the influence of the Missions. The station on the north branch stands in the way of any influence

[24] Hulbert and Hulbert, *Marcus Whitman*, III, 101.
[25] *Ibid.*, II, 329.

that may come in the Company's express route across the Mountains, the clear water Station is the most direct route from the upper Flathead to Vancouver, and Waiilatpu is to meet all influence that shall come in by way of the American Fur Company's route? [*sic*] As it is now situated it forms nearly a triangle and seems well located to exert the greatest influence upon the interests of the country. It seems as though providence had a wise design in our location. . . .

The opportunity in 1847 to take over The Dalles from the Methodists was seen as a windfall which would complete this new strategic concept. "It is a more important station than any in the country," wrote Spalding, "it is the keystone to the plain & mountainous countries, to the water & horse carriages." Whitman thought it essential to occupy The Dalles mission if the Methodists withdrew, for "should it fall into other hands it might at once either become a papal station or a petty trading post—if not a grog shop." To resist this trio of influences had become the main task; as for the local Indians, there was now only the hope of exercising some "restraint" upon that "low pilfering race." In September, 1847, the transfer was made. Whitman placed his newphew in charge and initiated a program of development. Within a month he had traced out a better wagon road well up on the plateau between the Umatilla and The Dalles, a route designed to circumvent many of the difficult tributary canyons and riverine sand dunes and also to avoid contact with the Indian encampments along the shore. "This I think now is to be our best station," he informed Boston; and he outlined the need for a school for whites, a boarding school for Indians, and gave new urgency to his plea for pastors and Christian settlers.[26]

By this time it was clear that the original Indian program had failed. In 1846 the situation at Lapwai had changed from one of material prosperity to near ruin. Spalding reported that there was no longer a school and "not the least probability that there will ever be one here again." The Indians' abandonment of their fields, vandalism of mission property, and personal threats against their teach-

---

[26] Phillips and Lewis (ed.), "Oregon Missions," p. 9. Walker was writing in 1842 to argue against the Board's abandonment order. The principal influence he was hoping to intercept was that of Roman Catholic priests; however, he did foresee the eventual influx of white settlers also. Spalding Letters, p. 322-e. Hulbert and Hulbert, *Marcus Whitman*, III, 225, 229-30, 235, 243-47. The Dalles was so important and the available staff so inadequate that Whitman urged that Tshimakain be abandoned and Walker take over the new station. After examining the situation, however, Walker refused. Drury, *Elkanah and Mary Walker*, p. 197.

ers revealed how complete was the loss of influence.[27] A similar change at Waiilatpu had been building up for a longer time; Tshimakain stagnated in its chronic ineffectiveness.

The reasons for failure were many. It is obvious, in retrospect, that the simultaneous conversion of the Indians to Christianity and an agricultural life in so short a time would have required a highly improbable set of skills in the missionaries and an almost impossible adaptability on the part of the Indians. This general difficulty, complicated by all the special features, such as the internal dissensions among the missionaries and within Indian tribes, the sinister counterinfluences of a few individuals—Indian and renegade half-breed or white—and the general disruptions and apprehensions of the natives stemming from their contacts with the emigrants, makes the over-all failure readily understandable.

THE CATHOLICS, THE COMPANY, AND THE END

The Catholic Challenge

Increasingly, however, one cause was magnified in the minds of these missionaries: the competitive influence of Roman Catholic priests. These Protestants had arrived in Oregon with the full measure of antipathy to "popery" characteristic of their time and sects. They were immediately placed on guard by their discovery that most of the fur company's personnel were Roman Catholic; and with the first appearance of priests in November, 1838, they began to gird for a relentless struggle for religious dominance in Oregon.

Father Francis N. Blanchet and Father Modeste Demers, traveling with the returning autumn express, enjoyed a warm reception from the post complements and local Indians at Colvile, Okanogan, Nez Perces, and Vancouver.[28] Unlike the Protestants, these priests had, in the French-Canadian *voyageurs,* latent congregations awaiting them at every company station. As most of these people had been long out of contact with their church, the priests were busy from the moment they arrived baptizing, solemnizing marriages, hearing confessions, celebrating Mass, and teaching prayers and catechisms. This is not to suggest a purely blissful reunion of priest and people;

[27] Drury, *Spalding,* pp. 323-26.
[28] *Notices and Voyages of the Famed Quebec Mission to the Pacific Northwest* (Portland, 1956), pp. 3-15; hereafter *Quebec Mission.* This source has been used for most of the local details of the Roman Catholic program.

Blanchet was initially shocked by the annual assault of the spring interior brigade upon the staid routines of Fort Vancouver ("a hideous assemblage of persons of both sexes, devoid of principles and morals"), and he was as distressed as Spalding by the casual indifference of both Indians and company personnel to the virtues of monogamy. Still, from the beginning of their work, the Catholics did have the advantage of a core of adherents at each post. Although such groups demanded much of their attention, the priests also viewed themselves as primarily missionaries, with a duty to carry the faith to the Indians.

For several years these two Canadian priests conducted an itinerant mission, traveling from post to post, making special journeys into various tribal areas, and covering a tremendous extent of country. Unencumbered by families, free of agricultural pioneering, drawing upon the resources and enjoying the confidence of the company, the overt challenge and obvious successes of these rivals embittered the struggling Protestants. For a time the competition was principally west of the Cascades, where it hastened, though by no means caused, the dissolution of the Methodist system.[29]

Actually, the first real challenge in the Columbia interior came from a different direction. Just as Protestant activity in Oregon functioned under separate controls (Methodist and American Board), so Roman Catholic missionary work came from initially separate and uncoordinated centers. Blanchet and Demers were sponsored by the Bishop at Red River settlement, operating under the jurisdiction of the Archbishop of Quebec. But in the early 1840's Jesuit priests from the Diocese of St. Louis crossed the plains and began work with the Indians in the forested regions east of the Great Columbia Plain. In 1841 Father DeSmet founded St. Mary's in the Bitterroot Valley to serve the Flathead tribe, and the next year his associate, Father Point, established Sacred Heart Mission on the St. Joe River in the midst of the Coeur d'Alene country (in 1846 this station was shifted to the Coeur d'Alene River and became known

[29] As evidence of the consciously planned competition, on a visit to Nisqually one of the priests discovered a Methodist constructing a chapel and promptly obtained permission from the local factor for a plot of ground for a Catholic chapel, for "his (the Methodist's) presence in that locality made necessary that of a Catholic missionary to save from the poison of error, natives so well disposed to accept the truth." *Quebec Mission*, p. 38. In the Willamette, rival services were held simultaneously side by side, competing for the attention and adherence of the amused or bewildered Indians.

as Cataldo Mission).[30] Thus one was a Canadian program closely geared to the British fur-trade system, the other an American venture related to the St. Louis–South Pass axis of American traders. Because the Jesuits on various occasions worked among the Nez Perces and the Spokanes, they directly encroached upon Lapwai and Tshimakain, and thus gave substance to the Protestants' fears of an enveloping attack.

In December, 1843, all the Catholic missions were united under Blanchet, now designated Bishop of Drasa. In 1844 the Jesuits initiated regular services at Fort Colvile and began further work in the Kalispell region. The following year Blanchet went to Europe to recruit priests and nuns for an enlarged program. While he was there, the Vatican responded to his firsthand accounts of the potential of his realm by creating an ecclesiastical province of Oregon, with Blanchet as archbishop and metropolitan. Eight dioceses were delimited within, although only Oregon City, Vancouver Island, and Walla Walla were established immediately. In October, 1847, the Bishop of Walla Walla (A.M. Blanchet, the Archbishop's brother) settled in the crude house of a Cayuse chief on the Umatilla, another priest was sent to the Yakimas, and the Roman Catholic program for the tribes of the Columbia Plain got under way.[31] The Protestants' worst fears now seemed confirmed. Anticipation of exactly this sort of invasion had shaped Walker's view of the need to counter "influences" at the strategic portals; had united all these dissident missionaries against the abandonment of any station, however difficult or discouraging its prospects; had prompted their insistence upon the necessity of taking over The Dalles; and had underlaid their fervent pleas for more helpers and more good "Christian" (i.e., Protestant) settlers.

And so once again the Columbia interior had become a zone of strategic rivalry. Despite the different motivation, there were, broadly, striking similarities with the rivalry of the previous genera-

[30] Hubert Howe Bancroft, *History of Oregon* (San Francisco, 1886), I, 325; *An Illustrated History of North Idaho* (Spokane, 1903), p. 756.

[31] *Quebec Mission*, pp. 211-12. Other dioceses contemplated for the interior were Fort Hall, Colvile, and New Caledonia. See also Sister Letitia Mary Lyons, *Francis Norbert Blanchet and the Founding of the Oregon Missions (1838-1848)* (Washington, D.C., 1940), p. 164. W. D. Lyman, *History of the Yakima Valley, Washington* ... (1919), I, 187-89. The exact location of St. Rose, the first Yakima mission, is not clear. Lyman suggests that it was either at "Chemna" (Shimnap) or Simcoe.

tion: a reminiscent competition for strategic sites and the establishment of near-duplicate posts; rivalry for the favor of the same Indian
tribes; the same connecting links with remote headquarters of finance and control, the one overland to Canada, the other by sea and
by South Pass to America. Furthermore, to the Protestants—who
increasingly viewed the Roman Catholics as conniving agents of a
foreign power and themselves as the valiant spearhead of American
destiny—it appeared to be, once more, a clear-cut competition of
nationalities. Ultimately the contest would also end with unexpected
abruptness, though more tragically than the capitulation of the Astorians in 1813.

Pressure on the British

A statement of such parallels is, of course, largely a summary expression of the degree to which all the missionary programs had
been hung upon the framework of the fur company. But in these
same years that monopoly was itself shaken by the complicated
events of the time and region, forced to adapt its program to meet
trends it could not control; and, surprisingly, also had its effectiveness sapped by internal dissension. No significant changes were made
in the pattern of operations within the Columbia interior through
the early 1840's. Men and horses, furs and goods continued to move
along the same routes in the same seasonal rhythms. But the profits
of old had dwindled. The three posts of Kamloops, Okanogan, and
Nez Perces together took in barely a thousand beaver annually; New
Caledonia and Colvile continued profitable, but the returns were
half those of a decade before (Table 1, p. 88). To offset depletion
in the core of its Pacific domain, the company sought to extend the
perimeter. Trapping parties were sent to probe the "Youta Country, south of Great Salt Lake," others ventured to San Francisco
Bay, and an agreement with the Russian-American Fur Company
gave the British the right to trade as far north as Mount Fairweather
in return for agricultural supplies.[32]

---

[32] There were a few local alterations. Fort Boise was shifted to the mouth of
that river in 1839; in 1843 Fort Kamloops was rebuilt on the west bank of the
North Thompson. An excellent summary of these developments as well as of the
other features of the time to be discussed is contained in W. Kaye Lamb's Introductions to the Second Series (pp. xi-xlix) and Third Series (pp. xi-lxiii) of
McLoughlin's Letters edited by E. E. Rich; and in Rich, *Hudson's Bay Company*, Vol. II, chaps. xxiv and xxv.

Such actions thus not only represented an almost desperate attempt to tap new fur districts but reflected a growing diversification of the whole economic program. By the early 1840's the company was caught in a crisis at both ends: a drop in production in the source regions and a decline in price in the market area. Beaver hats were going out of style and "unless the tide of fashion change," the Governor lamented, the future certainly "holds out no very cheering prospect."[33] Activities begun as ancillary supports to the fur business increasingly took on autonomous commercial significance. Vancouver became less a great fur entrepôt, more a producing center of grain, livestock, and timber products; farms and pastures were developed at Nisqually and Cowlitz, and milling expanded at Willamette Falls.

At the same time the relative positions of the British and Americans in Oregon were being transformed. In 1839 the first trickle of avowed American colonists arrived in the Willamette; with the missionaries active on both sides of the Cascades, and with the American public beginning to be "much attracted to this country by the overcharged pictures of its fertility and commercial importance," the company recognized a real danger. In 1841 the company sponsored a "counter-immigration" of former employees from their Red River colony to Cowlitz and Nisqually, designed to strengthen the British claim to the area north of the Columbia. The growing crisis prompted Sir George Simpson in 1841 to make the third of his personal visits to this distant and troublesome department. As before, the dynamic Governor initiated sweeping changes (though none directly affecting the Columbia interior), but the results of his personal touch were far different from those of previous inspections. This time there was no hope of rationalizing and revitalizing the realm. More serious, each of his major changes was a direct contradiction of McLoughlin's policies, and the antagonism which developed between the two ended in McLoughlin's retirement in early 1846.[34]

The company soon lost all control and influence over colonization. The counterimmigration failed, as nearly all the colonists left within a year or so to settle in the more attractive country of the

---

[33] Rich (ed.), *McLoughlin's Letters, Second Series*, p. 306.

[34] *Ibid.*, p. 226. The situation was deeply aggravated by McLoughlin's reaction to Simpson's handling of the investigation of the murder of McLoughlin's son, who had been in charge at Fort Stikine.

Willamette. McLoughlin's hope that these settlers might dilute the American flavor of the valley was doomed by the flood of migrants which began to flow along the Oregon Trail in 1843. By 1845 more than five thousand Americans were settled south of the Columbia. In 1842 Simpson had ordered the establishment of Fort Victoria at the eastern tip of Vancouver Island, and it was constructed the following summer; two years later, in response to the heavy American influx, he initiated operational changes to begin the shift of Columbia District headquarters to the new post.

As the Oregon question, under the forced draft of American political campaigns, suddenly flared into an explosive international issue, the British government became sufficiently alarmed to order a secret military reconnaissance of the region. Despite the far-flung network of company "forts," the report was not encouraging. Fort Nez Perces, which had burned and been rebuilt of adobe in 1841, was declared to be the stoutest of all, but none of the posts was a worthy military establishment: "They are calculated to resist a sudden attack of a band of Indians, but cannot be considered as works of defense against a disciplined force." To make matters worse, the Athabasca Pass route was considered impracticable for troop movements, in contrast with the thoroughly tested South Pass wagon road of the Americans. Nevertheless, the British drew up a strategic plan. The principal features were the fortification of the Columbia estuary, a strong post at Oregon City (Willamette Falls) to "overawe" the American settlers, and a central base at Fort Nisqually from which, in summer, troops could be dispatched to any part of the territory. The whole plan depended upon getting such garrisons established before the Americans did the same.[35]

Fortunately for all, this doubtful strategic scheme was never put to the test. In fact, it reached London too late even to be considered, for the boundary issue was settled upon the forty-ninth parallel in June, 1846.[36] The news arrived in the Columbia in November, along

[35] Joseph Schafer (ed.), "Documents Relative to Warre and Vavasour's Military Reconnaissance in Oregon, 1845-6," *Oregon Historical Quarterly*, 10 (March, 1909), 41-42. The report noted that Indian routes from Puget Sound to the interior via the Wenatchee and Yakima rivers could be used by troops. No personal reconnaissance of these was made, but it was stated that in 1841 "the Hudson's Bay Company made use of these routes to convey cattle to Nesqually"; *ibid.*, p. 43.

[36] A good coverage of the boundary crisis and settlement as it related to the company is in John S. Galbraith, *The Hudson's Bay Company as an Imperial*

with orders from Simpson for a complete inventory of property south of the line. The treaty specifically recognized the company's rights to the lands it actually occupied and to free navigation on the Columbia, but it was clear that the Columbia Department had been sliced in two and that the southern half would have to be evacuated.

An incidental result of the military reconnaissance of 1845 was a tabulation of the number of men, acres under cultivation, and livestock at each post west of the Rockies. It is possible thereby to gain a summary picture of the Hudson's Bay Company's development at the climax of their Columbia empire. The totals for the 23 posts were as follows: 484 men; 3,005 acres under cultivation; 1,716 horses; 4,430 cattle; 1,906 hogs; and 8,848 sheep. The distribution of these among the separate establishments reflected the functional geography of the system. Fort Vancouver, the Cowlitz station, and Fort Nisqually were the provision and commercial centers. Together they accounted for over half the personnel (200 at Vancouver), all the sheep, nearly all the hogs, over four-fifths of the cattle, more than half the horses, and 2,300 of the 3,005 acres under cultivation. In addition, there were two flour mills and three sawmills at or near Vancouver and another sawmill at Cowlitz. Forts Langley and Victoria, though of lesser development—with 55 men, 360 acres, and over 200 head of cattle between them—further emphasized the concentrated development of company activities in the Willamette–Puget Sound Trough as a result of the recent emphasis upon commercial trade. Elsewhere along the coast, Fort Simpson was the only northern station that remained after Simpson's 1841 reorganization; the meager relict of Fort George was still maintained, presumably as a symbol of company command of the Columbia; and Fort Umpqua, the former halfway station to California, marked the southern limit of occupation.[37]

Factor, 1821-1869 (Berkeley and Los Angeles, 1957), chaps. xi and xii. This book also contains a valuable analysis of the company's relations with the Russians and Mexicans.

[37] "Enclosure 2," Schafer (ed.), "Warre and Vavasour's Reconnaissance," p. 60. It is evident that some of the figures, especially acreages, are rounded estimates. More exact totals for cultivated land, which show a few marked discrepancies with the Warre and Vavasour compilation, are given for the posts south of the new boundary in the inventory of 1846-47, published in T. C. Elliott, "British Values in Oregon, 1847," *Oregon Historical Quarterly*, 32 (March, 1931), 27-45. Other sources continue to list fur returns from Forts McLoughlin and Stikine, so these must have been at least seasonally occupied as collection points.

The Columbia interior posts were listed with the following:

Post	Men	Acres	Horses	Cattle	Hogs
Colvile	30	118	350	96	73
Flathead	5	—	—	—	—
Okanogan	2	7	—	—	—
Thompson River	15	6	—	—	—
Nez Perces	10	12	68	23	12
Boise	8	2	17	27	—
Hall	20	5	171	95	—
Totals	90	150	606	241	85

Colvile's traditional role as the main provision center for the interior, as well as for the eight posts of New Caledonia, is illustrated (it also had the only flour mill), as is the more recent significance of Fort Hall as a supplementary supply station for the Snake country.[38]

Still a great system of remarkable dimensions and impressive strategic design, it was nevertheless fast losing its former means of support (see Table 1, p. 88). Thirteen thousand beaver from the entire Columbia Department were hardly adequate justification for such a vast, complex, and expensive establishment. It seems apparent that even without the complications of American settlers, missionaries, and political agitation, the Hudson's Bay Company soon would have been forced to shift more heavily into other economic activities and to withdraw from large sectors of now marginally productive fur country. With the boundary settlement, plans were drawn for a gradual evacuation from the Columbia country.

Disaster and Dissolution

The end of fur trade and missions alike in the Great Columbia Plain came abruptly. The disaster at Waiilatpu need not be examined in detail. It is of some importance to note that the Cayuse had been hard hit by scarlet fever the previous winter, and that in the late summer and autumn of 1847 they were devastated by measles. Some contemporary accounts estimated that as many as half the tribe

[38] In New Caledonia each post had a small plot of cultivation, but only Fort St. James, the local headquarters, had any livestock. It should be noted that the number of horses at a particular station is not too significant, as they were shifted about according to seasonal demands; none are listed at Thompson River, yet at times a great many horses were kept there to serve the New Caledonia brigades.

died from these virulent infections, which were introduced by emi-grant parties. These trials, added to all the festering grievances and fears which had been accumulating, help to account for the overt explosion of November 29, 1847, against the foreign doctor in their midst. Whitman, his wife, and seven others were murdered on that day, four more Americans were killed in the vicinity within a week. Forty-six women and children were held captive at the mission for a month until Peter Skene Ogden and a small armed party of Hud-son's Bay personnel ransomed them at Fort Nez Perces for five hun-dred dollars' worth of trading goods. Spalding escaped only by chance and left the interior with the rescued group which was escoted to the Willamette. The missionaries at Tshimakain stayed on for sev-eral uneasy months, then they left with a military escort for the lower country. The Roman Catholic missions continued for a while, with some adjustments, but the chain of events stemming from the Whitman massacre eventually disrupted much of that program also. Bishop Blanchet left the Umatilla with the Ogden party (two priests stayed on until February) and established St. Peter's Mission at The Dalles. In 1850 his Diocese of Walla Walla was dissolved; Blanchet was transferred to the newly activated Diocese of Nisqually, and ad-ministration of all interior missions was given to the Archbishop of Oregon City. Work in the Yakima area continued until 1855 when the more general Indian war caused a withdrawal.[39] Only Colvile and the Coeur d'Alene and Flathead stations continued without in-terruption.

This sudden eruption of Indian wrath, though focused upon Waiilatpu and confined for the time being to the Cayuse tribe, was a sufficiently ominous disturbance to cause an immediate shift in the Hudson's Bay Company's operations. Fortunately, under the spur of the boundary settlement, a feasible route connecting the Okanogan Valley with the lower Fraser via the Similkameen, just north of the forty-ninth parallel, had been reconnoitered in 1846 and 1847. Ra-ther than risk a run through the Fort Nez Perces danger zone, the interior brigade of 1848 used the new route to take out the returns from Colvile, Thompson River, and New Caledonia. In May the party of fifty men and four hundred horses broke the path across to the Fraser, where Fort Yale had been hastily constructed, and on down to Fort Langley. Later that summer the Snake country returns

[39] Lyman, *Yakima Valley*, pp. 188-89.

were forwarded, the last significant shipments to come from that old and troublesome sector. In 1849 a customs district for Oregon was established, imposing a duty on all British imports; American troops occupied rented quarters at Fort Vancouver; and American squatters began to swarm in upon the company's lands on the lower Columbia. By 1850 hope for a gradual, orderly withdrawal waned. The fur business had ended, the company was anxious to evacuate, and the only motive for staying was to sustain hope for an equitable liquidation.[40]

Thus the mission system was destroyed: Waiilatpu was now a charred ruin; Lapwai, Tshimakain, and Wascopam were empty shells; and the fur company was disrupted and dying. For the moment fewer emigrants passed through, for after 1848 gold diverted the main overland stream south and west along the Humboldt to California. Those who did come entered the region with a sense of danger and anxiety, and hurried through without hope of a restful pause and succor in the far-famed Walla Walla. The Indians had reacted to the impact of the white intrusion, and though actual violence had been precipitated by only a portion of one tribe, the shock waves of that explosion had rippled through the entire region, leaving a wake of instability and restlessness, igniting a smouldering tension of fear and defiance.

In the Great Columbia Plain, Fort Nez Perces remained as the only tangible evidence of the continuity of more than three decades of occupation and activity. But it was now an empty symbol of a bygone era, a useless pile in the midst of an apparently worthless area. The first stage of the invasion was over.

---

[40] Anderson, "Northwest Coast, pp. 110-13. About eight hundred beaver were sent out that year; in 1849 and 1850 only ninety-three and thirty-three pelts were forwarded, evidently the product of local trading at Boise and Hall. Ralph Richard Martig, "Hudson's Bay Company Claims, 1846-69," *Oregon Historical Quarterly*, 36 (March, 1935), 60-70.

CHAPTER SEVEN

Like an immense monster of desolation to these Indians the waves of civilization are fast approaching. . . .

LIEUTENANT JOHN MULLAN

How true it is that a stranger in a strange country is like an infant just opening its eyes upon the world. Everything has to be learned by observation and experience.

HENRY SPALDING

Preparations: Clearing, Organizing, and Evaluating the Land

CLEARING THE LAND

MID-CENTURY was a time of transition. One general pattern of human organization of the Great Plain built up over many years had been suddenly dissolved; it would take time to replace it with another. This intervening period had its own distinctive character. The most obvious feature was warfare: sporadic, but always imminent; at times confused and futile, at times orderly and effective, but ultimately decisive in its influence upon the region; the bitter harvest of the past which established the seedbed of the future.

Prelude: 1848-55

The shock of the Whitman massacre produced a demand among the American settlers of the Willamette for immediate revenge upon the Cayuse and for re-establishing security along the Oregon Trail. But Waiilatpu lay two hundred miles away in a wasteland; there were no federal troops in Oregon, and the settlers' numbers and resources limited the possibilities. In a few weeks a volunteer militia was formed, which arrived at The Dalles in January, 1848, erected a stockade, installed a single small cannon, and proclaimed it Fort Lee.

Guarding the strategic portal to the interior, the "fort" was designated as headquarters for the military operations.[1]

But the frustrations of their task were soon apparent. As the militia headed inland, they were harassed by small bands of mounted warriors, who scattered and disappeared in the hills when pressed. On March 2 they settled in among the ruins at Waiilatpu, dignifying the cluster of tumble-down adobe walls as "Fort Waters." Indian comissioners had been sent ahead to assure all other tribes that the Americans had come only to punish those Cayuse directly responsible for the massacre. But the longer they remained, the more clouded the issue became: how to know who the guilty ones were; how even to know who was a Cayuse among the intermingled peoples of the Walla Walla; where to seek those hiding out? After weeks of frustration, rumors that the guilty group had joined with the Palouses north of the Snake prompted a grand but fruitless sweep through the Palouse country; the Indians had fled undetected.

By late May it was clear that, for the time being, the task was beyond the resources, patience, and ingenuity of the militia. The volunteers were anxious to get back to their farms and families, ammunition was short, horses were travel worn, and the Indians could hide out all summer. Still, it seemed important to keep a grip upon the interior. To withdraw completely would be an admission of failure, and would leave the late-summer emigrant trains at the mercy of marauders. But these men were not professional soldiers, and the only inducement for them to stay was land. Accordingly, the Territorial Superintendent of Indian Affairs gave authority to colonize the Walla Walla Valley. This move contradicted the assurances which had been given the nonbelligerent Indians; the excuse was that, since the Cayuse tribe had refused to surrender their guilty members, it was proper that their lands be taken. The action was publicized in the Willamette as the "Forfeiture of the Cayuse Lands," together with glowing descriptions of the attractions of the area for settlement. Thus, about sixty men agreed to stay on and made arrangements to move their families that autumn. Whitman's grist mill was repaired, a store of seed wheat was made available, and the confiscated cattle and horses of the Cayuse provided the beginnings of herds.[2] The main body of the militia left for western

[1] Details of the campaign of 1848 have been drawn primarily from Bancroft, *History of Oregon*, Vol. I, chap. xxv.

[2] Thomas R. Garth, Jr., "Waiilatpu After the Massacre," *Pacific Northwest*

Oregon, accompanied by the missionaries who had been escorted down from Tshimakain. A few men stayed on at The Dalles, in the same fashion and for similar purposes as in the Walla Walla region. By their presence these soldier-settlers gave security to the emigrant trains of that summer, but as the travel season waned, the prospects of actual colonization and wintering in the interior caused many to reconsider their decision. Evidently no more than a dozen or so decided to stick it out on land claims in the Walla Walla area. Thus, the positive results of the "Cayuse War" were further diminished.

For the next five years the relationship between the two peoples was unmarred by major conflict. The emigrant trains descended the Blue Mountains and passed down the Umatilla through Cayuse territory only to find members of that dreaded tribe peddling potatoes from the scattering of garden patches along the river, or ready to trade cattle and horses.[3]

In June, 1851, the Territorial Indian Superintendent visited the tribe and established an agency on the lower Umatilla. Roman Catholic priests returned on occasion to this corner of the region, and continued in residence at Cataldo, Colvile, The Dalles, and in the Yakima Valley. In 1853 Theodore Winthrop visited two Oblate Fathers at their mission on the Ahtanum, which impressed this New Englander as "a strange and unlovely spot for religion"; while the priests had become "influential friends" of the Indians, he felt that they had dealt more successfully with potatoes than polygamy. White settlers remained few in number and impermanent in location. A handful held cattle herds in the Walla Walla and Touchet valleys and along the creeks just east of The Dalles. A few traders took up seasonal positions along the emigrant road to peddle fresh meat, flour, and other necessities. A ferry operated during the traffic season at the difficult Deschutes crossing. A few miners, drifting out from the Sierras, began to test some of the streams, but with little success.[4]

Quarterly, 38 (October, 1947), 315-18.

[3] P. V. Crawford, "Journal of a Trip Across the Plains, 1851," Oregon Historical Society Quarterly, 25 (June, 1924), 163; Eleanor Allen, Canvas Caravans (Portland, Ore., 1946), p. 99; Margaret Booth (ed.), "Overland from Indiana to Oregon: The Dinwiddie Journal," Sources of Northwest History, No. 2 (Missoula, Mont., n.d.), p. 12; Gwen Castle, "Belshaw Journey, Oregon Trail, 1853," Oregon Historical Quarterly, 32 (September, 1931), 234.

[4] Bancroft, History of Oregon, II, 213-14, 741. Theodore Winthrop, The Canoe and Saddle or Klalam and Klickitat, ed. by John H. Williams (Tacoma,

The only point of development which offered a solid hint of the future was at The Dalles. In May, 1850, a company of federal troops staked out a military reserve encompassing the old mission site and established Fort Dalles. Designed to police this strategic and troublesome point and also as a base for patrol of the Oregon Trail to the east, it was the kind of reliable fixture which fostered other developments. In the following year a steamboat began operating a shuttle between there and the Cascades. One immigrant arriving in September, 1852, found two stores "pretty well-stocked with provisions, dry goods, etc.," a blacksmith shop, a few houses, and a busy river landing where large flatboats capable of carrying thirty to forty dismantled wagons were available for hire. She thought it a meager little cluster, disappointing after long weeks of wilderness travel; nevertheless, for the region it was a significant nucleus.[5]

Although the scale of such developments was small, combined with other events of the time, their impact upon the Indians was large. The number of settlers was at most a few dozen, but they disdained Indian rights, locating where they pleased, quick to meet the slightest provocation with threats and force. Prospectors roamed peripheral stream valleys—the common sites of Indian summer camps—in increasing numbers. Whiskey sellers peddled their product indiscriminately, despite the opposition of many whites and Indians alike. And emigrant trains—whose straying stock, needs for supplies, and short-tempered defensiveness of families and property were always a fruitful source of conflict—continued not only to move through the region but to break new trails. In 1853 a large train decided to take a short cut to Puget Sound and traveled through the Yakima country and over Naches Pass. In the autumn of the next year, a party of Canadians bound for California from the Red River crossed the Rockies near Banff and arrived in the Spokane country, and some stayed to winter their livestock in that area and in the Walla Walla. And other trail searching, even more significant, was under way. In the summer of 1854 a military party surveyed a road from Puget Sound to Walla Walla via Naches Pass, and a group of parties under

Wash., 1913), pp. 171-73. "Great nos. went from this country [the Willamette] last June to explore the Spokane and Nez Perces countries for gold, they have returned unsuccessful," Spalding Letters, July 20, 1850, p. 357.

[5] Bancroft, *History of Oregon,* Vol. II, 91, 252-53, 256. The initial reservation was ten miles square, soon reduced to one. Conflicts over land claims arising from the mission era were to plague the town and vicinity for many years; *ibid.,* II, 290-93. Allen, *Canvas Caravans,* p. 103.

the direction of Isaac Stevens, governor of the newly created Washington Territory, crisscrossed the region reconnoitering feasible Pacific railroad routes. Finally, gold was discovered near Fort Colvile the following summer, and as the news spread the traffic to the diggings sharply increased.[6]

Thus, the volume and variety of contacts within the Great Columbia Plain was expanded during these few years, and every district, every Indian group, was directly touched. It was inevitable that fears, angers, and restlessness grew, and as the tensions increased it became apparent to many people that some decisive, comprehensive policy had to be implemented if an explosion were to be averted. Unfortunately, there was no agreement as to what that policy ought to be. And so, in the summer of 1855, the threshold of conflict was again reached (Map 14).

Most Indian leaders saw that it would be impossible to seal off the whole Columbia Plain, and they were willing to allow emigrants and other transients to pass through their lands; there were, in fact, good economic reasons for favoring such traffic. But fear of settlers was intense; the recent history of the Willamette and Rogue River areas undermined any confidence that a stable, mutually advantageous relationship could be established.

The Indians were not alone in this view. "If any country in the world has ever merited the title of 'Indian country', *this is it,*" wrote Major Gabriel Rains, commanding at Fort Dalles. He meant that it not only *was* Indian country but *ought to remain* so, and he went on to ridicule the recent establishment of Wasco County, complete with a set of officials, encompassing the whole of eastern Oregon ("the largest county ever known") and inhabited by perhaps thirty-five whites. He further described the mounting troubles, which in his view the whites had largely brought on themselves, and he predicted outright war if such deplorable conditions continued. It was the very kind of report which the man to whom it was addressed, General John E. Wool, commanding the Department of the Pacific from dis-

[6] David Longmire, "First Immigrants to Cross the Cascades," *Washington Historical Quarterly*, 8 (January, 1917), 22-28. John V. Campbell, "The Sinclair Party—An Emigration Overland Along the Old Hudson Bay Company Route from Manitoba to the Spokane Country in 1854," *Washington Historical Quarterly*, 7 (July, 1916), 187-201. They found five whites along the Spokane with four or five hundred head of cattle. Anderson, "Northwest Coast," pp. 117-18; J. Ross Browne, *Indian War in Oregon and Washington Territories*, 35th Cong., 1st sess., H. Ex. Doc. 38 (1857-58), p. 12.

tant Benicia, California, understood and with which he agreed. For
Wool, the Columbia Plain was but one far corner of a vast area
pockmarked with troubles and policed by limited forces of doubtful
effectiveness. The maintenance costs in the department were enormous, and campaign logistics were often circumscribed by the enormous distances, inadequate equipment, and scarcity of supplies.
Economy of action was a necessary principle. But more than that,
most army officers had little sympathy for either the means or the
objectives of many of their fellow citizens. Experience had taught
them that Americans often attacked and plundered the Indians for
no proper reason. Further, with the Willamette open for settlement
there was, in their view, no excuse for trying to seize this whole
barren interior country. Thus, the army viewed its role as one of
keeping the peace, stabilizing relationships, patrolling the trafficways
—in short, of protecting what it considered to be the legitimate
interests of Indian and white alike. During these years the troops at
Fort Dalles had made a couple of summer patrols along the emigrant
road to seek out and punish some Snake Indians who had attacked
wagon trains east of Fort Boise, but no overt show of force had been
made, no pressure exerted upon the tribes of the Great Plain.[7]

Obviously such a policy was anathema to most of the American
settlers and local leaders in the Northwest, who wanted freedom as
well as security to settle, travel, and do as they pleased wherever they
pleased. Isaac Stevens was the most vigorous and fair-minded advocate of the interests of the settlers. He had been impressed by the
mission accomplishments at Cataldo, and he was convinced that a
segregation policy (by which the Indians could be cleared from most
of the area but would be granted homesteads, taught the arts of
civilization, and given security within the confines of a reserved portion of land) was the only practicable solution to the problem.[8]

[7] 33rd Cong., 2nd sess., S. Ex. Doc. 16 (1855), pp. 16-17. See pp. 104, 119-21,
for an account of the 1854 patrol, and 34th Cong., 1st sess., H. Ex. Doc. 1, Pt. 2
(1856), pp. 78-79, for that of 1855. A fine, balanced treatment of army attitudes
and policies and of the bitter controversies between army officers and local officials is that of Robert Carlton Clark, "Military History of Oregon, 1849-59,"
Pacific Northwest Quarterly, 36 (March, 1945), 14-59.

[8] Thus the Washington Territorial Legislature memorialized Congress with
the plea that "the interests of this territory require that its citizens should be
allowed at once to occupy that portion of this territory [the Interior] for agricultural and especially for grazing purposes, without molestation." Quoted in
C. F. Coan, "The Adoption of the Reservation Policy in the Pacific Northwest,
1853-1855," *Oregon Historical Society Quarterly*, 23 (March, 1922), 13. 33rd

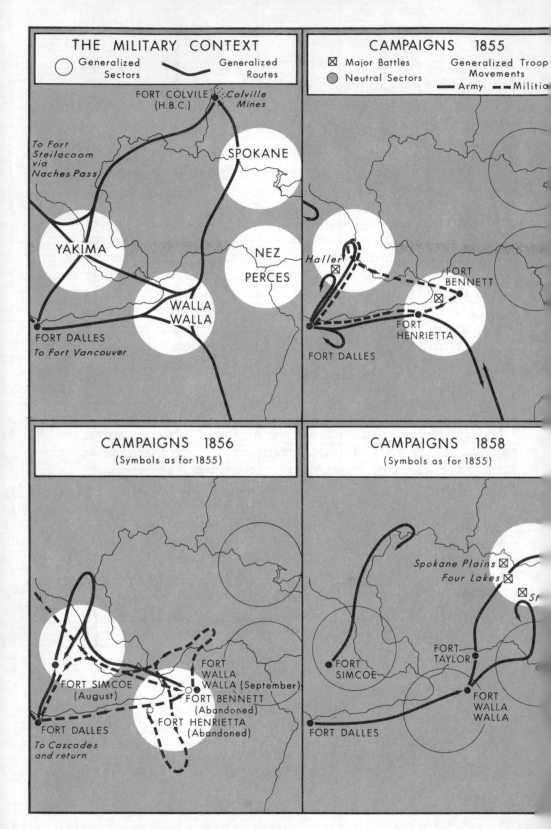

Map 14, upper left; Map 15, upper right; Map 16, lower left; Map 17, lower right

In the early summer of 1855, Stevens, in his capacity as superintendent of Indian affairs in his territory, and Joel Palmer, superintendent for Oregon, convened a council in the Walla Walla Valley to negotiate just such a reservation agreement. After two weeks of argument, a combination of persuasion, threats, and bribery yielded an agreement on three reservations, each to be supplied with schools and teachers, mills, millers, and mechanics. In addition, each tribe was to receive an indemnity in cash and goods for the land yielded. Following this, Palmer returned to The Dalles and persuaded the several bands of that vicinity to agree to a reservation.[9] The Indians were to be allowed a year to settle within these allotments, but Stevens and Palmer immediately declared all remaining land open to colonization.

If implemented successfully, these treaties would significantly alter the geography of Indian-white relationships. In the Yakima sector the several tribes would be so concentrated as to leave most of the trafficways to Colville and across the Cascades clear of Indian lands.[10] In the Walla Walla area, the Indians had been induced to relinquish the whole valley and to accept a reservation along the upper Umatilla. The Oregon Trail was to be relocated so as to bypass the Indians' lands. The Dalles bands were allotted lands in the Warm Springs area south of Tygh Valley. Although they retained certain fishing privileges, their home base was also to be shifted beyond the margin of the Plain well away from the emigrant road. The Nez Perces, being remote from areas of direct white interest, were given a

Cong., 2nd sess., S. Ex. Doc. 1 (1855), pp. 425, 455. See also the report of the Indian Agent of Middle Oregon, 33rd Cong., 1st sess., S. Ex. Doc. 1 (1854), pp. 486-93, for a similar view.

[9] The Indians, in anticipation, are reported to have held a strategy meeting the previous autumn in the Grande Ronde. In keeping with their view of how the problem ought to be solved, a clever scheme had been proposed by which each leader would describe his tribal boundaries and insist that the whole be made the reservation for his people; the tribal limits were to be coordinated so that together the entire Great Plain, excepting only the Walla Walla Valley, would be included. A. J. Splawn, *Ka-mi-akin, Last Hero of the Yakimas* (Portland, Ore., 1944), pp. 24-26. Dissension within and among some of the tribes defeated this plan. These negotiations are covered in detail in Hubert Howe Bancroft's *History of Washington, Idaho, and Montana*, and *History of Oregon*, Vol. II. The actual treaties, detailing the boundaries and all provisions, are published in C. J. Kappler, *Indian Affairs, Laws and Treaties* 57th Cong., 1st sess., S. Ex. Doc. 452 (1901-2), Vol. II.

[10] The "Yakima Nation" of the treaty included the Yakimas, Klickitats, Pisquouse, Palouses, and Middle Columbia bands.

large reservation, which included all the important districts of their homeland. As the local Salish tribes were not a party to these negotiations, the Spokane sector remained unaffected.

Explosion: 1855-65

The success of this bold initiative was astonishing but fragile. The bargaining and intratribal quarreling left many of the Indians more restless than ever, and within a few weeks the gold finds at Colville were attracting many miners across the region who, in the mild phrase of one observer, "were not always over-scrupulous in regard to the rights and property of the Indians." When an Indian agent, who had gone to investigate rumors that several miners had been killed in the Yakima area, was himself murdered, the spark of conflict was ignited. The Fort Dalles troops were on a punitive foray far east on the Oregon Trail, but upon their return an expedition into the Yakima area was organized. The plan was to send two companies north from The Dalles and another east from Fort Steilacoom via Naches Pass to meet in the middle Yakima Valley. Major Granville Haller left Fort Dalles on October 3, 1855, with 5 officers and 102 infantrymen; three days later several hundred Indians attacked them at Toppenish Creek, forced an immediate retreat, and harassed them all the way back over the ridge country (Map 15). The force from Steilacoom crossed the mountains, learned of the defeat, and quickly retired. It was an ignominious inaugural for the army, but, more important, what might have been a police action was transformed into a war.[11]

The southern half of the Great Columbia Plain was now aflame. Indian agents reported that the tribes of the Yakima and Walla Walla areas had formed an alliance and that there was coordination with tribes threatening Puget Sound. This ominous prospect unleashed a

[11] 34th Cong., 1st sess., H. Ex. Doc. 93 (1853), p. 57. The Klickitats were especially disgruntled because they had been forcibly repatriated out of some lands immediately west of the Cascades, and because they had been sold out by the Yakimas at the Stevens council. *Ibid.*, and Browne, *Indian War*, p. 9. Fort Steilacoom had been established on land leased from the Hudson's Bay Company near Fort Nisqually. Fort Vancouver was similarly established at the former fur post. These and The Dalles outpost constituted the federal army posts in the Pacific Northwest at the time. Haller lost five killed, seventeen wounded, many animals and supplies, and abandoned his only cannon. 34th Cong., 1st sess., H. Ex. Doc. 1, Pt. 2 (1856), pp. 80-89. For the subsequent campaigns in 1855-56, I have depended primarily upon 34th Cong., 1st sess., H. Ex. Doc. 93 and 118 (1856), and 34th Cong., 3rd sess., H. Ex. Doc. 1 (1856), pp. 147-203.

flurry of activities and plans among the Americans. The first important result of Haller's defeat was the abandonment of the Walla Walla area on orders of the local Indian agent, a withdrawal which finally ended the Hudson's Bay Company tenure at Fort Nez Perces.[12]

It was an act endorsed by the army and severely criticized by Stevens, and thus epitomized the sharp conflict in objectives of these two authorities. As Stevens was governor, Indian superintendent, and commander-in-chief of his territorial militia, the conflict was carried beyond mere argument into actual overlapping, conflicting strategies. The army continued to believe its task to be occupying the area and applying economic pressure to re-establish stability. The territorial authorities sought the decisive defeat and if necessary the destruction of any belligerent tribes. Thus, after an indecisive joint army-militia foray into the Yakima in November, General Wool began a careful build-up of men, horses, and supplies so that secure outposts could be established in the Yakima and Walla Walla valleys the next spring. But Stevens insisted on the need to occupy the Walla Walla immediately and wanted to undertake a winter campaign to drive all the hostiles into the Yakima for a decisive showdown.[13]

Bitter disagreement led to independent action.[14] The militia

[12] Palmer reported that the agent arrived at Fort Dalles on October 25 "with all the American and a part of the French settlers of the Walla-Walla, Toosha, and Umatilla valleys." The French were retired fur company personnel, most of whom had Indian wives; 34th Cong., 1st sess., H. Ex. Doc. 93 (1856), p. 82. Bancroft reported that about sixty whites were in the area. The Indian agent had a conference with the factor at Fort Nez Perces, and they decided to dump all the ammunition in the river and move what few supplies remained to Flathead post. Fort Boise had already been closed; Fort Hall soon would be. Bancroft, *History of Washington, Idaho and Montana*, pp. 139-40; and D. Geneva Lent, *West of the Mountains: James Sinclair and the Hudson's Bay Company* (Seattle, Wash., 1963), pp. 272-78.

[13] "They can only be conquered or brought to terms," General Wool explained to his superiors, "by occupying their country and such positions as would command their fisheries and valleys, where their cattle and horses must graze," 34th Cong., 1st sess., H. Ex. Doc. 93 (1856), p. 16. 34th Cong., 1st sess., H. Ex. Doc. 118 (1856), pp. 39-43.

[14] While Stevens' policies were representative and influential, he did not exactly mastermind all the movements of even his own militia; and, of course, that of Oregon was under separate command. It may also be noted that Stevens was a soldier as well as a political leader. He had graduated first in his class from West Point and had served a dozen years, including the Mexican campaign, before he was appointed governor.

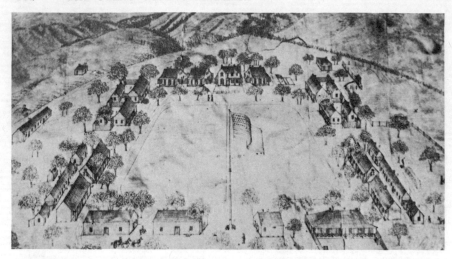

Fort Simcoe in the Yakima country, as sketched in 1858 by Captain Anthony Heger, assistant surgeon. *(Photo courtesy of Washington State University Library)*

headed for the Walla Walla. En route they built a stockade at the old Cayuse agency on the Umatilla, which they named Fort Henrietta. Nearing the valley, they were attacked by a band of Cayuse and their allies. When the battle was over the militia encamped and fortified a place two miles beyond Waiilatpu, which was called Fort Bennett. It was an unusually cold winter, and no further action was undertaken until March, 1856, when the militia, anxious to return to their families and farms, attempted a broad sweep to round up all the Indians of the area and drive them westward to confinement or destruction (Map 16). The only result was the plundering of a few Indians, surprised in their scattered winter camps; it was precisely the kind of disorderly, indiscriminate killing and scavenging that disgusted the army officers.

The army soon produced a similar disgust among the territorial officials by their own blundering strategy. Colonel George Wright, now in command in the Northwest, had been ordered to occupy the Yakima and Walla Walla sectors as soon as feasible. However, Wright believed that the former area had been pacified by the show of force the previous November, and he therefore decided that the main need was to occupy the Walla Walla Valley, primarily to replace the militia, which he viewed as a greater threat to the peace than the Indians. Accordingly, he left Fort Dalles for the Walla Walla in early April, with nearly all of his army. He was scarcely underway when he learned that the Yakimas and Klickitats had besieged the Cascade portage, a critical point on his supply and communications line which he had left virtually undefended. Thus, he backtracked, sent a force by steamboat to drive off the attackers, and revised his entire plan. The Yakima now had priority, and Wright spent much of the summer in a ponderous, deliberate sweep through the main valley, the Kittitas, and to the Wenatchee and back. On July 18, he announced that the "war" in the Yakima country was over. Actually there had been no war at all. The leaders of the Cascades attack had fled, and the tribes were peacefully congregating at their usual fishing sites.

As a result of this extensive reconnaissance, the Simcoe Valley was selected as the best location for a permanent post in this sector. It seemed to provide a good combination of local site and general strategic advantages. The valley was relatively warm in winter, there was grass for the animals, good land for gardening, and excellent pine a short distance to the west. It was on the main trail from Fort Dalles, in a position to command the whole Yakima Valley and also to keep a check on the troublesome Klickitats, who wintered in the valley beyond the ridge to the southwest. In August construction of Fort Simcoe was begun.[15]

The army was now ready to turn its attention once again to the Walla Walla, and in August four companies were detached under Colonel Edward J. Steptoe to establish a post in that sector. As usual the competitive strategies of the two authorities continued to complicate the over-all military design. When Stevens heard that Wright, after the Cascades episode, had moved his entire force into the Yakima, he feared that the Walla Walla sector might become a major rallying place for Indian retaliation; the possibility that the Nez Perces might join the conflict was an especially grave danger. Therefore he dispatched several companies of militia—some from The Dalles, some from Puget Sound by way of Naches Pass—to

[15] Wright's selection of this site is covered in two of his dispatches to General Wool in 34th Cong., 3rd sess., H. Ex. Doc. 1 (1845), pp. 168, 178. An excellent detailed and illustrated account of the construction and history of Fort Simcoe is that of H. Dean Guie, *Bugles in the Valley: The Story of Garnett's Fort Simcoe* (Yakima, Wash., 1956). All of the Yakima campaigns are also related in that volume, and it has proved a useful supplement to the government documents cited.

occupy the valley in June. Thus, the army objective, again, was not only to quell any Indian uprising but to replace the volunteer militia.

In September Colonel Wright reported that "The colonel [Steptoe] has selected a position on Mill Creek for the military post. It is five miles below Whitman's old mill-site, is directly on the trails from the Nez Perces, Spokane, and Palouse country, and controls the entire valley. Colonel Steptoe considers the position preferable to any other in that section of the country." If the two authorities clashed on policies, they did agree in their evaluation of this particular location, for Stevens had earlier summarized its advantages:

> Its position to overcome hostile Indians, and to protect the several immigrant routes is remarkably central. It is in direct connection with the great South Pass immigrant trail, and with all the northern routes explored by me from the sources of the Missouri. Roads run to the Nez Perces country, to the Yakima country, and via the Cascades to the Sound and to Colville. It is the central point of Indians within two to three hundred miles—. . . numbering some nine thousand.

He further detailed the favorable local features of mild winter climate, ample grass, good land for cereals, timber and fuel within easy distance, and, at that time, herds of beef cattle and a nucleus of settlers already established. That those settlers were no longer there was a raw issue between these leaders. Whereas Stevens insisted that the settlers should have stayed on and received the protection they were entitled to, and that their withdrawal had only spurred the Indians into overt hostility, the army publicly proclaimed its opposite view:

Fort Dalles, O.T.,
Aug. 20th, 1856

> The undersigned, having been designated to establish a military post in the Walla Walla country, and with a view to prevent all misunderstanding on the subject, believes it proper to make known the following instructions he has recently received from the Pacific Military Department.
>
> No emigrant or other white person, except the Hudson's Bay Co., or persons having ceded rights from the Indians, will be permitted to settle or to remain in the Indian country, or on land not settled or not confirmed by the Senate and approved by the President of the United States.
>
> These orders are not, however, to apply to the miners engaged in collecting gold at Colville mines.
>
> (signed)   E. J. Steptoe,
Brev't Col. U.S.A.

As Stevens' ill-fated reservation treaties had never been confirmed by the Senate and no lands had been opened by the federal government, this prohibition was absolute.[16]

The military occupation of the Walla Walla successfully stabilized that section, and in September the members of the militia left for their homes beyond the mountains. For the first time, the army was in sole command. The nearly eight hundred troops were soon distributed about equally among the three permanent posts. Fort Dalles guarded the strategic portal, the two new forts secured the troublesome Yakima and Walla Walla sectors, the Nez Perces and Spokanes remained quiet, and the army was determined to keep a firm grip on the interior until a comprehensive policy could be established. For General Wool, the whites, not the Indians, remained the principal threat to the peace. When Colonel Steptoe suggested that perhaps "a good, industrious colony at Walla Walla" would be advantageous, he received a vigorous rejoinder from his commander. Such a move would ignore those "natural advantages" of the Northwest "of which the army should avail itself"; the Cascade Range formed "a most valuable wall of separation between two races always at war when in contact," observed Wool. "To permit settlers to pass The Dalles and occupy the natural reserve, is to give up this advantage, throw down the wall, and advance the frontier hundreds of miles to the east, and add to the protective labors of the army." Prohibition of settlement was therefore to be strictly maintained; "the army cannot furnish guards to farm houses dotted among hostile tribes."[17]

General Wool realized that this was not a permanent solution, and he urged that new treaties be negotiated, but by impartial federal officials rather than by local authorities. Stevens' reservations were too severe, in Wool's opinion, and "the country is not worth

[16] 34th Cong., 3rd sess., H. Ex. Doc. 1 (1854), pp. 169, 194-95; *ibid.*, H. Ex. Doc. 76, pp. 337-38. An attempt was made in January, 1857, to extend federal land laws over the region east of the Cascades, but as the Indian treaties had not been ratified and therefore the Indian title had not been legally extinguished, the administration strongly disapproved this action. Thus, despite the independent measures of territorial authorities, for the time being "no public land, properly so called, exists *east* of the Cascade mountains." 34th Cong., 3rd sess., S. Misc. Doc. 28 (1857), pp. 1-4, dated Feb. 12, 1857.

[17] 35th Cong., 1st sess., H. Ex. Doc. 11 (1857-58), pp. 78-79. Wool's reply to Steptoe is included in 34th Cong., 3rd sess., H. Ex. Doc. 76 (1856), pp. 255-56, in a letter dated Jan. 1, 1857, signed by General Wool's adjutant.

the expense" of trying to force the Indians into acceptance. The Governor, on the other hand, opposed the army's grip upon the interior and tried to re-establish Walla Walla County ("the county the Military undertook to *keep rubbed out"*) and reopen the area to settlers; but to no avail. For more than a year the impasse remained.

Finale: 1858

The final phase of this era began in the spring of 1858. In April a band of Palouse Indians moved south and stole some of the army's cattle; rumors spread that whites en route to Colville had been killed in the scabland country, and petitions from the mining district asked for more protection. Accordingly, Colonel Steptoe left Fort Walla Walla on May 2 with four companies of dragoons and infantry to make a show of force through the Palouse country (Map 17).[18] Wanting to intersect troublemakers, Steptoe took a route eastward to Alpowa Creek and then crossed the Snake into the eastern Palouse country. The hostile Indians, as usual, had fled, and Steptoe decided to move on north toward Colville. But this was the first time that a military force had invaded the Spokane sector, and the Spokanes and Coeur d'Alenes became alarmed. Over a thousand Indians confronted the army just beyond Pine Creek, and their leaders asked for an explanation of this intrusion into their lands. Steptoe assured them that he was bound for Colville without hostile intentions; but he was off the main trail to that place, and the Indians, suspecting treachery, refused to offer boats and assistance to cross the Spokane River. When Steptoe, unprepared for a real battle, decided to withdraw, the Indians, now sure of their assessment, seized upon this indication of weakness to press an attack. After an all-day battle on the heights above Pine Creek, the army managed to sneak away in the middle of the night and flee southward to the Snake River.

A disaster had been narrowly averted, and Colonel Wright saw no choice but to retaliate in full force. Reinforcements were sent up from Fort Dalles, and by August the campaign was readied. During these summer weeks the number of miners traversing the region had been suddenly increased by the news of rich gold discoveries on the Fraser, and some prospectors had skirmished with the Indians in the

[18] The details of the 1858 campaigns are based upon 35th Cong., 2nd sess., S. Ex. Doc. 32 (1859).

Wenatchee area.[19] For this reason the army undertook parallel movements northward from Fort Simcoe and Fort Walla Walla.

Wright's Spokane operation was designed to insure a decision: twelve companies of troops, new rifles to replace the old short-range muskets, and ample quantities of ammunition and supplies. The strategic crossing of the Snake at the mouth of the Tucannon was fortified and garrisoned (Fort Taylor), and the eleven remaining companies and their large baggage train moved northward along the main Colville road. As they approached the tongue of open pine forest which projects southwestward along the scabland channels, a large force of Spokanes, Coeur d'Alenes, and Palouses began an intermittent harassment. On September 1 a more direct fight ensued, climaxed by an army charge which took a heavy toll of the Indians without the slightest casualty to the army. Disciplined, trained cavalry, armed with superior weapons, had shifted the usual indecisive balance between the two forces. Four days later an all-day skirmish further weakened the Indians without loss to the army, and with this the fighting was over. Departing from previous practice, however, Wright determined to insure his victory by inflicting a severe economic blow. Moving through the Spokane Valley to the Cataldo Mission, the soldiers captured and killed over nine hundred horses and destroyed whatever stores of grain, vegetables, dried roots, and berries they could find. Having intimidated the Indians by this trail of "slaughter and devastation," and having compelled them to sign peace treaties, Wright headed back to Fort Walla Walla, pausing to hang a few presumed ringleaders on the way. On the last day of September, 1858, he sent a succinct message to his superior: "Sir: The war is closed. Peace is restored with the Spokanes, Coeur d'Alenes and Palouses."

The sweep northward from Fort Simcoe reached as far as the Okanogan country and returned without encountering any concerted resistance, and it appeared likely that hostilities were at an end there, too. The permanence of the peace thus imposed was unpredictable at the time, but in fact, despite numerous petty incidents, the era of open warfare was over in the Great Columbia Plain.[20] Reviewed broadly, the sequence of action had spread step

[19] Rodney Glisan, *Journal of Army Life* (San Francisco, Calif., 1874), pp. 406-7, 413.

[20] Twenty years later the Nez Perces War would momentarily touch the mar-

by step into successive geographic sectors (following the initial punitive foray against the Cayuse): first the Yakima, next the Walla
Walla, finally the Spokane. That the Nez Perces, in the words of an
army officer, had remained one of the "oases in this desert of war,"
was of fundamental importance, for the neutrality of that large tribe
had sharply reduced the scale of conflict. The Stevens treaties were
reaffirmed and finally ratified by the Senate and signed by the President in 1859. Thus, the military era impressed important alterations
upon the human geography of the interior. Permanent army posts
now guarded three strategic locales; four reservations defined the
legally recognized tribal lands of the Yakima–Klickitat–Palouse, the
Cayuse–Walla Walla–Umatilla, the Nez Perces, and those of The
Dalles area. The Spokanes and Coeur d'Alenes, still free to live in
their homelands, were crippled and cowed by loss of property and
harsh punishment. Although there was no immediate forced removal of any of these Indians to their designated reservations, their
control over other lands and routes was ended and their influence
on patterns to come would be negligible.

ORGANIZING THE LAND

Politics

While the military branches of the national and territorial governments were busy "clearing" the land, the legislative branches
were busy organizing it.

Congress officially created the territory of Oregon in 1848, an
action which had been delayed two years after the boundary settlement when it became enmeshed in the slavery controversy. The
lands west of the Cascades were immediately apportioned into several counties, but those east of the mountains remained unorganized,
and before any action was taken at that level a new political par-
titioning of greater significance was effected.[21] The move to create a
new territory north of the Columbia began within two or three
years after the establishment of Oregon. The initiative came from

---

gin of the Camas Prairie, and in 1878 the Bannock War briefly affected the
Umatilla area.

   [21] Previous to their territorial status, the citizens of the Willamette had
formed their own famous provisional government. Under that earlier system,
the entire area was divided among four vaguely defined administrative districts,
but this framework was of no practical consequence in the interior.

the Puget Sound colonists who formed a secondary nucleus of Oregon settlement, but one quite inferior in numbers, accessibility, and prospects to the Willamette. Their feelings of isolation, separateness, and neglect were well founded, though whether such commonplaces of pioneering warranted so hasty a readjustment of the political map might be questioned. But the dichotomy seemed real enough, and the majority regarded the severance of the northern wilderness to be of such minor importance that the idea of partition was accepted with little debate by the Oregon legislature.

The memorial prepared for Congress in December, 1852, offered a concise geographical argument for the proposed division:

> Those portions of Oregon territory lying north and south of the Columbia River must, from their geographical position, difference in climate, and internal resources, remain in a great degree distinct communities, with different interests and policies in all that appertains to their domestic legislation and the various interests that are to be regulated, nourished, and cherished by it. The communication between these two portions of the territory is difficult, casual, and uncertain . . . .

This view was further buttressed by the observation that "Experience has proven that when marked geographical boundaries which have been traced by the hand of nature have been disregarded in the formation of local governments, that sectional jealousies and local strifes have seriously embarrassed their prosperity and characterized their domestic legislation."[22] As is so often the case in such matters, a clear statement of theory was followed by a contradictory proposal. The area of the new territory was to be all the land north and west of the main Columbia River. How that stream, cutting directly through the Great Plain, could be viewed as a more "marked geographical boundary" than the formidable Cascade Range, which separated two distinct physical realms, was not explained, although a countersuggestion that the whole of Oregon be divided along the crest of that barrier, when voiced in the legislature, received little support. The general reasoning evidently accepted the Columbia as a simple, clear demarcation which would enclose an area with "a sufficient number of square miles to form a state, which in point of resources and capacity to maintain a population will compare favorably with most states of the union."

[22] Bancroft, *History of Washington, Idaho, and Montana*, p. 60. The description of this action is based upon this volume, pp. 47-53, 58-63.

Actually, before receiving this official request from the territorial legislature, Congress began considering the issue on the basis of a local Cowlitz petition which had set forth similar arguments and advocated identical boundaries. And, again, as so often happened, the legislators played their own game of political geography and tinkered with the map until they came up with their own version of a proper division. They accepted the local demand for the lower Columbia as a southern boundary, but decided to extend that general east-west line along the forty-sixth parallel from its point of intersection with the river, just downstream from old Fort Nez Perces, east to the Continental Divide. The logic of this boundary lay in its more equal apportionment of area; clearly it could not stem from any relationship with the nature and prospects of the land itself. A change of another sort was also made. The original petition had suggested "Columbia" as a most appropriate name, but Congress, seated in the District of Columbia, was conscious of an incipient confusion of terms, and with all the illogic at its command substituted "Washington." Having been so perfected, the bill passed both houses, and Washington Territory came into being with the President's signature on March 2, 1853.

Territorial status was implicitly a transitory phase, and the boundaries had no necessary permanence. Yet, once established, such lines had a certain tenacity, and the pattern was more likely to be further subdivided within an initial framework than obliterated and redrawn. Even though this territorial division had been imposed upon the Great Columbia Plain prior to any real colonization, it became an invisible imprint upon the land which could be neither ignored without consequence nor altered without effort. And, indeed, the very vanguard of settlers sensed something of the implications of that line and immediately made the effort to change it. In August, 1855, the little cluster of residents at The Dalles called a convention to consider the creation of a new territory to embrace all the area east of the Cascades. Because they failed to attract a sufficient response from the Colville miners, the only other citizen group, nothing was accomplished. Two years later The Dalles settlers pressed a similar proposal upon the Oregon statehood convention, but again without success. In fact, there was more general interest in enlargement than in reduction, and the Willamette majority sought to make their northeastern boundary follow the lower Snake rather than the forty-sixth parallel, thereby annexing the Walla Walla country. This move failed, but in 1859 statehood was attained (with the loss of the easternmost section of former Oregon Territory), and that gave a greater rigidity to its boundaries. Thus that discordant political line across the Great Plain became still more deeply imprinted when colonization was just barely under way.[23]

Within these major political units, subdivisions were also soon established, the beginning of a complex evolution of county grids which exhibited even more intensely the same sequence: at first one or a few huge and largely empty units, with subsequent division and subdivision as the country became settled. In 1854 Wasco County, seated at The Dalles, was created to embrace the whole of Oregon east of the Cascade crest. Briefly it had a counterpart in Walla Walla County, established in 1853 to cover the whole of eastern Washington Territory, but that organization lapsed with the evacuation of settlers in 1855. By 1859 a new political ordering had divided the Washington sector of the interior among Klickitat, Walla Walla, and Shoshone counties.[24]

In 1855 a third element of political organization appeared with the platting of Dalles City (the legal, but never the colloquial, name) and the formation of a town government.[25] With this, the full hierarchical framework of state, county, and municipality had been initiated in the southern portion of the Columbia Plain.

Routes

Still another kind of order was also being elaborated upon the land in these years. Within the Great Plain all the principal trails of fur trade and mission days continued to serve emigrants, miners, and soldiers, but a number of other routes were either created or

[23] Merle W. Wells, "The Creation of the Territory of Idaho," *Pacific Northwest Quarterly*, 40 (April, 1949), 108-9. C. S. Kingston, "The Walla Walla Separation Movement," *Washington Historical Quarterly*, 24 (April, 1933), 91-92. The north-south course of the Snake, extended beyond old Fort Boise along the 117th meridian, became the eastern boundary, the detached section being lumped into Washington Territory for the time being.

[24] Throughout this study I have relied primarily upon the old county history volumes for the details of these highly unstable patterns. Such sources nearly always quote in full the legal boundary definitions of each change. As the relevant volume will be readily apparent for nearly every case and the appropriate section easily found, I have thought it overly cumbersome to give full citations in each instance.

[25] F. A. Shaver *et al.*, *An Illustrated History of Central Oregon* ... (Spokane, Wash., 1905), pp. 130-34. The legislative charter for town government was granted in 1857.

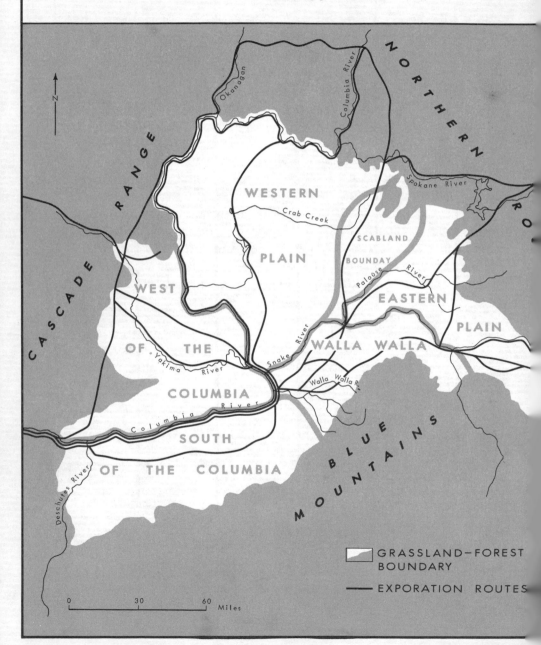

EXPLORATIONS AND REGIONAL DIVISIONS 1853-56

UNDER THE DIRECTION OF ISAAC STEVENS
AND AS DESCRIBED IN THE STEVENS REPORTS
1855-60

N

CASCADE RANGE

Okanagan

Columbia River

NORTHERN RO

Spokane River

WESTERN

Crab Creek

SCABLAND

BOUNDAY

Paloŭse River

PLAIN

EASTERN

WEST

PLAIN

OF THE

Yakima River

Snake River

WALLA WALLA

COLUMBIA

River

Walla Walla R.

Columbia River

SOUTH

Columbia River

Deschutes River

OF THE COLUMBIA

BLUE MOUNTAINS

GRASSLAND—FOREST BOUNDARY

—— EXPORATION ROUTES

0   30   60   Miles

Map 18

given new prominence. The most important additions to the old network were those leading through the mountainous borders. The Steilacoom–Walla Walla military road was surveyed in 1854; Naches Pass and the western section were most often barely passable, but at least the several militia, army, and survey parties kept a discernible line of travel hacked and trampled out. Its military value was proved in the campaigns, and the creation of Washington Territory gave it a civic significance as the most direct link between Puget Sound and the interior. A potential rival to this road had also received a good deal of attention, for both Stevens and the army surveyors recommended the Kittitas-Snoqualmie Pass route as superior.[26]

On the other side of the region, the broader mountain barrier was probed extensively by Stevens' railroad parties (Map 18). They reconnoitered each of the stream valleys leading from the Plain into the forested highlands. The southern three—the Salmon, Clearwater–Lolo, and Palouse—were dismissed as impractical, but the Coeur d'Alene and Clark Fork offered real possibilities. The latter was an old fur-trade route; Stevens traveled it several times and nominated it as the most feasible for a railroad (with the Spokane and tributary valleys linking it to the Great Plain). Although the Coeur d'Alene gave a more direct line to the east, its head was separated from the broad troughs to the east by the narrow but very high crest of the Bitterroot Range, which rendered its practicability for a railroad tentative. Yet the Coeur d'Alene Valley was selected for the military wagon road, which was to connect the head of navigation on the upper Missouri with the Columbia at old Fort Nez Perces. Lieutenant John Mullan, delayed a few weeks by Wright's final campaign, began construction of that road in early 1859.[27]

[26] 34th Cong., 1st sess., H. Ex. Doc. 1, Pt. 2, pp. 532-38; W. Turrentine Jackson, *Wagon Roads West* ... (Berkeley and Los Angeles, 1952), pp. 89-96. Stevens' proposed railroad routes are shown in his *Map No. 3, Rocky Mountains to Puget Sound, ... 1853-4*, accompanying *Reports of Explorations and Surveys, to Ascertain the Most Practicable and Economical Route for a Railroad from the Mississippi River to the Pacific Ocean*, Vol. XII (1860), 36th Cong., 1st sess., S. Ex. Doc. Captain T. J. Cram in his comprehensive report on military routes also endorsed it: *Topographical Memoir of the Department of the Pacific*, 35th Cong., 2nd sess., H. Ex. Doc. 114 (1859), p. 68.

[27] Mullan had made extensive surveys of the mountainous country as a member of the railroad survey team and tentatively selected this route in 1854. Cram, *Topographical Memoir*, p. 74, recommended this route for a military road. Even as he got under way with the specific wagon-road project, Mullan still held hope that a much shorter route via the Palouse Valley would prove

The significance of these new routes lay in their expression of new trends and potentials rather than in immediate practicalities. For half a century the trunk routes had been anchored upon the lower Columbia, Athabasca Pass, and South Pass; now portals had been opened leading directly to Puget Sound and the upper Missouri, heretofore areas of marginal importance to the realm as a whole. These two military roads were separate segments, each purposely bound into the older pattern at the persistent Walla Walla focus, yet at that point they linked into a new east-west routeway across the entire width of the Great Plain. If there was as yet little practical need for such a trunk line, Stevens' railroad map boldly proclaimed that here indeed was the main axis of the future. His recommended route for the northern "transcontinental," which he proclaimed as eminently suitable, entered the region in the Spokane country, bent southward toward the Columbia-Snake junction, and then bifurcated with one line up through the Yakima via Snoqualmie Pass to Seattle, and another down the north bank of the Columbia to Vancouver.[28] Through his efforts and enthusiasm, the railroad era had firmly arrived in thought if not in fact, and his geographic design was an important tool in shaping a new perspective upon incipient regional relations in the far Northwest.

It would be years before the steam engine would arrive on rails, but it came chugging up the Columbia powering the paddle wheel of a flat-bottomed riverboat in early 1859. Whether Stevens was the first to insist upon the practicability of using steamboats on the river above Celilo Falls is not certain, but at least he was urging their advantages upon General Wool in December, 1855, at the very time that Lieutenant Cram assured his superior that "I can confidently say that the river does not admit of steam navigation above the Dalles." Both men were familiar with the riverboats then operating on the two lower sections of the river, between Portland and the lower Cascades, and between the upper Cascades and The Dalles. When the campaigns had first been carried into the Walla Walla sector, the old Hudson's Bay Company bateaux were used to bring in some of the supplies and equipment. But their capacity and reliability was inadequate, and the chief quartermaster in charge of the

practicable; see 35th Cong., 2nd sess., S. Ex. Doc. 32, p. 50. See also Jackson, *Wagon Roads West,* chap. xvi.

[28] It is likely that he chose the north bank rather than the south simply because he was governor of Washington rather than Oregon.

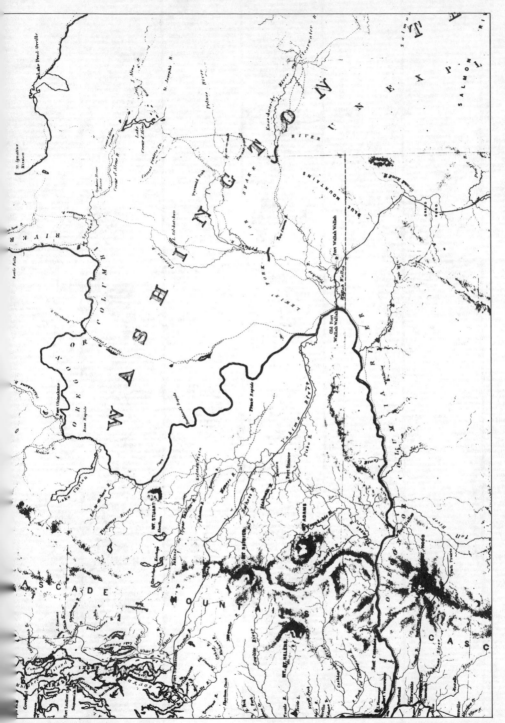

Map 19. Portion of "Department of Oregon Map of the State of Oregon and Washington Territory . . . 1859"

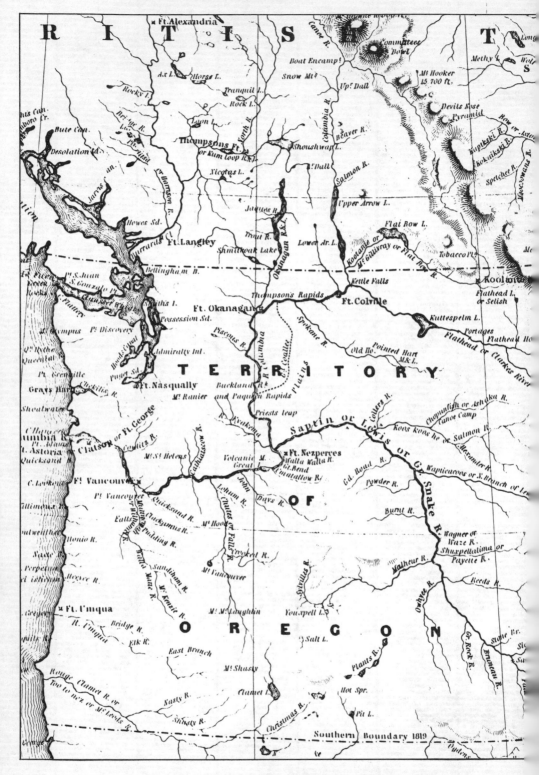

Map 20. Portion of "Map of the United States Territory
of Oregon West of the Rocky Mountains . . . 1838"

depot at Fort Nez Perces prevailed upon the freighting contractors to build a steamship. On October 24, 1858, the *Colonel Wright* was launched at the mouth of the Deschutes and made her first voyage upriver to the depot in May of the following year. An important corollary of this radical innovation was the improvement in portage facilities at the two downriver interruptions. At the Cascades a flimsy horse-powered railway gave regular service, while an organized system of teams and wagons bridged the dozen miles between The Dalles and Celilo Falls.[29]

Maps

A further achievement of these years was the development of a detailed and accurate base map of the Northwest. This, too, was an important part of the "organization of the land," of the gradual perfection of man's organized image of the land to fit the real patterns of nature. Inevitably a cumulative effort, with contributions from many sources, its best summary expression at this time was in the "Map of the State of Oregon and Washington Territory," compiled by the army's Bureau of Topographic Engineers and published in 1859 (Map 19). This map was important not only for its utility but for what it represented: the first reasonably accurate and detailed map of the whole region based largely upon direct American knowledge.

Some measure of that achievement can be gained by a comparison with the first map of the Oregon Country published by that same department in 1838 (Map 20). Issued near the beginning of the mission era, that earlier map vividly expressed the inadequacy of American knowledge and the necessary dependence upon the British, the fur traders, and sheer conjecture. Direct American involvement in the region gradually produced both the demand and the means for improvement. The first major advance was the Wilkes map of 1841 (Map 21). Drawn at a larger scale, it carried much

[29] Stevens' letter dated December 28, 1855, in *Message of the Governor of Washington Territory* . . . (Olympia, Wash., 1857), p. 135. 34th Cong., 2nd sess., S. Ex. Doc. 26 (1856), p. 40. E. W. Wright (ed.), *Lewis and Drydens Marine History of the Pacific Northwest* (Portland, Ore., 1895), p. 80; 35th Cong., 2nd sess., S. Ex. Doc. 32 (1859), p. 4. Frank B. Gill, "Oregon's First Railway," *Oregon Historical Society Quarterly*, 25 (September, 1924), 171-235; Oregon-Washington Railroad and Navigation Company, *Report to the Interstate Commerce Commission, Corporate History* . . . *1916*, compiled by F. B. Gill (mimeo), sheets 36, 56; hereafter cited as O.W.R.N., *Corporate History*.

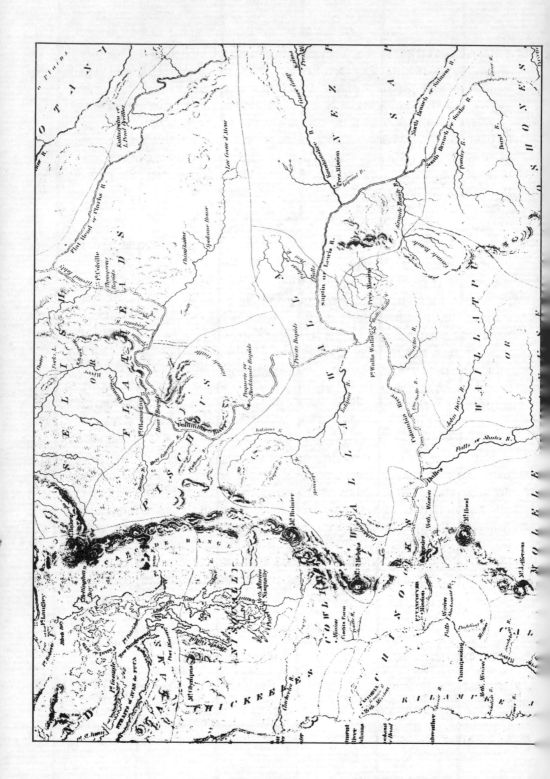

Map 22. Portion of S. Augustus Mitchell's Map of Oregon and Upper California, 1846

more detail; but although the Wilkes party gained considerable first-hand knowledge of the interior, no actual surveying was carried out, and, as acknowledged, for that area the map was basically British. The immigrations of the 1840's underscored the practical need for better maps. Fremont's careful survey of the Oregon Trail was a major contribution to western mapping, but related only to a narrow portion of the Northwest. Maps in guidebooks and separate sheets published for that market during the 1840's were small in scale and meager in detail, reflecting the inadequacy of basic sources. An interesting example is the Mitchell map of 1846, on which the Northwest is a reduced, slightly simplified copy of the Wilkes map with the addition of such features as the Oregon Trail and the new political boundary (Map 22).[30]

The entry of the army into Northwest affairs in the 1850's transformed this situation. To the need for good maps now was added the skills and equipment to make them and—especially with the addition of Governor Stevens and his Pacific railroad survey parties (which were largely staffed by army personnel)—the specific assignment to get them made. The army map of 1859 was a synthesis of the results of five years of intense activity.

For the most part that map speaks for itself. The immediate impression is one of accuracy; where knowledge is lacking, the map remains empty rather than filled with surmised streams and mountains; even a generally well-known river, such as the Snake, is given firm representation only where it has been crossed by actual surveys. Where knowledge is in hand, the detail of minor stream patterns suggests the accuracy of field work, in contrast to the wiggly stems of so many predecessor maps. The one curious aberration is the strange looping course of the Columbia through the center of the Great Plain.[31] Aside from that prominent (but hardly critical) inaccuracy, the map provided a reasonably reliable framework for thinking and practical planning. Designed primarily as a military tool, it would soon prove to be the kind of instrument useful to an array of other strategies.

[30] U.S. Dept. of War, Bureau of Topographical Engineers, *Map of the United States Territory of Oregon West of the Rocky Mountains* (1838). See Chapter 8 for further information on Wilkes's exploration. *Oregon and Upper California*, map published by S. Augustus Mitchell (Philadelphia, 1846).

[31] This portion of the Columbia had been navigated by a botanist of the Stevens party, but not by a surveyor. Inaccurate representation of this feature

One further feature of interest, the names on the map, is an essential part of this symbolic organization of the land. Such an authoritative map was both a display of current usages and an instrument for the stabilization of terms. That is was compiled from the archive as well as the field is suggested by the coupling of what were by now archaic terms with those current, as in *Oregon or Columbia River* and *Lewis' Fork or Snake River*. On the other hand there was the attempt to lend official prestige to the inadequate translation *Fall River* for the *Deschutes* of dominant local usage; also glaring are the misguided academic correction of *Tucannon* into *Two Cannon,* and the careless mistake of *Fort Dallas*. In general, however, the map accepts those names which carried the authority of selection and repetition over the years by residents and recurrent travelers; and, in general, that meant the triumph of Indian words for most of the streams (though only the phonetics and not the spellings were stabilized). The single exception was precisely the area where there had been the heaviest and most persistent contact by the British and Americans: along the Oregon Trail. There *Walla Walla* (the army still adhered to the more cumbersome *Wallah Wallah*) and *Umatilla* seem almost anomalous among *Burnt, Powder, Butter* (obscured on this map), *Willow, Rock, John Day,* and (on other maps of this time) *Mill, Pine,* and *Dry* creeks in the Walla Walla area, and the *"—Mile"* creeks near The Dalles. A sprinkling of other names around the Great Plain and its margins further hinted at the patterns and persons of the past: for example, *Kettle Falls* and *Ross Rapids* of early Anglo-American fur trade days; *Colville* (now firmly with two "l's") of the Hudson's Bay Company; and the French-Canadian *voyageur* legacy in *Dalles, Grand Coulee,* and *Coeur d'Alene.* The dominant character of the regional nomenclature, however, is Indian, in most instances so misapplied and so warped and shortened in transliteration as to obscure original meanings, but that in itself faithfully mirrored the contact between two disparate cultures. This dominance of Indian influence upon the base map of the moment merely reflected the fact that this half-century had been one of gradual, sporadic intrusion of alien minorities upon the region. With the triumph of the military, the balance had shifted wholly in favor of those intruders;

---

was common on early maps, and this fact further emphasizes the skill of David Thompson, for his map was remarkably accurate.

and just as new immigrations would soon begin to fill the region with a new population, so new maps would reveal an accompanying shift in nomenclature as the settlers veneered the land with their own characteristic terms.

EVALUATING THE LAND

Missionaries

These years of the mission and military eras also mark an important growth of knowledge about and changes in attitude toward the land. Whereas the missionaries had initiated their work with vague and fragmentary information about a distant unwanted wilderness, by 1858 a large volume of literature described an assuredly accessible and in some ways desirable country. Basic to this growth of information were the comments of the Protestant missionaries. As a group of dedicated Christians, who were cultivating the ground, experiencing the full cycle of the seasons, and working with the resources at hand, their ideas not only were given wide currency but carried an unprecedented reliability.

In general, in the first few years of missionary settlement the evaluations were but an elaboration of those of their perceptive forerunner, Samuel Parker, whose views were widely disseminated with the publication of *Exploring Tour Beyond the Rocky Mountains* in 1838. The picture of a vast grazing domain interspersed with a few suitable agricultural valleys, the whole enjoying a mild, dry, invigorating climate, was confirmed by the actual experiences at Waiilatpu, Lapwai, and Tshimakain. There were, however, differences of opinion as to how attractive such a combination of features would be to prospective settlers. Walker, for instance, stated in 1841 that the interior had "no natural advantages such as will induce emigration when it shall become fully known." It would never "become thickly settled" because there were too many deficiencies: summer drought, unseasonable frosts, poor soil, lack of timber, and isolation.[32]

Whitman, too, often suggested that the "upper Columbia" country would never be inhabited by a "Settled People," but he was far

[32] Parker's book was first published in Ithaca, New York, in 1838; the citations in the earlier chapter refer to an Irish edition of 1840. Walker Letters, Walker to the Reverend D. Greene, October, 1841. Some of his earlier letters had been more optimistic.

from negative about its possibilities. He believed that agriculture would be limited to those valleys where irrigation or natural sub-irrigation could overcome the long dry season, and thus the region could never become "settled" in the sense that easterners understood that term. But he became increasingly enthusiastic over the grazing possibilities. The excellent grass and mild winters seemed so great an advantage that "if the facts were known," he stated, in contra-diction to Walker, "I think very many would leave Vermont and all the eastern states and middle as well as the western in order to come to this country." In a letter to his brother in 1845, he explained that they had enjoyed "the best and handsomest butter" and "the fattest beef" all winter without any of the labor of hay cutting and stall feeding necessary back home, and urged upon him the advantages of such a country. Thus Whitman came to see this area as the *best* section of Oregon, where colonists could establish the very kind of combined irrigation and pastoral operation which he himself had so successfully developed at Waiilatpu. The country was not so much "limited" as simply "different."[33]

This view was readily endorsed by Spalding. "I know of no coun-try in the world so well adapted to the herding system," he wrote in 1843. Further, he recognized more explicitly that this different kind of country required a different kind of colonization procedure, for he stated that, because of the "scarcity of habitable places," regula-tions should first be adopted to insure that "no settlers shall be allowed to take up over twenty acres of land on the streams." Assum-ing that "habitability" was indeed so limited, this was the kind of sound local understanding which in later decades was to become common in the drier regions of the far West, and to be just as com-monly ignored by distant legislators who had control over such regu-lations.[34] In this same letter he listed the "habitable valleys"—in-cluding the Deschutes, John Day, Umatilla, Walla Walla, Tucan-non, Pataha, and Palouse—and in some instances he even estimated

[33] E.g., letter of 1841 quoted in Clifford Drury, *Marcus Whitman, M.D., Pio-neer and Martyr* (Caldwell, Ida., 1937), p. 251; Hulbert and Hulbert, *Marcus Whitman*, III, 131-32, 135-36.

[34] This observation puts Spalding in the vanguard of those Anglo-Americans who anticipated the need for a different land policy for such portions of the public domain. One is reminded of the persistent but unsuccessful labors several decades later of the famous John Wesley Powell to achieve this sort of regula-tion for the Great Plains and Rocky Mountain regions.

the number of families that could be "comfortably located" upon the available arable land: 150 along the Umatilla, 350 in the Walla Walla, and 60 in the narrow Tucannon-Pataha valleys. His over-all view, therefore, was of a vast, rich, pastoral domain sprinkled with a series of riverine oases of farmland.

Spalding's was the most detailed descriptive report given on the region by any of the missionaries, and it became well publicized. It had been solicited for a collection of information about the Oregon Territory to be presented to Congress, and was also included as part of two books. However, despite the wide audience ultimately reached by such means, the most immediately influential statements were the letters home to relatives, to former neighbors, to local church congregations, and to the sponsoring American Board (often published in *The Missionary Herald*). Hulbert has properly emphasized that "it was missionaries who first reported the soil and climatic conditions in the West which actually attracted immigration in bulk." However, he appended the important corollary that those physical conditions described had to be familiar kinds of conditions; the "unquestionable magnet" of immigration was always "the evidence that success with soil could be won on terms of farm or plantation life as the prospective emigrants knew it; that known reactions of soil to weather would be experienced; that wood with which they were used to working lay ready at hand; that all the old tricks of the trade would work in the new land."[35] The enthusiasm of Whitman and Spalding notwithstanding, it is clear that the Great Columbia Plain did not meet these terms. The physical conditions they described were new and strange, the "herding system" they advocated was unfamiliar, and thus, despite their fame, the volume, detail, and credibility of their reports, and despite their growing desire to recruit a nucleus of "good Christian" settlers, they were never successful in getting many others to see this region as they had come to see it. The positive lure of the Willamette, and the Indian situation and isolation of the interior, were significant factors, but most important was the fact that "the old tricks of the trade" would *not* work in this new land.

[35] Spalding's letter was dated April 1, 1843, and was included in Elijah White, *A Concise View of Oregon Territory* (Washington, D.C., 1846), pp. 19-24. It is also printed in A. J. Allen (comp.), *Ten Years in Oregon: Travels and Adventures of Doctor E. White and Lady West of the Rocky Mountains* (Ithaca, N.Y., 1848), pp. 201-12. Hulbert, *Where Rolls the Oregon*, pp. 27, 36.

Emigrants

The Willamette-bound emigrants (lured in part by the reports of other missionaries who *could* describe a familiar kind of land) soon became a greater source of information about the regions of Oregon. The first trickle of farmer-colonists in 1839 soon swelled into a flood; by 1843 "Oregon fever" was reported to be "raging in almost every part of the Union";[36] and by the latter 1840's several thousand a year were trekking the Oregon Trail. Nearly all of them no doubt reported their findings to the folks back home, and a considerable number sought to capitalize upon the mushrooming interest by publishing descriptions and guidebooks. These often very widely read accounts imprinted a picture of Oregon upon the minds of a large portion of the American public.

Among the most outspoken and oft-quoted interpreters of Oregon was Thomas J. Farnham, who arrived at Waiilatpu in September, 1839, and after a few days went on to the Willamette. His knowledge of Oregon was derived from his own limited contact, the missionaries, and the fur company people at Fort Vancouver; he was unfavorably impressed with what he had found, and his personal plans had gone awry, and he therefore departed by sea in December of that year. That Farnham's views were probably colored by his personal disappointments does not detract from their importance. The following general statement on the Great Columbia Plain is characteristic of his opinion and style:

> . . . a plain of vast rolls or swells, of a light, yellowish, sandy clay, partially covered with the short and bunch grasses, mixed with the prickly pear and wild wormwood. But water is so very scarce, that it can never be generally fed; unless indeed, as some travelers in their praises of this region seem to suppose, the animals that usually live by eating and drinking, should be able to dispense with the latter, in a climate where nine months in the year, not a particle of rain or dew falls, to moisten a soil as dry and loose as a heap of ashes.

Of the Walla Walla Valley, the area he examined most closely, he concluded that there were "scarcely 2,000 acres . . . which can ever be made available for the purpose of cultivation" because of the long drought and impossibility of irrigating any portion except the immediate stream margins. Thus, in effect, the concept of a "Great Columbia Desert," which had been diminished by reports of the

[36] Burlington *Iowa Gazette*, 1843, in "Documents Relating to the Oregon Emigration Movement, 1842-43." *Oregon Historical Quarterly*, 4 (June, 1903), 170-77.

1830's, now reappeared with an influential advocate. The distant compilers of information about Oregon who relied principally upon Farnham for their information never failed to give it emphasis: the area "lying between the Blue Mountains and the Cascade Range, is also but a succession of deserts, dotted it is true here and there with habitable spots, but still possessing no feature sufficiently indicative of being capable of wide agricultural exertions."[37]

Farnham's derisive theme that "Oregon Territory as a whole is, in its soil, the most cheerless and barren portion of the national domain" was certainly not echoed by others who wrote with personal knowledge of the Willamette,[38] but insofar as it applied to the Columbia Plain he had numerous supporters. For example, James Nesmith, as he moved through the region with an emigrant party in 1843, filled his journal with comments about "this country of sand and stone" which presented "but a dreary prospect to a man from the Western States." Not only was Fort Nez Perces surrounded by sand banks "not possessing fertility enough to sprout a pea," but "in fact this is too much the case with all the far-famed Walla Walla Valley." There were, indeed, a few "spots" of good soil along the streams, but "if this is a fair specimen of Oregon, it falls far below the conceptions which I formed of the country." Of course, it was not a "fair specimen" at all of the Oregon he was seeking. In the descriptions of these people the Columbia Plain suffered from a kind of "psychological–geographical" factor. These immigrants carried a mental picture which equated "Oregon" with the characteristics of the Willamette, yet they also understood that the Walla Walla Valley was a famed feature and the Columbia River the very symbol of Oregon. The resultant first impression was therefore often one of shock and disappointment. Farnham was apparently suffering from this kind of initial impact when he wrote of Fort Nez Perces:

[37] Farnham, *Travels in the Western Prairies*, pp. 80, 99. An earlier, somewhat shorter work similar in content was published in 1841, and several other volumes, each different but containing much of the same information, were published during the next several years. See Bancroft, *History of Oregon*, I, 227-34, and note 9, I, 230-31. Katherine Parr Traill, *The Oregon Territory* ... (London, 1846), p. 30; see also C. G. Nicolay, *The Oregon Territory* ... (London, 1846).

[38] This particular quotation is from Farnham's letter of May 20, 1843, published as "Products of Oregon Territory" in *The American Agriculturist*, 2 (November, 1843), 273-74. Farnham explicitly includes western Oregon as well in his denunciations, as he colorfully ridicules those who waxed overly enthusiastic over the vision of the "ideal, fig-bearing, orange-bearing, grape-bearing, wine-flowing soil of the Oregon."

The country around about has sometimes been represented as fruitful and beautiful. I am obliged to deny so foul an imputation upon the fair fame of dame Nature. It is an ugly desert; designed to be such; made such, and is such. . . . There is indeed some beauty and sublimity in sight, but no fertility. . . . Desert describes it as well as it does the wastes of Arabia.

Of course, that particular area *was* a desert, but his anger was ill-directed, for it would have been difficult to find any traveler of the past thirty years who had thought otherwise. This blurring of the regional distinctions between the lands east and west of the Cascades was not derived from the better guidebooks of the day, yet it was a common and persistent flaw, and at times explicitly expressed: "There is something grand and sublime in the scenery around it [the Columbia, east of The Dalles], yet I was disappointed in the scenery. Instead of trees with luxuriant foliage, you see massive rocks, pile upon pile, which have stood the wreck of time for centuries."[39]

Two other features combined to reinforce the emigrants' impression of this area as a desolate wasteland of little attraction. One was the season of contact, determined by travel weather and distance from the starting point in the East (commonly western Missouri). Therefore, nearly everyone crowded through in late summer, when the seasonal drought was nearing its maximum. "Barren," "parched soil," "withered brown grass," a "hot, dry, desolate waste" were vividly accurate descriptions of the appearance of the country. Those who visited Waiilatpu saw proof of the productivity of that spot, but that became simply the oasis which proved the desert. The second feature was the course of the main emigrant trail, which followed along or near the south bank of the Columbia and thereby took the travelers through one of the most barren, broken, rocky, sandy sections of the interior. Coming as it did near the end of a summer-long, difficult journey, it would have been remarkable for the weary travelers to see much good in such a land. Their journal entries suggest common agreement with the succinct notations of the grandson of one of England's most famous agriculturists: "Travelling through the most disgusting country. Exactly the old scene over again. Sage, sand, weeds—sand, weeds, sage . . . . Everything combined to make me sick and dispirited." Such impressions recall those of many of the early fur traders, and with good reason, for both groups were

[39] James W. Nesmith, "Diary of the Emigration of 1843," *Oregon Historical Quarterly*, 7 (1906), 355-57; Farnham, *Travels in the Western Prairies*, p. 85; Allen, *Canvas Caravans*, p. 101.

making contacts, similarly restricted in season and route, with an area unsuited to their economic interests.[40]

Although these were typical of the views of many travelers of the time, they were not the only ones. Some emigrants and visitors spoke more favorably of the pastoral resources. The thousands of Indian horses made this a logical inference for those who encountered them, but others who wrote encouragingly of the area did so because they were willing to rely upon the opinions of the missionaries rather than solely upon their own impressions.[41] Further, over the years several dozen families had encamped for weeks or even months with the Whitmans, and these persons no doubt came away with views similar to those of their host. Still, careful survey of a considerable volume of evidence suggests that Farnham and Nesmith spoke for a large share of the emigrants.

[40] Henry J. Coke, *A Ride over the Rocky Mountains to Oregon and California* (London, 1852), pp. 299-300. Coke, the grandson of "Coke of Norfolk," had ridden along the lower Umatilla to the Columbia on the days of these comments. W. H. G. Armytage, "H. J. Coke on the Oregon Trail," *Mid-America*, 31 (n.s. 20) (October, 1949), 258-69, gives a brief biography and sets the context of his journey. This unanimity in judgment of the area by such people still prevailed, as evidenced in the journal of Sir George Simpson on his 1841 trip down the Columbia "through dreary plains of sand"; in the detailed entries of the Canadian artist Paul Kane, who roamed about the Great Plain in 1845, "the country around, so far as the eye could reach, seemed to be a perfect desert of yellow, hot sand"; and in the descriptions of Lieutenant Henry J. Warre, who accompanied the eastbound brigade up the scabland trail in that same year "through a barren sandy desert, comparable only with the great Sahara...." Simpson, *Journey Round the World*, pp. 154-70, the quotation referring to the Columbia route below Fort Nez Perces; Kane, *Wanderings of an Artist*, pp. 189-210, quotation referring to the area around Palouse Falls; Henry J. Warre, *Sketches in North America and the Oregon Territory* (London, n.d.), pp. 2-4, comment referred to the first "200 miles" of the route from Fort Nez Perces to Fort Colvile.

[41] Hines, *Oregon*, p. 344; Palmer, *Journal of Travels*, pp. 232, 238. Such impressive herds were not always apparent. As the volume of emigrants increased, the Indians tended to keep their horses at a distance to avoid troubles. Further, when the main route was shifted down the Umatilla rather than through the Walla Walla, there was much less chance of encountering large herds. Also, as the traffic became heavier, the pasturage along the trail must have been greatly reduced, thereby causing the Indians to shun that locale and also giving the emigrants further reason to be unimpressed with what they saw of the country.

A good example of the missionary influence is Overton Johnson and W. H. Winter, *Route Across the Rocky Mountains, with a Description of Oregon and California* ... (Lafayette, Ind., 1846), reprinted in *Oregon Historical Quarterly*, 7 (1906), 62-104, 163-210, 291-327, wherein the guardedly optimistic view was explicitly derived from Spalding (see pp. 95-96).

Government Reports

National political interest in the "Oregon Question" flared concomitantly with these missionary and immigration activities, and here, too, reports on the character of the country were a natural by-product. A typical early example was the "Cushing Report" of 1839, a compilation of heterogeneous materials supporting America's legal rights to the territory, with an extensive supplement on the nature of the area. A number of familiar names appear among the contributors—Jason Lee, Congressman Albert Tracy, and Hall Kelley—but the only information on the Great Columbia Plain was supplied by Nathaniel Wyeth, who wrote a special "memoir." It was a well-organized description and appraisal, consistently recognizing the three "sections." The opinions were not new, but they were set forth clearly and forcefully. As for the "middle section," agriculture would always be limited to the irrigable valleys, but it was "perhaps one of the best grazing countries in the world." Wyeth described in detail the superior quality of the grass, emphasized how it remained nutritious throughout the dry season, how open grazing was available throughout the year, and stated unequivocally his opinion that "for producing hides, tallow, and beef" this section was "superior to any part of North America." He further pointed out that the area had been "much underrated by travellers who have only passed by the Columbia, the land along which is a mere collection of sand and rocks, and almost without vegetation." Such a view equaled the optimism of the missionaries, surpassed that of most of the emigrants, and was given considerable notoriety. Not only were ten thousand copies of this report distributed, but Wyeth's remarks were either quoted or drawn upon in similar compilations of the next few years.[42]

The prominence of Wyeth's testimony was partly an expression of the paucity of firsthand knowledge as yet available to Americans. However, in the early 1840's fresh information was acquired from the first official reconnaissance of the interior of Oregon since Lewis and Clark. The United States Exploring Expedition, under the command of Lieutenant Charles Wilkes, was designed to bring to

[42] 25th Cong., 3rd sess., H. Rept. 101, Appendix I of Supplemental Report, dated Feb. 16, 1839, pp. 6-22. See especially 27th Cong., 3rd sess., H. Rept. 31 (1843), pp. 24-33; and Robert Greenhow, *The History of Oregon and California, and the Other Territories on the North-West Coast of North America* (Boston, 1844), pp. 20-37.

the United States the same kind of scientific prestige that the voyages of James Cook and Jean de la Perouse had brought to their sponsoring nations. The vessels were dispatched from Norfolk in the summer of 1838, with a number of distinguished civilian and naval scientists on board. The next three years were spent in the South Seas and Antarctic margins. In the spring of 1841 the expedition sailed from Hawaii to obtain strategic, economic, and geographic data on the Oregon Territory. While most of the complement examined Puget Sound and the coastal regions, a small party was sent into the lands east of the Cascade Range. This group entered via Naches Pass and made a circuit around the margins of the Great Plain via Fort Okanogan, Tshimakain, Fort Colvile, Coeur d'Alene Lake, Lapwai, Waiilatpu, and thence up the Yakima to Naches Pass once more. Another member of the expedition accompanied Ogden's upriver brigade as far as Fort Nez Perces, made a few short side trips from there, and returned, while still another traveled the scabland "cut-off" between Waiilatpu and Fort Colvile.

A considerable portion of the region was seen directly by one or more of the members of the expedition, and contact was made with all of the missionaries and fur personnel in residence. The full narrative of the expedition was not published until 1845, but extensive extracts from a preliminary report to the Secretary of the Navy were made available in 1843 in a printing of five thousand copies. These contained a commentary on the general characteristics, climate, soils, vegetation, and productivity of each of the three usual sections, and also differentiated certain broad subsections. The evaluations of resources contained no surprises. Insofar as the Great Plain was concerned, aside from being able to testify as to the agricultural successes of the missionaries on the irrigated bottomlands, Wilkes added little to Wyeth's memoir. His general conclusion was very similar: little arable land (no more than ten thousand acres in the Walla Walla Valley), but excellent "natural hay" which was "capable of supporting a vast number of cattle."[43]

Another notable officer, Captain John C. Fremont, traveled

[43] 27th Cong., 3rd sess., H. Rept. 31 (1843), pp. 65-78; Charles Wilkes, *Narrative of the United States Exploring Expedition* (Philadelphia, 1845), 5 vols. and atlas. The Oregon material is contained in Vol. IV; the items cited on pp. 393-95. Wilkes was also able to give a more detailed and accurate picture of the climate, although this too did not alter the general view already well publicized. He reported that temperatures ranged between the absolute extremes of 108 degrees and minus 18 degrees.

through the region at that time; but in this area the famed "path-maker of the West" merely followed the Oregon Trail, and his narrative added nothing new, although his report on the route was widely used as a guide by many emigrants.[44]

This rapidly growing number of reports from missionaries, miscellaneous visitors, and official expeditions became the foundation for an even larger number of popular guidebooks and descriptive accounts,[45] and all these together shaped the public and official image of this far corner of the nation in the 1840's. In that emerging picture, the Great Columbia Plain was stabilized in the regional structure as part of (in some accounts the whole of) the "Middle Section." Its general character as a broad, undulating, barren, treeless expanse with a hot, dry summer climate was explicit in all accounts. But as to its value and attractions, the public was offered conflicting opinions: was it a desert with only a few habitable spots, or was it an unrivaled pastoral domain? Clearly, the actual resources of the Great Plain had not been tested on a sufficient scale to allow an unequivocal judgment.

Spalding's Revision

But experimentation was going on, and even as this great volume of accounts was publicizing a unanimous verdict on its severely restricted agricultural potentialities, a new and radical idea was being advanced from within the region itself. That its chief spokesman should be Henry Spalding is not surprising, for this dour, hard-willed missionary had from the start been an unusually keen and in-

[44] John C. Fremont, *Report of the Exploring Expedition to the Rocky Mountains in the Year 1842, and to Oregon and North California in the years 1843-44* (Washington, 1845), pp. 182ff. Fremont did explore south from The Dalles along the eastern side of the Cascade Range, and his reconnaissance of the western Great Basin and Sierra passes was his most significant contribution to western exploration.

[45] Among the best of these was Charles Wilkes's *Western America, Including California and Oregon with Maps of those Regions, and of the Sacramento Valley* (Philadelphia, 1849). Other prominent ones not already mentioned were Lansford W. Hastings, *The Emigrants' Guide to Oregon and California* (Cincinnati, 1845), and J. Quinn Thornton, *Oregon and California in 1848* (New York, 1849), 2 vols. These three were by Americans who had personally visited the region, although the latter two seem clearly to have drawn upon Wilkes for much of their information. An example of a British view by a former resident is John Dunn, *The Oregon Territory, and the British North American Fur Trade* (Philadelphia, 1845); a good illustration of a common kind of article compiled from various sources is "The Oregon Territory," *The Monthly Chronicle* (Boston), 7 (August, 1842), 337-50.

quiring student of the land. In the report solicited from him in 1843, he had attached to the usual observation that "the arable land . . . is confined almost entirely to the small streams" what, for that time, was an uncommon speculation: ". . . further observation may prove that many of the extensive rolling prairies are capable of producing wheat." In the next few years he had occasion to observe those "rolling prairies" in numerous localities and in various seasons and was impressed by the richness of the soil, the vigor of the bunch grass, and the superior attractions of such lands. Further, at Lapwai he began to experiment with raising crops without irrigation, and found that they succeeded. By 1846 he made a definite change in his judgment:

> . . . my views of the country have been materially changed by a more accurate acquaintance with its true nature. I once thought the valleys only susceptible of habitation; considering the plains too dry for cultivation. But I am now prepared to say this is not the case. The plains suffer far less from drought than the valleys. . . . The country, however, is no where peculiarly subject to drought, as was once thought— . . . my farm, though prepared for irrigation, has remained without it the last four years.

If correct, this was an astonishing discovery, for it would enormously expand the settlement and agricultural potential of the Great Columbia Plain. Spalding acknowledged that "timber is the great desideratum," but suggested that it could be rafted down the streams from the forested borders "so that but a very small portion of the country will be over ten or fifteen miles from the timber." He also expanded his previous arguments regarding the pastoral advantages:

> I cannot but contrast the time, labor, and expense requisite to look after herds in this country, with that required in the States . . . where two-thirds of every man's time, labor, and money is expended on his animals, in preparing and fencing pasture grounds and meadows, building barns, sheds, stables, and granaries, cutting and securing hay and grain, and feeding and looking to animals through winter. In this country all this is superceded by Nature's own bountiful hand. In this country a single shepherd with his horse and dogs can protect and look after five thousand sheep. A man with his horse and perhaps a dog can easily attend to two thousand head of cattle and horses, without spending a dollar for barns, grain, or hay. Consider the vast amount of labor and expense such a number of animals would require in the States.

With the additional attraction of a climate "peculiarly free from sudden changes of weather, or violent storms," Spalding was now prepared to state that "were I to select for my friends a location for a healthy happy life, and speedy wealth, it would be this country."[46]

It was a ringing endorsement, but a singular one. None of Spalding's colleagues ever expressed such comprehensive enthusiasm; no emigrant seems to have had such a vision; it would have delighted Hall Kelley, but apparently no propagandist after Kelley had dared to paint such a picture of the goodness of this "Middle Section."

It is ironic that Spalding had no sooner achieved this attractive vision of his adopted homeland than he was ejected from it. With the collapse of the missionary program and the general change in the patterns of contact with the region, there began a new phase in the evaluation of its resources. In the 1850's soldiers and surveyors replaced missionaries and emigrants as the leading students of the land.

Stevens' Reports

In fact, that decade was dominated by one student: Isaac I. Stevens. In the five years from 1853 to 1858 Stevens, as a result of his official duties, achieved a personal acquaintance with and acquired a detailed knowledge of the Great Columbia Plain far surpassing that of any other nonresident. Further, his scientific training, his contacts with other scientists, and the resources he was able to draw upon gave him a perspective and allowed him to assess the area at a level far beyond the reach of even such a keen and experienced local resident as Spalding. The contributions of his numerous coworkers and advisers must be acknowledged, but it was Stevens who synthesized this knowledge, added his own based upon both direct examination and scientific reasoning, and shaped the whole into a remarkable geographical study.[47]

[46] In White, *Oregon Territory*, p. 22. That the idea was not original with Spalding is suggested by his comment of the previous year that "it is thought by good judges that many of the high plains might produce wheat," Drury, *Whitman*, p. 252. For example, in a letter of February 12, 1846, Spalding stated: "I have traversed these plains in seven or eight different routs and find the country every where a rolling prairy, soil apparently of the best quality, covered every where with the excellent bunch grass which was just beginning to show the young blades.

"I took pains to examine the old stock which is every where about 2 feet, and found it grown halfway up from the bottom, consequently it is not a decayed material on which animals feed through the winter, but the very best of hay.... The country is every where well watered with springs & streams, very little timber upon the streams, many with none at all, but there is abundance upon the mountains from 3 to 20 miles distant." Spalding Letters, p. 261. Spalding Letter, dated April 7, 1846, in Palmer, *Journal of Travels*, pp. 285-86. See also pp. 288, 291-92.

[47] An evaluation of Stevens as a geographer, and a summary of his scientific background and experiences is presented in Donald W. Meinig, "Isaac Stevens:

When Stevens received his dual appointments as governor and as leader of the railroad survey, he had never been near the Oregon country, and he immediately sought all the available sources which might inform him of the character of his new territory. Years later he commented that he thereby obtained the impression "that the interior was worthless and uninhabitable." During the next two years he reconnoitered every large sector of the Great Columbia Plain, some more than once and at different seasons of the year. The published account of these efforts is dispersed in the several volumes of the Stevens Report, but the general conclusions are set forth in a "Geographical Memoir."[48]

One of the important contributions of the report was the delineation of five subregions within the Columbia Plain: (1) the Walla Walla Valley; (2) the eastern plain; (3) the western plain (separated from the eastern by the scablands of "trap and basaltic formations"); (4) the area west of the Columbia to the forested margins of the Cascades; and (5) the grasslands south of the Columbia in Oregon Territory (Map 18).[49]

Stevens characterized the nature and potential of each of these regions. To the Walla Walla he applied such uncompromising remarks as "a delightful rolling country, well grassed and arable, . . .a remarkably fine grazing and wheat country"; "its valley [the Pataha], as well as the table-land between it and the adjacent streams, is uniformly fertile"; "a most beautiful prairie country, the whole of it adapted to agriculture." The eastern plain, centered upon the

Practical Geographer of the Early Northwest," *The Geographical Review*, 45 (October, 1955), 542-58.

[48] "Speech of Hon. Isaac I. Stevens, of Washington Territory, in the House of Representatives, May 25, 1858," 35th Cong., 1st sess., Appendix to the Congressional Globe (1858), p. 428. Stevens was then territorial delegate to Congress, having resigned as governor.

The works specifically mentioned in his biography and narrative were those of Lewis and Clark, DeSmet, Simpson, Irving's *Astoria,* Fremont, Wilkes, and "many narratives" of the fur traders. Hazard Stevens, *Life of Isaac Ingalls Stevens* (Boston and New York, 1900), I, 291; *Stevens Report*, XII, Book 1, 154. The geographical memoir (XII, 226-331) is in four parts, of which only the second and fourth relate to the interior. The material in subsequent paragraphs is drawn both from this memoir and the narrative of exploration.

[49] Stevens was using the common term of Walla Walla Valley for the area between the Blue Mountains and the Snake River; he recognized that technically it ought to be restricted to the river valley. Stevens' discussion does not proceed systematically through each of these subregions, but his recognition of the divisions as a basic framework is always apparent.

Palouse country, was equally impressive. In his first crossing Stevens was "astonished, not simply at the luxuriance of the grass, but the richness of the soil. . . . The country is a rolling table-land, and the soil like that of the prairies of Illinois." Both of these sections had other requisites of settlement—ample water, wood along the streams, timber in nearby mountains—and therefore were "exceedingly well adapted to agricultural purposes."[50]

Stevens recognized that the drier western plain was less attractive, being

> rather sparsely grassed and scantily supplied with water for farming purposes. . . . Yet in this portion of the Great Plain and especially on the bank of the main Columbia, are many tracts and swales of good land. Indeed, there will always be found in this portion farming land enough to make practicable the occupation of the whole country by stock raisers and wool growers.

As for the area west of the Columbia, centered on the Yakima Valley, he insisted that "great injustice has been done this country by a want of patience on the part of gentlemen who have gone over it rapidly in the summer." Stevens pointed out that the Indians had raised crops and held large herds of stock, that the sagebrush was less extensive than commonly supposed, and he believed that "nearly every acre" of the grassy uplands was suited to cereal cultivation. Of the remaining area, Stevens joined Wyeth and Wilkes in stating that those traveling the main trail south of the Columbia got a wrong impression of the whole:

> . . . back a little distance the grazing is very luxuriant and excellent, and the soil rich, particularly in the river valleys. . . . When this interior becomes settled there will be a chain of agricultural settlements all the way from the Walla-Walla to the Dalles, south of the Columbia, along the streams. . . .[51]

Here was a radically different conception of the potentialities of the Great Columbia Plain. Stevens was ever aware that he was contradicting prevailing opinions. He pointed out reasons why others had come to different conclusions. Some of these were obvious, such as the limited regional and seasonal contacts of most travelers, but others were more deeply rooted in the common thinking of the time. There was, for example, the widespread prejudice against grassland soils; to the forest-bred American colonist, great expanses

[50] *Stevens Report*, XII, 197, 199, 252.
[51] *Ibid.*, pp. 253, 256, 257.

of treeless country seemed strange and doubtful. Proof of this belief would seem inherent in two notations by Stevens in the narrative of his journey across the Walla Walla and Palouse sections:

> I will here remark, to guard against misconception, that it must not be inferred, when I speak of a country as being covered with grass, that it is not an arable country. . . .
>
> . . . I will again remind the reader that it does not follow because the grass is luxuriant that the country is not arable.

In fact, rather than a reason for doubt, Stevens insisted that "a good growth of grass" was a reliable indication that "the allied cereal grains could be produced." Here, certainly, was the key to his radical assessment of the potential resources of the region. His source for this idea was not explicit, although certain inferences can be made. Both the botanist and geologist of the railroad survey concurred that wheat could be grown on the hills, though neither made clear whether they were using the presence of bunch grass as an indicator. Stevens' comparison of the Palouse country soils with those of Illinois was apt, for settlement was now being successfully advanced into the margins of the great prairie of the central states. But his perception was based upon a still broader perspective. In preparation for his survey of these western lands, Stevens turned to the Old World for comparison. His son and biographer reports that "he procured and studied all the available works on the steppes of Russia and Asia, as throwing light upon the formation and characteristics of the great plains." The significance of such information stemmed from the fact that this broadly analogous region was already extensively colonized and was being developed into a major wheat producer. Here was proof that grasslands of relatively sparse rainfall might be excellent grain-producing areas. Applying the comparison, Stevens concluded that much of the country along the northern route from Lake Superior to the Pacific

> compares favorably with the best portions of the empire of Russia for the cultivation of the great staples of agriculture, and west of the Rocky Mountains far surpasses them. . . . There is nothing in the soil of any portion, except the western part of the great plain of the Columbia, which forbids agriculture. . . .[52]

[52] *Ibid.*, pp. 142, 197, 199. J. C. Cooper, "Report on the Botany of the Route," *Stevens Report*, XII, Book 2, 16 (referring to the Yakima area); George Gibbs, "Report . . . upon the Geology of the Central Portion of Washington Territory," *Stevens Report*, XII, 485 (referring to the Walla Walla). Hazard Stevens, *Life of Stevens*, pp. 298-99. *Stevens Report*, XII, 331.

Stevens recognized that climate, and especially the long dry summer season, was commonly understood as the major obstacle to agriculture. He published weather observation data from Fort Dalles and Fort Walla Walla, which permitted a more accurate assessment, revealing the surprising mildness of the winters, and a total annual precipitation greater than popularly supposed: Fort Dalles, 14.32 inches; Walla Walla, 20.89 inches. Yet such totals were considerably less than those of the farming areas of the eastern states or west of the Cascades, and it was the deduction from just such comparisons that Stevens attacked as unwarranted. In a debate over the merits of the various Pacific railroad routes in which his opinions of his territory were sharply challenged, Stevens vigorously replied:

> Does it follow, because good crops are found on Puget Sound, in the Columbia and Willamette valleys, where forty to fifty inches of rain are deposited in the course of the year, that the fourteen to sixteen inches which fall in the interior are insufficient for crops? Is there anything to warrant such a deduction? Yet such is the deduction which has actually been made by some of our scientific men.
>
> Mr. Speaker, I think science would do well if it would go to work in a different manner. I would say ascertain all you can about our broad interior, about its soil, and about the amount of moisture deposited; and then go abroad to similar countries similarly situated, where they have raised crops, and see if you can infer anything.

Having "gone abroad" through his study of reports on the Russian steppes, he once again cited that comparison as proof of his judgment. It was a sound procedure, and it was this unprecedented combination of extensive personal reconnaissance, careful research, and logical reasoning which established the Stevens Report as the first *scientific interpretation* of the character and qualities of the Great Columbia Plain.[53]

[53] The summers were also milder than reported in at least one account: the erratic Hastings stated in his guidebook that the temperature in summer "frequietly rises to 180° (Fahrenheit), in the shade!" This is evidently not a misprint because elsewhere he mentioned 160 degrees in the eastern section. Hastings, *Emigrants' Guide*, p. 43. 36th Cong., 1st sess., *Congressional Globe* (May 29, 1860), p. 2414. He had made essentially similar statements on several earlier occasions. The influence of Lorin Blodget was probably very important upon Stevens' approach. Blodget was one of several prominent scientists Stevens consulted in preparation for his survey, and he also wrote an evaluation of the meteorological data accumulated (*Stevens Report*, I, 5-7, 566-71). Blodget's *Climatology of the United States* (Philadelphia, 1857) was the first comprehensive scientific treatment of the topic and had as one of its major themes the assessment of the potentialities of new regions through "comparative climatology" (*ibid.*, p. 27). Blodget recognized the Great Columbia Plain as a "climato-

Stevens was a vigorous protagonist of the attractions of his territory, but he could not work a revolution in attitudes by himself. Not
only were his ideas a sharp contradiction to those of nearly everyone
else, he was on other accounts so controversial a figure that his opinions were apt to be automatically dismissed by many people. This is
well illustrated in the reactions of various officials who had clashed
with Stevens on political matters. Jefferson Davis, who, as secretary
of war, directed the Pacific Railroad Surveys, is reported to have
stated that Stevens had "entirely misconceived and exaggerated the
agricultural resources of the Northern route. The fact is, he has no
knowledge of agricultural soils or conditions." The army officers
who wrote an over-all evaluation of these surveys pointedly contradicted Stevens' appraisals and made it clear that they regarded him
as a naïve and unreliable judge of the country. They spoke of the
necessity of "correcting those opinions formed from those appearances of fertility presented by the growth of grasses &c., which are
liable to mislead," and concluded that the "fertile or cultivable
areas" within the Columbia Plain were the "exceptions" and "of
limited extent." Locally, there was a similar clash in opinions. The
bitterly contradictory objectives of the Governor and the army were
rooted in part in this very difference in appraisal. Where Stevens
saw the inexorable necessity of clearing away the Indians in order
that the settlers might occupy this "delightful" and "fertile" country, the military saw the Columbia Plain as "a region fit, as a general
rule, for the occupancy of the nomadic tribes who now roam over it,
and who should be allowed peacefully to remain in its possession."[54]

---

logical basin," but his assessment was based upon more meager information than
Stevens' and therefore did not give as accurate a picture. He had monthly
temperature data from Lapwai (1837, 1840-41) and The Dalles (1850-55) and
precipitation data only from the latter (ibid., pp. 50-51, 62, 63). Presumably
much of the book was written before he had access to all of Stevens' materials.
Significantly, Blodget set forth a series of analogous climatic regions in America
and Eurasia, all at least broadly accurate, but he left out the Columbia Plain—
and it has no really close analogy elsewhere (ibid., p. 166).
    [54] Stevens, Life of Stevens, p. 430. The author insisted that Davis was predis-
posed in favor of a southern route for political reasons and wanted to destroy
confidence in Stevens' judgment. A. A. Humphreys and G. K. Warren, "An
Examination . . . of the Reports of Exploration for Railroad Routes . . . ," Stevens Report, I, 50-51. Stevens estimated that his northern transcontinental route
traversed but 320 miles of uncultivable land; these authors stated that, on the
contrary, it crossed 1,490 miles of such country. T. J. Cram, "Topographical
Memoir of the Department of the Pacific," 35th Cong., 2nd sess., H. Ex. Doc.
114 (1859), p. 56.

Soldiers' Experiences

These military officers had approached the area with the prevailing opinions of the time. The information available to them suggested a limited utility to the region, and their initial impressions were similar to those of most travelers. Yet through forced contact such men soon gained a better acquaintance. They not only kept records of the weather, but experienced the seasons and found much that was attractive in the climate. Their summer campaigns proved that water was available over most of the region. Their horses, mules, and cattle fattened throughout the year on the "celebrated 'bunch grass' " and their gardens and fields at Simcoe and Walla Walla yielded bountiful crops. As the military era lengthened, local army personnel began to see the region in quite a different light than did their distant superiors. The settlers' pressures upon this region could now be understood as something more than irrational acquisitiveness.[55]

Those very pressures were an indication that a change in attitude was permeating the whole Northwest. Insofar as the impact of the military era was concerned, the experiences of the volunteer militias were of greater consequence than the parallel experiences of the federal troops. Many of these farmers and stockmen returned to their Willamette and Puget Sound homes convinced that there was a better future east of the mountains. Add to these the experiences of Indian agents, surveyors, and various others who had contact with this land and saw something of the testing of its resources; add, further, the heightened attention given the region because of the

[55] See, for example, the comment of General Persifor T. Smith in 1849 regarding the whole interior: "This part of the country I have not seen, and only derive my knowledge from sources open to all. But it is clear, from universal report, that a large portion of this country offers no inducement to settlers; that there are some fertile districts of small extent; that there is pasture for immense herds of cattle." *Report of the Secretary of War ... Relative to Oregon*, 31st Cong., 1st sess., S. Ex. Doc. 47 (1849-50), p. 87. "Andrew D. Pambrun, The Story of His Life as He Tells It" (MS in the Eastern Washington State College Library, Cheney), p. 165. Pambrun, the son of the former Fort Nez Perces Factor and Steptoe's interpreter, described the crop trials at Fort Walla Walla in 1856-58. Steptoe's suggestion of an agricultural colony at Walla Walla, which was vigorously denounced by General Wool, is an apt illustration.

Perhaps the best indication of this change in attitude is the journal of Lawrence Kip, *Army Life on the Pacific ...* (New York, 1859). Kip was an officer in Colonel Wright's 1859 campaign, and although his comments by no means equal the enthusiasm of Stevens, he found much that was attractive and predicted an early influx of settlers. See pp. 26-39, 128.

Indian wars and peripheral mineral discoveries, and the reasons for a general change in attitude become clear.[56]

No evidence suggests that many were ready to echo the enthusiasm of Isaac Stevens, but a new perspective had been acquired and thereby the region was given new meaning. The reality and impact of that outlook was vividly expressed by Lieutenant John Mullan, a seasoned, careful, and normally matter-of-fact observer, on the occasion of his first glimpse of the Walla Walla in July, 1858.

> Below us some 1500 feet lay one of the most beautiful pictures that could break upon the view. . . . To our right lay the range of Blue Mts. viewed from summit to base, in front lay the ocean of rolling prairie . . . , while to our left lay the majestic Columbia traced from point to point by high bluffs & buttes that defined its course. While between them lay embossomed the beautiful valley of the Wallah Wallah. With the main river bearing the same name with its thousand feeders pouring down from the Mt. side in all directions each distinctly marked and traced by its line of verdure that skirts its border. Between each of these pitches preening in the distance the marks of civilized abode and the clouds of dust raised at different points in the valley bespoke the countless herds the valley was capable of supporting. With its mild and gentle climate, with its rich soil, abundance of timber of the first quality on the mountain tops and with its numberless streams affording mill sites at any point of the valley and an extent of land capable if fully cultivated [of supporting] . . . a population of 30,000 people. With the Columbia navigated for steamers drawing 3 to 5 feet of water to Old Wallah Wallah, what may we not anticipate from this valley as years shall fully develop up this region to our nation's notice![57]

Clearly this was a different valley from that seen by Thomas Farnham twenty years before, but the difference was more in the minds of the men than in the facts of the land.

[56] For instance, in 1854 the Indian agent in charge of eastern Oregon stated of the country east of The Dalles that "the hills are well adapted to the cultivation of the cereal grains," 33rd Cong., 2nd sess., S. Ex. Doc. 1 (1854), p. 489. A federal surveyor published a quite optimistic report on the nonirrigated agricultural potential of the Umatilla and Walla Walla valleys: A. N. Armstrong, *Oregon: Comprising a Brief History and Full Description of the Territories of Oregon and Washington* (Chicago, 1857), pp. 89-90.

[57] John Mullan, "Journal from Fort Dalles O.T. to Fort Wallah Wallah W.T. July 1858," in Pal Clark (ed.), *Sources of Northwest History, No. 18* (Missoula, Mont., n.d.), p. 10.

CHAPTER EIGHT

The experiment, so far as tried, has proved exceedingly gratifying, and many persons maintain that these uplands [of eastern Oregon] are destined to be the first grainlands of the State.

W. LAIR HILL

Colonization:

Gold, Grass, and Grain

INITIATION AND TRANSFORMATION

Influx

On October 29, 1858, the gates were officially opened. Just a month after Colonel Wright had announced his campaign to be over, General W. S. Harney, in command of the recently created Military Department of Oregon and Washington, proclaimed that peace was restored, and the land lay ready for settlers. In a way it was a rather precipitous action, especially in view of the federal government's opposition to settler intrusion during recent years. The Indian threat had been quelled by force, but was still unsealed by agreement, for none of the reservation treaties had been ratified; nor had any federal survey of public lands been initiated. But the pressures for land were apparent, and unlike most of his predecessors, Harney was an ardent expansionist, heartily in favor of advancing the wave of settlement.[1]

The initial influx into the Great Columbia Plain was not really a wave, but rather two narrow streams following well-worn channels, branching and spreading over the most favorable ground. The primary flow was eastward from the Willamette Valley to The Dalles,

[1] Robert C. Clark, "Military History of Oregon, 1848-59," *Pacific Northwest Quarterly*, 36 (March, 1945), 42ff. As Clark stated it, Harney's "conception of manifest destiny outstripped" even that of the local residents; his designs upon the San Juan Islands and Vancouver Island were sufficiently embarrassing to prompt his transfer from command in 1880.

partially halting in that vicinity, partially rushing far inland to the Walla Walla, with a trickle branching off into the Yakima Valley. The secondary stream was a diversion into the Walla Walla area of westbound transcontinental immigrants. The three localities had common attractions: grassy, well-watered lowlands already tested by gardens, fields, and livestock, readily accessible, and in the protective shadow of an army post.

As the principal portal, The Dalles, with its few years of headstart, experienced an immediate boom. Tents, log huts, and rough lumber shacks were hastily erected to serve as shops, taverns, restaurants, and hotels; crude corrals became livery stables for the influx of horses, mules, and oxen working the portage road and the inland trail. Ranch sites were quickly taken, forming a linear series along the largest of the "mile creeks" (Threemile, Fivemile, Eightmile, and Fifteenmile); others located along the lower Deschutes and to the south in Tygh Valley.

In the Walla Walla the military prohibition of settlement had not been absolute, for a few licenses had been issued to traders. Thus, two or three crude stores had been built adjacent to the fort, a postmaster had been appointed, and the unofficial titles of "Steptoeville" and "Waiilatpu" had appeared even prior to the lifting of the ban in October, 1858. Within a few months a townsite was platted, a grist mill begun, and a number of houses and stores erected (Map 23). Dr. Augustus Thibodo, arriving in December of 1859, found about fifty frame houses, two restaurants, a number of shops, and despite the high prices and unusual cold (minus ten degrees) promptly hung out his shingle as the first physician. A pack train of fifty mules demonstrated the new town's immediate role as an advance supply center for the Fraser mining region and for the prospectors who were already swarming over the peripheral mountain districts. Many freighting teams and a stage line connected with the river landing at old Fort Nez Perces. Another visitor of that year reported that "a great many are coming out here from Willamett and say they like this climate the best," and he thought it "a good stock country." He was not so certain about its agricultural future, but corn, wheat, oats, and vegetables did well "as far as they have been tried," and the only orchard old enough to bear fruit "bore full." The main valley with its network of small creeks was soon dotted with ranches, and a scattering appeared in the outlying valleys of

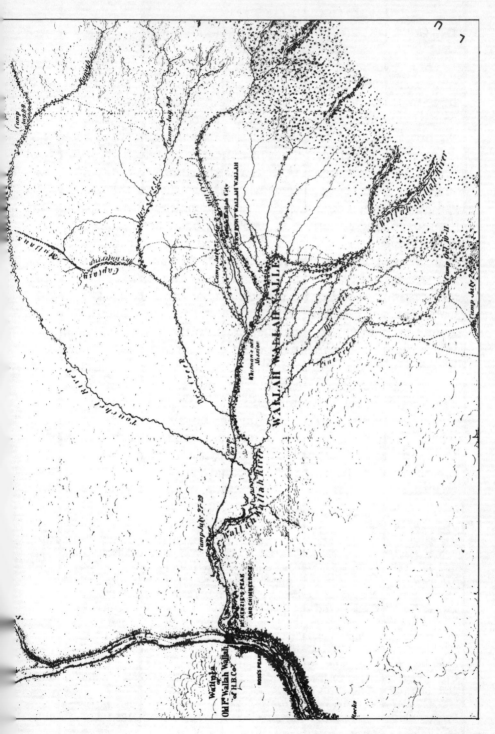

Map 23. The Walla Walla Valley, 1858. Portion of John Mullan's "Map of Military Reconnaissance . . ."

Dry Creek and the Touchet; more remote but still partially related were those along the Umatilla.[2]

These two pioneer colonization clusters were thus identical in type: each a budding town anchored upon an army post, surrounded by a small relatively densely settled, rural zone, and further encompassed by a much larger but very thinly occupied tributary area. At the first accounting they were also remarkably similar in scale. The 1860 census (which despite appearances must, given the context of things, be taken as no more than a reasoned estimate) listed the population of The Dalles cluster as 1,340 and that of the Walla Walla as 1,393 (not including the 155 counted along the Umatilla), and the "improved land in farms" as 6,057 and 6,902 acres, respectively.[3]

A number of stockmen quickly moved into the Klickitat country lying across the Columbia from The Dalles and south of the Horse Heaven Hills. Because that ridge carried a thin strip of pines a long way eastward, parallel to, though a good distance back from, the Columbia, some settlers hauled steamboat fuel by ox team to points along the river. Others ranged across into the Yakima Valley proper, where the first permanent settler of definite location is reported to have established a ranch near the mouth of Moxee Creek. The obvious deterrent in this area was the Indian reservation, which enclosed much of the best land and lay athwart the road to The Dalles. Unlike its counterparts, Fort Simcoe could not become a point of town development, for it was within the confines of the reservation; in the spring of 1859 the army turned it over to the Department of Indian Affairs to be used as the Yakima agency.[4]

That transfer was but one part of a general reorientation of mili-

[2] Frank T. Gilbert, *Historic Sketches of Walla Walla, Whitman, Columbia and Garfield Counties, Washington Territory* (Portland, Ore., 1882), pp. 297-98; Albert J. Partoll, "Frank L. Worden, Pioneer Merchant, 1830-1887," *Pacific Northwest Quarterly*, 40 (July, 1949), 189-202. Worden obtained a trading permit on February 1, 1858, and became the first postmaster on October 1, 1858. "Diary of Dr. Augustus J. Thibodo of the Northwest Exploring Expedition, 1859," *Pacific Northwest Quarterly*, 31 (July, 1940), 342-43. Thibodo entered the region via Canada and the Spokane Valley as a member of a party from St. Paul, Minnesota, bound for the Fraser gold mines. Joel Barnett, *A Long Trip in a Prairie Schooner* (Glendale, Calif., 1928), pp. 127-30.

[3] *Eighth Census, 1860* (Washington, 1864). No list of business houses is available, but it is reasonable to assume that these, too, were generally comparable in number and type; each town had a Methodist and a Roman Catholic church, and the Congregationalists were also established in The Dalles.

[4] *An Illustrated History of Klickitat, Yakima and Kittitas Counties* (Spokane, Wash., 1904), p. 94; 36th Cong., 1st sess., S. Ex. Doc. 2 (1859-60), pp. 94-96.

tary activities which followed immediately upon the conclusion of hostilities. As General Harney considered that the local tribes of the Plain had been fully pacified, Simcoe had no real purpose, and its winter isolation from Fort Dalles made it unattractive for any kind of depot. In February, 1859, he received an urgent request to provide escorts to the parties engaged in surveying the international boundary, and Harney then established Fort Colville about fourteen miles southeast of the Hudson's Bay Company post of the same name. Completed in the autumn of that year, it soon had a small civilian settlement adjacent, known as Pinkney City.[5]

On the other hand, Forts Dalles and Walla Walla still served as bases for patrols southward into the troublesome Snake country. The Indians on the Warm Springs Reservation suffered recurrent attacks from hostile Snakes, and Fort Dalles found a new focus of activity in that direction. Fort Walla Walla supplied patrols for the immigrant road beyond the Blue Mountains. Each fort also served as a base camp for the principal military activity of the day, the survey and construction of wagon roads. The Dalles–Great Salt Lake Wagon Road was authorized and initiated in 1859 to provide a more direct and easier immigrant route than the present Oregon Trail, avoiding the heavy grades over the Blue Mountains. It would prove to be an ill-conceived venture; the difficulties of the rough lands of the Deschutes and Crooked River areas and the inhospitality of the high desert country were surely underrated, and the surveyed route turned out to be considerably longer than the old trail. The second major project was the Fort Walla Walla–Fort Benton road to connect the Columbia with the head of navigation on the Missouri, via the Coeur d' Alene country. Lieutenant Mullan was in charge, and people soon conferred his name upon the road (Map 24). Fort Walla Walla served as the principal base, although in the summer of 1859 the *Colonel Wright* paddled its way up the Snake to the mouth of the Palouse, and that point became a useful advance depot.[6]

This flurry of progress by the whites was accompanied by the chaotic disintegration of the Indians. The reservation treaties were finally ratified in March, 1859, but any satisfaction from that be-

[5] 36th Cong., 1st sess., S. Ex. Doc. 2 (1859-60), pp. 94-95; W. P. Winans, "Fort Colville 1859 to 1869," *Washington Historical Quarterly*, 3 (October, 1908), 78-82.

[6] 36th Cong., 1st sess., S. Ex. Doc. 34 (1859-60), 51 pp. and map; 36th Cong., 2nd sess., H. Ex. Doc. 44 (1860-62), pp. 2-5.

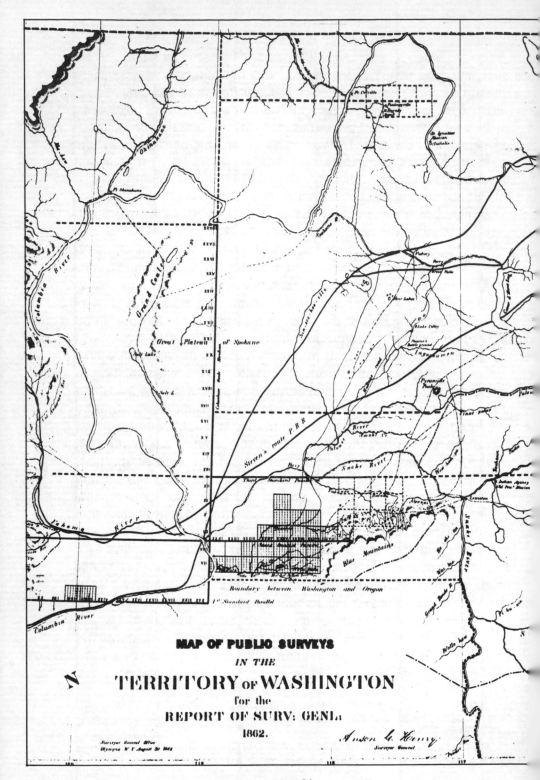

MAP OF PUBLIC SURVEYS

IN THE

TERRITORY of WASHINGTON

for the

REPORT OF SURV: GENL:

1862.

Anson G. Henry

Surveyor General

Surveyor General Office
Olympia W. T. August 30 1862

Map 24

lated move was one-sided. As the Walla Walla Indian agent reported: "There is an impression rife amongst them all that Agents are sent out to pacify them with kind words until such time as there will be soldiers and citizens enough in the country to drive them off their lands without paying them for them." There was ample precedent and current evidence to support their fears. Although their property outside the reservation was supposedly protected by law, their scattering of garden patches were often pre-empted and their horses and cattle stolen. The agency reports on tribe after tribe carry the same melancholy refrain: "very destitute," "impoverished," "much reduced" by war, disease, and starvation. For some, tribal life was completely shattered, and they led "a most dissolute and renegade" life, stealing, quarreling, selling their horses for whiskey. The winter had been harsh, supplies were low, and many died in the first year of "peace." The agents stressed the importance of getting the natives settled within their reservations, but many Indians resisted the idea of confinement, others sought to go to a different one from that assigned (the Palouse wanted to go to the Nez Perces instead of the Yakima), and for the time being not much was accomplished on the matter. There was much complaint from both sides about the Umatilla reserve being "too near a public highway," and although when the treaty was being negotiated it had been proposed to relocate the Oregon Trail, the local agent now recommended that the reservation be abandoned and the Indians be distributed elsewhere.[7]

The only exception to this general picture of misery and decline was the Nez Perces. Untouched by the recent wars, still remote from the areas of white settlement and traffic, with a reservation which embraced nearly the whole rather than but a small part of their homeland (Map 25), these Indians enjoyed a relatively stable and prosperous existence. They numbered between three thousand and four thousand, held an estimated ten thousand horses and two thousand head of cattle, and gave promise of becoming successful stockmen self-sustained upon their reservation.[8] For the moment

[7] "Records of the Washington Superintendency of Indian Affairs, Letters Received (Nez Perces), April 16, 1859" (MSS in the National Archives, Washington, D.C.). Hereafter cited as "Records of Indian Affairs." *Ibid.,* Sept. 20, 1958; Feb. 28, April 16, Aug. 2, Oct. 31, 1859.

[8] *Ibid.,* Aug. 2, 1859, and 36th Cong., 1st sess., S. Ex. Doc. 1 (1859-60), pp. 432-35. Other tribal populations listed in this latter document were Cayuse four hundred, Walla Walla eight hundred, Palouse four hundred, Coeur

they had escaped that "monster of desolation" which elsewhere had swept so heavily in upon the Great Columbia Plain.

Surge to the Mines

But such tranquillity was only momentary. In the summer of 1860 rumors turned attention to the Nez Perces country. The local Indian agent posted prominent notices of the law prohibiting unofficial entry into the reservation, but by November his fears were confirmed: gold had been discovered in the upper Clearwater country. As soon as the melting snows permitted, the uncontrollable influx of miners and traders flocked to the mountain meadow thirty miles east of the main Clearwater River, where a cluster of crude cabins had already been dignified as Pierce City in honor of the discoverer. Other opportunists were quick to see the junction of the Snake and Clearwater as an attractive site for a new trade center. The agent valiantly tried to uphold the law. On July 7, 1861 he issued a proclamation that this budding settlement was "in violation of United States law and cannot be permitted under any circumstances." The most apparent result was the appointment of a new Indian agent. He, too, tried to block the development, but the promoters simply ignored him and in October surveyed the town of Lewiston with a square mile of streets and lots. By December a dozen houses had been built, fifty tents occupied other lots, and the agent finally gave in and issued licenses to all who wished to trade.

The Superintendent of Indian Affairs, after consultation with the army, had, meanwhile, conferred with the Nez Perces chiefs and attempted to allay their fears. Privately, however, the local agent foresaw the worst. In an urgent demand for troops he described to his superior what seemed to be the inevitable outcome of it all:

> . . . the town of "Lewiston" will be built despite the laws and proclamations of officers—the rivers and streams will be cut up with ferries—"squatters" will settle down on every patch of arable land,—the fences of the Indians will be burned for firewood by travellers—their horses and cattle will be stolen without redress—wiskey [sic] is & will be sold to them without an effort at concealment, and the Indians will be overreached, plundered and destroyed and have but one defense,—that of taking up arms for their very existence.

All but the last point soon proved to be at least partly true, and

---

d'Alene six hundred, but various other reports are much at variance, and it seems clear that all of these groups were declining, some precipitously.

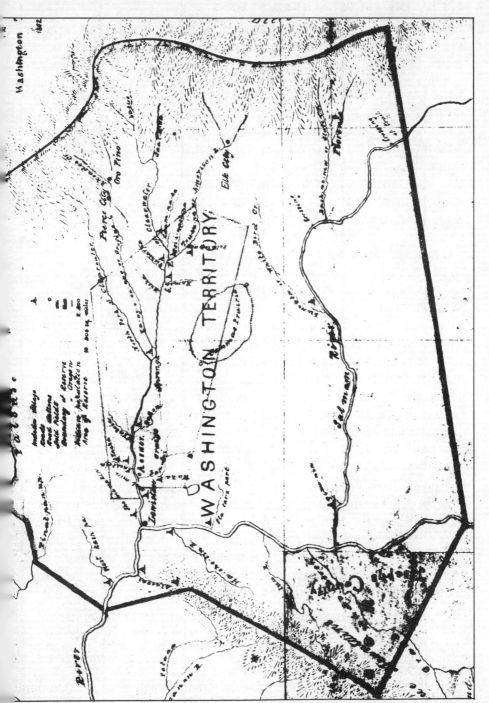

Map 25. Approximate Map of the Nez Perces Reservation, in Washington Territory, 1862 (reproduced from the original in the National Archives)

war was narrowly averted. At a major council in May-June, 1863, the Nez Perces were induced to accept a greatly reduced reservation which left all the mining lands outside, in return for guarantees of military protection (through the establishment of Fort Lapwai in Lapwai Valley above the old mission site); federal construction of mills, schools, churches, and houses; contributions of implements; and various cash indemnities covering past grievances and present relinquishments. As usual, though the Indians with considerable reluctance and dissension accepted the treaty, it was not ratified by Congress until 1867. Meanwhile, local whites acted as if the treaty were in force, while the government gave little indication of carrying out its promises, thus compounding the already well-merited distrust.[9]

The Clearwater discoveries were of major importance to the interior. They developed into the first mining district which could be reached only by way of the Great Columbia Plain (the Colville placers had proved too slight to sustain development; the Fraser districts could be reached more directly from the coast); and they set in motion an intense, widespread prospecting, which soon opened up an array of profitable districts peripheral to the Great Plain (Map 26).

Major extensions of mining activities began to develop with the first season in the Clearwater. In late 1861 discoveries on the South Fork gave rise to Elk City; by early 1862 the Florence and Warren diggings had opened up the lower Salmon River district. In that same year the Boise Basin (Idaho City), Powder River, and John Day (Canyon City) placers were discovered, to be followed by the Owyhee (Silver City) and Alder Creek (Virginia City) the next year. In 1864 important strikes on the lower Kootenay about fifty miles north of the border (Wild Horse Creek), and at Last Chance Gulch in Montana (Helena) completed the list of major districts, though in these frenzied years superficial finds had momentarily focused some attention on many other areas, such as the Wenatchee, Similkameen, upper Palouse, and Deer Lodge.[10]

[9] Material for this section has been derived from "Records of Indian Affairs," May 18, Aug. 28, Nov. 27, 1860; April 13, July 9, 1861; the last quotation is from a letter dated Jan. 4, 1862. Josephy, *Nez Perce Indians*, chap. x, gives a detailed account of the invasion of miners and negotiations leading to the treaty of 1863.

[10] Contemporary with the Clearwater was a major rush into the upper Fraser area, the Cariboo district. The best general source for the early history of these mining areas is W. J. Trimble, *Mining Advance into the Inland Empire* (Uni-

Such a series of sensational discoveries made the mountainous interior Northwest the first great successor to California as the preeminent locality of far western mining. In many ways it was an extension of the Californian experience and character. Initially, at least, most of the miners were Californians, and the regulations, methods, and manners were a direct transfer from that pioneering region.[11] Unlike California, mining was dispersed among a dozen important districts spread over a huge area, but Portland (like San Francisco) became the great entrepôt, and the Columbia Plain (like the Sacramento Valley) lay between the mines and the sea, and thus became directly bound up in the whole maelstrom of development.

For the Columbia Plain this new era was also reminiscent in geographic type with that of the fur trade, the region itself being primarily important for its trunk line and route focus, with activities concentrated upon a few strategic points, intermediaries between the resource-rich mountain lands and the great ocean depot (with Portland now serving in place of Fort Vancouver). Formerly the procurement ground for pack horses, the area now furnished quantities of beef as well. But the scale and implications of developments were of a different order: hundreds of stockmen and tradesmen and the spreading pattern of ranches and bustling towns instead of a handful of temporary agents and tightly clustered trading posts. Where the one had been but a superimposition upon alien Indian country, the other was a firm rooting in a new homeland.

The mines were entirely peripheral, and men, animals, and goods were channeled in turbulent streams through the region. But there were also junctions and eddies of intense activity. Lewiston was wholly a response to the mining trade, but although it had a rapid and prosperous development for a few years, its hinterland was largely restricted to the Clearwater and Salmon districts; as these soon leveled off and then declined in productivity, the town, though firmly established, stagnated. The major impact of this new era remained focused upon those two districts of persistent historic significance, The Dalles and the Walla Walla.

versity of Wisconsin Studies, History Series, Vol. III, No. 2) (Madison, 1914), esp. chaps. iv-v. Bancroft's various state and provincial volumes also document each in some detail. An excellent series of contemporary newspaper reports on the Clearwater and Salmon River rushes has been reprinted under various titles in *Idaho Yesterdays*, 3 (Winter, 1959-60), 19-29; 4 (Spring, 1960), 12-26; 4 (Winter, 1960-61), 14-22; 5 (Summer, 1961), 8-20; 6 (Spring, 1962), 40-48.

[11] Trimble, *Mining Advance*, p. 10.

The first influx literally overwhelmed The Dalles. The horde of adventurers who surged inland in early 1862 were held up by the ice and snow of the unusually severe winter. Before the river and trails were opened in late March, the pressures reached the breaking point, and The Dalles was plundered and ruled by a mob. A traveler later that year reported of Walla Walla that "the principal business appears to be selling horses at auction. Selling whiskey and gambling and worse." Another called it "a straggling, disorderly looking place, ... The dirty streets were crowded with freighting wagons and teams and pack animals and a considerable army of rough men." By all accounts there was plenty of business. [12] Simply catering to the elementary demands of the traffic with hotels and eating houses, brothels and saloons was enough to sustain a considerable town. Add to these the mushrooming business of outfitting newcomers and selling to the mining camps the basic essentials (bacon, flour, dried fruits, tea, coffee, whiskey, clothing, tools, and equipment), plus the necessary services of blacksmiths, saddle and harness makers, wheelwrights, wagon repairers, livery men, and livestock agents, and the bases for a vigorously diversified settlement are clear. And to this may be added an even greater array of other servants, idlers, drifters, and opportunists of many sorts. Each town, having a previously established small nucleus of businesses, burgeoned with this full array of activities with the first season of the mining boom.

The two towns had gotten their start in large part because of strategic positions on routes, and the enormous increase in traffic simply compounded that significance and function. As always, the river played a dominant role. The Dalles reaped the benefits of its position not only as the main portal to the interior, but, more importantly, as the essential transshipment point for all river traffic. The local company which operated teams and wagons along The Dalles–Celilo portage enjoyed an excellent business from the first opening of the interior. Even prior to the mining rush, it sold out on advantageous terms to the newly formed Oregon Steam Navigation Company, which also obtained title to the *Colonel Wright* and

[12] *An Illustrated History of North Idaho* (Spokane, Wash., 1903), p. 26. Helen A. Howard (ed.), "Diary of Charles Rumley from St. Louis to Portland, 1862," *Frontier and Midland,* 19 (Spring, 1939), 190-200. See also Doyce B. Nunis, Jr. (ed.), *The Golden Frontier: The Recollections of Herman Francis Reinhart, 1851-1869* (Austin, Tex., 1962). Randall H. Hewitt, *Across the Plains and Over the Divide* ... (New York, 1964), p. 463.

A view of The Dalles–Celilo portage railroad in the 1860's. The engine, the *J. C. Ainsworth,* was brought around Cape Horn in 1863; the track was of five-foot gauge and fourteen miles long. *(Photo courtesy of Union Pacific Railroad Company)*

the *Tenino* and thus gained full command of the river from Port-land to Fort Nez Perces. Even though the initial prospects of the company were very good, the sudden demands of the mining traffic were an enormous windfall to its promoters. The Dalles portage was swamped with business, and a broad-gauge rail line was under-taken and completed in the spring of 1863.[13]

Meanwhile, the steamboats on the upper river were producing far more gold for the company than any miner was getting from his placers. On one trip the *Tenino* took in over eighteen thousand dol-lars; in just two months in the spring of 1862 the three boats then operating garnered over fifty-six thousand dollars in upstream pas-senger fares alone. Such profits were a wonderful incentive, and along the banks at Celilo and just beyond at the Deschutes new boats were being constructed with the greatest possible haste. At least eight were completed during the first four years of the mining boom, two of these by independent operators each of whom soon sold out to

[13] The *Tenino,* built at Deschutes, had been launched in 1860. The O.S.N. acquired Olmstead's rail portage at the Cascades at the same time it purchased The Dalles Portage Company. The original O.S.N. was a Washington Territory corporation formed Dec. 16, 1860; it was succeeded by the O.S.N., State of Oregon, incorporated Oct. 21, 1862; see O.W.R.N., *Corporate History,* sheets 56-58.

the O.S.N. During the four years 1861-64 the latter company carried a total of ninety-three thousand passengers and over sixty thousand tons of freight on the stretch above Celilo.[14]

The river routes varied with the seasons and the boats. The latter ranged in size from the diminutive to the scale of the *Webfoot,* which was 150 feet long and had a displacement of 504 tons. Most were sternwheelers especially designed for extremely shallow-draft operations, yet numerous rapids and fluctuations markedly affected the service. The high water season, during which large boats could operate clear to Lewiston, generally ran from early May to early September; service on the Columbia prevailed without major difficulty for a month and a half prior and after that time. The low water season was usually from mid-November to mid-March, during which times the larger boats might be unable to pass above, or even attain, Umatilla Rapids. Ice interruptions varied considerably from year to year, from none at all to as much as sixty days. But at all seasons the rivers were treacherous, and damages and delays were not infrequent. The main line of upriver service was between the portage railhead at Celilo and Wallula, the river port which had sprung up adjacent to the site of old Fort Nez Perces. Service up the Snake to Lewiston was maintained in summer, but was hazardous and time consuming and therefore less frequent. In 1863, the tiny *Cascadilla* was plying the Clearwater between Lewiston and Lapwai, and the Snake between Lewiston and the sawmill at Asotin. Later she served as a shuttle between Wallula and White Bluffs Landing below Priest Rapids, the head of navigation on this section of the Columbia. Such local service was, however, sporadic.[15]

Networks and Competitions

As in previous eras, the whole interior was bound up in a network of routes focused upon the trunk line of the Columbia (Map 26). Most of the trails of fur trade, mission, and military days were

[14] Wright, *Marine History,* pp. 106-7. For details on names, dimensions, dates, and locations of construction, I have relied upon the carefully compiled list of Randall V. Mills, *Sternwheelers Up Columbia . . .* (Palo Alto, Calif., 1947), Appendix A, pp. 189-203. Mills's volume is an excellent coverage of the full history and flavor of the riverboat era throughout the Columbia Basin. 40th Cong., 2nd sess., H. Ex. Doc. 1 (1867), Appendix 8, "Letter of J. C. Ainsworth" (July 20, 1867), pp. 509-11.

[15] 40th Cong., 2nd sess., H. Ex. Doc. 1 (1867), pp. 509-11; Wright (ed.), *Marine History,* pp. 107-8.

in use, and a few new ones were added. Walla Walla and The Dalles had complementary and competitive positions within that network. Obviously both gained from the traffic along the main axis, of which each was a primary terminal; but they were competitive in their functions as inland mercantile supply centers for numerous mining camps. The principal area of competition was that reached *via* the Oregon Trail: the Powder River, Boise, and Owyhee districts. Although all Walla Walla merchandise came in by way of The Dalles, the more direct connection with the source offered by The Dalles was partially offset by the greater immediate accessibility and therefore better services offered by Walla Walla merchants. Much of the vigor of this competition was expressed in the bitter rivalry between the upriver towns of Umatilla and Wallula, each in a sense a satellite of its larger center. Here, too, was a reassertion of an older pattern, as when the "Umatilla cut-off" allowed the immigrants of the 1840's to bypass Waiilatpu. And, as before, despite the longer distance, the prospect of a stopover in the Walla Walla "oasis" was sufficient to divert much of the traffic to that route. A traveler of 1865 found Umatilla a dreary, windy and sand-choked hamlet, and although Wallula was little better, he reported that most of the Boise-bound passengers went that way because of the good road and stage line to Walla Walla and its good cheap hotels and provisions.[16]

The pretensions of Umatilla were but one of several irritants to Walla Walla's sense of rightful dominance of the interior trade. The Snake River service to Lewiston was a major bypass, but its seasonality and infrequency still allowed a considerable pack-train and stagecoach traffic between Walla Walla and the Clearwater. Fear of a rival town at Palouse Landing where the Snake River boats intercepted the Mullan Road proved unfounded; there was more substance to the rivalry of White Bluffs, from which point a road northeast across the Plain interconnecting with the Montana and Kootenay routes was laid out in 1863. Even its own port of Wallula hailed the "Wastuckna wagon road," leading directly northeastwardly beyond the lower Snake, as the most feasible route to Montana. Actually, none of these projects really depressed Walla Walla's business. It remained the focus of traffic for most of the interior, despite the fact that it lay thirty miles off the river and in some instances well off the most direct routes. The initial advantages of Walla Walla were simply too

[16] C. Aubrey Angelo, *Idaho: A Descriptive Tour and Review of Its Resources and Route* (San Francisco, 1865), pp. 39-41.

THE MINING ERA

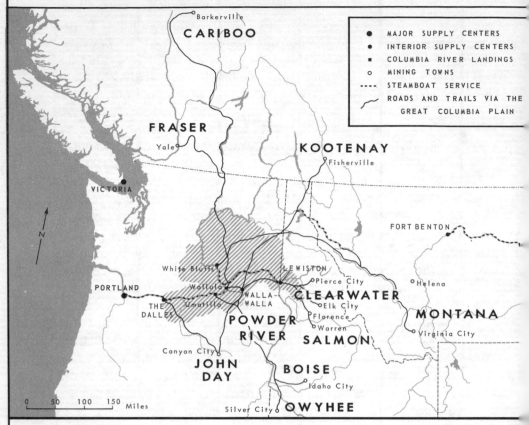

CARIBOO
Barkerville

FRASER
Yale

KOOTENAY
Fisherville

VICTORIA

N

FORT BENTON

White Bluffs
Wollula
PORTLAND
THE DALLES
Umatilla
WALLA-WALLA
LEWISTON
Pierce City
CLEARWATER
Elk City
Florence
Warren
SALMON
MONTANA
Helena
Virginia City

POWDER RIVER

Canyon City
JOHN DAY

BOISE
Idaho City

Silver City
OWYHEE

MAJOR SUPPLY CENTERS
INTERIOR SUPPLY CENTERS
COLUMBIA RIVER LANDINGS
MINING TOWNS
STEAMBOAT SERVICE
ROADS AND TRAILS VIA THE GREAT COLUMBIA PLAIN

0   50   100   150 Miles

PATTERNS OF COMPETITION 1858–187

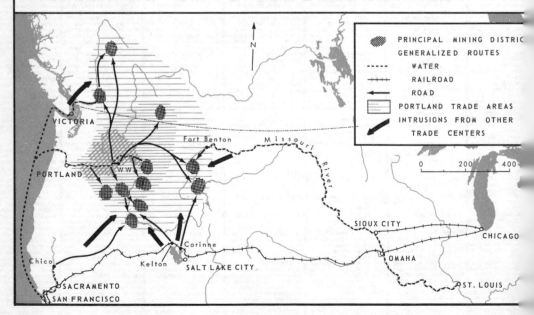

N

VICTORIA

Fort Benton
Missouri River

PORTLAND
W W

Chico

Kelton
Corinne
SALT LAKE CITY

SACRAMENTO
SAN FRANCISCO

SIOUX CITY

OMAHA

CHICAGO

ST. LOUIS

PRINCIPAL MINING DISTRIC
GENERALIZED ROUTES
WATER
RAILROAD
ROAD
PORTLAND TRADE AREAS
INTRUSIONS FROM OTHER TRADE CENTERS

0   200   400

Map 26, above; Map 27, below

great for any nearby rival to compete. To its headstart as a town and its location at the junction of all the best-known and proven routes it added an ever expanding scale and variety of businesses and services and tapped its hinterland with frequent and reliable tranportation facilities. Though the sternwheelers could probe well beyond Wallula in season, the Celilo-Wallula run gave the O.S.N. a quick turnaround and sure traffic over much of the year, and they therefore concentrated much of their means in that service. The volume of freight moved between Walla Walla and its port was prodigious for the time. Chafing under the exorbitant rates of the teamsters, local merchants began to talk of a railroad as early as 1862, and they induced the territorial legislature to request land-grant aid from Congress in the following year. Mullan even entertained the possibility of making Walla Walla a port by means of a canal, although he proposed this as a temporary expedient until a railroad might be constructed. It would be years before this kind of progressive thinking would ameliorate the costs and congestion on this route, but the business initiative was well expressed in the fact that by 1864 scheduled stagecoach service was available to The Dalles, Boise, Lewiston, and Fort Colville. At the height of the boom, pack trains, saddle trains, freighting wagons and stagecoaches combined to give at least occasional freight and passenger service from Walla Walla to every mining camp around the periphery, from the Cariboo to Alder Gulch to the John Day.[17]

Although Walla Walla easily outdistanced its local rivals, that was but one phase of the competition. In the larger pattern these towns, river landings, and transportation facilities were but elements in the over-all system of trade and transport radiating from Portland, and, on a still different scale, Portland was but one of several major

[17] The stage line was established in 1862; Gilbert, *Historic Sketches,* p. 303. William S. Lewis, *The Story of Early Days in the Big Bend Country* (Spokane, Wash., 1926), p. 8; Gilbert, *Historic Sketches,* pp. 237-38. *Walla Walla Statesman,* Feb. 23, 1867. All of these competitive landings and routes receive attention in various issues of this newspaper during the mid-1860's. Oscar O. Winther, *The Old Oregon Country: A History of Frontier Trade, Transportation, and Travel* (Indiana University Publications, Social Science Series No. 7) (Bloomington, 1950), p. 200; 38th Cong., 1st sess., H. Misc. Doc. 55 (1864), pp. 1-2. John Mullan, "From Walla Walla to San Francisco," *Washington Statesman* (Walla Walla), Nov. 29, Dec. 6, 1862; reprinted in *Oregon Historical Quarterly,* 4 (1903), 202-3. Gilbert, *Historic Sketches,* pp. 232, 303-4; Winther, *Old Oregon Country,* pp. 257, 282-83; W. D. Lyman, *An Illustrated History of Walla Walla County* . . . (1901), pp. 161-62.

entrepôts which sought to serve the Northwest mining region (Map 27). Though at first thought it might have seemed the logical commercial capital, its supremacy was sharply limited. In the Clearwater, Salmon, Kootenay, and John Day districts, Portland clearly dominated, working through its advance bases in Lewiston, Walla Walla, and The Dalles. It participated in the Fraser and Cariboo rushes also, but the rise of Victoria (dependent, in turn, as Portland partially was, upon San Francisco) soon undercut its position, and although in the first years numerous pack trains from The Dalles served those districts, no sustained commercial connection could be maintained. The Montana mines were among the richest, but here Portland encountered serious competition from St. Louis. The advantage to Portland of the pre-existing Mullan Road was counterbalanced by the proof of Missouri navigability to Fort Benton. Both of these links in this originally military scheme carried heavy traffic for many years. Portland, Walla Walla, and Lewiston interests rejoiced over the federal government's appropriation in 1865 for a direct wagon road between Lewiston and Virginia City, Montana. However, the amount was so small and the two possible routes (via Lolo or Nez Perces passes) were so rugged and forest locked that not even a pack trail was hacked through. In the late 1860's new elements entered the competition. Railroads across Iowa to the Missouri River gave Chicago, Omaha, and Sioux City entry into the Montana trade; and as the Union Pacific was pushed across the plains, freight and stage lines began to connect Virginia City with the ever approaching end-of-track. Once the transcontinental was completed, Corinne, Utah, became the freighting junction for the Montana trade; and by then Salt Lake City was aspiring to become the commercial center for more than just its Mormon hinterland.[18]

In the Boise and Owyhee districts Portland encountered competition from still another direction. Enterprising Californians laid out a number of routes linking some river or rail point in the Sacramento Valley with southwestern Idaho. The principal one was

[18] Winther's *Old Oregon Country* has an excellent general coverage of transportation, trade, and the competitions in the broad Northwest region. On the Fraser-Cariboo trade, see pp. 187-92; on Montana, see pp. 193-95, 198, 208-13, 223. The number of steamboat arrivals at Fort Benton jumped from four in 1864 to thirty-nine in 1867. See also Alton B. Oviatt, "Pacific Coast Competition for the Gold Camp Trade of Montana," *Pacific Northwest Quarterly*, 56 (October, 1965), 168-76. Jackson, *Wagon Roads West*, chap. xix. Winther, *Old Oregon Country*, p. 224.

from the steamboat landing at Chico by way of Honey Lake, touching the northwest bend of the Humboldt, and thence north to the Owyhee. Pack trains, freighting teams, and, in 1866, scheduled stage and mail service over this route indicated a considerable business. That the competition hurt was evident in the amount of derisive attention The Dalles newspaper gave to "The Cheeky Route," and in the obvious satisfaction the Umatilla paper derived from such reports as the following:

> Amongst the goods received this week there is about 100,000 pounds of Owyhee freight, part of which we notice is for the branch store at Owyhee of a house doing business in Sacramento. This looks rather bad for our neighbors of the Humboldt route.... Passengers can ... be hurried over alkali and sage brush day and night. But when it comes to the transportation of freight where short and good roads, water and wood at convenient distances, are required, the Humboldt route is *non est*.[19]

By 1870, however, there was no satisfaction whatsoever—with the completion of the Central Pacific, California as well as Salt Lake City and the East (via Kelton, Utah) had superior access to these southern Idaho districts.

Thus in this larger pattern Walla Walla, The Dalles, and Lewiston were but minor outposts within a competitive network that spanned half the nation. Their degree of success was merely an expression of Portland's success; their most direct competitors were their functional counterparts dotted widely across the whole far West. Ultimately Portland lost much of the trade of the "outer circle" (the Fraser, Cariboo, Montana, Boise, Owyhee), and retained dominance only in the "inner circle" (the Kootenay, Clearwater, Salmon, Powder, John Day) nearer the Great Columbia Plain.

To the extent that these Columbia Plain centers were merely marketing outposts of Portland, matters of distance, reliability, and efficiency of transport shaped patterns of competition. But they were more than mere outposts, and much of their success and significance stemmed from their function as production centers as well. The one great product of the Columbia Plain in the early 1860's was livestock, and in this it had, for a time, advantages far superior to any competitive area.

---

[19] *Columbia Press* (Umatilla), Oct. 5, 1867; references to the California competition are common in The Dalles paper throughout 1866-68, e.g., Jan. 27, 1867; see also Winther, *Old Oregon Country*, pp. 216-20, 259-60.

GRASS AND GRAIN

Stockmen

The livestock economy of the region was initiated prior to the main mining boom. The Fraser district and the scattering of prospectors in the mountain periphery could not provide much of a market, and those who came sought homesites and control of good rangelands without any certain idea of how they would dispose of future surpluses. The interior ranges were stocked primarily from the Willamette, which, with its herds accrued for twenty years from cattle brought across the continent by the immigrants and from imports from California, served as the "cattle nursery" for the entire Northwest. To these were added those brought by immigrants who came to the area directly from the East. It was an important coincidence that the mining boom immediately followed one of the worst winters ever experienced in the interior. A heavy blizzard was followed by weeks of alternating thawing and freezing which sealed the grass under an impenetrable icy crust. One pioneer recalled that of ten thousand head of cattle in the Walla Walla—Umatilla area in the fall of 1861, "not 1,000" were left by the following May. Whatever the exact numbers may have been, the losses were extremely heavy. The immediate result was that the demands of the incoming mining throng sent beef prices soaring, which in turn prompted heavy movements of cattle in from the Willamette. These either were driven in by way of the Barlow Road and other Cascade trails, or were shipped to The Dalles by boat. Some were trailed directly to the mining camps, others were used to restock and expand the range industry in the Columbia Plain.[20]

Stockmen soon scattered widely over the region, but not at random. Creeks, trails, and well grassed lowlands were attractive features. The Dalles vicinity, the several valleys spaced eastward along

[20] The phrase "cattle nursery" is J. Orin Oliphant's; see his "The Cattle Herds and Ranches of Oregon Country, 1860-1890," *Agricultural History,* 21 (October, 1947), 220. Daniel M. Drumheller, *Uncle Dan Drumheller Tells Thrills of Western Trails in 1854* (Spokane, Wash., 1925), pp. 63-65; J. Orin Oliphant, "Winter Losses of Cattle in the Oregon Country, 1847-1890," *Washington Historical Quarterly,* 23 (January, 1932), 8-9. The hardships of that winter are well described in Nunis, *Golden Frontier,* pp. 197-201; Reinhart's neighbor lost 435 out of a herd of 600 head of unusually fat cattle. Walter Bailey, "The Barlow Road," *Oregon Historical Quarterly,* 13 (September, 1912), 287-96; Earle K. Stewart, "Transporting Livestock by Boat Up the Columbia, 1861-1868," *Oregon Historical Quarterly,* 50 (December, 1949), 251-59.

the main trail, the Umatilla, Walla Walla, and Yakima areas were the main locales. For five or six years the demands were enormous, and a choice of markets was offered. A good illustration is provided by the activities of A. J. Splawn, a pioneer packer, trader, and stockman in the Yakima Valley. In 1861 he trailed a herd from Yakima to the Cariboo, during the next three years he ran pack and saddle trains to various camps, then in 1865 he drove cattle to the Boise district, in the next year he tended a herd on the Camas Prairie being held for the Salmon River market, in 1867 he drove a large herd from Yakima to Montana, and in the following year took another north into the Fraser country. The total volume of this kind of traffic is unobtainable. Newspaper and other accounts often list an estimate for a particular season and locale; for example, the Walla Walla paper reported in 1866 that five thousand head had been driven that year to Montana from the local area. A few more exact accountings are available for particular movements. Customs records reveal a total of 22,256 head entering British Columbia via the Okanogan Trail during the period 1859-70; peak years were 1862-66. During the spring shipping season of 1867 the O.S.N. Company reported that its boats had carried 11,978 cattle from Portland to The Dalles, and it was estimated that about half would be driven directly to the mines. One account suggested that "there has doubtless been an equal number driven across the Cascade Mountains." During the best years in the mid-1860's, exports must have approached twenty thousand head annually, and the total for the whole decade was perhaps well beyond one hundred thousand.[21]

This lucrative traffic did not end as abruptly as it began, but it tapered off rapidly. There were two simple reasons: first, the succession of major gold discoveries ended in 1865—even the best of the districts soon leveled off, many lesser ones were virtually abandoned, and even though most continued some production, populations stabilized at a level far below that of the initial rush; secondly, stockmen soon established herds in the local mountain valleys adjacent to the mines. There were many attractive locales, well grassed and watered, and with some care stock could be successfully wintered. The increase of these herds and the lessening of the demand soon

[21] Splawn, *Ka-mi-akin;* Trimble, *Mining Advance,* p. 108; F. W. Laing, "Pioneers of the Cattle Industry," *British Columbia Historical Quarterly,* 7 (October, 1952), 259; *Weekly Mountaineer* (The Dalles), May 15, 1867; A. J. Dufur, *Statistics of the State of Oregon* (Salem, Ore., 1869), p. 110.

made many of the mining districts self-sufficient in beef. Splawn states that after 1868 no Yakima cattle were driven to the mines. In that year a small herd of two hundred was trailed over Naches Pass to Puget Sound, and this marked the beginnings of annual exports in that direction; but the numbers and profits were pitifully small in comparison with the heyday of the mining trade.[22] Wasco, Umatilla, and Walla Walla stockmen continued to find some outlet in the old markets, but they, too, felt the changed conditions. The mines had proved a wonderful impetus for the establishment of a livestock economy in the Great Plain, but it was increasingly apparent that they could not sustain its further expansion.

There was more to the over-all livestock economy than cattle. Sheep, hogs, horses, mules, and burros (usually called "Mexican mules" or "pack mules") were also of some importance. All but the burros had been brought to the region primarily from the Willamette; the burros came from California. The draft and pack animals were of course capital equipment; thousands were wintered in the Walla Walla and The Dalles areas, but they were not a range stock in the same commercial sense or scale as cattle. The Walla Walla paper reported in 1866 that six thousand mules were in use and fifteen hundred horses had been sold to persons en route to the mines; that was probably the peak year. Many stockmen raised draft animals as a profitable adjunct to cattle, but it was not an expanding, specialized activity. Hogs were still a different matter. Salt pork and bacon were mining camp staples, but the Columbia Plain was far from an ideal hog-raising country, particularly before the grain economy was well established. Hogs were not a satisfactory range animal, were not well suited for droving over the rugged mountain trails, and required far greater facilities and care than cattle; thus, despite the market demand, they were not raised in large numbers. On the other hand, the sheep industry grew alongside that of cattle. The first large flock of forty-five hundred head was driven into the Yakima region in late 1861; by March only forty-five were left. However, one terrible winter was not a major deterrent, and numerous flocks were imported in the next few years. The Walla Walla paper reported that ten thousand had been wintered there in 1865-66 and then driven to Montana. But the mining market was not the major attraction. The expansion of farming in the Willamette and the Cali-

22 Splawn, *Ka-mi-akin,* p. 290.

fornia drought of 1864 brought in numerous sheepmen, who sought permanent ranges for wool growing. By the late 1860's numerous flocks of several thousand had become well established, especially in the Umatilla area. By the spring of 1867 wool was being shipped downriver, and a group of enterprisers at The Dalles had formed the Wasco Woolen Manufacturing Corporation to capitalize upon what seemed an obvious opportunity for industrial development.[23]

Farmers

Many of the earliest settlers had immediately prepared ground for grain, gardens, and orchards. This was done at a number of places, but by far the greatest efforts were concentrated in the Walla Walla Valley, where there had been ample publicized proof of productivity since Waiilatpu days, and where the largest body of attractive lowland soils lay. The exigencies of pioneering, shortage of labor, and the few and simple tools inevitably hampered expansion. Oats were the principal crop at first. The hundreds of pack mules, freighting teams, and cavalry horses provided an obvious market, and in the absence of adequate machinery oats could be cut and fed as hay. A few simple McCormick reapers were in use, but much of the grain was cut with cradles in the first few years; the first large threshing machine, an Aultman and Taylor powered by ten horses, arrived in 1861.[24]

Wheat was also sown from the first to meet local needs. In 1862 the demand for flour suddenly became immense, and by the end of the year three grist mills were in operation. However, the output was but a fraction of the need, and the mining districts had to depend primarily upon imports from the Willamette; furthermore, the quality of local flour was hardly the best. In 1863 a correspondent to the Walla Walla *Washington Statesman*, who signed himself simply as "Farmer," complained that Walla Walla flour was so poor that it was "scarcely salable anywhere"; which brought a sharp reply from the leading miller: " 'Farmer' has forgotten that to make first quality flour, the miller must have first quality wheat—the kind that one-

[23] On the use of burros see Winther, *Old Oregon Country,* p. 177. Trimble, *Mining Advance,* p. 108; John Minto, "Sheep Husbandry in Oregon," *Oregon Historical Quarterly,* 3 (September, 1902), 230, 232; *Walla Walla Statesman,* April 13, 1866; *Weekly Mountaineer,* June 15, 1867; Alfred L. Lomax, *Pioneer Woolen Mills in Oregon . . .* (Portland, Ore., 1941), pp. 285-96.

[24] Drumheller, *Uncle Dan,* p. 59.

horse Walla Walla farmers don't raise. I do not know of, nor do I believe there is a lot of 100 bushels [of] *pure wheat* in the county." No doubt both had ample reason for their opinions, but it was an inevitable pioneer situation; farmers and millers alike were still in an experimental stage, working with inadequate knowledge and crude equipment. "Farmer" expressed it well in his letter: ". . . up to the present time, farming has been merely experimental, and tens of thousands of dollars have been lost to the country by adopting a system of culture unsuited to the soil and climate; and even yet a great diversity of opinion exists as to which is the best crop to raise and how to raise it. . . ." He went on to call for the formation of a farmers' association so that experiences could be effectively shared. The editor agreed, and after the miller's letter offered his own critique and advice. He castigated the farmers for their slipshod methods and attitudes, which were fostered by the simple fact that they found a ready sale for whatever they raised regardless of quality. He urged that they stop raising spring wheat, obtain some pure white seed, and plant in the fall. Two years later he was urging June seeding (to be harvested the next spring) as having been proven to be "the safest and best plan."[25] Such contradictions merely revealed that the problem of how best to raise good wheat in the area was a complex one, and far more experience would be required before it would be solved.

While these experiments with the techniques of wheat raising were going on, experiments with the various lands of the area were also being made. The settlers generally believed that only the lowlands were suitable for crops, but in 1863 a few trial fields were sown on the "benchlands," which lay partially within but principally around the margins and above the main valley floor. The results were varied, but some yielded well enough to excite enthusiasm. "Farmer," for instance, was quick to claim that these areas were "the best wheat land we have," and saw as one of the purposes of his proposed farmers' association the contradiction of the prevailing impression "that all the good land in the valley has been taken up." In the following year the local editor hailed the results of a crop of thirty-three bushels to the acre from fifty acres of the upland as proof of the potential of that vast portion of the surrounding realm. He

<hr>

[25] Lyman, *Walla Walla County*, p. 186; *Washington Statesman*, Nov. 7, 21, 1863; July 7, 1865.

believed that, except for the lack of water for livestock, "thousands of acres that are now lying idle would be immediately put under cultivation." It is doubtful, however, if that deficiency were the only or even the principal deterrent to immediate expansion. Not all were ready to make such a radical revision of opinion on the basis of so few trials. Doubters continued to outnumber believers, and conversion would only come with accumulating proof.[26] Furthermore, testing of the moderately elevated benchlands and lower slopes was no reliable indication of the potential of the whole expanse of steeply rolling hill land. So the trials of the mid-1860's caused much interest and speculation, but no immediate land rush to the hills.

And there were other deterrents. The grain economy was not really flourishing. A shift in emphasis toward wheat was evident, but the reasons were not especially heartening. Just as with cattle, the mountain valleys were by now producing much more of their own hay and feed grains; oats, especially, were quite suited to the shorter seasons of the mining districts. Unfortunately the same trend was becoming evident with wheat and flour. Although the *Statesman* could confidently state that local products had "stopped the shipment of flour from below," it had to acknowledge the danger of "interception" by the increasing amount of wheat being grown in the back country districts nearer the mines. An estimated three hundred thousand bushels was produced in these areas in 1866. As the mining demands were also stabilizing, further expansion in the Walla Walla brought an inevitable result: wheat prices plummeted from $1.25 per bushel in 1865 to $.30 in 1867.[27] It was ironic that the glimpse of a vastly greater potential production coincided with a sharply contracting market.

Obviously, new outlets had to be sought, and Walla Walla's enterprising citizens were not long in seeking them. In the first week of March, 1867, the editor of The Dalles *Weekly Mountaineer* noted

[26] *Washington Statesman*, Nov. 7, 1863; Sept. 16, 1864; Lyman reports that at least one such trial in that year was a complete failure, and "hence the impression already common was confirmed that the upland was useless, except for grazing." He also reported that a crop of fifty bushels to the acre of oats in 1867 was not generally accepted as proof of the desirability of such lands. *Walla Walla County*, p. 181.

[27] *Walla Walla Statesman*, Feb. 3, 1865; Nov. 2, Dec. 7, 1866; Walla Walla production was estimated as two hundred thousand bushels; such figures cannot be relied upon, their importance stems only from the context of their use. Gilbert, *Historic Sketches*, pp. 263-64.

that a local mercantile house had received twelve thousand pounds of flour from Isaac's mill in Walla Walla, and the following week he reported on its excellent quality. It was pleasant news upriver, where the *Statesman* soon pointed out on April 5 that local flour was fast dominating the Umatilla and Wasco trade. But capturing such limited markets was hardly a major triumph; the exciting news came in June, when word was received that one thousand barrels had been sold in San Francisco at a profit. By the end of the spring season, the steamboat company reported the following shipments:

To: Portland	May 27-June 13	4,156½ barrels
The Dalles	April 19-June 2	578½ barrels
Lewiston	April 18-May 14	577¾ barrels

Overland movements would considerably raise the total sold inland to the mines, but whatever the exact proportions might have been, this new downriver outlet was of sensational importance. In that same June another twenty thousand barrels were reportedly awaiting transport, and the Wallula correspondent joyfully noted that "The road from Walla Walla to Wallula is literally lined with heavy freight teams, eight or ten yoke of cattle and four, six, eight and ten mule teams, all heavily loaded with flour are coming in every day." As both Portland and San Francisco had rich wheat-producing hinterlands, presumably the Walla Walla flour was being exported (New York is specifically mentioned in one account). In 1868 the first British vessel embarked from Portland with a full cargo of wheat and flour directly for Liverpool; in December the Walla Walla and Columbia River Railroad Company was incorporated, and, backed by the financial leader of the community, it gave every indication of opening a line to Wallula as soon as practicable. It would take time for the full implications of such developments to be felt; farm prices remained low, wheat that season was quoted at forty-five cents "and no sale at that," for as yet the downriver shipments were merely removing accumulated surpluses. But the outline of a fundamental economic reorientation was being drawn, and thereby the foundation of an expanding agricultural economy was being laid.[28]

[28] *Walla Walla Statesman,* June 7, 21, 1867; 40th Cong., 2nd sess., H. Ex. Doc. 1, Pt. 1 (1867-68), p. 510. The Wallula correspondent was quoted in T. C. Elliott, "The Dalles-Celilo Portage: Its History and Influence," *Oregon Historical Quarterly,* 16 (June, 1915), 169. John B. Watkins, *Wheat Exporting*

THE GREAT COLUMBIA PLAIN, *ca.* 1870

The Great Columbia Plain had thus been brought to the threshold of a new phase just ten years after the beginnings of permanent settlement. Gold had been a dynamic stimulus, but little more—by now there was "no longer any excitement about mining." Grass had been a bountiful resource, but cattle were now a glut on the market. By 1869-70 hope for future progress appeared to rest heavily upon grain, and especially upon wheat. These busy, turbulent ten years would in time appear to be but an introductory indication of the dominant emphasis and imprint of a long future. They were important years, and they had already clothed the region with a whole new character and significance. As a writer who set out on a descriptive reconnaissance of the area at this time stated, it was high time to correct those "effete notions" that "the whole of the North-west Territory was Oregon—that it had one river, the Columbia, and one town, Portland. . . ."[29] Inland lay a realm of fresh accomplishment and great promise.

The Dalles

To that same writer, The Dalles offered a pleasant introduction to the realm (Map 28). It had taken on a substantial appearance that seemingly belied its youth: a number of brick and stone business buildings, well-kept homes, churches, schools, gardens, and shade trees. Local pride fed avidly upon such favorable impressions, of course, yet local boosters were far from happy with their situation. Though famous for a decade, and the portal for thousands of travelers, the 1870 census recorded but 942 residents in The Dalles, and business was undeniably dull. What might appear to be an attractive stability to the visitor was an oppressive stagnation to many residents, and there was a strong nostalgia for the good rough days of the recent past. One did not merely sense this difference, it could be seen. Two derelict facilities, in particular, vividly expressed something of what had happened to the town: Old Fort Dalles had not

---

from the Pacific Northwest (Washington Agricultural Experiment Station Bulletin No. 201) (May, 1926), p. 10. E. A. Orcott, "Washington Territory Correspondence," *Dodge County Republican* (Minnesota, n.d.). This account is among a collection of newspaper clippings in the Northwest History Collection, Eastern Washington State College, Cheney; it is datelined "Walla Walla, W.T., Dec. 4th, 1868, a letter back home by a recent emigrant."

[29] Frances Fuller Victor, *All Over Oregon and Washington* . . . (San Francisco, 1872), pp. 8, 342.

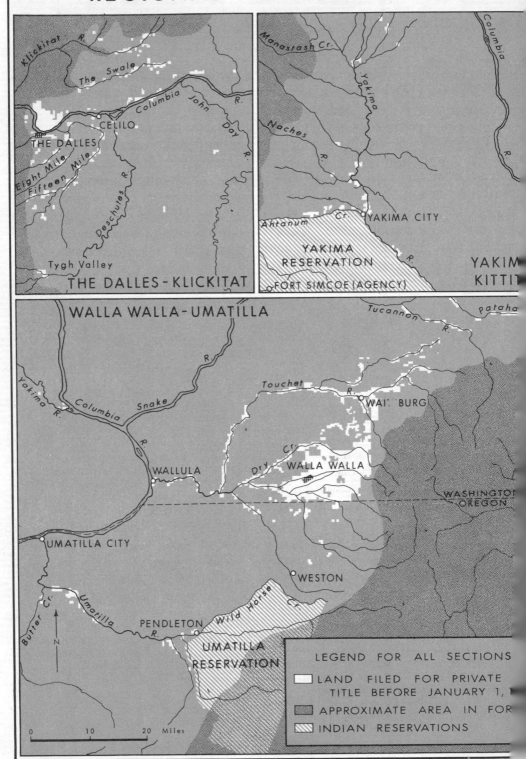

REGIONAL SETTLEMENT 1870

THE DALLES - KLICKITAT

Klickitat R.
The Swale
Columbia
CELILO
THE DALLES
Eight Mile
Fifteen Mile
Deschutes R.
John Day R.
Tygh Valley

YAKIMA KITTIT

Manastash Cr.
Yakima
Naches R.
Columbia
YAKIMA CITY
Ahtanum Cr.
YAKIMA RESERVATION
FORT SIMCOE (AGENCY)

WALLA WALLA - UMATILLA

Tucannon R.
Pataha
Yakima R.
Columbia
Snake R.
Touchet R.
WAITSBURG
Dry Cr.
WALLA WALLA
WASHINGTON
OREGON
WALLULA
UMATILLA CITY
WESTON
Butter Cr.
Umatilla R.
PENDLETON
Wild Horse Cr.
UMATILLA RESERVATION

N

0   10   20   Miles

LEGEND FOR ALL SECTIONS
LAND FILED FOR PRIVATE
   TITLE BEFORE JANUARY 1,
APPROXIMATE AREA IN FOR
INDIAN RESERVATIONS

Map 28

been garrisoned since 1867, it now received only intermittent use as a depot for supplies and animals in transit, some of the buildings had burned, all were in disrepair, and the army had recommended abandonment. The excitement and business of a critical military position had faded away; now the important outposts were those far to the southeast in the Snake country. The second evidence of change was the formidable stone edifice of the branch United States mint which stood half completed. Designed to coin the products of the Northwest mining regions when these were flowing so freely down the Columbia artery, its construction was canceled in 1866 when diverting bullion directly eastward toward the advancing railroads proved more advantageous. It was a bold symbol of how brief and capricious the mining traffic had been. Even what had seemed a more solidly based venture was an embarrassment to the town. The Wasco Woolen Manufacturing Corporation had begun operations in an imposing building in September of 1868. A flume from Mill Creek supplied the power to run the four hundred spindles, four looms, and fifteen knitting machines which turned out stockings, skirts, shirts, underwear, and blankets. But the history of operations was an almost incredible tale of woe: the reservoir embankment gave way twice, the water wheel broke, the boiler exploded, fire damaged a portion, low water caused a closing, and a mechanic's lien initiated a crippling legal tangle. It seems cruel to add that the quality of the products was so poor that they found little sale. Within a year the company was bankrupt, adding another all-too-prominent idle facility to the local scene.[30]

There were, to be sure, more flourishing, if less imposing, establishments. The O.S.N. shops at the mouth of Mill Creek and the warehouses and long incline at the boat landing (designed to serve through all the greatly varied seasonal water levels) were among the many tangible evidences of the town's key function in the river trade. A small flour mill had been in operation since 1866, and the editor of the local newspaper saw it as a symbol of the logical emphasis for the future. Walla Walla's downriver shipments had made a strong impression; why would it not pay Wasco farmers equally well? The editor insisted that, contrary to popular opinion, the local hill lands were well suited for grain production. By the spring of

---

[30] *Ibid.*, p. 92; 41st Cong., 3rd sess., H. Ex. Doc. 1 (1870), pp. 59, 94; Shaver *et al, History of Central Oregon*, p. 135; Lomax, *Pioneer Woolen Mills*, pp. 285-96.

1870 he could report that a number of farmers on the "Creeks" were giving the hills a trial, and that there was a general shift in emphasis to wheat, although the total grain crop was still remarkably small.[31]

The editor, in common with his counterparts in a thousand other American small towns of the time, liberally critized local farmers for neglecting a rich array of opportunities. "It would be but slight work," he claimed, to capture a share of Portland's vegetable trade with California; and again: " . . . every year we find in The Dalles market Eastern butter, California cheese, and many articles so easy of production right here." Any local gardener who raised a few grape vines or hops, or squeezed a few gallons of sorghum molasses was cited as pointing the way to assured riches. He dismissed the farmers' complaints that labor costs were far too high for such activities as but one of "a thousand valueless excuses for their delinquencies." He noticed that they seemed to have plenty of time to hang around town and that it took but "the least exciting news from the mines and every farmer is off on the road teaming, wearing out not only teams and wagons, but the personal vitality he may have." Particularly frustrating to him was the distortion of enthusiasm within the local agricultural society. Pride and improvement of products were the proper themes, but as the annual September fair days approached, the sponsoring group showed strong signs of being exclusively "a company of persons, associated for the trial of the speed of horses."[32]

Although such boosters were often discordantly shrill and quite unrealistic in their criticisms, the countryside clearly revealed that farming was as yet indeed in a raw, youthful, and indifferent stage of development. The county figure of seventeen thousand acres of "improved land" was a meager total, and much of this lay in widely scattered patches of creek-side pastures. For the majority of the rural settlers, farming remained secondary, as the look of their homesites revealed. Much of the fencing was a "frail and temporary . . . rickety boarding" (although stone fences and ditching were also used). Barns, stables, and other structures were said to be "criminally scarce and temporary." Editors might properly attempt to foster improvements, but the prevailing conditions were understandable. These settlers had come to raise stock and had been successful. The

[31] *Weekly Mountaineer,* March 15, 30, 1870. The Wasco totals in the 1870 census were: wheat 10,536 bushels; oats 26,593; barley 7,203.

[32] *Ibid.,* July 23, Sept. 3, 17, 1870.

combination of low beef prices and Walla Walla's downriver flour shipments might suggest that the future lay in farming, but that was not yet certain, and even if it proved true it would take time to make the shift. Meanwhile, the countryside continued to fill in with settlers from the Willamette. The best sites along the "Creeks" were by now taken, and across the river in adjacent Klickitat County the rich lands in "the Swale" were rapidly filling up. The influx would be even greater, the *Weekly Mountaineer* observed, if it were not for the prejudices built up by the impressions these people of the "Webfoot country" had gained in their original westbound transit twenty years before.[33]

Though business was rather dull, the common vision of the future was certainly bright. "The geographical position of the Dalles" guaranteed that it must serve as the trade center for the whole of eastern Oregon; what Portland was for the Willamette, The Dalles must become for all east of the mountains, and surely the younger city had as much potential as the older. The great incline warehouse at Celilo testified to the tribute that must necessarily accrue to the location, and there only needed to be better roads to Boise and Yakima to increase the flow.[34] If the scale of that vision was grossly exaggerated, the design was essentially accurate; The Dalles certainly had an assured function, and it had no local rival to dispute its leadership. A huge area lay beyond to serve, the only question was how soon and how fast it might need expanded servicing.

The Walla Walla Country

To the upriver visitor of 1870, Walla Walla offered some of the same impressions as The Dalles. It, too, had a surprisingly mature, substantial appearance, and its shade trees, ditches of running water, and flourishing gardens made it a true oasis, most pleasing after one had experienced the "dreaded" sand at Wallula, and the long dusty journey through the parched, barren land of the lower valley. Fort Walla Walla extended the parallel, for it also stood ungarrisoned, was used only for wintering stock, and had been recommended for disposal. Yet despite these similarities there was an unmistakable and important difference: Walla Walla was thriving. Actually, if one

[33] *Ibid.*, Feb. 8, 1870, a reprint of the Wasco County section in Dufur's *Statistics of Oregon.* Also March 22, Nov. 12, Dec. 10, 1870.

[34] *Ibid.*, Feb. 15, 1867; March 29, 1870; Victor, *All Over Oregon,* p. 96; George W. Pine, *Beyond the West* (2nd ed.; Utica, N.Y., 1871), p. 219.

toured both town and countryside the contrasts with the Wasco nucleus were far more striking than the parallels. The whole valley, from its Oregon corner north to upper Dry Creek, and from the lower foothills of the Blue Mountains nearly to the Touchet mouth, was almost solidly settled (Map 28). Stock raising remained important, but it was now merely an adjunct on many homesteads. Farming, though still experimental insofar as methods were concerned, was firmly established and expanding. The county produced five times as much grain as Wasco, and half of that total was wheat. Six flour mills (five powered by steam, one by water) were busy in the county, and a grain bag mill had also been started. Progress was equally evident in the tools of farming; the gang plow was beginning to replace the single-furrow "footburner," and the introduction of steam-powered threshing had increased efficiency and enhanced the quality of the product.[35]

Here, too, the local newspaper had for years been advising its readers of opportunities in a great variety of crops—Indian corn, sorghum, tobacco, grapes—and had urged the formation of an agricultural society to promote improvements in the quality of grains, fruits, vegetables, and livestock; but this was not a desperate attempt to get *something* started, for at least a few of these things were being energetically pursued. By the end of the decade dairy and garden produce were available in surplus, well established nurseries offered fruit and shade seedlings to new settlers, and thoroughbred livestock had been brought in.[36]

Despite this variety of activities, grain had always received primary emphasis, and the vigor of the local region in 1870 was directly related to the enlarged prospects for wheat. Flour was still freighted

[35] Victor, *All Over Oregon,* pp. 104-14; 41st Cong., 3rd sess., H. Ex. Doc. 1 (1870), p. 58. The 1870 census totals were: 110,905 bushels of wheat; 94,528 of oats; 17,459 of barley. *Walla Walla Statesman,* Aug. 30, 1867; Dec. 18, 1868; Sept. 3, 1869; Henry G. Langley, *The Pacific Coast Business Directory for 1867* (San Francisco, 1867); *Ninth Census of the United States, 1870,* "Manufactures."

[36] Indian corn was promoted from time to time (see *Walla Walla Statesman,* Feb. 3, 1865), but doubts that it would really thrive because of the coolness of nights and summer drought had often been expressed years before by such people as Charles Wilkes, Lansford Hastings, Isaac Stevens, and Lorin Blodget. Sorghum was persistently advocated; see May 16, Sept. 5, 1863; Aug. 22, 1865; Nov. 20, 1869; on tobacco see Aug. 1, Sept. 26, 1863. On the need for and purposes of an agricultural society, see Jan. 27, 1865. On dairy and garden activities, see Oct. 2, 1868; Jan. 8, 1869; Lyman, *Walla Walla County,* p. 189, reported that as early as 1865 the valley shipped twenty tons of onions to Portland.

to nearby mining regions, such as the John Day and those of north Idaho, and, fortuitously, to some of the more distant earlier markets, as in 1869-70 when the local Montana crop failed. But the new downriver export market was the real mainspring of expansion. A new outlook prevailed. Where in the recent past grain prices had fluctuated erratically with the rumors of the local mining trade, an unprecedented sensitivity to the larger world now ruled: the farmers were holding on to their 1870 harvest in anticipation that the Franco-Prussian war would cause a marked rise in grain prices. This kind of prospect, together with the excellent yields obtained and the growing realization that the rolling hills contained a vast acreage of potential wheatland, had caused a marked acceleration of immigration. Land was plentiful but the means to work it were not; good draft horses were selling for $100-$150 each, mules $125-$200, and oxen $80-$150 per pair. "Cayuses" (by now the common term for all Indian horses) could be had for a few dollars, but were not always a bargain: "They make good riding horses for *experienced* riders, but they will not do for 'raw emigrants.' " Other possible surprises awaited the newcomer: "A few days ago I saw a man putting pine timber into a wagon wheel. What would a Minnesotan think of filling a wagon wheel with pine?" Several sawmills were busy at the margins of the mountains supplying timbers and boards; however, fuel was rather scarce, and fencing was a serious problem.[37]

The influx of the last few years had already ranged well beyond the central valley. The upper Touchet was lined with farms; at its junction with Coppei Creek the first of the new agricultural towns, Waitsburg, now numbered 107 inhabitants, and the local mill was one of the leading flour exporters. Many of the best sites farther east along the Tucannon and Pataha were already taken, and in 1869 the first farmers had crossed the Snake and homesteaded along Union Flat in the Palouse country.[38] Walla Walla city persisted as the nexus of routes in all directions, passengers and traffic still moved along the roads and trails to the peripheral mining camps, but the spread of farm settlement made it the focus of a new kind of traffic serving a new hinterland, diminished in radius, but expansive in promise.

[37] *Walla Walla Statesman,* Aug. 6, 20, 1869; Aug. 20, 1870; Orcott, "Washington Territory"; Edward Young, *Special Report on Immigration,* 42nd Cong., 1st sess., H. Ex. Doc. 1 (1871), p. 197.

[38] Gilbert, *Historic Sketches,* pp. 345-46; Victor, *All Over Oregon,* p. 143; *Walla Walla Statesman,* Sept. 11, 1869; W. H. Lever, *An Illustrated History of Whitman County* (n.p., 1901), p. 104.

The town numbered 1,394 in 1870, the local trade area included another 5,500; both were being augmented every day.

Other Towns and Areas

Conditions at the third of the prominent inland trade centers were far different from either of the others. Lewiston had dwindled with the sharp decline in the Clearwater and Salmon mining districts. With neither the agricultural opportunities of Walla Walla nor the captive traffic of The Dalles, there was little prospect for any immediate growth. Indicative of the relentless shift that had taken place was the loss of the territorial capital to Boise in 1865, and Lewiston's complete failure to reorganize the political boundaries of the interior so as to create a new territory centered upon itself. The town population averaged perhaps four hundred, increased in the winter by the seasonal exodus from the mines. Nearly half of the Nez Perces County total of sixteen hundred were Chinese who worked the poorer placers and reworked abandoned claims. Agriculture was negligible; wintering of mining livestock was a principal activity. During the high water of late spring and early summer the steamboats came up from The Dalles, and when the shipping season ended, freighting teams from Walla Walla brought in further supplies, which were then packed across the Camas Prairie to the mines; but the traffic was a fraction of former times. The rich pastures of the prairie were still held by the Indians. Fort Lapwai was in good repair and garrisoned by a cavalry company.[39]

An "obstructive" Indian reservation and a declining mining trade were prominent features of another subregion also, but one which was rapidly adapting to new conditions. The Umatilla Valley, though relatively near to the Walla Walla, was never fully tributary to it, principally because it had its own direct route to the Columbia and The Dalles. Sheer distance from the latter, however, had prompted the splitting off of Umatilla County in 1862, the first of the numerous offspring from gigantic Wasco. This action also initiated the first of the many often chronic and bitter county seat rivalries, which would become prominent features of the evolving

[39] The county grain production was only eleven thousand bushels, mostly oats. In 1869 a farmer raised the first crop of wheat on the rim of the Palouse country overlooking Lewiston; *History of North Idaho*, p. 42. *Walla Walla Statesman*, Aug. 13, 1870. Fort Lapwai had been virtually abandoned during the latter part of the Civil War, then refurbished; 39th Cong., 2nd sess., H. Ex. Doc. 20 (1867), p. 11; 41st Cong., 3rd sess., H. Ex. Doc. 1 (1870), p. 57.

political geography of the Great Plain. As the county was established before any town existed, promoters were soon busy creating them in order to grab the prized seat. The first was Grande Ronde Landing on the Columbia, eight miles below the Umatilla, whose proponents claimed that the mining trade would soon make it the "Sacramento of Oregon." Within a few months Umatilla City was laid out at the mouth of the river, and when the southern Idaho mines boomed, it garnered the trade and lured the merchants of its rival. In 1865 it was granted, provisionally, the political prize. Meanwhile, the middle valley was becoming settled, and by the late 1860's the uplands toward Walla Walla were being colonized. In 1865 Weston became the second town of the county and soon voiced discontent with its distant river capital. In a lively and close election in 1868, a more central location in the Umatilla Valley was designated the permanent seat. As soon as the commissioners selected the exact site, the town of Pendleton was platted upon it (1869). Umatilla City tried to have the election invalidated, but failed, and that defeat was all the more bitter for it underscored the over-all decline which was already being felt. Only three or four years before Umatilla City had been a thriving place, with ten mercantile and grocery stores, three hotels, three forwarding agents, its own newspaper, and a dozen other businesses, but now several stores and houses stood vacant; and the general consensus within the whole Portland network was that "the Oregon trade with Idaho may be considered a thing of the past"; the new transcontinental railroad was rapidly drawing off the traffic. Local energies were directed toward getting a railroad from Umatilla to Utah, but even that doubtful prospect would hardly restore the glories of old. Without that traffic so miserable a location had little hope of recruiting business (with a kind of perverse pride the Umatilla paper periodically described its sandstorms as worthy of the Sahara).[40]

The decline at one end of the valley was more than balanced by the upsurge at the other. Stockmen were agitating for the unlocking of the fine pastures within the Umatilla reservation, and farmers were finding that their results and prospects were quite the equal

[40] This county seat rivalry is based upon William Parsons and W. S. Shiach, *An Illustrated History of Umatilla County and of Morrow County* (1902), pp. 134-41, 194. Langley, *Business Directory. Weekly Mountaineer,* June 21, 1870. *Proceedings of a Railroad Meeting . . . January 27th, 1868, on the subject of the Columbia Branch* (Umatilla, Ore., 1868), pp. 1-7. *Columbia Press* (Umatilla), March 21, May 30, 1868.

of neighboring Walla Walla. In contrast with other areas, the recent colonists were primarily Confederate Missourians, rather than from the Willamette, a feature imprinted upon the new county seat, where the street names commemorated such people as Lee, Beauregard, Jeff Davis, and Stonewall Jackson.[41]

After several years of slow infiltration, settlement in the Yakima Valley had also recently increased and begun to develop a focus. Ranches were scattered through the whole axis of the main valley, but the principal concentration was along Ahtanum Creek and around the main water gap (Map 28). At the latter point the first store was opened in 1869, a second was added the next year and, dignified with the name Yakima City, the site became the county seat. The area was far more isolated than the other settled locales. After the army withdrawal from Fort Simcoe, the road to The Dalles received so little maintenance that it became impassable for wagons. The Naches and Snoqualmie routes to Puget Sound were no better, although for two summers small herds of cattle had been driven westward over them. The first official mail link was that established with Wallula in 1870. Almost nothing had been attempted in the way of agriculture as yet, but its attractions as a cattle country were becoming well known, and some were ready to pronounce it superior to any other stock country in the nation, "even Texas not excepted."[42]

Cattlemen had located at a number of other points well beyond these several colonization clusters. A few had moved into the Kittitas, others ranged north of the Snake along the Mullan Road in the scabland country, and at least one was located at the margin of the prairies on the upper Palouse. The northern country between the scablands and the curving Columbia lay virtually untouched, but south of the river in Oregon the ranges between the Deschutes and Umatilla were becoming well stocked. Many of these operations were best described by the colloquial term, "cattle camp," denoting a rather transient use of the public ranges. Such camps might consist of little more than a crude shack and a makeshift corral of poles, brush, or rocks—a small "blind canyon" or steep-walled rock cove

<hr>

[41] *Columbia Press*, July 20, Dec. 14, 1867; Parsons and Shiach, *History of Umatilla and Morrow Counties,* pp. 159, 194. Pendleton was named after an Ohio Democrat, Weston after a Missouri town.

[42] Lyman, *Yakima Valley*, pp. 273-77, 285, 287; *Weekly Mountaineer*, March 29, Nov. 12, 1870; Splawn, *Ka-mi-akin*, p. 290.

with a narrow, easily fenced entrance was ideal.[43] Ranches were more permanent locations, and as the number of settlers increased a homestead or pre-emption claim would be filed to assure title. Units of a quarter section or more became the fixed base for utilization of the adjacent unclaimed public domain.

The cattle were almost entirely of the mixed English breeds common in the East and the Willamette, with some admixture of Spanish Californian stock. A few Texas longhorns had been brought into eastern Oregon, but because of fever (rinderpest) there was concern over their introduction, and they had already been prohibited from Washington Territory.[44] By 1870 there was little need for further importations of any kind, for how to dispose of the natural increase alone was problem enough. Yet settlers continued to come in, bringing more cattle with them, and the many fine ranch sites still available were, for the time being, a sufficient attraction to sustain expansion.

Connections and Boundaries

Improved communications were both a product of and an inducement to the generally quickened pace of development. The main centers of business were interconnected by scheduled passenger services, and the regularization, speed, and amenities of those services were one of the proudest expressions of the times. A man could leave Wallula at 3:00 A.M. and be in The Dalles before noon, and the next morning he could board the boat for Portland and arrive by midafternoon: total actual traveling time fifteen hours. It would take him nearly twice as long to return upstream, but to be able to travel 236 miles in two days for $12.00, and to be able to spend most of these hours lounging in the various bars of the boats and at The Dalles was a radically new and pleasant stage of progress. The steamboats and portages were a monopoly of the Oregon Steam Navigation Company, and although with the decline of the mining traffic "it was no longer possible in 1870 for an upper Columbia River boat to earn more than her original cost during a single trip," business was brisk and profitable. The frequency of service was

[43] Lyman, *Yakima Valley*, pp. 565-67; *Ritzville Journal-Times, Adams County Pioneer Edition*, Sept. 15, 1949, p. 3; *History of North Idaho*, p. 581. Cattle camps are mentioned in Parsons and Shiach, *History of Umatilla and Morrow Counties*, pp. 270-71.

[44] *Weekly Mountaineer*, Jan. 4, 1870.

adapted to the traffic of the several segments: daily between Portland and The Dalles; triweekly to Wallula; and weekly (in season) to Lewiston. Five boats, the *Yakima, Nez Perces Chief, Owyhee, Tenino,* and *Spray,* were available for service above Celilo.[45]

At the moment the most pressing deficiency in communications was the link between Walla Walla and Wallula. Stages connected with the river boats but took six hours—and usually six suffocating, dust-choked hours—to travel thirty miles. The right of way for the railroad had been obtained but as yet no construction begun.

There was another service which was new and exciting. One could leave the boat at Umatilla, board the stagecoach, and five days later be at the Central Pacific railroad station at Kelton, Utah, from where one could travel in comparative speed and luxury to Chicago and New York. En route the stage served Boise City and Silver City, and it was this connection that was allowing Kelton to replace Umatilla as the commercial outpost for southern Idaho. Although not of positive commercial importance for the Columbia Plain as yet, the marked improvement in mail service provided by this link was greatly welcomed.

The ease and speed of communications and the volume of traffic with Portland only served to magnify the internal disparity of Washington Territory; as the *Statesman* expressed it: " . . . the Western part of the Territory appears to the people of this valley like some foreign land, and it is about as little talked of or thought of by them as is the Chinese empire. No trade of any kind is carried on between the sections and there are no roads to offer inducement to trade or travel." It was hardly surprising, under the circumstances, to find strong support in Walla Walla for the shift of the northeastern boundary of Oregon to the Snake River. Naturally, the proposal was heartily endorsed by the Oregon legislature, but the issue became hopelessly entangled in other proposed realignments, all arising from the geographical peculiarities of Idaho.[46]

Idaho Territory had been hastily created in 1863 out of large

[45] Schedules, fares, and routes have been derived from *Bancroft's Guide for Travelers by Railway, Stage, and Steam Navigation in the Pacific States, No. 6, December, 1869* (San Francisco, 1869), and L. Samuel, *The Traveler's Guide and Oregon Railroad Gazetteer, August, 1872* (Portland, Ore. 1872). See also Wright (ed.), *Marine History,* p. 181.

[46] *Walla Walla Statesman,* Dec. 9, 1864, as quoted in Kingston, "Walla Walla Separation Movement," p. 94. 39th Cong., 1st sess., S. Misc. Doc. 83 (1866); 41st Cong., 3rd sess., H. Misc. Doc. 23 (1870).

chunks of Washington and Dakota because the political leadership in each of these was fearful of being overbalanced by the sudden influx of miners.[47] The choice of the western boundary was determined by Olympia's desire to retain the Columbia Plain but to "eject the new disquieting element east of Lewiston." The impossibility of maintaining any effective link between Lewiston, the temporary capital, and Virginia City, soon led to the further creation of Montana Territory (1864). With this move, northern Idaho was reduced to a narrow strip and, as it was equally isolated from the now larger population cluster in southwestern Idaho, it immediately sought to combine with eastern Washington and western Montana to form yet another territory. This proposed Columbia Territory, extending from the Columbia-Okanogan to the continental divide, certainly had greater logic than some existing units, yet it did not receive full support even within its area. Walla Walla opinion was much divided—some favored the new scheme, others continued to seek annexation to Oregon, while the most vociferous group sought the aggrandizement of their own city by working for the annexation of northern Idaho to the whole of Washington Territory, thereby making Walla Walla more central and thus the logical place for the eventual state capital. This latter possibility was quite enough to cause Olympia to oppose any such annexation. Ultimately, Lewiston was left as the only enthusiast for the proposed Columbia, and the geographical logic of her arguments was quite insufficient to overcome her political insignificance. When, in 1869, Nevada indicated a desire to annex southern Idaho, the specter of complete obliteration was enough to turn the majority of Idaho residents against any realignment whatsoever, and that closed the issue for the time being.

Despite this lack of unanimity on how to remake the political geography of the Northwest, the general issue at least revealed the widespread desire to recut the political pattern to fit more closely new regional realities. Among those new realities—though at the time by no means clearly discernible, perhaps, to most of its people—was the emergence of the Great Columbia Plain as a separate economic region. Through the early 1860's it had been closely bound up with the development of its mountain periphery, but

---

[47] This discussion is based upon two articles by Merle W. Wells, "The Creation of the Territory of Idaho," *Pacific Northwest Quarterly,* 40 (April, 1949), 106-23, and "Territorial Government in the Inland Empire: The Movement to Create Columbia Territory, 1864-69," *ibid.,* 44 (April, 1953), 80-87.

those ties had diminished, and the downriver orientation to a distant market had given the area a new pattern for development quite independent of those neighboring districts. The 1870 census counted about eleven thousand people in the region, with more than half of these in the Walla Walla. If nationally this was a tiny nucleus, it was nevertheless firmly established and growing. With a new basis for expansion, and with direct, continuous links to the west and east, the area was—for the first time—assuming a definite place in the rapidly evolving regional structure of the nation.

CHAPTER NINE

The question then of the profitable
production of wheat is simply a question of the cost of transportation.

C. H. DODD

Strategy:

Settlers and Railroads, 1870-90

GATHERING MOMENTUM, THE 1870'S

The Pace and Pattern of Expansion

TO DISCOVER the basis for a new economy was one thing, to realize
its promise was quite another. Wheat yielded beautiful crops, the hill
lands proved astonishingly productive, and Walla Walla grain was
being sold on the British market; yet although the acreage in crop
steadily increased, there was no boom, settlement expanded but
there was no land rush, downriver shipments mounted but there was
no prosperity.

The reasons for the paradox were readily apparent. It was no easy
task to create farms out of the rich bunch-grass prairies. Breaking the
sod was a slow and arduous work, few pioneers had sufficient work
animals or equipment to till their entire holding—or indeed to cultivate any part of it adequately—harvesting machinery was desperately short in all the newer localities. Although there was a steady
influx of people, nationally this was still a remote and little known
region. For the moment, the Midwest prairies and California were
more accessible and powerful lures for the land seeker. The journey
to the Northwest by wagon was nearly the longest, and by any other
means it was the most expensive to any of the active frontiers of the
time, and after the Panic of 1873 money was scarce and credit tight
throughout nation. Transportation was the principal root of the
problem, though the need for reducing cost was less important for
bringing people into the region than for moving produce out. Walla
Walla wheat was reaching the world market, but the facilities of

shipment were inadequate to support a major expansion of production and the costs too great to allow satisfactory profits to the producers.

The slow pace of developments was well illustrated—and in fact significantly controlled—by the difficulties encountered in the creation of the long-awaited railway from Walla Walla to the Columbia. Although incorporated in December, 1868, and granted a right of way three months later, the railroad encountered many problems. The original scheme for financing collapsed, and only after considerable delay was a new start made. The locomotives had to be ordered in Philadelphia and shipped by way of San Francisco. Logs for ties and bridge timbers were cut on the upper Yakima to be floated to a sawmill at Wallula; but the first drive failed for lack of water and caused a year's delay. Once construction was under way the makeshift wooden rails quickly wore out; plating them with strap iron also proved quite unsatisfactory. Ultimately, iron rails had to be sent from Wales. Not until March, 1874, were the first sixteen miles completed (to Touchet). It took over a year to build the next eight (to Frenchtown), three months for the next three (to Whitman), and service to Walla Walla was finally opened on October 30, 1875.[1] Though long abuilding, this little narrow-gauge was an instant success for its builder and an important stimulus to farming expansion. Settlers steadily moved south into the vacant lands in the Oregon sector of the valley and north toward Dry Creek and beyond.

On farther to the northeast, ranchers along the upper Touchet, Tucannon, and Pataha began plowing some of their pastures, while newer immigrants sought farm lands within the many gulches and hollows or gambled on the undulating surfaces lying high above the streams. The high prairies were regarded as a gamble because there was a persistent doubt about their productivity. Despite the fact that similar lands near the Walla Walla Valley had proved highly successful, pioneers in each of the newer localities showed the same

[1] Dates of construction are from O.W.R.N., *Corporate History,* sheet 83; descriptive details from Miles C. Moore, "A Pioneer Railroad Builder," *Oregon Historical Quarterly,* 4 (September, 1903), 195-201, recounting the career of Dr. Dorsey S. Baker, the Walla Walla merchant and banker who built the road. Moore states that Baker halted construction at Whitman, claiming his money was exhausted, and thereby induced Walla Walla citizens to raise a subsidy of twenty-five thousand dollars to complete the road out of fear that a rival town would arise at the terminus.

hesitancy and went through the same cycle of doubt, trial, and triumph that had occurred at Walla Walla a decade or more before. The usual concomitants of land settlement were also soon apparent. Everything east of Waitsburg was split off as Columbia County in 1876, with Dayton as its seat. Platted only four years before, Dayton soon had several merchants, a flour mill, a woolen mill, and in 1876 it became a corporate town.[2] Farther east, Marengo, Pomeroy, and Pataha City (the latter two bitter rivals, but three miles apart) were laid out in 1877 and 1878 and soon had their mills, stores, and optimistic citizenry. Farmers and grain merchants hauled the harvest over the rough, steep roads to the Snake River at New York Bar, and Hemingway's Landing (Illia).

As settlers began to fill this belt of rich prairie country skirting the northern margins of the Blue Mountains, attention was directed to readily accessible country north of Walla Walla between Dry Creek and the Touchet, and the broad surface of Eureka Flat beyond. However, despite gradual infiltration into the margins of these localities, they were apparently drier areas of lighter soil, with little surface water, and farther from the timber needed for fuel and fencing.[3] Because of these deficiencies the main vanguard of settlers in the latter 1870's probed northeastward across the Snake onto the high prairies of the Palouse country (Map 29).

Interest in the large expanse of richly grassed, steeply rolling country lying beyond the formidable canyon of the Snake lagged very little behind that given the area south of the river. Although farther from Walla Walla, the only regional supply center, in every other way the Palouse country was equally attractive. The land itself was almost identical in appearance and quality, and the river gave equal access to either side. Just as stockmen had settled along

[2] Both contemporary reports and pioneer reminiscences amply confirm this situation for all localities settled during the 1870's. E.g., *The West Shore,* 1 (December, 1875), 3; and J. O. Long, "Review of Stock Industry of Garfield County," *East Washingtonian Pioneer Edition* (Pomeroy), June 6, 1914. In Long's article, the first settler of Pataha Flat, a high prairie south of Pomeroy, states that it was commonly believed that no crops could be grown there. No doubt ranchers who wished to retain access to the public range were anxious to promote such beliefs, but they could only be effective if they built upon a pre-existent hesitancy about these hill lands. Gilbert, *Historic Sketches,* pp. 391, 398-99. The machinery of the woolen mill at Dayton had been purchased from the defunct mill at The Dalles.

[3] *The West Shore,* 5 (June, 1879), 187; *North Pacific Coast,* 1 (Jan. 15, 1880), 37.

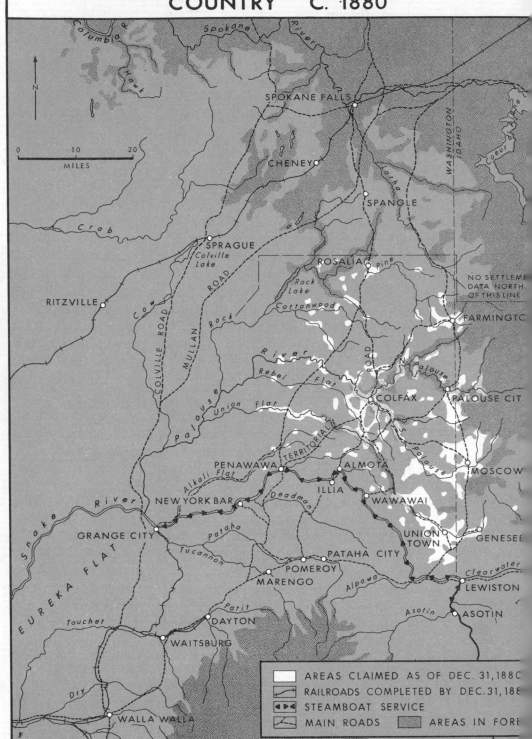

COLONIZATION IN THE PALOUSE COUNTRY C. 1880

N

0 10 20
MILES

Columbia R.

Cow Hawk

Spokane River

SPOKANE FALLS

CHENEY

SPANGLE

Crab

SPRAGUE
Colville Lake

Hangman

Latah

WASHINGTON
IDAHO

Coeur

RITZVILLE

COLVILLE ROAD

MULLAN

Cow

Rock

ROSALIA
Pine

Rock Lake

Cottonwood

NO SETTLEME
DATA NORTH
OF THIS LINE

FARMINGTO

Palouse

River

Rebel Flat

ROAD

N. Palouse

COLFAX

PALOUSE CIT

Union Flat

S. Palouse

MOSCOW

PENAWAWA
TERRITORIAL
ALMOTA

Alkali Flat

ILLIA

WAWAWAI

NEW YORK BAR
Deadman

UNION
TOWN

GENESEE

Snake River

GRANGE CITY

Pataha

Tucannon

PATAHA CITY

Clearwater

EUREKA FLAT

POMEROY
MARENGO

Alpowa

LEWISTON

Touchet

Patit

DAYTON

Asotin

ASOTIN

WAITSBURG

Dry

WALLA WALLA

AREAS CLAIMED AS OF DEC. 31, 1880
RAILROADS COMPLETED BY DEC. 31, 188
STEAMBOAT SERVICE
MAIN ROADS   AREAS IN FORE

Map 29

the Tucannon and Pataha, other settlers were soon locating along Union Flat Creek and the upper branches of the Palouse River. The influx of farmers was almost exactly concurrent with that into the lands on the other side of the Snake, proceeding slowly and experimentally in the early 1870's, then markedly accelerating toward the end of the decade.

Despite the fact that fewer than a hundred families resided there at the time, the area seemed so obviously set apart from the Walla Walla country by the physical barrier of the Snake River Canyon that it was organized as Whitman County in November, 1871. The next summer a territorial road was surveyed from Penawawa on the Snake to the Palouse forks and on north to Fort Colville. In the following year population was estimated to be about one thousand, and the country was reported to be "attracting much attention." In August, 1876, a federal land office was opened at Colfax, and land seekers no longer had to return to Walla Walla to file for homsteads, pre-emptions, or timber culture claims. There were still fewer than two thousand people in the area, but its reputation was steadily growing, and in 1877 the first real surge of immigration began. Regular wagon trains carrying whole groups of families began to move in, and the narrow little terrace cramped between the river and the towering canyon wall at Almota, the chief port of entry, was soon crowded with wagons, plows, threshers, and general merchandise. Landings were established at Penawawa and Wawawai also, and cable ferries were installed at the main crossings for wagons coming overland from Walla Walla. Local correspondents wrote of the "immense" volume of immigration and "vast numbers" of freighting teams traveling the roads between the Snake and the farming areas. The census of 1880 counted more than seven thousand in the Palouse country, and although small compared with other settlement frontiers of the nation, locally such growth was viewed as a genuine land rush.[4]

[4] The general progress of early settlement is well described in Gilbert, *Historic Sketches*, pp. 433ff., and Lever, *Whitman County*. C. S. Kingston "Territorial Road," *Spokesman-Review* (Spokane), Aug. 26, 1951; S. J. McCormick, *McCormick's Almanac for the Year 1873* (Portland, Ore., 1873), p. 48; 46th Cong., 3rd sess., H. Ex. Doc. 47, Pt. 3 (Dec. 1, 1880), p. 1016; Gilbert, *Historic Sketches*, p. 436; Elwood Evans, *Washington Territory: Her Past, Her Present and the Elements of Wealth which Insure Her Future* (address delivered at the Centennial Exposition, Philadelphia, Sept. 2, 1876) (Olympia, 1877), pp. 38-39. As an example of the new immigration, a train of eighteen wagons arrived at

The early stockmen found ideal ranch locations on the middle and lower reaches of Union Flat Creek: a small but perennial stream bordered by a narrow fringe of pine forest and by intermittent wet bottomlands where the grass grew high enough to cut for hay, the stream itself incised into the basaltic foundations of the country just enough to provide sheltered sites for homes and corrals. Above this shallow canyon to the north and south the bunch-grass hills rolled out to the horizon, a rich public range open to any who put it to use. This country lying just beyond the northernmost arc of the Snake was lower in over-all elevation than that land farther east and nearer the mountains. The risks of severe winters were significantly less, and if heavy snows or icy crust did come, cattle could be driven to the lower and drier country nearby to the west.

The farmers, on the other hand, feared not the winter with its snow and cold, but spring and summer, drought and hot winds. Moreover, they were still hesitant about farming the hills, and they had greater need of timber for fencing and fuel. Thus, as one pioneer put it succinctly, "the farmers were looking for flats, water, timber, and hay." They therefore sought out the scatterings of low level ground in the midst of the steeply rolling hills in the higher country to the east where the deep, dark soils and tall grass suggested greater rainfall and where tongues of forest projected out into the prairie along the higher ridges and larger streams. "We would say to the immigrant seeking a home, keep as close to the mountains as possible, for it requires considerable firewood as well as fencing material in this new country," advised the *Palouse Gazette,* and a pioneer of 1880 stated that "he was told that if he wanted to find good land, he should settle somewhere within fifteen or twenty miles west of the Idaho-Washington line." Thus the settlement frontier was never an expanding wave along a continuous front but rather a series of tiny nuclei as the earliest pioneers clustered upon those scattered locales of greatest attraction. The first of these was established at the forks of the Palouse River, and all the others lay to the east between that point and the mountains: upper Union Flat

Palouse City in September, 1877. Because of the outbreak of the Nez Perces War, they were escorted from Dayton by 150 soldiers from Fort Walla Walla. Garret D. Kincaid and A. H. Harris, *Palouse in the Making,* a series of articles collected in an unpublished pamphlet by the editors of the *Palouse Republic,* p. 1. *Palouse Gazette* (Colfax), Sept. 29, 1877; *Spokan Times,* March 16, 1878; Nov. 28, 1879; July 24, 1880.

Creek, Paradise Valley, the upper Palouse near the Idaho line, and on the broad flat about fourteen miles farther north along that political boundary. By the end of the decade most of the land in these districts had been taken, and settlers were already seeking out the many smaller spots with similar qualities. By that date, too, a score of tiny communities—with a post office, grist mill and general store —had gotten a start, but the largest and most promising were those established in the five earliest localities: Colfax (the first, and the county seat), Palouse City, and Farmington, Washington, and Genesee and Moscow, Idaho.[5]

The sudden appearance and the prospects for growth of so many new towns was viewed with jealousy by languishing older ones. "The great cry has been the Palouse," lamented the *Lewiston Teller,* "and emigrants painted on the wagons 'Palouse or bust' under the impression that the Palouse was all there is of the country." The writer insisted that the Asotin district and Clearwater country offered lands equally good in quality and accessibility to river service. But in fact these areas were more broken, drier, and more difficult to reach, while nearly the whole of the high Camas Prairie—which did have many of the qualities of the Palouse—was not only less accessible but was enclosed within the Nez Perces Indian Reservation.[6] Thus Lewiston, the old trade center which always viewed its river junction site as a natural guarantee of growth and greatness, found that, quite the contrary, it was almost completely bypassed by the new patterns of development.

Pendleton and The Dalles were in much more advantageous locations, but still had to be content for the time being more with the

[5] Fred R. Yoder, "Stories of Early Pioneers in Whitman County, Washington" (MSS of collected interviews, 1936-37, in the Washington State University Library, Pullman), pp. 63, 97. *Palouse Gazette,* Sept. 20, 1878, quoted in J. Orin Oliphant, "Notes on Early Settlements and on Geographic Names of Eastern Washington," *Washington Historical Quarterly,* 22 (July, 1931), 185; Oliphant's article is a useful compilation for dates, locales, and miscellaneous information about the earliest communities. Dates of the establishment of towns and facilities are found in Lever, *Whitman County,* and Gilbert, *Historic Sketches,* as well as in numerous less comprehensive sources.

[6] *Lewiston Teller* excerpt quoted in *The West Shore,* 11 (November, 1881), p. 279. Sister M. Alfreda Elsensohn, *Pioneer Days in Idaho County* (Caldwell, Ida., 1947), I, chap. vii. Far away in the southernmost corner of the prairie some farming was being done, the Patrons of Husbandry had built a hall, and around it the small community of Grangeville had developed, but although the mines offered an ample market for all the surplus of this small nucleus, under the circumstances there was no possibility of any significant expansion.

partial benefits of immigrant traffic than with the more enduring trade of local rural growth. The Oregon Trail was still a major highway: " . . . emigrant wagons, stock, etc. are arriving everyday in large numbers," noted the Pendleton *East Oregonian,* "some stopping with us while others move on further for other localities." In fact, the great majority did move on, and although Pendleton had indeed prospered, the main local agricultural frontier lay to the north where the upstart Weston had been narrowly defeated in its attempt to split off the richest portion of Umatilla County. But by far the most important entryway was up the Columbia through the historic portal, The Dalles. In the mid-1870's the town had still impressed the visitor with its "tumble-down and dilapitated appearance," but by the end of the decade it had once more become "a whirlpool" in the "great flood of emigration," with all the color and chaos of earlier days again apparent in the "motley throng of traders, land-hunters, cow-boys, speculators, saloonkeepers, Indians, Chinamen and cayuse ponies." But all the good ranch sites on both sides of the Columbia clear to Umatilla had been taken by now, and farming colonization expanded only slowly to the south of The Dalles and across the river in the Swale and other Klickitat localities. A stage line offered direct service to the Yakima and on to the new Kittitas community of Ellensburgh, but although stockmen continued to extend their operations there was little agricultural interest in these valleys. The main "flood" of land seekers flowed on eastward to the Walla Walla and the Palouse, giving a more solid boost to Walla Walla city (whose population of 3,588 in 1880 made it the largest town in the territory), and infusing the most rapid growth into such new centers as Dayton (996) and Colfax (444).[7]

This sudden spurt of immigration in the late 1870's coincided with the collapse of Indian resistance, though the two movements were more symbolically than causally related. The Nez Perces and the Bannock campaigns directly affected only the barest margins of the Great Columbia Plain, but each caused a considerable momentary scare. The Nez Perces finally expressed their wrath in 1877, after twenty years of provocation from their aggressive white neigh-

[7] *East Oregonian* (Pendleton), Sept. 18, Oct. 23, 1880; D. H. Stearns, *The Official Gazette, and Travelers' and Immigrants' Guide to Oregon and Washington Territory* (Portland, Ore., 1876), p. 109; W. D. Lyman, "Through Central Oregon on Horseback," *The West Shore,* 6 (December, 1880), 316-17; Lyman, *Yakima Valley,* pp. 565-77, 644. Walla Walla just barely surpassed Seattle's 3,533.

bors, and gave the residents of Lewiston and the Palouse some uneasy weeks. However, the principal source of dispute was the Wallowa country of eastern Oregon; most of the actual fighting took place south of the Camas Prairie in the Salmon River district, and culminated in the tactically brilliant retreat but ultimately pathetic surrender of Joseph and the remnants of his band in Montana. The Bannock outburst of 1878 had a more ominous portent but ended in a more ignominious collapse. The initiative came from the Indians of southern Idaho and eastern Oregon, whose plan was to join with the Umatillas and Cayuses and sweep the whites from the whole Columbia interior. But their leaders proved irresolute and the whole scheme foundered on the shoals of an age-old Indian rivalry; despite many common grievances, most of the Umatillas and Cayuses refused to join with the Bannocks and Paiutes, their long-standing enemies from beyond the mountains. As a result, although Indian warriors crossed the Blues, killed a few stockmen in the hills, and caused panicky settlers to crowd into Heppner, Pendleton, and Walla Walla, they failed to present a solid force and frittered away their momentary strategic advantage in useless scattered forays until confronted by federal troops. These soldiers, hastily assembled from Fort Lapwai and central Idaho, attacked and quickly routed the Indians near Pilot Rock, south of Pendleton, on July 7, 1878, and thereafter the Bannock campaign sputtered out in minor skirmishes far to the south beyond the mountains. These were the last of the Indian wars in the interior, and although hundreds of Indians still disdained to live on their assigned reservations, they were now regarded by the settlers merely as insufferable nuisances rather than potential enemies.[8]

The immigration of the late 1870's was more directly related to the growing realization that a huge productive grainland lay open for settlement. Despite the success of cultivation on the hills in the Walla Walla, and later in Columbia County, only after the same cycle of experimentation had been completed in the eastern Palouse did the general evaluation of the region undergo a change. In part this was because of the sheer scale of evidence, as district after dis-

[8] Parsons and Shiach, *History of Umatilla and Morrow Counties,* pp. 212-20. On the general problem of Indians and reservations in these and subsequent years, see Herman J. Deutsch, "Indian and White in the Inland Empire: The Contest for the Land, 1880-1912," *Pacific Northwest Quarterly,* 47 (April, 1956), 44-51.

trict from Pendleton to Palouse City showed the same result; in part, also, it was because the experiments in the Palouse were especially decisive. There the eagerly sought bottomlands lay higher and were closer to the mountains, and for the first time the pioneers encountered serious frost problems. Both grains and fruit were sufficiently damaged that a few of the earliest settlers gave up their claims and left for the "lower country"; others turned from wheat to oats as a more resistant crop.[9] Thus, when some of the settlers tested the hills and found them not only equally fertile but much less liable to frost and other problems and therefore not merely as good but *better* than the bottomlands, the final breakthrough into a new perspective on the potentialities of the region had been made.

Local newspapers quickly publicized this radical news. The *Palouse Gazette,* in the spring of 1879, explained "for the benefit of new settlers, who, seeing that the bottomlands have been taken first, may think that the hills or uplands have been rejected," that the hills were now preferred: "The bottoms grow too heavy straw, are more subject to frosts and, being usually more affected by late spring rains, the crop cannot be sown so early as on the uplands, and consequently cannot be harvested before the fall rains set in." Another Palouse paper noted that "it has required the strongest evidence to bring this fact to general notice," but soon this "marked peculiarity" would become an insistent refrain in the rapidly growing volume of literature emanating from or devoted to the region.[10]

Further, not only could wheat grow on these hills, it grew exceedingly well by any standard. Yields of thirty-five to forty bushels per acre were commonly cited as average, plus such remarkable results as forty bushels from a "volunteer" crop, or eighty-five bushels from a ten-acre field. Even if such reports were received with skepticism, as well they might be, an increasing volume of wheat was undeniably being floated down the Columbia to Portland for export. The shipments were tangible evidence where it would do the most good, for western Oregon had always been the principal source of migrants to the interior. It was a powerful lure and the relative merits of the lands east and west of the Cascades soon became a question which "taxes the best judgment of the old settlers." Whereas the first Oregon pioneers had scorned the east and sought the west, now "the

[9] Yoder, "Pioneers in Whitman County," pp. 50, 75, 80.
[10] Quoted in the *Spokan Times,* May 29, 1879; *North-West Tribune* (Colfax), Sept. 29, 1880.

sons and daughters and their families, and often their parents are seen moving east of the mountains." By the end of the decade a San Francisco paper described the immigration to "the Columbia Basin" as having "no parallel in the history of this coast since the influx into California during the early days of gold mining." "To the outside world," the whole Columbia interior was "known under the general name of the Walla Walla country," but in fact the pattern of development now extended beyond the limits of that subregion.[11] The census enumerations of 1880, which listed over 50,000 people, 360,000 "improved acres" in farms, and nearly 1,500,000 bushels of wheat, gave a firm measure of the new scale of developments, much of which had taken place during the last two or three years.

Deficiencies and Remedies

Throughout this period, however, there was one major deficiency of the region which was magnified precisely concordant with the success of the settlers. From the mid-1870's on, each successive colonization was farther from rail or river transport and each additional bushel of wheat became an added measure of the inadequacy of transport facilities (Map 30). The Walla Walla–Wallula railroad, by fostering a rapid increase in local production, merely compounded the problems on the river. In 1875 two small boats were making three round trips a week between Celilo and Walla Walla, but they could not handle the traffic. Two new and larger boats were built the following year, and two more the next, but by then not only had the Walla Walla trade increased, but the settlement of the Dayton, Pataha, and Palouse districts necessitated that service be extended along the entire lower Snake. The river service was not only slow and of inadequate capacity, it suffered from the fact that the low water stage coincided almost exactly with the period of greatest need, immediately following the harvest. Snake navigation was often suspended from late September until late March or April,

[11] See, e.g., Victor, *All Over Oregon*, pp. 23, 345; Stearns, *Official Gazette*, p. 117; Evans, *Washington Territory*, p. 38. "Volunteer" wheat was that which grew from kernels scattered in the field from the previous year. Any such yield would be as much the result of a variety of wheat which shattered badly before reaped and of extremely wasteful harvesting methods as of the fertility of the soil. G. H. Atkinson, "The Choice of a Home by Settlers in Oregon or Washington or Idaho," *The West Shore*, 6 (February, 1880), 38-40. *North Pacific Coast*, 1 (Feb. 15, 1880), 68-69, item reprinted from the *San Francisco Bulletin*.

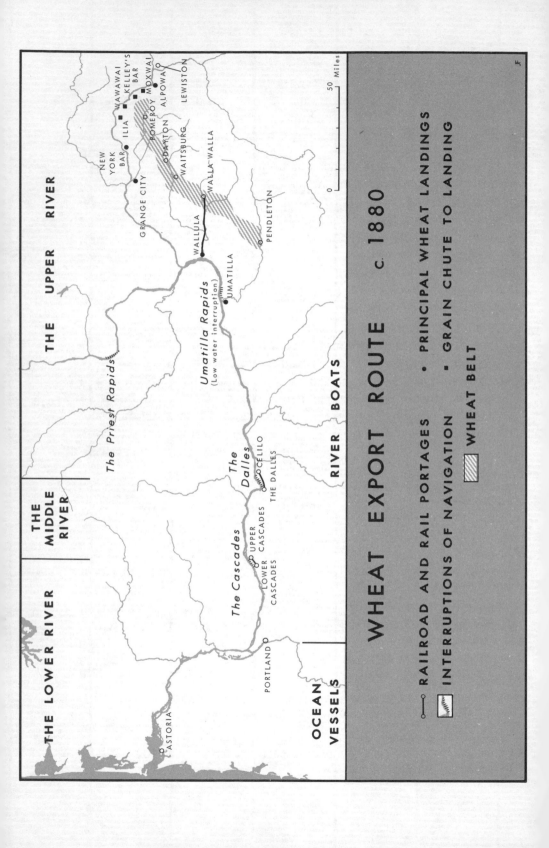

WHEAT EXPORT ROUTE c. 1880

• PRINCIPAL WHEAT LANDINGS

○〰️ RAILROAD AND RAIL PORTAGES

■ GRAIN CHUTE TO LANDING

🗻 INTERRUPTIONS OF NAVIGATION

▨ WHEAT BELT

THE LOWER RIVER

THE MIDDLE RIVER

THE UPPER RIVER

OCEAN VESSELS

RIVER BOATS

ASTORIA

PORTLAND

The Cascades

LOWER CASCADES

UPPER CASCADES

THE DALLES

CELILO

The Dalles

Umatilla Rapids
(Low water interruption)

UMATILLA

The Priest Rapids

PENDLETON

WALLULA

WALLA WALLA

WAITSBURG

DAYTON

GRANGE CITY

NEW YORK BAR

ILIA

WAWAWAI

KELLEY'S BAR

POMEROY

MOXWAI

ALPOWA

LEWISTON

0   50   Miles

and if the year had been more than usually dry, all navigation above Umatilla could be affected.[12]

Even when it was operating, the system was a cumbersome and inefficient procedure. A California reporter described it well:

> To give an accurate idea of the trouble of transportation from Walla Walla to the ocean, we will follow a sack of wheat from the field where it is grown. It is hauled to the depot at Walla Walla and there stored, to await its turn when the twenty-five thousand tons already ahead are taken away. Then it is put upon the cars and taken to Wallula; then it is put upon the boat and taken to Umatilla and transferred to another boat for Celilo; then it goes through the warehouse to the cars, taken to The Dalles and stored again; then it goes by boat to the Upper Cascades, and is then delivered to the railroad, by which it is taken to the Lower Cascades and transferred to another boat, by which it is taken up the Willamette to Portland. Here again it is stored, and thence sent down the river to Astoria and the ocean.

Little wonder that he concluded that "fortunes are being made slowly there now in wheat culture, with all the disadvantage of the isolated situation and an imperfect transportation." And for those utilizing the Snake, the situation was even more imperfect. The river lay two thousand feet below the uplands and could be reached only by way of short, precipitous, tributary canyons. To take a wagon load of grain down one of these steep trails was a rugged, time-consuming, and dangerous job. A few such trips were enough to set a man thinking of an alternative. Instead of wearing out teams, men, and brakes fighting gravity all the way down, why not let gravity do the job? In 1879 such thinking resulted in a grain chute constructed in the form of a wooden pipe, four inches square and thirty-two hundred feet long, from the canyon rim to the river landing. In the first trials gravity worked all too well: the wheat descended so rapidly that it was ground into coarse flour and soon wore through the pipe. The chute was then rebuilt with a series of upturns every hundred feet or so to reduce the velocity, and it worked so well that several others were soon built along this stretch of the river.[13]

---

[12] *Spirit of the West* (Walla Walla), Sept. 10, 1876; *Palouse Gazette,* April 16, 1880; *Spokan Times,* Sept. 11, 1880.

[13] James Wyatt Oates, "Washington Territory," *Californian,* 1 (Feb. 1, 1880), 117-18. The transfer at Umatilla was necessary only in very low water stages. Gilbert, *Historic Sketches,* pp. 290-91. The first chute was at Moxwai; the others, built in 1881, were at Kelley's Bar, Wawawai, and Illia, all on the south bank, which in this portion has almost no tributary canyons suitable for a road.

An ingenious device that saved much time and wear and tear on the farmers, their horses, and wagons, it did little to reduce the direct out-of-pocket costs of exporting. The wheat still had to be bagged at the landing and await the uncertain arrival of an empty boat. Complaints about the high costs and inadequacies of transportation continued to mount with every season, and with good reason. Indeed, wheat quotations in Walla Walla were usually only about half the prices offered in Portland. Ironically, the area now had the reputation of growing wheat "cheaper than in any other place in the United States" and transporting it "farther [and at greater expense] than any other wheat grown in the world."[14] Clearly something had to be done about it. A good deal of attention was directed toward navigation improvements, especially a means of eliminating the transshipments at the major portages at Celilo–The Dalles and the Cascades. But by far the best immediate hope was for a major extension of railroads.

Even before the acceleration of immigration there were numerous proposals, though little action, on railroad matters. After the Union Pacific and Central Pacific joined in 1869, a northern transcontinental seemed sure to follow; but the. Northern Pacific became bogged in a financial morass, and it did not necessarily promise to build along routes which would be of the greatest utility to the region. What was needed were railways specifically constructed to get Walla Walla wheat to the seaboard in the most direct and inexpensive manner; connections to the East were far less imperative. The first substantial proposal for such a line came from Seattle, whose citizens were so incensed at the Northern Pacific for selecting Tacoma as its western terminus that they undertook to build their own line. The Seattle and Walla-Walla Railroad and Transportation Company was formed in 1873; reconnaissances suggested the

---

A description and small sketch of one of these "grain pipes" is given in Cleveland Rockwell, "The Columbia River," *Harper's Monthly*, 66 (December, 1882), 6.

[14] *Memorial of the Legislative Assembly of Washington for the Improvement of the Navigation of the Columbia River*, 44th Cong., 1st sess., H. Misc. Doc. 17 (1875), p. 1; 45th Cong., 3rd sess., Ex. Doc. 1, Pt. 5 (1878), p. 5. The tariff on wheat from Walla Walla and all Snake River ports to Portland in 1880-81 was forty cents per hundred pounds, Oregon Railway and Navigation Company, *Local Freight Tariff*, March 20, 1881. William H. Brewer, "Report on the Cereal Production of the United States," *Tenth Census of the United States, 1880* (Washington D.C., 1883), III, 75. Hereafter listed as *Tenth Census*.

Walla Walla and Columbia River R. R. Co.

TIME TABLE NO. 1,

TO TAKE EFFECT THURSDAY, APRIL 1st, 1880.

This Time Table is in no case intended for the information of the public, nor as an advertisement of the times or hours of any train. The company reserves the right to vary therefrom at pleasure. It is for the information of the employes only.

ALL TRAINS DAILY.

EAST BOUND.		Miles from Wallula.	Main Line Stations.	Miles from Walla Walla.	WEST BOUND.	
FREIGHT.	MIXED.				MIXED.	FREIGHT.
No. 4.	° No. 2.				No. 1.	No. 3.
10:30 A. M. Ar.	9:20 P. M Arrives	32¼	**Walla Walla**.......... 5	0	Leaves 4:00 P M	1:00 P. M. Lv.
10:00..........	9:00.	27	Whitman (Junction)..... 11	5	4:20 "	1:30
9:00	8:10.	16¼	Touchet........... 7¼	16	5:10 "	2:30
8:30	7:40.	9	Nine Mile Tank........... 9	23¼	5:40 "	3:00
7:30 A. M Lv.	7:00 P. M Leaves	0	**Wallula**......... ...	32¼	Arrives 6:20 P.M	4:00 P. M. Ar.

NORTH BOUND.		Miles from Bl. Mountain.	Blue Mountain Extension Stations.	Miles from Walla Walla.	SOUTH BOUND.	
	FREIGHT No. 2.				FREIGHT No. 1.	
	3:00 P.M Arrives	19	**Walla Walla**........ 5	0	Leaves 9:30 A M	
	2:30	14	Whitman (Junction) ... 3	5	**10:00**	
	2:15	11	State Line................. 4	8	10:15	
	2:00	7	Milton 7	12	10:45	
	1:30 P. M Leaves	0	**Blue Mountain**.....	19	Arrives 11:30 A M	

* SPECIAL NOTICE.—Until further orders train No. 2 on Main Line will not leave **Wallula for Walla Walla** until the arrival of the O. R. & N. Co's steamers from Celilo and will have exclusive right to track against all other trains.

N. B.—Speed over all trestles and bridges must not exceed 4 miles per hour and no speed of any train exceed 20 miles per hour. Full face figures indicate meeting and passing points.

SIGNALS.

FIRST.—A stationary red flag by day denotes that the track is imperfect and must be run over with care. A red flag by day or a red lantern by night, waved upon the track, signifies that the train must come to a full stop. The waving of a hat or any like action should be regarded as a signal of danger, and NOT PASSED UNNOTICED.

SECOND.—A red flag by day, or a red lantern by night, displayed on the front of the engine, indicates that an engine or train is following, which has same rights as the engine bearing the signal.

THIRD.—A lantern swung across the track is the signal to stop. A lantern swung in a circle is the signal to go ahead. A lantern raised and lowered is to back up. If motion of lantern is quick, move quick, if slow move slow.

FOURTH.—One blast of the whistle is a signal to apply brakes. Two blasts to loose the brakes, and three blasts to back. Four blasts for switch or for calling in flagman, and five or more blasts for wooding up.

FIFTH.—A succession of short quick blasts is a cattle alarm. Brakemen must be promptly ready for any signals to be given.

GENERAL RULES.

FIRST.—All trains will be run on Portland time, and the clock in the office of the General Superintendent, at Walla Walla, will be the standard time, and Conductors and Engineers will regulate their time pieces by it.

SECOND.—Conductors will have charge of their trains and decide all questions relating thereto, except that directions given by them in conflict with these rules, or the safety of the road must not be obeyed and Engineers will be held equally accountable in these cases.

THIRD.—Conductors will be held personally responsible for the proper adjustment of all switches used by them.

FOURTH.—Conductors will not pass any passengers or employes over the road without a ticket from the General Superintendent.

FIFTH.—Conductors and Engineers must report to the General Superintendent all delays and accidents and the killing of stock of any kind during the trip, giving the locality and all the facts connected with the accidents, and kinds, and description of stock as fully as possible.

SIXTH.—Great care must be taken to prevent striking stock and trains must come to a full stop if necessary, to avoid doing so. Engineers will be held to strict account for any carelessness in killing stock.

SEVENTH.—Brakes must never be applied so tight as to slide the wheels. Conductors will be held responsible for train men in this respect.

EIGHTH.—No wood, freight, timber or other material of any kind will be allowed to be piled closer than 5 feet of the track. Section Foremen will see that this rule is strictly observed in all cases.

NINTH.—Section Foremen will not allow their Hand Cars to run over the road without being with them themselves.

TENTH.—Dampers of ash pans must in all cases be closed while engines are crossing bridges and trestles.

ELEVENTH.—Employes will see that all cars are secured against possibility of their being blown out on the main track by the wind.

TWELFTH.—Head lights on engines must be kept in good order and always lighted when running after dark.

THIRTEENTH.—Gravel and working trains will in no case carry passengers.

FOURTEENTH.—Engineers on approaching a station will sound the whistle at the distance of half a mile. When moving about stations the bell will be rung and all proper care used.

FIFTEENTH.—No notice will be given Station Agents or Trackmen of the passage of irregular trains, and they will govern themselves accordingly.

SIXTEENTH.—No irregular trains will be allowed to run over the road without written orders from the General Superintendent.

SEVENTEETH.—Engineers and Firemen should look back frequently to see that all is right when trains are likely to break apart. In such cases great care must be taken to keep the forward part out of the way of the detached part, and every precaution used to prevent a collision.

EIGHTEENTH.—All station service appertaining to the business of the W. W. & C. R. R. Co. at Wallula is to be done for said Company by the proper officers of the O. R. & N. Co. at that point.

NINETEENTH.—Train men must be at their posts 30 minutes before the time for starting their trains.

TWENTIETH.—Engineers must not leave their engines, nor permit any one to ride on them except the Road or Section Masters without permission from the General Superintendent.

TWENTY-FIRST.—The Road Master is authorized to direct the movement of trains in the absence of the General Superintendent.

UNION PRINT.

H. W. FAIRWEATHER,
General Superintendent.

feasibility of Snoqualmie Pass and produced glowing reports on the potential traffic between Puget Sound and the grain and livestock region of the interior. But, as with a hundred other schemes of the next thirty-five years, the financial resources proved inadequate to the task, and the line never crossed the mountains. The completion of the Walla Walla and Columbia River Railway was the first real step, even though it was but a fragment of the system needed. Built entirely by local capital, its profits were soon sufficient to attract wider interest. In 1877 it was purchased by the Oregon Steam Navigation Company, giving that pioneer firm an even tighter control of the transport system of the interior. Two years later eastern capitalists formed the Oregon Railway and Navigation Company, purchased control of the O.S.N. and the Oregon Steamship Company (Portland–San Francisco ocean service), and announced their intention of creating a regional railway system adequate to serve the mounting interior traffic.[15] Furthermore, the Northern Pacific was now showing definite signs of life. The surveyors had selected the final route between the Rockies and the Columbia River, and in the spring of 1880 construction timber was being felled on the upper Yakima, rails and equipment were being brought upriver, and the actual grading of this one of its several segments was begun.

"The American people have railroads on the brain," proclaimed a Yakima citizen in 1880, "why, you can count on railroads going anywhere and everwhere, . . . it would be hard to find a place where there isn't going to be a railroad."[16] This mania now swept in upon the Great Columbia Plain and gave every promise of quickening the pace and scale of regional development. From 1880 on the advance of settlers and of railways would be intimately interrelated.

[15] Thomas B. Morris, *Report of the Chief Engineer of the Seattle and Walla Walla Railroad and Transportation Company, to the Trustees and Stockholders, November, 1874* (Seattle, Wash., 1874), esp. pp. 25-29; 43rd Cong., 1st sess. S. Rept. 420, pp. 1-3. The Seattle and Walla Walla was the forerunner of the Pacific Coast Railway, which did build from Seattle to the coal mines around Newcastle. Oregon Railway and Navigation Company, *First Annual Report* (New York, 1880). This report gives a measure of the profits awaiting; the W.W.&C.R. returned a net profit of $269,004 in 1879-80, surely an enormous income from thirty-two miles of track. The profits of the O.S.N. over its twenty years of existence were of course even greater. Ainsworth, one of the early entrepreneurs who stayed on as an officer of the O.R.&N., stated that the O.S.N. paid $2,702,000 in dividends and sold out for $5,000,000. "Statement of Captain J. C. Ainsworth, October 27, 1883" (MS in the Bancroft Library, Berkeley, Calif.), p. 6.

[16] Quoted in the *Spokan Times*, Sept. 25, 1880.

Emergence of a Network

The new O.R.&N. undertook its program of linking the wheat country to Portland in a carefully planned sequence of constructions. Because the principal bottleneck in the river service was between Celilo and Wallula, where the boats had been able to move only half the harvest of 1879, this was the first segment undertaken. The work proceeded from both ends and was completed early in 1881; by linking the W.W.&C.R. (which had been relaid to standard gauge) and the portage railway, it gave through service from Walla Walla to The Dalles. Meanwhile, careful attention had been given to the best means of tapping the wheatlands beyond Walla Walla. In accordance with the recommendations of a special reconnaissance committee, a line north to the Touchet and on to the Snake River at Grange City was approved, with two short branches —one to Dayton and one up the Pataha. As for the Palouse country, the person in charge of that reconnaissance had proposed that the line

> ... should begin at a point on the Snake River, near the mouth of the Palouse, thence proceeding in a northeasterly direction towards Union Flat and thence in an easterly direction, crossing the South Fork of the Palouse into Idaho and terminate somewhere in the Potlatch country (southeast of Moscow) near the foot of the mountains. This with a branch road starting from a point near the Idaho line running north toward the Spokane country, would drain the most fertile region and become profitable feeders to the river. Any road west of that line would traverse a country not at all as productive, and would, moreover, entirely ignore that portion which is destined to be the granary of the Northwest.

Accordingly, the committee recommended a route from Texas Ferry (nearly opposite Grange City) to Colfax and Farmington, with a branch to Moscow. It was finally proposed that a line from the Columbia River through the Umatilla district and over the Blue Mountains into the Wallowa country be built, not only to tap present traffic but as a step toward an eventual transcontinental connection.[17]

[17] All dates of O.R.&N. construction are derived from O.W.R.N., *Corporate History*. These and the other lines proposed at this time are reported in Oregon Railway and Navigation Company, *First Annual Report* (New York, 1880), and "Report to the Stockholders of the Oregon Railway and Navigation Company by Committee to visit Oregon and Washington, 1880." "Walla Walla and the Palouse Country [1879]," in "Two Railroad Reports on Northwest Resources," *Pacific Northwest Quarterly*, 37 (July, 1946), 176-85, quotation on p. 185.

Unwilling to undertake all of these at once (a total of 285 miles), the O.R.&N. gave priority to the line from Walla Walla to the Snake. This plus the short branch to Dayton were completed in 1881, and the regular steamboat service between Celilo and Grange City was discontinued. In the following year the Umatilla branch from the Columbia to Pendleton was constructed. Then, on November 20, 1882, service was opened on the final downriver segment from Portland to The Dalles; the tedious portages had finally been overcome, and Walla Walla wheat could move without transshipment from the rural sidings to the ocean vessel docks.

Meanwhile, the "Pend Oreille Division" of the struggling northern transcontinental was also being built. Local headquarters were established at Ainsworth on the Snake, just above its junction with the Columbia. Construction was carried northeastward from that point toward eventual connection with the rails proceeding westward across the Dakota plains into Montana. Created by the railroad and thronging with activity, its locale and inhabitants quickly made Ainsworth notorious. "Built in the midst of a bleak, dreary waste," an army surveyor, Lieutenant Thomas W. Symons, pronounced it to be "one of the most uncomfortable, abominable places in America to live in," and another traveler stated that Ainsworth could "boast of a few of the best people, the largest number of bad men and women, and the greatest amount of sin, dust, and general disagreeableness, of any place of its size on the coast." Even Captain Ainsworth, who had not been consulted in the matter, decided that "it was anything but a compliment" to have "such a miserable place" carry his name. But such tumult was merely a measure of the scale and vigor of the long-awaited construction program. Despite "vexatious delays" in getting timbers down the Yakima, the line was steadily extended into the scabland country and reached Spokane Falls in June, 1881.[18] Beyond, the pace through the mountains was much slower, and not until September 8, 1883, were appropriate golden spike ceremonies staged at Gold Creek in western Montana to commemorate the first rail link between the Pacific Northwest and the eastern states.

Actually, it was as yet not quite the "transcontinental" that its earlier promoters had envisioned. Another segment had earlier been

[18] 47th Cong., 1st sess., S. Ex. Doc. 186 (1882), p. 50; *Spokan Times,* June 16, 1881; Ainsworth, "Statement," p. 20; Northern Pacific Railway, *Annual Report and Proceedings of Stockholders . . . Sept. 15, 1881* (New York, 1881), p. 27.

Ainsworth standing stark in the sand and sage in 1884. The bridge is across the Snake, which joins the Columbia in the right background. *(Photo courtesy of Washington State University Library)*

The junction of river and rail service at Riparia on the Snake River. The vessel tied up at the wharfboat is the *Almota*, a sternwheeler constructed at Celilo in 1876. *(Photo courtesy of Washington State University Library)*

completed from Kalama, on the Columbia below Portland, north
to its Puget Sound terminus at Tacoma, but no direct trans-Cascades
connection had been made. Indeed, it was the O.R.&N. line along
the Columbia that made it possible for Northern Pacific traffic to
move between Duluth and Puget Sound. A car ferry between Portland and Kalama and another across the Snake, with a short rail spur
to Wallula, served to connect the two systems. This connection was
possible because of a fact that would have great influence upon the
strategies of railroad construction in the Columbia interior: Henry
Villard, by means of daring financial manipulations, had obtained
control of both systems.[19] Indeed, it was Villard's dynamic leadership that had spurred this flurry of Northern Pacific development
and particular regional pattern of construction. Under the control
of his holding company, the Oregon and Transcontinental, the two
systems retained their separate corporate identities but were bound
together by traffic agreements.

During Villard's tenure an important apportionment of territory
was made, which changed the earlier proposals of branch-line strategy. On July 10, 1883, it was decreed that the Palouse country would
be tapped by the Northern Pacific. Accordingly, that year a line was
commenced at Palouse Junction (later Connell) and extended eastward up Washtucna Coulee, across the lower Palouse River, and on
to Colfax. Service was opened on January 1, 1884. South of the
Snake the O.R.&N. made minor extensions in its allotted territory.[20]

In 1884, Villard's vast railroad network was further elaborated
when the line across the Blue Mountains was completed from Pendleton to the Snake River at Huntington on the Oregon-Idaho border, where it connected with the Oregon Short Line, a subsidiary

---

[19] Villard was head of the syndicate that formed the O.R.&N., and in December, 1880, by means of his famous "blind pool," he secretly gained control of
the Northern Pacific. In the following year he was elected president of the N.P.
See James Blaine Hedges, *Henry Villard and the Railways of the Northwest*
(New Haven, Conn., 1930).

[20] O.W.R.N., *Corporate History*, sheets 5-6. A short line was built northeast
from Pendleton and another south from Walla Walla; in plan these were to
be joined, but the connection complicated matters. In 1879 the W.W.&C.R. had
built a branch from Whitman to Blue Mountain Station, fourteen miles to the
southeast. In 1883 that portion of this narrow-gauge between Whitman and
Barrett (seven miles) was abandoned and the remainder was widened and
linked directly to Walla Walla. This left a gap of ten miles between Blue
Mountain and the terminus of the new branch from Pendleton at Centerville
(Athena).

of the Union Pacific. With this, the steam engine could traverse the general route of the old Oregon Trail all the way from the Missouri to the Willamette at more miles per hour than the wagon trains had made in a day.

THE GREAT BOOM OF THE 1880'S

Proclaiming the Region

By 1884 the Great Columbia Plain was well into the railroad era (Map 31). In four years several hundred miles had been built, its most attractive settlement areas had been tapped, its imperative need of a line to the ocean port had been satisfied, and it was linked by two different routes to the rapidly evolving network of the nation. Historic entryways at three corners of the region were now overlain with steel rails. Not only could products be moved out, people could be brought in far more quickly, cheaply, and in greater numbers than ever before. The initiation of construction by major companies had already sharply accelerated immigration, and even before the golden spikes had been driven, the railroads themselves launched promotion campaigns designed to make the "Oregon fever" of an older time seem but a faint flush.

The railroads carried out this regional advertising with unusual intensity because they had not only an obvious interest in promoting settlement in order to generate traffic but also the added spur of profits to be gained from the sale of their enormous land holdings. The Northern Pacific had been subsidized by a land grant which included alternate sections (square miles) within a band eighty miles wide centered upon its main line from Lake Superior to the Pacific. In addition, the Villard roads formed the Oregon Improvement Company to promote certain townsites, develop coal and forest resources, and improve certain choice blocks of land for sale at higher prices. The scale and comprehensiveness of this propaganda campaign were enormous. In 1883 the president of the Northern Pacific reported to the stockholders that 2,500,000 copies of pamphlets and circulars had been printed, advertisements had been inserted in 167 newspapers in the United States and 25 in Canada, and an exhibit car sent into ten eastern states had been visited by 50,000 people. Liverpool had been established as European headquarters to serve a network of 831 agents in the British Isles and 124 on the continent, all of whom were well supplied with pamphlets, maps, and samples of grain to prove the wonders of the lands tributary to the northern transcontinental.[21]

Not all these materials, of course, were focused upon the merits of the Columbia interior, for the lands available reached from Minnesota to western Washington; but within the United States the greatest amount of interest was directed toward the Pacific Northwest. Immigrants arriving from the East and from California reported that Washington Territory was the best advertised region on the continent. The response was excellent, and the reasons for it were quite clear. As for the interior, it was not only the quantity of propaganda but the qualities of the region described which proved so persuasive. Further, the Northern Pacific literature was, for its time, unusually temperate and accurate in its descriptions and evaluations. Evidently the officials in charge realized that the actual attractions of the area were sufficient without gross exaggeration. Thus, for example, the principal early booklet issued on the region, while packed with alluring descriptions of the beauty of the country, the richness of its soil, and the profitability of its agriculture, nevertheless made distinctions between the better districts and the poorer, noted the scarcity of timber for fuel and fencing, and warned of the need to provide hay for livestock in case of unusually harsh winters. No doubt such literature reflected the fact that the railroad was making unusual efforts to garner the most accurate information. In July, 1881, it formed the Northern Transcontinental Survey and

[21] There has been much misunderstanding about the exact nature of the railroad land grants. In fairness to the railroads, it must be noted that although these lands were a subsidy to help finance the costs of construction, in return the railroads carried government freight at a reduced cost, a saving which in time more than equaled the amount received from the sale of lands. The geography of the land grants was complicated by the "lieu lands" provision, which compensated for lands that were already privately held when the grant was made. In that case, the Northern Pacific was allowed to select sections within additional ten-mile strips on either side of its original grant. Conflicts among the railroad, the settlers, and the government over this lieu land provision gave rise to extremely complicated litigations. For an excellent discussion of the general misunderstanding about these grants, see Robert S. Henry, "The Railroad Land Grant Legend in American History Texts," *Mississippi Valley Historical Review,* 32 (September, 1945), 171-94.

See Oregon Improvement Company, *Annual Report* and *(Special) Reports,* for the years 1881-88. Northern Pacific Railway, *Annual Report, Sept. 20, 1883* (New York, 1883), pp. 22, 38-39. European recruitment was aimed almost entirely at British and Germanic peoples. Materials were printed in English, Swedish, Norwegian, Danish, German, Dutch, and Finnish. See also Hedges, *Villard,* pp. 126ff.

RAILROAD STRATEGIES 1884–1890

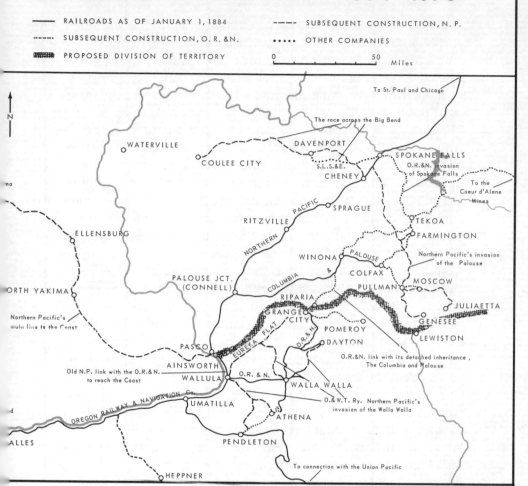

—— RAILROADS AS OF JANUARY 1, 1884   ----- SUBSEQUENT CONSTRUCTION, N. P.

..... SUBSEQUENT CONSTRUCTION, O. R. & N.   ••••• OTHER COMPANIES

▓▓▓▓ PROPOSED DIVISION OF TERRITORY

0 ——————— 50 Miles

To St. Paul and Chicago

The race across the Big Bend

WATERVILLE

COULEE CITY

DAVENPORT

SPOKANE FALLS
O.R.&N. invasion
of Spokane Falls

S.L.S.&E.

CHENEY

To the
Coeur d'Alene
Mines

ELLENSBURG

RITZVILLE

PACIFIC

SPRAGUE

TEKOA

FARMINGTON

NORTHERN

WINONA

PALOUSE

Northern Pacific's invasion
of the Palouse

ORTH YAKIMA

PALOUSE JCT.
(CONNELL)

COLUMBIA

COLFAX

MOSCOW

PULLMAN

Northern Pacific's
main line to the Coast

RIPARIA

GRANGE
CITY

EUREKA FLAT

POMEROY

O.R.&N.

JULIAETTA

GENESEE

LEWISTON

PASCO

AINSWORTH

O.&N.

DAYTON

O.R.&N. link with its detached inheritance,
The Columbia and Palouse

Old N.P. link with the O.R.&N.
to reach the Coast

WALLULA

O.R. & N.

WALLA WALLA

O.&W.T. Ry. Northern Pacific's
invasion of the Walla Walla

OREGON RAILWAY & NAVIGATION Co.

UMATILLA

ATHENA

PENDLETON

To connection with the Union Pacific

ALLES

HEPPNER

THE COLUMBIA RIVER
BETWEEN THE DALLES AND CELILO FALLS
SHOWING PROPOSED BOAT RAILWAYS

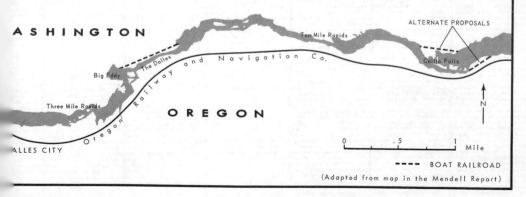

ASHINGTON

ALTERNATE PROPOSALS

Ten Mile Rapids

The Dalles and Navigation Co.

Celilo Falls

Big Eddy

The Dalles

Three Mile Rapids

OREGON

N

ALLES CITY

Oregon Railway and Navigation Co.

0 ——— .5 ——— 1 Mile

---- BOAT RAILROAD

(Adapted from map in the Mendell Report)

Map 31, above; Map 32, below

staffed it with some of the most eminent scientists of the time. The purpose was to map and evaluate carefully the qualities of lands and other resources of various regions. This information would give guidance to immigration, suggest industrial activities to initiate, and allow branch lines to be planned so as to tap districts of maximum potential.[22]

Primarily, however, it was not the opinions of scientists but of "practical farmers" that counted in recruiting settlers. Fortunately for the regional propagandists, they were served uncommonly well by these people. The farmers had demonstrated beyond doubt that the hill lands grew superb wheat, and the pampleteers could expound upon this peculiarity with complete confidence. And now, just as they were ready to spatter the nation and half of Europe with a barrage of information about the region, an even greater theme was emerging from the experiments of these practical men: the "well-known fact that wheat will grow and mature wherever the 'bunch grass' grows." Opening an even greater vision of the potentials of the region, it was a wonderful new refrain which the propagandists were prompt to sing. It was a bold idea, certainly as yet untested in many localities, yet it had come directly from the experiences of the settlers themselves. Lieutenant Symons had summarized the popular feeling of the time: " 'Bunch-grass' has become the synonym for things good, strong, rich, and great: the bunch-grass country is the best and finest country on earth; bunch-grass cattle and horses are the sweetest, fleetest, and strongest in the world; and a bunch-grass man is the most superb being in the universe." The stockmen had long known it, now the farmers were proclaiming the same, and the writers could give happy emphasis to the fact that there was room for many more thousands who might wish to turn the bunch-grass country into the finest wheat country on earth.[23]

[22] The Pacific Northwest ... (New York, 1882); Northern Pacific Railway, Annual Report, Sept. 21, 1882, pp. 37-39; Northern Transcontinental Survey, First Annual Report, Sept. 1882 (New York, 1882). The survey was directed by Raphael Pumpelly, and included E. W. Hilgard of the University of California, the most eminent soils scientist of his time.

[23] Frank J. Parker, Washington Territory (Walla Walla, ca. 1882), p. 3. E.g., The Pacific Northwest, p. 20, for propaganda about bunch grass. 47th Cong., 1st sess., S. Ex. Doc. 186 (1882), p. 111.

A few persons had a larger vision, insisting that even the sagebrush lands were suitable for wheat growing. Symons thought that some of it at least was, and W. McMicken, after observing a few trials in the Yakima and Kittitas, announced that he felt 'warranted in making the assertion that there is no

Opening New Districts

Such enlargement of the agricultural potentials, together with the recent expansion of facilities, gave the land seeker of the mid-1880's a choice of many districts. In the Walla Walla and Palouse countries, the influx caused but an acceleration of the settlement expansion already well under way. In both areas there was an almost immediate filling in of the vacant lands within the more humid belt near the mountains and some expansion westward into drier districts. The northernmost Palouse particularly benefited from the completion of the Northern Pacific, as the farmers around Rockford, Spangle, and Pine City could now haul to the railroad at Cheney and Sprague, instead of far south to the Snake. The most radical impact, however, was upon the Big Bend, the vast expanse of rolling country lying between the scablands and the great arc of the Columbia. The southern sector had long been within reach of the riverboats, but it was so obviously a treeless sandy desert that it received no interest whatsoever from settlers. On the other hand, the higher lands of the northern portion had most of the qualities of the Palouse but were so remote from shipping facilities as to remain virtually uninhabited throughout the 1870's. The building of the Northern Pacific along the entire eastern margin of that country altered the situation.

Even as the railroad was being graded, the first testing of the land for crops was being made. Philip Ritz, a stockman who had settled on the broad undulating country just west of upper Cow Creek in 1878, encountered a small group of immigrants in Walla Walla and induced them to stake out claims in his district. Ground squirrels ate the first sowing of wheat, but in 1880 a small patch yielded well. Such trials were probably critical to the sudden emergence of the idea that bunch grass was a reliable indicator of wheatland. In the following year the rails were laid, townsites were platted at Ritzville and Sprague, and interest in the area greatly increased. At first it suffered, as had much of the whole interior for many decades previously, from the fact that the main line of travel followed the rocky, basaltic coulees and scabland channels, and therefore provided hardly a glimpse of the grassy plains. The view was not an enticing

---

desert land in this Territory." However, as Symons noted, the popular view was that "sage-brush" was "almost a synonym for worthlessness." See 47th Cong., 1st sess., S. Ex. Doc. 186 (1882), and 46th Cong., 2nd sess., H. Ex. Doc. 1, Pt. 5 (1879), p. 898.

one to the summer traveler. "I am told there is 'lots of water' away from the railroad," reported an easterner, who went on to say: "I hope so most sincerely, for the sake of present inhabitants and future settlers. . . . The colonists in that region would need a Moses at every mile-post to smite the black, ugly rocks with his rod and make the water gush over all the parched land. . . ." But one need not search far for a good homesite. Within the general scabland belt itself, there were numerous "islands" of rich, grassy soil with timber and surface water nearby. These locations were almost immediately settled, and as soon as the daily passenger train began to offer through service from Portland and the East, the depots at Spokane Falls, Cheney, and Sprague became crowded with land seekers who pushed out onto the margins of the prairies to the west. Indeed, by 1884 the regular train was already supplemented by daily immigrant trains which, like the wagon trains they replaced, carried not only the colonists but all their household goods, farm machinery, and livestock at a low fare.[24]

In 1883 the whole area was detached from Whitman and Spokane counties and subdivided into Lincoln, Douglas, Adams, and Franklin counties. Of these, only Lincoln had a substantial number of settlers. Sprague, with the division offices and shops of the railroad, was the largest of its towns, but Davenport and Harrington were already sufficiently developed to cause a spirited three-way contest for the county seat. Sprague won the honor, though not without being accused of counting the votes of the cemetery, little children, and passengers on through trains.[25] The intensity of these rivalries among communities but two or three years old was a sure sign of the vigor of settlement expansion and of the confidence in the agricultural future of the district.

Elsewhere the railroads had not as yet had such a marked effect upon farming expansion. The high plateau south of the Columbia remained a stronghold of stockmen. Experiments with wheat growing were being carried out in the early 1880's in a number of scattered localities, most notably in the Grass Valley district between

[24] *Ritzville Journal-Times, Adams County Pioneer Edition,* Sept. 15, 1949, p. 5; *Spokan Times,* June 5, 1880; "The Far Northwest," *Chicago Times* (Sept. 30, 1881); see also "Cheney and Medical Lake," *The Northwest,* 2 (September, 1884), 4-6; *The West Shore,* 9 (April, 1883), 73; Northern Pacific Railway, *Time Table,* August, 1884.

[25] Richard F. Steele and Arthur P. Rose, *An Illustrated History of the Big Bend Country* . . . (Spokane, Wash., 1904), pp. 76-83.

the Deschutes and John Day rivers, south of Alkali toward Rock Creek, and in the Blackhorse district along Willow Creek, but despite the generally good results obtained, developments were gradual. One special complication was the uncertainty over the legal availability of lands, arising from disputed claims of the Northern Pacific and of the Eastern Oregon Land Company (the latter held title to alternate sections within a six-mile strip which had been granted a decade before to The Dalles Military Wagon Road Company).[26]

When the Northern Pacific showed the first signs of activity in the interior, interest in the Yakima country picked up, for it was well known that the surveyed route of the transcontinental ran through the entire valley toward a pass across the Cascades to Tacoma. Merchants and speculators soon appeared, a federal land office was opened in Yakima City in June, 1880, and all prepared for the inevitable boom. But these hopes were premature, for in the following year Villard gained control and diverted the N.P. to a connection with the O.R.&N. at Wallula rather than constructing his own trans-Cascade line. With this the two clusters of settlement, around Yakima city and in the Kittitas around Ellensburgh (which had been platted in 1875), lapsed into doldrums. A few local experiments with irrigation were being made, but the whole area west of the Columbia, valley as well as upland, largely remained cattle and sheep country. A stage line offered service between Ellensburgh, Yakima, and The Dalles, but it was a poor substitute for the railway so eagerly anticipated. No one doubted, of course, that the steam cars would eventually arrive. The stage men were well aware of impending ruin and looked "gloomily forward to the time when they can no longer crack the whip over a six-in-hand and prance up to the roadside hotel as the chief event of the day." However, as the same writer noted, "the passengers do not share their gloom, and there are always more passengers than drivers."[27]

[26] Shaver *et al., History of Central Oregon,* pp. 430-31, 439-42, 560-61; Parsons and Shiach, *History of Umatilla and Morrow Counties,* p. 272; "From Eastern Oregon," *The Northwest,* 2 (February, 1884), 6. The last item reports with surprise the fact that experiments on the uplands in Rock Creek district yielded better than the bottomlands. Thus even at this date the old prejudice had to be broken by actual local test, not by inference from the by now comprehensive successes over so much of the land to the east. *The West Shore,* 13 (December, 1887), 844. After lengthy litigation, the courts finally sustained the Eastern Oregon Land Company in 1893.

[27] *Kittitas Standard,* July 28, 1883, as quoted in Lyman, *Yakima Valley,* p. 594.

Actually neither passengers nor drivers had to wait long for that time to come. In January of 1884 Villard's empire collapsed and the N.P. and O.R.&N. reverted to separate control. This left the northern transcontinental but an overly long and unprofitable line terminating in the bleak wastelands of Wallula, and construction of the Cascade division was hastily undertaken. The Ainsworth ferry was now shifted over to the Columbia to serve the new landing at Kennewick. At the same time, the railroad laid out the new town of Pasco on the north bank of the Columbia, which would serve as the junction of the Wallula and Yakima lines, and the operational terminus of the Idaho and Cascade divisions. As a result Ainsworth quickly faded away to an unlamented death. As soon as the grading commenced, the Yakima country was again the focus of great interest. Speculators began to swarm over the valley seeking attractive townsites, and farmers began to look over the bottomlands and the grassy slopes of the Horse Heaven and Rattlesnake hills. The first train arrived at Yakima city on Christmas Eve, 1884, but, to the consternation of local citizens, a month or so later the railroad laid out a new town beyond the gap four miles to the north and made clear its intentions of developing North Yakima as the commercial center of the valley. It was an old railroad trick, prompted usually by a refusal to pay the prices demanded for station and yard land and by an interest in the profits from town lot sales on their own lands. In this instance the former was evidently the main factor, for the company offered free lots in the new town to those businesses that would move. The response was fairly good and a number of houses and stores were loaded intact onto the cars or dragged along on rollers to their new locations; some, indeed, reportedly staying open for business en route. However, not all citizens enjoyed having the railroad dictate the destinies of communities so decisively, and the net result was a bitter rivalry between the old town and the new.[28]

Construction of the remainder of the Cascade division was a difficult, slow, and costly job. Service was opened to Ellensburgh in 1886, and a tortuous, temporary switchback completed over Stampede Pass in the following year. In May, 1888, the tunnel under the

[28] "North Yakima and the Cascade Branch," *The Northwest*, 2 (September, 1884), 7-8; Lyman, *Yakima Valley*, pp. 337-41, 394-95, 401; "The Yakima Country," *The Northwest*, 2 (February, 1884), 14.

Cascade crest was finished, and the first adequate through service to Puget Sound initiated.[29]

Collusion and Competition

The divorce of the O.R.&N. from the N.P. directly affected regional as well as transcontinental strategies. The traffic of the rich Palouse country became the main focus of interest. The railroad situation there was peculiar; in the separation of the companies, the O.R.&N. gained control of the Columbia and Palouse, even though that line was physically a branch from the N.P. and could be reached by the O.R.&N. only over the N.P. tracks between Wallula and Palouse Junction (Connell). Nevertheless, the new parent was quick to further the development of its isolated child. In 1885, following the original strategy suggested to tap the best portions of the Palouse, the line was extended from Colfax to Moscow, and in the following year a branch was built from Colfax to Farmington. Because the O.R.&N. had also, as part of the separation agreement, received title to the huge block of Palouse lands held by the Oregon Improvement Company, it was now in an excellent position to capitalize upon the fast-mounting wealth of this area.[30]

The Northern Pacific, on the other hand, suddenly found itself almost closed out of its most promising tributary territory, and soon decided that it was "compelled for the protection of its interests," not only to build into the Palouse but to invade the Walla Walla country. A line was surveyed from Marshall, near Spokane Falls, into the apex of the Palouse grainlands at Spangle and on south, bisecting the richest part and cutting diametrically across the extending tentacles of its rival. By the time the O.R.&N. had opened service to Farmington, in the autumn of 1886, the N.P. had reached nearby Belmont.[31]

[29] Northern Pacific Railway, *Annual Report, Sept. 16, 1887*, p. 14. The bridge across the Columbia at Kennewick was opened also in that season; Northern Pacific Railway, *Annual Report, Sept. 20, 1888*, pp. 16, 83.

[30] The original Oregon Improvement Company holdings totaled 149,011 acres in the Palouse. The O.R.&N. received 112,408 acres in the allocations of 1884. See Oregon Improvement Company, *Second Annual Report*, 1882, p. 16; Oregon Improvement Company, *Report, June, 1884*, p. 25; and Oregon Railway and Navigation Company, *Annual Report, June 30, 1884*, p. 11.

[31] "The Railroad Situation in Washington and Oregon," *The Northwest*, 3 (December, 1885), 11. All dates of construction of N.P. branch lines have been derived from an official unpaged mimeographed report, "Branch Line Data,

In January, 1887, a new corporate situation developed when the O.R.&N. was brought under the control of the Union Pacific. To the N.P. it was a change at once ominous and hopeful. If the competition continued, it now promised to be even more intense, with the O.R.&N. able to draw upon the resources of its giant parent; yet a new directorate also opened the possibility of new territorial agreements.[32] And in fact such an agreement was proposed by the Union Pacific and readily accepted by the N.P. The pact covered numerous relationships, but the principal regional result was the allocation of all the area north of the Snake to the N.P. and the preservation of all south for the O.R.&N. It was a decision with immense strategic implications to the Northwest. The Columbia and Palouse would be transferred to the N.P., and the whole northern portion of the interior would be diverted from its historic focus down the Columbia and oriented instead to Puget Sound. On the other hand, the threatened invasion of the Walla Walla by the N.P. was stifled, and the whole southern sector of the interior would remain entirely the sphere of the Portland line. To Wall Street directors this kind of domination of areas was more satisfactory than competitive constructions from which neither company might garner an adequate traffic.

What was good for the companies was of course not necessarily good for the regions affected. Farmers and tradesmen in the Palouse and Walla Walla were vehemently opposed. With as yet no form of government regulation of freight rates, competition was the only means of achieving reductions, and local people could only regard such an agreement as a vicious expression of monopolistic exploitation; for them, not only the more miles of track, but the more companies, the better. But the most effective cry came from Portland, where the business interests strenuously objected to the prospect of losing the entire trade of the Palouse. Further, the Coeur d'Alene district was rapidly becoming a major mining region. Gold had been

---

Western District, May, 1922," made available to me by the office of the Assistant General Passenger Agent, N.P. General Offices, St. Paul, Minnesota.

[32] The ensuing situation is generally well covered by Hedges, *Villard;* however, I have relied primarily upon the detailed presentation by Paul Rigdon, in his "Historical Catalogue, Union Pacific Historical Museum," an encyclopaedia of Union Pacific history available in the Office of Public Relations, U.P. General Offices, Omaha, Nebraska. The pertinent materials, gathered by Rigdon from company records and other historical sources, are found in Vol. VIII, and as these can be readily located in the comprehensive index under the general item "Villard–O.R.&N.–Oregon & Transcontinental," detailed citations are omitted.

discovered there in 1882, causing a small rush, but now large silver deposits had also been found and the prospects greatly magnified.[33] Because of these railroad manipulations, Portland would not be able to serve this first big revival in the mining hinterland which had been the basis of its greatest prosperity twenty years before. Whereas local citizens might be ignored, the Portland interests could not. In fact, some were directors of the O.R.&N., who felt that their New York overlords in the Union Pacific had badly abused their profitable child in the Northwest.

Under such pressures the issue was reopened. To modify the territorial allocations, the O.R.&N. was given authority to build a line along the north bank of the Snake from Riparia to Lewiston, thus allowing it contact with the southern margins of the Palouse. But the relationship between the companies soon became tense and suspicious. In the Walla Walla, a man named George W. Hunt was busy surveying a series of rail lines; though Hunt was ostensibly a local entrepreneur, there was good reason to suspect that he was secretly sponsored by the N.P.[34] When the federal government also showed signs of clamping down on this type of corporate collusion and dominance, and when a private legal opinion suggested that the joint agreement could not be upheld in court, the scheme collapsed and the leadership of the companies became mutually antagonistic.

To the joy of local residents, these Wall Street antagonisms unleashed a veritable frenzy of competitive building in the Palouse and Walla Walla. The first and imperative move by the O.R.&N. was to connect its isolated Palouse lines to the rest of its system. This was achieved by bridging the Snake at Riparia (Texas Ferry) and building up Alkali Flat to a junction with the old Columbia and Palouse line at La Crosse. While this was being completed in the summer of 1888, other construction crews were busy extending the Farmington branch—north along the margins of the Palouse through Rockford and down into the valley to Spokane Falls. In the few years since the completion of the Northern Pacific, Spokane Falls, which was virtually created by the railroad, had become the largest city in the interior and seemed destined to become the trade focus of a huge hinterland. Further, a branch from this new extension was

[33] *History of North Idaho,* pp. 984-94.

[34] The importance of these regional questions and the way in which the N.P. was poised for action in case of a breakdown in negotiations is evident in the Northern Pacific Railway, *Annual Report, Sept. 15, 1887,* pp. 56, 67-68.

constructed east from Tekoa, across the Coeur d'Alene Indian Reservation, to Wallace in the heart of the new mining district. Finally, a line was built from Winona, on the lower Palouse River, along a northeasterly arc to Seltice, just beyond Farmington. This was designed to enlarge its command of the burgeoning Palouse traffic. The general manager of the O.R.&N., who had made a personal reconnaissance, reported to the President of the Union Pacific that every mile of this latter line passed through "as fine wheat, stock, and fruit land as I ever saw east or west, rapidly settling up with thrifty intelligent farmers, the O.R.&N. cannot occupy this territory too quickly."[35] All these branch lines were completed by the end of 1889. Thus, in two years the O.R.&N. had not only furthered its position in the Palouse grainlands, but had reached out to challenge the Northern Pacific at Spokane Falls and in the Coeur d'Alene, two valuable areas which the N.P. had regarded as properly part of its inviolable domain.

But the Northern Pacific just as vigorously responded to that challenge. Its Palouse line, previously halted at Belmont, was pushed on through Palouse City to the Genesee district. When completed, in June of 1888, it provided a north-south trunk line through a hundred miles of the richest lands, cutting directly across the earlier O.R.&N. branches to Farmington and Moscow. In 1890 a branch was sent east from Belmont toward the timber lands of the upper Palouse River, but only the six miles to Farmington were completed. A more significant construction begun in that same year was a branch east from Pullman to Moscow, thence curving southward down into the Potlatch Canyon toward the Clearwater River. The ultimate objective was Lewiston and a position from which eventual penetration of the Clearwater and Camas Prairie districts could be made, although for the time being construction was halted at Juliaetta, where service opened in July, 1891.

South of the Snake the competition was equally intense, though there it was largely a matter of a Northern Pacific invasion of an area in which the O.R.&N. felt that it had a sufficient system to command the major part of the traffic. Prior to the outbreak of this rivalry, the O.R.&N. had constructed its Pataha branch to Pomeroy, in conformance with its original strategy. Now it built only the

[35] Union Pacific Railway, *Letters Received*, W. H. Holcomb to Chas. F. Adams, Farmington, W.T., May 1, 1888, Vol. 83 (Union Pacific Archives, Omaha).

short link necessary to complete the Walla Walla and Pendleton route and then held on while the N.P. busily conspired to steal as much traffic as possible. The N.P. instrument in this region was the Oregon and Washington Territory Railway, popularly known as the Hunt system. The O.&W.T. was designed to be primarily an agricultural line, and it made no attempt to give the most direct connections between towns but sought to cut through farming districts in such a manner as to garner the maximum grain traffic.[36] The first segment constructed was that from Attalia (near Wallula) northeastward along the entire axis of Eureka Flat. From Eureka a branch was angled southward through the Touchet district to Walla Walla and then looped on northeastwardly to Waitsburg and Dayton. Only that portion between Waitsburg and Dayton was directly parallel with the O.R.&N. Further penetrations were made from Wallula southeastward to Centerville (Athena) and to Pendleton. Each terminus was already served by the O.R.&N., but the lines cut through farming country some distance from rival stations. The Hunt system was completed in 1889.

The fact that the O.R.&N. stood by and did not engage in competitive construction while these 160 miles of new railway were built in its heretofore private domain was the result of its assessment of the qualities of the main areas involved. The O.R.&N. did in fact have construction crews poised for action, and when they discovered Hunt's intention of tapping Eureka Flat a counterinvasion was immediately considered. However, a reconnaissance of that district in the spring of 1888 was enough to dissuade the move. It was an unusually dry year even for that dry area, the wheat crop was withering in the fields, and the settlers were all hauling domestic and stock water in from the Touchet River. In the opinion of the O.R.&N. general manager, "it would certainly seem to be wrong to have two parallel lines anywhere" in any of the lands west of Walla Walla city, which appeared to offer "scarcely business enough to support one." Thus, content that his company was already sufficiently entrenched in the good lands to the east, he urged that "they turn their attention as rapidly as possible to the Palouse country, . . . which every well informed person will tell you is far superior to all other wheat country in Washington Territory, or Oregon."[37]

[36] On the strategy of the Hunt system, see *The Northwest*, 7 (October, 1889), 16.
[37] Union Pacific Railway, *Letters Received*, W. H. Holcomb to Chas. F. Adams, May 17, 1888. See also letter of May 1, 1888.

Although the strategic battleground between these two giant systems was limited (within the Great Columbia Plain) to the two oldest and richest farming districts, there were other areas beyond the scope of this rivalry which could be advantageously tapped by railway extension. For the O.R.&N., the whole of northern Oregon between The Dalles and Pendleton was a tributary region whose citizens were anxious for branch lines that would eliminate the long hauls from the plateau down into the Columbia canyon. However, these districts were not developing with the rapidity of the Walla Walla or Palouse; and they were so isolated by several deep canyons that a series of feeder lines would be necessary, no one of which seemed likely as yet to garner a heavy traffic. Accordingly, only the least expensive and most promising was built at this time: the line up Willow Creek, passing through the expanding wheat district around Lexington and terminating at Heppner, a major wool shipping point.[38]

The Northern Pacific, on the other hand, was in an ideal position to expand into the Big Bend, a huge area of far greater potential which was rapidly being colonized. Moreover, although that country seemed beyond the aspirations of the O.R.&N., there were dangers from other sources. In 1888 the Seattle, Lake Shore and Eastern Company began grading a roadbed between Spokane Falls and Davenport, which was to be part of a trunk line across the Big Bend and over Snoqualmie Pass to Seattle. Northern Pacific surveyors had already located a route for a branch in this direction, and the N.P. quickly dispatched a small crew far to the west to grade a roadbed through the "middle pass" across the Grand Coulee, in order to establish a prior claim at that strategic point. Then construction was begun on a branch from the main line at Cheney toward Davenport and points beyond. In itself, the S.L.S.&E. was not a grave threat, for it was an independent company with meager resources. It reached Davenport in October, 1889, but only with contributions of land, labor, and money from local citizens, and by this time the N.P. was in Almira, forty-six miles west, and was preparing the way to the Grand Coulee. The danger was that a major rival would get control and make the S.L.S.&E. an instrument of invasion. By the end of

---

[38] For a description of this area and its need for a railroad, see J. W. Redington, "Heppner and Morrow County," *The West Shore,* 13 (November, 1887), 773-74. This branch was completed in December, 1888.

1890 the N.P. could be well satisfied with its efforts and strategy in the Big Bend. The branch known as the Washington Central was now completed to Coulee City, the pass across the Grand Coulee was graded, and extension on to the Columbia could be made "as fast as circumstances will justify." Furthermore, much to the dismay of local citizens who had subsidized it as a competing line, the N.P. had gained corporate control of the S.L.S.&E.[39]

Further Stimulus

This last outburst of railway building in the late 1880's, like those preceding it, had a marked impact upon the pace and direction of settlement expansion. The Walla Walla and Palouse countries, though the focus of the great rivalry, were less directly affected than other areas simply because the best lands had already been taken. Only those lines which tapped the drier western margins, such as the Pleasant Valley line north from Winona, and the O.&W.T. lines in Eureka Flat and Oregon, directly stimulated further colonization. The Big Bend was the most active frontier, expanding concurrently in two divergent directions, each prompted by different circumstances (Map 33). One area of interest was the land along the N.P. main line southwest of Ritzville. Here the railroad had been in service for several years, but farming had expanded only by gradual experimentation. It was dry country, sparsely grassed and treeless, yet wheat appeared to be moderately successful, and year by year the farmers were finding "that the arid belt begins a little further west than had heretofore been supposed." By 1888, the Ritzville district had become sufficiently developed for the town to seek incorporation, and in that same year a store and post office were opened at

---

[39] Steele and Rose, *Big Bend Country*, pp. 86, 88-89. Another segment of the S.L.S.&E. was also being built east from Seattle. Northern Pacific Railway, *Annual Report, Oct. 17, 1889*, pp. 11, 43.

And in fact agents of the Great Northern were known to be making reconnaissances through the Big Bend. The N.P. had good reason to fear that this line, steadily pushing across Dakota and Montana, would transform the Big Bend into another costly battleground. Further, if the Great Northern built across the Big Bend to Puget Sound, it would have a much shorter route than the N.P., which looped far south and up the Yakima Valley. Thus the N.P. line from Cheney westward was designed not only to capture a rich and rapidly developing area but also as a segment of a possible short cut which would be important if competition "in the matter of time of through trains to the Pacific Coast" became a reality. Northern Pacific Railway, *Annual Report, Sept. 15, 1887*, p. 68.

EXPANSION INTO THE BIG BEND

BASED UPON MAPS OF LAND STATUS WITHIN THE LAND GRANT
OF THE NORTHERN PACIFIC RAILROAD CO.

LAND SOLD OR CLAIMED AS OF

■ AUGUST 1, 1884   ■ APRIL 1, 1887   ■ JULY 1, 1891

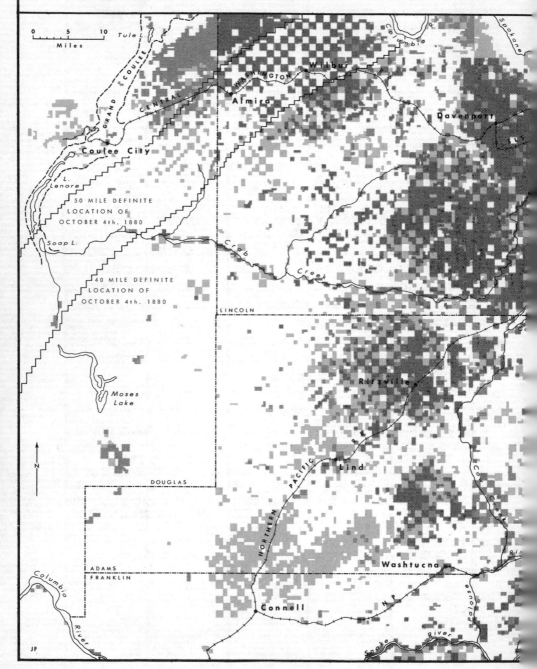

Map 33

Lind, seventeen miles down the track in the heart of Adams County.[40]

Claims were being taken up all over the country, even well to the south where the bunch grass began to give way to sagebrush. Prudent observers regarded this expansion as a gamble, but there was a mounting enthusiasm for taking the risk. The most vigorous extension of the farming frontier, however, was directly westward across the northern Big Bend. This was higher, wetter, obviously richer country, and landseekers and townsite promoters swarmed out ahead of the railroads building west of Davenport. By the time the N.P. completed its Washington Central branch, almost the entire band of country from Davenport to the Grand Coulee had been taken up, and a series of towns—most notably Wilbur, Almira, and Coulee City—were booming with activity. Well beyond, a wholly new nucleus of colonization was developing in the Badger Mountain district, a fertile, attractive country lying high above the Columbia. The southern slope of Badger Mountain (which was not much of a mountain but merely an upturned edge of the plateau surface) was steep, cut with ravines, and forested. The timber, plus nearby springs, provided the requisites of colonization around Waterville, the seat of Douglas County. The town was not platted until 1886, but underwent an unusually vigorous promotion which attracted much attention to the whole district. As yet it was the "Ultima Thule of the Big Bend," remote from adequate transportation facilities, but the residents were certain that the N.P. would soon arrive, while local entrepreneurs in Ellensburg were busy with a scheme to build a railroad to the Columbia and tap the district by means of riverboats. In the summer of 1888 the "City of Ellensburg" made a successful ascent over Priest Rapids and on up to the mouth of the Okanogan, apparently assuring the soundness of the idea.[41]

The aggressiveness of Ellensburg interests was a good expression of the stimulus given to another area by the most recent railway constructions. Long poised for a boom, the arrival of the trains set off a vigorous promotion in the Kittitas Valley. However, the pattern here was different. This was not regarded as dryland grain

[40] "New Regions for Farmers," *The Northwest*, 6 (August, 1888), 2; Steele and Rose, *Big Bend Country*, pp. 775, 782.

[41] Steele and Rose, *Big Bend Country*, pp. 541-44, 572; *The Northwest*, 6 (September, 1888), 29; "Ellensburg, in Central Washington," *The Northwest*, 7 (April, 1889), 16. (Note that by now "h" had been dropped from the name of Kittitas community.)

country, and landseekers confined themselves rather closely to the half dozen small creeks which focused into the central valley. Irrigation of orchards, grains, and hay would be the basis of agricultural wealth, but it would take time to develop major facilities. Thus the boom was much more an urban than a rural one, and the railroad was of especial importance. The N.P. made Ellensburg the headquarters of the Cascade division, thereby giving it a major payroll, and also began to exploit the coal and timber resources along the upper Yakima River, making both readily accessible to local merchants. With the completion of the Cascade line, Ellensburg became another portal into the Great Columbia Plain; not a major one, for western Washington and its ports were a poor source of immigrants as compared with Portland and the Willamette, and the best farming lands were a long distance from the Kittitas Valley; yet freighting teams were following trails to the Columbia, and land seekers began to use the town as a base for reconnaissance of the Wenatchee and Badger Mountain districts. If the volume of such traffic was as yet small, the aspirations of Ellensburg to become the metropolis of central Washington were not.

Despite the fifteen hundred miles of line built in this decade, there were still several areas beyond the reach of the iron roads. The center of the region, lying between the Rattlesnake Hills and the Grand Coulee, was a void, but of course its dry character made it unattractive to settlers. Had it been better country, it certainly would have been opened up early by means of riverboats on the Columbia. The Lewiston hinterland—the Asotin ' country, Clearwater Valley, and Camas Prairie—was also untapped. But the river boats did provide some service, and the comparative stagnation of this corner was more the result of the imprisonment of the best block of lands in the Nez Perces Reservation than of inadequate transportation. Likewise, the districts lying back from the Columbia east of The Dalles had been bypassed by the railroads, and this had retarded the pace and scale of their settlement. Yet neither side was utterly remote, and although agriculture development progressed more slowly than in more favored areas, by the end of the decade most of the good land had been taken. The older settled portions of the Klickitat country had only a relatively short haul to the river, and the newer districts of the Horse Heaven Hills to the east could haul either to the Columbia or over to Mabton or Prosser stations on the N.P. Yakima line.[42] Settlers on the high plains on the Oregon side had a longer haul, but when they did reach the Columbia they could load directly on to the railroad rather than the much less adequate ferries.

Aside from these few corners of the region, railroads and pioneers had proceeded together in the astonishingly rapid development of the Great Columbia Plain. Their interdependent relationship in the settlement process was complex. In most of the best farming districts, the settlers had come first and the railroads had followed; along some of the trunk routes, the railroad was the pioneer and lured the farmer after. Certainly, transportation was a critical factor, and wherever the farmers did range beyond the reach of existing facilities, they did so in confident expectation that they would soon be served.

Old Problem—New Form

But if gaining a railroad was essential, that alone was not regarded as sufficient. While it was obviously necessary to have the facilities to move the harvest, it must be done at a rate profitable to the harvesters. One railroad was essential, two were regarded by the shippers as highly desirable, and a competing river service along the trunk route to the sea would be ideal insurance against collusion between the railroad managements. While the 1880's mark the emergence and triumph of the railroads and the sudden decline and near demise of the riverboats, interest in the historic waterways remained high, and in fact the first real efforts toward navigation improvement were made concurrent with this burgeoning railroad era.[43]

Actually, authorization of the first major aid to navigation, the construction of a canal around the Cascades, was made in 1877, prior to any definite railroad invasion of the interior. That facility, long sought by most Northwest interests, was finally approved in response to the steadily growing traffic and the burdensome costs. But in fact the work proceeded so slowly, being dependent upon

[42] Robert Ballou, *Early Klickitat Valley Days* (Goldendale, Wash., 1938), p. 476.

[43] This situation was common elsewhere in the country. In the East the railroads had usurped the traffic of the extensive canal and river systems, but the problem of rates and need for competition were intensified. See *Report of the Select Committee on Transportation—Routes to the Seaboard, April 24, 1874,* 43rd Cong., 1st sess., S. Rept. 307, Pt. 1 (1894), pp. 237-39 on the Columbia interior; and 45th Cong., 3rd sess., Ex. Doc. 32, Pt. 3 (1879).

meager annual appropriations, that, far from a satisfaction, it became a source of chronic frustration through the years when it was most needed. Numerous other surveys were also made of the regular navigation routes, and attention was even extended to waterways well beyond existing services. Lieutenant Symons made a detailed reconnaissance of the upper Columbia between Kettle Falls and the Snake in 1881, and even at that early date he was so sanguine of the settlement prospects of the Big Bend that he recommended a boat railway be constructed around Priests Rapids and other lesser improvements be made in order that service could be extended as soon as necessary.[44]

By far the greatest attention, however, was logically focused upon The Dalles–Celilo, where, as John H. Mitchell phrased it in good senatorial language, "nature has with unmerciful and unsparing hand placed an absolute embargo on the navigation of the waters of this the second river on the continent." The spectacular series of falls and rapids at this gateway to the interior had now been studied and tested in detail. The low falls, the narrow troughs, and the extremely high velocity of the river precluded the feasibility of mere channel improvement, and all engineering studies reported the need for some sort of bypass. A canal would be an obvious remedy, but there were also recommendations that two boat railways be constructed to carry the riverboats around the principal obstructions (Map 32). Whatever the means, the need for a solution to this "key point in the commercial strategy of the Pacific Northwest" was widely understood.[45]

[44] 47th Cong., 1st sess., S. Ex. Doc. 186 (1882), esp. pp. 61-62 on Priest Rapids.

[45] 50th Cong., 1st sess., S. Rept. 859 (1888), p. 10. The total fall over the 13 miles varied from 81.4 feet at extreme low water to 56.5 feet at extreme high water (the flood of 1876). The narrowest trough varied from 125 feet at low water to 1,250 feet at high. River steamboats had actually been taken down over the falls and through the rapids, but only at high water seasons and at great risk; all were damaged, and these trips were made not to bring down cargo but only the boats themselves, which had become surplus on the upper river after the railroad had been built. Charles F. Powell, *Survey of the Columbia River at The Dalles in Oregon*, 47th Cong., 1st sess., S. Ex. Doc. 184 (1882), pp. 6-7; Mills, *Sternwheelers,* pp. 131-32.

Suggested designs for the railways called for a carriage of 190 x 48 feet dimensions, rolling on 21 sets of wheels on a track of 25½ feet gauge, to be pulled by a cable from a stationary steam engine. The fact that the riverboats were flat-bottomed and lacked keels would make such devices rather simple to

The experiences in the Northwest now proved, as was already evident in the East, that railroads were not enough, and that "competing water-ways only can keep freight and passenger rates within reasonable bounds. . . . The water may not carry the freight, but it forces the railway to a reasonable rate." The O.R.&N. had withdrawn its boats on the upper Columbia trunk line, but it was not enough merely to replace these boats by those of another, competing company. Through water service was essential, not only because of the inevitably high costs of transshipment but simply because the O.R.&N. controlled the strategic portage right of ways at both The Dalles and the Cascades. This profitable position had always brought that company ample abuse, but none more resounding than this denunciation by Senator John H. Mitchell in the late 1880's:

... the Columbia River being the only real pass through which the productions of the Great Columbia Basin or inland empire can find their way to the seaboard, it has been made possible for one corporation engaged in the business of transportation to intrench itself as a powerful tax-gatherer and collector of tribute at these gates of commerce on this grand river, and thus absolutely control the navigation of the waters of the Columbia and its tributaries from their source to the sea, and dictate the terms of its commerce.

It has been made clear ... that ... from the earliest period of the establishment of civilization in the far West, a corporation, the Oregon Railway and Navigation Company, and its immediate predecessor, the Oregon Steam Navigation Company, have held undisputed sway over the waters of the Columbia and its tributaries, with no restraint or restriction whatever on their power, discretion, or disposition in the establishment of rates of transportation to which the producers and shippers are subjected, save and except one, the ability and willingness of the producer or shipper to respond to their demand. . . .

That the waters of any one river on God's green earth, much less one so grandly magnificent in volume, length, and every other respect as the Columbia, endowed with all those elements of greatness and grandeur and moral and physical power that constitute and characterize the greatest of the great internal water-ways of the world, should be dom-

construct. William A. Jones, *Annual Report on River Improvements in Oregon and Washington Territory, for the year ended June 30, 1885,* 49th Cong., 1st sess., S. Ex. Doc. 114 (1886), pp. 16, 32-34. Strongly built barges that could carry a load of wheat right through these obstacles were also suggested, but apparently the idea was not endorsed by any responsible engineer or steamboat captain; testimony of C. H. Dodd, vice-president of the Portland Board of Trade, in G. H. Mendall, *Obstructions to Navigation in Columbia River,* 50th Cong., 2nd sess., H. Ex. Doc. 73 (1889), p. 51.

inated and controlled by any one man or any set of men, or corporation, or company, is a standing reproach to the people or nation that
tolerates or permits it. . . .[46]

But such spirited outbursts proved of no more avail than the
chronic and less eloquent grumblings of farmers and merchants.
Neither canal nor boat railway was authorized at this time. By 1890
over a million and a quarter dollars had been expended on the
Cascades Canal, but it was still far from complete. A few minor
obstructions—sandbars, boulders, and reefs—had been cleared on
the Snake, but the "through waterway" so urgently demanded
seemed a long way off. The O.R.&N. boats still served the wheat
landings on the Snake, shuttling between Lewiston and the railroad
at Riparia, and service was still offered on the two sections between
Portland and The Dalles, but only to serve the Washington side and
the tourist business. Elsewhere the railroad ruled unchallenged.[47]

There was another hope, however, which for the first time waxed
strong in the late 1880's.The Oregon State Railroad Commission was
formed on April 1, 1887, and immediately undertook to investigate
the widespread complaints about exorbitant rates on wheat and wool
shipments from the interior. Two months later it requested the
O.R.&N. to make reductions of about 25 per cent. The railroad
agreed to reduce its tariffs but not so drastically, and although the
commission strongly protested this failure to comply fully, it was not
as yet empowered to enforce its recommendations. However, a group
of Walla Walla citizens immediately filed protests with the newly
formed Interstate Commerce Commission in Washington, and the
railroad was thereby ordered to make further reductions. These
were still not to the level desired by the local commission, but the
battle had been joined, some amelioration achieved, and the railroad placed upon the defensive. Now forced to file with a public
commission not only its rates but its whole financial position, the
railroad came under continuous scrutiny, and charges and profits
were revealed to be well above those prevailing in most other parts

[46] 48th Cong., 2nd sess., H. Ex. Doc. 7, Pt. 3 (1885), p. 556. See also Watson
C. Squire, "Resources and Development of Washington Territory," *Message and
Report of the Governor of Washington Territory to the Legislative Assembly,
Session 1885-6* (Seattle, Wash., 1886), p. 21. 50th Cong., 1st sess., S. Rept. 859
(1888), p. 11.

[47] Summary of expenditures on various sections of the river is included in
51st Cong., 2nd sess., H. Ex. Doc. 6, Pt. 2 (1891), p. 992. See also T. S. Lang,
"Oregon," in 51st Cong., 2nd sess., H. Ex. Doc. 6, Pt. 2 (1891), p. 809.

of the nation. At least a beginning of public curbs upon the independent power of such corporations had been made.[48]

The whole problem of transport charges would remain a matter of general interest for decades, but in broader perspective, while important, it was not a really fundamental matter to regional development. That the high rates charged at this time reduced the prosperity of individual farmers and merchants seems apparent; that they markedly stifled enterprise and retarded expansion, as was so widely insisted, seems doubtful. The population of the region had increased by more than a hundred thousand in twenty years, dozens of new towns had been founded, and hundreds of local businesses initiated; improved acreage in farms had increased twenty-five fold, and "Walla Walla" wheat had become a staple on the world market. Immigrants were pouring in and the produce was pouring out, each in ever increasing volume. Despite monopolies, collusions, and high charges, a radically enlarged and improved system of physical facilities of transport was in being; every established district touched had been enormously stimulated, and whole new districts of great promise created. Railroads and settlers had together ushered in a new age in the Great Columbia Plain.

[48] This discussion is based upon Lang, "Oregon," pp. 784-86.

CHAPTER TEN

By a curious coincidence it appears...
that over the greater part of this region of small rainfall wheat is grown
without irrigation.

A. W. GREELY

A peculiarity of the soil of eastern
Washington is its apparently inexhaustible fertility.

MILES C. MOORE

Conquest: Some Patterns, Methods, and Ideas, 1870-90

DECLINE OF THE STOCKMEN

From Open Range to Ranches

THE 1880's marked a final shift in the balance of relationships and regional dominance between the stockmen and the farmers. It was a gradual change, extending over a period of three decades, though the ultimate result could readily be foreseen well before 1890. In the 1860's while agriculturists slowly established a small nucleus in the Walla Walla Valley, the stockmen had expanded over the whole southern half of the region and confirmed its qualities as a superior grazing country. In the 1870's the range cattle industry reached its peak, as the farmers, now discovering a much greater potential than heretofore known, began to establish numerous other clusters of set-tlement. Finally, in the 1880's the open-range cattle industry came to an end and was succeeded by smaller ranching operations and a still vigorous sheep industry, but the whole was rapidly being confined to those marginal districts unattractive to the extending wave of farmer colonists. In 1890, whereas the farmer could look ahead to a profit-able future in his enlarging new realm of conquest, the stockman, his ranks reduced and squeezed upon a dwindling portion of his old rangelands, knew that he had to look back to view his expansive years.

The depression of the early 1870's afflicted the stockmen even more than the farmer, for it was a prolongation of difficulties which had been developing for several years. There was no sufficient outlet for the expanding herds of cattle. The mining camps continued as the chief, but steadily dwindling, market. As large herds were held on the ranges, the older districts became heavily overstocked, and their quality began to deteriorate. The ranchers gradually entered new localities, but it was an expansion powered more by desperation than a vision of enlarged opportunities.[1]

The first indication of a change came in 1875 when buyers from Wyoming appeared and began to purchase cattle to be driven to the northern plains. In the following year this market proved even better, and over the next few seasons the cattle industry of the interior enjoyed a spurt of prosperity based largely upon the demands of Wyoming, eastern Montana, and the Dakotas. The sudden development of this new outlet was related to the final Indian wars of the northern plains. After the Black Hills gold discoveries, the whites moved relentlessly into this last home of the Indians in the mid-continent grasslands. A treaty with the Sioux and Cheyennes in 1876 prepared the way for the opening of a huge area, a new addition to the public domain available to any who could get cattle onto it first and establish their positions on the range. Thus stock was needed quickly and in large numbers. There were several possible sources. The farmers of the Midwest held large numbers of good quality cattle, but they were distributed among thousands of farms and not easily assembled into large herds; nor were they obtainable at cheap prices. The ranges on the periphery of the new area—in western Montana, around Cheyenne, and in Nebraska—contributed but were so new that they lacked large surpluses. The two major areas where cattle were both plentiful and cheap were Texas and the interior Pacific Northwest, and thus the historic cattle drives of each area—the one north to Kansas, the other east to the mining districts —were revived and extended until they met in the northern plains.[2]

[1] On the status of the stock industry at this time, see Splawn, *Ka-mi-akin*, p. 291; Lewis, *Big Bend Country*, p. 10; J. Orin Oliphant, "The Eastward Movement of Cattle from the Oregon Country," *Agricultural History*, 20 (January, 1946), 23.

[2] Splawn, *Ka-mi-akin*. On the history of the cattle industry in the northern plains, see Harold E. Briggs, *Frontiers of the Northwest: A History of the Upper Missouri Valley* (New York, 1950), chap. iii, and Ernest Staples Osgood, *The Day of the Cattleman* (Chicago, 1929).

The "Oregon cattle" (as all the herds from the Northwest were called in the markets to the east) had certain definite advantages over Texas stock. They were largely of Durham (or shorthorn) type and were much better beef producers than the wild, rangy longhorns, yet they were hardy, proven range animals. Further, they were free of disease, and tick fever was proving to be a problem with Texas cattle. Thus, each spring the buyers swarmed into Walla Walla and out over the ranges of the Palouse, Yakima, and northern Oregon to recruit large herds for the drives eastward.[3]

Some cattle were trailed over the old Mullan Road through western Montana, but much the greater number were driven along the old Oregon Trail into Wyoming. Buyers in the Palouse country commonly assembled their herds in the southwest corner, there to swim them across the Snake at Lyons Ferry. Yakima cattle and those from the Big Bend were driven to the Columbia-Snake junction. These herds then converged upon the Walla Walla Valley and were driven over the Blue Mountains to Baker City, Oregon, another major assembly point for ranges south of the mountains. From there they were trailed in herds of various sizes on across the Snake River Plains. A typical report of one of the larger drives illustrates something of the outfit and procedures:

> Messrs. Lang & Ryan recently purchased in Eastern Oregon, Washington and Idaho, for the Cheyenne market, 23,800 head of cattle, paying an average of $13 a head for them. . . . The outfit to drive these cattle East consists of 120 men, 40 wagons and 800 horses. The drive will be about nine miles per day, and will finally decrease to five miles per day as the hot weather approaches. They expect to be ready to "go East" by the 25th of April.

The total volume of this eastward movement is unrecorded, but it is clear that it was increasing rapidly in the late 1870's and was by far the most important outlet. The census of 1880 reported that a total of seventy-two thousand head had been driven during the previous season from Washington Territory to Wyoming, far more than to any other interstate market. Several thousand head were sold in the mining districts each year, and a few thousand were driven

[3] The general history of this movement is drawn from Oliphant's two articles, "Eastward Movement of Cattle" and "The Cattle Trade from the Far Northwest to Montana," *Agricultural History*, 6 (April, 1932), 69-83; and John K. Rollinson, *Wyoming Cattle Trails: History of the Migration of Oregon-raised Herds to Mid-Western Markets* (Caldwell, Ida., 1948).

across the Cascades to Puget Sound, but all of these together were but a fraction of the export to the East.[4]

The scale of individual operations remained rather small compared with those in Texas and the Great Plains. The total area of the range country was much less, and it was further segmented by major rivers, canyons, and ridges which cattle would not readily cross. Probably typical of the more permanent operations was one in the Klickitat country described in 1879.[5] The range consisted of about 12,500 square miles of public domain, all of it by now heavily overgrazed. The herd numbered about 5,000, including 1,725 calves branded during that year. Five hundred head were marketed, mostly steers which brought an average of twenty dollars a piece. Natural losses ran about 10 per cent. The only land owned was 160 acres upon which a house, two barns, and corrals were located. None of the land was cultivated, nor were any of the meadows cut for hay. Because the rangeland was relatively rough country, the cattle tended to group into numerous small herds each grazing in a restricted locality, and there was no general cooperative roundup. Many calves were missed during the spring branding season, and once weaned these "slick-ears" (or "sleepers" or "mavericks") became open game for anyone who could put a brand on them. The number of calves branded "depends wholly upon one's vigilance," and some stockmen were known to brand more calves than they had cows. This particular operator employed six men; others often kept fewer regularly and more during the branding and marketing season. Whatever the practice, wages were low, the investment in property and equipment (chiefly horses and saddles) was small, and so long as the market held, such cattle raising was profitable.

The very nature of the new market made it a temporary one, but an event in the interior sharply altered the situation even before the northern plains became fully stocked. Severe winters had occasionally caused losses of stock during the 1870's (1871-72 and 1874-75, especially) but the industry was naturally resilient, and these

[4] Lewis, *Big Bend Country*, p. 11; Viola Lawton (ed.), "History of Grazing in the State of Washington" (WPA MS in the Washington State University Library, Pullman), p. 19; *The West Shore*, 6 (March, 1880), 69; Clarence Gordon, "Report on Cattle, Sheep and Swine," *Tenth Census*, III, 139. See J. Orin Oliphant, "The Cattle Trade on Puget Sound, 1858-1890," *Agricultural History*, 7 (July, 1933), 129-49. *North Pacific Coast*, 1 (December, 1879), 7, reported that four thousand head had been driven over Snoqualmie Pass that year.

[5] *Tenth Census*, III, 135-36.

setbacks were no real deterrent to expansion. The disastrous season of 1861-62 so firmly fixed in the memory of the oldest settlers was only a legend to most of the present stockmen. The winter of 1880-81, however, proved a worthy rival of that famed year; if meteorologically it was not quite an equal, economically it was far more calamitous. Estimates of losses varied with different reports and localities, but typically ranged from 30 to more than 50 per cent, and thus totaled in the tens of thousands.[6] The main export surpluses were thus wiped out, many a stockman was financially ruined, and the whole industry was severely shaken.

This catastrophe marked the virtual end of the open-range cattle industry; ranching continued, but in the face of mounting difficulties. Anyone who wished to do more than engage in hazardous speculation now considered access to protected winter ranges and supplemental winter fodder to be essential precautions. Such stabilization required investment. Further, most of the ranges were now seriously depleted, and the over-all scale of stock raising would have to be adjusted more narrowly and closely to the sustaining qualities of the land. The Oregon, Klickitat, and Yakima areas were specifically noted as having been heavily overgrazed, and in the older districts the area available was also being reduced by the encroachments of the farmers. Barbed wire fences were beginning to cut up the ranges and the stock routes, and the controversy between farmer and stockman now flared over "herd law" legislation. Without fences, wandering stock damaged crops; with them they were themselves injured by the dangerous barbs—who was responsible for the damages in either case? Hardly had the argument become heated before it was ended by passage of "herd laws" which placed liabilities for damage upon the owners of trespassing livestock and gave full support to the fence builder. It was a perfect expression of the decisive shift in balance between the farmers and the stockmen in the region.[7]

[6] Oliphant, "Winter Losses," p. 13; Splawn, Ka-mi-akin, p. 291, estimated that 50,000 of a total of 150,000 head in the Yakima country perished.

[7] Stearns, Official Gazette, p. 54; Tenth Census, III, 135. For farmer-stockman controversy, see, e.g., the North-West Tribune (Colfax), Sept. 8, 1880; East Oregonian (Pendleton), Jan. 10, Feb. 28, April 10, 1880; North Pacific Coast, 1 (December, 1879), 10 (quotation from the Walla Walla Union). About herd laws, see, e.g., the Washington Territory law, which read, in part:

"Any person letting stock run loose shall be held accountable for all damages said stock may commit upon cultivated land when stock shall be found on or about the premises where damage was committed. It shall be lawful

The winter of 1880-81 had severely weakened the livestock industry precisely at the time when agriculture was being given a tremendous boost. In the Palouse country experimentation had given way to full confidence; the railroads had just now opened the Big Bend and seemed certain soon to tap every district. Indeed, at this very time it was finally being realized that wherever bunch grass would grow wheat would grow, which in general could mean only that wherever the stockman was the farmer would soon follow. The graziers had long disparaged the experiments of the farmers and were likely an important factor in prolonging the doubts entertained about the agricultural potential of the region. Their general theme was simply that when the farmer turned under the bunch grass and sowed wheat he destroyed a better crop than the one he raised. Their argument was well put by a Yakima spokesman in 1880:

> Farming must be confined to localities especially favored by nature, ... Yet we have those among us who are already trespassing on the stock range, regardless of nature, vainly endeavoring to achieve success, with prospects more futile than had the farmers of western Kansas and Nebraska, where for the past decade they have constantly battled against nature, even, with weapons to destroy the countless millions of grasshoppers, and with prayers long and loud to the end that the drouths might be choked off. . . . So with Yakima county and much . . . of the great Columbia Basin. It is true that certain portions of Walla Walla, Columbia and Whitman counties, and in a few other localities, oasis like spots are well adapted to agriculture and yield largely. But some of the antagonistic features are these: there is danger of getting only partial crops; the good and suitable land lies in too small patches for the most advantageous use and convenience of machinery; it takes one-half or more to shove the residue over the succession of portages up to Portland and down the slough to market. Whereas, on the other hand, in stock we never fail. Our machinery is simple, our conveyance is furnished by the marketables, the demand for our stock increases two fold, as California and other localities increase their population and diminish their stock ranges. In short we, the Columbia Basin, shall

---

for the owner of the premises to take such stock into custody and keep the same until such damages shall have been ascertained and established by court, when such animals by the order of the court be sold and after satisfying the judgment, the balance shall be turned over to the owner with certain reservations."

Laws of Washington Territory (Olympia, 1883), p. 55, as quoted in Todd Vernon Boyce, "A History of the Beef Cattle Industry in the Inland Empire" (M.A. thesis, State College of Washington, 1937), p. 106.

soon be obliged to furnish the Pacific slope with stock, without a note-worthy competitor. Hence would it not be advisable to farm a few of our most favored spots, just enough to amply supply home demand, and make all other pursuits subsidiary to stock raising?[8]

But by that time the evidence for rebuttal was already at hand. Nature clearly had not confined farming so narrowly, the railroads were readying to overcome the portages, and the great markets for livestock were an assumption as yet unsupported by the facts. And, indeed, a few months after this was written nature would give pow-erful evidence to suggest that the region might be better suited to wheat than cattle.

In the 1880's it was stock raising rather than farming which was being confined to a few "especially favored localities"—but favored only by being outside the realm of agricultural interest. In the Walla Walla and the Palouse, ranching become limited to the west-ern margins and along the Snake River: drier country, rough and broken by canyons, sparsely grassed but well sheltered in the winter. The scablands continued as an excellent ranching district, though now more cramped by farmers on either side and scattered within. The northernmost Big Bend was hardly grazed at all before the settlers moved in, but the southern portion—from Crab Creek to Pasco—was a lingering stronghold of open-range operations. Annual spring roundups were held, starting at the far south and working north. The cattle were sorted and branded and the surplus formed into trail herds or loaded at Northern Pacific stations for shipment east.[9] West and south of the Columbia much rangeland also re-mained, but again confined largely to the drier and rougher areas. The Yakima, Klickitat, and Oregon sections had the advantage of good summer pasture in the nearby mountains, but utilization of these grazing grounds required more attention to herding, and thus they were more readily occupied by the sheepmen than the cattle-men. And in these districts the competition from sheep was often more severe than that from farmers.

[8] *North-West Tribune,* Aug. 4, 1880; this letter was also reprinted in the *Spokan Times,* Aug. 14, 1880.

[9] Boyce, "Beef Cattle," p. 86; Fred R. Yoder, "Pioneer Social Adaptation in Lincoln County, Washington, 1875-90," *Research Studies of the State College of Washington,* 10 (September, 1942), 183-84. On rail shipments east, see Oli-phant, "Cattle Trade from the Northwest," and Joseph Nimmo, Jr., "The Range and Ranch Cattle Business of the United States," 48th Cong., 2nd sess., H. Ex. Doc. 7, Pt. 3 (1885), p. 170.

Sheep and Horses

The sheep industry, though in general contemporary in the region, tended to expand in the wake of the cattle industry. No actual warfare broke out between the two, but there was a constant antagonism marked by occasional threats and actions to drive the sheepman off what the cattlemen deemed to be their rightful ranges. A Yakima resident reported disgustedly that "cattle owners are running from a pestilence—sheep, . . . my range . . . has a band of scabby sheep at every watering-place." There ought to be law to confine sheep to certain localities, he insisted, or the cattlemen would be ruined. But the public range was as open to the one as the other, and though often temporarily deterred, the sheepmen gradually took command of a major portion of the remaining federal domain. There were several reasons for this. For one thing, the cattlemen so persistently overgrazed the land that its carrying capacity was steadily reduced; but even when it became only marginally profitable for cattle, it was in many cases adequate for sheep. Also, once grazed heavily by sheep, the grass was so closely cropped that cattle could not thrive (hence the eagerness of the cattlemen to prevent the slightest entry or passage of flocks). Further, while the market for cattle was erratic, that for wool was steadier, and there was the added advantage of being able to sell surplus sheep for slaughter when an outlet was available. Moreover, it appears that the sheep industry was better organized and managed. It had, certainly, its "tramp" operators who roamed over the public range without any permanent base, but the work itself was far more of a drudgery, the herder shared none of the glamour associated with the cowhand, the whole industry had none of the prestige of cattle raising, and therefore it did not attract nearly so much improvident and unlearned speculation.[10] Thus, while the fortunes of the cattle industry fluc-

---

[10] *Tenth Census*, III, 136. One of the few areas from which the sheepmen were successfully barred was the Badger Mountain district. When flocks were driven in in 1886, local farmers and ranchers held a meeting and demanded that the herders leave, which they did, though they were blamed for setting fire to much of the local timberland out of spite. They never returned to this area. Steele and Rose, *Big Bend Country*, p. 539.

Mutton sheep were often trailed eastward in large herds in the 1880's. *Tenth Census*, III, 139; Minto, "Sheep Husbandry," pp. 232-33. See also the financial records of sheep operators in Umatilla and in Walla Walla, detailed in *Tenth Census*, III, 133, 138-39. In the eleven years, 1870-80, the Umatilla firm had

tuated erratically, the sheepmen steadily expanded, invading boldly where possible, encroaching marginally where not, making good use of the mountain pastures in summer and the sagebrush in the winter, neither of which were highly valued by the cattlemen.

The scabland country and southern Big Bend became an important sheep area in the mid-1880's. Sprague was the major shearing center, as the bands could be driven there in late spring and then on to the mountains. The Snake River and Palouse flocks were herded east into Idaho, those of the Big Bend were mainly taken to the Colville uplands north of the Spokane and Columbia. Bands varied in size from about fifteen hundred to three thousand, and were principally hardy, thick-wooled grade Merinos or coarser-wooled Rambouillets. But even as the herder was replacing the cowboy, the farmer began to cramp his movements. Not only were the home ranges heavily stocked and being reduced by the expansion of farming, but access to the summer mountain pastures necessitated crossing an ever widening, ever more densely settled agricultural belt. When asked what his greatest difficulties were, a Sprague sheepman promptly replied, "The farmer and his shotgun."[11] The "great antipathy toward the sheep man" brought chronic harassment, and, together with the reductions in the available lands, soon caused many sheepmen in this area to shift their operations to Montana.

Elsewhere in Washington, the Yakima and Kittitas were the principal sheep areas, neither of which was as yet faced with severe restrictions. However, by far the most important sheep country was in northern Oregon between The Dalles and the Umatilla. The low-lying sand plains and canyons provided excellent wintering grounds, the plateau good transit grazing, and the open or thinly forested highlands to the south offered easily accessible summer pasture. Large bands were also ferried across the Columbia and driven into the Klickitat uplands for the summer season. Here, too, farming

---

sold ninety thousand dollars worth of wool and eighty-five hundred head, and had steadily raised its average numbers from fifteen hundred to twenty thousand. *The West Shore*, 7 (March, 1881), 82, expressed hope that the heavy winter losses would drive out "tramp" herders.

[11] Barton, "Washington," p. 994. My discussion of the sheep industry in this area is based primarily upon this source and Lawton, "Grazing in Washington," pp. 20-26, 43. For an additional report on Sprague as a wool shipping center, see "The Present and Future of Sprague," *The West Shore*, 13 (September, 1887), 658.

was expanding, but not on the same scale as eastern Washington, and the upland wheat districts were so fragmented by intervening rough country that they could not coalesce into a barrier separating the seasonal grazing grounds. The building of the railroad branch to Heppner made that place an ideal shearing point, midway between the winter and summer ranges, and it quickly became a large wool-shipping center. Pendleton, Arlington, and The Dalles were also important.[12]

Horses were yet another of the range animals of the interior at this time. Cattlemen necessarily kept large number for their own needs and often had surpluses for sale. More important were the wild bands of "cayuses" which roamed the more arid country of the middle Columbia. When crossed with "American" sires, these Indian horses produced an excellent hardy animal suitable for saddle, driving, or light farm work. Farmers throughout the Northwest offered a considerable market, and in the latter 1880's several hundred horses were annually shipped or trailed to the East.[13] Though never a large activity, the annual roundup and shipment of horses remained a vestige of the range operations for many years.

By 1890 the livestock industry of the interior had nearly completed a full phase of change and was very different from that of twenty years before. The open-range cattle era was virtually past, and ranching, restricted to a few locales, was now a relatively minor part of the over-all regional economy. Cattle were being sent to the rising cities on the Pacific coast, but shipments to the East had almost ceased. The range sheep industry of eastern Washington was nearly gone, and the more permanent operations were narrowly confined. West of the Columbia sheep remained more important but with little room for expansion. On the other hand, south of the Columbia in Oregon the sheepmen were becoming established on a major scale: over half a million head were held, the industry was becoming better organized, and wool was more important than wheat over the country from The Dalles to the Umatilla. Aside from these areas, the gleaning of the freely offered bounty of nature had been but an initial, preparatory phase in the full "domestication" of the Great Columbia Plain.

[12] *Klickitat, Yakima, and Kittitas,* p. 107; Redington, "Heppner and Morrow County," p. 773; Minto, "Sheep Husbandry," pp. 232-35, 242.
[13] Yoder, "Lincoln County," p. 184; Ballou, *Klickitat Valley,* p. 193.

THE FARMERS

Obtaining Land

The plow steadily turned under the bunch grass, not simply because the land produced excellent crops but because the stockman had no legal means of resistance. By any of the various federal land acts he could gain title to a quarter section to insure his homesite. He might file for two or three times as much land by taking advantage of the several different acts, although to fulfill their legal requirements he would have to become something of a farmer himself and demonstrate certain "improvements." Such technicalities were no doubt successfully avoided in numerous cases, and by an even bolder flaunting of the law more area might be acquired through bogus filings by hired hands and with the assistance of corrupt, gullible, or simply overworked government officials. But there was no sure way of acquiring sufficient acreage for a successful range livestock operation. The earning capacity of grazing lands was too small to warrant outright purchase in any quantity from either the government or the railroad, and neither offered any type of long-term lease. Thus, although the stockman was widely regarded by others as a parasite who gathered his profits from lands he did not own, he could do nothing else. Once the farmer, land company, or speculator began to move in upon his range, he had no means to impede them. No doubt much of the heavy overstocking of the ranges was simply a frantic attempt to make the most of an opportunity that was rapidly disappearing.

The farmer, on the other hand, had an increasing number of choices in the method of obtaining clear title. In most localities, the homestead and the pre-emption were the principal means of acquiring government land. Under the former any citizen (or anyone declaring his intention of becoming one) who was head of a family or a single man over 21 could obtain 160 acres free (except for a modest filing fee) by residing "continuously" on the claim for five years and making certain minimal "improvements." Under the pre-emption law anyone with the same qualifications could acquire 160 acres after but six months of residence, at a cost of $1.25 per acre. In 1873 Congress added a third method by passage of the Timber Culture Act, designed specifically to benefit settlers upon the western prairies. Title to 160 acres was to be granted to any settler who planted 40 acres (reduced in 1878 to 10 acres) with a prescribed number of trees and maintained a certain portion over a period of ten years (later reduced to eight years). Finally, in 1877 the Desert Land Act allowed the purchase of 640 acres at $1.25 per acre upon proof that it had been placed in irrigation within three years after the original filing.[14]

The full details of these laws revealed an even greater flexibility. Certain types of claims could be converted from one form to another, and as "permanent" residence was required only on homesteads, a settler could file for more than one type of claim simultaneously. More significantly, there were innumerable ways in which the letter of the law—the meaning of which was often far from clear even to those who tried to administer it—could be evaded. The Timber Culture and Desert Land acts were notoriously abused, but the fault was as much that of naïve legislators as of conniving land seekers. The former law was admirable in purpose but disadvantageous in practice. The types of trees specified were not always the most practicable for a particular district,[15] but more important, the cultivation of trees produced no immediate income and the pioneer necessarily had to devote most of his time to preparing his land for annual crops. The Desert Land Act was ill conceived and mirrored the ignorance of the lawmakers of the nature of irrigation agriculture. Irrigation was a more intensive mode of farming, requiring much less land but far more labor and capital than dry-land grain agriculture. Yet the law apparently intended that an entire square mile must be put under ditch within three years, a ludicrous impossibility for the pioneer settler. This situation prompted extreme liberality in interpretation by claimants and officials alike.

How extensively the settlers evaded the technicalities of the law can never be measured, but it was not very fundamental. To the extent that they built homes, plowed the land, and raised crops they carried out the basic intent of the government policies anyway. That speculators, individual and corporate, reaped profits in this grandiose national transaction was certainly not in accordance with the popular will, but, in this region at least, they do not seem to have

[14] See Roy M. Robbins, *Our Landed Heritage: The Public Domain, 1776-1936* (Princeton, N.J., 1942), for an excellent survey of the sequence, provisions, and problems associated with these various laws.

[15] 47th Cong., 1st sess., H. Ex. Doc. 1, Pt. 5 (1881), p. 916, in which McMicken objected to the exclusion of the aspen and Lombardy poplar, both of which would well serve the settlers of eastern Washington.

impeded the progress of the legitimate land seeker. No considerable block of good farmland came under the control of such persons, and though they were no doubt much in evidence in every new district, they seem to have been no more than petty, parasitic intermediaries in the colonization process.[16] The acquisition of government land was, almost literally, only half of the story, for the Northern Pacific Railroad held title to every odd-numbered section within the limits of its large land grant, a swath forty miles wide looping through most of the best agricultural districts.[17] Because the first wave of settlers tended to select government land, the pattern of settlement within this strip was often momentarily a checkerboard. However, the railroad's terms of sale were far from exorbitant. Throughout the 1880's agricultural lands were priced at from $2.60 to $6.00 per acre, with provisions for contracts of five years or ten years at 7 per cent interest. Nominally a maximum of 320 acres was available to any one settler, and if it was purchased on the ten-year credit plan, residence and cultivation were required.[18] No doubt there was room for evasion of these requirements too, with or without the approval of the railroad, but again the important fact is that in all the better districts most of these lands were rapidly sold to legitimate farmers.

Both the government and the railroad sought to serve the land seeker with convenient offices of application and sale, where they could consult maps and have all the detailed provisions explained.[19]

[16] This conclusion is not based upon a detailed study of the actual processes of land alienation but is an impression gained from the whole range of materials reviewed in the course of this work. These include not only government reports and newspaper accounts but some familiarity with federal land office records and private abstract and title insurance company records for certain districts. Insofar as the history of land tenure is concerned, the subsequent role of banks and various credit agencies would prove to be of much more significance to the economic history of the region than the operations of initial frontier speculators.

For a detailed study of the actual operation of these land laws, with vivid stress upon the considerable legal, illegal, and financial hazards of acquiring so-called "free" or "cheap" land, see Walter M. Yeager, "The Pioneer's Problems of Land Acquisition Under the Public Land Laws in Southeastern Washington, 1850-1883" (M.A. thesis, Washington State University, 1961).

[17] Plus the "lieu lands" strips on either side, as noted in the preceding chapter.

[18] These provisions appear in numerous N.P. pamphlets of the time.

[19] During these years federal land offices were opened at one time or another in The Dalles, Walla Walla, Lewiston, Colfax, Spokane Falls, Waterville, and North Yakima. At the end of this period the Northern Pacific was directing migrants to authorized agents in Walla Walla, Colfax, Spokane Falls, Cheney,

Despite the fact that under almost any provision the settler might risk the dangers of rival claimants and corrupt or overly rigid officials, in general land was readily available, conveniently obtained, and modestly priced. The important thing was not just to get it, but to live by it.

Wood and Water

Certainly the most serious problem facing the pioneer in the Great Columbia Plain was the dearth of timber for buildings, fencing, and fuel. It was a deficiency which could not be glossed over, even in the most intemperate promotion literature, although much was made of the fact that it was cheaper and easier to import wood than to clear it from the land. So it was, but the argument gained force only after it became possible to import in quantity. That time came when dozens of sawmills were eating away at the bordering forests and their produce was being sent forth by log drives, flumes, and railroads, and thus it was a far more persuasive argument in the 1880's than in the 1870's.[20] Both the larger and the local geographic patterns of colonization were significantly shaped by these needs, though fortunately for the early landseekers much of the best farmland lay adjacent to the forests. The first arrivals in these districts often chose claims which contained some timber, but this was usually gaining a short-term advantage at the cost of a long-term loss, for when cleared, such timberlands were almost invariably poor farmland and often reverted to little more than waste. A better choice was good prairie land within easy hauling distance of timber, and such lands were soon taken by the early wave of land seekers. Those who came later and had to settle farther from the forests might still be able to select lands that had a bit of wood—a thin line of willow, alder, or cottonwood along the small creeks, patches of heavy brush in the concave north slopes—and would make good use of anything that could be made into a board, a post, or kindling.

All of the early main settlement clusters lay near to the fringing forests. Particularly advantageous were those locales where a narrow strip of pines was carried well out into the prairies along a stream or

---

Sprague, Davenport, Wilbur, Ritzville, Hatton, Pasco, North Yakima, Ellensburg, and Goldendale; see text of Northern Pacific Railway, *Sectional Land Map of Eastern Washington and Northern Idaho* (Buffalo, N.Y., 1892).

[20] See Atkinson, "Choice of a Home," p. 39; "A Canadian in Eastern Washington," *The Northwest,* 2 (August, 1884), 13.

ridgetop, as in the Walla Walla, the Klickitat, and the eastern Palouse. The broad tongue of forest in the scablands was especially important to the northern Palouse and eastern Big Bend. Settlers of northern Lincoln County obtained timber from the canyons along the Spokane and Columbia rivers, and the Badger Mountain colonization demonstrated how important the lure of a mere patch of good trees could be.

The earliest settlers might cut their own needs, but commonly the sawmill operator was an important if unsung member of the pioneer vanguard. In either case, like the stockmen, they exploited the free gifts of nature without bothering about title to the land or trees. And, again, it was not altogether conscious thievery, for there was little choice. Depredation of federal timber lands was an old practice in the nation, but was long virtually unchecked because the government failed to provide any reasonable alternative. In June, 1878, the Timber Cutting Act finally recognized the imperative needs of settlers by authorizing legitimate colonists to cut timber for their own needs without charge.[21] But this too was far from adequate. The settler needed boards and shingles as well as logs and firewood, and thus he needed a sawmill, not just access to a woodlot. Such mills could operate under the Timber and Stone Act of that same year, which allowed the purchase of 160 acres of uncultivable timbered land at $2.50 per acre, but because the demands of a new district were so imperative and because policing the forest lands was nearly impossible, the law was almost completely ignored. Trespass was the rule and was well supported by popular opinion.[22]

Even with dozens of small sawmills scattered around the periphery, the problem of delivery remained. A prairie settler might easily make a few trips to the woods to get enough boards for a house, but to haul sufficient for fencing and a winter's fuel supply was another matter. A few streams, most notably the Palouse and Yakima, were early used to float logs to sawmills located well beyond the main forest zone. In the Walla Walla country several long

[21] Robbins, *Our Landed Heritage*, pp. 287-88. Five years before this, the surveyor general of Washington Territory had urged that the homestead law be amended to allow settlers to claim a detached portion of timberland also; 43rd Cong., 1st sess., Ex. Doc. 1, Pt. 5 (1873), I, 237.

[22] For example, when two sawmill operators were arrested for cutting the government timber on Badger Mountain, the settlers were so insistent upon the necessity for lumber that the charges were dismissed; Steele and Rose, *Big Bend Country*, pp. 551-53.

flumes were built to bring logs from the highlands. Those terminating at Milton, Dixie, and Dayton served large mills which supplied heavy construction beams, bridge timbers, and railroad ties, as
well as boards, posts, and firewood.[23] As the railroads advanced in the
1880's, the general problem was eased in most districts. Still the
costs of importing lumber and fuel remained high for the pioneer
and were apparently a factor in causing some settlers to select partially timbered and poorer farmlands in the Potlatch and Clearwater
districts rather than a quarter section of rich prairie in the Big
Bend.

Under these circumstances, that stereotyped landmark of the
American pioneer, the log cabin, was a rarity. Anywhere except
along the margins of the forest, the use of logs was an extravagance.
By far the most common structure was a simple box house of broad,
rough-cut boards, with the cracks covered by battens or stuffed with
mud, grass, newspapers, or any other handy material. Another famous American pioneer makeshift, the sod house, was even less evident. One reason was that even where the bunch grass was a heavy
growth, the fine-textured soil quickly dried and crumbled. More
important was the fact that almost no one wanted to live in a sod
house if he could help it, and by the time the pioneers were venturing far out onto the prairies, where such houses might have been
logical temporary shelters, sawmills and railroads together made it
possible for most to obtain enough boards to build at least a small
hut. In fact most of the really crude housing was used only briefly,
and a more striking feature of the housing during the general colonization period was how quickly it was characterized by neat, well-
built structures, complete with split shingles, porches, and even a
bit of gingerbread trim, all of which reflected the pioneer role of
numerous sawmills, railroads, and craftsmen, and the quickly developing prosperity of the general citizenry.[24]

[23] The one at Dixie was owned by Dr. Baker of W.W.&C.R. Railway fame,
who built a narrow-gauge railroad from Walla Walla to connect with the flume.
This line was later sold to the O.R.&N. and ultimately was transferred to the
N.P. The other two flumes, each eighteen miles long, were operated in the
1880's by the Oregon Improvement Company. The Milton flume timberlands
had been stripped. See O.W.R.N., *Corporate History*, sheet 26; Moore, "Pioneer
Railroad Builder," p. 200; Oregon Improvement Company, *Annual Report,
Nov. 30, 1886*, p. 15, *ibid., Nov. 30, 1888*, pp. 16-17.

[24] Materials on housing are numerous but so widely scattered through contemporary accounts, pioneer reminiscences, and local histories that documentation would be cumbersome. Interesting sketches of Big Bend claim shanties

Although the most immediate need of timber was for a house, fencing posed a more chronic and laborious difficulty. Almost any kind of makeshift would do for a corral for farm animals and to protect the first few acres broken out. For such purposes the spindly poles of creekside willows or even piles of thornbrush from the hillsides might serve. But as the fields were expanded, the amount of timber needed for posts and rails became enormous and impossible to obtain for those who lived far from the woodlands. Yet in any district with more than a mere scattering of settlers, the horses and cattle roaming the prairies made it necessary to fence if a crop was to be harvested. Fencing was an onerous burden on the pioneer and slowed the pace of farming expansion during the 1870's. Local newspapers of the time carried much discussion of the problem, and early settlers who later reflected upon their pioneering trials almost invariably gave it emphasis. The immigrant was "compelled to waste two or three years in struggling along from hand to mouth trying to support his family and fence his place," complained a correspondent in the Pendleton *East Oregonian;* a Dayton farmer reported an outlay of $600 to enclose his 160 acres and build a few cross fences within; farmers on the lower Klickitat prairie were proposing "to form a joint fence company," to reduce these heavy burdens. However, unlike the previous decade, by this time there was little talk of "live fences"—thorn hedges of various types—or other possible but untried devices, because the physical means for efficient fencing had already been developed. Some settlers used smooth wire to a limited extent, even though it was not wholly effective against horses and cattle, but after 1874 the newly invented barbed wire at last gave the prairie farmer an efficient tool of colonization. Barbed wire was manufactured in the Midwest though, and the cost of shipping it to Portland and up the river on the boats was prohibitive for most settlers. By 1880, however, it was becoming fairly common in the older districts, and two or three years later the problem neared a solution, for as other manufacturers began to compete with the original patent holders, the volume of wire production increased, and the entry of the railroads into the interior reduced the shipping charges. As the costs were brought within reach of most settlers, a network of barbed wire soon spread over all the farming districts.

---

made of logs, sod, and boards are found in *The Northwest,* 4 (September, 1886), 6.

Most of the rail fences disappeared from the landscape, as they offered a ready supply of posts for the new style. Thus a major impediment to colonization in the 1870's faded into a minor problem in the 1880's, and barbed wire must be listed along with many other features of that decade as a factor in the acceleration of settlement.[25]

Water was another problem for the pioneer, but one which in general was not a major restriction upon early colonization in the Great Columbia Plain. Most of the first districts settled were relatively humid, with numerous small creeks, and even though many of these dried up in the summer, water could usually be obtained from shallow, hand-dug wells. In drier areas, such as the Yakima and parts of Oregon, the early settlers kept close to the rivers or the perennial creeks flowing from the mountains. In any of these areas the unlucky pioneer away from a stream might find that he had misjudged the availability of water on his land and be forced to haul from a neighbor's well or creek, but he would probably not have to journey far nor do so except during the driest weeks of late summer. Only when colonization began to push in toward the more arid center of the interior did domestic water supply become a serious difficulty. For many years it was a major problem in the country northwest of Walla Walla, and especially on Eureka Flat. Here the water table was usually beyond the reach of hand-dug wells. Rainwater and snow melt were stored in cisterns, but nearly all had to haul from the Touchet or the Snake during the summer. After the railroad was built in 1888, water was shipped in by tank cars and sold for half a cent per gallon, and the farmers might still have to haul it several miles from a station. By this time, also, wells were being drilled or driven with some success, but the general deficiency afflicted the area for many years.[26]

[25] *East Oregonian,* Jan. 10, April 10, 1880; *The West Shore,* 8 (May, 1882), 84-85; *North Pacific Coast,* 1 (Jan. 15, 1880), 37. On the fencing problem and development of barbed wire, see Walter Prescott Webb, *The Great Plains* (Boston, 1931), pp. 280-318; and Earl W. Hayter, "Barbed Wire Fencing—A Prairie Invention," *Agricultural History,* 13 (October, 1939), 189-207. One early settler reported that barbed wire cost fifteen to twenty cents per pound, W. G. Victor, "Pioneers of the Mayview Country," *East Washingtonian Pioneer Edition* (Pomeroy), June 6, 1914. For other pioneer comments on wire fencing, see Yoder, "Pioneers in Whitman County," pp. 53, 103. Lyman, *Yakima Valley,* p. 668, see quotation from the Kittitas newspaper of December, 1883.
[26] *Walla Walla Daily Statesman,* Jan. 1, 1883; F. H. Newell, "Report on Agriculture by Irrigation in the Western Part of the United States at the Eleventh Census: 1890," *Eleventh Census of the United States, 1890,* p. 245.

Tools and Techniques

The earliest settlers of limited means often started farming with the same primitive type of tools and methods which had been used by generations of farmers before them: a heavy, single-furrow plow, broadcast seeding by hand, scythes and cradles for reaping, and flails or the trampling of horses for threshing. But this kind of preindustrial pioneering was temporary. Sulky plows, mowers, rakes, reapers, and steam- or horse-powered threshers were in common use even in the newest districts in the 1870's. Grain binders using wire were introduced in the latter part of that decade, those using twine appeared in the next, but the principal harvesting implement was the header. The costs of machinery were high, fully twice that in the East, reported one traveler in 1884, but credit, though also costly, was readily available from dealers. Some machinery was imported all the way from the East, some from California, but by this time western Oregon firms were turning out a considerable array; and as agriculture expanded, local blacksmiths and machinists began to manufacture many of the less complicated items. The railroads, again, reduced costs and made a wider variety available, stepping up competition among dealers. But even in districts still untapped by railroads, there was soon no lack of machines offered for sale. A typical example of the selection available may be seen from the advertisement of an Ellensburg establishment in 1883, which listed itself as the local agency for such items as the following:[27]

Celebrated Bain Wagon
Buffalo Pitts' Farm Engines
Buffalo Challenger Thresher
New Buffalo Vibrating Thresher
Imperial Oregon Header
McCormick Harvester and Twine Binder
McCormick Combined Mower and Reaper
Champion Combined Mower and Reaper
Tiger Self-Discharging Sulky Rake
McCormick Daisy Reaper
Thomas Sulky Plow
Hollingsworth Sulky Plow
McCormick Iron Mower
New Champion Mower

[27] Lyman, *Yakima Valley*, p. 647. Yoder, "Pioneers in Whitman County," is full of notes on this topic, which are succinctly summarized in his "pioneer social adaptation" studies of the Palouse country and Lincoln County. Ernest

Although this land held the promise of excellent yields, its potentials were not released by the first touch of the plow. The bunch grass, thick and wiry above the ground and supported by a deep, dense root mass below, was not conquered so easily. The Walla Walla newspaper warned new settlers that ordinarily they could not expect a really good harvest for three years after turning the sod. The common practice was to burn off the cover, plow in the fall, again in the spring, and then harrow and seed the following fall or spring. The newspaper suggested that a good deep first plowing and then shallow tillage for a few seasons would hasten the decay of the grass and roots and keep them from interfering with the crops.

Even when the land was well prepared for grain, the working out of the best seasonal cycle and methods of cultivation remained a matter of experiment and discussion for many years. The most prominent topic of dispute was over the respective merits of fall or spring sowing. During the early years of Palouse settlement, the Colfax *North-West Tribune* pointed up the question in the following manner:

> Will some of our successful farmers give us their views as to the best time to sow grain in this country, together with some practical results? Judging from all we can see and learn, it will be positively settled that Fall sowing is much more advantageous for many reasons. If given an opportunity of doing that part of the Spring's work in the Fall, the yield will, in our judgement, be much greater and of superior quality of grain, the grain can be harvested so much earlier that it can be sold when the market is better, and it will also escape the warm, dry weather that often proves the only damage to the wheat crops in this country.... The *Tribune* would be glad to publish the opinions of some of our farmers on this subject.

At this time spring seeding was much more common. The season of 1882 gave added emphasis to the issue, for the spring rains were unusually light and the long dry season reduced the yields. It was not a crop failure, but it was a severe disappointment. The Walla Walla *Daily Statesman* thought it a good lesson for those whose routine had been "to plow and sow in the spring and expect 40 bushels to the acre." The results of those who farmed differently pointed the way for all, the writer went on to say, for "the fact is beyond question that wherever good cultivation was had and wheat

Ingersoll, "Wheat Fields of the Columbia," *Harper's Monthly*, 69 (September, 1884), 510.

was sowed in early fall on summer-fallow, the crop was good." Apparently the lesson was heeded: in 1884 it was reported that about 80 per cent of the wheat in the Walla Walla area was fall sown, "and farmers are universal in the statement that the fall planting is decidedly the most favorable." In the following year a special study of wheat farming in the interior confirmed that fall wheat was much the most common.[28]

Even though fall seeding normally returned the best yields, it did not become universal. This fact, and the fact that the general shift to fall wheat was gradual, was an indication that the issue was complicated and could not be decided by a general comparison of yields. For one thing, the rhythm of field work made it difficult to make the shift in some areas. In the Palouse and Big Bend, the harvest might extend well into September, or even to October if interrupted by rain; and if the autumn rains were persistent, the small capacity of the equipment commonly used (for example, two- or three-furrow plows) might make it impossible to get the stubble burned off, and plow, harrow, and seed before winter set in. Larger equipment would obviously speed the process, but in the 1880's it was only gradually being made available. More equipment would do the same, but required an investment in machines, horses, and hired labor beyond the means of many farmers. The practice of summer-fallowing half of the grainland would entirely overcome the difficulty, as such land was ready for immediate seeding after the first good soaking rain. But for several reasons, summer fallowing was by no means a universal practice.

Even more important, probably, was the danger of winter kill. If the fall-sown grain did not get a good start before winter set in, it might be killed by a severe frost. The danger was serious under two types of circumstances: in the higher country of the Palouse and eastern Big Bend where winter temperatures were lower than in the Walla Walla and Umatilla, and in any of the drier areas where frost was likely to be unaccompanied by an insulating blanket of snow. These weather problems were not consistent nor did they

---

[28] *Walla Walla Daily Statesman,* Jan. 1, 1883; E. W. Hilgard reported that trials in the Big Bend also had shown that three years were needed to subdue the grass; *The Northwest,* 2 (April, 1884), 4. *North-West Tribune,* July 28, 1880; *Tenth Census,* III, 75; 48th Cong., 2nd sess., H. Ex. Doc. 7, Pt. 3 (1884), p. 536; Frank Greene, *Report on the Interior Wheat Lands of Oregon and Washington Territory,* 50th Cong., 1st sess., S. Ex. Doc. 229 (1888), p. 16. Greene's survey was made in 1885.

cause widespread failures, but it was not unusual for the farmer to have to reseed the bottomlands and wind-swept slopes the following spring.

The problem of winter kill was basically a matter of weather and wheat varieties, and if nothing could be done about the one, there was certainly hope of improving the other. The principal variety of wheat grown over most of the interior was a white club type, commonly known as Little Club. The ancestry of this wheat was traceable from Spain to California, from where it was introduced into the Willamette. Aside from those of the missionaries, the first crop sown in the interior was from Little Club seed brought to Walla Walla from California in 1859. It was an excellent wheat for the first districts of the new region in every respect but one: its Mediterranean heritage had given it little resistance to cold weather. When the farmers began to shift from spring- to fall-sown wheat, they continued to use this variety, and thus they subjected it to entirely new stresses. The *Daily Statesman* in its argument for the necessity of fall seeding after the experience of 1882, recognized the problem and suggested that it would be "advisable to introduce hardy winter varieties from the Northwestern States" (Minnesota-Dakota). Within a few years some of these varieties were being tested, most notably Scotch Fife from Dakota. Indications were that it would yield better, but it was as yet not clear that its other qualities were adequate.[29]

The question of varieties was complicated by the fact that the ideal wheat needed a special combination of qualities. It was not enough to find a wheat that was cold resistant; it had to be resistant to drought in the summer, to rust and smut, be able to stand in the field after ripening without shattering, and give a heavy yield to the farmer and a high-quality flour to the miller. Although hardy wheats could be obtained from colder regions, they were not ideally suited to the peculiar summer conditions and harvesting system of the in-

[29] Carleton R. Ball, "The History of American Wheat Improvement," *Agricultural History*, 4 (April, 1930), 53; Barton, "Washington," p. 1001. In time Little Club became regarded as properly a "spring wheat" in the interior, though in the warmer climates of Spain, California, and western Oregon, it was a "winter wheat," that is, one sown in the fall. *Walla Walla Daily Statesman*, Jan. 1, 1883. Emma H. Adams, *To and Fro, Up and Down in Southern California, Oregon, and Washington Territory, with sketches in Arizona, New Mexico, and British Columbia* (Cincinnati, Chicago, St. Louis, 1888), p. 343; "Eureka Flat," *The Northwest*, 7 (October, 1889), 20. The Saskatchewan Fife noted in Barton, "Washington," p. 1002, was evidently the same variety.

terior. Because the summers were normally almost completely dry, the wheat was allowed to ripen fully in the field and was then cut by a header and immediately threshed. Because of the limited amount of harvesting equipment, a ripened field might stand for many days, even weeks, and under such circumstances even a slight wind would shatter the kernels from the heads of some varieties. Little Club, evolved in Mediterranean environments, was excellently suited to these conditions, whereas the wheats from the humid eastern states were not.[30] Thus, despite its deficiencies, Little Club was not quickly displaced and continued to be an important wheat, both spring- and fall-sown, for many years.

Further complicating the issue was the fact that in the 1880's it became apparent that no single wheat variety would prove ideal for the entire region. The yields from Little Club were markedly less and its quality often much lower in drier districts, regardless of the season of sowing, and trials of more drought-resistant varieties were soon made. By the end of the decade Pacific Bluestem, an Australian wheat, was becoming the leading wheat in such areas as Eureka Flat and the Ritzville district.[31] Yields were said to have increased by 25 per cent, and Pacific Bluestem was being hailed as the means of advancing farming much farther into the arid core.

Local writers praised not only the wonderful yields but the general market quality of the grain. However, Little Club was a soft white wheat, which did not command top prices beyond the region. Relatively low in both protein and gluten, it was excellent for pastry flours but not ideal for the best bread. Milling and baking qualities were not as yet of much concern, but as new wheats were introduced, they became factors in evaluation.[32]

[30] Adams, *To and Fro,* p. 343; and 48th Cong., 2nd sess., H. Ex. Doc. 7, Pt. 3, p. 536. In the East the wheat was cut by binders before it was completely ripe and remained stacked in the field for some time before threshing. The idea that wheat must go through this "sweat in the straw" (a drying of the kernels after reaping) before threshing cast some doubt upon the header system when it was first being tried in the Walla Walla; see *Spirit of the West* (Walla Walla), Aug. 7, 1875.

[31] "Eureka Flat," p. 20; *The Sentinel* (Asotin), Jan. 25, Feb. 15, 1889; *Ritzville Journal-Times, Adams County Pioneer Edition,* Sept. 15, 1949, p. 17; *Report of Washington State Grain Inspector, 1898-1900* (Olympia, 1900), p. 20.

[32] It seemed apparent that the hard wheats from the northern Great Plains became softer when grown in the interior. Northern Pacific Railway, *The Palouse Country* (ca. 1890), p. 2. For general comments on quality, see *Tenth Census,* III, 75. Nimmo, "Range and Ranch Cattle," 48th Cong., 2nd sess.,

The search for wheats better adapted to the peculiar conditions of the region and the use of different varieties in different localities was an important sign of a maturing wheat economy. In 1890 Little Club and Bluestem were by far the most important, but they were merely the pioneers in an experimentation which would continue into the present.

THE PUZZLE OF SUCCESS

While the general success of agriculture in the interior was a source of pride and satisfaction, the underlying reasons for that success were a puzzle to many persons. For half a century there had been speculation as to whether agriculture could ever become established in such a dry region; now a decade of experience had proved beyond doubt that it could. But what was the cause? Could wheat really thrive under conditions so radically different from farming elsewhere, or had the area itself undergone change?

Has the Rainfall Increased?

There were those who thought that this dry interior country was no longer as arid as it once had been. "An old fashioned States rain" in the Walla Walla Valley in late August, 1875, the heaviest of a number of unusual showers that season, was enough to set off discussion of the question:

> That memorable personage, "the oldest inhabitant," says he has never seen so heavy a rainfall, in the same length of time.... Some persons, philosophizing upon the subject, attribute the change to the breaking up and cultivation of so much of the soil. That has a tendency to attract the clouds; and that the planting of fruit and ornamental trees contribute likewise to produce the same result.

The idea that such actions could in fact change the climate was not new in the area. Several years before, in a pamphlet published "for the benefit of those who are inquiring for new homes in the far west," Selucius Garfielde, congressional delegate from Washington Territory, noted that while the eastern part of his territory was dry

---

H. Ex. Doc. 7, Pt. 3 (1885), p. 60, states that "Oregon" wheat was rated slightly better than that of California in Liverpool; however, in a careful test of wheats in 1883-84, Oregon wheat was rated very low; see "Investigations of American Cereals and Their Products," *Report of the Commissioner of Agriculture for the Year 1884,* p. 83.

through the summer months, "spring showers mature most of the crops," and "it is probable that tree-planting may increase the amount of summer precipitation." He was merely echoing a belief widely held over the country and indeed in many parts of the world. In the older eastern states many people were sure that extensive cutting of the forests had diminished the rainfall, while in the central plains the rapid extension of plowing and planting was popularly thought to have caused a beneficial increase. To be sure, the topic was controversial and not all were convinced, but even scientists were giving the matter attention, and there seemed to be evidence in support.[33]

Proponents of the Timber Culture Act had often cited these climatic benefits, and locally the surveyor general of Washington Territory lamented that the settlers of the interior were neglecting to use that method of land acquisition because "the value of the timber for wood alone should not be the first consideration in encouraging the growth of timber in a treeless country. The wonderful atmospheric changes, . . . more abundant rainfall being the most important of these, is of much greater importance to the settler." Philip Ritz stated in 1878 that the rainfall in the Columbia Plain was "very much greater than it was ten years ago," and because he was not only a strong advocate of the Timber Culture law but a leading nurseryman who had furnished thousands of trees to the settlers, he felt that he "might be entitled to a little credit" for such climatic improvement. Statements to the effect that "as cultivation increases moisture will correspondingly increase," did not necessarily mean that it would come in the form of rainfall, but that was the usual implication. Lieutenant Symons cited evidence from Nebraska, where the westward-advancing settlers had been "carrying along an increased rainfall," to suggest that the same thing was happening in the Great Plain of the Columbia.[34]

[33] *Spirit of the West* (Walla Walla), Sept. 3, 1875; Selucius Garfielde, *Climates of the Northwest* (Philadelphia, 1871), p. 16. The contemporary evidence of such beliefs is extensive. Among the best sources are the annual volumes of the *Report of the Commissioner of Agriculture,* e.g., 1869, p. 516; 1870, p. 508; 1871, pp. 233, 354-55; 1873, pp. 384-86. I have examined the existence and importance of such ideas in a wheat region of Australia during this same time in *On the Margins of the Good Earth: The South Australian Wheat Frontier, 1869-1884* (Chicago, 1962), esp. pp. 70-71, 87.

[34] 47th Cong., 1st sess., H. Ex. Doc. 1, Pt. 5 (1882), pp. 898, 916. Philip Ritz, "Settlement of the Great Northwest Interior, San Francisco, Jan. 4, 1878" (MS in the Bancroft Library, Berkeley, Calif.), p. 6. For an extensive statement of

Whatever the exact cause might be, numerous people advanced the idea that the rainfall in the interior had been increased in some manner during the 1860's and 1870's. Yet their case was not entirely convincing, for neither the evidence that it had increased nor the explanation as to how this had been accomplished was satisfactory. The meteorological records were too scanty to be conclusive, but not even fragmentary statistics were cited in support. Locally the idea rested upon the memories of the "oldest inhabitants," the impressions gained from "unusually" wet weather, the opinion that the soil seemed to be more moist, the belief that springs flowed more freely, and the fact that the crops seemed to get better each year. Such evidence, joined with the general theories abroad in the nation about the climatic effects of trees and cultivation, made a sufficient argument for those so inclined. On the other hand, summer was still a dry season, and while some were talking about an increase in rainfall, others were emphasizing the fact "that there is scarcely a shower between May and the following October, and . . . the average rainfall for the year does not exceed twenty inches." When the same writer acknowledged that wheat farming in such a climate was "so at variance with common experience that it might well be questioned," he had focused attention upon the critical matter. The remarkable fact was that year after year good yields were being obtained from *spring-sown* crops in a *summer-dry* climate. Such a phenomenon was completely outside the experience of farmers anywhere else in the nation.[35] Thus it was understandable that the early immigrants settling in this peculiar region might at first try to account for their success by assuming that an increase in moisture had taken place, for surely the "natural" conditions seemed insufficient to produce such results. In time, however, it became apparent to some that there was no change in the climate—the summers remained dry and the total rainfall remained low.

Theories and Facts

One man who had a ready answer to the question was the Reverend G. H. Atkinson, an avid amateur meteorologist with a keen

---

Ritz's ideas on the topic, see the *East Oregonian,* Jan. 17, 1880. 47th Cong., 1st sess., S. Ex. Doc. 186 (1882), p. 112.

[35] *The Pacific Northwest,* p. 19. It may be noted that the summer dry season in California is even longer and more severe, being a typical "Mediterranean" climate, but in that older farming region all of the nonirrigated grain crops

interest in regional progress. He gave much attention to the weather and climate of the Pacific Northwest, and his views were widely publicized. Although never directly contradicting those who believed that there had been a marked increase in rainfall, Atkinson stressed the fact that the summers were dry ("there is absolutely no rain from June to September"), the total precipitation "does not exceed 20 inches," and "if successful farming depended upon the limited rainfall there would be poor harvests." His explanation was that cultivation and planting did indeed increase the moisture, but primarily in the form of "dew" rather than rainfall:

> The clouds supply only in part the moisture which is needed. The warm air currents, surcharged with vapor, which sweep inland from the ocean up the channel of the Columbia River prevent drought. . . . The moisture with which they are laden is held in suspension during the day, diffused over the face of the country. At night it is condensed by the cooler temperatures and precipitated in the form of a fine mist on every exposed particle of surface which earth and plant present. The effect is that of a copious shower.

It followed, therefore, that the primary need was to create a greater exposure of surface for cooling and absorption, and, happily, every farmer had the ideal tool: "The plow proves to be the cooler. It opens the light, porous soil to the air, which enters it freely, and parts with its moisture to nourish the plants." Here was a ready explanation for the remarkable success of agriculture on the high dry hills, for as the plow "moved up the hill sides" and opened the soil, the wheat was able to "absorb its full supply of moisture every cool night," and "the higher the hill, the quicker the cooling process occurs in the still air." Orchards, groves, and crops also increased the cooling surfaces, and thus his admonition was "plow and plant" to "restore" the arid lands "that have for ages abounded in the bunchgrass."[36]

---

were necessarily seeded in the late fall or early winter to take full advantage of the winter rains.

[36] Nancy Bates Atkinson, *Biography of Rev. G. N. Atkinson, D.D.* (Portland, Ore., 1893). Atkinson came to Oregon in 1848. For several years he collected weather data at Oregon City. Later he became chairman of the Committee on Meteorology of the Portland Board of Trade and was the author of most of the material on climate in the descriptive literature on the Pacific Northwest sponsored by that agency and Portland newspapers; *ibid.*, p. 132. He did directly refute those who had suggested that "electrical charges caused by the telegraph" had produced an increase in moisture. This, too, was an idea which had been put forth in other parts of the country, although some persons blamed the telegraph for causing droughts rather than wetter weather; e.g.,

With such an explanation, the "paradox" of harvests from an arid land was resolved, and it could be confidently stated that "a summer drought . . . which in most climates is a calamity, is here a benefit," for the wheat ripened in the field and stood awaiting the harvest without fear of damage from rain. Atkinson's theory of how cultivation increases moisture was widely publicized and gave powerful support to the important idea that "wherever bunchgrass grows wheat will grow."[37]

In the 1880's the rapid settlement and wide publicity given the region attracted increasing attention from scientists. The leader of a group studying the "arid regions of the Pacific Slope" regretted that he was unable to examine in detail "the peculiar conditions governing agriculture" in the Great Columbia Plain, but a distinguished member of his committee, E. W. Hilgard, was soon able to do so as one of the scientists with the Northern Pacific's Northern Transcontinental Survey. While making a midsummer reconnaissance north of Crab Creek in the Big Bend country, Hilgard was struck by the appearance of scattered clumps of giant ryegrass on the

---

Scientific American, 192 (March, 1955), 14, quoting an item from the March, 1855, issue. Another bit of folklore of the time was that the building of railroads had changed the climate by a vague "electrical" process. The only expression I found of this belief in the interior was by a resident of The Dalles, who stated that whereas previously there had always been a difference in the barometric readings at The Dalles and Portland, since the railroad had been built between the two the readings were about the same. He concluded that, "acting as a conductor," the iron track "may have drawn off and diffused over Eastern Oregon some of the conditions of humidity in the atmosphere of Western Oregon." J. P. Killinger (comp.), *Dalles City Directory, 1884-85* (The Dalles, Ore., 1885).

The Pacific Northwest, p. 20. Atkinson was the author of this part of this descriptive pamphlet. This discussion of his ideas is based upon this source and his own booklet, *The Northwest Coast* (Portland, Ore., 1878), pp. 45-51. Many of the statements in the two are nearly identical, as they are also with those in several of his speeches and articles reprinted in his biography. Like many others writing on the topic, Atkinson was not always consistent in his statements. In some places he does state that "summer showers" will be increased, despite his emphasis upon the absolute drought of that season; the full context of his statements suggests that despite his use of "precipitation," he nearly always meant "condensation."

[37] See especially Atkinson, *G. H. Atkinson,* p. 373. His theories were not only given wide currency in the volumes previously cited, but in such publications as Northern Pacific Railway, *Annual Report, 1877,* pp. 11-12; "Report of the Governor of Washington Territory," in *Report of the Secretary of the Interior,* 48th Cong., 2nd sess., H. Ex. Doc. 1, Pt. 5 (1884), p. 581; *Eastern Washington Territory and Oregon* (Farmington, W. T., 1888), pp. 25ff.

high hills, a plant which he had heretofore seen only in the Yakima valleys and had thought to be an indicator of poor, excessively alkaline soils. A careful examination revealed an important feature:

> ... these tufts of grass are always located on ground either heretofore or at present occupied by colonies of badgers, which have given the ground a most thorough subsoiling and tilth. In other words, it shows that the rye-grass follows *not* the alkali, but moisture; and its existence here points the way clearly for the operations of the farmer. Cereal crops will grow wherever rye-grass will, provided the tillage be as deep and as thorough as in these badger colonies, where moisture can always be found at ten to twelve inches in depth.

Thus, in a sense, he gave support to the idea that an "increase in moisture" did indeed "follow cultivation," but not, as many others believed, in the form of rainfall or dew, but in making use through proper tillage of that which was already stored in the soil—a subsurface rather than an atmospheric change.[38]

Interest in the peculiar circumstances of wheat raising in the Great Columbia Plain culminated in the order for a special government investigation. The survey was carried out in 1885 by Lieutenant Frank Greene of the Signal Corps, and the results were published three years later. The opening statement of the report succinctly stated the features of interest:

> The interior wheat lands of Oregon and Washington Territory have attracted attention by their unfailing crops, the large average yield, the comparatively small amount of precipitation, and the general dryness of the summer months. The latter feature has gained for these districts the erroneous name of the rainless regions of Oregon and Washington.

Greene made extensive use of a questionnaire to gather the opinions of the farmers "as to why wheat can be successfully grown under these conditions." A few suggested heavy dews as the important

[38] E. W. Hilgard, T. C. Jones, and R. W. Furnas, *Report of the Climatic and Agricultural Features and the Agricultural Practices and Needs of the Arid Regions of the Pacific Slope, with notes on Arizona and New Mexico* (U.S. Dept. of Agriculture Report No. 20) (Washington, D.C., 1882), p. 5. E. W. Hilgard, "Report of E. W. Hilgard to Professor R. Pumpelly, Director" (June 4, 1883, MS in the Land Department, N.P. Railroad, St. Paul). This particular portion of Hilgard's report is reprinted in *The Northwest,* 2 (April, 1884), 1-4. It is interesting to note that nowhere in his Pacific Northwest reports did Hilgard suggest that the rainfall might be increased by man's actions, even though a year or so before he gave support to the idea that forests had a definite effect upon climate; see Hilgard, Jones, and Furnas, *Climatic and Agricultural Features,* pp. 17-18.

factor, but the majority emphasized the high moisture retentiveness of the soil. On the basis of his own examinations, Greene disposed of the "dew theory," for he found that, contrary to Atkinson's belief, there was "a marked absence of palpable dew in the spring and summer months."[39]

Greene's conclusion was that crop success could only be explained by taking into account several factors which together formed a unique environmental complex:

1. A soil of great fertility.
2. A friable soil which readily absorbs moisture.
3. An underlying stratum of clay hardpan which arrests percolation within reach of the plant roots.
4. A rainfall of low intensity, an important part of which falls during the very early growth of the wheat, which, together with a gradually melting snow cover, is nearly all absorbed by the soil rather than running off the surface.
5. A nearly dry ripening and harvesting season, but rarely with severe desiccating winds.
6. Perhaps to a slight extent, a latitudinal advantage which gives longer hours of sunlight during the maturing period.[40]

Although subsequent studies would modify and refine this analysis, Greene's report stands as by far the most careful and reasoned explanation to that time.

In the same year that these results were published, reports were also issued on the climate of this and other regions of the far West. Such studies, made under the direction of General A. W. Greely, were designed in part to provide reliable information to prospective settlers. Common opinion over the nation that "the interior portions of Oregon and Washington were almost rainless" was specifically mentioned as one that needed correction. The residents themselves were aware of this fallacy, but the data also suggested that the average total rainfall of some districts was larger than commonly believed. Stations at Walla Walla, Dayton, Pomeroy, and Colfax reported averages of between twenty and twenty-seven inches annually. The smallest amount was seven inches recorded for Kennewick. The length and severity of the summer dry season was also less than commonly represented. Several stations reported completely dry periods of as long as a month in exceptional years, but the data

---

[39] 50th Cong., 1st sess., S. Ex. Doc. 229 (1888), pp. 5, 11, 18-21.

[40] These factors are not listed in quite this manner in Greene's own summary, *ibid.,* p. 16, but they appear in the report.

did not seem to verify the idea of a completely rainless season from May to October for any place. Nevertheless, compared with nearly all of the older agricultural areas of the nation, the interior was obviously a "dry" region—relatively so throughout the year, remarkably so in the summer. But such studies began to verify with statistics what local farmers had already demonstrated: that wheat could succeed with much less rainfall than commonly supposed. As a general rule of thumb, it had been assumed by those concerned with the over-all patterns of regions and resources in the nation that areas receiving less than twenty inches annually could be labeled as "arid," meaning incapable of agriculture without irrigation. Now it was suggested that fifteen inches would be a better figure.[41]

These investigations were important contributions to both scientific and public understanding of the nature of agriculture in this unusual regional environment. The farmers themselves were not much concerned about such studies, for they merely explained the results already obtained. But there was still much vacant land in the core of the region, and this change in ideas about "arid" regions might well become a subtle but important factor in the further advance of colonization. Certainly as each year passed, the "peculiarity" of the interior was becoming more familiar and commonplace, and ideas about the need for changing its natural conditions gave way to a simple acceptance of the conditions that did prevail. In the older districts there was no longer much talk about increasing the rainfall. By now the farmers had experienced a good many yearly cycles; some seasons had been unusually wet, some unusually dry, but it was becoming possible to get a notion of what was unusual and what might be generally expected. As in most regions,

[41] A. W. Greely, *The Climate of Oregon and Washington Territory*, and *Rainfall of the Pacific Slope and the Western States and Territories*, 50th Cong., 1st sess., S. Ex. Docs. 282 and 91 (1888). The quotation is from p. 5 of *Climate*. The literature frequently related that good harvests had been obtained from wheat which had not received a drop of rain from the time the first shoots had broken through the surface; e.g., *The Northwest*, 2 (February, 1884), 3; *Eastern Washington* (Walla Walla, *ca.* 1885), p. 2. Greely, *Rainfall*, p. 8. It was recognized that no such figure could be taken as absolute, as there were many other factors which affected the efficiency of the rainfall for agriculture. The fifteen inches figure was based primarily upon findings in Dakota. No doubt the Columbia interior information was a useful corroboration that wheat would grow with that amount, and in fact it was already being raised in districts which, according to the isohyetal map accompanying the Greely report, received less that fifteen inches.

there were not only the regular variations of seasonal weather, but highly localized caprices. The most spectacular were the occasional summer "cloudbursts" or "water spouts." These brief but intense downpours, sometimes accompanied by hail, could be devastating. Such powerful convectional storms could pound a swath of grain into the earth and send a swirling wall of water down the local canyons, sweeping along barns, wagons, and livestock. The areas along the deep Snake River Canyon were especially afflicted.[42] But if not perfect, there was no doubt that the weather in general was very good. Certainly the most important fact was simply that—so far—the region as a whole had never experienced anything like a real crop failure.

An "Inexhaustible" Soil

The excellent yields obtained were obviously an expression of soils as well as climate. And as with climate, the soils of the interior seemed so different from those of other agricultural regions of the nation that they aroused much interest and led to extensive speculation and analysis.

The summer newcomer found that not only was the climate astonishingly dry but the soils had a drab, parched appearance which offered little sign of fertility to anyone accustomed to the moist dark

[42] Because of the wide interest in areas of colonization, the results of such scientific investigations were quickly communicated to the public. Thus, for example, materials from the Greely reports were quoted in such literature as the *Minneapolis Tribune,* April 4, 1889; *The Northwest,* 7 (May, 1889), 14; Northern Pacific Railway, *The Palouse Country,* an advertising folder. Mention of fifteen inches of rainfall as adequate for wheat appears quite commonly in the general literature from this time on.

Lang, "Oregon," p. 716, reported in 1890 that old settlers in the Umatilla area believed that the rainfall had increased; however, this was associated with wheat trails on some of the lower lands toward the Columbia. In the Walla Walla and Palouse there was evidently little concern about the theory. Such ideas were also being undermined by experiences in the Great Plains, see *The Northwest,* 7 (October, 1889), 31. The Greely reports did not take a firm stand on the issue, but stated that "The weight of opinion and of accumulative evidence tends to confirm the theory that forests do slightly increase the mean rainfall." Greely, *Rainfall,* p. 9.

These weather peculiarities also caught the attention of the amateur theorists. Ritz hoped that the thousands of trees planted over the region might in time mitigate "those fearful water-spouts that are becoming such a terror to our prairies," *East Oregonian,* Jan. 17, 1880. Atkinson also was certain that they were caused by the absence of the "cooling action" of trees and fields; G. H. Atkinson, "The Water-Spouts of the Upper Columbia Basin," *The West Shore,* 5 (October, 1879), 290-92.

earths of the East. There must be a peculiar nutrient in these western soils. Attention was at first directed to the presence of alkali, a well-known feature of desert lands. Although it was long believed to preclude agriculture, experiences in Utah and California had proved that some of these desert soils were very productive when irrigated, and it was now suggested that the fine yields in the interior were because of the alkali which "acts as a sort of fertilizer and partially renews the soil." Although the term "alkali" was obviously being employed in a broad and vague sense, chemical analyses performed a few years later did reveal the presence of large amounts of alkaline elements, such as soda and potash.[43]

However, the main public interest in soils was not directed so much toward their specific chemical composition as to more general ideas about fertility and durability. The scientists themselves disagreed as to the implications of soil chemistry,[44] but another approach yielded results which were much more readily understood. Sometime in the late 1870's Senator John H. Mitchell gave a sack of soil from near Weston in Umatilla County to a professor at the Smithsonian Institution. The senator summarized the findings of the analyst as follows:

He ... stated that he regarded the soil as the best wheat-producing soil he had ever examined; that it contained properties very similar to the soil of Sicily, where wheat had been raised for 2,000 years without exhausting the soil. The report further stated that the soil was of such character that it would fertilize itself as cultivated; that it would not be necessary to let it rest after a crop or two....[45]

[43] *Spirit of the West*, Aug. 7, 1875; also Victor, *All Over Oregon*, p. 100. See "Horse Heaven," *The Northwest*, 3 (October, 1885), 17, for a reprint of a letter from the Department of Agriculture reporting on an analysis of a sample of Walla Walla soil. E. W. Hilgard wrote on the general nature of these soils, in "The Yakima and Klickitat Regions," *The Northwest*, 2 (March, 1884), 2, but his detailed reports evidently remained unpublished until 1892; see E. W. Hilgard, *A Report on the Relations of Soil to Climate* (Weather Bureau Bulletin No. 3), Washington, D.C.: U.S. Dept. of Agriculture, 1892), pp. 26-30.

[44] See Edward A. Schneider, "An Analysis of a Soil from Washington Territory and Some Remarks on the Utility of Soil-Analysis," *American Journal of Science*, 3rd series, 36 (October, 1888), 236-47. Schneider analyzed a soil sample from near The Dalles, but he insisted that there were certain flaws in the common techniques employed and that it was not possible to determine the fertility of a soil by chemical test alone.

[45] John H. Mitchell, "Oregon, Its History, Geography, and Resources," *National Geographic Magazine*, 6 (April 20, 1895), 276-77. The exact date of this event is not given; the *Nimmo Report* of 1885 (48th Cong., 2nd sess., H. Ex. Doc. 7) reported it as having taken place "several years ago."

That the Great Plain of the Columbia was underlain with a vast basaltic platform of great depth had long been known. The rock exposed in canyon walls, coulees, and scablands made that clear to any knowledgeable observer. Samuel Parker, Captain John Fremont, and Lieutenant J. Drayton of the Wilkes expedition had all commented upon it many years before. The "volcanic" origin of the soil was understood, and thus the comparison with Sicily was eminently suitable in every respect: it was simple, readily believable, and its implications could hardly have been more satisfying.

So satisfactory was it that probably no scientific report on the region ever had such immediate and widespread currency. It was repeated in one form or another in practically every speech, newspaper, pamphlet, book, and official document which offered a descriptive account of the qualities of the region. A reporter visiting Walla Walla soon after this wonderful intelligence found that not only did people know of it, they were overbearingly outspoken about it: "Everyone in Walla Walla knows (and has a tendency to remark on all occasions), that there is only one place in the world which has a soil exactly like that of Walla Walla, and that place is Sicily." This tie with Sicily, he went on to explain, was

> ... regarded by Walla Walla much as a connection by marriage with a family which came over in the "Mayflower" might be by a man who lacked ancestors of his own. But if the similarity is not much to be proud of merely as a similarity, it is worth a good deal for what it implies, for as Walla Walla is once more aware (and terribly aware), "Sicily was for hundreds of years the granary of Europe," etc. etc.[46]

Such implications, so widely accepted, had a profound effect upon the attitudes toward and methods of farming. The farmers needed no scientist to tell them that their soils were immensely fertile, but it *was* nice to know that such fertility was everlasting. And if the example of Sicily were not comforting enough, further evidence in the region itself could be marshaled in proof. The Reverend Mr. Atkinson addressed himself to the matter in characteristic fashion. If the soils had been derived from the decomposition of the underlying basalt, the important question, he stated, was whether that

[46] Senator Mitchell's actions may not have been the first to produce such an Old World comparison with these implications. Atkinson credited James Tilton with having made a similar comparison, though no date is given; Atkinson, *G. H. Atkinson*, p. 389; see also Ritz, "Settlement"; *Tenth Census*, III, 18, 111. After about 1881, however, it is usually clear that the views expressed are directly drawn from Mitchell's report. *The Northwest*, 2 (February, 1884), 3.

same process was continuing, and if so could the rate of decomposition be increased so that the mineral nutrients locked in the rocks were constantly made available to the soil. Reasoning from all the signs at hand, he concluded that this was precisely the case, that the process did continue, and that the enrichment of the soil was speeded by cultivation. "The basalts are our treasure house," he proclaimed, a "constant and ever-present" source of fertility which will in all probability "replace the annual losses of the mineral elements of our soil." Thus, for Atkinson, the plow not only proved to be the "cooler," increasing the moisture, but was the "fertilizer" as well. Such a wondrous feature quickly became the chorus to the "Sicily refrain," varied in words but constant in its theme: a soil of "inexhaustable fertility"—"the lava fields of this region are vast and inexhaustible manure heaps"—soils which are "reproducing themselves constantly as the processes of decomposition... proceed"—a "marvelous fertility [which] is only increased by use."[47]

Inevitably the propagandists who popularized this theme supported it further with statements that farms had grown wheat continuously, year after year, for fifteen, twenty, or even thirty years without a break. While as yet very few acres had been cultivated for thirty years, it was certainly true that many fields had been cultivated continuously for well over a decade. Such facts could quite honestly be cited, but they did not present a balanced picture. By the latter 1870's some farmers in the Walla Walla area began to fallow their older fields in alternate years, and the practice gradually became more general. In 1884 the reporter who was so impressed with Walla Walla's obsession with the analogy of Sicily, noted that nevertheless it was beginning to be recognized that "this pounding away at the land year after year with wheat, wheat, wheat, and never a rest or intermission" was not the best policy, and that the "larger and wiser" farmers were summer fallowing in alternate years. Greene

[47] G. H. Atkinson, "The Increase of Soil from Basaltic Rocks—The Source and Extent of the Basalts," the *Oregonian* (Portland), n.d., reprinted in Atkinson, *G. H. Atkinson*, pp. 387-92. The fragmentary quotations are from, respectively, Miles C. Moore, *Report of the Governor of Washington Territory to the Secretary of the Interior* (Washington, 1889), p. 26 (and quoted also in *The Spokesman*, Spokane Falls, Aug. 3, 1880); *The Oregonian's Handbook of the Pacific Northwest* (Portland, 1894), p. 22; Barton, "Washington," p. 1002; *Historical and Descriptive Review of the Industries of Walla Walla, 1891* (Walla Walla, Wash., 1891), p. 18.

found that fallowing was generally regarded as desirable after ten or fifteen years of continuous cultivation.[48]

The fact that the land did yield so well for so long without any interruption of cropping meant that fallowing only gradually became part of the normal wheat farming routine. And even as the general merits of fallowing every other or every third year became more widely appreciated, the exact reasons for its success were neither understood nor of much concern. Yields seemed to be improved, but whether because of plant nutrients, an increase in soil moisture, or some other factor was not clear. The main idea was the need to "rest" the land to "renew its strength,"[49] and thus fallowing usually consisted only of plowing, without any further tillage until the land was prepared for seeding the following year.

Those few writers who expressed concern about prevailing practices often advocated a rotation of crops as well as fallowing in order to maintain fertility. But there was little that could be suggested as practicable. Oats and barley were grown in some quantity throughout the wheat region, largely as hay and grain for work horses and other farm stock. But these made the same demands upon the soil as wheat and could not be regarded as "rotation" crops in the full sense of the term. Flax had received considerable experimental attention, especially in the Palouse and Walla Walla, but it proved to be harder on the soil than grain, besides having other difficulties in cultivation and marketing, and by 1890 it had practically disappeared from the region. In the several small irrigation districts— most notably the central Walla Walla, the upper Touchet, and the middle Yakima—a considerable variety of crops was being cultivated and a wider assortment being tested or vociferously advocated by local enthusiasts. Inevitably, some persons saw this diversity on small irrigation holdings as a model for the region and urged the wheat farmer to add orchards, vegetables, dairying, and other intensive activities. Many of the grain farmers did have an orchard, a garden, a few milk cows and poultry to meet their own family needs, but

[48] References to fallowing in that decade are very scarce. Oates, "Washington Territory," p. 116, wrote in 1880 that its value had been discovered "by late experience." *The Northwest*, 2 (February, 1884), 3. 50th Cong., 1st sess., S. Ex. Doc. 229 (1888), p. 15.

[49] E.g., W. H. Ruffner, *A Report on Washington Territory* (New York, 1889), p. 83.

few showed any interest in expanding these into commercial mainstays.[50]

Indeed, the tendency in the region was toward greater rather than lessened emphasis upon wheat. While local propagandists proclaimed the region's perfection for a long list of crops and implied that diversification was a logical and desirable goal, the wheat farmer increasingly regarded himself as a specialist. The struggling pioneer might peddle any kind of produce he could raise and find a market for, but the compelling goal was to raise wheat and more wheat. Wheat was proven profitable, its cultivation was simple, and it had prestige. Throughout these two decades wheat had been the decisive instrument of conquest and measure of value. Wherever wheat had succeeded, the farmers had rapidly replaced the stockmen; they had broken, fenced, and domesticated the land; towns had sprung up, railroads entered, and the life and landscape of the district had been quickly transformed. Wheat had brought the region its fame; wheat had lured its colonists, delighted its publicists, puzzled its scientists, and attracted national attention. In the perspectives of the moment, the history and destiny of the region seemed bound up with this "standard cereal of the world,"—everything seemed to have been leading slowly, experimentally, but inevitably, toward this conquest, and the future seemed to promise an enlargement and celebration of that triumph. In 1890, clearly "wheat was King."

[50] See, e.g., *Spirit of the West*, Sept. 10, 1875; *North Pacific Coast*, 1 (Jan. 15, 1880), 37; Parker, *Washington Territory*, p. 11; *The Pacific Northwest*, p. 24. The last-mentioned pamphlet praises flax as a rotation crop, but admits the greater labor required in production and the lack of any local processing mills. G. H. Atkinson, "The Model Farm of Eastern Oregon and Washington," *The West Shore*, 8 (May, 1882), 84-85.

CHAPTER ELEVEN

> We have witnessed the field grow up
> now called the Inland Empire, which
> used to be called "The Great Interior
> Desert."
>
> L. F. GROVER

Empire: Town and Country, ca. 1890

LOCALITIES

EVEN the most discerning and optimistic predictions of 1870 fell short of the nature and magnitude of actual developments over the next twenty years. Potentials dimly discerned at the outset had not only been realized but extended. Population had increased tenfold to more than a hundred thousand, "improved" farm acreage had surpassed two million, and the regional geography had taken on some unforeseen patterns (Map 34). Although in detail there had been much unevenness in scale and tempo, every corner of the region had felt the touch of change, and over-all it was an era of accelerating progress. By any measure or comparison it was "boom" time in the Great Columbia Plain in 1890.

In the markets of the world such progress would most likely be measured in bushels of wheat which flowed out in an annually increasing flood. Local citizens, however, would point with as much pride to their towns as to their farms, for these were even more vivid expressions of achievements and prospects. Certainly the easy creation and rapid development of towns was astonishing: "Nothing in all the strange ways of the wild West strikes the Eastern visitor as more curious than the manner in which cities are planted and grow out here. A man plats a townsite much as he would break a few acres of farm land, and then proceeds to raise a city as if it were a crop of potatoes."[1] If there were as yet no real "cities" in actual size, there were several in name and scores in aspiration. Moreover, there was one genuine city, which, if not exactly in this region, was certainly of it.

[1] H. P. Robinson, "Spokane Falls," *The Northwest*, 2 (July, 1884), 11-16.

Spokane Falls

The meteoric rise of Spokane Falls was surely the most remarkable phenomenon of its time in the interior. The falls on the Spokane River was a fine site for mills, and it was long assumed that a settlement would eventually arise there. But during the first twenty years of colonization it was a remote corner, well away from the main avenues and areas of development. The Mullan Road passed by to the south and crossed the river nearly twenty miles upstream, and there was no need for mills with no population to serve. Only as farmers began to move into the northern Palouse was a town initiated, and even then its prospects were by no means clear. "Our star shines brighter and brighter every day," exclaimed a Spangle correspondent, "if Spangle had not been built Spokane Falls might have made a fair country village, but now this is destined to be the city of the upper country." If this was a bit of typically extravagant boosterism, it was not as yet foolishness, for although the newer town had already surpassed Spangle in size, neither was more than a "fair country village." Even his rival correspondent in Spokane Falls expressed no more than a cautious optimism. He could boast of 350 people, but his town had "a painfully new look," and there were no good farm lands in the immediate vicinity. It did have wonderful water power, however, and he tried to bolster the faith of his fellow citizens by insisting that "the permanency of the town does not turn altogether on the question of the county seat as many suppose." The bitterness of the rivalry with Cheney for that political plum was a good expression of insecurity, however, and in 1880 Spokane Falls lost the first round in that struggle by a margin of 563 votes to Cheney's 680.[2]

Gaining a railroad would prove to be far more important than becoming a petty political capital, but that, too, did not at first bring all the advantages hoped for. The Northern Pacific established its division point and shops at Sprague and thereby seemed to have given Spokane Falls another ominous rival for leadership. Still, the town did grow in size and confidence. The first issue of one of its early newspapers stated unequivocally that Spokane Falls was "bound to be the chief metropolis not only of eastern Washington, but of that vast extent of territory, now being rapidly peopled,

---

[2] *North-West Tribune* (Colfax), Aug. 4, 1880; Jonathan Edwards, *An Illustrated History of Spokane County . . .* (1900), p. 290.

known and suggestively spoken of as the 'Inland Empire.' "[3] If at the moment this might be dismissed as another trite burst of enthusiasm, it was soon confirmed as a prescient view. While many a town could see in the wonderful fertility of the Columbia grainlands its own promise of greatness, Spokane Falls, clustered on the gravelly, thin-soiled, pine-clad floor of an unpromising valley, dared to dream of a whole new regional concept.

That new region had emerged quite suddenly in the 1880's. The completion of the Northern Pacific had set the axis and was soon followed by development of a diverse array of districts to the north and south. The Coeur d'Alene mining rush was the first big event, and it was soon followed by lesser but profitable discoveries to the north in the Colville and Metaline districts. Railroads sent out to tap these areas further opened the superb white pine forests to easy exploitation. To these were added the branch lines reaching through the whole Palouse country and deep into the Big Bend. In less than a decade Spokane Falls found its position changed. On the far periphery of the old region, it was now at the very center of the new. It was sustained not merely by the wheat of the Columbia Plain, but by minerals, lumber, and livestock as well, gathered from the whole of northeastern Washington, northern Idaho, and even western Montana. By 1890 the "Inland Empire" was no mere dream, and the Spokane Falls newspapers could record the events of that region under the heading "News From Tributary Towns." By every local measure it was properly a "metropolis"; with twenty thousand people it was the largest inland city north of Salt Lake City and west of Minneapolis, and could boast of all the contemporary marks of urban progress—the best in electric lights, nearly eight miles of street and cable railways, and an array of handsome brick structures in the central city lying between the river and the railroad. A new region had emerged, and Spokane Falls was its undisputed capital.

Walla Walla, City and Country

The triumph of Spokane Falls was obviously a matter of dismay to local pretenders such as Cheney and Sprague, but the rise of such a city anywhere in that area was a shock to an older "capital." Until this late frenzy of development, the events of half a century had

[3] *Spokane Falls Review,* May 19, 1883, as quoted in Ralph E. Dyar, *News for an Empire: The Story of the Spokesman-Review* . . . (Caldwell, Ida., 1952), p. 5.

seemed to indicate that Walla Walla would dominate the interior. Its citizens assumed that destiny to be so logical, so inevitable, that they could smugly eschew the strident boosterism that was endemic among the many upstart communities. As a discerning visitor of 1880 reported, "The people were bright, intelligent, and pleasant to meet, but not with the ambitious and progressive natures of other places we had visited. The feeling of self-satisfaction, possessing the thought that Walla Walla was the hub of the universe, was like the old feeling of the Bostonian for his beloved Boston." The whole aspect of the community confirmed its position: well-graded streets, business blocks of cut stone four stories high ("marvels of beauty"), neat and "elegant" homes embowered in shade trees and creeping vines.[4] This was no raw, struggling frontier town, but a solid community well rooted in the past and confident of the future. It had always been the center, its farmers had discovered the wealth in this land, its grain merchants and millers had established the export lifeline, its citizens had built the first railroad, and all regional progress was but an emanation from its own.

Such a satisfying position did not make it wholly immune from the infectious optimism that swept over the region when the railroad companies began to build in earnest and the settlers began to pour in in unprecedented numbers. "Caught in that cyclone of enthusiasm, Walla Walla laid foundations for metropolitan size."[5] Unfortunately, it soon became apparent that all regional developments did not naturally focus upon Walla Walla. The critical flaw was the failure to gain a central position within the railroad network. Once the Northern Pacific was linked with the O.R.&N. at Wallula, Walla Walla was no longer the terminus of the main axis, but merely on a branch from the trunk line. Several lines did tap its immediate hinterland, but the decision to extend the Columbia and Palouse east from the N.P. rather than north from the O.R.&N. severed most of the trade of the rich country beyond the Snake. Walla Walla's connection northward was belatedly made, but by then the N.P. had focused much of the Palouse traffic upon Spokane Falls. The com-

---

[4] Carrie Adell Strahorn, *Fifteen Thousand Miles by Stage* (New York, 1911), pp. 304-5, 308. The author was the wife of Robert E. Strahorn, who was for many years one of the leading "on the ground" railroad strategists of the nation. The title of the book was no exaggeration, for Mrs. Strahorn accompanied her husband on most of his journeys and was no doubt one of the most widely acquainted and best informed persons of the far West.

[5] Adams, *To and Fro*, p. 346.

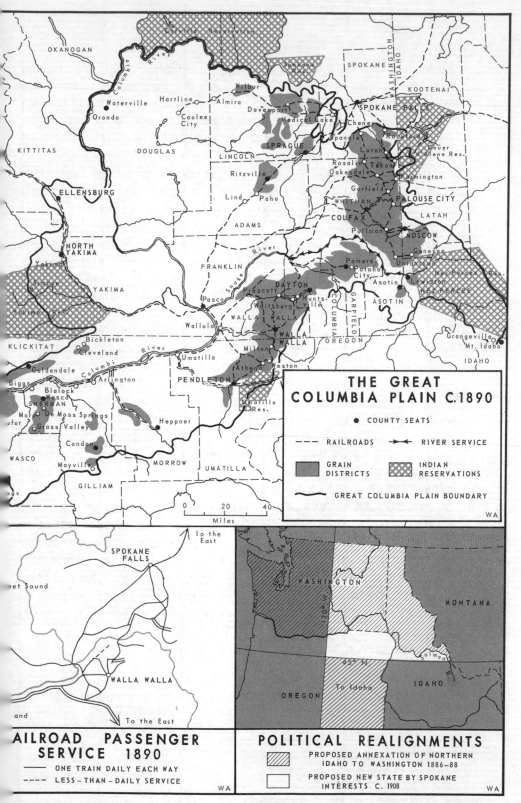

THE GREAT
COLUMBIA PLAIN C.1890

- ● COUNTY SEATS
- --- RAILROADS   ➤ RIVER SERVICE
- ▨ GRAIN DISTRICTS   ▨ INDIAN RESERVATIONS
- —— GREAT COLUMBIA PLAIN BOUNDARY

0   20   40
Miles

WA

RAILROAD PASSENGER SERVICE 1890

—— ONE TRAIN DAILY EACH WAY
--- LESS-THAN-DAILY SERVICE

To the East
SPOKANE FALLS
et Sound
WALLA WALLA
and
To the East

WA

POLITICAL REALIGNMENTS

▨ PROPOSED ANNEXATION OF NORTHERN IDAHO TO WASHINGTON 1886-88
☐ PROPOSED NEW STATE BY SPOKANE INTERESTS C. 1908

WASHINGTON
MONTANA
OREGON
To Idaho
IDAHO
120° W
45° N
Salmon

WA

Map 34, above; Map 35, lower left; Map 36, lower right

pletion of the N.P.'s Cascade line to Puget Sound and of the O.R.&N.'s connection from Umatilla to the East via Pendleton left Walla Walla off all the railroad thoroughfares except the O.R.&N.'s rather devious and belated Portland-Spokane route. With everything north of the Snake being usurped by Spokane Falls, everything west of the Columbia within easy reach of Tacoma and Seattle, and with Portland and The Dalles, as always, in command of the downriver country, Walla Walla merchants found it quite impossible to reach out and serve all the new districts of the Great Columbia Plain. It had been left in an eddy off the mainstream, important locally—in fact, no other town was the focus of so many short branch lines—but closed off from direct access to the region as a whole (Map 35).

This "geographical defeat" was a bitter blow. It was not pleasant to be toppled from an eminence so long enjoyed. After the initial disappointment, however, it was concluded that "all was not lost." Walla Walla was surrounded by the richest and best-developed wheat-land in the Northwest, and it had by no means been completely by-passed by the progress of the times. About five thousand people lived within the town in 1890, and the immediate countryside was the most thickly populated in the interior. Its big mercantile houses, two major banks, and three daily newspapers were a good measure of the size and prosperity of its hinterland. The scale of its farm implement business and its six flour mills were good evidence that it was still a leading center of the grain country, and the establishment of the Hunt Threshing Machine Company, the first major implement factory in the interior, was an important enhancement of that position.[6] Old Fort Walla Walla, now somnolent but tidily maintained, occupied its square mile at the outskirts; and through action of the late territorial legislature, Walla Walla could also boast of "a fine new penitentiary," within which the addition of a jute mill for the manufacture of grain sacks allowed the prisoners to pay their debt to society in a manner unusually practical and satisfactory to local citizens.

Having never been in a position of regional dominance, most

[6] *Ibid.* Throughout this chapter details about the type and number of various establishments in the towns have been derived primarily from R. L. Polk and Company, *Oregon, Washington and Idaho Gazetteer and Business Directory, 1889-90* (Portland, Ore., 1889). Here and there this has been supplemented by an item from one of the many contemporary sources.

other towns of the local area could be well pleased with their progress of the past few years. Dayton, with 1,880 residents, was the largest of these, and its local support was as diversified as any center in the interior: wheatlands of unsurpassed richness, a valley given over to orcharding and other intensive activities, and, despite heavy cutting in the mountains, sufficient forest resources to support two fair-sized sawmills. Huntsville, founded by a United Brethren group as a site for an academy, Waitsburg, the oldest town on the Touchet, and Prescott, laid out by the O.R.&N., were other well-established communities closely spaced in this productive district. Farther east, Pomeroy's triumph over Pataha City seemed fully assured. Gaining the county seat and the railroad terminus were probably the most decisive reasons why its population of 661 was three times that of its bitter rival three miles farther up the flat. At the other end of the Walla Walla country, Milton dominated the upper main valley and Weston and Athena shared the rural trade of the higher wheatlands up on the divide toward the Umatilla. All of these towns had enjoyed a growth well beyond that of a dozen or more others, which may have been initiated as early but had never gotten more than a post office and general store, and perhaps a blacksmith shop and stagecoach inn.

The railroad was the most decisive arbiter of these competitions and at times could affect the prospects of a town even well after it had been granted its coveted facilities. Wallula, with no farmland at all nearby, had always been dependent upon its strategic traffic position. The railroads had made it "pretty much all 'junction'"—the connecting point of the N.P. and O.R.&N., a focus of the O.&W.T., and the base of the important Walla Walla branch. The N.P. established a roundhouse, car repair shop, and coal bunkers, and the O.R.&N. made it a division point, with a ten-stall roundhouse and machine shops. However, in 1889 all of these facilities were moved—those of the N.P. to Pasco, and those of the O.R.&N. to Umatilla—in each case to serve the new mainline traffic—the one across the Cascades, the other across the Blue Mountains. Wallula's population was thereby cut in half, and it was changed from a thriving railway center to a mere focus of tracks, and once again was notable to the traveler for being as much an unlovely "junction of sand dunes and sand ridges" as of routeways. The young town of Pasco, having completely replaced Ainsworth, now inherited part of Wallula's functions and began to see in its position at rail and river junctions a destiny as the "center of the great inland empire." A flour mill, tannery, sawmill, foundry, and meat packing plant were being "talked of" as the new decade was greeted.[7] Actually, Pasco as yet had little more than a newspaper to do the talking and the railroad facilities to support the three or four hundred people on the sandy banks of the Columbia. Certainly nothing in the immediate hinterland would foster much growth, and the central position claimed was a misreading of the new regional patterns that had emerged.

Aside from railroad towns, all others were dependent primarily upon local rural trade, and therefore upon wheat. The Walla Walla country was by far the greatest grain district of the interior. Yet local promoters, especially in Walla Walla city, were now giving much attention to other possibilities in agriculture. After all, practically no good wheatland remained unclaimed, and if the district was to continue to grow, it must turn to more intensive activities which would support a larger rural population. Thus Walla Walla, which had set the pattern for the present farming in the interior, now sought again to lead the way for the next phase. Irrigation was, of course, the oldest kind of agriculture in the area, but it had long languished. There were many small farms scattered along the dense network of creeks, but no comprehensive system of water management had been developed. Each farmer, or perhaps two or three together, had dug small ditches to serve an immediate riverine strip, but on much the same scale and fashion as Marcus Whitman had done half a century before. In view of the potential, it seemed a meager accomplishment to local boosters: ". . . there is room to settle 500 families tomorrow, along Mill Creek alone." Likewise, Walla Walla nurserymen had supplied seeds and seedlings for many of the farm orchards and gardens of the region, but the full commercial possibilities were far from realized.[8]

Yet it was claimed that "this is, *par excellence,* a fruit country." The wonderful success of apples, pears, apricots, quinces, plums, prunes, and berries of almost any kind had been "perfectly demon-

[7] George A. Crofutt, *Crofutt's Overland Tours* (Chicago and Philadelphia, 1889), p. 219; R. C. Julian, "Wallula, Washington," *Pasco Express Souvenir Illustrated Edition,* July 19, 1906; *Spokane Falls Review,* Jan. 1, 1890, p. 31.

[8] The small town of Starbuck was also something of a railroad town, as the helper engines serving the steep Alto grade were stationed here. Newell, *Agriculture by Irrigation. The Wealth and Resources of Oregon and Washington, The Pacific Northwest* (Portland, Ore., 1889), p. 90.

strated," and a greater emphasis upon such products was trumpeted as the road to riches and the trend of the future.[9] It was acknowledged that exceptionally severe weather had on occasion damaged the infant industry (particularly in 1882-83), but every country had such risks, and the general climate was better than that of some of the world's most famous fruit districts. Walla Walla boosters, fond of Old World comparisons, now added another; not only were they favored with a Sicilian wheat soil but their district was destined to become "the Rhineland of America": the "topography is much like it," the location inland from the "westerly ocean currents is hopefully analogous," and the latitude was lower, the climate even less rigorous, and the soil more productive. Such a comparison suggested ideal conditions for more than just the usual fruits: "If wine-growing will not in time be the leading industry of this region, then are indications and presumptions from analogies of soil, climate and location worthless." Considering the fame of Champagne, the Palatinate, and Franconia, it seemed "remarkable" that viticulture had not already become established in the Walla Walla by experienced wine growers. So far, "only enough has been done to demonstrate perfect adaptability."

And the list of opportunities was much longer: tobacco, hops, sorghum, sugar beets, sweet potatoes, broom corn—any one of these, it was claimed, would bring ample rewards, and their success would likely set a pattern for the whole district. Dairying, too, was certain to become a mainstay. Timothy, clovers, and alfalfa thrived and, together with the mountain-fed streams, would allow production of butter of a quality to attract dealers from "as far east as Chicago." Although the need to expand irrigation was emphasized, none of these crops necessarily required it, and many of the promotion writers set forth a scene of slopes and hilltops as well as valley bottoms covered with orchards, vineyards, beet fields, and sown pastures. The aim was the diversification and intensification of all farming.

If the actual picture in 1890 little resembled this vision, it did offer a basis for speculation. The wheat farmers steadfastly rejected any suggestion of change, but in the Walla Walla Valley and along the narrow bottoms of the upper Touchet many of these crops had

[9] Such a view and the subsequent material on this general topic are based primarily upon *Wealth and Resources,* cited above, and another pamphlet, *Eastern Washington,* published by the Watchman Press (Walla Walla, *ca.* 1885); the statements in these two are often nearly identical.

been tested with encouraging results. Orchards had proved profitable for those who gave them adequate attention, dairy products were in short supply throughout the region, local breweries had expressed satisfaction with the few bushels of hops, and analyses of local sugar beets seemed favorable.[10] The mere fact that these things could be grown and marketed in the local towns was no proof that they could be raised on a scale, with a quality, and at a cost sufficient to become regional specialties, which could compete in national markets. On this point the assurances of the local boosters were extravagant, but experimentation was taking place and a nucleus of intensive agriculture was becoming established.

The Palouse Country

The Palouse country in 1890 was an excellent expression of the achievements of twenty years. In 1870 stock raising had only begun, farming had hardly been initiated, and there were few settlers and no real settlements. Two decades later practically all the land had been taken, the eastern portion was a grainland, and the farmers were replacing the stockmen in all but the roughest lands along the western and southern fringes. Although colonization in the 1870's had focused upon a few attractive localities, during the next decade the eastern Palouse proved so uniformly productive, was settled so rapidly, and was so extensively served by railroads that no one community emerged as the dominant trade center of the area. Between Spangle, on the edge of the prairies overlooking the pinelands of Spokane Valley, and Uniontown, a few miles from the brink of the Clearwater Canyon, there was a score of bustling communities which had been adding new businesses and services with every year, each hoping to outdistance its nearest neighbor, all confident of continuous progress.

Colfax, the oldest town, was no longer the largest but was still among the most important. It was the Whitman County seat because no other community had existed to challenge it, and its farmlands and the timber resources along the upper Palouse had sustained its growth. The first railroad surveyors had given it cause for alarm: some persons had derided it as "a mere crack in the ground," strung out along the narrow canyon floor of the south Palouse, and there was fear that the railroad would bypass it entirely. The Ore-

[10] See Hilgard *et al.*, *Climatic and Agricultural Features*, pp. 88-89, for an assay of sugar beets grown at Dayton.

gon Improvement Company did lay out a new center called Plainville three miles south, in the midst of the good wheat country, but the O.R.&N. built into the canyon; and thus Plainville was stillborn and Colfax thrived. In 1890 it was the focus of a number of routes. Railways connected Colfax to Walla Walla, Moscow, and Spokane Falls, stage lines gave service to Palouse City and to Pomeroy, and there had been much talk of other railways to connect with the Northern Pacific somewhere to the north, and to tap the Union Flat district to the south. Its scale and variety of businesses were quite impressive for the time; among the most notable were four hotels, five groceries, six implement houses, two hardwares ("with mammoth stocks"), two newspapers, three banks, a flour mill, a foundry, a pork-packing plant, and a Baptist academy. Its two sawmills were the largest in the interior, with a combined daily capacity of seventy-five thousand board feet. The thin strip of forest along the river had long since been denuded, and these mills depended upon log drives from the Idaho mountains. (Unfortunately, the Palouse was a small and erratic stream, far from ideal for this purpose, and in 1890 a legislative appropriation to improve its channel was requested.) Though proud of these facilities, local promoters were quick to insist upon the opportunities yet remaining. "The chief need of Colfax at present is small manufacturing establishments," reported one booklet, which went on to suggest a linseed oil mill, beet sugar factory, twine mill, woolen mills, and agricultural implement factories. If the prospective investor found that practically no flax, beets, hemp, or wool were being raised in the vicinity, he no doubt would have been assured that they had all been proved "especially adapted" to the area and needed only his initiative to become staple products.[11]

Palouse City, another of the older communities, had had a more colorful and erratic history than its neighbors. Loggers, mill work-

[11] *North Pacific Coast*, 1 (March 1, 1880), 90. *Palouse Gazette* (Colfax), July 30, 1886, announced the intention of the Washington Railway and Transportation Company to build lines from Colfax to McCoy (near Rosalia), Genesee, and Central Ferry. *Spokane Falls Review*, Jan. 1, 1890. Barton, "Washington," pp. 975-76, lists the locations and capacities of the sawmills in Washington as of 1890. 51st Cong., 1st sess., S. Misc. Doc. 68 (Jan. 28, 1890). It was claimed that over twenty million board feet of logs had been driven to Palouse City and Colfax during the previous year. Oregon Railway and Navigation Company, *Eastern Washington Territory and Oregon* (Farmington, W.T., 1888), p. 24.

ers, and miners had long mingled with farmers on its muddy, saloon-lined main street. Gold discoveries in the Hoodoo district near the sources of the Palouse River had prompted a considerable rush in the early 1880's, and though it was not rich enough to sustain much development, the town was the main supply center for what remained. Wheat and timber, however, became more important with each year, and together made it the busiest shipping point and headquarters of the train dispatcher on the N.P.'s important Palouse branch. Three sawmills operated in or at the outskirts, and Palouse City served as outfitting center and off-season residence for most of the logging operations upriver. The arrival of the railroad had caused a rapid growth. In 1890 it had well over a thousand people and the city fathers proudly advertised that its combination of wheat ("2,000,000 bushels this year"), timber ("20,000,000 feet cut this year"), and mining ("$100,000 in gold dust per year") offered "better opportunities for investment here than anywhere else in the state."[12] Certainly the town was beginning to present a more substantial picture to any would-be investor. Ten years before, the community had decided that its original site, on the shoulder of a steep hill above the first mill on the river, was no proper place for a growing town, and had elected to move, buildings and all, to a narrow flat just downstream on the north bank. The new location was roomier but also muddier, and every spring the main street became almost impassable ("not even jackassable"—as a crude sign one year expressed the old western cliché). When Palouse City was finally incorporated in 1888, the chief municipal desire was to extricate itself from its mudhole, a project hastened by a momentary disaster—a fire which burned out half of the business district. Typical of the times, optimism was undaunted and rebuilding began immediately. Main Street was filled in and raised six feet, and this improvement, together with water lines, sewers, and sidewalks, began to rescue the town from its bog. As numerous new brick buildings—including the elaborate three-story St. Elmo Hotel— began to replace the ramshackle wooden false fronts, Palouse City took on a respectable civic appearance.

In the Idaho corner of the Palouse country, Moscow was "rapidly assuming the proportions of a substantial city." With about two

[12] Kincaid and Harris, *Palouse*, pp. 13-15. Most of the following details on Palouse City are derived from this source. *Spokane Falls Review*, July 20, 1890, p. 15.

thousand population, it was the largest town in the area. Unlike its rough neighbor to the north, it was "well drained and well arranged" and was about to assume an even more civilized air as "plans and specifications for the erection of suitable buildings" to house the territorial university had just been accepted and construction would soon begin.[13] Several small sawmills in the nearby mountains supplied local needs, but the main basis of prosperity was the rich farmland on all sides. Two modern flour mills served the export market, and a second railroad, the Northern Pacific's Lewiston line, arrived at 1890 to tap the heavy grain traffic.

That railroad branch, after various surveys, was built east from Pullman, and real estate in that town "took a sudden rise."[14] Established several years after its larger neighbors, Pullman had grown rapidly after garnering two railroads in as many years, which made it an important wheat shipping point.

These four towns, with an aggregate population of over fifty-five hundred, could be encompassed within a circle of little more than ten miles radius. Had all their activities been concentrated within a single city, the Palouse would have had a major regional center, comparable to Walla Walla in the area south of the Snake. As it was, most functions were shared and duplicated among the four towns, no one of which performed as a single focus for any activity for the Palouse country as a whole. Beyond this central cluster there were at least ten communities rather evenly spaced within the railroad net, generally similar in size, character, and prospects: Spangle, Rosalia, Oakesdale, Garfield, Farmington, Tekoa, Latah, and Rockford to the north; Uniontown and Genesee to the south. In each a weekly newspaper vigorously promoted its fortunes, attempting to attract people, businesses, and industries. All had grain merchants and the usual nucleus of stores, blacksmith shops, and implement dealers, but only two had banks, three had flour mills, and none had the full array of services and industries which might give it confident expectations of garnering a larger trade and surpassing its nearby rivals. Any activity which would lure people, advertise its opportunities, or keep the name of the town before the public was eagerly sought, and thus in 1890 Garfield enjoyed a wonderful Fourth of July when a celebration staged by

[13] Alanson Smith, "Idaho," 51st Cong., 2nd sess., H. Ex. Doc. 6 (1890), p. 550; also *Spokane Falls Review,* Jan 1, 1890, p. 27.
[14] *The Spokesman* (Spokane Falls), July 4, 1890.

the Whitman County Farmers' Alliance, assisted by the W.C.T.U., drew six thousand people for an all-day gathering:

> From early morning to 10 o'clock farmers' wagons, hacks and buggies rolled into town from every hill in a continuous stream. There were excursion trains on both the Union Pacific and Northern Pacific. . . . It was a great opportunity for them to talk "crops and things.". . . Every local office seeker was on hand and the poor farmer was waylaid on every turn.[15]

Certainly Garfield residents had talked about Garfield as well as "crops and things." No doubt every orator had praised the town's handsomeness, prosperity, and promise, and if in the days following it was no different than before, at least it had enjoyed a magnificent bit of publicity.

The Big Bend

Whereas the Palouse exhibited the developments of twenty years, the Big Bend bore the marks of no more than ten. Indeed, the visitor of 1890 would have found himself in the midst of a swirling land rush. New settlers were arriving daily, dismounting stiffly from the wooden seats of the immigrant trains to scatter out in search of farms, while promoters, tradesmen, and speculators were sizing up the prospects of the new towns. The Washington Central branch of the N.P. provided the main entryway and set the principal axis of settlement. A trip westward along that line in the spring of 1890 would have displayed in its succession of communities the whole process of town development—though in reverse sequence—from Cheney, with all its substance of ten year's growth, through a half dozen others, each newer than the last, on out to the end of track where the terminus town was yet but a pattern of stakes on the ground.

Cheney, with a population of 647, though secure as a local trade center and "the gateway to the Big Bend," was a disappointed town. Spokane Falls had obviously triumphed in their keen rivalry, and had recently capped its success by capturing, once again and irrevocably, the county seat. Cheney still dreamed of retribution. The current hope was that the Northern Pacific would extend its Big Bend line on west to Ellensburg and then build directly east from Cheney to Missoula to form a new and much shorter transcontinental trunk route. This would relegate Spokane Falls to a branch line,

[15] *Ibid.*, July 5, 1890.

while at the same time making Cheney the logical new location of the division point and railroad shops.[16]

The first village along the Washington Central branch was not a typical wheat country settlement at all. In the 1870's the peculiar qualities of Medical Lake had become part of the folklore of the region. The first local resident claimed that he had cured his sheep of the scab and himself of rheumatism by a plunge into its waters, and soon others reported fine effects from bathing or drinking. As a visitor of 1890 reported:

> The fame of Medical Lake soon extended through Washington and Oregon, and every summer invalids came to camp upon its pine-clad shores. A village sprang up, hotels of a simple country type were built, and a building with apparatus for hot baths was put up. Next followed a concern for evaporating the water and obtaining from it the mineral salts, which, ground to a fine white powder, were put up in tin boxes and sold by travelling agents to the drug stores on the Pacific Coast, and later in the East. A rival salt-making factory was soon set up and in recent years the competition has been sharp enough to bring the price at times down from two dollars per pound, to fifty cents. It now rests at the golden mean of one dollar. . . .[17]

Thus Medical Lake became the first resort town in the interior. In 1890 it numbered 617 residents and had ample accommodations for many more seasonal visitors.

Davenport regarded itself as the main town within the real wheat country of the Big Bend. It was the oldest, but only by a few months, and although small was growing rapidly. In the summer of 1890 it celebrated the entry of its second railroad, the S.L.S. & E., which was soon offering a daily train direct to Spokane Falls, covering the forty miles in only two hours and thirty-five minutes. However, Davenport's jubilation was stifled when it became known that the N.P. had assumed control of its rival, to which was added the further indignity of losing another county seat election to Sprague. Moreover, other towns along the line had suddenly emerged to compete for settlers and businesses. Wilbur, platted only the year before, was

[16] *Spokane Falls Review*, Jan. 1, 1890; *The Spokesman*, Aug. 3, 1890. The Cheney Academy had been established in 1883 with a gift of land and cash from the Northern Pacific, but it was not a flourishing success and in March, 1890, was deeded to the state to become a normal school; J. Orin Oliphant, "The Benjamin P. Cheney Academy," *Washington Historical Quarterly*, 15 (April, 1924), 106-16.

[17] E. V. Smalley, "In the Big Bend Country," *The Northwest*, 8 (May, 1890), 15; see also *The Spokesman*, Aug. 3, 1890.

advertising itself as certain to be the largest town of the area, and had already incorporated, organized a board of trade, and gained the promise of a flour mill. Wilbur boosters argued that because it was located "in almost the exact geographical center" of the agricultural region between the scablands and Grand Coulee, it was as natural for the trade of that country to focus upon Wilbur as "for stock to go to water when they are dry or to seek shelter in a storm."[18]

But "nature" did not confer leadership so inevitably, the situation was wholly in flux, and no town could be fully assured of its future. At that very moment Almira, a few miles down the track and only ninety days old, was boasting of fifty "good, substantial business houses and dwellings of people full of thrift and industry." Immigration was at flood tide, and soon, so it was claimed, a new county would have to be formed and Almira would "fall heir to the county seat without any strife or doubt, which, with other combined advantages and surrounding influence, will make her one of the future cities of Central Washington." Her claim to be the natural trading center for "about 350,000,000 acres of splendid farming country" was either an outrageous exaggeration or a ludicrous misprint, but in either case could serve as an apt display of the boundless enthusiasm of the times.[19]

By midyear the railroad had reached Coulee City, and another infant town joined in the rivalry. Although only put on the market in April, by August its promoters could point to a wonderful growth: four general merchandise stores, one ready-made clothing and furnishing house, two "first class" hotels, two bakeries, three lumber yards, a blacksmith and wagon shop, two livery stables, and three real estate agents. These together with a roundhouse, coal bunkers, "and all that belongs to a division station" seemed to assure a much greater future, whether or not the railroad was built on farther toward Badger Mountain or the Okanogan. These people "think they have the world by the tail, and are bound to have a city second hardly to Chicago," wrote one disenchanted visitor who thought Coulee City "a little miserable town," and was more im-

[18] *The Spokesman,* July 5, 1890; Steele and Rose, *Big Bend Country,* pp. 94-96, 145-50; *Spokane Falls Review,* Jan. 1, 1890, p. 24.

[19] *Spokane Falls Review,* Jan. 1, 1890, p. 23. Wilbur, with the same idea, joined Sprague to defeat Davenport's bid for the Lincoln County seat. By retaining the seat in the far southeast corner, Wilbur hoped to become central within this new proposed county. *The Spokesman,* Aug. 3, 1890.

pressed by the scarcity of water and the clouds of dust in his mid-summer journey through a country he thought "should be called the Great American Desert."[20]

These little towns were "all wild over railroad matters," reported the same man, and none equaled the frenzy of Waterville, still far-ther west and as yet beyond the magic touch of the iron track. Although the census had granted it a population of but 293, its two newspapers and energetic citizens saw greatness in its future. Not only could they claim the usual array of business houses, but other and better measures of civic progress, including "a live board of trade, a good brass band, a good church building and three ministers of the gospel, a singing school, fire company, skating rink, three benevolent organizations, and numberless progressive euchre parties for the entertainment of the fair sex." No town was more addicted to geographical reasoning. Because of the "peculiar topographical formation," all the trade of the area between the Grand Coulee and the Columbia would be "forced into the lap of Waterville," but more, it was "near the west end of the farming country and the nearest point to tide water on the prairie. It is the beginning of the mining and lumbering country just such a position as is occupied by Denver, Rapid City, the peerless Spokane Falls and other won-derful and rapid-growing cities of the West." And, even better, it was located "in the same range of townships" midway between the "Queen City of the Sound" (Seattle) and the "Minneapolis of the West" (Spokane Falls), and that alone ought to be "sufficient to make Waterville the great railroad center of the Big Bend." Al-though at the time the railroad was reached only by stagecoaches to Coulee City (daily) and Ellensburg (twice weekly), the prospect was enough to spur metropolitan dreams. There was talk not only of a water system and electric lights but of a streetcar system as well.[21] The outermost ripple of this wave of frenzied activity rolling out in advance of the iron rails had reached the banks of the Colum-bia. At the foot of a steep canyon trail under the brow of the Waterville plateau an energetic pioneer had established a store and post office in 1888, added a grist mill, and in 1890 had the *Orondo News*

[20] *The Spokesman*, Aug. 3, 1890; Daniel C. Haskell (ed.), *On Reconnais-sance for the Great Northern: Letters of C. F. B. Haskell, 1889-1891* (New York, 1948), pp. 25-26.

[21] *Spokane Falls Review*, Jan. 1, 1890, p. 26. *Morning Review* (Spokane Falls), May 12, 1889; Steele and Rose, *Big Bend Country*, p. 572.

proclaiming the assured future of this "natural junction" of river and rail, the coming port for the Big Bend and the Okanogan.[22] As yet he had few neighbors, but he was confident that he would soon be surrounded.

On the other side of the region another string of communities along the main line of the Northern Pacific skirted the southeastern border of the Big Bend between Spokane Falls and Pasco. However, these were rather different in character from the towns along the Washington Central branch. Sprague, the first one beyond Cheney, had metropolitan pretensions as great as any of its contemporaries and a population and development which surpassed most of them, but its line of brick business blocks, handsome residences, opera house, city hall, electric light plant, and Roman Catholic school were an expression not of its farm trade but of its forty thousand dollar monthly payroll. It was almost wholly a creation of the railroad. The N.P. had selected its site, bestowed its name, and then established the division headquarters, yards, and shops ("the largest and best equipped west of Brainerd, Minn.") in its support. Although Sprague did have rural contacts, its location in the midst of the scabland corridor did not favor it with an immediate hinterland comparable to those of its rivals to the northwest and southeast. That very site was both a joy and embarrassment to its boosters. While they might brag of its picturesque setting in the shallow coulee with running water and lakes nearby, the land seekers more likely agreed with the traveler who thought it a "peculiarly unattractive town . . . in a narrow valley, sultry and desolate and hemmed in by black ledges of volcanic rock." But if Sprague had little prospect of becoming a premier agricultural center, it had its own kind of dreams. The summer of 1890 brought an exciting batch of rumors: The N.P. was going to enlarge its facilities greatly; the O.R. &N. would build through to tap the Big Bend; a smelter would be established (presumably for Coeur d'Alene ores). The prospects never seemed brighter, lot prices were soaring, and the city council had happily granted a franchise for a streetcar line.[23]

A trip farther down this line would reveal little of the scale and

[22] Lindley M. Hull, *A History of Central Washington* . . . (Spokane, Wash., 1929), pp. 410-11, 523.

[23] *Spokane Falls Review,* Jan. 1, 1890, p. 28; "Sprague and the Big Bend Country," *The Northwest,* 2 (September, 1884), 6-7; Steele and Rose, *Big Bend Country,* pp. 173-79..

bustle of the developments elsewhere, for the results obtained by the earliest pioneers had been insufficiently promising to attract the main surge of immigration. By the end of the decade, wheat raising had become well established in the Ritzville district, but it had been a difficult struggle and the achievements in general would hardly bear comparison with those in the Walla Walla or Palouse. There was one exceptional locale, however, which seemed to demonstrate what might be accomplished over a much wider area. A short distance west of Ritzville a group of German families had settled, each purchasing a half section of land. Though literally scraping the earth to get started—living in dugouts and gathering cow dung and sagebrush for fuel—through hard work and good management (especially in tillage and fallowing) they had achieved unusual success. Good houses, orchards, windbreaks, and windmills already made them a distinctive island in the semi-arid pioneer landscape of Adams County. However, the average farmer elsewhere had accomplished much less, although the area was not wholly bypassed by the land seekers. Just prior to 1890 a substantial number of claims had been taken up even along the southern margin of the county. But the subdued nature of development was well expressed in the towns. Recently incorporated, Ritzville was a decade old with a flour mill and a newspaper, but its three hundred people were considerably fewer than several younger towns in the interior. On down the track, Paha, originally a private promotion which had failed, was replatted by the N.P. in 1889, and Lind was staked out (four blocks of sixteen lots each) in the following year.[24] But none of the three displayed much of the bustle and boosterism so endemic elsewhere. The agricultural development of this droughty fringe was obviously still in an experimental stage.

Beyond these agricultural margins in the Big Bend, it would have been unusual in 1890 to have encountered even a guarded optimism. It was not just that the stockmen had now yielded all of their best rangelands to the fence and plow—that was neither new nor unexpected—but that they had been staggered by another blow from nature. A cold and snowy January which had weakened their herds was not too uncommon, but a heavy blizzard followed by a bitterly cold spell in March proved devastating. Local estimates that only a

[24] *The Northwest*, 10 (May, 1892), 35; Steele and Rose, *Big Bend Country*, pp. 782, 788; *Ritzville Journal-Times, Adams County Pioneer Edition*, Sept. 15, 1949, p. 39.

quarter of the sheep and cattle had survived even in the warmer desert of Franklin County were perhaps exaggerations, but it was clear that many a stockman had been ruined and that the whole industry had yet to be placed on a sound sustaining basis.[25] Local commentators stated that a good lesson had now been learned and that the necessity of putting up hay for such winter emergencies was clear to all. But this was an old refrain, the same lesson had been taught every few years over the past three decades, and it was still not clear that such harsh teaching had at last been accepted.

Yakima, Kittitas, and Klickitat

West of the Columbia the pattern of communities was different from that in the grainlands to the east. The railroad paralleled the Yakima River for 130 miles, from its mouth to the mountains, but instead of a series of aggressive towns, most of the names spaced along the track were little more than just that—a siding and a signpost. The fact that town development and competition was largely focused upon but two centers—Ellensburg and North Yakima— reflected the pattern of development of the countryside. Although much of the valley land was now in private title, agriculture was confined to irrigated flats and subirrigated stream margins. The territorial legislature had cleared the legal obstacle to expansion by approving the doctrine of appropriation for the waters of Yakima and Kittitas counties, and more than a score of irrigation companies had filed for incorporation. But development was costly; some of the companies had already failed, most soon would, and very few could show any visible measure of accomplishment.[26]

The most reassuring exhibit of the time was the Moxee ranch in the small valley just east of North Yakima, where a company had about five hundred acres under irrigation. Most were in barley and alfalfa but great publicity was being given to the fifty acres in tobacco and to the product of the four cigar makers, which "experts" claimed was "nearer to Havana flavor than anything they had ever smoked."[27] In the Kittitas Valley the town canal which opened up a block of land east of Ellensburg was the major accomplishment. The

[25]Steele and Rose, *Big Bend Country*, pp. 90-92; *The Spokesman* (Spokane Falls), July 22, 1890.

[26] Lyman, *Yakima Valley*, pp. 350-52, 354-56; 51st Cong., 1st sess., S. Rept. 928 (1890), I, 304-5.

[27] Barton, "Washington," pp. 1026-28; 51st Cong., 1st sess., S. Rept. 928, Pt. 1 (1889-90), pp. 266-75; *The Spokesman* (Spokane Falls), Aug. 3, 1890.

A sketch of North Yakima which appeared in *The West Shore* in 1887, a view appropriately focused upon the new depot and a Northern Pacific train, which company was responsible for the town's founding and early growth. *(Photo courtesy of Northern Pacific Railway Company)*

Typical of the most common industrial activity in the region, the Palouse City Roller Mills was a water-powered establishment at the rapids just across the river from the upper end of Main Street. The railroad was a spur to a sawmill just upriver. This 1889 view also offers a good sample of residential architecture on the North Hill. *(Photo courtesy of Washington State University Library)*

total acreage under ditch from these and all of the smaller projects was certainly not large, but there was good reason for optimism because the achievements were obviously so far short of the potential.

There was, however, a serious problem in attracting the interest of investors and land seekers. As one local resident put it, while a man from California or Nevada "knows just how to go to work at and what to do with" a plot of Yakima sagebrush and will have it "irrigated in three weeks and . . . blooming in a very short time," most of the newcomers were from the East and knew nothing about irrigation. Such a person "comes out here and looks over the country and concludes that starvation stares him in the face, and if he has money enough to go back, he does."[28] First these people must be educated on the merits of irrigation agriculture. But there were also the obstacles of cost and the complications of organized development. At the moment there was hope that the federal government, which had held hearings on irrigation problems through the West during the previous summer, would soon make surveys of reservoir sites, irrigable areas, and related matters. Few believed as yet that the government ought to build dams and dig canals, but the provision of reliable basic information would be a proper service. It was felt that such information, combined with the crop results already obtained, ought to be a convincing lure for private development.

Ellensburg and North Yakima were similar in many ways, each the focal point of a small irrigation district and of a broader encompassing ranching area. Each was a county seat and a boom town of considerable substance, with scores of business houses, several hundred homes, and an expanding pattern of new subdivisions staked out upon its margins. Although the intervening ridges and narrow canyon set them apart physically, each in a local compartment, their aspirations could not be so contained. These wider visions were inevitably competitive, for each community saw itself not only as the logical metropolis for the whole Yakima country but as the central city of the entire state. This latter rivalry had caused them to split the east-side vote for the location of the capital of the newly admitted state and thereby make certain that this political prize would go to Olympia. Ellensburg was allocated one of the state normal schools, a modest consolation prize, but North Yakima was

28 Testimony given in 51st Cong., 1st sess., S. Rept. 928, Pt. 1 (1889-90), p. 283.

still locked in a struggle with Spokane Falls and Colfax for the agricultural college.[29]

As for enlarging their regional positions, North Yakima's hopes at the moment rested primarily upon a projected railroad link with Vancouver, opening up a new route to the sea, and agricultural, pastoral, and timber districts enroute. Ellensburg was still determined to capture the Okanogan trade with a combined rail and riverboat service. No rails had yet been laid, but ten miles of roadbed had been graded, and the project seemed so certain that even some of the most accurate maps of the time showed the Tacoma, Ellensburg and Conconnully Railroad and Navigation Company as a reality.[30]

In 1890 the Kittitas community had an edge in this competition. The census recorded 2,768 people, compared with 1,535 for North Yakima, whose civic leaders were demanding a recount. The principal factor in this advantage was probably the Northern Pacific, which had selected Ellensburg as the headquarters of the Cascade division operating between Pasco and Tacoma. On July 4, 1889, Ellensburg had been nearly leveled by a devastating fire, but within a week reconstruction had begun, and by 1890 the town was already so much larger and better than before that its citizens might remind the visitor with pride that Spokane Falls and Seattle had suffered in the same way in that very same year, and broadly imply that a great fire was itself an indicator of great progress.[31]

In the lower Yakima Valley a falls in the river had prompted a vigorous promotion of the townsite of Prosser. An irrigation and power company was formed and plans laid for a dam, canal system, electric lights, and industrial development;[32] but little had as yet been accomplished. A generous estimate of the population was one

[29] The first vote, in 1889, was: Olympia 25,490; North Yakima 14,711; Ellensburg 12,833; others 2,139. As Olympia did not have a majority, a second vote was held in 1890 with the following result: Olympia 37,413, North Yakima 6,276, Ellensburg 7,722. Arthur S. Beardsley, "Later Attempts to Relocate the Capital of Washington," *Pacific Northwest Quarterly*, 32 (October, 1941), 401-47. Lyman, *Yakima Valley*, p. 710; *The Spokesman*, July 15, 1890. The three-man legislative committee had so far balloted twice, with one vote for each town each time. In 1891 a new committee selected Pullman.

[30] Lyman, *Yakima Valley*, p. 694. An example of such a map is Northern Pacific Railway, *Sectional Land Maps of Eastern Washington and Northern Idaho* (1891).

[31] *The Spokesman*, Aug. 3, 1890; Lyman, *Yakima Valley*, pp. 691-93.

[32] Lyman, *Yakima Valley*, pp. 830-31.

hundred, and if the future hung promisingly upon the falls, the present hung precariously upon the meager rural trade with the wheat farmers of the dry hills south of town.

Beyond those hills lay Klickitat County, an elongated strip between the ridge and the river wherein the farmers were even more narrowly confined between the edge of the forest on the north and the rough and rocky margins of the Columbia canyon on the south. In the east Cleveland and Bickleton had been platted almost simultaneously and only three miles apart in an area that held little promise of sustaining even one town. Each had a store, post office, and sawmill gnawing at the fringe of the forest, but both were so remote from the arteries of trade and traffic and so much of the surrounding land seemed more appropriate for sheep than wheat that they lay untouched by the town boom prevalent elsewhere. Goldendale, the county seat thirty miles to the southwest, was the only center of growth. Here the countryside was becoming well settled, local demands kept four sawmills busy nearby, and the bank, newspaper, flour mill, and fervent interest in railroads gave it an air comparable to towns in the larger agricultural districts. Wheat was hauled to the river at Columbus, and there was a daily stage to The Dalles, but a railroad was deemed an imperative need. A local group had formed the Columbia Valley and Goldendale Railroad Company in 1889 but had accomplished little more. Typically, they could not confine their plans to a mere feeder to the river, but talked grandly of a line from the Columbia through the Yakima and on to the Colville Valley.[33]

The Dalles and Its Hinterland

This lack of a railroad on the Washington side was sheer gain for the Oregon side, as all traffic was thereby focused toward the river and mostly funneled through The Dalles. And in fact this old gateway town was thriving on just such a situation—a quickened pace of settlement, but a lagging rate of railroad extension—throughout its hinterland. In 1890 the general appearance of the town—its shade trees, dwellings, and air of maturity—was likely to leave a favorable impression upon the casual visitor as it had twenty years before, but the vigor of its economic life had been greatly improved. A decade ago the new tide of immigration and the construction of the O.R.

[33] *Klickitat, Yakima, and Kittitas*, pp. 109-10, 139, 142.

Despite the frenzy of railroad building in the 1880's, a few districts remained dependent upon other facilities, as these photographs vividly illustrate: *Upper*—A trail wagon and its hitch of twelve horses unloading at The Dalles after a long haul from the tablelands to the south. *Lower*—The *Spokane* loading at Waha Landing, on the Snake above Lewiston. *(Photos courtesy of Northern Pacific Railway Company)*

&N. along the Columbia had rescued it from its doldrums, and the establishment of the railroad division point and car shops, employing over two hundred men, had done much to sustain its new level.[34] Once revived it attracted other activities: a sawmill and woodworking plants served by a timber flume from the mountains, a salmon cannery served by several large fish wheels along the Columbia, a modern roller-process flour mill served by the wheat districts opening up on the plateau. And the new era was even more apparent in such signs of civic improvement as sidewalks, water works, electric light system, "an elegant brick opera house," and two private and three public schools. As local citizens looked out upon a hinterland —stretching east to Willow Creek and far south, even beyond the margins of the Great Plain—and saw what was happening, they were certain that the recent growth was only the first step toward a greater future.

The patterns and processes evident at the moment in that hinterland represented another local variation within the over-all regional colonization movement. Except for the country near The Dalles, it was, like the Big Bend, largely a new area of agricultural development. Although the farmers had reaped some good crops, there had been some poor ones also, and there must still be much experimentation to determine where and how wheat might be an assured success. In contrast to the Big Bend, however, no railroad cut through the fertile districts to serve a broad swath of rural colonization and a string of bustling towns. No railroad did because no railroad could: the agricultural area was a scattering of plateau fragments, each lying well back from and above the Columbia and separated from one another by rugged canyons. The steady increase in the number of wagon trains which brought the harvest down off the tableland to Blalock, Rufus, Biggs, and The Dalles was a good indication that railroad branches might be worth building; but the traffic was tributary to the O.R.&N., and since there was no threat of invasion by a rival, the company was in no hurry to undertake the task.

Because farm development was so new and no railroads had been built onto the plateau, the pattern of towns was unstable. Dufur, much older than most, was a firm fixture in the Fifteenmile Creek district back of The Dalles, but east of the Deschutes the situation was in flux. Wasco, Moro, and Grass Valley in Sherman County,

[34] Adams, To and Fro, p. 390. Most of the following is based upon Lang, "Oregon," pp. 705-840, and Shaver et al, History of Central Oregon.

and Olex, Condon, and Mayville in Gilliam thought of themselves as competing for supremacy in their general districts. As one pioneer recalled, some of these had barely become "enough of a town so that you could see it with the naked eye," and none had the number of citizens or services to give it a clear-cut advantage.[35] The creation of these two counties was political recognition that colonization was fragmented by the Deschutes and John Day canyons, and had set off the usual intense rivalries for the county seat. Wasco and Condon held the coveted prize at the moment, but with little sense of security; Gilliam County, only five years old, had already held three elections on the issue, and a slight increase in the population or importance of some locality would probably be sufficient to revive the question. Arlington (formerly Alkali) had been Condon's bitterest rival and was certainly the most substantial town of the area. However, it was not in the wheat country but only a shipping point along the dry rocky river margins. The town was incorporated and had a bank and newspaper, but it could hardly dress up the site and surroundings as easily as the name, and it seemed unlikely to be in a position for any considerable growth.

Although the merchants of The Dalles were certain that the growth of these localities would magnify their trade and prosperity, it was the relative meagerness of development which kept the outlying areas firmly bound to the old river town. The towns had no railroad, and they lacked the variety and scale of stores, banks, wheat agents, implement dealers, and other necessary services; therefore the settlers had to look to the nearest center offering these things. There was, however, ample evidence elsewhere in the interior that such a situation was unlikely to endure.

In fact one need only look east to Morrow County to realize what was likely to happen in Sherman and Gilliam. This Willow Creek country had once been as firmly a part of The Dalles trade area as the lands to the west, but when the railroad branch was completed up the valley to Heppner that town "brightened up and started on a new growth," and began to perform many of the functions that had heretofore been performed by The Dalles. In 1890 it had two banks,

[35] De Moss Springs was even less notable in size but was certainly distinctive in character. It was founded by James M. De Moss, the head of a family of touring evangelists and musicians, who camped on the site, decided to make it a permanent home, and laid out a town with streets named for poets and composers. Giles French, *The Golden Land: A History of Sherman County, Oregon* (Portland, Ore., 1958), pp. 145-47.

several mercantile houses, a flour mill, implement dealers, wheat and wool agents, and numerous other facilities, none of which was subsidiary to the older center. The railroad was the key; once goods could be shipped directly to and from Portland, once buyers and salesmen could ride the coaches right into Heppner and put up at the new Palace Hotel (three stories, "practically fire-proof, provided with water, baths, and electric lights"), local services from The Dalles were superfluous. Morrow County citizens had had to donate the right of way and depot grounds as an inducement to the O.R. &N., but it is unlikely that in 1890 many thought of these as other than a gift well repaid.[36]

Pendleton and the Umatilla

Still farther east in the next valley, Pendleton was one of the most prosperous and progressive towns of the interior. A "handsome, large, and commodious" ninety thousand dollar brick courthouse represented its hold upon Umatilla County. Well-graded streets and a new electric light system displayed its civic improvement, while its eight churches, two church academies, fine public school system, and twenty fraternal organizations were proud demonstrations of its religious, intellectual, and social progress. More basic to its actual growth were its flour mills, planing mill, foundry, and two large woolen mills. Midsummer of 1890 was enlivened by rumors that a paper mill and a street railway might soon be established, and the demonstrated willingness of local citizens to support such projects gave more substance to these reports in Pendleton than in many another town. The wool scouring company had been lured by a successful stock promotion undertaken by the local Commercial Association, and a year or so before eighty thousand dollars had been raised to help obtain a second railroad.[37]

It was evident that growth had been rapid, and the more avid boosters were certain that it had been greater than preliminary census figures indicated: "...that Umatilla county has only 12,000 or 13,000 inhabitants is simply an absurdity," declared the editor of the East Oregonian, who demanded a recount. But the final figures

[36] The West Shore, 15 (April, 1889), 190; Parsons and Shiach, History of Umatilla and Morrow Counties, p. 296.

[37] Parsons and Shiach, History of Umatilla and Morrow Counties, pp. 173-81; East Oregonian (Pendleton), Aug. 12, 1890; The West Shore, 15 (June, 1889), 348. The townspeople wanted to get the Oregon and Washington Territory, the "Hunt system," to build a branch from Wallula.

of 2,506 for the town and 13,381 for the county were not over-shadowed by many others in the interior. Aside from Spokane, only Walla Walla and The Dalles, both much older, surpassed Pendleton by a significant amount, and only Whitman had a larger county population. Considering the fact that much of Umatilla was locked up in the Indian reservations—a galling disability which it was hoped would soon be overcome—it was, all in all, a hopeful position.[38] A considerable portion of the county was more focused upon Walla Walla than upon Pendleton, but the fine wheatlands to the north, the excellent situation for stockmen, with wintering grounds down the valley and summer grazing in the mountains, and the un-surpassed railroad situation on the main line, and with direct connections to Portland and to Puget Sound—together with the demonstrated progressiveness of its citizenry, seemed to offer the town an unusually firm basis for optimism.

Lewiston and Vicinity

Pendleton's cry for the opening of her bordering Indian reservation to white settlement brought an echo from another town similarly aggrieved: "Lewiston like Pendleton is hemmed in and hampered by the Indian reservation question. Our best land is under lock and key." Unfortunately for Lewiston, this statement was no editorial exaggeration. The high-lying Camas Prairie, almost completely enclosed by the Nez Perces Reservation, was the only good agricultural area tributary. The fertile Palouse lay just to the north, but was reached only by a tortuous steep grade up over the canyon rim and was already tapped by railroads and firmly focused in other directions. The Asotin country, across the Snake, was more accessible but less productive. It was one of the few districts which had lost population recently. A few good harvests in the mid-1880's had attracted an influx, but the crops had been near failures for the past three or four years. By August it was clear that 1890 would show little improvement there or anywhere in the low country around Lewiston. There was hope for change in this limiting situation, however, because the federal government had initiated its new policy of allotting each Indian family a farm and setting aside pasture and timber reserves, after which, presumably, the remainder would be opened for white settlement. Many persons had already arrived in the vicinity in anticipation, but had found the process

[38] *East Oregonian,* July 10, Aug. 12, 1890.

proceeding at a typically bureaucratic pace, with no indication as to when Indian lands would be available.[39] Sixty miles to the south, at Grangeville on the southern margin of the prairie, others hovered in similar hope and frustration.

Important as that issue was, 1890 found Lewiston far more excited about railroads than reservations. No town had been more anguished over the matter, for no town had been so certain of the inherent superiority of its position and yet so completely ignored. In the first years of the railroad excitement, a local editor assured his readers that Lewiston was "the key" to the over-all strategies simply because "Lewiston is not an accidental location . . . it exists through the inexorable operation of natural laws." Unfortunately, the railroads persistently defied nature, lending their magic touch to dozens of upstart towns while leaving historic Lewiston completely "shut off from the newly awakened life of the west." Instead of the "rush and roar of the steam car" and "the warning jingle of the street-car mule," Lewiston had only the "rumble and dust of the primitive stage coach" and "the tinkle-tinkle of the pack train." But suddenly that "strange anomaly" seemed near an end. In April it was announced that negotiations with the Northern Pacific had been completed. Lewiston was to furnish a subsidy of sixty-five thousand dollars, plus a free right of way and depot grounds in the city, and the N.P. would extend a branch from its Palouse line by way of the Potlatch Canyon.[40]

"Have you bought a lot in Lewiston yet?" asked the *Teller*, "There is going to be a big boom here this summer; don't you forget it. You can buy a lot right now for $150 that will be worth $500 in a year's time." That may have been fair advice. In May the contracts were let, final surveys run, and everything began in earnest. At Latah, where the line would reach the bottom of Potlatch Canyon, a town was formally platted, its name changed to Kendrick in honor of the chief engineer of the N.P., and fifty-two hundred dollars worth of lots were sold in three hours one May afternoon. And if anyone had any doubts about Lewiston finally getting the attention her position deserved, these might have been dispelled a few days

[39] *Lewiston Teller*, Aug. 7, 28, 1890; Newell, *Agriculture by Irrigation*, p. 240; *The Spokesman*, Aug. 20, 1890; *History of North Idaho*, p. 88; *The West Shore*, 15 (July, 1889), 381-82.

[40] *The West Shore*, 7 (September, 1881), p. 241, quoting the *Lewiston News*; *Lewiston Teller*, April 10, 24, 1890.

later when Charles F. Adams, president of the Union Pacific, together with a host of other U.P. and O.R.&N. officials, stepped off the *Annie Faxon,* arriving from Riparia on its upriver run. One official was quoted as believing it likely that the U.P. would build from Huntington all the way down the Snake River Canyon to avoid "the snow blockades" on the Blue Mountains. It was also well known that a line west to Pomeroy had been surveyed a few years before. It seemed logical that the O.R.&N. would need something better than the *Annie Faxon* and her sister sternwheelers to compete with the N.P. for the trade of so important a center. From this time on railroad rumors gained in strength and variety through the year: the Burlington would build to the coast via Lolo Pass, the Midland Pacific was surveying a Sioux City–Seattle route, the Seattle and Salt Lake would come through via the Snake River (and no enterprise "has started out with so much assurance of success and stability").[41] It seemed that those "inexorable natural laws" were at last prevailing and would bring the railroads as they had the rivers into one grand junction at Lewiston. With such a solid boom under way, the official census (849) need not be accepted as a humiliation nor dismissed as inaccurate, but simply ignored as anachronistic. Iron strands would soon be weaving this neglected corner into the fabric of the new empire.

GENERALITIES

The Harvest of 1890

In the long hot days of July the harvest began in the Walla Walla and Umatilla. While the towns displayed the progress of twenty years or more, the measure of each year was first taken on the farms. The headers opening their swaths around the grainfields marked the onset of an annual pulsation of activity. A view from the summit of one of the high rounded hills might reveal a half dozen or more such machines at work, each with six horses shoving a twelve-foot cutter bar tilted high against the tall wheat. Large wagons with ungainly "header boxes"—high on the left side, low on the right— received the cut grain from the moving headers and carried it away to a stack or directly to a thresher. From a distance the thresher

[41] *Lewiston Teller,* April 10, May 1, 8, 15, 29, 1890. On the railroad rumors, see *ibid.,* Oct. 9, Dec. 25, 1890; and Smith, "Idaho," 51st Cong., 2nd sess., H. Ex. Doc. 6 (1891), p. 535.

might seem merely a blot of billowing dust, smoke, and chaff, but a closer view would reveal the huge machine, powered by a belt from a steam engine, around which a dozen men worked in the dust and heat, stoking and stacking, tending the machinery, filling and sewing the sacks of fresh wheat. Water wagons stood near by; some distance off—and hopefully upwind—was the mobile cookhouse, mounted on wagon wheels, where three or four women prepared the meals in a furnace-like atmosphere. Working from dawn to dark these men and women, horses and machines, provided the real measure of the yearly increment of basic wealth in the region.

And as the sack piles beside each thresher grew wider and longer, it became clearer with each day that 1890 was going to be a good year. In August the harvest reports from the Palouse and the northern Big Bend country began to confirm that optimism for the region as a whole. By September the last of the crop—late spring-sown wheat in some localities and the grain in the higher eastern Palouse, which had been cut by binders instead of headers—was all that remained to thresh, and within a week or two it was apparent that these, too, had given excellent returns. As always, there were a few localities which fell short of the average: the Asotin country and Tammany, the western fringes of the Big Bend in Adams County, some of the Horse Heaven slope, and the lower country just back from the Columbia on the Oregon side. But all of these were in drier areas which had rarely yielded well. In total, these districts were but a small portion of the wheat country and therefore could not markedly detract from the region-wide satisfaction with the harvest.

Once the grain was in the sack the most important thing to the farmer was the railroad. Through the rest of the year he might complain of high rates, poor service, and arrogant officials, but at this moment to have a railroad nearby was the greatest possible advantage. If the closest siding allowed several trips a day, four horses and a big wagon might be enough to get the wheat out of the field in a reasonable time. A greater distance necessitated greater facilities. The farmers on the Oregon tableland back of The Dalles, Biggs, and Blalock had the longest hauls. Here a dozen horses might be hitched to four or five "trail wagons" in order to get several hundred sacks to the warehouse in a single daily trip. The most difficult hauls were those down into the Snake River canyon to the steamboat landings, though several grain chutes on both the Garfield and Whitman County sides had alleviated that problem. In general the wheat country was by now fairly well served by the rail network. The majority of the farms were within ten miles of a siding, and a large proportion were within five.

Because all the grain was marketed in sacks, the towering elevator was not the distinguishing landscape symbol of the Columbia wheat country. Long low warehouses or simple open platforms lined the railroad every few miles. Platforms could serve, because normally the railroads could move a major portion of the harvest before the onset of the autumn rains. However, the bumper crop of 1890 strained every facility. Storage space was soon jammed full, wheat agents gave up buying until they had room available, and the farmers themselves had no adequate place to keep the grain and were anxious to get the sacks out of the fields before the rains. Inevitably everyone's wrath was directed against the railroads. These, in turn, insisted that they could handle a normal crop in proper time and that they were doing everything possible to move this one: "Every locomotive that could be repaired so as to haul a train was put to use and all the cars that could be made to hold wheat—even coal cars and flat cars—were rigged up."[42] But despite these efforts, by the end of the year it was expected that the last of the crop would not be sent to market before April.

Normally to be "sent to market" meant sent to tidewater as the next major step, but six thousand carloads of the 1890 harvest were sent east to Minneapolis and Duluth, a movement "rendered possible by the unusual condition of the market." However, the majority did go to Puget Sound and Portland. Competition between these ports had increased from the moment the N.P. had completed its Cascade line from Pasco to Tacoma. Even Portland newspapers had to acknowledge that their shipping costs were higher because of towage and pilotage fees on the lower Columbia.[43] Still, port competition for the grain traffic was dependent primarily upon the railroad pattern in the wheat districts. Because nearly all wheat loaded by the N.P. was hauled to Tacoma and that by the O.R.&N. to Portland, only the wheat from the vicinity of the eleven towns with competitive service, or from farms which were equidistant from the country sidings of the two companies, was really affected by this

[42] *The Northwest,* 9 (January, 1891), 36.

[43] Northern Pacific Railway, *Annual Report, Oct. 15, 1891,* p. 16; Barton, "Washington," p. 1004.

rivalry. The farmers, of course, were concerned only with the price they received, and thus the direction of grain movement from such competitive points was dependent upon the actions of wheat buyers, the availability and costs of storage, and railroad rates and service as well as the shipping costs of the ports themselves.

In 1890 twenty-five grain vessels loaded in Puget Sound, fifty-three at Portland, but because the Willamette Valley was a large exporter, such numbers are not indicative of traffic movements from the interior.[44] At whichever port the wheat was loaded virtually all of the grain exported from the American Pacific states was sent to the United Kingdom, although some might then be forwarded to continental ports. Thus, the economic tie established more than twenty years before was now the one absolute life line of the Columbia Plain.

Towns and Services

Such a harvest was as good news for the townsmen as for the farmers, for most of the money which flowed back along that economic life line was in the hands of the growers only briefly. Thus, the prosperity of 1890 merely compounded the already great surge of optimism and growth characteristic of the towns. There were now forty-one formally incorporated communities within the Great Columbia Plain, and probably a dozen more in which there was talk of such a move. The former ranged in size from Walla Walla with 4,709 to Yakima (the old town) with a mere 196 according to the 1890 census, though the citizens of each would no doubt have insisted that the enumeration had been inaccurate and was already out of date, which was probably true but not by the margin claimed.

Legal status and population were not the only measures of the relative positions of these many centers. The distribution of banking facilities was perhaps the most useful single indication of local business developments, for the lack of a bank was a serious handicap to townsmen and farmers alike. In 1890 only twenty-one towns had banks, eight of which had more than one (Appendix). Despite the considerable differences in the size and solvency of these institutions, they did serve to set their communities significantly apart from all others.[45] Newspapers were also a useful indicator. The fact that

[44] Wright (ed.), *Marine History*, p. 381.

[45] The information on number and location of banks, newspapers, and flour mills is derived from R. L. Polk and Company, *Oregon, Washington and Idaho Gazetteer and Business Directory, 1889-90* (Portland, 1889).

Ellensburg, Pendleton, and The Dalles were each supporting one and Walla Walla three *daily* papers was certainly some measure of the scale, importance, and stability of these places. Forty other towns had weeklies (nine of which had two), although such a paper could be merely an indication of hopes (as at Orondo) rather than of actual developments (as at, say, Colfax). Nevertheless, a local newspaper was regarded as an indispensable agent of progress and gave each of these communities a degree of satisfaction denied those without.

Still another mark of development was a flour mill. Because the entire population made use of locally milled products, such a facility was considered almost indispensable to any aspiring town. In 1890 there were sixty-one such mills, distributed among forty-eight localities, though, again, there was a wide range in scale and quality.

For the region as a whole these particular distributions of town populations and facilities in 1890 represent only a momentary glimpse of a rapidly changing scene. The current surge of colonists into the Big Bend, the evident growth in the Yakima and Kittitas valleys and on the Oregon uplands, and the probable expansions into numerous other localities seemed certain to alter these patterns. Yet in the older zones of colonization, it was clear that significant differentiations had been established. Barring some new kind of resource development, it seemed unlikely that Pendleton, Walla Walla, and Dayton would ever be surpassed by any other communities in their respective localities. In the eastern Palouse the situation was less stable, but it was obvious that Colfax, Moscow, and Palouse City had a significant edge on their rivals. The Dalles and Ellensburg also appeared to have assured dominion over their local districts, but as each was aspiring to be the focus of a much wider realm, which was still in the flux of developments, their relative positions were by no means so clear. North Yakima's future was even more problematical; despite its obvious head start, the eventual spread of irrigation over the whole valley might radically alter the situation. Elsewhere the extent of colonization, the fertility of the soil, and the pattern of railroads were as yet so uncertain as to give any local predictions of growth the taint of hopeful boosterism.

Remnants

While the varying density of towns over the region was an accurate reflection of the density of farm colonization, it did not reveal the full extent of conquest. Every locality had been brought into use. The arid rocky Middle Columbia country, beyond Moses Lake and across to Saddle Mountain and the Rattlesnake Hills, though devoid of farms and towns, was the last refuge of the stockmen, who also held out on the Cascade foothills and in the canyon country and higher slopes south of the Columbia. Even the Indian reservations within and around the margins of the Great Plain could not escape this comprehensive invasion. "The intruding whites held as many cattle on this reservation as the Indians, and possibly a larger number," reported the Lapwai Agent on the Nez Perces Reservation, and his complaint was applicable to all the others. The settlers were quick to answer that "hundreds of Indian ponies" were a constant nuisance in their ranges and fields, which further confirmed that while reservation boundaries were barriers by law they were certainly not in fact.[46] Yet even though the ranges could not be adequately policed, no one but Indians (or those married to Indians, a means beneath consideration by all but a few "renegade" whites) could settle on reservation lands, and thus the rapid spread and growth of agricultural colonization had served to magnify the ever greater contrast with these large blocks of "virtually empty" land. The pressures mounted for the "opening" of the reservations, by which was meant allocating farmlands to each Indian family and allowing white colonists to file claims upon the remainder.

This agitation was directed primarily against the Nez Perces, Umatilla, and Yakima reservations, each of which was adjacent to areas already colonized, obviously included much good farmland, and which together were accommodating fewer than forty-five hundred Indians. Most of the remaining Indians once associated with the Great Plain were distributed among the Colville, Spokane, Coeur d'Alene, and Warm Springs reservations, each more peripheral to the zones of colonization and in relatively unattractive country. Indeed, the last named was in such a sterile location that the agent recommended that it be abandoned and the Indians sent elsewhere to avoid starvation. The total population of all the reservations was about nine thousand. That figure does not suggest any reduction in numbers since the onset of the Indian wars, but that there had been a real reduction in the viability and cohesiveness of the old tribal life was clear from all the agency reports. Their enum-

[46] *Report on Indians Taxed and Indians Not Taxed in the United States at the Eleventh Census* (Washington, 1894); *The Sentinel* (Asotin), May 31, 1889.

The *Hassalo* at The Dalles wharfboat, *ca.* 1890. *(Photo courtesy of Union Pacific Railroad Company)*

A wagon train of wool arriving at an Oregon rail siding. *(Photo courtesy of Washington State University Library)*

erations could list houses, farms, schools, and churches, but their descriptions were a melancholy review of crudeness, filth and disease, sloth and indifference. Because these conditions were well known in the region, it would be unfair to suggest that all of the pressures of the whites for the abolition of the reservations stemmed from a simple greed for land. Greed there was, in ample amount, but there was also reason to view the reservation policy as worse than a failure —as nothing less than a wellspring of corruption which, under the guise of Christianity (and despite the earnest labors of several dedicated missionaries), had yielded a pathetic travesty of the intended "civilization."[47] Because "civilization" could only mean the white man's civilization, the proposal that the Indians be allocated farms and the rest of the reservation land be opened to colonization could be accepted in the region in good conscience as an honorable and rational reform. At the moment only the Nez Perces was being surveyed for that purpose.

Names on the Land

The confinement of the Indians, their rapidly dwindling proportionate strength, and their seemingly incipient fusion into the over-all settlement patterns were mirrored in the names on the maps of 1890. Those mundane "tools of organization" were a revealing expression of the degree of conquest and domestication attained. Agricultural colonization had necessarily clothed the variations of nature in a more close-fitting garment, rescuing small streams, valleys, and buttes from their primeval anonymity or obscurity. For the most part these were given prosaic labels. *Dry, Rock, Clear, Alkali, Spring, Willow,* were commonplace adjectives appended to creeks, canyons, flats, and hollows over many parts of the region. On the other hand, such subjective terms as *Pleasant, Paradise,* and *Eden* must have been initiated in a more self-conscious manner. Many towns took their names from established local features—*Spokane Falls* was the most obvious new example, as *The Dalles* was of the older centers; more often than not, to serve convenience or pretension, a clarifying noun was appended, as in *Palouse City, Pataha City,* and *Coulee City.*

But personal names were sprinkled ever more thickly over the map, through the simple processes of colonization. Common use of the most convenient means of reference gradually confirmed the

[47] *The Sentinel,* May 31, 1889.

name of many local settlers upon local features, such as *Hinton* Creek, *Corbett* Draw, *Clark's* Canyon, *Sweeney* Gulch. Towns were also often denoted in equally commonplace fashion: after a pioneer *(Wilbur)*, an early merchant *(Heppner)*, a town promoter *(Hartline)*, or a wife *(Almira)*. As founders of towns and sidings, the railroads logically conferred many names of their own choosing. A few, such as *Reardan* and *Sprague,* honored local officials, but others honored men who might never have set foot in the region. *Starbuck, Endicott, Pullman, Prescott,* and *Oakes*dale represent a good portion of the board of directors of the O.R.&N., and thus also the indelible imprint of a historic and critical link between eastern finance and western development.

Compared with other areas, there was relatively little commemoration of famous persons or events. The history of the region itself yielded few prominent personalities; settlement had been abrupt and rapid, and the migrants were mainly from far away. *Lewis*ton and *Whitman* County preserved the names of widest local fame, *Steptoe* Canyon and *Hangman* Creek more recent and colorful local events.[48] However, *Missouri* Flat and *Tennessee* Flat in the Palouse suggest why nearby *Union* Flat and *Rebel* Flat represented a more direct, fresh, and vivid memory for many of the settlers. National history was otherwise most commonly expressed in the names of political figures. *Lincoln, Douglas,* and *Garfield* are here, as in many other parts of the West, while *Colfax* and *Pendleton* honor politicians whose distinction was so small that, in time, even such small towns could become better known than their namesakes. Taken together, such names were an accurate though increasingly cryptic expression of the context of colonization.

Political Geography

A more obvious kind of organization of the land was the evolution of its political framework. By 1890 the region had been parceled among twenty-one counties, as compared with eight of twenty years before. In their varying scale these reflected the uneven age and density of colonization, as the size of Walla Walla and Columbia compared with Douglas and Yakima might suggest. But a nearly empty Franklin County, and an Asotin County which was very small in size and population alike, also indicated that other factors were

[48] Hangman Creek, still an alternative name for Latah Creek, recalls the execution of several Indian leaders by Colonel Wright in 1858.

involved. In fact, counties were to a considerable degree the formalization by the territorial legislature of local designs and desires. Whenever a local district could marshal a convincing argument as to the need and express a near unanimity as to the design for a new county, action was not often long delayed. As colonization spread, mere distance to the county seat became a common basis for agitation; but the difficulties of travel and the evolution of divergent orientations were often more potent arguments. For example, the successive segmentation of old Walla Walla County into four increasingly smaller units was less a matter of distance than of the difficulties of travel "across the grain" of the valleys and canyons along the north slope of the Blue Mountains. Thus, although Asotin County had few settlers when it was created in 1883, its communications were so completely focused upon the Snake that its citizens could express a unanimous relief that "no more will we be compelled to climb the Alpowai hill and trudge across the country for the sake of paying our taxes at Pomeroy." Similarly, Morrow, Gilliam, and Sherman each enclosed a settlement district oriented directly to the Columbia, with little contact across the canyons and ridges between them. Although most of the county boundaries in both of these subregions followed the geometric lines of surveyed sections, they were more closely concordant with terrain features than the simple political map would indicate. This is not to suggest, however, that the gross lineaments of the land were always accepted as the proper pattern for the political framework. Despite the obvious hardships that its canyon site imposed upon the residents of the Moscow district, Lewiston so persistently opposed the formation of a new county that Latah was finally created only as the result of an extraordinary appeal to Congress.[49]

. Where disagreements did appear over the proper design of this political evolution, they hinged, more often than not, upon the intense rivalries of towns over the location of the county seat. Although convenience was an obvious part of the prize, the belief that it would markedly affect property values ("every man of reason and experience knows that property is made valuable in proportion to its relative distance from a county seat"), and that it might give that "shadow of an advantage in the first lap" of the "headlong, neck-and-neck race for cityhood and prosperity" were often more power-

[49] An Illustrated History of Southeastern Washington ... (Spokane, Wash., 1906), p. 655; History of North Idaho, p. 587.

ful incentives in the struggle.[50] Indeed, a substantial courthouse gave such an important measure of security in this first frantic phase of town competition that some were built in whole or in part out of money locally donated rather than tax funds. While a few of these rivalries took place within counties whose boundaries were already accepted by the majority of its residents, in most cases some realignment was desired, and as the expansion of colonization and the growth of towns were still in progress, the local political patterns of 1890 were far from stabilized.

Political geography on a larger scale had also been a lively concern, but by 1890 it had, rather suddenly, assumed a new level of stability. The admission of Oregon as a state in 1859 had impressed a firm political boundary across the southern portion of the interior, but the territorial status of Washington, Idaho, and Montana kept open the possibility of major alterations elsewhere. As population growth carried all of these steadily toward statehood, local interest in realignments had mounted in the 1880's.

The idea of a new state in the interior had again been proposed, this time as a more modest unit comprising only eastern Washington and northern Idaho, but had received little support. Perhaps the previous failure to create Columbia Territory was a deterrent; more likely the impending rail link with Puget Sound, the desire to retain an ocean frontage, and the need for western Washington's population to insure early statehood were more important considerations. Whatever the reasons, the movement that did gain widespread allegiance was a much simpler design: the annexation of northern Idaho to the whole of Washington (Map 36). This scheme would impose only one new boundary and that along what everyone acknowledged as being an "almost impassible barrier." The idea had been vigorously promoted by a Lewiston editor and had soon gained a remarkable unanimity from other local spokesmen, political parties, and territorial delegates. Presented to Congress with the concurrence of both Idaho and Washington legislatures, it had seemed certain of passage.[51]

[50] *North-West Tribune,* Oct. 13, 1880; Robinson, "Spokane Falls," pp. 11-16.
[51] Herman J. Deutsch, "The Evolution of Territorial and State Boundaries in the Inland Empire of the Pacific Northwest," *Pacific Northwest Quarterly,* 51 (July, 1960), 130. *Congressional Record,* 17 (Feb. 23, 1886), 1706-10. The proposed division followed the east-west course of the main Salmon River, with short direct links to the Montana and Oregon borders at either end. Merle W. Wells, "Politics in the Panhandle: Opposition to the Admission of

But no sooner had the outline of the idea been stated in the halls of Congress than a dissenting voice was raised. A new petition had arrived from the Coeur d'Alene district asking for annexation to Montana. That seemingly minor bit of discord was enough to set in motion a jumble of conflicting forces. Heartened by this collapse of panhandle unanimity, southern Idaho renewed its opposition, playing upon the vague danger of being gobbled up by a greedy Nevada, the bitter internal problem of the growing Mormon preponderance in the southeast, and the fear that any reduction in population would long delay Idaho's admission to statehood.[52] Despite these and other issues, the bill to annex northern Idaho to Washington was passed by Congress, yet the political pressures and complexities it had unleashed doomed it to die unsigned on the desk of President Grover Cleveland in 1888.

The failure to alter these territorial divisions was almost immediately followed by positive moves to stabilize the political map as it stood. In Washington Territory the desire for immediate statehood was now given firm priority over any enlargement scheme. Sentiment in the Lewiston and Moscow districts remained strongly in favor of annexation, but the admission of Washington and Montana simultaneously in 1889 made any boundary change so unlikely that the offer of the state university of Moscow was enough to undercut the last stronghold of internal resistance to the confirmation of the existing unit, panhandle and all.[53] On July 3, 1890, Idaho became a full-fledged member of the union, and any lingering regret in Lewiston and vicinity was smothered by the upsurge of new pride and allegiance. Moreover, the promise of a state-constructed wagon road and the lively rumors that the O.R.&N. would build a line all along the Snake River Canyon allowed some optimism that even so "unnatural" a creature might be sufficiently bound together that it might not only live but thrive in harmony.

A Discordance of Regions

The hardening of these political lines diminished any likelihood that the Great Columbia Plain would ever form the core of a single political region. But even though the political map was discordant

Washington and North Idaho, 1886-1888," *Pacific Northwest Quarterly*, 46 (July, 1955), 79-89.

[52] Wells, "Politics in the Panhandle"; *History of North Idaho*, pp. 74-76.
[53] *Ibid.*, p. 89; *ibid.*, p. 610.

with the patterns of settlement and economic development, these too no longer fit within the regional framework which had seemed obvious in decades before. That they did not was hardly recognized at the time, much less a matter of any concern. It was a case of new patterns imposed upon the land leading to new patterns of thought about the regionalization of the area.

Many factors had contributed to this change. Political divisions had such actual precision and common prominence in the public mind that "eastern Washington" was an attractive, even if inaccurate, substitute for the "Great Plain of the Columbia," and the stabilization of the political boundaries in the area enhanced this kind of usage. At a different scale, the spread of settlement had given sharper and more widespread recognition to local subregions. Through these past twenty years the *Walla Walla Valley* had been augmented by a broadened concept of the *Walla Walla country;* the *Palouse* and the *Big Bend* had become commonly recognized and consistently defined areas; and *Camas Prairie, Clearwater Valley,* and *Asotin country* were only slightly newer and less well-known. There were many others, not all of which were precise, stable, or widely employed, but each representing a part of the same process of organizing the land in the minds of men.

Inland Empire was broader in connotation. If still rather vague in delimitation, its central concept was becoming increasingly clear. Spokane Falls had in a remarkably short time turned her commercial pretensions into a reality. In 1890 it was apparent that a half dozen more local districts had been encompassed within this new focal region. The railroads had made possible this kind of reorientation, and the patterns of lines and the circulation of traffic within the company networks revealed how great the alteration had been (Map 35). For decades the Plain had been focused internally upon the Walla Walla Valley and externally along the lower Columbia trunk line. Now Spokane, Puget Sound, and Portland gave a powerful divergence to the patterns of traffic and thinking alike. The stronger the concept of an *Inland Empire* was superimposed upon the Palouse and Big Bend, the stronger the idea of *Central Washington* as a distinct region between the Cascades and the Columbia took hold in Ellensburg and the Yakima. And from the day that a throng of stockmen, cowboys, and merchants from east of the mountains took the "Stampede Tunnel Special" through the Cascades to trod the sidewalks of Tacoma in celebration of the perfection of that rail link, the habitual idea of a region wholly bound to Portland was no longer tenable.

The term *Great Plain of the Columbia* was still employed in general descriptive accounts of the far Northwest,[54] but it was no longer so common in use nor so clear in concept. Whereas in 1870 that region, long recognized as a distinct physical area, had appeared to be developing into a distinct economic region within the national framework, in 1890 it was fading away as a public image. The patterns of nature remained as before, but they were becoming obscured by the superimposition of divisive and divergent patterns of man.

[54] E.g., M. F. Sweetser, *King's Handbook of the United States* (Buffalo, N.Y., 1891). P. 868.

CHAPTER TWELVE

For the first time in the harvest history
of the Walla Walla Valley, the new
"caterpillar" traction engines...have
been given a trial..., and there is every reason to believe that in a few
years horses will be almost eliminated
from the harvest fields.

PACIFIC FARMERS UNION

Elaboration:

Some Patterns and Methods

SETTLERS AND RAILROADS

Depression and Resurgence

THE BOOM days of 1890 were exhilarating but they were also deceptive. With wealth and progress so evident, it was easy to assume
that it was the natural, inevitable result of an industrious progressive people and a richly productive region. It was soon made clear,
however, that a fertile soil, an excellent climate, and bountiful
harvests were not in themselves enough—that high wheat prices,
vigorous railroad expansion, and a growing tide of immigration
were essential concomitants of natural endowments. With the onset
of the depression of 1893, wheat prices plummeted, railroads became
insolvent, and immigration dwindled. All over the region banks
and stores closed their doors, land sales were drastically slowed, and
although there was little exodus from the farms, "hard times" had
set in. It was a severe reminder that wealth was not simply a local
product, and that the region was merely a small corner of a national,
indeed international, economic world.

Moreover, the severity of this nationwide economic debacle was
compounded locally by its coincidence with a peculiar natural event.
The spring of 1893 was so unusually cool and wet that crops were
seeded later than usual throughout the region, and a full month
later in the Palouse. The extra moisture promised excellent yields,

but in late September "a rainy spell the like of which had never been heard of within memory of the oldest inhabitant set in," lasted for two weeks without interruption, and was followed by sporadic rains on through October. Because the crop was so retarded, only about half of the grain in the Palouse had been threshed, and even some of that was still piled in the fields and could not be hauled because of the mud. The Big Bend and Walla Walla districts suffered only lightly, but in the Palouse, generally the most productive area, an estimated 40 per cent of the crop was a total loss, and much of the grain finally marketed was damaged. Several warehousemen set up steam dryers to salvage as much as possible.[1]

The heavy autumn rains were a prelude to an unusually wet season, which lasted into the following spring and resulted in further, if more localized, damage: the greatest floods on the Snake and Columbia since colonization began. Half of Lewiston and The Dalles lay under water for weeks in May and June and then had to be excavated from a thick layer of mud and debris. For a time train service was entirely suspended between Portland and Umatilla.

The crops of 1894 were rather good, but in the following year nature shifted to another extreme. This time the dryness of spring and the heat of summer, while not unprecedented, resulted in a much lighter harvest than usual, which coupled with low prices to magnify the severity of the general depression.

The first break in this stagnation was local, and the result of special circumstances. The new program for the Nez Perces Reservation (Map 37), initiated by the pressures of the expansive years, was gradually brought to a climax in 1895. The land had been surveyed, the Indians allocated their farms and special reserves, and at noon on November 18 the remainder was thrown open to public selection. Spectators who came to enjoy a good land rush, "with the firing of cannon and firearms, the shouts and execrations of those who were ahead and behind in the race for the coveted goals," were disappointed. There was no great rush onto the Camas Prairie because the government had made no attempt to keep the claimants off before the opening ("the lack of soldiers has robbed the event of a great many of its exciting features"), and thus the area had been thoroughly reconnoitered and choice sites already staked out. In

[1] *Agricultural Notes* (Washington Agricultural Experiment Station Bulletin No. 10) (December, 1893), p. 27; *Palouse Republican* (Palouse City), Oct. 13, Oct. 20, Dec. 22, 1893; *Spokesman-Review* (Spokane Falls), Oct. 25, 1893.

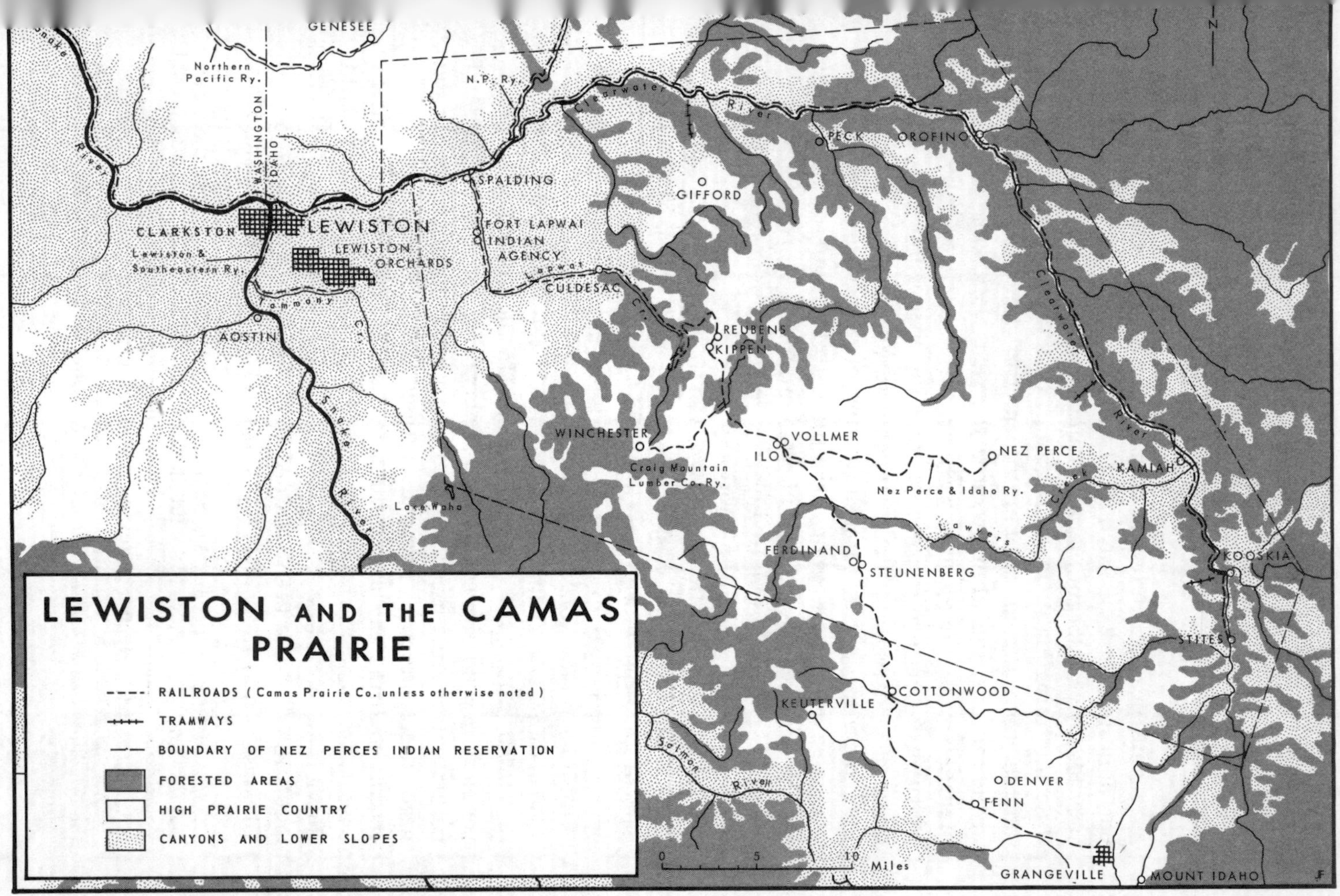
LEWISTON AND THE CAMAS PRAIRIE
RAILROADS (Camas Prairie Co. unless otherwise noted)
TRAMWAYS
BOUNDARY OF NEZ PERCES INDIAN RESERVATION
FORESTED AREAS
HIGH PRAIRIE COUNTRY
CANYONS AND LOWER SLOPES
GENESEE
Northern Pacific Ry.
N.P. Ry.
WASHINGTON
IDAHO
Snake River
Clearwater River
PECK
OROFINO
SPALDING
GIFFORD
CLARKSTON
LEWISTON
LEWISTON ORCHARDS
Lewiston & Southeastern Ry.
FORT LAPWAI INDIAN AGENCY
Lapwai
CULDESAC
Cr.
Tammany Cr.
AOSTIN
REUBENS
KIPPEN
WINCHESTER
VOLLMER
ILO
NEZ PERCE
KAMIAH
Craig Mountain Lumber Co. Ry.
Nez Perce & Idaho Ry.
Lawyers Creek
Lake Waha
FERDINAND
STEUNENBERG
KOOSKIA
STITES
COTTONWOOD
KEUTERVILLE
Salmon River
DENVER
FENN
GRANGEVILLE
MOUNT IDAHO
0 5 10 Miles
N

Map 37

fact, there was more of a rush *out* of the area than *in,* as many settlers had been camped on their land for days in order to hold it and then hurried to Lewiston on November 18 to make their legal filing.[2]

The absence of a dramatic climax to this long-awaited event did not indicate a lack of interest. Hundreds of claims were immediately filed, homes begun, fences strung, and sod broken. There was little intermingling of the two groups of settlers, as each sought a different kind of country. The Indians had chosen their allotments in the canyons; the whites wanted the rich black soils of the high prairie. Because the opening was late, the settlers had little time in which to build adequate shelter, and the first winter was a harsh experience. According to the *Spokesman-Review* of November 13, 1897, there had been a "transformation of this country from a cayuse-dotted wilderness to an agricultural district producing 300,000 bushels of splendid grain." There were about thirty-six hundred settlers, twenty-eight hundred quarter sections under fence, and over twelve thousand acres in cultivation.

The excellent yields obtained, even from the first "sod-sown" crops, immediately emphasized the problem of transportation. The haul to Lewiston, down over Craig's Mountain—the rough northern edge of the Camas Prairie—was too long and difficult to serve an expanding production. Railroads were needed, and there was soon good indication that they would come. At the time of the opening, the closest rail point had been Juliaetta, in the lower Potlatch Canyon just beyond the edge of the reservation. To the disgust and frustration of Lewiston, the N.P. had gotten no farther, despite the negotiations, promises, and preparations which in 1890 had seemed certain to bring the first train into Lewiston before its "citizens have eaten their Christmas dinners."[3] Gaining clearance to build through the northwest corner of the reservation had caused a delay, and hardly had this been obtained than the depression had canceled all construction programs. Not until 1898 was action renewed. By

[2] *Spokesman-Review,* Nov. 19, 20, 1895. Several reporters covered the event, and one attempted to give it the full drama of men with "jaded horses, rumpled clothes, and bloodshot eyes" locked in a desperate scramble. The others not only offered little evidence of this but specifically emphasized its absence.

[3] A good résumé of the preliminaries, delays, and final triumph is given in the *Lewiston Centennial Edition* of the *Lewiston Morning Tribune,* July 16, 1961.

Railroad promotion of the Northwest: *Upper*—A traveling exhibit car used to advertise all lands tributary to the Northern Pacific to prospective home seekers (1895). *Lower*— An exhibit in Kansas City sponsored by the Northern Pacific stressing the virtues of "The One only Palouse Country on Earth." *(Photo courtesy of Northern Pacific Railway Company)*

then business conditions had improved and the obvious potentialities of the Camas Prairie made it a district worth controlling.

On September 15, 1898, Lewiston began a three-day celebration of the arrival of the first passenger train. In the following year a sixty-three-mile branch line was started along the Clearwater to Stites, and a short stub was built twelve miles up Lapwai Creek along the best entryway to the Camas Prairie. In this way the railroad controlled—although it did not directly serve—the new region, and the company felt no urgency to undertake the costly construction up out of Lapwai Canyon on to the tableland.

The farmers on the prairie were unhappy, but because the N.P. gave no sign of further action, they made the best of a situation which was at least somewhat improved. The main problem was getting the wheat down into the canyons to a siding; however, examples of how to solve it were at hand. Grain chutes and tramways had operated for a decade along the Snake River downstream from Lewiston. In 1892 an elaborate tramway had been completed at Juliaetta to serve the Potlatch tableland to the east, and three years later a steel grain pipe half a mile long was in operation at Kendrick. By 1903 the Camas Prairie farmers had three tramways sending grain down to the Clearwater rail line; two served the eastern side of the prairie (terminating at Kooskia and Pardee) and one the northern (at Lenore).[4] They were a poor substitute for a local railroad, but a welcome relief from the tedious, difficult, and dangerous wagon haul down the side of the canyon.

Upon the basis of these developments Lewiston began to grow in the manner it had long anticipated. In 1900 it had a population of 2,425, and there were another 1,100 in Concord, the new model town and irrigation development being promoted by eastern capitalists just across the Snake. A steel bridge had just been completed, and a franchise for a streetcar line between the two had been granted. The growing grain trade, new mining discoveries in the Buffalo Hump district, and the anticipated exploitation of the timberlands of the upper Clearwater provided a solid basis for Lewiston's hopes in the new century. Its hinterland now contained a

[4] *The Northwest*, 10 (November, 1892), 20; *Spokane Review*, July 13, 14, 1892, May 25, Nov. 1, 1903, Jan. 28, 1904; *Spokesman-Review*, Oct. 1, 1895. The Juliaetta scheme used twenty-foot cable cars running on rails, drawn by a thirty horse power engine, and could carry passengers as well as grain. Elsensohn, *Idaho County*, pp. 451-52.

dozen infant towns. Many of these were along the rail lines and were so new and closely spaced that there was little indication of which ones would thrive. At the moment Stites and Mellon (later Culdesac), each a terminus of a branch, seemed to have a special advantage, but one which could be eliminated by further railroad extension. Up on the prairie the situation was even less stable for no one knew the exact route of the railroad, when and if it was built. Grangeville had a head start, as well as a location which could serve both the farming and mining trades, and in 1902 it also got the county seat away from Mount Idaho. But still Grangeville could not be confident of its position. The community already had a vigorous rival in Denver, created by a townsite company in 1892 to be the metropolis of the Camas Prairie. The promoters had built stores, established a newspaper, lured several other businesses, and their advertising literature implied that their hopes were already a reality by showing a plot complete with a courthouse, agricultural college, schools, and churches. It was enough to worry Grangeville or any other aspiring town.[5]

By the turn of the century, five years after the last means of Indian resistance had been broken, this far southeast corner of the Columbia Plain was well into the cycle of development which the neighboring Palouse and Walla Walla had experienced two to three decades before. It was often spoken of as another Palouse—a "complement, or twin"—and in terms of soils and yields, if not in total product, that was a reasonable comparison.[6] Isolation seemed the only drawback, and that was a matter which could be overcome. If the N.P. was content to stay in the canyons, another company would have to be sought. There was always hope that the O.R.&N. would challenge its rival here as elsewhere, and there was serious talk of a local effort to build an electric line from Lewiston via Tammany and Waha to Grangeville. If that could be accomplished, the Camas Prairie could assume its "rightful" place as one of the most fertile and prosperous districts of the interior.

By this time, also, the tide of hope and progress was running

[5] E. H. Libby, "Lewiston Valley and the Buffalo Hump District," *The Northwest,* 17 (March, 1899), 11; Robert G. Bailey, *River of No Return . . .* (Lewiston, Ida., 1947), p. 447; *The Northwest,* 17 (June, 1899), 38; W. S. Brackett, "An Exploring Expedition in Northern Idaho," *The Northwest,* 19 (January, 1901), 7; Elsensohn, *Idaho County,* pp. 460-67.

[6] Brackett, "Exploring Expedition," p. 7.

strong again in many other parts of the Columbia Plain. From 1897 onward "good times" prevailed; wheat prices rose sharply, railroads —reorganized and refinanced—were again ready to build wherever necessary to compete in or control a promising district, and land seekers began to flock in. Most of them came from the Midwest, and many arrived with a good deal of money, ready to buy a farm rather than create one. Spokane reporters were assigned to keep a close watch on the depots, and the newspapers gave prominence to these signs of progress. The *Review* estimated that thirty thousand had arrived in March and April of 1901, and this did not include those arriving in Pendleton and Walla Walla on the O.R.&N., nor those coming east from Portland and Puget Sound.[7]

The Big Bend was the major area of new colonization because good land was available, recent harvests had been excellent, and the Great Northern had created a new axis of settlement through the most attractive country. That new transcontinental, following along Crab Creek, almost exactly bisected the area lying between the Northern Pacific's main line through Ritzville and its Washington Central branch to Coulee City. Completed through the Big Bend in 1892 (and across the Cascades to Seattle in 1893), its impact was delayed by the great depression. A series of sidings was laid out, such as Harrington, Mohler, Odessa, and Krupp, and a division point established at Wilson Creek, but there was little or no growth before 1900. Then began a surge of settlement; all of the land in the Crab Creek country was quickly taken, and the frontier was pushed on west and south into the sagebrush plains. Ephrata, platted in 1901 at Beasley Springs, an old roundup campsite, reported fifty-four teams lined up at its two warehouses on an October day of 1902, and in that same year the town of Quincy was laid out on the dry flats eighteen miles farther down the track.[8]

None of this seemed speculative, for excellent crops were being obtained in all the Crab Creek country. A measure of the prevailing

[7] *Spokesman-Review*, May 2, 1901. It was estimated that this immigration had dispersed over the Inland Empire in the following proportions: 30 per cent to the Lewiston and Moscow areas (which included the Camas Prairie, Clearwater, and Potlatch districts); 25 per cent to the Big Bend; 15 per cent to the Palouse; 5 per cent to the Colville Valley; and 25 per cent either remaining in the Spokane area or scattered widely to such locales as the Newport and St. Joe timber areas, or the Okanogan.

[8] Steele and Rose, *Big Bend Country*, pp. 158-69, 577-82; *Big Bend Chief* (Wilson Creek), Oct. 10, 1902.

confidence was the fact that much of this colonization was in the form, not of homestead filing, but of larger purchased tracts. In fact, it was here that "corporation farming" first appeared in the region. Initiated in a small way near Harrington in 1882, a successor organization, the California Land Company, greatly enlarged its holdings after the advent of the railway and by 1904 had nearly twenty-five sections of wheatland in cultivation. Individuals could not handle that scale of operations, but a 2,100-acre farm north of Wilson Creek, with an expected harvest of 25,000 bushels from the 1,200 acres in wheat was closer to the norm here than the old 160-acre homestead.[9]

The influx of settlers also spread beyond those lands readily accessible to the new railroad. The Waterville tableland, from the rim of the Grand Coulee to its western edge along the Columbia, was so rapidly filled that on April 4, 1904, the Douglas County Agricultural Society published an "open letter" in the Waterville *Big Bend Empire* advising homeseekers that "there is no longer any homestead land worth taking" and almost no "raw land" to be bought from individuals or the railroad. There was no desire to discourage newcomers, however, as improved land could be had for fifteen to twenty-five dollars per acre. Furthermore, there was an unusual opportunity of leasing land. A considerable amount of empty land had been available here at the time the state of Washington was formed, and several large blocks had been set aside by the state, the eventual income from which was to be used to support colleges, reformatories, and other public institutions. Interest in these lands picked up as the rest of the area became settled. In 1903 a local group announced that they had leased seventeen thousand acres of state land and were ready to "colonize the same with eastern settlers" under subleases.[10]

This Waterville district was good farming country but poorly served by transportation. One rail line was poised at the base of the "pass" onto the Plateau (Coulee City) and another ran deep in the bordering canyon (the G.N. in the southwest corner), but there was none on to the high-lying wheat country itself. One wheat grower claimed that it cost him twenty-three cents a bushel to deliver his sacks twenty-five miles to Coulee City. But although the situation was inadequate, it had somewhat improved. The Columbia and Okanogan Steamboat Company offered daily river service between

[9] *Ibid.,* pp. 158-62; *ibid.,* Aug. 1, 1902.
[10] *Big Bend Empire* (Waterville), Oct. 29, 1903.

the new town of Wenatchee and Brewster, near the mouth of the Okanogan, with a twice-weekly boat as far as Bridgeport. In 1903 a tramway two miles long was built from the canyon rim to Orondo, the chief shipping point for the immediate vicinity of Waterville. But the real need was a railroad, and the hopeful had plenty of rumors to feed upon. Unfortunately, the only construction caused more alarm than hope. In 1903 the N.P. built a short line south from Coulee City to connect with the G.N. at Adrian. As both companies were then under the control of James J. Hill, the link allowed the N.P. to avoid the "long dead haul" of grain eastward to its own main line at Cheney and thence to the coast. However rational that might be for the railroads, it could only blunt Waterville's long-standing hopes that the N.P. would build across its area into the Okanogan country or toward a trans-Columbia link with the N.P. main line in the Cascades. A G.N. branch along the Columbia toward the Okanogan seemed the most likely prospect; although better than the present steamboat service, it would not improve the farmers' situation at all.[11]

In the opposite corner of the Big Bend the problem of development had been the reverse of that in the Waterville district. Instead of obviously good land and poor transport, the country south from Ritzville had long been served by a railroad but had been plagued by marginal crops. Now that too had dramatically changed. The harvests of 1897 and 1898 were superb, and the remaining railroad land in the vicinity was quickly grabbed. By 1902 Ritzville, having marketed just under two million bushels from the previous crop, was claiming to be "the largest primary wheat shipping station in the world." By this time land was being taken up clear to Franklin County, and long-desolate rail sidings had sprouted into towns. Cunningham, Hatton (formerly Two Wells), and Connell (formerly Palouse Junction) were platted in 1901-2, and Lind incorporated in the midst of a sudden spurt of growth.[12]

Speculation was rife in farmlands as well as town lots.[13] By 1903

[11] *Davenport Tribune*, Nov. 5, 1903; *Wenatchee Daily World*, Oct. 27, 1905. For an earlier report of river service, see *The Northwest*, 20 (March, 1902), 14. *Big Bend Empire*, Nov. 5, 1903, July 14, Aug. 4, 1904; *Big Bend Chief*, Aug. 8, 1902; Steele and Rose, *Big Bend Country*, p. 118.

[12] Steele and Rose, *Big Bend Country*, pp. 770-71; *Spokesman-Review*, July 25, 1901; *Ritzville Journal-Times*, Sept. 15, 1949, pp. 33-39.

[13] A good measure of the speculative fever was its attraction of some skillfully fraudulent promoters. One got hold of a tract of barren ground nine miles

Franklin County had become the focus of interest. Nearly all the railroad sections were purchased by land companies at the usual rates of $1.50 to $2.50 per acre. In that year such sections near Eltopia, hardly beyond the sand dunes, were selling for $6.50 per acre, and three years later the Ashley-Burnham Land Company, the largest of the promoters, was advertising "60,000 acres in the Great Central Washington Wheat Raising Belt" all with "very productive soil, good water, and no irrigation" for eight to fifteen dollars per acre. Most important, these lands were being put into wheat, and with results that seemed to prove that such a purchase was not speculative at all. The 1903 crop was light, but the next years were excellent, and Franklin County became famous for having developed from a sagebrush wasteland to a production of one and a half million bushels of wheat in five years. In light of that fact, the local claim that "we consider an investment in Franklin County wheat land at the present prices to be the most profitable investment that can be made" did not seem wildly extravagant. Nor did the claim of "good water" stretch the truth, though the costs of obtaining it were not emphasized. By this time wells were being drilled into the basalt and good water was being tapped, on the average, at about three to four hundred feet at a cost of about eight hundred dollars.[14]

A portion of this influx of land seekers spread across the Columbia into the Rattlesnake and Horse Heaven districts. Here, too, good crops already obtained were a strong attraction. Relatively little new land was available from either the government or the railroad, but private grazing land was being marketed. The Horse Heaven Land Company, for instance, had twenty-eight thousand acres available at prices of six to ten dollars per acre. Difficulties in obtaining water were a deterrent; many settlers on the south slope of the Horse Heaven Hills hauled water from the Columbia and that was hardly

west of Lind and drew up a beautiful paper plan of "Cascade City," complete with public parks, churches, and schools, and served directly by three railroads and Columbia River steamboats. Lots were peddled all over the East for prices "ranging from a gift, with the purchase of $2.50 bottle of patent medicine, to $250." Steele and Rose, *Big Bend Country*, pp. 788-89.

[14] *Klickitat County Agriculturist* (Goldendale), March 7, Oct. 3, 1903; *Pasco Express*, July 19, 1906. A survey of the records of local abstract and title companies confirms the fact that this company had purchased many sections from the Northern Pacific. *A Review of the Resources and Industries of Washington* (Olympia, Wash., 1907), p. 117; Frank C. Calkins, *Geology and Water Resources of a Portion of East-Central Washington* (Water-Supply and Irrigation Paper No. 118) (Washington, D.C., 1905).

a good advertisement to the easterner. Still they came to look the country over. In the spring of 1902, the Goldendale newspaper reported almost weekly on the stream of arrivals there and at Prosser and Mabton; by April the N.P. was running extra sections to accommodate the crowds. In the following year at least some of the Klickitat area transportation problems were solved. In April the Columbia River and Northern Railway completed a line from the river landing at Lyle to Goldendale. It was of little use to farmers east of Rock Creek, and some west of that canyon continued to haul directly to the Columbia and ferry their grain across to the O.R.&N., but the road did make a loop through the Swale and thereby served the older and richest district. The railway had also purchased control of The Dalles, Portland and Astoria Navigation Company, and with the Cascades Canal completed, it could offer a complete shipping route to the export docks.[15]

Further Pressures on the Stockmen

Taken together, these colonizations were an almost encompassing movement in upon the dry core of the region. As the farmers took up the last of the bunch-grass prairie lands, they forced the cattlemen into the sagebrush country and they in turn pushed in upon the arid wintering grounds of the sheepmen. By 1905 the Moses Lake–Lower Crab Creek country was the only unmolested stock district east of the Columbia; elsewhere the stockmen held out only on scattered nonarable patches of scablands, coulees, and canyons. In the following year a roundup was staged to clear that area of the last herds of wild horses, which were more numerous than cattle on the open range. The riders swept through the Potholes and Frenchman Hills, and moved the herds north toward Ephrata to be loaded for shipment to North Dakota, where they would be turned loose and disposed of in small lots. The drive took several weeks, garnered several thousand head, and made Ephrata a lively place. But the fact that at the climax of the roundup the town was as crowded with reporters and photographers as with stockmen and buckaroos was an indication of how rare and anachronistic this corner of the "Wild West" had become. Even on those sagebrush flats, the wheat

---

[15] *Spokesman-Review,* Oct. 23, 1900, July 25, 1901; *Klickitat County Agriculturist,* Dec. 1, 1900, March 15, April 26, May 3, 1902; Sept. 26, 1903; *Tri-City Herald* (Pasco), Dec. 12, 1958, quoting a newspaper account of 1903.

warehouse was a more commonplace feature than a horse roundup.[16]

Most of the cattle in the area were sold off in the fall of that same year, leaving the sheepmen to make a last stand. But they had other problems. Even if they could retain their winter range, they were faced with new difficulties in their summer pastures. The federal government was establishing national forests, eliminating grazing from some and beginning, in 1906, charging pasturing fees in the remainder. Chelan County was the principal summer range for Big Bend flocks, and the sheepmen had protested to the government supervisor, but to no avail. As one stockman put it, the important question had become "How much stock can you carry through the summer?" instead of the old commonplace, "How are you fixed for hay?" for winter.[17]

The Oregon sheepmen were much less afflicted by the developments of this period. They had already lost control of much of the most fertile tableland areas by 1890, and the further influx of settlers (much smaller here than in Washington) did not significantly reduce their ranges. Indeed, the geographic situation was the reverse of that in the Big Bend, for the farmers were confined to a few discontinuous areas while the stockmen were left free to dominate the more extensive rough broken country and thin-soiled highlands. Because of this, railroads built primarily to serve the wheat areas could not become avenues of relentless agricultural advance and therefore could serve the stockmen as well as the farmer. The Heppner branch had been the first of the feeders to function in this manner, and by 1905 similar lines had been built up onto each of the disconnected tablelands. In 1897 the Columbia Southern Railway was completed from Biggs to Wasco, was extended to Moro two years later, and in 1900 was pushed onto Cross Hollow seventy miles south of the Columbia. There a townsite company laid out Shaniko,

[16] *Big Bend Chief,* Oct. 3, 1902. The prevalence of horses and the badly deteriorated condition of the rangelands is described in Calkins, *Geology and Water Resources,* pp. 23-24. *Wenatchee Daily World,* May 14, 1906; *Spokesman-Review,* May 1, 1906.

[17] *Big Bend Chief,* May 31, 1907; *Wenatchee Daily World,* March 9, 1907. The sheepmen at this particular meeting were from Ephrata, Krupp, Wilson Creek, and Kahlotus, and owned a total of about thirty thousand head. The question was quoted in David Griffith, *Forage Conditions and Problems in Eastern Washington, Eastern Oregon, Northeastern California, and Northwestern Nevada* (Bureau of Plant Industry Bulletin No. 38) (Washington, D.C., 1903).

established a bank and a hotel, and induced some merchants to set up in business. The company also built the largest wool warehouse in the region, and in the next year eastern buyers purchased 1,360,000 pounds at the June sale. In 1905, after several years of survey rivalry with another company, the Columbia River and Central Oregon Railroad built from Arlington to Condon. In that same year the Great Southern was completed from The Dalles up Fifteen-mile Creek to Dufur, and two years later the O.R.&N. built a short branch south from near Pendleton to Pilot Rock. These railroads were primarily wheat feeders, but each terminus was an outpost in or near the pastoral frontier. Because of the system of sales, only Shaniko became a major wool shipping point, but the others could serve the stockmen in other ways. Although there were problems with increasing government restrictions on the summer ranges, the Oregon sheepmen were not seemingly doomed by the irresistible course of general regional development.[18]

The major problem within these pastoral districts was long recognized but ever worsening—overgrazing. By 1905 scientific study was confirming in detail what every stockman knew in general. In the driest areas the perennial grasses (sand grass or needle grass [*Stipa comata*], Indian millet [*Ericoma cuspidata*], woolly or bearded wheatgrass [*Agropyron subvillosum*]) had been nearly destroyed, leaving only the desert shrubs (white sage or winterfat [*Eurotia lanata*], antelope bitterbrush [*Purshia tridentata*], spiny hopsage [*Grayia spinosa*]); in the less arid lands, the nutritious wheatgrass *(Agropyron spicatum)* and giant wildrye *(Elymus condensatus)* had given way to June grass *(Pao sandbergii)*, which furnished only a brief spring pasture, and such areas being steadily invaded by sagebrush *(Artemisia tridentata)* and rabbitbrush *(Chrysothamnus nauseosus)*. It was reported that there was "considerable difference of opinion among the stockmen as to whether or not the native

[18] Shaver *et al, History of Central Oregon*, pp. 170-71; Wallis Nash, *The Settler's Handbook to Oregon* (Portland, Ore., 1904). For an unenthusiastic report on the site and prospects of Shaniko, see the *Klickitat County Agriculturist*, April 29, 1900. The name was derived from Scherneckau, an early settler. Both the C.R.&C.O. and the Columbia Southern were formally absorbed by the O.R.&N. in 1906. The C.R.&C.O.'s rival was the Arlington and Pacific Coast, a Portland financed venture which was thwarted by the refusal of the O.R.&N. to grant it a suitable traffic agreement; on this, see Shaver *et al., History of Central Oregon*, pp. 566-68; also see p. 166; *Condon Globe*, June 27, 1901; *Moro Bulletin*, July 23, 1902.

grasses, especially bunch-grass will restore themselves if given an opportunity."[19] Experiments suggested that they would, with proper care, and that bunch grass could also be raised on cultivated ground. Further, the scientists believed it unlikely that any exotic grass would yield as well or have the high feeding value of the best of the native growths. But even though the need for range rehabilitation was readily apparent, the will and the means seemed irresolute and indecisive.

Irrigation Projects

There was still another kind of encroachment upon the stock-man's last refuge. Smaller in scale, more restricted in locale, but as inexorable in process as the spread of wheat farming, irrigation agriculture shared in the boom that ushered in the new century. The largest project was designed to bring water to the east side of the main valley between Yakima and Prosser. A private company had begun this in 1892, but was ruined by the depression. Revived in the next decade, the company continued to extend the Sunnyside Canal until 1906, when it sold out to the federal government.[20] This assumption of federal control was one of the first fruits of the Reclamation Act of 1902 and marked the beginnings of planned, coordinated survey and development of the irrigation potentialities in the region. The federal government also paved the way locally by opening the Yakima Reservation, after land allocations to the Indians, to farm, townsite, and irrigation developments. A series of short canals on the west side, in the Wapato-Toppenish district, was soon initiated. Local schemes also enlarged the area under ditch in the Moxee and Ahtanum valleys.

A second major focus of irrigation promotion and development encompassed the lowlands around the mouths of the Yakima, Snake, and Walla Walla rivers. On the west side of the Columbia, a project begun in 1892 to build a canal from Horn Rapids along and beyond the west bank of the lower Yakima had been halted by the depression. In 1902 the Northern Pacific formed a subsidiary to complete that undertaking. This company also laid out the townsite of Kennewick once again, and several hundred residents were on hand to celebrate the arrival of the first water in the ditch in 1903. Two

[19] J. S. Cotton, *Range Management in the State of Washington* (Bureau of Plant Industry Bulletin No. 75) (Washington, D.C., May 23, 1905), pp. 14-16.
[20] Lyman, *Yakima Valley*, pp. 359ff.

years later the Richland canal was constructed to serve the peninsula between the Yakima and Columbia. East of the Columbia and
south of the Snake, two canals—the Columbia and the Two Rivers
—were also completed at this time in the western edge of Walla
Walla County; the former drew from the Walla Walla River and the
latter pumped from the Snake. North of the Columbia-Snake confluence, above Pasco, the situation was quite the opposite. After
long agitation and several attempts, a more ambitious scheme was
apparently dead. This project planned to divert water from the
Palouse River above the falls into a storage reservoir in Washtucna
Coulee, with a canal south from near Connell to irrigate the triangle
between Eltopia and Pasco. Tacoma capitalists initiated the project
in 1892 but soon withdrew; a successor company formed in 1904
accomplished little before the federal government undertook a full
study of the scheme. The adverse decision, announced in 1906, was
greeted by local persons with anguish and accusations of jealous
political intrigue, but it seemed to put an end to the idea.[21]

There were numerous other irrigation developments. Several additional canals were constructed in the Walla Walla and Kittitas
valleys, and there was expansion in the lower Umatilla area around
Hermiston and Irrigon. An ambitious project, in an area previously
untouched by agricultural progress, was the Hanford canal, taking
water from Coyote Rapids on the Columbia to the terrace opposite
White Bluffs. There were also two developments in the Lewiston
area, one across the Snake on the Washington side, the other on the
slope above the city. The first, begun in 1896 and promoted by the
president of the Union Pacific, brought water from Asotin Creek to
a new town, Concord (incorporated as Clarkston in 1902), and its
suburban tracts. The other, Lewiston Orchards, was initiated in
1905, drawing from Lake Waha near the edge of Camas Prairie.
Subdivided into five-acre tracts, with water delivered under good
pressure to each by underground pipes, this project was "pronounced by engineers to be one of the most highly developed in the
West in point of general efficiency."[22]

[21] *Ibid.*, pp. 849-52. Kennewick, started when the N.P began its Cascade line,
nearly disappeared when the railroad bridge was completed, then revived with
the 1892 project, only to falter again when that collapsed. *Pasco Express,* July
16, 19, 1906; Steele and Rose, *Big Bend Country,* pp. 795-96, 946.

[22] The most significant canals were the Burlingame ditch in the former and
the Cascades Canal, supported by a dam on Kachess Lake, in the latter; Lyman,
Yakima Valley, p. 357; James Stephenson, Jr., *Irrigation in Idaho* (Office of

The total area that could be irrigated under these projects was only a small proportion of the agricultural acreage of the region, and the total actually in production was an even smaller fraction, for it took time to complete the full network of facilities. But these figures or proportions provide no measure of the significance of irrigation activities. Once in full production, these lands would give high returns and support relatively dense rural populations. Moreover, together these projects represented an important phase in the elaboration of the geographic patterns of colonization. In a few of these areas there had been earlier attempts to raise wheat, usually with marginal results, but for the most part they were in arid sections which had not been farmed before. The spread of irrigation agriculture was therefore complementary rather than competitive with the advance of the dry-land frontier. By 1905 at least a beginning had been made in nearly all of those districts which could feasibly be developed on the basis of local water supplies. Closely associated was the establishment of many new towns, most of which were platted and promoted by the irrigation companies themselves. Further, these farm and town developments gave rise to agitation for and some actual construction of new railroads.

Railroads and Towns

The Yakima Valley was the area most affected by these changes, and here the Northern Pacific was in an excellent position to take advantage of them. New towns arose from mere sidings along its main line, as at Toppenish and Wapato. But the major irrigation development was on the other side of the valley, across the Yakima River, and this prompted the building of a branch line to Sunnyside (in 1906) and Grandview (1907), tapping the best of that area. North Yakima was the focus of other railroad developments. The North Yakima and Valley railway built a line to Naches in 1905, and four years later to Moxee. In 1908 the Yakima Valley Transportation Company began building lines to provide the environs of North Yakima with rapid and efficient electric railroad service.[23]

Experiment Station Bulletin No. 216) (Washington, D.C., 1909), pp. 40-41; also Bailey, *Rivers,* pp. 435-40, 447.

[23] Northern Pacific Railway, *Annual Report, 1906,* p. 6; *1907,* p. 6; Northern Pacific Railway, *Branch Line Data,* Western District (1922). These lines did not become part of the N.P. system until 1914. Lyman, *Yakima Valley,* p. 344.

Electric railways became a topic of great interest at this time. Because they could provide a different kind of service—frequent, rapid, with as many stops as needed—they injected a new complication into the railroad situation. As they were most feasible in areas already well developed, the Walla Walla and Palouse received greater attention from promoters than any of the newer areas, which were simply anxious for any kind of railroad service. In the Walla Walla there was much talk of a line from Dayton to Wallula or Pasco, passing through all of the principal communities.[24] Difficulties in raising capital retarded that scheme, but a less ambitious project to connect Walla Walla with Milton was completed in 1909 by the Walla Walla Valley Railroad Company.

In the Palouse, Spokane capitalists pushed forward a much longer program with unusual dispatch. The surveyors for the Spokane and Inland Empire were in the field in late 1904 seeking "a route which would be the shortest, give the easiest grades and reach the largest number of people"—a worthy aim for any railroad. By the summer of 1907 lines had been completed to Colfax and Palouse City, and a year later the latter was extended to Moscow. Further surveys were also made, and it was believed that the S.&I.E. would eventually offer rapid transit to Lewiston.[25] It completed directly with the older railroads, whose lines it contacted at eight points and ran adjacent to through most of its extent. Although it was responsible for the rise of only one new town (Steptoe), it did lay out country sidings every few miles and thus drew trade directly from the rural area as well as from the established centers.

An electric railroad for the Camas Prairie was also initiated at this time. Like many others, it was never put in service, but unlike most it showed such tangible signs of life that it prompted action from an older railroad. The Lewiston and Southeastern was locally financed, and it ran out of money in the brief depression of 1907, having only graded its roadbed into Tammany, ten miles south of town, along its surveyed line via Waha to Grangeville. That was enough to spur the Northern Pacific into building a tortuous line up out of the canyon from Culdesac and onto the plateau toward

[24] "Our New Era in Transportation," *Up-to-the-Times Magazine,* 1 (December, 1906), 11-13; *Spokesman-Review,* Nov. 13, 1908, p. 18; *The Touchet Valley* ... (Waitsburg, Wash., *ca.* 1909), p. 52.

[25] *Weekly Commoner* (Colfax), Jan. 27, 1905, Jan 5, 1907; descent into the canyon to Lewiston was to be made along either Steptoe or Hatwai creeks.

the same objective; the first train reached Grangeville on December 1, 1908.[26]

The Camas Prairie finally had not only its long-awaited railroad but also, as the result of an unusual arrangement, a degree of competitive service. After several years of sparring with rival surveys and rumored plans over the Clearwater-Snake country, the N.P. and O.R.&N., confronted by the huge costs of construction in difficult terrain, signed a contract for joint action. While the N.P. was building to Grangeville, the O.R.&N. was laying rails along the north bank of the Snake in the canyon between Lewiston and Riparia. In 1909 these two lines were leased to the Camas Prairie Railroad, an operating company owned equally by the two major railroads, and using their rolling stock. The unusual feature was that although the C.P. was constructed and operated jointly, the N.P. and O.R.&N. competed for the trade of local shippers because beyond Riparia they offered rival connections to the Pacific ports. The O.R.&N. route to Portland followed the south bank of the lower Snake to Wallula. This line had been completed ten years before to avoid hauling the ever increasing Palouse and Spokane traffic over the heavy grades south of Starbuck on the old Walla Walla line. The N.P. connection was by way of the north bank of the lower Snake to Pasco and Puget Sound, or via a new half-owned subsidiary, the S.P.&S., to Portland.[27]

A railroad also reached the Waterville plateau at this time. In 1909 the Great Northern opened service on a long branch leading up Moses Coulee and into the heart of the wheat country, terminating at the new town of Mansfield.[28] Half a million bushels of grain were said to be awaiting shipment, and the long hauls to Coulee City or the Columbia would be over for most of the farmers.

Important as these branch lines were to local districts, these years were a new era of railroad construction which was characterized more strikingly by the building of two new trunk lines across the entire region. The Spokane, Portland and Seattle was a joint crea-

[26] Elsensohn, *Idaho County*, pp. 148-51; *Lewiston Morning Tribune*, July 16, 1961; Northern Pacific Railway, *Annual Report, 1909*, p. 6.

[27] The contract for joint action is noted in Northern Pacific Railway, *Annual Report, 1905*, p. 12, further details are found in those for 1906 and 1909, and the exact dates and matters relating to the several subsidiary construction companies involved are contained in the special O.R.&N. and N.P. reports of 1916 and 1922, respectively, previously cited.

[28] *Wenatchee Daily World*, Oct. 9, 1909.

tion of the N.P. and G.N., each of which wanted a direct outlet to Portland for the burgeoning traffic of Spokane and the interior. Because they desired a railroad of high capacity and minimum operating costs, they elected not to make use of the existing N.P. line from Spokane to Pasco but to build a new roadbed of even grade and optimum curvatures. This new route led through the scabland channels, Washtucna Coulee, and the lower Snake, made use of N.P. tracks only across the bridge to Kennewick, and then followed the north bank of the Columbia to Vancouver, crossing there to Portland. The other new trunk line was an invasion of the Northwest by a fresh competitor. The Chicago, Milwaukee and St. Paul had long been a major "granger" road, serving a large part of the agricultural Midwest. Now, in the early years of the new century, it bridged the Missouri in South Dakota and headed for Puget Sound along the most direct route. Entering the Columbia Plain at Tekoa, it cut across the northern Palouse, bisected Adams County, followed lower Crab Creek to the Columbia, thence directly west to Ellensburg, up the Yakima to Snoqualmie Pass, and on to Seattle. Both of these trunk lines were opened for service in 1909, the S.P. &S. in early May, the C.M.&St.P. just two months later.[29]

Although these new companies laid several hundred miles of track in the Columbia Plain, the primary purpose of each was service across rather than within the region; and although each was competitive with earlier railroads, such rivalries were interregional rather than local in nature. Nevertheless, each new line did enhance the transportation facilities of some districts, though this was incidental to its over-all strategy. The S.P.&S. roadbed was within sight of the O.R.&N. nearly the entire way from the Palouse River to Vancouver, but the fact that a river separated the two was locally important. The eastern Klickitat was especially benefited; sidings were now spaced along the Columbia, and the wheat no longer had to be ferried across the river.[30] The C.M.&St.P. brought service closer to a few areas in the northern Palouse and to a broader area south of Ritzville, and it became the pioneer line in the wheat frontier west of Lind.

Logically, the impact of these trunk lines upon town develop-

[29] Northern Pacific Railway, *Annual Report, 1909,* p. 15; F. H. Johnson, *Brief Record of the Development of the Milwaukee Road* (Chicago, 1935), p. 38.

[30] The C.R.&N. railway from Lyle to Goldendale now came under S.P.&S. control.

ments was also minor. The most important new communities were those established by the railroads to serve their own internal purposes as division points—Malden and Othello on the C.M.&St.P., Cliffs on the S.P.&S., each with an operations office, roundhouse, and maintenance and repair shops. Even those local branch lines designed to tap wheat districts unserved by railroads had less effect upon the pattern of towns than had similar constructions in the decades before. Douglas, Withrow, and Mansfield were new sites on the G.N. feeder, but only Mansfield, at the terminus, had much prospect for development, for Waterville, even though bypassed, had had a solid head start. The situation on the Camas Prairie was more unstable (Map 37). Grangeville's already dominant position was firmly buttressed by becoming the terminus, the Denver's aspirations were as firmly undermined by being left off the route. However, in several cases older communities that were not bypassed found themselves suddenly faced with severe competition from new sites adjacent. As soon as the railroad route had been decided, J. P. Vollmer, a wealthy Lewiston resident and a director of the N.P., purchased land at several points, laid out new towns, and energetically promoted their development. Reubens was platted near Kippen, Vollmer a mile east of Ilo, and Steunenberg a quarter of a mile up the track from Ferdinand, each designed to replace the older site. Although Vollmer invested heavily in these new places and offered advantageous terms to lure people already established in the old, the high prices of lots and local resentment against the idea of his scheme hindered its success.[31]

Railroads strongly affected a few other towns also, and none more drastically than Sprague. In 1894 the local railroad laborers staged a strike, and in consequence the N.P. temporarily shifted its division headquarters to Spokane Falls. However, in the next year a fire destroyed the roundhouse, shops, and twenty-four locomotives, as well as a large part of the business district of Sprague. Three months later the N.P. moved all its activities to Spokane Falls, now clearly the most important city of the interior, and Sprague was left maimed and half deserted. Nor was that an end of its suffering for the following year Davenport, capitalizing upon this disaster, forced the issue

[31] Chicago, Milwaukee, and St. Paul Railway, *Washington* (*ca.* 1910), pp. 17, 19; Ballou, *Klickitat Valley,* p. 313; Elsensohn, *Idaho County,* pp. 446-49; Vollmer also founded Fenn and sought to lure the residents of Denver, three miles to the east and completely off the railroad.

of the Lincoln County seat to another vote and easily won the prize away from its old rival.[32] Sprague, reduced to 695 people in 1900, could only look to its rural trade for sustenance and even that was diminished in the next decade when the S.P.&S. established wheat sidings nearby.

Palouse City was also affected by railroad and industrial developments, though the impact was as yet not drastic. In 1903 the Weyerhaeuser interests purchased a large tract of timberland in the upper Palouse watershed and beyond, and also bought the facilities and timberlands of the big mills in the town. In 1905 the Washington, Idaho and Montana Railway was constructed east from Palouse City to tap those areas, and a large new mill and model company town were established near the edge of the forest eight miles upriver. With the completion of the railroad, mill, and town of Potlatch in 1906, the plant in Palouse City was to be phased out and the log drives on the river discontinued.[33] Although Palouse City was destined to lose a major payroll, for the time being it continued to thrive, not only on its good rural trade but also because the expanded developments in its lumbering hinterland continued to draw some of their services from the older town, despite the rise of Potlatch.

These setbacks and a scattering of lesser ones in other communities notwithstanding, generally in the towns the first years of the twentieth century were a time of growth and undiminished confidence. Although the land seekers coming by the trainload and the march of the farming frontier in upon the remnants of the rangelands were often touted as the surest indicators of regional progress, the greatest actual increment of growth was in the towns. And the patterns of that growth were becoming more stabilized. As the countryside filled and the railroads penetrated throughout each major district, the spacing and elemental character of these communities became more firmly set. Local trade areas were sharply defined, prospects for local industry clearly apparent, and the comparative position of each town with its neighbors certainly evident. Thus, although

[32] Steele and Rose, *Big Bend Country*, pp. 106-10, 181-86; the election results: Davenport 1,582, Sprague 537, Harrington 240.

[33] Ralph W. Hidy, Frank Ernest Hill, Allan Nevins, *Timber and Men: The Weyerhaeuser Story* (New York, 1963), pp. 254-60. A rival scheme to accomplish a similar purpose had been promoted by Moscow interests, who got a secret Union Pacific subsidy to survey the Moscow and Eastern Railroad, and hoped to establish a large mill on the outskirts of their town; see the *Daily Idahoan* (Moscow), Sept. 29, 1961, for a brief account of this venture.

these years were marked by a flurry of developments in town and country alike, it was less an extension of fresh patterns into new lands and more an elaboration within established frameworks.

A MEAGER DIVERSITY

Other Grains and Livestock

Wheat remained king through all these years, enlarging the extent of its realm and increasing the magnitude of its presence. Pastoralists had yielded ground to the continued encroachment, while irrigationists expanded onto a scattering of lands which had never been brought into its domain. Yet wheat was not the sole ruler of the dry-land farming area. Two other grains were also evident over much of the region, and were significant in some districts. Barley had proved to be an excellent crop in the foothill belt of the Walla Walla country and in the Camas Prairie. The yields and quality were high. Some of the crop was used for stock feed, some was sold to breweries in the Pacific Northwest, and an increasing portion was being exported to Europe.[34] In most of the wheat districts oats were used as feed for work horses, but they were especially important as a commercial crop in the eastern Palouse. In these more humid districts it was common to fallow every third year, and oats and barley were spring-sown crops which yielded better than a second successive wheat crop. In such circumstances these grains were more complementary than competitive with wheat.

Although wheat was dominant, there was a growing sentiment that it ought not remain so, at least to its present degree. The reasons and motives for this belief were varied. The near disaster of 1893 in the Palouse led to suggestions that a more diversified agriculture would provide a much needed security, although exactly which other crops would not have been damaged by such heavy rains was not made clear. Much of the literature advocating diversification came from the promoters and propagandists of towns, who had an obvious self-interest in enlarging the rural population and trade. While there was still vacant land, they had been content to celebrate the magnificence of the wheat yields; now, however, they must urge subdivision of large farms and intensification and diversification of production if more people were to be attracted and

[34] *Report of the Washington State Grain Inspector,* 1898-1900, p. 7; *Up-to-the-Times Magazine,* 1 (May, 1907), 470.

accommodated and the towns continue to grow. It was common to point out that this was inevitable, a "natural evolution of farm life" promoted by rising land prices and the need for rising incomes, and was in no way the result of diminished yields or any other inherent deficiency. Others, however, warned that "this country will not raise wheat always, any more than any other country will." They insisted that all older wheat regions had had to diversify and "if Washington is an exception, it will be the first one."[35] Such opinions were as common among the few agricultural scientists of the time as they were apparently rare among the many farmers.[36]

As nearly every farm had livestock—a few cows for milk, some for beef and veal, perhaps a few hogs—greater emphasis in that direction was often viewed as a logical and advantageous shift. That it would require a change from present practices, however, was also apparent. Many of the cattle lived on stubbleland in the fall, a threshing straw stack in the winter, and the weeds of the fallowed ground in the spring and summer. It was common to cut some grain green for hay, and a few farmers had a bit of meadowland. Obviously, these animals were rarely fattened, indeed many were half starved through much of the year, and the system provided no basis whatsoever for commercial beef production. Cultivated fodder was needed, but exactly what plant might answer was not clear. Corn was suggested, and one agricultural scientist thought he discerned a "deep undercurrent of interest" in that crop stemming from the midwestern heritage of many of the settlers. Although many had planted a few acres of corn when they had first arrived, and perhaps had done so because they were "homesick for the miniature dark-green forest of the 'Corn Belt,' " the fact that they had not continued to raise it was strong evidence against the opinion that it was well-suited as a rotation crop in the wheat belt. In fact, there had

[35] *Palouse Republican*, Nov. 3, 1893, Jan. 12, 1894; *Touchet Valley*, pp. 37, 41; J. O. Scobey, "Farm Resources," in *Report of Farmers' Institute . . .* (Washington Agricultural Experiment Station Bulletin No. 5) (May, 1892), p. 91; and Scobey, "Dairy Farming in Washington," in *Report of Farmers' Institute . . .* (Washington Agricultural Experiment Station Bulletin No. 2) (January, 1892), p. 24. See also Byron Hunter, *Farm Practices in the Columbia Basin Uplands* (Farmers' Bulletin No. 294) (Washington, D.C., 1907), pp. 27-28.

[36] For an example of a farmer who agreed, but acknowledged that practically all others thought of nothing but wheat, see the statement of A. D. Thayer in *Proceedings of the Convention of Producers, Shippers and Millers, otherwise known as the Wheat Convention* (Pullman, Wash., 1906), pp. 10-11 (hereafter cited as *Wheat Convention*).

been experimentation with corn for forty years or more, with little success. A few fields were still raised in the Walla Walla country, but the cool nights and drought of the summers made it "a treacherous crop, in the main." Some farmers thought it better than bare fallow despite the risks, but there was neither a "deep undercurrent of interest" nor a secure potential for a major livestock industry based upon corn. Experimental plots of sorghum seemed to offer greater hope, but it was an exotic plant unfamiliar to the farmers and was not given extensive field trials at this time.[37]

The most promising forage crop was alfalfa. For years it had been thought suitable only for moist bottomlands and irrigated ground, but after the turn of the century experiments by scientists and farmers alike proved that it would yield well on the drier uplands (a better appreciation of its origin in the semi-arid districts of the Old World might have suggested this fact earlier). By 1910 alfalfa acreage was increasing in the Walla Walla, Palouse, and Big Bend, but primarily in place of timothy or other grasses in the bottomlands, or of bunch grass on thin-soiled upland areas.[38] Nowhere was it regarded as either a replacement for or complement of wheat, and thereby as a tool of diversification.

Despite the disinclination of the majority, a few farmers were as interested in raising meat as wheat, and the local literature often gave prominence to the fact and urged others to follow their example. A report in the *Spokesman-Review* described a German farmer in the Potlatch country who mowed ripe barley, burnt it over to remove the straw and beards, and turned hogs in upon the fields to fatten. In the eastern Palouse hogs were often fed on small fields of standing grain and used to clean up the sometimes extensive patches of wheat or barley flattened by wind and rain, which could not be harvested with a header. Although local reporters rarely failed to

[37] G. A. Crosthwait, *Indian Corn, Its Production and Improvement* (Idaho Agricultural Experiment Station Bulletin No. 57) (April, 1907), pp. 5-6; *Illustrated History of Southeastern Washington*, p. 169; S. G. Cosgrove, "Valuable Opinions on Farming Our Lands," *East Washingtonian Pioneer Edition* (Pomeroy), June 6, 1914. This article was written in 1903. Thomas Shaw, *A Farmers Paradise* ... (St. Paul, Minn., 1898), p. 14; *Spokesman-Review*, Oct. 5, 1900, p. 4. See also *Crop Tests* (Idaho Agricultural Experiment Station Bulletin No. 24) (May, 1900), p. 17, for a report on experiments with "Russian millet."

[38] *Spokesman-Review*, Oct. 5, 1900; E. E. Elliott, *Growing Alfalfa Without Irrigation* (Washington Agricultural Experiment Station Bulletin No. 80) (1907); Cosgrove, "Valuable Opinions"; *Pacific Farmers Union*, 1 (July 23, 1909), p. 1; *Big Bend Chief*, April 26, 1907.

insist upon the profit and advantages, these practices did not in themselves provide a foundation for a meat industry. The hog might be a cheap and efficient harvester, but he had to eat in other seasons too, and he needed more water, shelter, and general care than most farmers could or would provide for any large number.

Dairying had its proponents, but rarely among the farmers. Regional promoters thought it disgraceful that dairy products had to be imported, while some college "experts" saw the milk cow as the best means of diversification. The promoters insisted that conditions were favorable, the farmers replied that no suitable fodder was available, the experts warned that one had better be found. Yet all recognized that there was a powerful "disinclination of the farmer to subject himself to the annoyance of milking and caring for his stock," and that fact was perhaps enough to explain why on most farms milking remained a small family chore instead of a large business enterprise.[39]

Root Crops and Orchards

No crop or activity received such intensive promotion as the sugar beet. In 1892 at a meeting in Garfield, a college speaker urged the farmers to consider the crop, stating that "a description of the soil and climate best adapted to the production of the sugar beet is an accurate description of the soil and climate of the Palouse country." He went on to "assume the role of prophet and predict that the present generation will see the Palouse Country sown to beets." During the next few years further tests were made at both Pullman and Moscow, and the merits and suitability of the beet were widely advertised. While it would cost three times as much as wheat to raise, the profit would be five times greater. In 1899 "the beginning of a new epoch in the industrial development of the 'Inland Empire' " seemed at hand when the last obstacle, the need for a sugar refinery, was overcome. Spokane promoters built a mill at Waverly with a daily capacity of 350 tons of beets, and experts from France were brought in to supervise the planting and cultivating of 1,400 acres. It was to be expected that "to raise a new crop with strange habits—a crop which demands an entirely different system of farming—very naturally involves more or less disappointments." Some of these difficulties were overcome, and some farmers did decide that

[39] *Touchet Valley*, pp. 40-41; Scobey, "Dairy Farming in Washington"; *Walla Walla Valley, Washington* (Walla Walla, 1910), p. 41.

beets provided an excellent rotation with wheat, better than fallow. Yet in 1909 the total acreage of sugar beets was only 1,363, an indication of the failure of this "new epoch" to materialize.[40]

Potatoes, widely grown for domestic use, were often advocated but rarely attempted as a specialization. Some viewed them as a replacement of fallow in the wheat cycle, and saw a great market for potato alcohol to be used in "automobiles, farm engines, stoves and for lighting purposes." Orcharding, well established as a specialty in the Walla Walla, Touchet, and Yakima valleys, was also promoted as an advantageous combination for the grain farmer. Wheat and fruit were raised side by side on many sunny slopes in the eastern Palouse, though the acreage in trees was a small portion of the total in cultivation, and even here grainfields and commercial orchards were not commonly on the same farm. Apples, plums, and prunes were the principal products and were marketed widely through the Northwest. A horticulturist had predicted that the Palouse would "one day be the most famous apple country in the United States," but it was already feeling the competition from the expanding irrigation districts. Local boosters insisted that the fault lay with man and not with nature:

> Fruit raising is a business. We do not make it a business. When we learn to plant our lands and to cultivate, and prune, and spray, and thin, and pick, and pack as does the orchardist of Yakima and Wenatchee, then and only then will the Palouse apple take its proper place as the first in quality.... It goes without saying that an apple raised without irrigation is superior to the irrigated product.

Unfortunately for the future of the Palouse apple, such superiority was by no means so obvious to others.[41]

But it was certainly true that successful commercial orcharding

[40] C. A. Gwinn, *The Sugar Beet* (Washington Agricultural Experiment Station Bulletin No. 3) (February, 1892), pp. 44-45; *Sugar Beet Investigation in 1898* (Idaho Agricultural Experiment Station Bulletin No. 18) (1899), p. 51; see also *Sugar Beets in Idaho,* Bulletin No. 12 (1898) in the same series; *Northwest Magazine,* 17 (July, 1899), 26; Edwards, *Spokane County,* pp. 286-87. Waverly was chosen as the site for the mill because of the water power from Latah Creek; the O.R.&N. constructed a short railroad branch from Fairfield to serve the factory. *A Review of the Resources and Industries of Washington* (Olympia, Wash., 1901), p. 87; see remarks of A. D. Thayer of Waverly, *Wheat Convention,* pp. 10, 11; see John Fahey, *Inland Empire: D. C. Corbin and Spokane* (Seattle, Wash., 1965), pp. 197-201, for a succinct history of this enterprise.

[41] *Davenport Tribune,* Aug. 9, 1906; *Northwest Magazine,* 19 (February, 1901), pp. 21, 40; Palouse as apple country reported by Shaw, *Farmers Paradise,*

was an intensive, painstaking task, as was dairying, beet farming, potato raising, and almost every other agricultural activity advocated for the region. That fact made it not only unlikely that the wheat farmer would take on any of these as a major sideline, but even more certain that few would have the slightest interest in shifting from grain to another kind of agriculture. That "Eastern farmers with ideas of intensive farming can make these lands yield far greater returns," *might* be true, and here and there "along the line of the Spokane & Inland the size of farms is being reduced," but the man who made these observations had just reaped forty-six thousand bushels from one thousand acres of wheat near Garfield, and he gave no indication that *he* was considering a change. Why would such a person want to prune, spray, thin, pick, and pack fruit, or thin beets, or milk cows morning and night, day after day, month after month? When an advocate of dairying told a farmers' meeting that he "was quite willing to admit that a harvest of forty, fifty and sixty bushels of wheat to the acre is a temptation that has strong tendencies to lead most of us astray from a desire to be troubled with any other branch of farm work . . ." he made a gross understatement. When he told another similar group that wheat was a "lazyman's crop" which took little intelligence to raise he revealed his own lack of tact and strong bias.[42] While such persons talked of future profits from untested markets for new activities which required far greater effort, the wheat farmer was making a profit in an established market from familiar routine with ever greater efficiency. Good wheat farming was becoming a more specialized task, too; it required larger and more complicated machinery, better understanding of soils and tillage, greater care in seed selection and treatment. But good wheat farming gave good returns, and so long as these continued there was little room for dissatisfaction and little interest in diversification.

THE WHEAT INDUSTRY

New Machinery

Improvements in machinery enhanced the efficiency of every phase of wheat raising during these years. Many of the changes were

p. 27; S. J. Chadwick, "Whitman County, Washington," *The Coast,* 14 (December, 1907), 368.

[42] *Spokesman-Review,* June 17, 1909; Scobey, "Dairy Farming," p. 24; Scobey, "Farm Resources," pp. 91-92.

A steam-powered combine "at work near Walla Walla." This is probably the Eureka Flat machine mentioned in the text. *(Photo courtesy of Northern Pacific Railway Company)*

One of the big Holt combines at work near Walla Walla about 1900. *(Photo courtesy of Northern Pacific Railway Company)*

merely a matter of better designs, more careful workmanship, or higher quality materials applied to implements long familiar. Better iron and steel made possible lighter frames, shares, and moldboards and thus larger plows for the same number of horses. The double disc came into more common use, particularly in the preparation of uncultivated fallow for seeding and sometimes in place of the plow in areas of light crops and thin stubble. Greater attention to the tillage of fallow to control weeds and conserve moisture gave rise to various types of cultivators, of which the rod weeder was the most important innovation. Improved seed drills, fitted with shoes or discs, completely replaced the wagon-mounted broadcasters once commonly used.

In harvesting equipment, however, there was a different order of change. To be sure, binders, headers, and threshers were altered in dozens of details designed to enhance efficiency, reduce breakage, and simplify repairs, but these were overshadowed in interest and significance by the development of the "combine." The first of these spectacular machines was evidently brought in from California in 1888. Farmers reportedly came as far as seventy miles to watch it cut a swath twenty feet wide around a large grainfield northwest of Ritzville. It was powered by a huge ground wheel, operated by five men, and pulled by thirty-two horses. Two years later the California Ranch near Harrington obtained a similar machine and attracted a similar crowd, and a few years after that the O.R.&N. ran a special train from Pullman to Endicott to let the farmers watch the first such trial in the Palouse country. Inevitably there was much diversity of opinion as to the practicability of such a radical innovation. One of the most obvious problems was overcome almost immediately, however, when in 1891 the Holt Company, a leading California manufacturer, marketed a "sidehill combine" with a leveling device especially designed for the peculiar needs of the region. Within ten years combines were not uncommon in any of the drier wheat districts. By 1902 the Holt Company had established a large distributing warehouse in Walla Walla and in that year reported eighty-eight sales and a greater demand than they could satisfy.[43]

It was by then clear that there was no serious drawback inherent

[43] *Ritzville Journal-Times*, Sept. 15, 1949, p. 19; *Weekly Advertiser* (Sprague), July 24, 1890; Kincaid and Harris, *Palouse in the Making*, pp. 5, 42; the authors are uncertain of the exact year of the trial of the combine. *Fifty Years on Tracks* (Peoria, Ill., 1954). See the *Weekly Advertiser*, July 24, 1890, on the farmers' con-

in the use of the combine in the Big Bend, the more level sections of the western Palouse and Walla Walla, the Horse Heaven, and the Oregon wheat districts. But in the eastern Walla Walla and Palouse and the Camas Prairie real problems remained. In the latter two, especially, fear of early autumn rains made the farmers reluctant to leave grain to ripen in the fields, and therefore reluctant to abandon the binder. Furthermore, much of the oats in these areas was bound for winter feed. The combine could not be used for that purpose, nor would it leave a straw stack to winter livestock.[44] Furthermore, the average farm was much smaller in these districts than in the drier country. Because most were only a quarter to a half section in size, the advantages of being able to harvest thirty to forty acres per day were less impressive, and the cost of such a machine seemed inordinately great. Further still, these farmers did not normally keep half enough horses to pull a combine, and because of the steeper ground and smaller fields it was not certain that even the usual number could handle a machine which already had a reputation as a "horse-killer," even in less hilly terrain.

One obvious means of meeting many of these problems was to design a smaller combine. In 1907 a local company was established to do just that in the area which most needed such a machine. The first product of the Idaho National Harvester Company of Moscow was not very successful, but by 1909 its diminutive combines were selling well. In appearance and size they resembled a push-binder; they had a six-foot cut and needed only two men and four horses to harvest fifteen acres a day. About the same time machines of an intermediate size (ten-foot header, three men, fourteen horses) were being shipped in by a California manufacturer also. Although such combines seemed to answer many of the special needs of these districts, there was no immediate indication that they would cause a general change in harvesting practices.[45] There was still the problem

cern over the sidehill problem; also Lyman, *Walla Walla County*, pp. 144-45. The Holt Company advertised that its machines had been used in the Big Bend since 1893; see *Big Bend Empire*, June 30, 1904; *Spokesman-Review*, June 15, 1902.

[44] One proponent of the new machine suggested that it would thereby "aid in building up a better grade of stock" because the farmers could no longer get by with that kind of feeding, but such an argument was unlikely to bring about change; see remarks of Oscar Young of Pullman, in *Wheat Convention*, pp. 15-16. Young's statement contains interesting measures of the costs and other advantages of the combine he had been operating for three years.

[45] State of Idaho, *Commissioner of Immigration, Labor and Statistics, Fifth Biennial Report* (Boise, 1907-8), p. 90; *Pacific Farmers Union*, 1 (June 25,

of climate, the investment in headers and binders, and the view that the binder would be needed anyway, and that grain bound and ripened in the stack gave a heavier, high-quality product.

Elsewhere experimentation was under way at the opposite end of the scale. In 1902 a wheat grower on Eureka Flat tried out a gigantic steam-powered combine which cut a swath forty-two feet wide and was reputedly capable of harvesting a hundred acres a day. His success was not reported, but the machine was even potentially feasible only for the largest farms on almost level terrain. This was not the first use of steam traction for field work. Farmers near Harrington and in Umatilla County were plowing with huge steam tractors as early as 1893, and several were reported in operation in Adams County a few years later. These, too, were obviously limited in their regional adaptability, but the very idea of replacing the horse by mechanical power was even more obviously of enormous portent. Steam tractors could not work such a revolution because they had far more problems than advantages. Heavy fuel and water requirements were a serious handicap, they were useless in a hilly terrain, and easily mired in any soft ground whether wet or dry. Furthermore, they were far too expensive and huge for any but the largest farms; as one historian put it, "the engines were built in such ponderous weights and elephantine proportions that it seemed the designers intended to plow all the land in sight in one day's operation."[46]

1909), and 2 (March 17, 1911), 7. The intermediate-sized machines were the "Betty Best" combines of the Best Manufacturing Company of San Leandro. In J. S. Jones, H. P. Fishburn, and C. W. Colver, *A Report on the Milling Properties of Idaho Wheat* (Idaho Agricultural Experiment Station Bulletin No. 72) (December, 1911), p. 7, it is stated that despite a few headers and combines the great majority of northern Idaho wheat was cut with a binder.

[46] *Moro Bulletin*, Aug. 12, 1902; *Spokesman-Review*, Feb. 21, 1893, p. 6, Jan. 1, 1903. A similar combine was in operation near Quincy, the only two in the region at the time. *The Northwest*, 11 (July, 1893), 37; Steele and Rose, *Big Bend Country*, p. 792. An excellent account of the history and problems associated with these and other steam engines is that of Reynold M. Wik, *Steam Power on the American Farm* (Philadelphia, 1953). These engines in the Columbia Plain were almost certainly imports from California, where there had been much experimentation and where both the Holt and the Best companies had developed steam tractors and harvesters; see also *Fifty Years on Tracks* and R. B. Gray, *Development of the Agricultural Tractor in the United States, Part I: Up to 1919 Inclusive* (U.S. Dept. of Agriculture, Agriculture Research Service, Agric. Engineering Research Branch, Farm Machinery Section, Information Series No. 107) (Beltsville, Md., June, 1954). Also see especially Wik, *Steam Power*, p. 64.

But innovations came in rapid order after the turn of the century. In 1904 the Holt Company fitted a steam tractor with "caterpiller" tracks, which began to solve the problem of traction. Experiments with gasoline tractors had been going on for years, and in 1906 Holt produced the first gasoline-powered caterpillar tractor. With this, fuel and water were no longer limitations, the efficiency of the gasoline motor allowed a smaller machine, and the caterpillar tracks made it the first tractor usable in hilly terrain (though these first machines were by no means ideal for hillside work). In 1904 Holt also pioneered in adapting a gasoline motor to run the internal machinery of a combine. This eliminated the huge ground wheel, making the machine lighter and easier to pull, and allowed the threshing machinery to run at a constant speed whatever the rate of travel. With this combination of innovations, the Holt Company had paved the way for a revolution in harvesting methods especially well adapted to the peculiar needs of the Columbia wheat country. By 1910 more than a hundred tractors had been produced, many had been tried in the region and pronounced a success, and Holt was confidently promoting their new idea in combines, admonishing local farmers to "have your old machine changed to gasoline drive." How long that revolution might take and to what extent it might reach was far from clear, but that it was under way seemed apparent. The header and the binder had been faced with a steadily improved combine for twenty years, but for the first time the horse had a real competitor. Not only a new scale but a new means of farming was clearly possible.[47]

Marketing Problems

In contrast with such remarkable innovations in getting the crop off the ground, the methods of getting it to market had not changed at all. Yet there was interest in that phase, and many were certain that the means of a radical improvement had been clearly demonstrated for years. The issue was an old one: sacks versus bulk handling. The several wheat regions of the nation provided a convenient comparison of the two systems: the Pacific coast areas (California and the Northwest) had always used sacks, while all of the main

[47] *Fifty Years on Tracks;* Gray, *Agricultural Tractor,* pp. 40-46. Speed had been a serious problem with combines, because when the ground wheel ran at a slower rate on turns and uphill, it did a poor job of threshing. *Pacific Farmers Union,* 1 (July 23, 1909), 6; *Up-to-the-Times Magazine,* 4 (September, 1910), 2787, 2791, and 4 (October, 1910).

Midwest regions had shifted to bulk facilities years before. The disturbing fact was that a comparison of costs made it seem "nothing less than . . . astonishing" that any grain district would continue to use sacks. Computations of the annual expense of the sacks, of the labor and time required for sacking and handling, of the losses from breakages, field rot, rats, and mice, suggested that Columbia wheat growers paid an enormous penalty for persisting in their old ways. Such figuring indicated that the savings from a change to bulk would pay for all the necessary new facilities in two or three years.[48]

Such a comparison made sacking appear to be inordinately costly and clumsy, but a full exploration of the matter soon revealed that the problem was much more complicated. The most commonly cited reason for the resistance to change was the fact that all of the grain was shipped around Cape Horn; the sailing ships would handle only sacks because bulk cargo might shift violently in rough seas, and there was also the problem of overheating and spoilage during the two long, slow passages through the tropics. It was stated that disastrous experiences had caused marine underwriters to set insurance rates at prohibitive levels on bulk shipments. Granting the validity of these arguments, the farmers could still ship in bulk to the ocean terminals, where the grain could then be sacked for export. But this plan encountered serious objections also. Smut, a wheat fungus, was a widespread problem in the Columbia Basin, though one whose seriousness varied greatly from farm to farm depending upon the efficiency of the preventive measures taken by the individual grower. Grain dealers pointed out that storage in elevators distributed the smut through all the wheat, blackening the entire lot to the point that it would be graded down at terminal markets. Thus sacks were a protection for the careful farmer and original buyer; an exporter put the issue succinctly to the Wheat Convention: "Gentlemen you cannot get rid of the sacks until you get rid of the smut." And there were other reasons for keeping local shipments separated. The Columbia grain region was peculiar in the great number of varieties grown. There was a marked price differential among these wheats, which reflected the differences in milling qualities and various market preferences, and thus farmers, buyers, and millers had an interest in keeping them segregated. The need to achieve greater regional uniformity in grain was often cited but not easy to achieve.

[48] S. C. Armstrong, "The Elevator vs. Warehouse System," *Wheat Convention,* pp. 30-34.

It was not so much a simple matter of education and cooperation as a matter of local differences in climate, methods, and agronomic problems.[49]

It was common to point out that the long summer dry season, a major climatic difference between the Columbia region and those east of the Rockies, *allowed* the use of sacks, as wheat could be left in the field or stored on open platforms with little fear of rain damage. It was not common but perhaps basic to the question to cite a positive if subtle advantage of this situation to certain middlemen:

> From the climatic condition arises another peculiar situation which makes for the retention of the sack-handling method. During the period of farm or warehouse storage, the sun's heat dries out the grain. When sold, it is sold by weight rather than by measure. If, however, the sacked grain be shipped to terminal points on the seacoast, it will absorb moisture. The gain in weight from this source more than counterbalances the cost of the sacks, additional handling expense, and often the entire cost of storing.[50]

Thus when the problem was examined more closely, the possibility of a simple change faded. There was no agreement as to the desirability, no mutual understanding of why sacks continued to be used, and therefore no focus of effort to overcome particular obstacles. The impressive computations of the savings to be achieved by the abandonment of sacks did not take into account such matters from the other side of the ledger as the lowering of average grade through mixture, the resultant problems of the millers, and the unearned "moisture increment" of dealers. Certain groups evidently had a vested interest in the existing system but its exact basis and value was never clear, and so the issue remained one of persistent concern but little action.[51]

[49] H. A. Haring, *Warehousing* (New York, 1925), pp. 577-79, has a good summary of all of the leading reasons for the continued use of sacks. A Tacoma exporter insisted that the installation of bulkheads would easily overcome the danger of shifts; see *Wheat Convention,* p. 35; also see Haring, *Warehousing,* p. 579. The problem of grain uniformity is examined in the next chapter. See *Wheat Convention,* pp. 53-60, 65-71, for a discussion of prices and milling qualities.

[50] Haring, *Warehousing,* p. 578.

[51] See, for example, the report of a debate in Davenport, growing out of the discussions of the Wheat Convention, in the *Commercial Review,* 32 (Feb. 23, 1906); Rollin E. Smith, *Wheat Fields and Markets of the World* (St. Louis, Mo., 1908), p. 216; John F. Carrere, *Spokane Falls, Washington Territory, and Its Tributary Country . . .* (Spokane Falls, 1889), p. 33; Albert C. Moore, "The Grain Bag Problem," *Up-to-the-Times Magazine,* 1 (May, 1907), 357. Those

Other problems associated with marketing received about as much attention and as little result. National comparisons demonstrated that Columbia growers received lower prices for their wheat than those in any other region. There were a number of reasons for this situation, but the fact that Columbia farmers netted an unusually small proportion of the initial European sale price inevitably focused attention upon the problems of transportation. A study reported that one year the prices received at various points along the marketing system were as follows:

At the farm	59¢ per bushel
Local market	66.2
Portland	78
Liverpool	96

This price to the farmer was ten cents below the national average.[52] As ocean shipping was highly competitive and costs at that end could presumably be reduced only by radical improvements, such as a Panama Canal and larger and faster ships, complaints were principally directed at the railroads.

Despite an increase in governmental powers of regulation during these years, there was little faith among the general public that adequate restraints had been achieved. There were, however, some demonstrations of various new governmental interventions. The most famous of these was the breakup of the Northern Securities Company, a holding company which had brought the Northern Pacific and Great Northern under a single control. Formed in 1901, it was dissolved by order of the Supreme Court in 1904, and certain railroad constructions in the Big Bend were directly related to these actions.[53] But chief concern was focused upon the Columbia, for a

who understood that sailing vessels and the Cape Horn route were the main problems could take heart in the report that the new transcontinental, the C.M.&St.P., was giving consideration to the construction of elevators along its line because the Panama Canal, now under construction, would eliminate the need for sacks; see the *Weekly Commoner* (Colfax), March 22, Dec. 20, 1907. Meanwhile, a few of the larger farmers experimented with bulk tanks on combines, but these added weight to an already heavy machine and their feasibility remained in doubt; see *Wheat Convention,* pp. 31ff.

[52] Frank Andrews, "Freight Costs and Market Values," *Yearbook of the U.S. Department of Agriculture* (Washington, D.C., 1906), pp. 381-84.

[53] The Coulee City–Adrian line, tying the N.P.'s Washington Central branch to the G.N. main line, was built upon the formation of the holding company; the extension from Adrian to Connell to tie into the N.P. main line was a response to its dissolution.

waterway was still regarded as the only certain means of effective competition with a railroad.

The portages remained the crux of the problem. The state of Oregon, impatient at the unconscionably slow progress by the federal government on the Cascades Canal, built a portage railroad there in 1891. The completion of the canal in 1896 ended that bottleneck and prompted a significant rate reduction by the O.R. &N. However, there could be no full waterway competition so long as The Dalles–Celilo interruption remained. In 1900 a private company undertook to build a portage railway along the north bank and to operate a line of boats on the upper river. However, its first vessel, the *Frederick K. Billings* (originally used as a transfer boat by the N.P. before the completion of the Pasco-Kennewick bridge), ran aground and damaged its bow on its initial run, the company soon ran short of money, its railway construction was halted, and by 1902 it was bankrupt. In the following year the state of Oregon authorized a portage railroad along the south bank between Big Eddy and Celilo. Completion of this line in 1905 prompted a Portland group to organize the Open River Navigation Company to operate a connecting boat service on the upper river. For the first time the possibility of real competition seemed at hand, and to meet the threat the O.R.&N. again reduced its rates. Actually, the steamboats carried little grain except from the Klickitat country, and the completion of the S.P.&S. soon took away most of that. A Dalles-Celilo canal remained the great hope but was yet far from a reality. Meanwhile, the reduction in railroad rates indicated that although they carried little freight and few passengers the reappearance of the stately stern-wheelers on the upper Columbia was not only a nostalgic sight but an economic benefit.[54]

But even if the railroads could by various means be brought under greater regulation, the farmer would apparently still be at the mercy of other profiteers. W. H. Reed, the Washington State Grain Inspector, tried to alert the Wheat Convention to connivance of the "Portland-Tacoma-Seattle grain buyers' combine" which set a

[54] This account is based upon Mills, *Sternwheelers,* chap. vi and xi, unless otherwise indicated. *Klickitatat County Agricultirist,* Feb. 17, Aug. 4, Sept. 1, 1900, March 22, 1902. In 1909 the state authorized an extension of its portage railway from Big Eddy to The Dalles to facilitate downriver loadings and the steamboat company announced that it was considering the towage of large wheat barges between Pasco and Celilo; *Pacific Farmers Union,* 1 (Aug. 27, 1909), 1.

single ocean terminal price, wiping out the "God-given advantage of a better harbor" which gave Puget Sound lower ship charter rates than Portland.[55] There were so many other kinds of presumed discriminations cited at such discussions that the farmer might well have viewed the whole marketing system as one designed and operated more as a conspiracy to extract money from his pockets than to facilitate the shipment of wheat from the grower to the consumer.

And if the farmer rarely understood the amount and purpose of these many charges along the way, he likely had even less comprehension of the complexity of forces which actually set the day-by-day prices offered for his grain. At the Pullman convention Inspector Reed made a valiant try at explaining that situation:

> Pretty much of everything affects the market price of wheat: a larger or a smaller prospective yield of the greater wheat producing countries, such as the United States, Russia, France, Argentine, India and Australia; a general rainfall in harvest time in any of these agricultural domains; the discovery that rust is devastating large districts ...; the advent of the festive grasshopper or the predatory cinchbug and other like banes; an earlier than usual winter-closing of the Russian sea of Azov, and the Black Sea at Odessa, or of our own great lake ports which is always a precursor of an advance of the competing railroad's freight rates to seaboard; the unexpected addition or reduction of the import duty on wheat by Germany, France, or to a minor degree, as in this present month, by smaller countries like Mexico and Brazil; the outbreak of a war, or threatening outbreak of one involving any extensive wheat producing or buying country; the murder of a ruler in any of them; the development of a monetary panic or money market stringency; the general prosperity or poverty of the consuming masses; the accidental or possible prearranged disposition of the producers to sell early, or to hold their grain; an official estimate on the crop of a nation or even of one of our largest wheat growing states, which is different from the prognostications. All of these and many, many other legitimate factors are constantly protruding themselves to affect the daily market price of wheat.[56]

Taken altogether this wheat business was a bewildering affair. While it was laudable to try to extend their comprehension, it appeared that the farmers, as a group, would never understand, or even attempt to understand, much beyond how to grow and harvest it. That was their end of the business, and that was something they could talk about with confidence. Even there a growing number of

[55] W. H. Reed, "Influences Affecting Markets and Prices," *Wheat Convention,* p. 81.

[56] *Ibid.,* p. 78.

"experts" insisted that they could help and that the farmers had much to learn about their soils, crops, and methods. But this was the one place where the farmer could be a teacher as well as a learner. Any suggestion that came out of the laboratory or the experimental plot would not be convincing until it had been mass tested in the field. The advantages of any change would have to be measured against the cumulative experiences of thousands of men who had raised hundreds of millions of bushels of wheat over a full half century in the Great Columbia Plain.

CHAPTER THIRTEEN

> We wheat farmers have been called
> land robbers and it has been said that
> the father was robbing his son, but I
> believe that our children's children
> will be raising wheat here in this Pa-
> louse Country.
>
> J. S. KLEMGARD

Inquiry: The Farmer
and the Scientist, ca. 1890-1910

IMPROVING AGRICULTURE

IN THE late spring of 1890 a farmer of Umatilla County wrote to
the Signal Service Officer (under whose name a weekly weather and
crop bulletin was issued) to ask why his wheat was doing poorly
despite an apparently favorable season. His inquiry was passed on
to a professor at the agricultural college in Corvallis, who concluded
from the farmer's description that he had planted his wheat too
deeply, and he explained why this was detrimental. Publication of
this exchange in the *Pendleton-Tribune* prompted a correspondent
from nearby Helix to point out what a valuable service this kind of
advice was and to report that the local chapter of the Grange had
gone on record in support of the need for local agricultural experiment stations in the wheat regions.

The Helix Grange was merely endorsing an idea which had been
discussed for some time. Not long thereafter the first such station
was established at Pullman in conjunction with the State College of
Washington. Soon Idaho and Oregon undertook similar work, and
the range of activities of all of these institutions was steadily increased.[1] The results of these efforts were soon on display in experi-

[1] *Pendleton-Tribune*, July 17, Aug. 7, 1890. The Pullman station was estab-
lished in 1891, the one at Moscow in 1892; Alfred Charles True, *A History of
Agricultural Experimentation and Research in the United States, 1607-1925*
(U.S. Dept. of Agriculture Miscellaneous Publication No. 251) (Washington,
D.C., June, 1937), p. 131. Oregon began field station work in eastern Oregon at

mental plots on their model farms and were also described in handy pamphlets, in speeches before local farm societies, and in special farmers' institutes which were held in various communities from time to time. The most spectacular means of bringing together the farmer and the scientist was the farm demonstration trains sponsored jointly by the schools and the railroads. Carrying a faculty of lecturers, fitted with elaborate displays, and including flatcars loaded with the latest machinery, these trains were hauled from town to town and drew large crowds.[2]

Despite such facilities and efforts, however, a close working relationship between scientist and farmer was neither easily nor quickly formed. Farming was an ancient and practical art which one learned by doing, not by reading books or listening to lectures. Unlike the Umatilla farmer, most who sought advice talked things over with their neighbors and would never have considered asking a government official. Disdain for self-styled experts was deeply ingrained, and the follies of impractical theorists were a familiar theme in rural humor. Furthermore, it was soon apparent that these agricultural scientists were not only willing to answer the farmer's questions but equally ready to question some of his practices. Whereas the farmers were primarily concerned about yields, costs, and prices, these advisors talked and wrote about soil exhaustion, the overemphasis upon wheat, and the need for the farmer to change his ways of doing things. It would not be surprising under the circumstances if many farmers came to regard such a person as more a meddlesome nuisance than a scientific partner.

Better Wheats

Nevertheless these years do mark the beginnings of an alliance. The farmers were more receptive to certain kinds of help than others, and the problem of wheat varieties provided the easiest means of

Moro in 1899, French, *Golden Land*, pp. 176-77. In addition to these government-sponsored programs, the O.R.&N. railroad established an agricultural research station near Walla Walla in 1898 and began experiments with grasses and grains. This station is described briefly in Shaw, *Farmers Paradise*, p. 2, and in the *Spokesman-Review* (Spokane), Oct. 5, 1900, p. 4, and is mentioned in several other accounts of the time. A brief search at the Union Pacific archives in Omaha and an inquiry at the Portland offices of the company failed to uncover any reports or further information on this project.

[2] *Pacific Farmers Union*, 1 (April 2, 1909), has a photograph and description of a typical example. In the library of Washington State University in Pullman

establishing a link. Because of the perennial search for the ideal wheat, many varieties from many sources were tried. There was little system to such introductions; they were brought in by farmers, railroad companies, grain buyers, milling companies—by anyone who had an interest in the matter. A few did prove successful enough to compete with Little Club and Bluestem, and by the early 1900's the grain region was divided into three "wheat belts" equivalent to three rainfall zones, each characterized by certain principal varieties.[3]

In the eastern and most humid zone, Little Club was still an important wheat but two winter varieties were also popular. Fortyfold (also called Gold Coin), from the Genesee Valley of New York, was a good milling wheat which yielded well and matured a week or two earlier than others, an important feature in this area where wheat was at times damaged by early fall rains. Unfortunately, it shattered easily and was often badly affected by smut. Red Russian, of English origin despite its name, gave excellent yields, did not shatter easily, and was favored by many farmers because its heavy stem growth crowded out weeds, especially wild oats. However, its flour was so poor that it brought a considerably lower price.[4]

Little Club was also still grown in the "middle zone," those areas receiving about fifteen to twenty inches of precipitation, but here, too, it had new competitors. Red Chaff, a similar club-type wheat, was preferred by many but suffered from the same deficiency of being easily winter killed. Jones Fife, a hybrid developed by a New York farmer and introduced into the Walla Walla region about 1900, proved to be a hardy and good-yielding wheat, but it shattered

---

is a brief typed report entitled "The Practical Value of the Farming Demonstration Train especially the Northern Pacific, 1910, *Dry Farming Special,*" which gives a more detailed description as well as some opinions as to the value of such efforts.

[3] Much of the agricultural literature of the time refers in some way to these zones and varieties. The best single source is Hunter, *Farm Practices.* Also useful are Ball, "Wheat Improvement," and J. Allen Clark, John H. Martin, and Carleton R. Ball, *Classification of American Wheat Varieties* (U.S. Dept. of Agriculture Bulletin No. 1074) (November 8, 1922).

[4] "From the flour standpoint, this wheat [Red Russian] staggers the miller. It is not and never will be classed with milling wheats.... We have outlived the time when it is profitable to grow a poor breed of wheat because it is a weed killer." J. T. Bibb, "What Is Milling Value in Wheat?" *Wheat Convention;* the same speech is printed in the *Commercial Review,* 32 (Jan. 26, 1906).

easily and had a long drooping head which made it difficult to harvest. Bluestem was also grown extensively in this belt and was the leading wheat in the third and driest zone, that receiving less than fifteen inches. There its chief rival was Turkey Red (which at this time was grown to some extent in the other zones as well), a bearded wheat of high quality related to a famous variety introduced into Kansas by Mennonite emigrants from the Volga-Don area of Russia. Its principal disadvantage was its beard, which made horses' mouths sore (it was common to cut some wheat for hay, especially along the fencerows to open the fields for reaping machines) and also made it disagreeable to work with. And in the Pacific Northwest it commanded a lower price than Bluestem.

Many other wheats were tried. Each year brought optimistic reports about some new variety, and it might enjoy local prominence for a time, only to respond poorly to a particularly cold winter or a dry spring or a hot early summer and thus cause the farmers to shift back to a more proven wheat or try a still newer one. It was obvious that government supported agricultural stations could render a valuable service by a more systematic selection, testing, and distribu-

Some wheats of the Columbia Plain. From left to right: Little Club, Pacific Bluestem, Red Russian, Turkey Red, Hybrid 128 (by Spillman). (Photo reproduced from J. Allen Clark, John H. Martin, and Carleton R. Ball, *Classifications of American Wheat Varieties* [U.S. Dept. of Agriculture Bulletin No. 1074])

tion of new varieties.[5] But the agricultural scientists knew that they could do more than that: they could *create* new varieties especially adapted to the peculiar needs of these regions. Such efforts would take time, but little was lost in getting started. A program was begun in 1899 at Pullman by W. J. Spillman. First he found out from the farmers what they wanted in a wheat. The chief demand in the eastern Palouse was for a hardy, nonshattering, stiff-strawed winter wheat, which in general could be taken to mean essentially a winter variety of Little Club. By 1905 Spillman had a hybrid deemed worthy of extensive field test by farmers, and in the next few years several others were released.[6] No quick miracles were to be expected, but progress was made, some of the results were quite encouraging, and an important tie between the scientist and the farmer was being established.

Better Tillage

It was the easiest sort of link to form because the scientist was merely producing a superior product for the farmer to use in his own way. But there was much more to raising wheat than having good seed, as both the farmer and the scientist well knew, and when the scientist began to broaden his concerns and his prescriptions, when he began to tell the farmer how to farm, it is not surprising that he encountered resistance. That resistance stemmed more from a common human resentment of and skepticism at being told how to do things by "experts" and "outsiders" than from a deeply ingrained routine of farming in the region. Indeed, the farmers themselves were always experimenting, and farming practices had never become wholly stable.

This fact was well illustrated by the chronic controversy over spring versus fall seeding. For years most of the grain was spring-sown. Gradually it seemed apparent, however, especially in the more humid sections, that fall-sown grain usually gave a better yield. But

[5] The Washington State Grain Inspector wanted his own department expanded to undertake such efforts, citing the introduction of Bluestem wheat as an example. Bluestem had been introduced by an individual and was only gradually spread from one locality to another. For several years probably many a farmer who desperately needed such a drought-resistant wheat either had never heard of it or was unable to obtain enough for seed. *Report of the Washington State Grain Inspector*, 1899-1900, p. 20.

[6] W. J. Spillman, *The Hybrid Wheats* (Washington Agricultural Experiment Station Bulletin No. 89) (1909); see also the identical articles in the *Washington Agriculturist*, 2 (May, 1909), and *Pacific Farmers Union*, 1 (July 23, 1909).

this was not always the case, and the issue was complicated by problems with smut, weeds, and the vagaries of the seasons. The situation remained unstable throughout these years. Thus, for example, a report from Dayton in the fall of 1910 stated that "the old method of seeding grain in the Spring is giving place to Fall seeding, due to the fact that Fall grain yields heavier, is a surer crop, and usually tests higher." But this kind of shift had been reported annually for thirty years. One of the reasons why spring wheat continued to be planted in areas such as the Camas Prairie was the inability to get all of the land plowed and seeded during the interval between harvest and winter weather. That problem varied from year to year, but was in part caused by the fact that many were farmers trying to work too many acres with too little equipment. And there were other factors. Weeds were a stealthily spreading menace, but there seemed to be no agreement as to the best means of combating them. One report stated that the shift from spring to fall sowing in the Palouse was done "as a means of checking the foul growth that is creeping over the fertile fields," yet a few years later a Winona correspondent reported that the trend was now back to spring wheat because with fall seeding "the mustard, china lettuce and thistles come up early in the Spring and seem to get the start of the wheat, damaging it materially. . . ."[7]

The oldest and most widespread of the common weeds was wild oats *(Avena fatua)*. After 1900 several others began to cause concern, especially Russian thistle *(Salsola kalitragus)*, China lettuce or compass weed *(Lactuca scariola, L.)*, and Jim Hill mustard *(Sisymbrium altissimum)*. Jim Hill mustard was commonly considered as the "most dangerous weed" in the region, though in 1909 at least one observer considered a newcomer, morning glory *(Convolvulus arvensis)*, to have characteristics so ominous as to make Jim Hill mustard seem "a tame weed of trifling importance."[8]

[7] *Klickitat County Agriculturist* (Goldendale), July 4, 1903; *Commercial Review,* Sept. 15, 29, Oct. 12, 1910. Cf. "Owing to the prevalence of 'Jim Hill' mustard in Western Whitman County little wheat is planted in the fall," *ibid.,* Dec. 1, 1910.

[8] *Twelve of Idaho's Worst Weeds* (Idaho Agricultural Experiment Station Bulletin No. 14) (1898), p. 103; C. V. Piper, *The Present Status of the Russian Thistle in Washington* (Washington Agricultural Experiment Station Bulletin No. 37) (October, 1898), found that weed chiefly in the Walla Walla, in the initial stages of its invasion, probably having been brought in by railway cars from the Dakotas or Colorado, where it was already a bad pest. The very name given to the mustard suggests that it was first noticed about the time of and attributed to the entry of the Great Northern Railway in the early 1890's. Also see editorial, *Pacific Farmers Union,* 1 (June 18, 1909), 4, and 1 (Aug. 13,

The season of sowing and the weed problem were both closely related to the extent and character of fallowing. The early years of continuous cropping had given way to periodic "resting" of the land. The rhythm varied among various districts: in the relatively drier areas a simple wheat-fallow sequence was generally followed; in the more humid areas a three-year rotation of winter wheat, a spring crop (most commonly oats), and fallow was widely used; in the eastern Palouse country many farmers raised two successive crops of winter wheat, then followed with a spring crop and fallow. But even though the practice of fallowing was nearly universal within the area, there was no unanimity as to its purpose, value, or proper methods. At the very least fallowing was regarded as a means of "resting" the land and curbing the weeds. It seems clear that many had only the vaguest notion of how "resting" improved the land. Agricultural scientists and the more knowledgeable farmers talked of moisture storage, decomposition of organic matter, and bacterial life, but they too exhibited an uncertainty and differences in emphasis about such matters. As for weed control, the crudest form was to run livestock on the stubble fields and plowed ground to keep the growth down. Though widespread, this practice was strongly criticized by all concerned with improving agriculture.[9]

The most common pattern in the preparation and treatment of fallow was to burn off the stubble in the fall, a practice condemned by most agricultural scientists.[10] Plowing was begun immediately

1909), a report from Fairfield in the northern Palouse, which described this weed as new, of unknown origin, but flourishing.

[9] Such practices are mentioned in many kinds of literature. A spot survey of the whole wheat region of eastern Washington in 1913-14 revealed that these three systems were practiced by 52 per cent, 35 per cent, and 13 per cent, respectively, of the farmers; see Homer Gregory, "A Study of the Cost of Wheat Production in Eastern Washington," *Washington Agriculturist,* 8 (April, 1914), 28. Hunter, *Farm Practices,* contains the most complete descriptions and discussion of fallowing in the area, but again it is a topic treated in some degree in many other publications. "Don't fallow so as to make pasture for your stock. If you do you will be feeding them at a very expensive rate out of your next crop"—remarks of R. C. McCroskey to his fellow farmers, see *Wheat Convention,* p. 10.

[10] Hunter, *Farm Practices,* p. 28, represented the majority, stressing the serious loss of organic matter and deterioration in the texture and moisture-holding capacity of the soil. However, Hunter acknowledged that heavy stubble was difficult to plow under, an important practical fact which farmers in the more humid sections well understood: trying to get a light, horse-drawn plow

after the first fall rains had softened the ground. Bad weather or lack of equipment might cause some stubble land to be left until the next spring. In either case, plowing was followed by disking or harrowing at least once and usually two or three times during the late spring and summer to check the weed growth. But there were many variations of this pattern, reflecting differences of opinion, circumstance, and little certain knowledge as to what was best suited for any particular district.

Byron Hunter, who made an extensive study of the methods used in this wheat region, concluded that the best procedure consisted of "disking and harrowing in the early spring before plowing, packing the subsurface immediately after plowing, and following this by sufficient surface cultivation to retain moisture and keep the weeds under control." He stated, however, that this sequence was not as yet in general use. To those interested in such matters at the time, it must also have been clear that this recommendation bore the mark of a distinctive agricultural system called "dry farming." That system had been recently developed in the Great Plains and was being promoted in that broad area with evangelistic fervor as the road to agricultural salvation for all who struggled to wrest a living from the earth. Often called the "Campbell system," after Hardy W. Campbell of Nebraska, its principal advocate and propagandist, its most distinctive feature was an emphasis upon the necessity of subsurface packing after deep plowing followed by frequent tillage to pulverize the surface into a fine "dust mulch" which would both absorb summer rainfall and inhibit the evaporation of soil moisture.[11]

News of the Campbell system was not long in reaching the far Northwest, and it quickly found local advocates. Soon trials were being made by farmers and scientists with sufficiently good results

---

through "40-bushel stubble" on the steep north slopes of a Palouse hill could be an exasperating job. On the other hand, a professor of agriculture at Pullman in describing fallowing in Umatilla County noted that stubble plowed under tended to dry the ground out, which might be taken as implicit approval of burning, although disking the stubble was another possibility; see *Pacific Farmers Union,* 1 (Jan. 22, 1909), 3.

[11] Hunter, *Farm Practices,* p. 29; see Mary Wilma M. Hargreaves, *Dry Farming in the Northern Great Plains, 1900-1925* (Cambridge, Mass., 1957), for an excellent study of the origins, sources of support, methods, characteristics, and significance of this movement.

to encourage further promotion of the idea.[12] Actually, in the drier districts the common fallowing practices did not differ greatly from this new system. Subsurface packing was the chief missing ingredient, and it required special equipment. The need for repeated fine tillage of the surface also spurred demands for more efficient implements and soon resulted in the perfection of the rod weeder.[13] It would take time for such equipment to be widely adopted, and newspaper references to particular farmers who were raising wheat "in strict accordance with the methods of the Campbell dry farming system," obviously suggest that by 1910 such strict accord was uncommon. Yet there was a more general acceptance of the importance of moisture conservation, and farming practices were being more and more adapted to that purpose.[14]

More dramatic evidence of the encounter between this remarkable movement and the far western corner of the nation's farmland was the fact that in early October of 1910 Spokane was host to the Fifth International Dry Farming Congress. Though the choice of site was certainly dictated more by outside sponsors and by local business and civic organizations (especially the various railroads which had an interest in promoting dry-land settlement) than by

[12] E.g., *Big Bend Chief* (Wilson Creek), Sept. 19, 1902, described the system and stated unequivocally that "the same rule will apply to Washington soil that applies to the Nebraska or Dakota crop land." In order to test this system as well as conduct other experiments in districts drier than those near Pullman, the state college established experimental farms near Ritzville and Quincy. The March 9, 1907, issue of the *Wenatchee Daily World* carried a report of Professor E. E. Elliott's visit to the Quincy district to discuss the possibility of such an experimental farm. Elliott had recently visited the Great Plains, was impressed with the dry farming system, and saw great possibilities for it in the Big Bend.

[13] The rod weeder is nothing more than a light wide frame connecting two wheels which are geared to a square rod that is rotated just under the surface. It proved very effective in cutting weeds at their roots, did not clog, and was so light that several could be hitched together to till a very broad swath and thus greatly increase the efficiency of farming. I am not certain just when and where this simple but important machine was invented. The earliest reference discovered was a description of those made by the Washington Weeder Works of Walla Walla in *Up-to-the-Times Magazine*, 4 (August, 1910), 2753-55.

[14] *Weekly Commoner* (Colfax), July 15, 1910; the evidence is scattered through much of the regional literature; among the most interesting sources is the study by Lon L. Swift, "Land Tenure in Oregon," a Master's thesis published in the *Oregon Historical Quarterly*, 10 (June, 1909), 31-135. Swift describes in detail typical leases in the wheat country; each includes quite specific requirements as to tillage and some include an explicit reference to moisture conservation; see esp. pp. 112-20.

the lure of widespread interest from farmers and landowners within the region, the convention did in fact receive a great deal of publicity and must have fostered a greater awareness of the topic.[15]

In retrospect, locally the most significant if probably not the most popular paper on the topic had already been published by the congress earlier in that same year. In it, R. W. Thatcher, the director of agriculture at the state college in Pullman, strongly implied that "dry farming" was becoming a fad, a universal prescription backed by little scientific evidence of success. He warned of the "very real danger that the present tide of popular enthusiasm in and for dry farming will result in attempts to extend these areas far beyond the limits to which results of former studies will apply." Furthermore, far too little was yet known about soils, climate, and the effects of tillage in any area to be confident of results. Later that year, in releases to local papers publicizing the upcoming Spokane congress, he emphasized that "owing to the great variation in conditions in different parts of the country no set rule could be laid down for all." Not only was Washington different from North Dakota, but "even in the Inland Empire no hard and fast uniform rule may be followed with equal success in all localities."[16] In response to these interests and needs, the agricultural college announced a new program of basic research on the soils and climates of the wheat region.

That response and Thatcher's frank statements were an illustration of science at its best in the wheat country, serving as a caution to enthusiasts, insisting upon the need for knowledge, and showing a readiness to undertake a careful, unhurried search for answers to practical problems.

MEASURING THE RAINFALL

In order to study "dry farming" it was critical to know just how dry each locality was. Thatcher decried a still too heavy dependence upon that famous folk source of climatic history, "the memory of

[15] Hargreaves, *Dry Farming*, pp. 109-10; previous congresses had met in Denver, Salt Lake City, Cheyenne, and Billings. Many of the country newspapers gave publicity to the Spokane session both before and after. The complete report of that congress is in the *Dry Farming Congress Bulletin*, 3 (Dec. 1, 1910).

[16] R. W. Thatcher, "Some Recent Results of Dry Farming Investigation in Washington," *ibid.*, 3 (Feb. 1, 1910), 240-46; *Spokesman-Review*, July 3, 1890, p. 8; see also a similar lengthy article in the *Weekly Commoner*, Aug. 26, 1910. In neither case is the article signed, but both originated in Pullman and clearly are expressions of Thatcher's ideas.

AVERAGE ANNUAL PRECIPITATION

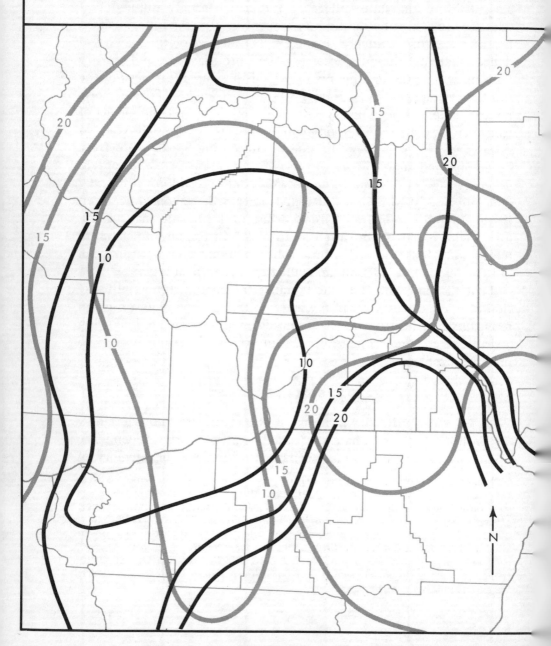

ISOHYETS FROM A.W. GREELY, "The Climates of Oregon and Washington Territory", 1888.

ISOHYETS BASED UPON ANNUAL AVERAGES AS OF 1910.

Map 38

the oldest inhabitant," and announced plans to establish thirty new weather stations in eastern Washington. Although more detailed knowledge was needed about localities, much more was already known about the region in general than twenty years before. Whereas in 1890 there were fewer than a dozen stations with lengthy records of precipitation, twenty years later half a hundred were sufficiently well placed to give at least some standardized measure for every important district.[17]

One striking fact revealed by the available figures was that wheat farmers in the Columbia region had penetrated far into rainfall areas which would have been considered to be outside the safe limits of agriculture elsewhere in the nation. Not only had the frontier of settlement advanced beyond what it had been in 1890, but the more extensive data revealed that the extent of the drier districts was greater than previously thought (Map 38). Excellent crops had repeatedly been raised in areas averaging no more than fifteen inches of rainfall, and paying crops had been harvested in parts of the Crab Creek country, Adams and Franklin counties, and in the Horse Heaven Hills which received hardly half that amount. Indeed, the opening sentence in a contemporary study which stated that "there is probably no other region in the United States where dry farming is successfully conducted with so low a rainfall as in the Columbia Basin" was remarkably similar to that of Greene's "rainless regions" report on the Walla Walla and Palouse of twenty-five years before. Although a harvest of wheat from such land might still astonish anyone unfamiliar with the region, there was no longer any mystery about the factors involved. Local scientists were well aware of these, and general national reports now routinely recognized the area as a distinctive agronomic province which demanded different methods than those of other grain regions. Though it was still common and convenient to use a particular "line of rainfall" (isohyet) to demark the safe limit of agriculture—and in the Columbia interior it was now suggested that a profitable crop might be obtained from as little as eight and a half inches—the new climatic data now allowed a more scientific study in particular of what every experienced farmer knew in general: that it was not the yearly

[17] Thatcher, "Dry Farming"; *Weekly Commoner*, Aug. 26, 1910; cf. "Eastern Washington," "Eastern Oregon," and "Idaho" in U.S. Dept. of Agriculture, Weather Bureau, *Climatic Summary of the United States* (Washington, D.C., 1936).

total of precipitation that mattered so much as the right amount at the right time. By 1910 scientists were attempting to find out exactly what these amounts and times were and how the tools and methods of tillage could best be adjusted to take maximum advantage of them.[18]

The lengthening climatic record also provided a firm contradiction to popular ideas about climatic change. The notion that cultivation or "settlement" was responsible for an increase in rainfall was still alive in the region but the scientists were ready to marshal a great array of statistics in contradiction. Such data invariably showed that while rainfall fluctuated irregularly from year to year, the climate was clearly not changing. Wheat harvests in the seeming "deserts" might indeed reveal a marvelous change in the face of nature, but "the western man who has observed the wilderness blossom as the rose decries his own power when he charges to the account of change of climate the blessings resulting from his own initiative."[19]

These blessings were sufficiently apparent in the Columbia wheatlands that only the farmers in the driest districts had reason to be particularly interested in the topic. If to the scientist climate was a statistical average of weather conditions over a period of years, to the farmer it was something averaged in his experience and inseparable from the remembrance of his crops. Though the scientist was

[18] Lyman J. Briggs and J. O. Belz, *Dry Farming in Relation to Rainfall and Evaporation* (Bureau of Plant Industry Bulletin No. 188) (Washington, D.C., 1910), pp. 8, 24, 25; published annual rainfall figures were always deceptive because it was not the calendar year that mattered but the crop year, especially the period from October through June.

[19] E.g., *Spokesman-Review*, Jan. 1, 1903, p. 1; Steele and Rose, *Big Bend Country*, p. 794, quoting the *Ritzville Times*, 1902; Lever, *Whitman County*, p. 188; Richard H. Sullivan, "The So-called Change of Climate in the Semiarid West," *Yearbook of United States Department of Agriculture, 1908*, p. 296. Sullivan's remarks were directed especially to those in the Great Plains, but an information book published by the Oregon State Immigration Commission was equally direct, noting that in view of common misleading impressions, "it is well to state that the climate of any locality does not change"—*Oregon Farmer* (Portland, 1913), p. 36. The fact that this book was written "under the direction of an advisory committee from the faculty of Oregon Agricultural College, Corvallis" was also a good indication of how the scientists had replaced earlier self-trained or self-styled experts in such propaganda work. Another important scientific report on this subject at the time was Willis L. Moore, *A Report on "The Influence of Forests on Climate and on Floods,"* published by the House of Representatives, U.S. Committee on Agriculture (Washington, D.C., 1910). Moore was chief of the U.S. Weather Bureau and made his report in response to interest in the topic expressed by congressmen.

gathering ever more data, these were of little direct use or interest to the farmer. The scientist was not as yet able to offer a daily weather bulletin, and so the farmer was still his own forecaster, reading the signs in the sky each day and planning his work accordingly as farmers had always done; and any reflection upon a season past was not in terms of inches or degrees Fahrenheit but in the homely terms of everyday experience.

The August 26, 1909, issue of the *Davenport Tribune* provided an unusually rich example of how a season was remembered in just such terms, and the very fact that such a lengthy "history of the weather" was featured on the front page was also a measure of how the country press still served as the mirror of country life:

On the 20th of March the heavens were swept clean of their snow flakes and a few scattering flakes of snow fell, after which the sun came out and the winter was over. By the 22nd of March the hilltops were drying nicely and the ambitious farmer was seeding the warm ground of the south hill slopes. For the next 20 days the weather was alternately sunshine and clouds, warm days being followed by cold windy ones. But no rain fell and the ground was becoming dry and the grain was laying dormant in the soil. By the 10th of April the greater part of the seeding was done and the last ones to sow planted their seed in the dust.

The outlook during the following days was not bright. Dry day followed dry day and although on the 10th and 15th of April there were slight showers, the dust was scarcely laid in the roads and still the seed upon which so much depended, rested in the soil and waited for the signal from the skies.

On the 26th of April, the month supposed to be the month of showers, the population of the Big Bend went to bed feeling rather blue. But during the night the cool gusts of air and the awakening of the wind called the sleepers from their dreams and all night long the gently falling rains gave drink to the thristy soil.

The first day of May was the finest of the year and the sun following the shower, coaxed the tiny green sprouts up here and there over the fields. The weather following the early part and middle of May was too cold for the tender crop and the grain was not coming up well. On the 19th of May the temperature became warmer and in a few days all the grain was up except that sown late, in the dust.

The last few days of this month will be remembered with pleasure by our people for many years, until other rich days lavished upon us by nature have crowded the recollection of them from our minds. At 10 p.m. on the 26th day of May rain began falling and continued steadily all night and all the next morning. The afternoon of the 27th the clouds cleared away and the sun came swinging out. But on the

28th the heavens were torn by lightning and riven by thunder and great torrents of rain fell upon the already drenched fields. When the deluge was over a sheet of water one and three quaters inches deep had fallen over the land, enough to make a fair crop without another drop, provided excessive heat was not visited upon us.

On the first day of June the heavens were again darkened as also were the brows of some of our people who said too much rain was a possibility. In the evening we had a fine rain but more fell in the districts to the south and west than in our immediate vicinity.

On the night of the fourth a cold wave swept over the land slightly yellowing the tips of the grain here and there but close examination showed that the fears of frost were ungrounded.

The following days until the 29th of June were ideal for the growing of wheat. The weather was warm but not windy and an occasional warm shower revived the growing fields. But the 29th and 30th of the bridal month, these are the dark days in the season of 1909. The stalks of grain stood silent and still in the unmoving air. Then quietly, slowly, silently, the air began to move. Farmers began to look uneasy for the breath of the earth was warm. Slowly, softly, came the air from the south. The green ends of the leaves curled and then dried. The milky fluid in the heads that was to turn into kernels of wheat began to dry. The green grain on the south slopes and in the lighter or rocky soil took on a yellow tinge, but the farmers knew it was not the yellow that precedes the ripening grain.

For two days nature breathed her hot breath over the growing fields and then she stopped. But the damage was done. How much nobody knew or will ever know, but by the threshing machines the story is now partly being revealed. Any grain grower will tell you that a Big Bend crop can stand two days of the dreaded hot wind and still yield a bountiful supply. The early days of July were ideal for a fast maturing crop and the heavy rains of the 5th, 6th and 7th of July partly atoned for the damage done.

From the 8th day of July to the middle of the present month there has been an unbroken succession of warm, with an occasional shower, and clear days. Close observers claim that this period has been one of the most perfect for the ripening and maturing of wheat ever experienced in this country.

Now the crop is made. Enough rain fell. Frost was not encountered and hot winds were of short duration.

The editor thought that his readers would enjoy this review of "just what kind of weather made just this kind of crop," but he prefaced that remark by stating that "with less or more rainfall, or with less or more hot winds and with warmer or cooler weather, we would have had a crop anyway." That was the most telling conclusion, even though one his local readers took for granted. That was the general sum of experience in this Columbia wheat country and was, after all, why the farmers and the townsmen need not feel overly concerned about climatic statistics or climatic change.

STUDYING THE SOILS

In farming, "dry" was a matter of soils as well as climate, for some retained moisture better than others. The unusually high moisture capacity of the finely textured soils of the Columbia wheatlands was well appreciated as a general fact, but it required knowledge of a different order to understand it as a fact of soil physics, and knowledge at a different scale to understand how it varied among the several types of soil to be found in any one locality. The topic of moisture was only one of many related questions about soils being investigated at this time, and the studies undertaken within the region were but a small part of a national effort during an important formative period in the history of American soil science.

As is not uncommon in such early stages of investigation and formulation in any science, it was an era dominated by a few major figures and sharp controversy. When Thatcher posed the question, "Are the principles of soil fertility which have been worked out in regions of greater rainfall applicable to semi-arid districts?" he was probably aware that it had already been answered by eminent authorities. The problem was that they disagreed. Hilgard, the University of California expert, had given a resounding "No" to the question, a conclusion based principally upon chemical analyses of a wide variety of soils in the American West and in fact supported at certain critical points by evidence gathered in the Columbia interior.[20]

But Milton Whitney, in the recently established Bureau of Soils of the Department of Agriculture in Washington, D.C., had initiated a program of studies which evaluated soils on a different basis. Whitney supported a theory about soil fertility which placed much greater stress upon soil structure and texture with reference to soil

[20] *Weekly Commoner,* Aug. 26, 1910. Thatcher is inferred to be the author. See Hilgard, *Relations of Soil to Climate,* and E. W. Hilgard, *Soils, Their Formation, Properties, Composition, and Relations to Climate and Plant Growth in the Humid and Arid Regions* (New York and London, 1906); on the significance of his Columbia investigations, see Hans Jenny, *E. W. Hilgard and the Birth of Modern Soil Science* (Pisa, 1961), pp. 62-63.

moisture than upon soil chemistry, and therefore did not differentiate between humid and arid soils on the same basis as Hilgard. Both of these concepts were represented in the work of soil scientists in the region. The national bureau undertook detailed studies which described, classified, and mapped the soils of portions of the Yakima and the Walla Walla valleys and the Lewiston area; chemical analyses of the mineral constituents, with special attention to those regarded as critical plant nutrients, were more in the Hilgardian tradition.[21] Because of this theoretical conflict the practical implications of such studies were inherently uncertain, and although they provided important additions to information, they did not as yet represent sure advances in understanding. But the fact that scientists disagreed among themselves about the most fundamental principles of their own work did not always deter them from advising and warning the farmer about his.

Actually as far as "dry farming" was concerned the local scientists recognized the need for practical tests, and they tried to exercise caution as to the likely results. There was a candid admission that the relationship between soil tillage and soil moisture was as yet uncertain, and while some practices did seem preferable to others much more experience was necessary to be sure. Such caution was no doubt engendered in part by the knowledge that any recommendation would quickly be put to a severely practical test by farmers all along the frontier of settlement which was advancing toward the desert center of the region. While it seemed apparent that in all districts yields were principally determined by moisture, in most areas there was always enough rainfall for a reasonably satisfactory harvest. But in this central district the farmers were near the limits of agriculture; crops were at best marginal, at worst failures; and any means of increasing moisture was desperately important. Experience had undermined any hope of changing the climate, but the dry-farming enthusiasts now offered hope of changing the soil so as to conserve and yield more moisture. If the scientists could confirm and extend that program, they would gain greatly in local favor;

[21] Jenny, *Hilgard*, chap. vi; C. A. Jensen and B. A. Olshausen, "Soil Survey of the Yakima Area, Washington," and J. Garnett Holmes, "Soil Survey of the Walla Walla Area, Washington," in *Field Operations of the Bureau of Soils* (Washington, D.C., 1902), pp. 392-419 and 711-28, respectively. E.g., G. A. Crosthwait, *A Soil Fertility Text* (Idaho Agricultural Experiment Station Bulletin No. 59) (May, 1907).

if they could not they would be a disappointment; and if they were proved wrong they would be discredited. The clarity and impor-portance of the problem was no doubt a strong deterrent to dog-matic assertions.

In the older, more humid districts, however, the agricultural ex-perts were quite ready to warn of dangers, criticize common meth-ods, and suggest changes. The first intimation of concern about erosion, a topic which would in later years become almost an ob-session with local scientists, appeared about 1910. For the first time certain tillage practices were recommended partly because "the land won't wash so badly," and the farmers were admonished that "pre-cautionary measures should be taken against heavy cultivation of steep hillsides where there is danger of washing if you loosen the soil too much."[22] That the evidence of erosion was only very recent is strongly suggested by the fact that so careful an observer as I. C. Russell was impressed in 1896 with the

> striking fact, especially on the hilly portion of the plateau, that even the steepest slopes, in many instances having an inclination of from 20° to 30°, are without rill marks. This is not because there is a mat of roots binding the soil together and thus preserving it from washing for the surfaces of the plowed hillsides are smooth and unscarred by gullies.[23]

But even though the scientists could point to the signs, they could only predict the problem for erosion was as yet of no direct con-sequence to the farmer. There were no gullies, rills were easily smoothed over with a harrow or seed drill, and if there was any sheet erosion it would cause no alarm, for the soil was deep and that which was newly exposed could be considered as good as that which slipped downslope.

Another topic, however, was far more important to the agricul-tural experts. Despite the fact that the Columbia soils were unusu-ally fertile, the scientists insisted that a cycle of nothing but wheat and bare fallow could not continue without a sharp decline in yields. Tests which showed marked reductions in organic matter and nitrogen were offered as testimony from the soil itself of impending

[22] *Washington Agriculturist*, 3 (October, 1909); article by C. C. Thorn, agron-omist, in the *Weekly Commoner*, Aug. 12, 1910; similarly, the remarks of R. W. Thatcher, *Pacific Farmers Union*, 2 (Aug. 12, 1910), 5.

[23] Israel Cook Russell, *A Reconnaissance in Southeastern Washington* (Water Supply and Irrigation Paper No. 4) (Washington, D.C., 1897), pp. 68-69.

difficulties.[24] There was general agreement among such men that the danger was clearly apparent and imminent, and that counteractions should be initiated without delay.

There was also a general awareness, however, that such warnings were unlikely to be heeded very promptly. The farmers' complacency was usually deplored as a lamentable lack of foresight and a defiance of the lessons of history, but the issue was not that simple and the accusation not quite fair. Again, the power of the scientists' case was weakened by the fact that it was a prediction and not a reality. Although the earlier adoption of the fallow system had at least partly resulted from a presumed decline in yields, there was no clear evidence that yields were now declining anywhere in the Columbia wheatlands. Thus Samuel E. Robinson, more candid than most critics but as certain as any of the ultimate consequences, opened his argument of the case with the frank admission that "we cannot point to an actual falling off in the yield per acre . . ."—and he was referring to the eastern Palouse, which had been cropped for more than thirty years. He completed that sentence by insisting, nevertheless, that "this is no proof that there will not be such a falling off as other states have experienced at a time not far distant." But he recognized, too, that this idea was directly challenged: "It is true that men of experience do now assert that our soil will produce increasingly large crops year after year without deterioration; and they point to the fact that with one exception ours is not comparable with the soil of other regions, being a volcanic ash. . . ." And so it all led back to the question of soil origins, and inevitably to the wondrous fame of Sicily, an analogy which had been established by even more eminent scientists. The argument of impoverishment could therefore be dismissed as deficient in both evidence and logic; the yields had not declined in the Columbia, and the fact that they had declined in every older region in America was irrelevant, for the only comparable soils had been producing wheat for two thousand years. Those who sought to awaken the farmers to impending danger were therefore not combating, as some implied, merely a stolid indifference rooted in ignorance and greed, but rather a solid

[24] E.g., Shaw, *Farmers Paradise*, p. 26; Hunter, *Farm Practices*, p. 27; Crosthwait, *Soil Fertility*, p. 3; R. W. Thatcher, *Washington Soils* (Washington Agricultural Experiment Station Bulletin No. 85) (1908), p. 54; R. W. Thatcher, "The Fertility of the Palouse Soils," *Pacific Farmers Union*, 34 (Sept. 3, 1909), 8.

confidence, supported by experience and widely heralded scientific testimony.[25]

The topic of soil origins was basically a geological matter and thus the realm of another group of scientists. Here, too, these years constituted an important period in the expansion of knowledge and were marked by controversy, though in this case the dispute centered upon conflicting interpretations of local evidence rather than upon more general principles. That local geological problem, however, had important implications for those interested in the qualities of soil and agriculture. Much of the regional geological work undertaken at this time was prompted by the practical problems of water supply. Data were collected on wells, the possibilities for artesian supplies, and the practicalities of irrigation. Much of this work necessarily focused attention upon the character of the soil mantle, of the immediately underlying beds, and thus inevitably upon the relationship between the two.

The geologist who made the first extensive but fairly detailed reconnaissances in the region during this period gave strong implicit endorsement to the Sicilian analogy. Israel Cook Russell marshaled an array of field evidence and mechanical and chemical analyses in support of his conclusion that "the deep, rich soil covering the basaltic plateau . . . is a residual soil formed by the disintegration and decay of the lava rocks on which it rests." "This is the justly celebrated soil of the wheatlands," Russell went on to say, and he vividly stressed the geological foundations of agriculture: "The sending of wheat from the State of Washington to the famishing people of India, which has recently been done, is rendered possible

[25] Samuel E. Robinson, "The Improvement of the Wheats of Eastern Washington by Selection" (unpublished thesis, State College of Washington, 1905), p. 4. There was no diminution of the publicity about the Sicilian qualities of these soils. Newspapers and promotional literature continued to exploit the analogy and to employ such terms as "inexhaustible" and "perpetually fertile"; e.g., *Big Bend Empire* (Waterville), April 4, 1904; *Klickitat County Agriculturist,* Jan. 29, 1910; *Spokesman-Review,* Jan. 1, 1903, part 5, p. 1; E. A. Davis, *New Commercial Encyclopedia, Washington, Oregon and Idaho; the Pacific Northwest* (Berkeley, Calif., 1909), p. 56. Even local scientists acknowledged the analogy and the unusual durability, though generally insisting that an eventual reduction in yields was inevitable; see Elton Fulmer and C. C. Fletcher, *Washington Soils* (Washington Agricultural Experiment Station Bulletin No. 13) (1894), p. 40. Thatcher was concerned about the loss of organic matter but thought that "with proper attention to the humus needs" this basaltic soil would "doubtless maintain its reputation for high fertility indefinitely," Thatcher, *Washington Soils,* p. 54.

because ages ago volcanic rocks capable of furnishing a wonderfully rich soil inundated the tertiary lowlands where now 'rolls the Oregon.' " While he neither stated nor clearly implied that the surface soils were being so constantly and sufficiently replenished as to make them inexhaustible, it was possible to interpret his report as powerful and comforting support for that belief.

Like any good scientist, Russell did not ignore alternative hypotheses. He acknowledged that "the close similarity between the soils of the basaltic plateau and the loess of China . . . has led some careful observers to conclude that the soil of eastern Washington is really a deposit of dust that has been drifted from a distance by the prevailing winds." Russell then demonstrated how his own observations had convinced him that the wind was no more than a superficial agent. But although his report was influential, it did not settle the matter.[26]

While the scientists argued among themselves about the question of origin, certain implications of the loess theory received wide publicity. The fame of the "China analogy" was in origin and degree remarkably similar to that of the Sicilian comparison. Sometime in the 1890's Mark W. Harrington, who had been chief of the Weather Bureau of the United States Department of Agriculture, visited the Columbia country and later gave his impressions to a Seattle newspaper. He explained how the character of the soil and the shape of the hills made a loessal origin very probable, and then went on to say, as reported by the press:

> This fine soil is very fertile. It seems to be of a kind which is perpetually fertile. In the whole world, I know of only one locality which has a similar soil. This is the north of China, in the two Provinces of Shansi and Shensi, west of Pekin. This is the original home of the Chinese, from which they spread out over the rest of China. This soil is wonderfully fertile; for, though it has been cultivated for four thousand years, it remains unchanged. And to me the Palouse soil seems to be the same; from which I am led to believe that it is inexhaustible.[27]

How wonderful for the regional boosters to have a distinguished man of science utter those magic words "inexhaustible" and "per-

---

[26] Russell, *Southeastern Washington*, pp. 58-60, 93. Russell made a similar statement in an earlier survey but did not at that time elaborate upon his reasoning and evidence: Israel Cook Russell, *A Geological Reconnaissance in Central Washington* (Bulletin of the U.S. Geological Survey No. 108) (Washington, D.C., 1893), p. 19.

[27] As quoted in Henry C. Shaver, "In the Famous Palouse Country, Idaho," *The Northwest*, 19 (June, 1901), 31. I have not tracked down the original pub-

petually fertile," and to offer an analogy which bettered that of Sicily by two thousand years! China now became as prominent as Sicily in the promotional literature, and, unbothered by any possible incompatibility, some cited both comparisons in testimony of the perfection of the region.[28]

Significant support for the loess theory came from Frank C. Calkins, who made an extensive reconnaissance of the Big Bend in 1902. Calkins offered a point-by-point critique of Russell's views and explained how his own field observations coupled with further chemical analyses led him "to believe that the wheat soils are not residuary, but wind deposits."[29] Such a theory inevitably raised questions about the source of the loess and the era and rate of deposition, but as the topic was peripheral to his main assignment, Calkins did not give lengthy consideration to these matters.

The Calkins report served to clarify the dispute, but it would take much more research to resolve it. To those interested in the surface geology of the region, it was an intriguing question. To those whose concern was more with soil fertility and management than with origins, it was at least indirectly relevant. Certainly the matter had some bearing upon popular notions. If, for example, the soil was in fact imported rather than residual, it might be well to stop thinking of those layers of underlying basalt as vast "manure heaps" supplying constant replenishment. But the topic was so clouded with uncertainty that any implications, cautionary or reassuring, were purely speculative. And although the scientists debated and the boosters swelled their chorus of praise, the topic was utterly beyond the interest of the farmers. One writer, after explaining in detail why he supported the residual rather than aeolian theory, put that point very well: "The farmers of the county, however, do not exercise themselves as to how their lands were originally made, whether from rock erosion remaining *in situ* or from rock eroded at some distant place and carried and deposited by the winds

---

lication of these remarks, but numerous references to them in the literature of the time suggest that this is an accurate quotation.

   [28] A good example among many is S. H. Soule, *The Rand-McNally Guide to the Great Northwest* (Chicago and New York, 1903), in which the Harrington interview is quoted on p. 222 and referred to again at the end of the volume in an advertisement sponsored by the Colfax Chamber of Commerce. Also see *Touchet Valley*, pp. 15, 21.

   [29] Calkins, *Geology and Water Resources*, pp. 45-49.

where it now is. They know that they have them and are mighty well satisfied with them."[30]

Because that satisfaction was derived from experience, the farmers could understandably resent those who presumed to criticize their ways. At the wheat convention in 1906, a prominent Pullman farmer acknowledged that he and his fellow farmers were being called land robbers, then offered in rebuttal the fact that in 1904 he had leased 320 acres, plowed it, pastured cattle on it, without further preparation sowed the seed in ground which was by then so cloddy that it "would almost shake the drill to pieces," and reaped a crop of more than 40 bushels to the acre.[31] Such a harvest from land that had been tilled for thirty years by methods that defied recommended practices was the kind of evidence which gave the farmer good reason to be skeptical of or at least indifferent to the advice and warnings so freely offered by the scientists. The simply fact was that year after year good crops had been obtained by a variety of methods. If some were better than others, it was difficult to demonstrate why; if yields were certain to diminish soon, it was difficult to worry about problems that did not as yet exist.

By 1910 the scientific study of these Columbia wheatlands was being carried on by a variety of specialists in different locations. But the link between the scientist and the farmer was rather slight. A large portion of the data being gathered and the experiments undertaken simply accounted for the routine results of the farmers. The fact that those results were so satisfactory to the farmers no doubt dulled their interest in explanations which could be regarded as "academic" rather than "practical." It was, of course, only the practical that could bring the two together. If the scientist could create a better wheat, the farmers were willing to try it, as they had tried countless others of unknown origin. If the experts recommended a better procedure for conserving moisture, those farmers struggling to make a living in the drier districts were ready to listen and to give it a try. But when the scientists castigated the farmers for their sloppy care of the land and their blindness to eventual results, the farmers who were reaping a handsome harvest each year were quite as ready to dismiss such experts as meddlesome impractical theorists.

[30] State of Idaho, *Fifth Biennial Report, Commissioner of Immigration, Labor and Statistics* (Boise, 1907-8), p. 261.

[31] *Wheat Convention*, p. 12.

Each of these groups in its own way was engaged in the study of the land, and each had much to learn. But in some ways the farmer was still well ahead of the scientist. Both came to this region as much handicapped as helped by knowledge gained elsewhere, for this was an unusual land which was not like any other they had known. The farmers' advantage was in experience. Many had the benefit of a generation or more of dealing with a particular piece of ground which they might know, even though intuitively and inarticulately, quite as effectively as the scientist knew his test plot. At this stage in regional development, the conscientious farmer was as much an agricultural expert as any of the scientists.

CHAPTER FOURTEEN

Late in June the vast northwestern desert of wheat began to take on a tinge
of gold, lending an austere beauty to
that endless, rolling, smooth world of
treeless hills, ... miles of fallow ground
and miles of waving grain ... a lonely,
hard, heroic country ...

ZANE GREY

Culmination:

The Great Columbia Plain, ca. 1910

THE YIELDS OF THE LAND

Harvest

BY LATE June of 1910 it was clear throughout the wheat country
that the crop was going to be very different from that of the year
before. Such a change was as satisfying to some farmers as it was disappointing to others. It all depended upon where one lived. For
the prospects, as always somewhat varied among the several districts,
were in most cases exactly the opposite of the previous year. It was
as if the season of 1910 had been carefully designed to counter-
balance the inequalities of 1909.

The harvest of 1909 had been a poor one in most of Oregon,
sufficiently so to induce some Sherman County farmers to hire a
rainmaker from California to try to work a beneficent change. Rains
in the late spring were regarded as an essential finishing touch for
a good crop, and the rainmaker arrived in Wasco at the end of
April, ready with his chemicals and electricity to persuade "the
vagrant moisture to come down to earth." No subsequent reports on
this venture were found, and it is therefore not clear how much
credit he received for the good showers spaced through May and
June over all the higher benchlands on either side of the Columbia
from The Dalles to the Walla Walla country. A month of hot
weather ripened the grain very fast, and by the end of July the first

harvest reports from Moro, Condon, and Ione confirmed the expectations of a fine crop. Across the river a similar return from the Horse Heaven slope was especially gratifying following a year in which part of the wheat had been so poor it was left in the fields and some of that harvested had yielded as little as three or four bushels to the acre. Around Echo and Holdman, in Umatilla County, areas which had often averaged no better than eight bushels were returning nearly twenty, and the Pendleton correspondent who reported the good news added that as a result "the farmers of the county were never in a more happy frame of mind, and automobiles are being ordered by many."[1]

In the Walla Walla country there was less cause for celebration. It had been an unusual spring: the winter snows had disappeared early, and there followed a warm and dry period broken by only a few light showers. The fall wheat came through without serious damage but spring-sown crops were poor. Over-all the harvest was a fair one, better in many cases than had been predicted in early summer, though not equal to that of the year before, which had not been especially good. On the Camas Prairie conditions were better, chiefly because the farmers there grew little spring wheat; but in the Palouse the situation was worse, both because of a larger acreage of spring grain and because of an even drier season. It was commonly regarded as the driest spring and summer in memory, with no general rain after mid-April. The fact that yields reported in the eastern Palouse ranged from twenty-five to thirty-five bushels per acre revealed how far from actual failure a mediocre crop was in this unusually productive area. But spring crops were much poorer (and included more oats and barley than in other districts), and the total production was well below that expected from the Palouse.

The Big Bend was the most sharply afflicted by these vagaries of the weather, though the result was tempered by the fact of a bumper crop the previous year. Everywhere the harvest was light, and in

[1] *Heppner Gazette*, April 28, 1910. The rainmaker was Charles Mallory Hatfield, the most famous in the far West of a number of such practitioners; see Clark C. Spence, "A Brief History of Pluviculture," *Pacific Northwest Quarterly*, 52 (October, 1961), 135-36. *Pacific Farmers Union*, 1 (Aug. 27, 1909), 4. *Commercial Review*, 41 (Aug. 4, 1910). Most of this description of farm conditions in 1910 is based upon the local reports published in various issues of the *Commercial Review* of Portland, a weekly devoted to the grain trade of the Pacific Northwest, and of the *Spokesman-Review*, the leading daily newspaper of Spokane.

some localities much of the wheat was too short to be cut with a header. The area as a whole reaped only half as much as the year before. Although the crop on the Waterville Plateau was somewhat better than elsewhere, even there the unusual dryness of the season was vividly emphasized in late August when threshing was interrupted for four days because of blowing dust.

By September 1 the harvest was virtually over, except for a few higher districts, principally the Camas Prairie, which were always later. It was the earliest finish ever—"something never before accomplished in the history of the country"—and caused considerable comment. Partly, of course, it was the result of the light crop in all Washington regions; and also, the warm dry season had caused the grain to ripen faster than usual. But it was also because of more harvesting machinery. The farmers were estimated to have ordered 125 new threshers and 250 new combines for 1910 from the big Walla Walla distributors and manufacturers, considerably more of both types than in any previous season.[2] There were 20 per cent more machines reported in the Dayton area, and the average run there of the big itinerant threshing outfits was only twenty-two days, half what had been common in recent years. The large increase in the number of combines was, of course, a major factor in shortening the harvest period. They were being used in every district, though much more extensively in the drier areas than in the Camas Prairie and eastern Palouse. A Pullman correspondent reported that the crop in that vicinity was being threshed by half a dozen stationary machines and a dozen combines. Some of these latter were probably the little Moscow-built harvesters; another report from Pullman that one day three combines had tipped over on steep hillsides was good evidence of why the big machines were less prominent and the steam thresher was still supreme in the Palouse.

The horse dominated the scene, whatever the method of harvesting. The big stationary outfits used twenty to thirty teams to haul the bundle wagons and water tanks, while hitches of twenty-six or thirty-two horses were commonly used to drag the big combines over the rolling hills. But here and there the horses were gone, and a steam or gasoline tractor pulled the combine. These too helped speed the harvest, as some of the newspaper discussants of the 1910

² *Spokesman-Review*, June 11, 1910. The Brown-Lewis Manufacturing Company, established in 1909, built thirty-two combines for the 1910 season; *Up-to-the-Times Magazine*, 4 (July, 1910), 2699-2701.

A header delivering grain into a header box amidst a fine stand of wheat in the Swale, near Centerville, Klickitat County. The header was the most widely used harvesting machine until well after 1910. *(Photo courtesy of Northern Pacific Railway Company)*

The "Pride of Washington," the product of Walla Walla's leading factory, was typical of the general type of thresher used in the region. *(Copied from W. D. Lyman, An Illustrated History of Walla Walla County, State of Washington [1901])*

season pointed out. Yet it is also clear from those reports that this was a very early phase in the history of tractor farming in the Columbia country. After more than a decade of trial, the steam tractor had made little headway as a mobile field machine, while the gasoline track-type tractor had not as yet been sufficiently demonstrated to spur wide adoption.[3]

By September 1 the annual result was reasonably clear. Over-all production of the region would be at least 15 per cent below the fifty-two million bushels of 1909, and the contrasts in proportions of those totals between the two years provided a good illustration of how the vagaries of a season's weather could alter the fortunes of the various localities:[4]

District	Approximate Proportion of Total Wheat Production	
	1909	1910
Oregon, Klickitat, Horse Heaven	9%	20%
Walla Walla (Umatilla through Asotin counties)	23	26
Camas Prairie	6	9.5
Palouse	27	22.5
Big Bend	35	22
	100%	100%

Shipment

The hauling season started with the harvest but lasted into late fall as many of the farmers and their teams were hired as part of the threshing crews. Where the distance was far the great trail wagons were still a familiar sight, but by 1910 the railroads had spread their tentacles into every important district, and most farmers were now less than five miles from a siding and could make several trips a day with four horses and a wagon (Map 38).

Railroads were still being built in the region to capture some part of the wheat traffic. Although the Northern Pacific's Adrian-Connell

[3] A land company purchased eight hundred acres near Ione and planned to experiment with the use of gasoline power instead of horses for all field operations. If successful, as seemed probable to the correspondent who reported it (he noted that such machines were already being used in Gilliam County), it was expected that others would soon make the change also. That was typical of the way such innovations were spread over the farming country: gradually, district by district, by ample demonstration in the hands of practical farmers. *Heppner Gazette,* Jan. 27, 1910.

[4] Total for 1909 calculated from the U.S. Census; 1910 from the *Commercial Review,* 49 (Sept. 1, 1910).

In the eastern Palouse many farmers used binders instead of headers. Here is a harvest landscape dotted with "shocks" of grain bundles a few miles south of Palouse City, with the rocky south slope of Kamiak Butte forming the background. *(Photo courtesy of Northern Pacific Railway Company)*

A push-binder working an oat field in Eden Valley, about four miles west of Palouse City, *ca.* 1910. This machine was in effect the application of a binder mechanism to a header and had advantages of a wider swath and better handling on steep ground than the standard binder. *(Photo courtesy of H. L. Linden)*

link was conceived principally as a means of more direct shipment of grain from the Davenport–Coulee City line to the coast, when it was opened in the fall of 1910 it gave important local service to a broad strip of new farming country, and a short branch up Bowers Coulee to Schrag tapped a wheat district lying midway between the two new lines of the Milwaukee Railroad. Together, the constructions of these two companies of 1909 and 1910 radically improved the transportation situation in the central Big Bend, to the satisfaction of the recent pioneers in that region, some of whom had had to haul their wheat twenty miles or more.

Even a very short branch could make a welcome difference. The embarrassment and consternation in Waterville over the refusal of the Great Northern to build into the town was soon translated into action. Businessmen and farmers raised eighty thousand dollars to construct the four-and-a-half-mile connection, the Great Northern agreed to furnish the ties and rails, and on August 28, 1910, the Waterville Railroad opened for business, just in time to take care of the harvest. Similarly, a farmer on the Camas Prairie obtained enough local support to build the Nezperce and Idaho Railroad over the fourteen miles from Nezperce to Vollmer. Completed in June, 1910, it was expected to handle more than a million bushels of grain that autumn. Interest was keen in a few other localities that felt need of closer rail service. Farmers in the Union Flat area of Whitman County, for example, hoped to induce the Spokane and Inland Empire Company to extend their electric railroad from Colfax southwest to the Snake River. At a mass meeting at Dusty in 1909 they agreed to offer a subsidy in land and money, and their spokesmen were ready to assure that such a line would garner two million bushels of wheat annually, which now had to be hauled over difficult roads to the O.R.&N. However, those areas remote from service by 1910 had usually been ignored because their volume of traffic was insufficient to warrant costly construction, and their chances either of attracting a major company or of financing a local concern were not good.[5]

[5] *Spokesman-Review*, June 17, Nov. 17, 1909, Aug. 21, 1910. *Commercial Review*, Sept. 8, 1910; *Lewiston Morning Tribune,* July 16, 1961. *Pacific Farmers Union*, (June 25, 1909), 1.

The Mayville district, an upland "island" in southern Gilliam County, was an example of a good wheat-growing locality severely handicapped by isolation. But the total production was so small and a connection with the Condon terminus of the O.R.&N. branch would require such costly construction across

A few districts still depended upon the waterways. Steamboats plied the upper Columbia between Wenatchee and Bridgeport, but the Mansfield branch had taken away much of the former wheat trade. Similarly the completion of the railroad along the north bank of the Snake between Lewiston and Riparia in 1908 took away more than half the usual river trade although the O.R.&N. boats continued to call at the wheat landings along the south bank between Asotin and Riparia.[6] Boats from Pasco to Priest Rapids carried some wheat from Franklin County, but there too most of the farmland was now better served by rail. The Open River Company offered service from Pasco to Portland but with little effect, for the rivers were paralleled by railroads on *both* banks from Riparia to Portland.

At most of the shipment points the farmer had a choice of warehouses to receive his grain, and at some of the larger stations half a dozen or more companies competed for his trade. In 1910 there were more than 400 warehouses (including a few elevators) distributed among about 150 grain handling points. The majority of these establishments were affiliated with some type of chain, most commonly as a line warehouse of one of the big Portland or Puget Sound milling and exporting companies,[7] or with a more local system, such as the Vollmer-Clearwater Company which operated fourteen warehouses serving the Camas Prairie, or of a cooperative, such as the Farmers Grain and Supply Company with nine houses in the eastern Big Bend.

Most of the grain was shipped out of the region as wheat, but an increasing amount was milled in the interior. The country grist mill was still in evidence but new roller-process electric mills built primarily to serve the rapidly growing Oriental export market were now much more significant in the regional economy.[8]

---

the broad canyon of Thirtymile Creek that hopes for a railroad were dim. See *Heppner Gazette*, May 12, 1910. The Horse Heaven country was similarly handicapped by heavy grades to connect with a main line along the Columbia or in the Yakima Valley, and, as with Mayville, the major railroads had no incentive to build, since the farmers had no choice but to haul to their sidings anyway.

[6] *Wenatchee Daily World*, July 11, 1910; *Spokesman-Review*, Aug. 20, 1910.

[7] The most extensive systems were those of Kerr Gifford and Company, Interior Warehouse Company, Pacific Coast Elevator Company, Puget Sound Warehouse Company, and Seattle Grain Company with forty-four, thirty-nine, thirty-two, twenty-nine, and twenty-seven houses in the region, respectively; data from Polk directories.

[8] Locations of mills in 1910 are in the Appendix. The growth of the Oriental trade and its stimulation of the local milling industry is apparent from the various issues of the *Commercial Review* of Portland.

The movement of that flour and wheat to the ocean terminals was, over-all, a more complex pattern than twenty years before. The elaboration of the railroad network had intensified competition in some areas and allowed a greater flexibility as to shipment route and destination. Though the region was now served by four major railroad systems, the incidence and character of competition were quite different in the several grain districts. Local competition was greatest in the Palouse and portions of the Walla Walla, where numerous towns were served by two or three railroad companies. In such cases the farmer did not directly choose among the railroads but his choice of grain dealer usually had the same effect, for the warehouses of any one were usually located on the sidings of a particular line. The Big Bend was crossed by three transcontinental systems. The building of the Great Northern and the Milwaukee had cut heavily into the Northern Pacific's position in this increasingly important area, and few farmers or dealers had a choice for shipment. The Klickitat and the Oregon districts across the Columbia were each the private preserve of a particular railroad, with only a rather ineffective steamboat line as a possible alternative for those near the river.

Such patterns of service were directly relevant to the larger order of competition between the grain terminals of Puget Sound (Tacoma, Seattle, Everett) and those on the lower Columbia (Portland, Vancouver, Astoria). In this, too, there was now more flexibility than before. The Milwaukee and the Great Northern were focused upon Puget Sound, but the building of the S.P.&S. now gave the Northern Pacific a choice of either export outlet. Joint ownership of the Camas Prairie Railroad gave three alternatives to the grain dealers in that region: to ship to Puget Sound via the Northern Pacific, or down the Columbia via either the S.P.&S. or the O.R.&N. Rates on the last two were necessarily equal, but the costs of export from the Columbia River and from Puget Sound were not, and in September of 1910 the O.R.&N. felt compelled to offer the same rate for Walla Walla–Tacoma shipments via Portland as the Northern Pacific charged on its more direct Cascade route. This action was considered to be an advantage for the farmers, because Puget Sound exporters usually paid two or three cents a bushel more than those of Portland.[9]

[9] *Up-to-the-Times Magazine*, 4 (September, 1910), 2787. The Portland price was lower because of the pilotage fees and delays on ocean shipping in the lower Columbia.

A Case steam threshing engine of about 1910 at work in the Palouse. *(Photo courtesy of E. A. Malsed)*

A pair of water wagons kept in steady use by the demands of the steam threshing engine. *(Photo courtesy of W. A. Meinig)*

In 1910 the triumph of Puget Sound over Portland and the river ports was clearly mirrored in the volumes of shipment of the annual crop:[10]

	Wheat	*Flour*
Columbia River	6,339,972 bushels	556,113 barrels
Puget Sound	8,787,752 bushels	1,439,398 barrels

As a barrel of flour was the equivalent of four and a half bushels of grain, the total quantity of wheat sent through Puget Sound was nearly double that sent down the river. Three mainline railroads spanning the Cascades had more than offset "nature's gravity route" to the sea. In addition to these totals, a small amount was probably sent to California and to the East by rail. The rest of the crop was used locally in the Pacific Northwest for flour and seed.

The price of wheat at any point within this network of movements and markets was an unfathomable calculus of all the factors of production and consumption in all of the wheat regions and markets of the world. Rarely steady for even a few days at a time, it annually provided another seasonal measure of satisfaction or disappointment among the farmers. The pattern of 1910 was not unusual. The first sale of new wheat at Walla Walla, a load of Bluestem from Eureka Flat, brought ninety cents a bushel in late July. That was a very good price, but it held for only a week or so. By September it was below eighty cents, by late autumn it hovered around seventy cents. Club wheat, the other of the two standard market classes, was always lower, and by December was bringing as little as sixty cents. As a result the farmers held large stocks in the warehouses, hoping for a rise and complaining bitterly at the connivance of millers and exporters. Such complaints were expectable but wholly ineffective and not a little naïve. The pattern of 1910 was a forceful example of the fact that price was determined in the world rather than in the region and thus even a short crop in the Columbia country had no discernible effect upon the price received.

As the year ended the wheat farmers could total the results and file

[10] Calculated from tables in the *Commercial Review*, 43 (June 22, 1911), 7-8. The Columbia River export includes some from the Willamette, but the distortion is not great, as wheat production in that area was less than 7 per cent of the Northwest total. A small amount of wheat from the Grande Ronde and southern Idaho is no doubt also included in the figures for the Columbia trade.

them in their memory of crops and conditions accumulated over the years. Most of them probably considered 1910 a disappointment in yield or price, but except for a few on the driest margins of settlement, it was far from a failure. Although the price had slipped badly as the harvest waned, it did not fall much below that received in recent years; and although the spring wheat had been damaged, the over-all crop in most districts still gave a decent return. After all, measured against the perennial hope for a truly bumper crop, most harvests were a disappointment, and prices were always lower than the farmers thought they should be. And, as always, memory of the past quickly gave way to hope for the future, for while one crop was still being put in the warehouse the next was being put in the ground. Indeed, the unusually early and short harvest season of 1910 allowed earlier, better, and more extensive preparation, and as the autumn rains were favorable, plowing and seeding went forward very well, and more land was sowed to fall wheat. The crop of 1911 was off to a good start.

Other Products

The fame and fortune of the region was so bound up with wheat that it is easy to overlook the local significance of other grains. Barley had become an important crop in two areas. Columbia County was the heart of the most productive district, which extended along the foothill belt from the Walla Walla Valley to the upper Pataha. The Camas Prairie production was essentially a continuation of that same belt beyond the interruption of the lower and drier lands of the Asotin-Lewiston area. Most of this grain was sold as brewing barley and was marketed through the same dealers and facilities as the wheat. Oats was an important crop in the eastern Palouse and to a lesser extent in the Camas Prairie as well, but it was not an important item of commerce. Most of this production was consumed in the Northwest, much of it on the farms that raised it, the rest of other farms and in the logging and mining camps, wherever large numbers of work horses were used. These two grains were prominent only in the more humid eastern districts of the interior, a pattern displayed in the varied proportions of the grainland devoted to wheat and to other crops among the several areas:[11]

[11] Calculated from the 1909 crop year as given in the U.S. Census of 1910.

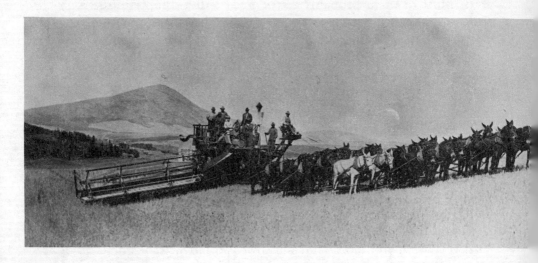

The most dramatic sight in the Columbia wheatlands, locally a proud symbol of power and progress, was the sweep of the great horse-drawn combines over the rolling golden hills. But this one, hauled by thirty mules and posed in front of Steptoe Butte a few miles west of Garfield, already carried evidence of important changes, for the combine was gasoline powered, and the gasoline tractor was but a few years in the future. *(Photo courtesy of Northern Pacific Railway Company)*

This remarkable outfit was more a symbol of farming failure than of machine progress. A fourteen-foot header is feeding directly into a twenty-foot Best combine as they jointly skim the few heads off a crop barely worth harvesting in the arid fringe of the wheatlands west of Eltopia in Franklin County, *ca.* 1912. *(Photo courtesy of James Wysong)*

	PROPORTION OF TOTAL GRAINLAND	
District	*Wheat*	*Other Grains*
Oregon, Klickitat, Horse Heaven	90.5%	9.5%
Walla Walla	77	23
Camas Prairie	42	58
Palouse	73	27
Big Bend	94	6

Certainly little else was being produced in these grain districts, despite the urgings and warnings of those who, for whatever reason, advocated a diversified agriculture. A few hundred scattered acres—of sugar beets around Waverly, of potatoes around Garfield and Palouse, of prunes at Elberton, of apples and other fruits in the Touchet Valley, or of dry navy beans on the ridges above Kendrick[12] —these and others were but an infinitesimal sprinkling of variety within the grainlands.

That variety which the proponents of diversification so vociferously desired was to be found not in the grainlands but on the irrigated farms. There was land under irrigation in all of the major districts: in tiny creekside strips, patches of greenery on bars and terraces within the basaltic canyons of the Columbia and Snake, or small oases in the midst of or on the margins of the wheat country. But such situations were only minor variations within the uniform pattern of the grainlands. However, west of the Columbia the scale and situation was different. In the Yakima country the patterns were reversed: irrigation was the mainstay, and the scattering of wheat farms on the lower slopes of the ridges seemed a precarious anomaly. This main dominion of the ditch farmers would appear on a general map as a series of misshapen beads of quite different sizes strung along the river: the Kittitas Valley, the Selah, Ahtanum, and Moxee areas, the big Reservation district on the west side and bigger Sunnyside downstream on the east, the tiny Prosser and Benton City acreages, and Richland and Kennewick near the junction with the Columbia. Together these Yakima areas contained about two thirds of the total land which was or could be irrigated by all of the present projects of the interior.[13] Much of that acreage was not yet

[12] University of Idaho agronomists had advocated experimenting with the navy bean as a leguminous alternative to fallow. By the summer of 1910 there were about three thousand acres of beans in the area, the first large bean thresher was on order, and the warehouses had installed cleaning equipment to process the crop; *Spokesman-Review*, Aug. 6, 1910, p. 5.

[13] O. L. Waller, *Irrigation in the State of Washington* (Office of Experiment Stations Bulletin No. 214) (Washington, D.C., June 22, 1909).

actually under ditch, but the product and the promise of the Yakima in 1910 were sufficient to prompt the O.R.&N. to build a branch of a hundred miles from near Wallula across the Columbia to Kennewick and up the east side of the valley to North Yakima, with a short spur to Sunnyside. Opened for service in March of 1911, this line not only ended the general Northern Pacific monopoly over the Yakima Valley, but because of the narrow shape of the agricultural district brought competitive service into or near most of the communities.

The remaining third of the irrigable domain was divided unequally among a dozen areas. In these, as well as in the Yakima, hay (chiefly alfalfa) was the principal crop, but better known were the apples, cherries, peaches, pears, berries, and grapes, the peas, beans, and potatoes and other fruits and vegetables which served not only the grocers of the Columbia interior but to some degree those of the whole Northwest. Certain choice products were shipped to more distant markets. These products were both an important addition to the region's resources and a severe deterrent to the success of those diversification schemes which sought to promote the same crops on the nonirrigated grainlands.

In most of the larger districts comparisons of the current harvest with those of previous years was a different sort of thing than in the wheat country. Each year was better than the last, in that every harvest was bigger because more land was being watered, young orchards were more mature, and the farmers were more experienced in a type of agriculture that was new to most. In 1910 many of these farms were still in the process of development, there was a continuing influx of people and a considerable speculation in land; an expansive optimism pervaded the Yakima, Umatilla, and other major irrigation districts.[14]

In some communities in Oregon the measure of any year was taken well before the harvest seasons of field or orchard, for the commercial life of most of the towns between the Umatilla and the Cascades was quickened more by the annual wool sales of late spring than by the wheat harvest of late summer. Wheat and sheep were for the most part raised by different men who were often neighbors.

[14] Much of this inflow of people and money came from the Puget Sound area; Guy Vernon Bennett, "Eastward Expansion of Population from the Pacific Slope," *Washington Historical Quarterly*, 3 (April, 1912), 115-23, provides a useful summary.

By 1910 this propinquity of fields and flocks was a pattern based not upon the preferences of individuals but upon the potentials of the land, for by that time all of the fragments of tableland big enough for a farm with soil deep enough to plow had been broken and sowed to grain. The general character of a terrain which rimmed such uplands so extensively with sandy flatlands, or thin-soiled, sparsely grassed canyons and mountain flanks allowed the farmer and the sheepman to share a general district in a stable, noncompetitive manner.

Shearing usually began in early April, as soon as the danger of cold wet weather was past. On April 7, 1910, for example, the *Arlington Record* described the beginnings of shearing by Smythe and Smith, local sheepmen who expected to put forty-five thousand head "through the machine." A month later the *Heppner Gazette* reported on the "wool pouring into Echo"—a million and a half pounds so far from the Umatilla and Butter Creek districts. By late May the shearing was about completed, the yield being lighter than usual. Then the wool buyers from Boston arrived and the sales began. Pendleton, Pilot Rock, Echo, Heppner, and Shaniko were the chief market points, and scouring mills at Pendleton and The Dalles prepared the wool for rail shipment east. The Pendleton Woolen Mills Company was the only local consumer.

These Oregon woolgrowers kept about seven hundred thousand head of sheep. There were only about half a million in all the rest of the interior, distributed among several districts. The Yakima and Klickitat area was the most important of these, with good local wintering grounds and excellent summer pastures in the Cascades. East of the Columbia the stockmen were still in retreat before the farmer. Along the Snake the sheepmen had been pushed off all but the canyon lands, but in the center the pressure was still on as the homesteaders moved into the arid reaches west of Moses Lake, and on to the Frenchman Hills and the gentle Wahluke Slope. By the close of 1910 little land remained here for the sheepman except the most rugged of the coulees and canyons and the steep face of Saddle Mountain. In all of these portions of the Columbia Plain, sheep and wool were of minor and lessening economic importance.

By 1910, however, there were indications that these pressures might slacken and that the line separating the domains of farmer and stockman might soon stabilize. The most obvious sign was the failure of crops all along the encroaching margins of the crescent of wheatlands from the Quincy Flats and lower Crab Creek country, through the western parts of Franklin and Walla Walla counties to the Horse Heaven hills. One bad year would not halt the advance of settlement, but in fact there had not as yet been a really good year. Even the Big Bend bumper crop of 1909 had been poor along this fringe. A less obvious but no less significant symptom was the fact that many homesteads in this area had been abandoned before completion, indeed some quarter sections had been taken up and abandoned twice within a span of five or six years. The passage of the Enlarged Homestead Act of 1909, which allowed claims of half a section (320 acres) in certain semiarid areas designated by the Secretary of the Interior, may have given some encouragement, for it was a long belated recognition by the federal government that larger farms were necessary in the drier regions.[15] But even though the act was applied to numerous blocks of government land in the Columbia country, it could have little effect unless the farmer reaped at least marginally profitable crops. In these lands this would mean a doubling of the bushels per acre as well as of the acres per homestead to improve the situation. Land seekers were still coming into this arid center, but most were filing on land already once claimed and abandoned, and that, plus the fact that much of the land claimed had never been sown, and much of that sown had never been reaped, furnished relatively recent but reasonably certain signs that the march of the frontier in these Columbia wheatlands, after a half century of expansion, was slowing to a halt.

THE PATTERN OF TOWNS

Towns

While the quality of the land was measured every year, that of the towns was measured every ten. Of course, each tradesman had his annual accounting of the season's returns, but these computations were essentially private matters, and thus the boosters in every town based their claims chiefly on the sheer number of citizens. Once every ten years there was the opportunity to match their optimistic estimates and rounded totals of the advertising tracts against the stark authority of the federal census. Almost invariably the actual

[15] The statement about abandoned homesteads is based upon a spot check of the Federal Land Office records for several localities; Louise E. Peffer, *The Closing of the Public Domain* (Stanford, Calif., 1951), pp. 147-48.

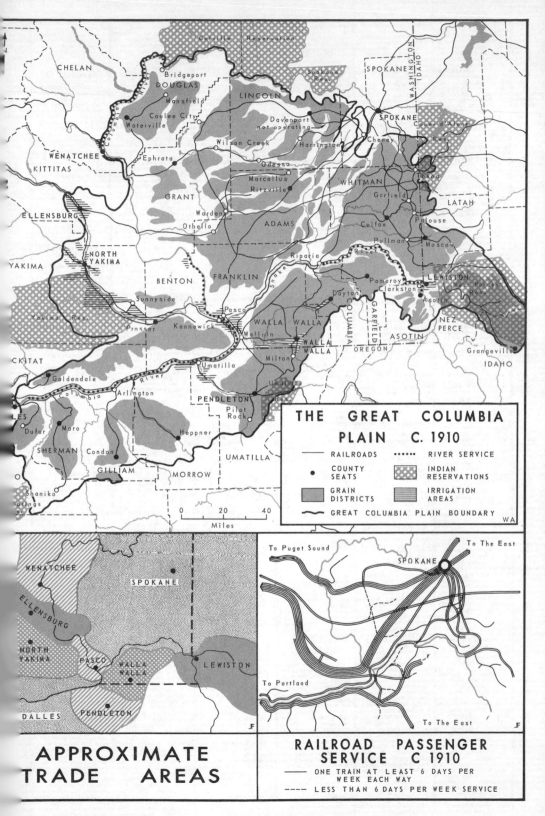

THE GREAT COLUMBIA PLAIN C. 1910

— RAILROADS ⋯⋯ RIVER SERVICE
• COUNTY SEATS ▨ INDIAN RESERVATIONS
▨ GRAIN DISTRICTS ▤ IRRIGATION AREAS
GREAT COLUMBIA PLAIN BOUNDARY

0   20   40
Miles

APPROXIMATE TRADE AREAS

RAILROAD PASSENGER SERVICE C 1910

— ONE TRAIN AT LEAST 6 DAYS PER WEEK EACH WAY
--- LESS THAN 6 DAYS PER WEEK SERVICE

Map 39, above; Map 40, below left; Map 41, below right

count was well below local claims, but disappointment could be mitigated if size and growth rate were greater than those of rival towns.

As the figures of the decennial poll became known in 1910, there was ample reason for general satisfaction within the region as a whole. Population was now more than three hundred thousand, about three times what it had been in 1890, there were nearly a hundred incorporated towns and villages, and almost every one had grown considerably, and some phenomenally, during the past twenty years. Among the various districts there were of course many variations in scale and pattern. In the older areas the proportionate position among the several towns was quite stable, little changed over a decade or two, and in the newer areas a similar type of pattern was now quite discernible. Expectedly, the Big Bend and the Yakima displayed the greatest changes.

In the eastern and longer settled part of the Big Bend country, Davenport (population 1,229) and Wilbur (757), Harrington (661) and Odessa (885),[16] Sprague (1,110), Ritzville (1,859), and Lind (831) appeared firmly established in a clear lead over neighboring towns along their respective rail lines. Farther west along these routes, however, while the spacing was now set, some of the rivalries were still keen. It was clear that Coulee City (276), a raw creation at the terminus of the Washington Central branch in 1890, was unlikely to acquire even a hint of the greatness logically expected by her founders. The immediate country was only marginally productive, and the Mansfield branch of the Great Northern had not only taken away a large trade area but threatened to sever the vast Okanogan country from any future connection (Map 41). Hopes that the Northern Pacific might compete for the Okanogan trade by an extension from Coulee City were not dead, but as a result of the Mansfield line, the Coulee City—Brewster stage, the only tangible connection in that direction, had been discontinued after twenty years of service.[17]

Waterville, one of the most strident of the contenders in 1890, had reason for greater satisfaction with the census results, for her popu-

[16] Odessa was the most prominent of the Russian place names in the Big Bend. Others were Batum, Tiflis, and Moscow (soon changed to Bluestem). It is tempting to assume that these are directly related to the considerable number of settlers from Russia in the district, but that may not be correct.

[17] *Wenatchee Daily World,* July 11, 1910.

lation of 950 was far ahead of any nearby town of the wheatlands. Yet most of the grandiose hopes of an earlier day were also irrevocably gone. The little five-mile spur of her own construction was a meager substitute for the strategic position within contending railroad networks envisioned by her promoters, and the Mansfield branch and its several stations took away considerable local trade. But much more ominous had been the rapid rise of a major rival, which had hardly existed twenty years before. The building of the Great Northern had made Wenatchee a junction of rail and water lines, irrigation developments soon gave it an expanding basis for local growth, and the town quickly became the focus of a widening trade area. Waterville interests were alert to the danger but relatively helpless. They did their best to rally Douglas County opposition to the construction of a bridge across the Columbia at Wenatchee; when that failed they tried to insist that it be a toll bridge instead of free, all in fear of losing the trade of the "Southside," the southerly portion of Badger Mountain and adjacent river country.[18] By 1910 it was clear that their fears were well grounded, for such trade had indeed been lost, and the only rail service in Douglas County was a daily (except Sunday) train directly to and from Wenatchee, which with its population of 4,050 was clearly the leading center of a large area.

As the seat of Douglas County, Waterville in 1910 presided over a political area which had also recently been much diminished. Agitation for division inevitably followed hard upon the recent influx of settlers; a bill to create Big Bend County out of the country south and east of Grand Coulee was introduced in the legislature early in 1909. The need for a more reasonable size and convenience were powerful arguments. It was pointed out that existing rail, boat, and stage schedules made a trip of thirty hours from Ephrata by way of Wenatchee and Orondo to Waterville. The bill was passed on February 20, 1909, after being altered to read Grant County, as a more fitting companion to bordering Douglas, Lincoln, Adams, and Franklin. Ephrata (1910 population 323) was named the temporary county seat, and as usual other towns immediately began campaigns to capture that prize permanently. Wilson Creek (405) laid claim as a more substantial community, while Adrian was soon able to insist that, as the point where the new Northern Pacific line crossed

---

[18] *Ibid.*, March 9, 1907. The bridge was completed in December of that year.

the Great Northern, it was the logical focus of the whole county. Other nearby communities were also striving for recognition, such as Quincy (264) and Soap Lake. The latter was the newest health resort of the region; a correspondent reported that a hundred tents lined the shores in July, 1910, every train was bringing in more people, and there were "wonderful tales to tell of cures effected."[19]

All of these communities lay along the Great Northern and had started some years before, but in the southern part of the country the towns were as new as the railroads. Wheeler was born in 1910; numerous lots were sold and a bank and several stores established even before the railroad was put into operation. Warden, where the Northern Pacific crossed the Milwaukee Road, was a year older but as yet had a more impressive network of tracks than of trade. Othello, just beyond in the "panhandle" of Adams County, was not in a more productive locale, but as a railroad division point it had sufficient sustenance and confidence to incorporate as a town in 1910. All of these tiny communities expected to thrive on the rural trade of the wheatlands and the extensive irrigation districts which were anticipated from the water of Moses Lake.[20] In 1910 such expectations were enough to support considerable speculation in town lots but little volume of town business, for the wheat farmers had yet to raise any wheat and the irrigation development totaled only a few hundred acres.

Other patterns which were largely new since 1890 were those of the irrigation districts, and especially the Yakima Valley below North Yakima city (Map 42). By 1910 a string of bustling towns wound through the narrow corridors of irrigated farmland on either side of the river, each with its commercial club proclaiming its unrivaled advantages for settlers and investers. In many cases their very names had been chosen to prompt attractive visions of handsome settings and bucolic bounty: Sunnyside, Grandview, Richland, Midvale, Fruitvale, Pomona. Sunnyside and Toppenish were two of the best examples of the rapid growth characteristic in the valley during this boom era. Sunnyside (colloquially known as the "Holy City" because of the imprint of Protestant morality stamped upon it by its founder, who tried to focus community life upon a federated church and wrote into the deed of every lot a prohibition of drinking, gambling, and prostitution) was solidly established as the lead-

[19] *Ibid.*, Feb. 2, 1909, July 22, Aug. 3, 1910.
[20] *Ibid.*, March 25, 1909, July 2, 1910.

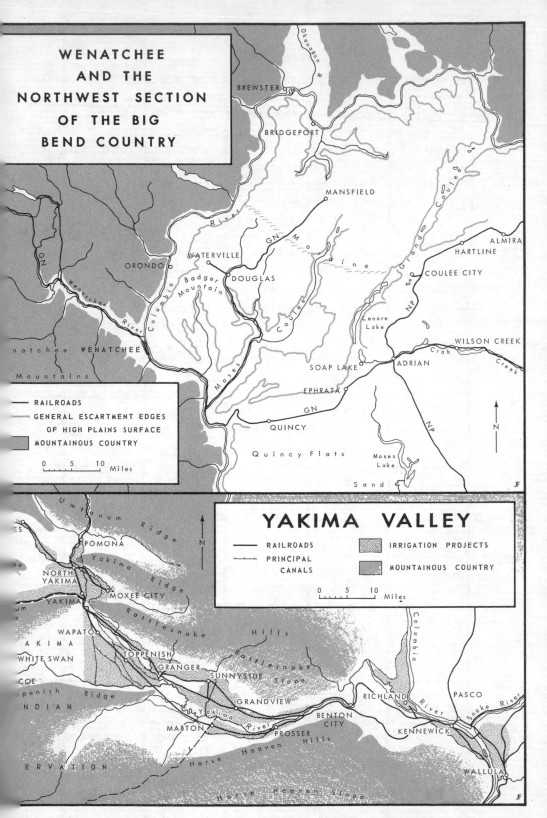

WENATCHEE AND THE NORTHWEST SECTION OF THE BIG BEND COUNTRY

BREWSTER

BRIDGEPORT

Okanogan R

Grand Coulee

MANSFIELD

GN Moraine

River

ALMIRA
HARTLINE

ORONDO
WATERVILLE
DOUGLAS

Badger Mountain

COULEE CITY

NP

Lenore Lake

WENATCHEE

WILSON CREEK

Crab Creek

Moses

Coulee

SOAP LAKE

ADRIAN

natchee
Mountains

Wenatchee River

Columbia

EPHRATA

GN

RAILROADS

GENERAL ESCARTMENT EDGES
OF HIGH PLAINS SURFACE

MOUNTAINOUS COUNTRY

QUINCY

NP

N

0   5   10 Miles

Quincy Flats

Moses Lake

Sand

JF

YAKIMA VALLEY

Umtanum Ridge

POMONA

N

—— RAILROADS

Yakima Ridge

++ PRINCIPAL
CANALS

IRRIGATION PROJECTS

MOUNTAINOUS COUNTRY

NORTH
YAKIMA

MOXEE CITY

0   5   10 Miles

YAKIMA

Rattlesnake

WAPATO

Hills

Columbia

AKIMA

WHITE SWAN

TOPPENISH

Rattlesnake

GRANGER

SUNNYSIDE

Slope

COE

penish Ridge

GRANDVIEW

RICHLAND

River

PASCO

NDIAN

Yakima River

BENTON
CITY

Snake River

MABTON

PROSSER

KENNEWICK

ERVATION

Horse Heaven Hills

WALLULA

Horse Heaven Slope

JF

Map 42, above; Map 43, below

ing community on the east side, with a fine new hotel, high school, a municipal water system, and electric arc lamps along Main Street. Toppenish, only seven years old, but with 1,598 inhabitants, was the largest of the new settlements on the other side; however, it had quite a different character for it was a "reservation town" with an ample supply of all those features banned by Sunnyside. Of the approximately 3,000 Indians on the Yakima Reservation, about 225 were doing "more or less farming," a few had herds of cattle or sheep, a good many owned range horses, but an increasing number were to be found in and about Toppenish and the other new towns along the railroad, doing day labor, freighting or some sort of team work, or little at all. Practically all of the productive land of the reservation was occupied by whites, either through lease of Indian allotments or homesteads on the unalloted remainder; the Indian was subservient and marginal even within his own reserve.[21]

Prosser (population 1,298), a considerably older center than most, still pointed to its water power as an unrivaled asset. An earlier judgment that such a site "ought to make this the best town between Tacoma and Spokane" was increasingly difficult to sustain, but the town had added a thousand to its population during the last ten years and had successfully led the fight to create a new county for the lower end of the valley. When Benton (after Thomas Hart Benton) County was established in 1905, Prosser became its seat, but only provisionally, for Kennewick (1,219), another of the upstart irrigation communities, had strongly challenged; by 1910 the issue was unresolved, and no permanent county buildings had been built.[22]

In most of the older farming districts the pattern of towns across the land had been set well before 1910. In the Walla Walla country the older towns continued to prosper, and the settlement of drier sections, such as Eureka Flat, was so sparse as to sustain no more than a few tiny hamlets. In the Palouse, colonization of western

[21] Lyman, *Yakima Valley*, pp. 554-60, 907-9; and Roscoe Sheller, *Courage and Water . . .* (Portland, Ore., 1952), p. 23.

[22] Lyman, *Yakima Valley*, quoting the *Prosser Bulletin* of June 26, 1902; also see pp. 739-40, 757. Another new county movement, initiated in the central section, would split off all below Union Gap from the North Yakima nucleus. The *Yakima Herald* (North Yakima), May 18, 1910. Similarly, a move to carve "Orchard County" out of northern Umatilla was being pushed in the vigorous irrigation nucleus around Milton and Freewater. *Heppner Gazette*, May 5, 1910; *Up-to-the-Times Magazine*, 4 (September, 1910), 2787.

Whitman County after 1900 resulted in a few more substantial centers, such as St. John (421) and Endicott (474). Colfax, the county seat, had grown steadily (2,783 in 1910) but no more dominated the Palouse country than it had twenty years before. Moscow (3,670) was larger, and Pullman (2,602) was nearly equal in size, sustained not only by highly productive farm lands but by the steady expansion of the university and the state college. Among the dozen smaller towns, Tekoa (1,694) had shown the most vigorous growth, an expansion related to its railroad facilities and to the recent development of farming and lumbering on the adjacent Coeur d'Alene Indian Reservation. On the Camas Prairie the census of 1910 was reporting conditions only a little more than a year after the completion of the railroad. Grangeville (1,534) remained largest in size and importance, while Nezperce (599), now a terminus of its own little spur, was well established in the midst of some of the best of the farmlands. In most cases the rivalry between new townsites and adjacent older ones along the new railroad had not as yet resulted in much development in either. An exception was at Vollmer and Ilo, where the new (Vollmer, population 332), a half mile east on the other side of the tracks, had a slight edge over the old (Ilo, 209), but only taken together did they represent a substantial town.

Goldendale in the Klickitat country was in size (1,203) and position rather similar to Grangeville: a rail terminus drawing the trade from nearby farming, grazing, and lumbering districts. Across the Columbia, Dufur, Shaniko, Condon, and Heppner were in some degree analogous. The first two were considerably smaller than the others, and their hopes for growth were severely dampened by what was taking place deep in the Deschutes Canyon in the summer of 1910. There the Oregon Trunk and the O.R.&N. railroads were blasting passageways on either side of the river in a frantic race to tap the vast new frontier region of central Oregon. In March a promoter laid out a townsite at Mopins Ferry (Maupin) in expectation of drawing much of the trade of Tygh Valley, Juniper Flat, and the Shaniko area.[23] The upland block of wheatland in Sherman County, bisected by a railroad, was served by three small towns of remarkably similar size, Wasco (386), Moro (378), and Grass Valley (342), while Gilliam County had Condon (1,009) and Arlington (317) at either end of the railroad branch, with not even a

[23] *Grass Valley Journal*, April 1, 1910.

substantial hamlet serving the more dissected lands in between. The fact that Arlington was the largest town along either bank of the Columbia between The Dalles and Pasco was a measure of how barren was the swath cut by the great river and how effectively the railroad branches had tapped the tablelands beyond. Along the lower Umatilla, just back from the Columbia, a small portion of that barrenness had been made to bloom, however, and within that irrigation district the new budding towns of Hermiston (647) and Stanfield (318) were a sharp contrast with their historic but relict neighbor Umatilla (198).

The distribution and number of newspapers and banks (see appendix) continued to offer additional indications of community developments. Of course many more of each existed than in 1890, and the fact that more places had banks than newspapers, in marked contrast with the situation twenty years before, was perhaps an indication that local economic development was now actually more comprehensive than local boostering, though some of the banks, like some of the newspapers, were insubstantial operations at best. Seven of the small cities of the region supported daily newspapers, in two of these as well as in two smaller towns semi-weeklies were published, and nearly a hundred other places had a weekly paper. There were 188 banks distributed among 122 cities, towns, and hamlets, and though these differed greatly in size and security, together they brought financial services into every farming locality.

Cities

The presence of a daily newspaper and of banks with large assets, combined with the census figures on population, gave a clear indication of which of these centers had already achieved some degree of the status to which most had once aspired. Such characteristics were merely a hint at a more critical difference in function. The variety and quality of professional services—medical, legal, and in some cases educational and governmental—were usually greater in these centers, while their business was not only more diversified but reached beyond immediate localities to serve as suppliers for larger districts. In fact all of these larger commercial centers were near the borders of the Great Columbia Plain, and their hinterlands extended well into neighboring grazing, timber, and mining districts (Map 40).

Walla Walla and North Yakima were much the largest of these

centers and were the best illustrations of continuity and of change, respectively, the one the historic leader of the oldest productive district of the Columbia Plain, the other a remarkable growth amidst one of the newest. Walla Walla had more than doubled in size in the decade after 1890 and then doubled again by 1910. Its twenty thousand inhabitants now drew sustenance largely from within the same geographical limits as had the fewer than five thousand in 1890 but from a realm thoroughly settled, with some of the richest of the grainlands and a much expanded irrigation agriculture. But the census figure of nearly a million dollars in "value added by manufacture" was perhaps the most significant measure of the eminence of Walla Walla's position. Most prominent were the three farm machinery factories whose products, together with those of assembly and distributing warehouses such as that of the Holt Company, were marketed over the whole of the grain country. Flour milling, fruit and vegetable packing, and many smaller consumer industries completed the total of forty-eight manufacturing establishments, a greater number and variety than any other city in the region. Commerce was handled by several large mercantile houses, wholesalers, and banks, and promoted by an extremely active Board of Trade, three daily newspapers, and the *Up-to-the-Times Magazine,* one of the most ambitious organs of its type in the whole Northwest. Furthermore, Walla Walla enjoyed a far better array of educational and cultural facilities than others. Local citizens had recently contributed two hundred thousand dollars to support an expansion of Whitman College, and the community had another college, two Roman Catholic schools, an Episcopal girls' academy, a business college, and a school of music, as well as a small symphony orchestra and a concert band. These schools and the homes ("more fine homes in proportion to size than any city in the state"), parks, and tree-lined streets in which her citizens took such pride still prominently displayed Walla Walla's relative maturity as well as her prosperity. That air of complacent superiority which Mrs. Strahorn had found thirty years before still enveloped the city, and her spokesmen were anxious to emphasize the surprise of newcomers, who found not "a new, wild and wooly Western town" but an "old, well-settled, rich, intelligent, prosperous, happy, and up-to-date community, knowing of the good things of life, and determined to have and enjoy them." It was fitting—indeed a generation overdue—that on October 1, 1910, the federal government closed old Fort Walla

Walla as a needless post in the midst of a thoroughly domesticated region.[24]

If Walla Wallans thus smugly exaggerated the charms and culture of their city, the general contrast in character with other places was nonetheless real, as a glimpse of North Yakima would have quickly revealed. It was largely new and, if not "wild and wooly" in the romantic western sense, it had no lack of bustle and commotion. For North Yakima was in the midst of a great boom. A population of 14,082 represented nearly a fivefold increase in ten years, and thus most of its people and most of its businesses were new and the city was engulfed in speculation and change. North Yakima was sustained not only by the richness of her immediate environs but by the whole Yakima Valley, for it had clearly emerged as the commercial capital of a large district. That district was still rapidly expanding in productivity, and there was almost no limit to the expansive visions of Yakima publicists. In late 1910 the city was preparing to celebrate the arrival of a major new railroad (something Walla Walla had not enjoyed for twenty years) and the prospect of more to come looked entirely favorable. It seemed "without question" that the O.R.&N. would push on across the Cascades to Puget Sound and almost as likely that some company would build southwest to the Columbia River via Fort Simcoe and the Mount Adams district, "tapping an undeveloped country of vast potential resources." Such lines would make Yakima a major focus and handsomely enlarge her tributary region. A similar optimism confidently anticipated that the local electric railroad would eventually knit the entire Yakima country into a network of "over 250 miles of road."[25] Internally, the city's industries employed more people and produced goods of greater total value than did Walla Walla's, but there was less di-

[24] Norman Olaf Forness, "The Up-to-the-Times Magazine, 1906-1911: A Promoter of Enterprise and Reflection of Culture in Walla Walla" (M.A. thesis, Washington State University, 1960), p. 57, quoting from Vol. V (September, 1911), p. 4632, also pp. 63-68. The second college was Walla Walla College, founded in 1892 by the Seventh Day Adventists.

[25] Lyman, Yakima Valley, p. 343. The excitement over railroad matters was heightened by mystery surrounding the surveys and constructions of the North Coast Railroad Company, which built the Wallula-North Yakima line. Not until late 1910 was it made public that the company was an instrument of the Union Pacific. Ellis A. Davis, New Commercial Encyclopedia ... (Berkeley, Calif., 1909), p. 58. The Union Pacific acquired a controlling interest in this Yakima Valley Transportation Company in June, 1909; Helen W. Gouldin, "Here's Our Little Electric Brother," Union Pacific Magazine, 7 (June, 1928), 9.

versity and greater seasonal fluctuation, as the majority were related to fruit and vegetable marketing, such as fruit drying, canning, box-making plants, and cold storage facilities. While Walla Walla reflected upon its age and beauty, North Yakima pointed to the scale and rate of its growth and to many buildings which were newer, bigger, and costlier—civic pride could flourish as well on the one as the other. Though North Yakima had failed to get the State Agriculture College, it did become the seat of the annual State Fair.

The rapid rise of North Yakima was in contrast with Ellensburg, and in some measure a triumph. Ellensburg, with 4,209 people, could appropriately be grouped in size and function with the larger centers of this Columbia country; but whereas in 1890 it had been larger in population and quite the equal of North Yakima in the geographical extent of its commercial pretensions, it was now smaller by ten thousand and had clearly lost its bid for the Okanogan trade. Kittitas County was now essentially the commercial as well as political limit of Ellensburg's dominance, and while that included a diversity in grazing, lumbering, and mining activities equal to or even surpassing that of Yakima County, it encompassed an irrigation district so much smaller in production and potential as to offer no hope of comparable growth. And though Ellensburg got its second railroad a year earlier than North Yakima, the C.M.&St.P. did little to enhance the town's commercial position. To the west it simply paralleled the Northern Pacific, without opening a new Cascade district; and although it followed the old route of the railroad eastward to a Columbia port which had been partially constructed and ardently desired in 1890, by 1910 there was no port to serve and no boats to connect with along this barren stretch of river. The railroad continued east into the Big Bend but through a country so poor and sparsely settled as to offer no trade expectations for Ellensburg merchants. Even the State Normal School, a well-established source of pride and the one means by which Ellensburg drew upon and served an area far beyond the Kittitas, was much the smallest of such schools, far surpassed in enrollment by the one at Cheney.[26]

The building of the Great Northern railroad and the consequent rise of Wenatchee had completely severed Ellensburg from the

[26] Frederick E. Bolton and Thomas W. Bibb, *History of Education in Washington* (Office of Education Bulletin No. 9) (Washington, D.C.: U.S. Dept. of the Interior, 1935), pp. 303, 311. Ellensburg had 175 regular students in the 1910-11 academic year, Cheney 914.

Okanogan country, and by 1910 Wenatchee, though much younger, with 4,050 people, was already equal in size and clearly had good prospects for further growth. The Mansfield branch had insured that the whole of Douglas County would be in some degree tributary. Whether the Okanogan would be tapped by an extension of that line or one along the Columbia was as yet uncertain,[27] but that a much increased traffic would soon be flowing into Wenatchee from the Okanogan, Methow, Chelan, and Entiat valleys seemed inevitable. Meanwhile the river steamers to Bridgeport brought down whatever was presently available, and the irrigation and orchard developments in the lower Wenatchee Valley alone seemed sufficient to sustain further growth.

North Yakima, Ellensburg, and Wenatchee each served a diversified trade area combining some portion of the western Columbia Plain with the mountain country beyond; and The Dalles, Pendleton, and Lewiston (and to a much lesser extent Walla Walla) performed the same function along the southern borders of the region. Of these The Dalles had perhaps the least reason to celebrate its level of achievement in 1910. It had grown steadily but not rapidly, and a population of 4,880 must have seemed a disappointing total for a settlement half a century old and occupying what was regarded as a most strategic position. In fact the qualities of that position were persistently exaggerated and misread. Once the railroads took the traffic away from the river boats, the transshipment business— the impetus and mainstay of the early years—was irrevocably gone. The plan to have the federal government build a canal around the rapids and Celilo Falls, long endorsed by local leaders as the only means of reviving the river traffic, had been approved, but it was not clear how opening the river to through traffic would enhance the commercial growth of The Dalles. At the moment the hotly competitive construction of the two railroads up the Deschutes Canyon had quickened business and renewed confidence in further expansion, for The Dalles would be near the junction of these new lines with the main routes along the Columbia. But again it remained to be seen whether these railroads to central Oregon would provide greater impetus to The Dalles than had the shorter branches to Shaniko, Condon, and Heppner. The Dalles liked to think of it-

[27] Fear that the mysterious North Coast Company planned to build north toward the Okanogan prompted the Great Northern to run a number of different surveys; *Wenatchee Daily World,* Oct. 9, 1909.

self as a naturally strategic site, the portal to the interior and the funnel to the coast, but that alone had not proved sufficient to insure command of a major region. The situation was shaped by the fact that Portland was so near, so accessible, and so many times larger that it overshadowed all, holding The Dalles to a minor regional trade center, the biggest within a large area to be sure, but smaller than if it had more fully dominated the commercial life of the area.[28]

None of these budding cities could take less pleasure from the census of 1910 than Pendleton. The total of 4,460 was barely larger than that of 1890. The geographical limits of its trade area had been stable for a good many years, for Walla Walla and LaGrande firmly dominated the most productive bordering districts. But its position and historic pattern of development had never been favorable to extravagant geographical dreams, and it was well recognized in 1910 that growth must rest largely upon a more intense development of local resources. There was strong interest in the latest proposal for a city and suburban electric railway, and its advocates stressed that such a line would, "by economizing and facilitating commercial transportation, tend to break up the large farms and encourage diversified and intensified farming, thereby securing a thick settlement for an almost depopulated country."[29] The most positive signs of these trends were to be found in the new Umatilla irrigation projects down stream. Although mercantile firms in those towns would no doubt depend upon Portland for supplies, most of the people would find Pendleton the nearest source of many retail and professional services. Thus there was hope that the present stagnation was only a brief phase in the continued progress of the community.

Lewiston had long been afflicted with geographical dreams of grandeur and had suffered grievously from the difference between expectations and reality. But in 1910 it appeared that the natural logic which Lewiston had always seen as inherent in her river junction site was beginning to take effect. There was nothing inevitable about growth at such a location, and indeed the river traffic was

[28] The carving of Hood River County out of the northwest corner of Wasco in 1908 represented no real loss of trade, for everything to the west of The Dalles had always looked to Portland; more ominous was the long-standing agitation in the Shaniko and Antelope districts for subdivision, which would probably be intensified by any new settlement attendant upon the new railroads farther south.

[29] *Inland Herald* (Spokane), Feb. 11, 1910.

much reduced from a few years before—though United States Senator Weldon B. Heyburn's forthright statement that "Idaho has one seaport, Lewiston, and we intend to maintain it," was comforting assurance that her natural gift was not to be neglected. But Lewiston had doubled in size when the railroad opened up Camas Prairie, and the line down the Snake, completed in 1908, had provided more direct connection with the outside world. Far short of being a junction of transcontinentals, it at least gave overnight Pullman service to Portland and Seattle. Moreover, there was talk of more lines to come: the Spokane and Inland Empire electric was expected soon, and it was reported that the Northern Pacific "plans constructing its main line through the Clearwater country from Missoula, Montana, surveys having been completed."[30]

Actually Lewiston's growth to a population of more than six thousand was primarily the result of local developments. The Lewiston Orchards tract on the high terrace to the south was flourishing; the new town of Clarkston across the Snake already had 1,257 residents, and the bridge made them part of a greater Lewiston commercial center; in 1910 one could even ride in a new Ford taxicab between the two. There was room for more growth in these irrigation projects, but Lewiston's vision of an expansive future could draw upon a much wider realm. Not only was it the hub of a rich corner of the Columbia Plain, but beyond there was a vast country assuredly rich in forests and hopefully rich in minerals which had as yet barely been tapped. With a little more time and the proper railroad connections, the prospect of a real metropolis in this strategic southeastern border zone—"portal to an empire of wealth"—might seem as well assured as the fact of a metropolis in what appeared to be an analogous situation in the Spokane Valley—portal to a well-acknowledged "Inland Empire."[31]

That these larger centers had developed along border zones of the Columbia Plain was a persistent defiance of the logic of nature as interpreted by the boosters of Pasco, who were sure that nature intended all to be tributary to this greatest junction. "Every stream, canyon, coulee and valley" of a tremendous region reaching from

[30] State of Idaho, *Sixth Bienniel Report, Commissioner of Immigration, Labor and Statistics* (Boise, 1909-10), p. 223; *Great Facts About a Great Region* (pamphlet issued by the Lewiston Commercial Club, *ca.* 1909).

[31] *Lewiston Morning Tribune*, July 16, 1961); State of Idaho, *Sixth Biennial Report*, p. 225.

the Kittitas to Colville and the Clearwater country "tend to a common center at Pasco," the promoters of *The Pasconian* had insisted nearly twenty years before, and now the new *Columbia Journal of Commerce* was singing the same refrain. "Here at the junction of the Columbia and Snake Rivers, at the crossings of the great railroads, and at the point of the greatest area of irrigable land in one body, with every advantage of soil, climate and transportation, there is bound to be in the near future a large city." But even though it was an impressive junction of rails as well as rivers, nothing of the sort had as yet happened. The population of 2,083 was supported largely by servicing those railroads rather than the country they gave access to. Kennewick, like Clarkston, had developed out of the irrigation projects across the river and added another 1,257 people to the cluster, but unlike Lewiston there was no tributary district of any wealth. For to be central within the Columbia Plain made Pasco peripheral to all its productive districts. Only if it could bring those districts into focus and develop a higher level of function than Walla Walla, Lewiston, or North Yakima could its dreams be fulfilled. In 1910 there was no evidence that Pasco could do this, though local boosters seemed unshaken in their faith that it would. The *Inland Empire,* the new Open River Transportation Company stern-wheeler plying between Pasco and Celilo, was in function as well as name perhaps the best basis for those hopes. Once the Celilo Canal was completed, the waterway to the sea would lie open, with surely great consequences for the commerce of the interior.[32] Just what those consequences would be was uncertain, but no place was better situated to partake of them than Pasco.

Spokane Falls and the Inland Empire

All these centers which had triumphed over local rivals in the struggle for the dominance of more than local areas were still minor in size and significance compared with the one real metropolis of the Columbia Interior. The city at the falls was now simply Spokane, shortened in name as if its lengthened fame had made it no longer necessary to reiterate its greatest natural asset (which "grand

[32] *The Pasconian*, 1 (December, 1892); *Columbia Journal of Commerce*, 1 (Jan. 4, 1909); W. D. Lyman, *The Columbia River: Its History, Its Myths, Its Scenery, Its Commerce* (New York and London, 1909), p. 327. See p. 9 for a report on the maiden voyage of the *Inland Empire* on Dec. 27, 1908, and the plans for future service.

spectacle" was now "alas, ... cribbed and cabined ... by the march of industrial and electrical power"[33]), and the city was an even more wondrous phenomenon than twenty years before when it had suddenly emerged from village obscurity to regional leadership. Its growth was astounding: from 20,000 in 1890 to the 104,402 of the census of 1910. The first hundred thousand had come so quickly that more hundreds of thousands seemed sure to follow. On February 8, 1910, a new daily newspaper, the *Inland Herald,* confidently assumed half a million by 1920, and to progressive minds this fivefold increase would hardly seem unreasonable for a city which had already tripled in the last ten years.

Moreover, Spokane was five times larger than Walla Walla, the next largest in this Pacific Northwest interior, and it had more than five times as many manufacturing establishments, which employed ten times as many people. But more important, Spokane could look down upon Walla Walla not only as smaller in size and product but subservient in position and function. Although Walla Walla was the focus of a large and prosperous region, that whole region was, in the eyes of Spokane, but a small though valued part of the *Inland Empire,* that rich interior domain which the Chamber of Commerce was equally fond of calling more explicitly the *Spokane Country* (Map 43). Developments within that realm had been so rapid and varied over the past twenty years that it was easy to predict as phenomenal a growth for that entire region as for its capital. It was confidently anticipated that, with fully half a million population now, "in a generation the Inland Empire will be the home of ten millions."[34]

The extent of that empire was often described in the literature of the day: it reached from the Cascades to the Rockies, and from the Blue Mountains to (in some versions well into) British Columbia. That was the common claim, but such a geographical vision overreached the actual situation. The fact that Spokane was the largest city within those bounds did not make every district actually tributary to it. And tribute was the proper measure, for the Inland Empire was by now clearly a euphonious term for the "sphere of influence," the commercial realm of Spokane—in the jargon of modern geography it was a "nodal region." And while Spokane was

[33] Lyman, *Columbia River,* p. 315.
[34] *Inland Herald,* Feb. 8, 1910.

certainly the geographical center of the region so described, it was not the functional focus of all that was thereby included.

The impress of its influence was in fact quite uneven. Its dominion over everything north to the international boundary was complete. A local entrepreneur had initiated the Spokane Falls and Northern Railway, which first tapped the Colville Valley and Boundary mining district, and that line was now part of a larger system of Great Northern branches which reached beyond to the Republic, Kootenay, and other areas. The southeastern section of British Columbia had better direct access to Spokane than to any Canadian city, and although the political boundary was a commercial impediment, the common network of mining interests strengthened this international tie. To the east, Spokane commanded much of the trade of the rich Coeur d'Alene district, as well as that of the Idaho panhandle timber country. Beyond the Bitterroots, however, its commercial influence faded well to the west of the Rockies. The Flathead and Missoula districts were part of the Spokane trade area in only a very minor way; it was not merely a matter of distance but of direction, for most supplies could be obtained more readily and cheaply from St. Paul and Minneapolis.

But it was chiefly to the south and west of Spokane, on the Great Columbia Plain, that the concept of a single mountain-girded trade area was more extensive and simpler than warranted by the actual situation. In fact, only two of the half dozen major districts—the Palouse and the Big Bend—were actually dominated by Spokane (Map 39). These two were adjacent and readily accessible by several railroads, and the routes and number both of lines and actual trains offered the best indication of metropolitan influence and extent. Thus the map of the service routes, of daily communications on the Columbia Plain, gives the best clue to the patterns of contact with and competition among its bordering metropolitan centers (Map 40).[35]

[35] As I was unable to locate time schedules for each railroad company for the same date, it was necessary to make certain interpretations in the compilation of this map. Northern Pacific and Camas Prairie trains were based upon the official *Time Table,* June, 1910; the Adco-Connell line was not in service until October, and I have added the train which appears in schedules of a few years later. Great Northern and Spokane and Inland Empire trains are from the official Great Northern *Time Table,* October, 1910. O.R.&N. trains are derived from the *Time Table* of June 24, 1916, from which I have subtracted trains on lines not in operation in 1910. A comparison of Northern Pacific train service in 1910

Anyone in the Palouse country could get to Spokane within two or three hours after boarding a train. Most towns had at least two trains a day, and some had a remarkable variety of service. Garfield could brag of the most—six trains a day each way—and the traveler had a choice of the regular steam trains of the N.P., or the new boat-nosed, porthole-windowed, gasoline-powered McKeen railcars of the O.R.&N., or the electric cars of the S.&I.E. These last were clean and speedy in sprints but liable to many stops, for true to its design the "Inland" was in effect a streetcar service through the country-side, with neat little platforms and shelters every mile or two along its tracks, ready to stop for a passenger or a milk can. The situation was different in the Big Bend. Several trains a day ran along the main lines of the N.P. and the G.N., but not all actually served to connect the region with Spokane. The luxuries of the *North Coast Limited* and the *Oriental Limited* were not designed for the farmer or small-town merchant; other through trains usually carried a coach or combination car to accommodate local passengers at larger towns such as Ritzville or Odessa, but smaller centers were served only by a daily "milk-run," which paused at every siding. Towns along the Washington Central branch of the N.P. to Coulee City and Adrian had the limited choice of riding the single passenger train or the coach hauled along at the tail of the local freight to and from Cheney. But whatever the qualities of these services, they were a means by which anyone on any day could get to the metropolis in a few hours, and they well represented the close ties between these two districts and Spokane.

But beyond these undoubted realms, other trains revealed the weakness of Spokane's grasp upon areas claimed within its empire. Beyond the Grand Coulee, for example, the daily (except Sunday) mixed train on the Mansfield branch turned everyone westward to Wenatchee and, if need be, beyond to Seattle. Even in the southern Palouse the O.R.&N. locals carried passengers to Walla Walla almost as readily as to Spokane. Lewiston was perhaps the best example of divergent orientations. There were two trains every day to and from Spokane but it was a long slow haul up out of the canyon, the trip

and 1916 indicated almost no change, and thus I assumed that the O.R.&N. service shown is nearly accurate for 1910. No schedules for the C.M.&St.P. were available; it was assumed that this transcontinental provided at least two daily trains across the region. Likewise, short lines were assumed to provide at least one daily train each way.

The Northern Pacific's Spokane-Lewiston passenger train wheeling through the Palouse country, *ca.* 1905-10. *(Photo courtesy of University of Idaho Library)*

A view of Moscow, Idaho, looking northeast from the college campus on a late winter day, about 1900. *(Photo courtesy of University of Idaho Library)*

took almost six hours, and the Lewiston passenger who sought a metropolis might well prefer to board the evening Pullman for the longer and more costly but far more comfortable journey down along the river to wake up the next morning in Portland. Walla Walla enjoyed similar services to the coast, while Spokane could be reached only via Pasco or the devious O.R.&N. route through the Palouse, an even more tedious trip than the Lewiston-Spokane run.

Thus in both Walla Walla and Lewiston the *Oregonian* competed with the *Spokesman-Review* as the metropolitan daily, and business houses advertising in the latter were often at a serious disadvantage in this rivalry. For Spokane's central position in the interior was an advantage only in the provision of services and of goods manufactured there from local products. Everything else had to be shipped in, and, much to Spokane's distress, even goods arriving from the East were likely to cost more in Spokane than in Seattle or Portland because the rates on shipments destined for ocean ports were often lower than on those to nearer but inland points (a practice made necessary, so the railroads claimed, by the competition of ocean shipping). Thus Spokane could dream of, but not really dominate, an Inland Empire extending clear to the Cascades and the Blue Mountains. Costs and convenience, as well as distance, made the area south of the Snake and west of the Columbia turn more readily to Portland and Puget Sound. Forty trains every day crossed or cut through the Cascade barrier, each a service in the ever more efficient linkage of coast and interior.

Such a pattern helps to explain another: the fact that all of the smaller cities—Wenatchee, Ellensburg, North Yakima, The Dalles, Pendleton, Walla Walla, Lewiston—were along the western and southern borders of the Great Columbia Plain. Each was in an intermediate commercial zone, protected by distance, terrain, and patterns of contact from the direct influence of either Spokane or the coastal cities. Each thus dominated a considerable local district, though each was in turn ultimately dependent upon the commercial, financial, and other services of metropolitan centers. And in fact Spokane's position within such a hierarchy was ambiguous: much larger and the focus of a greater, more diverse and productive area than any of the other inland cities and indeed the focus to a certain extent of some of them and of others in the mountain country, yet itself dependent to a degree greater than it would like to admit upon those still larger cities on the coast.

Despite these realities Spokane was not ready to concede that she must accept an empire so far short of her pretensions. The competition of Seattle and Portland, the discrimination of railroad rates, and the persistent and obvious dichotomy in so many interests between the coastal region and the interior prompted Spokane to raise once again the cry for a realignment of the political geography of the Pacific Northwest. The present boundaries were "so unnatural" as to cause "much injustice" and give rise to "a remarkable condition," claimed important spokesmen for the cause. "It is a singular fact that the people of the Inland Empire center their pride in the term 'Inland Empire' and hold the Inland Empire in their affections above their affections for their state." Not, it was hastily explained, because of any disloyalty to their state, but because they had an "identity of interests and resources" and a natural focus. Although it was commonly assumed that mountain ranges provided obvious boundaries, the Spokane Chamber of Commerce supported the idea that a boundary be established along the 120th meridian north from California, and another east from that line along the 45th parallel (Map 36). All south of 45 degrees would become the new state of Lincoln, Jefferson, Whitman, or some other appropriate name. Even though historical evidence of a long-standing desire for a separation, the legal possibilities, and much current enthusiasm could be marshalled in its support, such a change inevitably fostered dissention. For example, although Wenatchee, Ellensburg, North Yakima, and The Dalles might have good reasons to be reluctant about a state dominated by Spokane, the proposed boundaries would leave them as underprivileged stepchildren within their old states, which would be so altered as to make the coastal interests overwhelmingly dominant. And while most districts within the new state might be better served than before, the Umatilla and Grande Ronde could certainly wonder whether Spokane would be a better focus and capital than Portland and Salem. There were in fact so many issues and opinions, as well as technical problems, raised by the proposal that its chances for success were never very great. It was nonetheless an important expression both of the persistent division between coast and interior and more specifically of the newer patterns of organization created within the interior.[36]

[36] *Report of Committee on New State, Submitted to the Spokane Chamber of Commerce* (unpaged pamphlet; Spokane, *ca.* 1909). The use of straight lines for state boundaries was quite as "unnatural" in terms of terrain as those they

REGIONS AND LANDSCAPE

In none of these discussions, arguments, and claims did anyone speak of the Great Columbia Plain. The name was not quite gone nor the concept dead, but it had faded from common parlance and memory. It was likely to be used only by someone who had a geographical eye that searched for broad regions in surface and structure, such as the geologist, Frank Calkins, who accepted it as the proper name for a "broad topographic province" and explained the suitability of the century-old label: ". . . the inequalities of the surface, while relieving the monotony of the landscape, do not determine its character, nor make its designation as a great plain seem inappropriate to one familiar with the region." But by this time most people who lived in it or wrote about it were not familiar with it as a region. For the *Great Plain of the Columbia,* which for half a century had seemed so obviously a unit to most of its travelers and temporary residents, had gradually disappeared in the following half-century. Everything had worked against its integrity as a region. It had been parceled among three states, in a different pattern among three metropolitan spheres, and in a still different way among the three economies of the wheatlands, irrigation districts, and grazing areas. By 1910 most residents, whether engaged in politics or promotion, journalism or commerce, farming or stock raising, were likely to think of themselves as living in the *Inland Empire,* or the *Wheat Belt,* or the *Columbia Basin,*[37] or perhaps simply as in *Eastern Washington, Eastern Oregon,* or *Northern Idaho.* Even more commonly recognized were a group of smaller regions, essentially subdivisions of the Columbia Plain but parts so well established in the public mind as to obscure the whole: the *Palouse,* the *Walla Walla Country,* the *Big Bend,* the *Yakima,* the *Horse Heaven Coun-*

would replace, but the incongruous Idaho panhandle would be abolished and the choice of the 120th was commercially more realistic than the Cascades because it more nearly coincided with the western limits of Spokane's trade. For a useful general discussion of the idea, see W. F. Meier, "Will There Be a New State—Lincoln?" *World Today,* 12 (April, 1907), 400-403.

[37] Calkins, *Geology and Water Resources,* p. 14. This was written in 1902. The prominent and ambiguous modern term, *Columbia Basin*—used for the actual hydrographic region of the Columbia River system, for the areas directly affected by the Grand Coulee reclamation project, and for a more vaguely defined irrigation and hydroelectric realm—was not in common use in 1910. It seems at that time to have been used to refer to that portion of Oregon between the Columbia and the Blue Mountains, but it was a term used more by writers than by residents; e.g., *Oregon Farmer.*

try, the *Camas Prairie,* or the *Umatilla.* All of these designations, and especially the last set, were commonly regarded as more or less "natural" units and to those familiar with them connoted a particular landscape as well as location.[38]

And everywhere the visible scene was now to some degree a product of man as well as nature. It was a varied blend which reflected in innumerable details the differing character and age of settlement. The impress of man was most obvious in the small cities and towns spaced every few miles over the countryside, a few old enough and well placed that they seemed pleasantly embowered islands blended into the gross texture of nature, others such an ungainly jumble of bricks and boards standing starkly upon a plain that they seemed a harsh intrusion. Most of these settlements were connected one to another by steel rails, a pattern of lines now firmly etched into the face of the earth, curving in conformity with the greater shapes of its surface and cutting through and across more gentle swellings and swales. These clusters so laced together formed the grossest of man's visible networks upon the land, but this system was enveloped within the more subtle but comprehensive patterns of the rural countryside. Farmsteads dotted the landscape, thickly in the humid districts, more sparsely in the drier, in a fashion as varied as the towns: some nestled in a hollow of the hills, or shaded in a mature grove or orchard tract, or sheltered in a narrow canyon so as to seem a pleasing blend of man and land, while others, even in the best of country, appeared so crude, unsheltered, and unkempt as to suggest a poverty of pride and spirit amidst a bountiful nature. All around them the monotony of the prairie had been replaced by the variations of crop and fallow, field and pasture. The fences—brush lined in the older districts, naked posts and wires in the newer— marched straight across the steepest slopes, stamping a rectangular order upon the curving symmetries of nature, while the roads, dirt tracks for the most part—parallel strips of brush, weeds, and ruts— cut across the countryside to form a grid larger and less complete but expressing as vividly the relentless geometry of the national design. Such patterns were almost everywhere visible, though but

---

[38] This was true not only of residents but of the scientists who studied the patterns of physical and agronomic conditions. A good example of the recognition of such "more or less natural sub-divisions" is C. C. Thorn, "Moisture Conditions and Climatic Regions of the Inland Empire," *Washington Agriculturist,* 5 (November, 1911), 5-8, reprinted in *Pacific Farmers Union,* 3 (Dec. 8, 1911).

faintly in those last parcels which had been selected but never settled. Yet even there corner markers, claim shacks, and wagon tracks offered an incomplete but characteristic tracing of the same orderly plan.

Though it might have escaped the untrained eye, every foot of ground had been affected, if only indirectly, by the activities of man. Even those unwanted remnants of coulee and canyon, mountain slope and sandy waste, which not only had never been claimed but had apparently never been touched, were not quite the same, for the motley band of men's companions—plants, animals, birds, and insects—had penetrated every nook and cranny. The generations of horses, cattle, and sheep which had nibbled at every accessible browse, the cheat grass waving amidst the bunch grass, the ring-necked pheasant crowding the sharp-tailed grouse, the rat and the mouse, the earwig and the housefly, these and a host of others—some purposely imported, some unwanted, some as yet unnoticed—were agents in or adjuncts of the process of domestication.[39]

In the long view that process began when man first trod upon this part of the earth several thousands of years before; but its most significant phase began when Meriwether Lewis and William Clark looked upon and wrote about these "Wavering plains." A century later that process had so completely affected their region of the "Grait Plains of Columbia" that, while its form was still discernible in the patterns of the earth, it was disguised from the modern traveler and resident alike by many remarkable differences in dress, character, and name.

[39] See Buechner, "Biotic Changes in Washington," for an excellent review of such changes.

CHAPTER FIFTEEN

> But the more meaningful divisions are
> the fusions of people and place, of en-
> vironment, stock, economics, dialect,
> history, consciousness, and ways of life,
> which are called "regions" and "sub-
> regions."
>
> MAX LERNER

Perspectives:

History, Geography, and Culture

TRANSITION: 1910 TO THE 1960'S

DECEMBER 31, 1910, was certainly not the end of an era; yet changes
of major significance were under way. Some of the signs were at
hand, though probably largely unnoticed or unappreciated by residents of the region, other evidence would appear only when the
characteristics of this particular time were measured against trends
and developments of later years. Taking all of these things together,
the years on the eve of the First World War can be regarded as an
important transition from one era to another.

Stabilizations

One feature was apparent to anyone who could view the region
as a whole: little land remained unclaimed. Except for the irrigation districts the colonization era was at an end. All of the good land
had long since been settled, and any worth holding even on speculation had been snapped up during the first decade of the new century. The exact limits of successful farming were not as yet certain,
and indeed could be expected always to differ a bit from year to
year because of variations in the weather, prices, or farming practices, but recent crop failures all along the present frontier suggested
that further advance was unlikely. In that way the arid portion of
the Great Plain was being defined in the center of the region, a
"Columbia Desert" much smaller than the one encountered by fur

traders and thirsty travelers many decades before, but nonetheless real.

The fact that the region was running out of land carried a series of implications. The rural population was probably near its maximum, and indeed it might even decline, for despite vigorous promotion subdivision and diversification had not taken place in the grainlands, and the general trend was quite the opposite. Half a section (320 acres) was now an average-sized farm in the more humid districts, double that and more was common in the drier areas. And if the rural population was no longer expanding, then the towns dependent upon them were unlikely to grow. Larger farm incomes from better farming and higher prices could increase local trade, but there seemed little immediate prospect of either. Certainly the trade areas of most of the towns were by now pretty well defined, the outcome of town rivalries reasonably clear. New counties or railroads might alter the fortunes of a few places, but in view of other trends, despite the current agitations and rumors, these too might be more nearly stabilized than commonly realized.

Anyone who pondered these matters at the time did not have to wait many years for decisive evidence. All of those optimistic predictions of town and city expansion so prevelant around 1910 were doomed. The decade 1911-20 marked the peak of growth and the beginnings of decline in rural and town populations in the wheatlands, and the end of county formation and railroad construction. During the First World War wheat prices were high, times were good, and those farmers and townsmen well established in the region prospered, but the census of 1920 revealed clearly that the general expansion was at an end and the boom was over. Perhaps the most telling evidence was the fact that the city of Spokane, far from mushrooming on toward half a million, was stagnant: a growth of 67,554 during the previous decade was followed by an increase of 35 persons in the ten years after 1910. Even more shocking perhaps to those who had been so confident of perpetual progress was the actual reduction by 3,861 in Walla Walla's total, a loss of 20 per cent. All over the grainlands the trend was similar, if not always as severe. County populations were everywhere lower, those of the towns varied, some markedly decreased, most were stable, and only a few significantly increased. Almost every town in the Palouse lost population, with some of the larger ones in the best farming dis-

A townscape typical of the region and era. A view south along Third Street in Garfield, 1906. The three-story brick building shared by the First State Bank and the Garfield Mercantile Company (with the Knights of Pythias hall on the third floor) would surely have been regarded as a satisfying symbol of the progress of the town, as would the fresh poles ready to receive the lines of a new electric system. The teams farthest down the street are gathered at the town watering trough. *(Photo courtesy of Washington State University Library)*

Colfax, strung out for a mile along the bottom of the shallow canyon of the South Palouse, was recurrently plagued by floods, and this one of March, 1910, was one of the worst, making the new Whitman County courthouse seem like a moated castle as the waters swirl right over the Spokane and Inland Empire yards. *(Photo courtesy of Washington State University Library)*

trict, which had been well settled for twenty years or more, showing the greatest change. The Palouse had been particularly affected by speculation, not merely in real estate but in businesses and professions. The boom times after the turn of the century, the promise of diversification, the prospects for local industry, the assumed impact of electric railroads, and related movements, seem to have attracted more people to the towns than the trade of the ensuing years could sustain. Certainly the exodus was greater than could be accounted for by larger farms and a reduction in rural populations. The phenomenon was a kind of internal secondary wave of town speculation, which was not directly reflective of what was actually happening in the countryside.[1]

The fact that a number of towns in the drier districts increased in population during that same decade reflected the fact that in those areas town development in 1910 had not yet caught up with rural development, but it is evident from other data that by 1920 they were as clearly at or past the peak of their growth as were those in the Palouse. This change in the historical pattern of development was most vividly illustrated along the very edge of settlement. The census figures of 1920, which showed a marked reduction in the acres in grain in Grant, Adams, Franklin, Walla Walla, and Benton counties as compared with those of 1910, provided bland statistical evidence of the harsh fact of chronic failure all along that arid fringe at the center of the Great Plain. The entire inner margin of the wheatland crescent had shriveled in the perennial drought, and although the retreat was generally a matter of a few miles, it left behind not only a narrow swath of abandoned farms, moribund towns, and a weedy wasteland even poorer than the niggardly cover of the unplowed desert nearby, but also a broader belt in which settlers still worked the earth but with hopes subdued and progress stilled by the seeming certainties of nature's limitations.

Only where those limitations could be radically altered by man was growth continued and optimism sustained, and thus the Yakima Valley and Yakima city (the "North" now dropped from its name) emerged in that next decade as the leading area and center of what now seemed an anomalous progress. The city grew by another third

[1] The shrinking of Palouse City from 1,549 to 1,179 reflected the closure of the big lumber mill and shift of all its operations to Potlatch, but the declines in such substantial places as Genesee, Pullman, Garfield, and Oakesdale, as well as in nearly all the smaller towns, suggested a more general factor at work.

during those years, Wapato and Grandview tripled, Toppenish doubled in size, nearly all valley towns showed some gain, and the total population of Yakima and Benton counties increased by twenty-five thousand. Most of the lesser irrigation districts displayed a similar trend, with consequent increases in Wenatchee, Lewiston-Clarkston, and, less directly, Pendleton. Ellensburg was a conspicuous exception; centered in an irrigation district which had not expanded and which was more suited to hay than to horticulture, its small loss in population reflected the more general regional pattern.

Irrigation developments were also responsible for the only additional railroad branches. The Northern Pacific expanded its Yakima network with lines to Tieton and White Swan, and by an extension of the Grandview branch east to a connection with the main line below Prosser. In 1913 the Milwaukee built a branch along the Columbia to Hanford and another short stub to tap an anticipated development at Moses Lake. But in that same year the O.-W.R.R. &N. pulled up their spur to Waverly, a response to the failure of the sugar beet promotion in the Palouse, and although the Great Northern graded a line through Davenport and down Hawk Creek to the orchard tract near the mouth of the Spokane River, no steel was ever laid upon it. In 1914 a hundred miles of main track were built from Ayer Junction on the lower Snake up through the scabland channels to Spokane, but that tapped no new districts whatever and was simply the O.-W.R.R.&N.'s response to the challenge of the S.P.&S., for its old connection through the Palouse—piecemeal in origin, devious in route, and severely limited in capacity—could no longer compete for the Spokane-Portland traffic. But other often discussed cutoffs were never built, nor did any of the rumored invasions of the Pacific Northwest by other major companies come true.[2] As late as 1920 maps were being published showing new electric railroads as if they actually existed, but in fact none were built after 1910, and the largest in operation, the S.&I.E., was almost immediately in serious financial difficulties. Thus the era of railroad construction ended concurrent with the end of colonization, after forty years of closely related expansion.

[2] In December, 1910, the O.R.&N. was reincorporated as the Oregon-Washington Railroad and Navigation Company, still a Union Pacific subsidiary. Examples of the unrealized cutoffs were a Ritzville-Ellensburg line and one from Pullman westward down Union Flat Creek, each part of a Northern Pacific strategy to expedite shipments to the coast.

In 1915, as if carefully timed to be a symbol of, as well as a practical facility in, a new era, the long-awaited Celilo Canal was completed. But it proved a false sign and an ineffective agent, for although the waterway was now open from Pasco and Lewiston to the sea, the railroads remained in control of the traffic. To eliminate the portages was not enough; it would also be necessary to develop some facility of greater capacity and efficiency than the stern-wheel steamboats, which were a picturesque tie with the past rather than a promising hint of the future.

The stabilization of these patterns of settlement, population, and transport had certain political results. The idea of a new state for the Inland Empire floundered and soon faded again from public concern (to be revived as a topic, though not as a serious political agitation, in the 1930's); however, not only did the sense of a separation of interests between coast and interior remain, but the political tensions arising therefrom were accentuated by divergent population trends. While the interior stabilized, the coast continued to grow and logically sought a commensurate increase in political representation. Reapportionment became an especially important concern in Washington state, where the historic balance between the sections on either side of the Cascade had been relatively close. The shift in trends after 1910—the actual declines in population in all of the grain country—started a mounting pressure for change, but not until 1930, and then only by a public initiative rather than a dutiful legislature, was a change made. In the east only Yakima and Chelan were given increased representation, Spokane was left unchanged, all other areas lost. This reduction in political power was the inevitable price of population decline, given the political geography of the state. Locally the culmination of rural development was reflected in the stabilization of the county pattern. Despite several vigorous agitations for subdivision current in 1910, the creation in Idaho of Lewis County out of Nez Perce in 1911 was the only significant change thereafter.[3]

[3] The margin of victory for the initiative was fewer than 1,000 votes out of more than 230,000 cast. In eastern Washington, only Yakima, Kittitas, and Chelan counties cast majorities in favor. See J. Orin Oliphant, "Legislative Reapportionment in Washington," *Washington Historical Quarterly*, 22 (January, 1931), 3-25; and J. F. Roush, "Legislative Reapportionment in Washington State," *Pacific Northwest Quarterly*, 28 (July, 1937), 263-300.
Continued shift in regional population patterns resulted in a major political contest for reapportionment again in the 1950's; see Gordon E. Baker, "The

Transformations

Quite apart from the stabilization of broad patterns, signs of change of a very different sort were visible in 1910, quite obviously new, and certainly the focus of great interest, yet their implications could not be generally appreciated. The tractor was one. That the successful trials of the gasoline-powered track-laying machine marked the beginning of a new era in farming operations was suspected by some but could only be confirmed by the actual results. It took twenty years or more to complete that change, but when it was finished virtually everything about agriculture—its costs, scale, and methods, its labor requirements, rhythm of operations, and effects upon the soil—had been altered.

The passing of the work horse from the scene released several thousand acres in every district from the raising of fodder crops, which allowed a significant increase in the land devoted to wheat and barley. It was largely this internal expansion in acreage rather than any new colonization or improvement in average yields which accounted for the greater productions and exports during the 1930's. In those same years farmers in the more humid districts increasingly included field peas as a rotation crop, a leguminous plant which not only enlarged their incomes but helped to maintain the fertility of their soils. Peas are still part of the farming scene in those areas, but they have been reduced in importance by the more recent trend of direct nitrogen application and annual cropping. This substitution of fertilizer for fallow has so sharply increased both yields and acreages in crop that wheat production is now double what it was in 1910 with no increase at all in farming area. Such changes are the fruits of the formal research begun in the region more than half a century ago, and of the formal education of two generations of farmers' sons. The collaboration of scientist and farmer is now so close

---

Politics of Reapportionment in Washington State," *Eagleton Institute Cases in Practical Politics, Case 3* (New Brunswick, N.J., 1960).

Though Lewis County enclosed only a relatively small area, it reflected the local feeling of separateness of the residents of the Camas Prairie and the difficulties of communication with and the desire to be free from Lewiston. The town of Nez Perce was named the county seat, which probably accounts for the fact that it was the only agricultural community on the Prairie to gain rather than lose population during the period 1910-20. Clearwater County (with a seat at Orofino) was created in 1911 and Benewah County (St. Maries) in 1915 in response to developments in the lumber districts of northern Idaho and only barely touched the eastern margins of the Columbia Plain.

that one can glimpse the ideal of the future when every field is a test plot, every farm a laboratory, and every farmer a scientist.[4]

The automobile was a contemporary of the tractor but was the cause of far greater excitement, speculation, and interest to farmer and townsman alike. By 1910, for example, the *Up-to-the-Times Magazine* of Walla Walla, in keeping with its name, featured a special page each month entitled "Automobile News," full of information on new models, useful hints for owners, and the feats of local drivers. Although by then the automobile was a proven machine, it was not as yet a satisfactory vehicle. The biggest problem had nothing to do with motor or chassis but was simply the lack of decent roads, and this limitation was serious enough to keep the automobile an expensive gadget rather than a routine convenience. Even in the cities, where the taxicab had recently become an established service, a rainy spell might suspend operations, while in the country the roads were impassable for weeks at a time. The need for improvement was a matter of perennial concern. "Straw day"

[4] Figures and trends in wheat acreages, yields, production, shipments, and so forth, from about 1880 are presented in *Wheat Supply and Distribution in the Pacific Northwest* (Oregon Wheat Commission Statistical Bulletin No. 1) (Pendleton, December, 1956). For a more intensive geographical analysis of the 1930's, see Ben H. Pubols and Carl P. Heisig, *Historical and Geographical Aspects of Wheat Yields in Washington* (Washington Agricultural Experiment Station Bulletin No. 355) (December, 1937). The literature emanating from these recent decades of research is large. The most comprehensive summation is found in Carlton Raymond Schroeder, "The Physical Geography of the Palouse Region, Washington and Idaho, and Its Relation to the Agricultural Economy" (Ph.D. dissertation, University of California, Los Angeles, 1958); although focused upon one subregion, much of it is relevant to all the grainlands. An interesting brief review of trends in the rangelands, which describes the strong recovery of areas so seriously overgrazed by 1910, is G. John Chohlis, "Range Conditions in Eastern Washington Fifty Years Ago and Now," *Journal of Range Management,* 5 (May, 1952), 129-34. Schroeder's study is also a useful guide to the expanding literature on more basic matters of geology, as is C. D. Campbell, "Washington Geology and Resources," *Research Studies of the State College of Washington,* 21 (June, 1953), 114-53. The loessal character of most of the soil mantle of the grainlands is now generally accepted, but the source, time, and pattern of its deposition and the ways in which it has been reworked by other agents remain less certain. J. Harlan Bretz's theory on the origin of the scabland is commonly accepted, but with controversy on many of the details. Knowledge about these physical, as well as meteorological and biological, features has been greatly advanced in recent decades, yet each advance has raised new questions, and these detailed problems are no less puzzling to the scientists of today than were the larger general ones which faced those explorer-scientists who first reconnoitered the region a century and a half ago.

was an annual event in some counties, usually near the end of harvest when plenty of fresh material was available to scatter upon the "dust cursed" roads of late summer,[5] but it could be no more than a temporary expedient and was aimed as much at preventing the near suffocation of travelers as improving driving conditions for vehicles.

Nothing less than the reconstruction of the entire road network in the region, with careful attention to camber, drainage, and macadamized bed, would be necessary if the automobile were to become anything but a fair-weather luxury. But such a program was a staggering prospect. Roads were the responsibility of the counties, and the costs of comprehensive improvement seemed to these rural-dominated governments to be far out of proportion to any possible benefits. It was difficult to envision even a small part of the potentiality of the new instrument. The railroads so completely dominated all beyond mere farm-to-town movements that the very idea of through traffic on the roads was only gradually accepted as an important possibility.

And, again, not until 1910 and the years just after were the signs of a new era in transportation discernible. In that year, for example, the directors of the Washington State Good Roads Association decided that the state would have to assume the leading role and began a campaign for the creation of a state highway department. In 1912 the first map of the state showing "roads open to automobile travel" was compiled (Map 44), and the new department undertook to define a set of interregional routes and to begin their improvement. In the spring of 1910 the Oregon State Automobile Association and the Portland Motor Club, noting that "reliable road information" was "very scarce," jointly sponsored a reconnaissance of eastern Oregon in order to compile the first accurate map. The maps produced by such surveys vividly illustrated the fact that the first "through routes" were merely a series of local county roads, an alternating sequence of section-line straightaways and square corners zigzagging across the countryside. There were no markers, and the motorist venturing beyond his own locality had to consult his map at every crossroad. The first tour book of the American Automobile Association to include a traverse of the Columbia Plain was issued in 1912; its detailed map showed almost mile by mile those individual

[5] *Northwest Magazine*, 20 (August, 1902), 53.

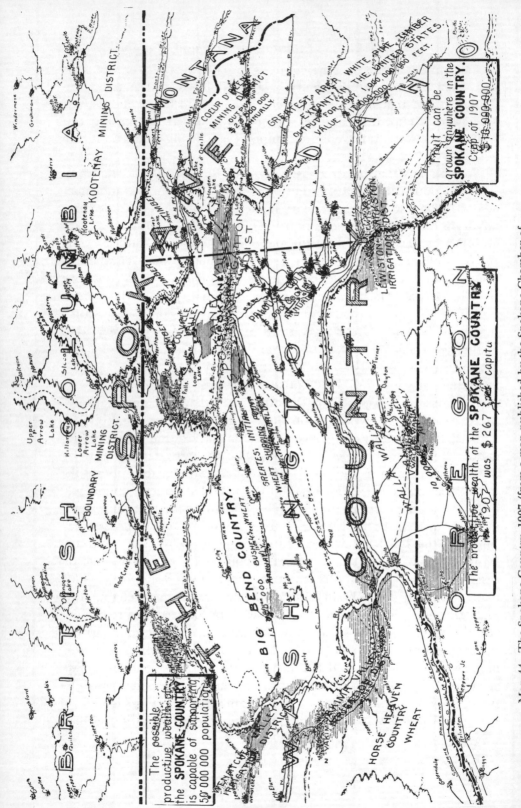

Map 44. The Spokane Country, 1907 (from a map published by the Spokane Chamber of Commerce in *Spokane and the Inland Empire*, N. W. Durham, *The Spokane and Inland Empire Commercial Encyclopedia*, 1909)

features needed to guide a driver between Spokane and Wenatchee (Map 45). That entire route was over unimproved roads, but such maps emboldened an ever increasing number of motorists to try them and thus began an ever greater demand for something better.[6]

While the application of the internal-combustion engine to field and road profoundly altered the character of life, permeated every corner of the Great Columbia Plain, and thus marked an important historical change, the geographical changes directly associated with those instruments were not radical. The enlargement of farms, reduction of rural populations, demise of hamlets, decline of small towns, and growth of cities, the expanding network of paved roads and competition of autos, buses, and trucks for the traffic of the railroads—these and a host of related changes were essentially no more than gradual modifications worked out within the basic spatial framework of local patterns established before 1910.

Yet there have been other kinds of changes, largely unforeseen fifty years ago and unrelated to any specific developments of that time, which have so drastically altered the geographical character of so large a portion of the Great Columbia Plain as to make present patterns seem discordant with that past. The arid center has undergone a remarkable transformation (Map 46). There some of the worst land of the region has been converted into some of the best, and the area afflicted with despair and decline in 1910 is now the locale of greatest confidence and growth.

Irrigation, which provided the first impetus for this change, was far from new to the region as a whole, but the Columbia Basin Project was so far beyond any of the other irrigation schemes in concept, size, and cost that it was hardly envisioned in 1910. Construction of Grand Coulee Dam was begun in 1933, but twenty years passed before the first commercial harvest was gathered from the initial block of lands irrigated by its waters.[7] A decade before

[6] Leon Starmont, "50 Years of the Good Roads Fight," *Spokesman-Review*, Oct. 10, 1948; *Arlington Record*, April 28, 1910.

[7] The first formal study of the idea of irrigating the Columbia Basin was undertaken in 1903, when the U.S. Reclamation Service began evaluation of proposals to bring water from the Spokane or Pend Oreille rivers. Such projects were generally regarded as beyond feasibility and excited little public interest, and after several years the government declared them unsuitable. About 1918 the Pend Oreille proposal was revived, and study of the Grand Coulee as another possibility was initiated. From that time on proponents of these two vied for recognition, and the prospect for some sort of Columbia Basin Project steadily gained assurance.

the first of these new farms were established a completely unforeseen development was suddenly added to part of the same area. In 1943 the federal government began the emergency construction of the Hanford Project to manufacture plutonium for atomic weapons. This huge operation was not only continued but has been enlarged and diversified since World War II, and the almost instantaneous emergence of a sprawling urban complex of nearly sixty thousand people out of what had been a hamlet and two towns totaling about six thousand is an indication of what the sudden injection of more than half a billion dollars and the provision of nine thousand jobs in one plant can do to a locality. Even more recent than Hanford are the dozen huge dams across the Columbia and lower Snake, all built since 1945, and more are definitely scheduled for the near future. These together with Grand Coulee Dam have made this arid stretch of the rivers the greatest producer of hydroelectric energy on the continent.

Because even in this arid fringe the initial colonization movement touched every locality and left at least a thin sprinkling of settlers and the beginnings of a few hamlets, the modern urban pattern shows—with few exceptions (such as Grand Coulee)—the same names and places, but all in radically different scale and proportion. Hamlets such as Warden, Quincy, and Othello, which for half a century struggled desperately to stay alive on the edge of the desert, were suddenly transformed into thriving towns; former small towns, such as Ephrata and Moses Lake, became small cities competing for commercial leadership of the whole basin. The Tri-City complex (Richland, Kennewick, Pasco) reflects the stimulus of all the forces of change—Hanford, the Columbia Basin Project, electric power, and navigation; while several older cities on the river (Wenatchee, The Dalles) or on the borders of this emergent central region (Walla Walla, Pendleton, Yakima) have been touched by one or more of these factors. The completion of dams already authorized will bring slack-water navigation to the mouth of the Clearwater and finally make the "Port of Lewiston" a reality instead of an empty pretension. Already downriver other historic ports of brief but lasting fame, such as Wallula and Umatilla, have been relocated in site and re-established in service, and similarly Almota and Penewawa may soon reappear in modern dress to serve the Palouse.

None of these developments is yet complete, but their combined

ROADS OPEN TO AUTOMOBILE
TRAFFIC 1912

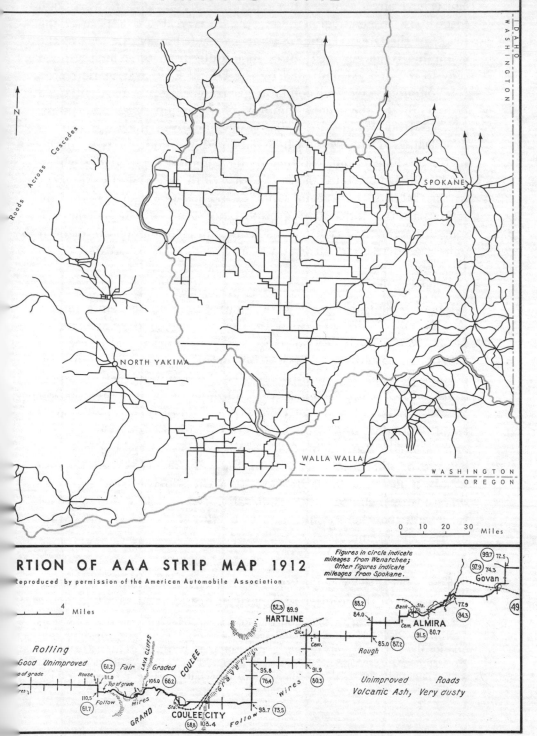

Map 45, above; Map 46, below

effects have already altered the general geographical patterns enough to give rise to new regional concepts. Fifty years or more after the image of the Great Columbia Plain had faded away, the idea of the Columbia Basin emerged out of its middle districts. At first applied only to the area encompassed by the Grand Coulee irrigation project, common usage and common geographical sense have enlarged it to embrace the whole complex of irrigation areas and power projects from Yakima to Walla Walla and from the Okanogan to The Dalles. That region which emerged so suddenly is so prominent, productive, and exciting in its potentialities that the wheatlands, which were once the source of wealth, pride, and excitement in this interior, now seem a narrowing periphery of staid towns, stable patterns, and lessening importance. And so it is by comparison, although a half century of science and technology have made it more productive than it ever was in the days of its greatest fame.

CONCLUSIONS

There remains the need to summarize some of the more important general features revealed by this century of development, to display more clearly certain sequences, continuities, and changes in geographic patterns. It will also be useful to review the more important external relationships, to assess the significance of influences from and ties to other regions. Beyond these, there is the temptation to set forth a kind of summary interpretation of the over-all character of the region, to try to determine its position within the patterns of a national culture. This last is a hazardous undertaking, not only because of difficulties inherent in the very objective but because ideally it demands an evaluation of matters beyond the limits of this study or included only peripherally. Nevertheless, so much here is relevant that there would seem to be almost a scholarly obligation to make the attempt.[8]

Frontiers

Ever since Frederick Jackson Turner spoke so eloquently of the significance of the frontier in American history, and subdivided the

[8] Anyone interested in this kind of panoramic perspective on the course of man in the Pacific Northwest should read Herman J. Deutsch, "Geographic Setting for the Recent History of the Inland Empire," *Pacific Northwest Quarterly*, 49 (October, 1958), 150-61; 50 (January, 1959), 14-25. These richly documented studies abound with fresh insight and are especially pertinent to some of the themes in this section.

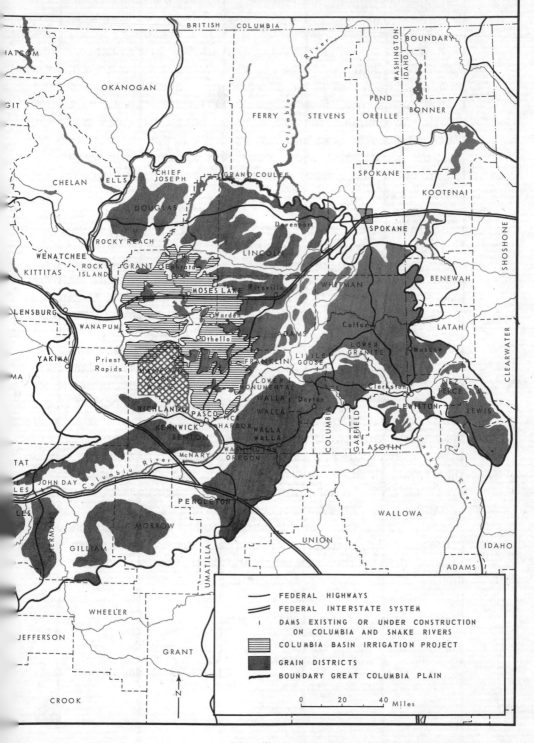

GREAT COLUMBIA PLAIN 1960

BRITISH COLUMBIA

WASHINGTON
IDAHO BOUNDARY

HATCOM

GIT

OKANOGAN

FERRY STEVENS PEND OREILLE BONNER

CHELAN WELLS CHIEF JOSEPH GRAND COULEE SPOKANE KOOTENAI

DOUGLAS

ROCKY REACH Davenport SPOKANE

WENATCHEE LINCOLN SHOSHONE

KITTITAS ROCK ISLAND GRANT Ephrata BENEWAH

MOSES LAKE Ritzville WHITMAN

LENSBURG WANAPUM Warden ADAMS Colfax LATAH CLEARWATER

YAKIMA Priest Rapids Othello LOWER GRANITE Moscow

MA FRANKLIN LITTLE GOOSE NEZ PERCE LEWIS

LOWER MONUMENTAL Clarkston LEWISTON

RICHLAND PASCO ICE WALLA WALLA Dayton GARFIELD

KENNEWICK HARBOR WALLA WALLA ASOTIN

BENTON WASHINGTON OREGON COLUMBIA

TAT McNARY

JOHN DAY Columbia River WALLOWA

LES PENDLETON

SHERMAN MORROW UNION IDAHO

GILLIAM ADAMS

WHEELER

JEFFERSON GRANT

N

CROOK

	FEDERAL HIGHWAYS
	FEDERAL INTERSTATE SYSTEM
I	DAMS EXISTING OR UNDER CONSTRUCTION ON COLUMBIA AND SNAKE RIVERS
	COLUMBIA BASIN IRRIGATION PROJECT
	GRAIN DISTRICTS
	BOUNDARY GREAT COLUMBIA PLAIN

0   20   40 Miles

Map 47

westward movement into the traders' frontier, the ranchers' frontier, the miners' frontier, and the farmers' frontier, his concepts have provided a framework for presentation and a challenge to analysis.[9] Each of these "frontiers" was apparent in the history of the Columbia Plain, though, as may be expected for any specific region, with numerous variations from a schematic sequence. Although the trader, the rancher, the miner, and the farmer represented groups differing in economic purpose, they did not in every case represent discrete phases in economic development. It may be useful to review the particular sequence which does appear in the region and to summarize the general geographical character of each developmental era (Map 47).

The very nature of the traders' frontier suggests continuity with, rather than an abrupt alteration of, previous geographical patterns. Such was the case in the Columbia interior, though the fact that most of the posts in and near the Great Plain were established more to guard strategic junctions and passageways than to trade with the natives prompted a selection of sites somewhat discordant with the pattern of Indian settlement. Had the main purpose of the companies in this area been to trade with the largest and wealthiest tribes, they would have been obliged to establish posts within the Nez Perces and Yakima areas, whereas Forts Okanogan and Nez Perces (Walla Walla) lay within the realm of relatively minor tribes (the latter post, despite its name, being a hundred miles west of the main grounds of the Nez Perces). Likewise, the shift from Fort Spokane to Fort Colvile was a move away from the main Indians in that sector to a site more advantageous for communications. Nevertheless, though these posts were no more than a group of connected points widely scattered within the region, together they drew upon and influenced all the Indians of the interior.

The missions represented a similar kind of pattern, but one more concordant with that of the tribal areas. That was to be expected in view of their purpose, although the most direct contact with the Indians was not always the controlling factor in choosing a location. The military posts, too, were necessarily related to the principal

[9] Frederick Jackson Turner, "The Significance of the Frontier in American History," *American Historical Association Annual Report for 1893* (Washington, D.C., 1893), pp. 199-227. The subsequent literature on the "Turner Thesis" is enormous. A recent useful guide to the main topics commonly treated, together with an extensive bibliography, is Nelson Klose, *A Concise Study Guide to the American Frontier* (Lincoln, Neb., 1964).

Indian areas and sought locations which combined some of the attributes of those of the two preceding systems: as with the missions, a patch of cultivable ground was important; as with the fur posts, command of communications was essential.

Thus the first half-century of white activity resulted in the establishment of nearly a score of settlements which were superimposed upon, and functioned in direct relationship to, the Indian pattern. Though varied in purpose, the fur, mission, and military settlements were of the same geographical type, each group being a series of separate but interconnected locations with no attempt at comprehensive occupation of the region. They were also sufficiently bound to similar factors (including one another) as to form a number of clusters: Fort Dalles-Wascopam; Fort Nez Perces-Waiilatpu-Fort Walla Walla; Lapwai-Kamiah-Fort Lapwai; Fort Spokane-Tshimakain; Ahtanum-Fort Simcoe; Fort Colvile (Hudson's Bay Company)–Fort Colville (United States Army). Of the others, Fort Okanogan stands most conspicuously alone, a testimony of the relative insignificance of the local Indians and of the singular importance of the New Caledonia connection.

Each of these posts was in some way designed to minister to the Indians, even if for very different purposes: one set established to placate and exploit, one to convert and civilize, and another to chastize and control. In no case (excepting only the local militia, who established a series of ephemeral camps) was there an intent to destroy. Yet viewed over the span of those years, from the standpoint of the Indians all of these points of contact take on the appearance of festering sores whose influences spread gradually and insidiously to infect whole tribes with disease, economic distortion, and social disintegration. In time these tribal areas, which provided the general framework for the basic human geography of the region, would be largely dissolved, leaving only the several Indian reservations scattered along the margins of the Columbia Plain, persisting as deformed remnants of that long-established pattern.

The miner, the stockman, and the farmer appeared simultaneously in the region. All were in the vanguard of that general colonization movement which would result in a comprehensive spread of settlers over the countryside. Each group can be viewed as representing a separate sequential phase in the history of development only in terms of relative importance and the differing length of time it took each to become firmly established. The miners swarmed through the region and stamped their mark immediately upon certain localities; stockmen and farmers came along with them, anxious to serve their needs; but it took several seasons to stock the ranges and even longer to get an agricultural nucleus implanted. Although in the usual schematic presentations of the frontier sequence, the initiation and development of towns is considered to be a phase which follows in response to agricultural colonization, here the merchants and townsmen or other professions accompanied the miners, and the towns grew as a concurrent part of the whole process.[10]

The mining frontier was of the same geographical type as that of the fur trade, mission, and military systems. The mines themselves were beyond the margins of the Plain, and thus the imprint was one of a few points connected across the region. Although it had no necessary tie with the Indians (whose patterns of regional distribution had been largely, but not wholly, disrupted by 1859), there was a close geographical continuity with the earlier systems because of the obvious value of their facilities and the legacy of their experiences. The river and the paralleling wagon road between The Dalles and the Walla Walla Valley had been the basic axis of all. The army had initiated steamboat navigation on the upper river just in time to demonstrate its utility for the mining rush; near each end of that segment Fort Dalles and Fort Walla Walla became obvious sites for towns, providing security and positions as strategic for servicing interior mining districts as they had been for commanding military operations. The focus of activity upon these sites and the demands of garrisons and townsmen offered a logical impetus to stockmen and farmers. Of the two locales, the Walla Walla Valley was physically superior for ranching and agriculture, and its location was closer to and generally more advantageous for contact with the various mountain mining districts which actually provided the main market. Thus there was an important degree of historical continuity in geographical patterns, linking through various intermediate activities such seemingly disparate groups as fur traders and farmers.

The Walla Walla Valley was the principal nucleus of both the ranchers' frontier and the farmers' frontier, and these two were not

[10] This does not make the Columbia Plain unusual but is further evidence that the stereotyped sequence does not fit much of the American frontier. Richard C. Wade, *The Urban Frontier: The Rise of Western Cities, 1790-1830* (Cambridge, Mass., 1959), which opens with the statement, "The towns were the spearheads of the frontier," is a prominent example of the growing volume of studies emphasizing the role of speculators, planners, and merchants.

only similar in specific locale of origin but were of the same general geographical type—each a comprehensive use of area, tending to spread contiguously outward from a center rather than to be merely an occupation of selected points. But they differed one from another in detail, and though simultaneous in their initiation, they were unequal in the rate and pattern of their expansion. The stockmen spread out quickly while the farmer followed slowly, and although the farmer ultimately overtook the rancher in all but the most arid and rugged sections, it was not simply a case of identical regional patterns unfolding at different rates of expansion, for there were significant differences in the sequence of districts occupied by the two frontiers. The principal discordance arose from the fact that the Yakima Valley and the various canyons and valleys tributary to the Columbia below Walla Walla provided ample grass and especially good wintering grounds for livestock, but were much too arid and barren in appearance to attract early agricultural colonists. Thus, while the stockman quickly occupied much of the southern portion of the Great Columbia Plain and later expanded northward (though skirting the arid center until last), the farmers clung to the humid eastern margins and expanded in a kind of arcuate pattern across the whole northern part before gradually probing inward upon the drier western districts. The desire for access to the most favorable combination of soil, terrain, water, and timber, plus the pressing need for transport facilities, led also to a more discontinuous pattern of expansion. At almost any scale the map of agricultural colonization would display several nuclei rather than a continuous outward spread from a single major center.

The general rural colonization movement cannot be regarded as one great inflow of settlers continuing until the region was filled. The cattlemen stocked at least the best of the ranges of the southern districts within ten years after entry and most of the remainder of the region in another ten, but the farmers took almost fifty years to occupy their smaller portion of the same realm. Nor was this latter by any means a steady expansion. Rather it was characterized by a slow experimental beginning, which gathered strength as the richness of the rolling hills was realized and the possibilities of downriver export were demonstrated, then was sharply accelerated in the late 1880's in conjunction with the rapid extension of railroads, reached a peak around the turn of the century as speculators and farmers competed for the remaining unplowed lands, and then came to an abrupt halt in the face of sustained crop failures along the margins of the last remnant in the arid center. Examined in greater detail, this over-all sequence is punctuated by pulsations of varying strength resulting primarily from national economic forces which affected prices and the inflow of people and capital.[11]

These general patterns of expansion of the ranching and farming frontiers were a reflection not only of the differing attractiveness of the various districts within the Columbia Plain, but also of the particular portals through which the colonists entered the region. As long as the Columbia Gorge and the Oregon Trail across the Blue Mountains were the chief avenues, the Walla Walla Valley persisted as the principal focus of development and point for dispersal into new lands. Once the railway spanned the Northern Rockies, however, the Spokane Valley became a second and rival center. The almost instantaneous rise of Spokane Falls as the largest city in the interior was a vivid measure of the abrupt alteration of regional orientations. Within the wheatlands perhaps the clearest expression of that impact upon the geography of colonization was the expansion of settlers westward across the northern Big Bend along the axis provided by the Washington Central branch from Cheney to Coulee City. Had there been no heavy inflow through the Spokane portal and no booming city in that valley, the northern Big Bend would almost certainly have been colonized more slowly, tapped by feeder lines from the south, and become oriented directly toward the Pasco–Walla Walla area.

Portals and Routes

A review of the portals and routes by which the Great Columbia Plain was linked to regions beyond its mountainous borders during the course of these several frontier eras reveals persistence, change, and fluctuation (Map 48). The Columbia Gorge, nature's breach through the Cascade barrier, was consistently important, a major trafficway in all eras, its significance modified only in the railway age by competing lines across the mountains to Puget Sound. The Oregon Trail across the Blues was an avenue little less continuous

[11] The clearest example of a special factor which distorted the "natural" flow of settlers was the Nez Perces Indian Reservation. Enclosing a rich humid country reasonably accessible to water transportation, it delayed the colonization of most of the Camas Prairie by as much as twenty years. Its sudden opening precipitated the best example of a genuine "land rush" in the interior.

FRONTIER PATTERNS
AND MOVEMENTS

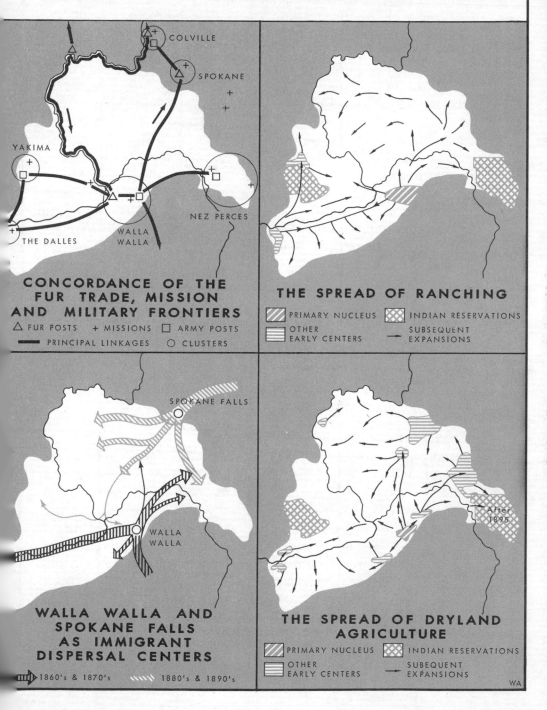

CONCORDANCE OF THE FUR TRADE, MISSION AND MILITARY FRONTIERS

COLVILLE

SPOKANE

YAKIMA

THE DALLES

WALLA WALLA

NEZ PERCES

△ FUR POSTS   + MISSIONS   □ ARMY POSTS
━━ PRINCIPAL LINKAGES   ○ CLUSTERS

THE SPREAD OF RANCHING

PRIMARY NUCLEUS   INDIAN RESERVATIONS
OTHER EARLY CENTERS   SUBSEQUENT EXPANSIONS

WALLA WALLA AND SPOKANE FALLS AS IMMIGRANT DISPERSAL CENTERS

SPOKANE FALLS

WALLA WALLA

▶ 1860's & 1870's   1880's & 1890's

THE SPREAD OF DRYLAND AGRICULTURE

After 1895

PRIMARY NUCLEUS   INDIAN RESERVATIONS
OTHER EARLY CENTERS   SUBEQUENT EXPANSIONS

WA

Map 48

in use, if not quite equal in importance. It was never more than a branch line for the British fur trade (and some of the Snake country expeditions used alternate routes), but once opened to wagon traffic it became the major American passageway, briefly (before the California gold rush) the actual main line of the westward movement, and thereafter the Pacific Northwest's principal link with the main transcontinental trunk line of the nation.

On the other hand, the historical role and importance of the Spokane portal varied greatly. The scabland channels and connecting glacial valleys provided easy natural passageways linking the Great Plain with the labyrinthine trenches of the northern Rockies, but the fact that they did not provide a direct link with the Columbia left the Spokane Valley eccentric to the main waterway. Because of the importance of the Columbia for the fur trade, Fort Colvile provided a more convenient junction of land and water routes than Spokane, even though the latter offered more direct access to several important districts to the northeast. Had the transcontinental axis of that system crossed the Rockies at a point south of Athabasca Pass, the importance of the upper Columbia would have been much reduced and that of the Spokane Valley correspondingly magnified (the original Fort Spokane was founded under such circumstances, before either Athabasca Pass or the upper Columbia had been tested). Similarly, had the Mullan Road become a major trafficway between the upper Missouri and the Columbia, the Spokane Valley would have been a rival of the Walla Walla from the beginning of farmer colonization instead of having to wait a quarter of a century for the railroad to make it so.

When the Northern Pacific did arrive, it provided the nearest parallel to the original Missouri-Columbia link marked out by Lewis and Clark, but the fact that its builders chose to follow the easier grades of the Clark Fork rather than the shorter but more difficult route across Lolo Pass to the Clearwater condemned Lewiston to continued insignificance, while it revived and accentuated the importance of Spokane. Had the international boundary been farther north, Spokane would probably have become an even greater focus of traffic in the railway age, drawing trade along the route of the present Spokane International in greater volume from a wider area. Similarly, the position of that boundary no doubt reduced the flow along the Okanogan Valley. However, here the interdiction was probably not great, for although nature provided a broad north-south trench, there was little basis for traffic after the diversion of the New Caledonia brigades. The cattle drives to the Cariboo mines in the 1860's marked the only revival. After the fur era no use was made of the Columbia upriver from its junction with this route, which meant that no town ever arose upon the site of old Fort Okanogan, despite Ross Cox's expectation. The situation was similar directly south at the opposite corner of the Plain. The Deschutes, like the Okanogan, was unnavigable, and although it flowed through a narrow deep canyon instead of a glacially broadened valley, the trail southward along the edge of the forested Cascades was no more difficult than that in the north. The fur parties probed this route, and Fremont tested and mapped it for hundreds of miles on along the base of the Sierra Nevada, but it led to nothing. The fact that trails branching westward threaded the ranges to the Sacramento Valley was of little import, for there was no economic basis for direct trade or travel overland between California and the Great Columbia Plain. What traffic there was moved more cheaply and conveniently by water or by way of the Willamette Valley. The frantic construction of parallel railroads up the canyon of the Deschutes in 1910 was a competition for traffic envisioned on this "inside route," but not actually awaiting at the time.

The Cascade pass routes to Puget Sound were entirely a product of the railroad era. Despite an occasional early traveler, company of troops, or emigrant wagon, they were of no general significance until the 1880's. Although such abortive schemes as the Seattle and Walla Walla Railway tried to reach eastward specifically to tap the Great Columbia Plain, that region was relatively incidental to the three companies which finally did link it to Puget Sound. Each of these was headed across the continent to a Pacific port, and thus they cut more or less directly across the Plain along routes which for the most part had never been used before.

Viewed broadly, therefore, these transcontinental railroads introduced the first basic departure from the route patterns of the fur-trade era. All before them was reflective of the basic Columbia system: major branches from the northeast and the southeast joining in the interior to form a single trunk line through the Columbia Gorge. Even the first railroads (The W.W.&C.R., O.R.&N., and the Wallula-Spokane segment of the N.P.) followed this pattern.

The old and the new gathered to meet the Northern Pacific passenger train at the Lewiston depot in 1909. On streets like this the automobile would quickly replace the horse-drawn carriage; on country roads it would for some time yet be of limited practicality. *(Photo courtesy of Northern Pacific Railway Company)*

The later northern transcontinentals opened new avenues to the sea and suddenly brought the Columbia Plain into the sphere of Puget Sound as well as the lower Columbia, cementing a new geography of competition which has been as important to the development of the region as it has to the ports which have sought its trade.

This review of routes and portals offers ample evidence of how "accidental," "illogical," and unpredictable is the impress of man's patterns upon the lineaments of nature. Had American companies rather than British dominated the fur trade of Oregon, had the Blackfeet and Sioux not impeded the advance up the Missouri, had the international boundary been drawn along another line, had any number of human circumstances been other than they were and the patterns of development in the Great Columbia Plain would have been different. Despite the bold relief of nature's frame of mountains and valleys, passes and canyons, the resultant human geography is explicable only in terms of particular groups of people working out their particular programs of action within the particular circumstances of their history.

Cultural Influences

The significance of these routes must be measured in terms of what has moved along them. The main commodities for any particular era are sufficiently obvious as to require no summation. What may be loosely termed "cultural influences" ("culture" in the broad anthropological sense) are more elusive, but so significant that an attempt must be made to interpret how they are related to these various interregional connections and how they have left their mark upon the patterns of development in the Great Columbia Plain. The attempt will necessarily be suggestive rather than definitive, a general schematic framework for thinking rather than a final distillation from detailed analysis (Map 49).

At the time of the arrival of the first white explorers, the Indians of the Columbia interior had two major interregional contacts with other Indian cultures. One was stable in type and fixed in place, the other relatively new and dynamic in impact, but intermittent and diffuse in point of encounter. The first centered upon The Dalles–Celilo Falls, that old, narrowly focused conjunction of coastal and interior peoples; the second refers to the contacts maintained by the Indians of the southeastern border of the Columbia Plain with those of the Plains culture far to the east. Influences carried into the region along the several trails from the upper Snake River country were powerful in effect, promising in time to revolutionize the life of all of the tribes of the interior as they had already transformed those of the Nez Perces and Cayuse. In a broad view, that inexorable wave of change spreading across the Columbia Plain at the beginning of the nineteenth century was but an outer ripple from the impact of a dramatic new encounter between cultures which had taken place in central Mexico nearly three centuries before. It was in fact the ramification of a single element introduced at the time. The horse had been diffused slowly northward, had become a catalyst for change among the Indians of the southern Great Plains, and was then spread on from tribe to tribe, each incorporating the animal into their own patterns largely in imitation of those from whom they received it. The horse reached the Columbia country by way of the Snake River Plains, and the cultural influences from that direction were thereafter sustained by the seasonal forays of the Nez Perces and others to the buffalo country. In this way, life in this far northwestern region was being remolded into patterns similar to those of the Indians east of the Rockies. Culturally the Great Columbia Plain was becoming a distant western compartment of the Great Central Plains.

The fur trade, as it finally developed in the Columbia interior following the brief competitive opening phase, represented a cultural importation from the northeast. The North West Company and Hudson's Bay Company were similar in character, a distinctive complex which may appropriately be termed "Canadian Northwoods culture," an amalgam of English capital, Scottish leadership, and French-Canadian–Indian labor. Developed empirically in the wooded, water-laced country east of the Rockies, it was not so well suited to conditions, natural or human, on the Pacific slope, as was evidenced by nagging problems with equipment, diet, transportation, and relations with local Indians. The North West Company exhibited the strains of these incongruities between the old cultural system and the new region, Simpson's energetic reforms were in part a calculated response to them, and the result was a "Pacific subculture," which became stabilized as a special variant within the general Canadian pattern.

The phase and area of operations most radically affected were those involved in the Snake country expeditions, and that change was a direct response to the influences and threat from contacts with the quite different "American fur trade culture." Those ponderous annual Snake country parties were a blend of Canadian and American characteristics: carefully organized and cohesive, as might be expected of the former, but mobile, trapping rather than trading for furs, and ruthless in their exploitation, as was characteristic of the latter. Here the Canadian system took on features of the American in order to compete, and it was an interregional contact not unlike that of the Indian pattern it overlapped. In each case the encounter between cultures took place in the same general locality, and while the impact of the American fur trade upon the Canadian system was nothing like that of the horse upon the Columbia Plains Indians, it was a diffusion along the same corridor, and it could be viewed as the prelude to other American influences which would force change upon and finally oust Canadian culture from that region.

The lower Columbia was also a focus of interest to both the fur traders and the Indians but with an important difference in location and character; Forts George and Vancouver represented a shift downriver, away from the age-old environmental boundary between coastal and interior regions and cultures, to a convenient transport contact between riverine and oceanic shipping. Though vessels from

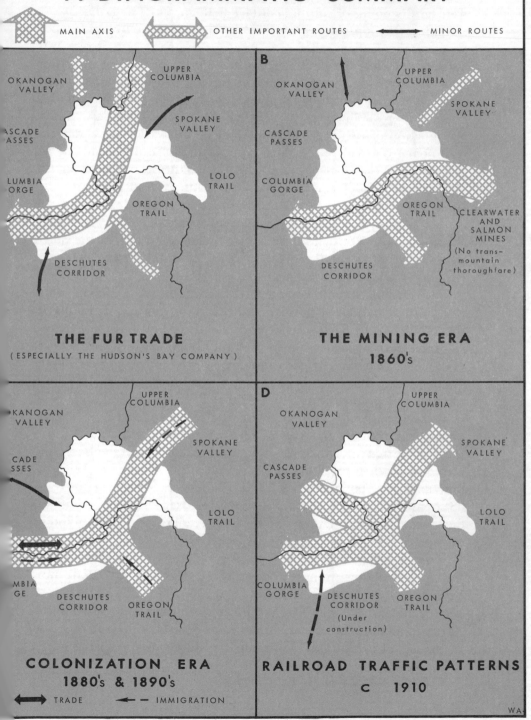

ROUTES AND PORTALS
A DIAGRAMMATIC SUMMARY

MAIN AXIS   OTHER IMPORTANT ROUTES   MINOR ROUTES

A

OKANOGAN VALLEY

UPPER COLUMBIA

SPOKANE VALLEY

CASCADE PASSES

COLUMBIA GORGE

LOLO TRAIL

OREGON TRAIL

DESCHUTES CORRIDOR

THE FUR TRADE
(ESPECIALLY THE HUDSON'S BAY COMPANY)

B

OKANOGAN VALLEY

UPPER COLUMBIA

SPOKANE VALLEY

CASCADE PASSES

COLUMBIA GORGE

OREGON TRAIL

CLEARWATER AND SALMON MINES

(No trans-mountain thoroughfare)

DESCHUTES CORRIDOR

THE MINING ERA
1860's

C

OKANOGAN VALLEY

UPPER COLUMBIA

SPOKANE VALLEY

CASCADE PASSES

LOLO TRAIL

COLUMBIA GORGE

DESCHUTES CORRIDOR

OREGON TRAIL

COLONIZATION ERA
1880's & 1890's

TRADE   IMMIGRATION

D

OKANOGAN VALLEY

UPPER COLUMBIA

SPOKANE VALLEY

CASCADE PASSES

LOLO TRAIL

COLUMBIA GORGE

DESCHUTES CORRIDOR (Under construction)

OREGON TRAIL

RAILROAD TRAFFIC PATTERNS
c 1910

W.A.

Map 49

America and other nations occasionally called, these fur-trade ports were hardly points of cultural contact analogous to The Dalles.

Within this superimposition of the patterns of the fur trade upon those of the Indians, there was one especially critical direct link between the two: the horses of the Nez Perces, Cayuse, and Yakima which became an essential resource for the Columbia interior fur trade. It was an intercultural connection formed near the junction of the two great branches of the Columbia, and it was, essentially, the junction of two streams of cultural influence flowing across the continent from widely separated sources and spreading into the region along those branches: a north-woods culture nurtured in the St. Lawrence Valley and Hudson's Bay country, and the horse culture of the Indians, diffused north and west from Mexico and the central plains. Because the physical environment of the Columbia Plain was more like that of the central plains than that of the north woods, the animal of the plains became essential to the success of the north-woods system in that area.

The missionaries also represented the influx of a pair of distinctive cultural influences through those same entryways, stemming in this case from the St. Lawrence and New England, but their tenure was sufficiently ephemeral as to warrant no emphasis in this general assessment. The soldiers who came after stayed longer but were soon so completely enveloped in the swirl of the mining rush and colonization as to leave no distinctive impress.

Those abrupt new movements of the 1860's opened new interregional connections, and the pattern of cultural importations was thereby shifted in emphasis. The mining era bore the stamp of California. When the *San Francisco Bulletin* of November 13, 1862, described the population at The Dalles as being composed of "Saxon, Celt, Teuton, Gaul, Greaser, Celestial and Indian," it was describing a medley familiar to its local readers, and probably most of those described, excepting only the Indians, were actually from California. There were many from the Willamette also, and some of the annual inflow from the East along the Oregon Trail now branched off into the interior, but "a stratum of Californians was to be seen everywhere, and these produced throughout the region a similarity in methods of mining, in manners of society, in interests, and in the sort of institutions that tended spontaneously to spring up."[12]

[12] Trimble, *Mining Advance*, pp. 10, 140-41.

California also contributed to the cattle industry of the Columbia Plain, although not so directly or comprehensively as to the mining industry. At first the ranges were stocked primarily with cattle driven in from the Willamette Valley, which were a mixture of Spanish longhorns from California and "American" (largely British) stock which had been driven overland (and the Hudson's Bay Company had brought in some by sea). The Californian element in these herds was definite, for Ewing Young's famous northward drive of several hundred head (630 arrived safely) from the Sacramento Valley in 1837 provided the first large nucleus for western Oregon herds. Nevertheless, while there were also later increments from the south, the continual mixing of these two strains altered both into a general type of "Oregon" cattle in which the Spanish ancestry was subdued by the British. In general, this geographical and historical sequence of expansion of the range and ranch cattle industry in the Pacific coast region paralleled developing patterns east of the Rockies. The Spanish cattle were derived from a common nucleus in central Mexico; California and south Texas were analogous frontier compartments of Mexican ranching; northward drives from those areas brought Spanish herds into contact with American cattle along the eastern wooded margins of the central plains in Kansas, Missouri, and Iowa just as in the Willamette Valley; and the resultant blended stock was spread onto the open ranges of Nebraska and southeastern Dakota, just as it was taken from wooded western Oregon eastward into the Columbia grasslands. Ultimately these two separate streams were brought together when the east-moving trail herds from Oregon encountered those from Texas and the Midwest in the northern plains of eastern Montana and North Dakota.[13] The principal contrast was in the continuous importation of Texas stock northward to the Great Plains, as compared with the insignificance of California stock after the very early period of Oregon developments.

Examined as a "culture" the cattle industry was a matter of methods and equipment as well as animals. Here the detailed characteristics, sources, and diffusions are not quite so clear, but certain general patterns seem apparent. Few, if any, elements of Mexican ranching culture came north from California along with the Spanish cattle.

[13] Osgood, *Day of the Cattleman*, pp. 27, 92-93. It should be added that there was also a continual importation of Midwest breeding stock into the Pacific Northwest, a movement especially important in quality if not in numbers after the completion of rail connections.

The drives were sporadic buying trips rather than annually recurrent encounters and involved no sustained intermingling of the two peoples. Furthermore, upon arrival the cattle were distributed among the farmers. No open range or extensive ranching industry was established in the Willamette, and even if attempted the differences in physical conditions would have precluded close similarity with Mexican operations. The stockmen who first occupied the ranges of the Columbia Plain were largely Willamette farmers who had managed cattle—often half-wild stock left to roam in the woods —as a common part of their routine, and their methods in the interior were empirical adaptations to local conditions and larger numbers. So, too, the trailing of herds to the mining camps was learned by doing, and served as good preparation for the larger movements eastward in the 1870's. Exactly when and to what extent the use of the rope as a lasso, the horned saddle, high-heeled boots, and other practices and regalia of Spanish origin appeared in the region is not clear, but they were almost certainly derived from Texas rather than California. The cooperative roundup was not a common feature until the stockmen had moved in upon the more arid central district of the Big Bend, and that technique may have been learned from contacts with the Texas-trained Wyoming cattlemen who were teaching those from the mountain valleys of western Montana how to operate on the open ranges of the high plains in eastern Montana.[14] It seems plausible to suggest that the methods, equipment, dress, behavior, and lingo commonly considered to be characteristic of the American cowboy and the cattle industry (nearly all of which were borrowings or adaptations from a Mexican pattern), were only gradually spread into the Columbia interior. It was probably long after the peak of the "cattleman's frontier" in that area that the "cow camps" became "ranches," and some (but not all) "stock pens" became "corrals," while a "string" of Columbia saddle horses never did become a "remuda." Such a cultural diffusion—spreading westward along the general path of the Oregon Trail, following the initial contacts with the cattlemen of the plains along the North Platte, Big Horn, and Powder rivers—is reminiscent in pattern if not in impact of that of the Indian era and of the spread of the horse culture northward and westward from those same Texan and Mexican sources.

The first farmers of the 1860's, like the stockmen, were from the

[14] *Ibid.*, pp. 48, 88.

Willamette. They brought with them seeds, cuttings, nursery stock, and equipment, and set about to farm in eastern "Oregon" just as they did in western. Theirs was the agriculture of Midwestern emigrants, modified only by the failure of Indian corn to thrive in the cooler and drier summers of Oregon. Corn failed in the interior also, though it was tested annually for many years by new immigrants directly from the Midwest; despite the absence of that staple, however, the initial agriculture in the Walla Walla Valley was largely an unconscious imitation of that of Kentucky, Illinois, or Missouri: a small farm of varied crops and livestock, garden, orchard, and shade trees centered in the rich bottomlands along a running stream. The failure of corn magnified the emphasis upon wheat from the beginning, and discovery of the fertility of the hills and of an expanding export outlet made possible the rapid emergence of a wheat-specialty region which bore little resemblance to its midwestern antecedents.

As a result of the emphasis on wheat, the influence of California became ever more prominent. The first standard variety, Little Club, was a Spanish wheat introduced by way of California, as was Australian Bluestem, the first staple of the drier districts. The whole system of the wheat economy was largely an imitation of that in the Sacramento Valley, which had gone through a sequence of trial and expansion about a decade in advance of the Columbia Plain. When a local editor, in a reply to prospective immigrants, stated that "Eastern machinery is useless here," he was merely giving cryptic and exaggerated emphasis to that fact. The plows, harrows, seed drills, mowers, rakes, and wagons were basically no different from those used east of the Rockies, but the larger farms and one-crop emphasis fostered the development of much larger implements and a system of gang farming (that is, three, four, eight, or a dozen plows working the same huge field) which had become symbols of Californian grain agriculture. Twine and wire binders of eastern manufacture were common in the eastern Palouse and Camas Prairie, but the header system, which was the standard harvesting method everywhere else, was a Californian borrowing. So, too, was the combine (needing only the attachment of leveling devices to fit it for work on the rolling Columbia hills) and the track-laying "caterpillar" tractor, which together provided the essential instruments for a revolution in the agricultural economy. The marketing system was also an extension of practices already established in California: the use of sacks instead of bulk shipments, the long low warehouses or platforms instead of the towering elevator, the early importance of the sternwheel riverboats, and the ocean wheat fleet of sailing vessels connecting directly to the English market.[15]

Not only was the wheat economy an expression of Californian influence, but this was also probably true of the program of those who preached the need for and virtues of diversification and the transforming glories of irrigation. Although the small mixed farm was an old American ideal, the Columbia Plain as a potential cornucopia of sugar beets, wine grapes, fruit, truck, and dairy products could best be illustrated by the actualities of California, where by 1910 diversification and irrigation had reduced bonanza wheat farming to a minor part of the agricultural scene.

The most obvious influence of the Middle West upon the mature grain agriculture of the Columbia Plain was the dry farming movement. But although that distinctive product of the Nebraska and Montana plains was received with enthusiasm by many, it was soon discovered that the system of tillage devised for east of the Rockies could not simply be imported and applied in the far West but had to be experimentally adjusted to the peculiarities of local conditions.

In these ways the "farming culture" of the Great Columbia Plain evolved as a distinctive blend of Californian and middle western elements. The physical characteristics of the region would accommodate some imports from both regions but not the transfer of a complete agricultural system from either. In its most critical physical feature, the seasonal rhythm of winter moisture and summer drought, it was more like California; but in the cold of its winters and the thick grass and deep soils of its wetter districts it was more akin to the humid prairies of Illinois and Iowa. Yet in detail—and a successful agriculture requires a close adjustment to those details— in each of these and other features, as in the whole, the region was unique.

[15] F. Dale Higgins, "John M. Horner and the Development of the Combined Harvester," *Agricultural History*, 32 (January, 1958), 14-24. The riverboats themselves represented the Hudson and Mississippi traditions adapted to California conditions. As Randall Mills put it, "the gold rush that made steamboating on the Sacramento necessary, made steamboats on the Columbia and Willamette practicable," *Sternwheelers*, p. 14. The engines for the first such vessels built in Oregon were imported from San Francisco. The first downriver export in 1867 was sent to San Francisco to tie into the established California export network.

Comparisons with the Middle West

The geographical sequence of agricultural colonization in the Columbia Plain was in many ways an enactment on a smaller stage of that same drama of pioneering so famous in the Central Grasslands of the Middle West: settlers from the woodlands first occupying the more humid borders of the grasslands, then gradually spreading ever farther, until finally halted by the arid region whose margins they defined by their own failures (Map 51). All the familiar problems characteristic of the larger region appear in the smaller also, but the difference in scale usually mitigated their severity in the Columbia Plain. The scarcity of wood and the consequent problems of housing, fuel, and fencing were common to both, for example, but even though in the Columbia Plain there was considerable talk and some experiment with thorn hedges, and some use of makeshift dugouts and a few sod houses, the rich pine forests fringing every side were so accessible to the best prairie lands that the early settlers were not seriously handicapped; and by the time later home seekers were pushing deep into the Big Bend country, the railroads were marketing lumber and barbed wire at every station.[16] Similarly, although the first colonists spread out a decade ahead of the railroad, there was ample good farmland within twenty miles of the Columbia and Snake (waterways at least equal to the lower Missouri, and far superior to the Kaw, Platte, or any river of the Central Grasslands) and the rails arrived in time to join with the settlers in the advance into lands farther away from the rivers. Thus, although transportation was long considered a chronic problem, it was never a crippling deficiency. Similarly, when homesteads were established in districts beyond the immediate reach of living streams or shallow, hand-dug wells, water could usually be hauled from a river or small lake a few miles away, and later it was imported and peddled by the railroads, until finally deep well-drilling machinery and windmills provided a local solution.

Barbed wire and the light, efficient steel windmill were famous industrial tools developed in response to the needs of pioneers in the grasslands of the Great Plains. In the Columbia Plain the different scale softened the severity of the problem and allowed colonization

[16] The sod house of the Great Plains became more famous than important; as James C. Malin put it, "the prevailing house type would be more accurately described as the sawed house, rather than the sod house," *The Grassland of North America: Prolegomena to Its History* (Lawrence, Kan., 1948), p. 268.

to proceed by the use of substitutes until such equipment could be imported from the East.[17]

Finally, some general parallels in attitudes toward grasslands as a type of country may be noted. Long before the entry of the farmers, both regions had been condemned as wastelands: the concept of a "Great Columbia Desert" was a precise parallel in root and time with that of the "Great American Desert." Such generalizations were gradually modified in both areas by proof of their value for grazing, but their suitability for farming was less easily demonstrated. In large part, of course, those who pronounced judgment upon the Columbia Plain had already crossed the Great Plains east of the Rockies en route to the Northwest, and a parallel in verdict was to be expected. Ralph Brown stated that for the northern Great Plains, "signs of the breakdown of the desert idea first appeared officially with the railroad surveys of 1855, when at last the High Plains were compared to the steppes of Russia,"[18] and thereby Isaac Stevens becomes a perfect example of how the ideas of the same person might affect both regions. But the test of the more humid prairies had by then already been under way for a decade or more in Illinois, northern Missouri, and eastern Iowa, and the expansion of the farming frontier westward from there into drier districts continued to be about ten or fifteen years ahead of the advance in the Columbia Plain across similar environmental gradations. Thus the farmers swarmed into eastern Colorado in the late 1880's and soon defined the limits of agriculture by their crop failures, whereas the comparable movement and experience in the core of the Columbia Plain took place after the turn of the century. That lag was beneficial to the smaller region insofar as it made such tools as the railroad, barbed wire, and windmill more readily available to the vanguard of colonists, but it does not seem to have enhanced the ability of the Columbia pioneers to judge virgin ground. Here the critical physi-

[17] See Webb, *Great Plains* (New York, 1931), chap. vii; Hayter, "Barbed Wire"; Clarence H. Danhof, "The Fencing Problem in the Eighteen-fifties," *Agricultural History*, 18 (October, 1944), 168-86. One might speculate that had the Columbia Plain been colonized before the central grasslands, this difference would have made it unlikely that barbed wire would have been invented in the Pacific Northwest, for the severity of the need and the potentialities of the local market would likely have been insufficient to prompt the interest and competitive experimentation which did produce that solution in the Midwest.

[18] Ralph H. Brown, *Historical Geography of the United States* (New York, 1948), p. 370.

cal differences between the two regions, especially the sharp contrast in summer precipitation, prohibited a simple transfer of knowledge from one region to the other, and the farmers in each case had to learn year by year from their own labors.

The interest in the seeming "anomaly" of the summer dry season was itself an expression of both the direction and timing of the settlement of the Columbia Plain. This feature was a "marked peculiarity" only to those who took for granted an opposite condition. It was a clear representation of the middle western view, for had most of the settlers and prospective immigrants been Californians, this feature would have been regarded as commonplace, although the success of spring-sown crops under such conditions might still have been puzzling. In any case, the theories that cultivation, tree planting, or the building of railroads might influence the rainfall, and the lively interest in various rain-making devices, represented the importation of ideas developed from experiences east of the Rockies.

The Great Columbia Plain differed from the Great Central Plains not only in size and in certain important physical details but also in national location. Some effects of its relative isolation from sources of supply and markets were evident and realized. Farm machinery was more costly, for even that manufactured within the region had to be built largely from materials imported from the East, and the same was true as well of most consumer goods. At the same time the prices received by the farmer were nearly the lowest of any wheat-raising district in the nation, although yields considerably higher than the national average helped to offset that disadvantage. Isolation from the national market strengthened the regional emphasis upon a one-crop foreign export economy. Much that was advocated by the promoters of diversified agriculture was unrealistic because of the vast distance from any large market. As the orchardists learned in time, only by producing a superior product rigidly graded and efficiently marketed could this handicap of distance be overcome. Similarly, many of the industries so avidly sought by the boosters for their towns and cities were or would have been doomed by the absence of adequate outlets within the region or nearby. In this feature the contrast with the Middle West is striking and instructive. Although the wheat regions of Kansas and North Dakota were as devoid of manufacturing centers as the Columbia Plain, the urban-industrial belt of the nation was not only more accessible to all, it actually overlapped the prairie lands of Illinois, reaching into

Minnesota, Iowa, and Missouri to form a combined agricultural-industrial, rural-urban complex of great diversity and productivity. Thus, in general the middle western farmer had a greater choice of crops, markets, and suppliers, and the middle western town had better chances of luring specialized businesses and industries.[19]

Sources of Population

All of these specific elements, comparisons, and factors help to define and illuminate the particular characteristics of cultural developments in the Columbia Plain, but the dominant "culture pattern" was primarily determined by the kind of people who came in and the mundane way of life they represented. The geographical patterns of population provenience show two relatively distinct historical stages: the first from 1859 to about 1885, dominated by the inflow from western Oregon, the second, from about 1885 until about 1910, dominated by migrants directly from east of the Rockies.[20]

The population of the Willamette Valley, the first main source of colonists, was drawn almost entirely from a large block of the states bounded by New York and Virginia on the east and Iowa and Missouri on the west.[21] Missouri, Iowa, and Illinois were the most important specific sources, but many of those emigrating from there had been born in states to the east. Thus, early Oregon was a distant transplant of a Middle West broadly defined to include the transappalachian extensions of the older "middle states" and "Border South," with an ingredient of New Englanders, minor in num-

[19] L. B. Zapoleon, *Geography of Wheat Prices* (U.S. Dept. of Agriculture Bulletin No. 594) (Feb. 21, 1918), esp. Map 1. The lowest prices were paid in southern Idaho and central Montana; Blackfoot, Idaho, was the dividing line between equal shipping charges east and west to Liverpool. The frantic competition among the midwestern towns to attract industry has been carefully examined and richly presented by Lewis Atherton in *Main Street on the Middle Border* (Bloomington, Ind., 1954).

[20] The determination of source areas in the ensuing discussion is based upon a wide variety of materials, most especially the published data in the United States censuses and tabulations and close analyses of the biographies in several of the older county histories. Both of these sources require a good deal of interpretation which has been aided by much fragmentary evidence. The result is necessarily in the form of general conclusions, but they are put forth with considerable confidence, even though they cannot be refined into absolute quantities.

[21] See Jesse S. Douglas, "Origins of the Population of Oregon in 1850," *Pacific Northwest Quarterly*, 41 (April, 1950), 95-108.

bers but important in influence, who had come directly to the lower Columbia by sea or indirectly as part of the movements westward from upstate New York and Ohio. The Willamette was the area in the far West physically most suitable to receive such a direct transfer with a minimum of change, and the earmarks of the culture of that source region were evident in such varied features as the style of architecture and the layouts of farms and towns, the methods of farming and the promotion of agricultural societies and county fairs, the concepts and structure of town and county governments, the role of churches and the denominational academies and colleges, and— as expressed in all of these things and many more—in the whole intricate set of values, attitudes, and behavior.

And yet this patterned complex had been loosened and altered in its new setting. Not quite all of the familiar crops and methods worked in this new land, larger land allotments fostered a greater dispersal of settlement, the much greater isolation and slower infiltration of settlers retarded the pace of development, lessened competition, and narrowed the possibilities for commerce and industry. In short, this Willamette pattern was an isolated, provincial, frontier copy of the culture of the American midlands steadily being adjusted to new physical surroundings and a very different national location.

It was primarily representatives of that Willamette pattern who formed the first cadre of farmers and townsmen in the Columbia Plain. Californians were also a prominent part of the initial surge into the interior, but the mining rush dispersed into many mountain localities and lasted only a few years, and they became only a minor part of the permanent population.[22] There was also an annual inflow from the east by way of the Oregon Trail, drawing from the same general middle western states (although the proportion from south of the Ohio River was significantly less than during the earlier Oregon migration). Despite a steady increase in this traffic, however, the influx up the Columbia, composed both of easterners who had come by ship and, primarily, those who had been born in western Oregon or had resided there for some time, remained the largest source throughout the 1860's and 70's.

[22] The Chinese, at first a drifting group, but later settling in the river towns and Walla Walla (the census of 1880 recorded 1,158 in Wasco County, 530 in Whitman, 512 in Walla Walla), were the most visible legacy of the Californian influx, and they became a permanent if tiny segment of the population composite.

Inevitably that basic western Oregon pattern was further loosened and altered in this new setting, an area very different in climate, soil, and appearance, and one which, after the initial stimulation of the mining districts, was even more remote than the Willamette from any other market connection. Here agriculture differed even more from its Ohio Valley antecedents and gradually took on important Californian characteristics. Yet the over-all culture pattern remained essentially that of its original colonists, and thus the Columbia Plain was a variant of the Willamette pattern, a regional compartment of a now enlarged, transplanted, provincial "middle western" culture.

The completion of the transcontinental railroad connections in the middle 1880's brought an abrupt shift in the patterns of immigration. Most of the colonists now came to the Columbia Plain directly from the Middle West and especially from those areas which were in the first generation of development: western Iowa, Nebraska, Minnesota, and Dakota. Increasingly the expansion of settlement was also supported from within by migrants from older districts; much of the Big Bend was settled by people who had lived, at least briefly, in the Walla Walla or Palouse.[23] The proportion of colonists from west of the Cascades became minor during these years, though briefly enlarged in the early 1900's by the influx from the Puget Sound area into the booming irrigation developments.

Although the population of the Columbia Plain was derived largely from the Middle West, it did not represent a typical middle western population. One major difference appears: the relatively small proportion of foreign-born colonists. Here again the factor of isolation seems to have had a marked effect. Despite the mass European propaganda campaigns of the railroads and the states, there was virtually no direct migration of Europeans into the Columbia Plain. Those who did come had settled at least briefly in other states, principally in the farming regions of the Middle West, and when they moved on to the Pacific Northwest most of them came as individuals or families and not in groups. This produced a sharp con-

[23] For example, analysis of the 195 biographies of Adams County residents in Steele and Rose, *Big Bend Country*, revealed that 79 came directly from the Middle West, 72 from elsewhere in the Columbia interior (chiefly from the Columbia Plain but a few from Coeur d'Alene, the Grande Ronde, and so forth), 12 from western Oregon or Washington, 7 from California, 2 directly from Europe, and 3 from other parts of the United States; 14 had been born or raised in Adams County; the origin of the remaining 6 was not given.

trast between the cultural geography of colonization in the Columbia Plain and that in the Central Plains. In the latter region from the 1840's on Europeans as well as American born were part of the frontier movement. Toward the end of the century 40 to 50 per cent of the population in many of the newer areas of Minnesota, Dakota, and Nebraska were immigrants directly from overseas, and they often clustered in cohesive groups imprinting upon much of the rural Middle West a loose mosaic of ethno-religious compartments.[24]

In the Columbia country there was little that was comparable. In time a number of European-born immigrants filtered in, but their proportion of the population was rarely half what it was in areas of concurrent colonization east of the Rockies. After 1890 a few Jews, Italians, Greeks, Slavs, and others from eastern and southern Europe began to appear in the towns and small cities, the first largely as peddlers, tradesmen, and in various professions, the rest chiefly as railroad workers and migratory laborers, but in different proportions and patterns than in the Middle West. The one important example of a foreign group colonization was that of the Volga German Lutherans, who came west from Nebraska in 1883 and settled around Ritzville in Adams County. [25] Elsewhere one might encounter a loose cluster of German Catholics, Norwegian Lutherans, or similar group, but invariably they were intermingled with other peoples, and the compartmentalization or at least general dominance of countryside and towns by a particular ethno-religious group did not exist in any degree equal to that of the Middle West. Isolation—the greater distance, cost, and effort, and the intervening opportunity of good land readily available in the Central Plains—would seem to have been the main cause of that difference as it was of the economic contrasts previously noted.

[24] I know of no single work which offers a general analysis of this important cultural characteristic of the Middle West, though there is a huge literature bearing upon it. J. Neale Carman, *Foreign-Language Units of Kansas*, Vol. I: *Historical Atlas and Statistics* (Lawrence, Kan., 1962), is an amazingly detailed and effective presentation, county by county, of ethnic groupings. Hildegard Binder Johnson's several studies of German colonization are especially useful, for example, "The Location of German Immigrants in the Middle West," *Annals of the Association of American Geographers*, 41 (March, 1951), 1-41.

[25] Elmer Miller, "The European Background and Assimilation of a Russian-German Group" (M.A. thesis, Washington State College, 1929). At the time of Miller's study, this group totaled 787, 46 per cent of whom still spoke German as the language of the home; about half had split from the Lutheran faith and had formed German Congregational churches.

INTERREGIONAL CULTURAL INFLUENCES

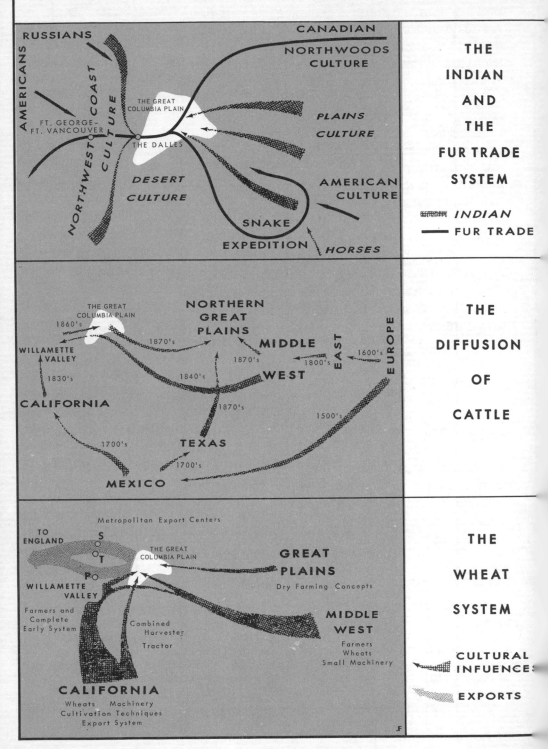

THE INDIAN AND THE FUR TRADE SYSTEM

RUSSIANS

AMERICANS

CANADIAN

NORTHWOODS CULTURE

THE GREAT COLUMBIA PLAIN

NORTHWEST COAST CULTURE

FT. GEORGE–FT. VANCOUVER

THE DALLES

PLAINS CULTURE

DESERT CULTURE

AMERICAN CULTURE

SNAKE EXPEDITION

HORSES

INDIAN

FUR TRADE

THE DIFFUSION OF CATTLE

THE GREAT COLUMBIA PLAIN

NORTHERN GREAT PLAINS

MIDDLE

EAST

EUROPE

1860's

1870's

WEST

WILLAMETTE VALLEY

1870's

1800's

1600's

1830's

1840's

CALIFORNIA

1870's

1500's

1700's

TEXAS

1700's

MEXICO

THE WHEAT SYSTEM

Metropolitan Export Centers

TO ENGLAND

S
T
P

THE GREAT COLUMBIA PLAIN

GREAT PLAINS

Dry Farming Concepts

WILLAMETTE VALLEY

Farmers and Complete Early System

Combined Harvester Tractor

MIDDLE WEST

Farmers Wheats Small Machinery

CALIFORNIA

Wheats   Machinery
Cultivation Techniques
Export System

CULTURAL INFLUENCES

EXPORTS

Map 50

Regional Relationships

These same two historical phases of population provenience can also be seen, in a somewhat larger perspective, as distinct eras in more general relationships between the region and the nation which had great bearing upon the cultural and economic situation of the Columbia Plain (Map 51). During the first period that interior region was part of a larger "Oregon," which was a kind of functionally autonomous, locally organized province in an isolated corner of the nation. The Oregon Steam Navigation Company was a good symbol of that period: a product of local initiative, a trunk line binding the several local regions into an isolated provincial system, its financial and corporate power a product of its own local success. The Walla Walla and Columbia River Railroad was another example: the creation of a local entrepreneur with locally founded capital responding to a local need and profitable opportunity. Virtually all industry, commerce, and merchandizing in the Willamette as well as the interior could be similarly characterized: local enterprises bound into a network focused upon a single center, Portland, the provincial capital through which the limited economic and cultural contacts with the outer world were maintained.[26]

The completion of the two transcontinental railroads in the 1880's was both a primary cause and a perfect symbol of an important change. They drastically altered the old degree of isolation and spurred integration into a rapidly evolving national system. The transformation of the Portland-owned O.S.N. into the O.R.&N., which then became merely a regional piece of a transcontinental network and a corporate subsidiary of national financial interests, was a vivid indication of the change. The Northern Pacific was perhaps an even better symbol of the outreach of national power, for it was a notorious creature of "Wall Street," an example of a distant arbitrary control which subordinated any regional interest to national financial manipulations. Later railroads, too, came to the region, not primarily to compete for its traffic, but as transcontinentals involved in larger strategies. Once these links were formed, national interests worked to capture and integrate this outlying provincial district into the larger pattern. In grain marketing, flour milling, lumbering, and agricultural machinery sales, local enterprise

[26] Lancaster Pollard, "The Pacific Northwest," in Merrill Jensen (ed.), *Regionalism in America* (Madison, Wis., 1952), p. 195, effectively states a similar interpretation, and his whole chapter is relevant to this concluding section.

COMPARATIVE SEQUENCES
OF COLONIZATIONS

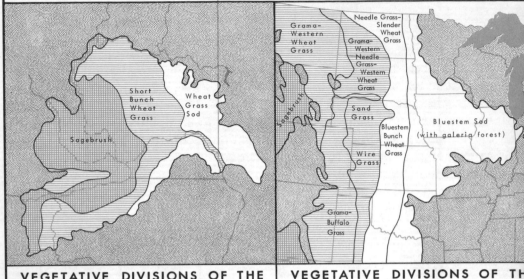

VEGETATIVE DIVISIONS OF THE COLUMBIA GRASSLANDS

(DOMINANTS ONLY)

GENERALIZED FROM VARIOUS SOURCES

| | TALL GRASS | | SHORT GRASS | | FOREST |

VEGETATIVE DIVISIONS OF TH CENTRAL GRASSLANDS

(DOMINANTS ONLY)

GENERALIZED AFTER SHANTZ AND ZON "ATLAS OF AMERICAN AGRICULTURE"

| | TALL GRASS | | SHORT GRASS | | FORE |

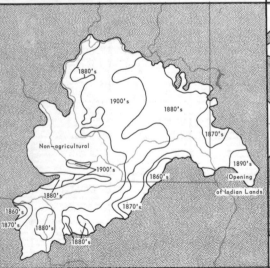

EXPANSION OF DRYLAND AGRICULTURAL SETTLEMENT

(MOST OF THE 1890's EXPANSION TOO SMALL AND SCATTERED TO BE SHOWN EFFECTIVELY)

EXPANSION OF AGRICULTURA SETTLEMENT

GENERALIZED AFTER MARSCHNER "LAND USE AND ITS PATTERNS IN THE UNITED STA

Map 51

gave way to larger concerns. Chicago mail-order houses brought small-town merchants under heavy competition. Portland's hold was broken and even its regional position was compromised by the rapid emergence of Seattle and Tacoma. In the interior the rise of Spokane and eclipse of Walla Walla was more than just a dramatic change in magnitudes and geographical orientations, it was a symbol of the submergence of local control and the ascendency of national interests.

That national ascendency was more than a linkage of communications, capture of resources, control of commerce, and domination of finance, for along those same steel rails came less tangible and more subtle influences. These brought no abrupt changes in culture patterns, for they had already been primarily derived from that same general source region. But this Northwest provincial culture of an older Missouri–Ohio Valley ancestry, which had grown up in isolation, was now brought into closer contact with the dynamic culture of a broader American midlands and thereby became more quickly and exactly responsive to national movements. In so many ways the Columbia Plain seemed to reflect a clear image of the Middle West: in its town and country architecture, in its general agrarian character and attitudes and organizations, in its solid republicanism (after a brief but fervent affair with populism), in the whole style of life and outlook of the times. This last was an intricate blend of many things, but in retrospect many of the more attractive qualities of life during the first decades of this century seem to be overshadowed by the massive influence of a crass materialism, strident boosterism, and frantic concern to be in the forefront of "progress." Although these features permeated the nation, they were most clearly expressed in the Middle West and seem to have had their most perfect far western reflection in the Great Columbia Plain; which is to say that "Main Street" was to be found in the Palouse hills as well as in the great prairies, and that Babbitt lived in Walla Walla, too, where the *"Up-to-the-Times Magazine* was his fervent servant and perfect symbol.[27]

Yet despite all the obvious ties of parentage, parallels in development, and later pervasive influences, the Great Columbia Plain was

---

[27] This is, of course, caricature, but Elkins and McKitrick's stress on the importance of the fact that in the Middle West "every town was a promotion" seems equally appropriate for the Columbia Plain; Stanley Elkins and Eric McKitrick, "Turner Thesis: Predictive Model," in Edward N. Saveth (ed.), *American History and the Social Sciences* (Glencoe, Ill., and London, 1964), pp. 379-99, quotation from p. 393.

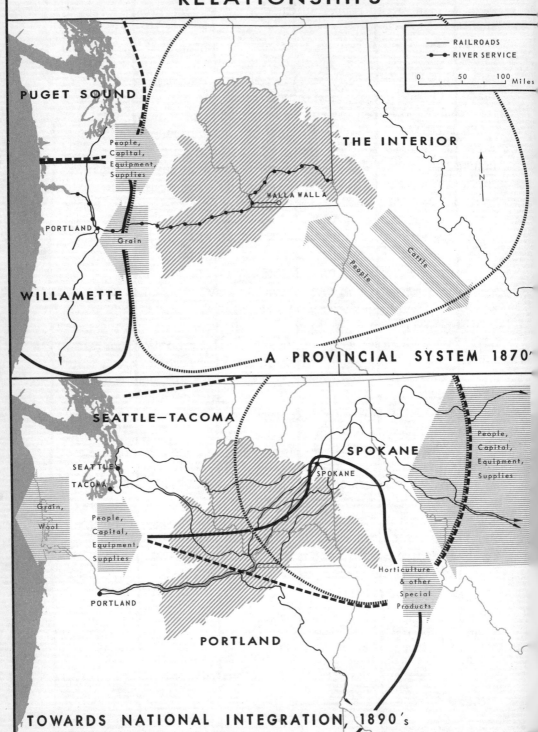

SOME INTER-REGIONAL
RELATIONSHIPS

RAILROADS
RIVER SERVICE

0   50   100 Miles

PUGET SOUND

THE INTERIOR

People,
Capital,
Equipment,
Supplies

WALLA WALLA

N

PORTLAND

Grain

People

Cattle

WILLAMETTE

A PROVINCIAL SYSTEM 1870'

SEATTLE—TACOMA

SPOKANE

People,
Capital,
Equipment,
Supplies

SEATTLE
TACOMA

SPOKANE

Grain,
Wool

People,
Capital,
Equipment,
Supplies

Horticulture
& other
Special
Products

PORTLAND

PORTLAND

TOWARDS NATIONAL INTEGRATION, 1890's

Map 52

never merely a far western transplant of the Middle West. Such a characterization provides a useful general classification but an inadequate description; it suggests a type but obscures the reality, for it glosses over the differences arising from the smaller size, from the relative isolation and particular national location, and from the peculiar physical conditions. Furthermore, such a comparison could not be pushed much further without careful consideration of larger settings. For the Columbia Plain has been an integral part of Oregon or the Pacific Northwest. Despite sharp differences in landscapes and economies, the several regions of this larger realm have always had much in common in people and heritage and have been closely interlocked. To residents of the Columbia Plain, the wet valleys, dense forests, high mountains, and seashore have not been strange environments of distant lands, but reasonably familiar country nearby and accessible. The links between coast and interior have always been apparent, binding together like people of unlike work. Salem and Olympia have each been the focus of formal ties; but far more important have been Portland, Seattle, and Tacoma, serving to link the grain dealer with his export house, the local merchant with his suppliers, the rural resident with urban life, the provincial townsman with the cosmopolitan world.

Some degree of regional consciousness, some sense of belonging to a broader Pacific Northwest community, has long been apparent in this far corner of the nation, even if there might be little understanding of or agreement about its most characteristic features or geographical limits.[28] The stark physical and economic diversities defy any simply summation of the whole, a problem which plagues today's propagandist and interpreter no less than it did their counterparts a century ago. The wheatlands, coulees, and sagebrush plains are as anomalous within a modern "Evergreen Land" as the Great Columbia Desert was in an Oregon presumed to be a land of ceaseless rain and impenetrable forests. Such a realm, especially, needs careful study and interpretation of each of its parts as well as the whole.

A more local regional consciousness has long been apparent east of the Cascades also, but it has been little more clearly formulated than that of the whole. Although grounded in that gross physical

[28] Pollard, "Pacific Northwest," and V. L. O. Chittick (ed.), *Northwest Harvest: A Regional Stock-Taking* (New York, 1948).

contrast between coast and interior, it has failed to coalesce around a stable regional entity. That is not surprising, for the successive prominence of the Great Columbia Plain, the Inland Empire, and the Columbia Basin as major regional identities is merely expressive of recurrent changes in ecology and strategy—in the alteration of the earth and the organization of area—which have taken place over the past century and a half. The Great Columbia Plain was clearly recognized for more than half that span, but it was never famous nationally and has been so long obscured locally that it is not likely to be resurrected into public prominence, even within its own bounds. For despite the richness of its history, the area once encompassed is now so transformed by new forces of growth, so assured of greater development, so confident of continuing progress, that its residents and visitors alike are more fascinated with speculative projections of its future than by reflective interpretations of its past.

Appendix

TABLE 2
Populations and Facilities of Towns, 1890 and 1910

Town	Population* 1890	Population* 1910	Banks† 1890	Banks† 1910	Newspapers† 1890	Newspapers† 1910	Flour Mills† 1890‡	Flour Mills† 1910
WALLA WALLA COUNTRY								
College Place, Wash.						1		
Dayton, Wash.	1,880	2,389	1	1	2	2 SW	1	3
Freewater, Ore.		532		2		1		1
Huntsville, Wash.							1	2
Lamar, Wash.								1
Milton, Ore.	544	1,280	1	2	1	1	2	2
Pataha City, Wash.		176	1				1	1
Pomeroy, Wash.	661	1,605	2	2	2	1	1	1
Prescott, Wash.		502		1		1	1	1
Starbuck, Wash.		761		1				
Touchet, Wash.				1				
Waitsburg, Wash.	817	1,237		2	2	2	1	1
Walla Walla, Wash.	4,709	19,364	2	2	3 D	3 D; 1 W	6	4
Wallula, Wash.	518				1	1		
PALOUSE COUNTRY								
Albion, Wash.		276		1				
Almota, Wash.							1	
Colfax, Wash.	1,649	2,783	3	4	2	2	1	1
Colton, Wash.		393			1	1	1	1
Elberton, Wash.		330		1			1	1
Endicott, Wash.		474		1		1		
Fairfield, Wash.		308		1		1		
Farmington, Wash.	418	489	1	1	1		1	1
Garfield, Wash.	317	932		2	1	1		1
Genesee, Ida.	282	742		2	1	1		1
La Crosse, Wash.				1		2		1
Latah, Wash.	232	339		1	1		1	1
Malden, Wash.		798						

Town	Population*		Banks†		Newspapers†		Flour Mills†	
	1890	1910	1890	1910	1890	1910	1890‡	1910
Moscow, Ida.	2,000	3,670	3	3	2	2	2	1
Oakesdale, Wash.	528	882	1	2	1	1		1
Palouse City, Wash.	1,119	1,549	1	2	2	1	1	2
Pine City, Wash.							1	1
Potlatch, Ida.				1				
Pullman, Wash.	868	2,602	1	2	1	2		1
Rockford, Wash.	644	663		2	2	1	1	
Rosalia, Wash.	248	767		2	1	1		
St. John, Wash.		421		1		1		
Spangle, Wash.	303	299		1	1			
Steptoe, Wash.						1		
Tekoa, Wash.	301	1,694		2	1	1		1
Thornton, Wash.				1				
Troy, Ida.		543		1		1		
Uniontown, Wash.	279	426		2	1	1		
Waverly, Wash.		318		1		1		
Winona, Wash.				1				1

THE CAMAS PRAIRIE, ASOTIN, AND CLEARWATER AREAS

Town	Population*		Banks†		Newspapers†		Flour Mills†	
Alpowa, Wash.							1	
Anatone, Wash.				1		1		1
Asotin, Wash.		820		1	1	1	1	1
Clarkston, Wash.		1,257		2		1		
Cottonwood, Ida.				2		1		1
Culdesac, Ida.		436		2		1		2
Denver, Ida.								1
Ferdinand, Ida.				1				1
Gifford, Ida.		153		1				
Grangeville, Ida.	540	1,534		3	1	2	1	2
Juliaetta, Ida.		414		2		1	1	1
Kamiah, Ida.		324		2		1		
Kendrick, Ida.		543		1				1
Kippen, Ida.		111						
Kooskia, Ida.				1		1		1
Ilo, Ida.		209		1		1		
Lapwai, Ida.								1
Leland, Ida.								1
Lewiston, Ida	849	6,043	3	5	1	2 D	2	2
Mohler, Ida.								1
Mt. Idaho, Ida.							1	
Nez Perce, Ida.		599		3		1		2
Orofino, Ida.		384		2		1		
Peck, Ida.		236		1				1
Reubens, Ida.				1				
Steunenberg, Ida.				1				
Stites, Ida.		300		1		1		
Summit, Ida.								1
Sweetwater, Ida.								1
Vollmer, Ida.		332		1		1		4
Westlake, Ida.								1
Winchester, Ida.				1				

THE BIG BEND COUNTRY (INCLUDING WENATCHEE) (ALL IN WASHINGTON)

Town	Population*		Banks†		Newspapers†		Flour Mills†	
Almira		368		1		1		1
Brewster				1		1		
Bridgeport		431		1		1		1
Cheney	647	1,207	1	1	1	1	1	1
Connell				1		1		
Coulee City		276		1		1		
Creston		308		1		1		1

Town	Population* 1890	Population* 1910	Banks† 1890	Banks† 1910	Newspapers† 1890	Newspapers† 1910	Flour Mills† 1890‡	Flour Mills† 1910
Cunningham		153	1			1		
Davenport	396	1,229	1	1	1	2		1
Downs			1					
Edwall			1			1		
Eltopia			1			1		
Ephrata		323	1			1		
Harrington		661	2			1		1
Hartline		237	1			1		1
Hatton			1			1		
Kahlotus		132	1			1		
Krupp			1					
Lind		821	2			1		1
Marengo							1	
Medical Lake	617	1,730			1	1		
Odessa		885		2		1		1
Orondo					1	1	1	
Othello			1			1		
Paha			1					1
Quincy		264		2		1		
Ralston			1					1
Reardan		527	1			1		
Ritzville		1,859		3	1	3	1	1
Sprague	1,689	1,110	1	2	1	1	1	1
Washtucna		300		1		1		
Waterville	293	950		2	2	1		1
Wenatchee		4,050		3		1 D		2
White Bluffs						1		
Wilbur	410	767		2	1	1		1
Wilson Creek		405		1		1		

THE YAKIMA AND KITTITAS VALLEYS (INCLUDING PASCO) (ALL IN WASHINGTON)

Town	Population* 1890	Population* 1910	Banks† 1890	Banks† 1910	Newspapers† 1890	Newspapers† 1910	Flour Mills† 1890‡	Flour Mills† 1910
Ellensburg	2,768	4,209	1	3	1 D; 2 W	1 D; 1 SW 1 W		4
Grandview		320		1		1		
Granger		453		1		1		
Kennewick		1,219		1		2		
Kiona				1		1		
Mabton		666		1		1		
North Yakima	1,535	14,082	2	4	2	2 D; 3 W	1	1
Pasco		2,083		2	1	2		
Prosser		1,298		2		2	1	2
Richland						1		
Sunnyside		1,379						
Toppenish		1,598		1		1		
Wapato		400		1		1		
Yakima (Union Gap)	196	263					1	1

THE KLICKITAT AND NORTHERN OREGON

Town	Population* 1890	Population* 1910	Banks† 1890	Banks† 1910	Newspapers† 1890	Newspapers† 1910	Flour Mills† 1890‡	Flour Mills† 1910
Adams, Ore.		205						
Arlington, Ore.	356	317	1	3	1	1		
Athena, Ore.		586		1	1	1 SW		1
Bickleton, Wash.				1				1
Boyd, Ore.							1	1
Condon, Ore.		1,009		3		2		1
Dufur, Ore.		523		1		1	1	
Echo, Ore.		400		1		1	1	1
Goldendale, Wash.	702	1,203	1	3	1	2	2	2
Grass Valley, Ore.		342		2		1		
Helix, Ore.		109		1				1

Town	Population* 1890	1910	Banks† 1890	1910	Newspapers† 1890	1910	Flour Mills† 1890‡	1910
Heppner, Ore.	675	880		2	1	2	1	
Hermiston, Ore.		647		2		1		
Ione, Ore.		239		1		1		
Irrigon, Ore.						1		
Lexington, Ore.		185			1		1	1
Mayville, Ore.								1
Moro, Ore.		378		1		1		
Olex, Ore.							1	
Pendleton, Ore.	2,506	4,460	2	3	1D; 1W	1D; 1SW	2	1
Pilot Rock, Ore.		197				1		
Rufus, Ore.							1	
Shaniko, Ore.		495		1				
Stanfield, Ore.		318						
The Dalles, Ore.	3,029	4,880	3	2	1D; 1W	1D; 1W	1	2
Umatilla, Ore.		198						
Wasco, Ore.		386		2	1	1		2
Weston, Ore.	568	499		1	1	1	1	

* Populations are from the U. S. Census, and thus are for incorporated towns only, except for Moscow in 1890, which is an estimate based upon a precinct population of 2,861.

† Figures for banks, newspapers, and flour mills for 1890 are from R. L. Polk and Company, *Oregon, Washington and Idaho Gazetteer and Business Directory, 1889-90* (Portland, Ore., 1889); banks, newspapers, and flour mills for 1910 for Oregon and Washington towns are from Polk's *Oregon and Washington Gazetteer and Business Directory, 1909-10* (Seattle, Wash., 1909); newspapers and flour mills for 1910 for Idaho are from Polk's *Idaho State Gazetteer and Business Directory, 1910-11* (St. Paul, Minn., 1910); banks for Idaho, 1910, are from State of Idaho, *Sixth Biennial Report, Commissioner of Immigration, Labor and Statistics* (Boise, 1909-10). All newspapers are weekly except those marked D (daily) or SW (semi-weekly).

‡ One flour mill at Crab Creek not included in list.

Bibliography

I. Books, Articles, Pamphlets, Bulletins, Manuscripts, Newspaper Accounts, Unpublished Materials

Adams, Emma H. *To and Fro, Up and Down in Southern California, Oregon, and Washington Territory, with sketches in Arizona, New Mexico, and British Columbia.* Cincinnati, Chicago, St. Louis, 1888.

Agricultural Notes. (Washington Agricultural Experiment Station Bulletin No. 10.) December, 1893.

Ainsworth, J. C. "Statement of Captain J. C. Ainsworth, October 27, 1883." MS in the Bancroft Library, Berkeley, Calif.

Allen, A. J. (comp.). *Ten Years in Oregon: Travels and Adventures of Doctor E. White and Lady West of the Rocky Mountains.* Ithaca, N.Y., 1848.

Allen, Eleanor. *Canvas Caravans: Based on the Journal of Esther Belle McMillan Hanna, Who with Her Husband Rev. Joseph A. Hanna, Brought the Presbyterian Colony to Oregon in 1852.* Portland, Ore., 1946.

Anderson, Alexander Caulfield. "History of the Northwest Coast." 1878 MS in the Bancroft Library, Berkeley, Calif.

Angelo, C. Aubrey. *Idaho: A Descriptive Tour and Review of Its Resources and Routes.* San Francisco, 1865.

Armstrong, A. N. *Oregon: Comprising a Brief History and Full Description of the Territories of Oregon and Washington.* Chicago, 1857.

Armytage, W. H. G. "H. J. Coke on the Oregon Trail," *Mid-America,* 31 (New Series 20) (October, 1949), 258-69.

Atherton, Lewis. *Main Street on the Middle Border.* Bloomington, Ind., 1954.

Atkinson, G. H. "The Choice of a Home by Settlers in Oregon or Washington or Idaho," *The West Shore,* 6 (February, 1880), 38-40.

———. "The Increase of Soil from Basaltic Rocks—The Source and Extent of the Basalts," *The Oregonian* (Portland), n.d. Reprinted in Nancy Bates Atkinson, *Biography of Rev. G. H. Atkinson,* pp. 387-92.

———. "The Model Farm of Eastern Oregon and Washington," The *West Shore,* 8 (May, 1882), 84-85.

———. *The Northwest Coast.* Portland, Ore., 1878.

———. "The Water-Spouts of the Upper Columbia Basin," *The West Shore,* 5 (October, 1879), 290-92.

Atkinson, Nancy Bates. *Biography of Rev. G. H. Atkinson, D.D.* Portland, Ore., 1893.

Bailey, Robert G. *River of No Return: A Century of Central Idaho and Eastern Washington History and Development.* Rev. ed.; Lewiston, Ida., 1947.

Bailey, Walter. "The Barlow Road," *Oregon Historical Quarterly,* 13 (September, 1912), 287-96.

Baker, Gordon E. "The Politics of Reapportionment in Washington State." *Eagleton Institute Cases in Practical Politics, Case 3.* New Brunswick, N.J., 1960.

Baker, O. E. (ed.). *Atlas of American Agriculture.* Washington, D.C., 1936.

Ball, Carleton R. "The History of American Wheat Improvement," *Agricultural History,* 4 (April, 1930), 48-71.

Ballou, Robert. *Early Klickitat Valley Days.* Goldendale, Wash., 1938.

Bancroft, Hubert Howe. *History of Oregon, 1834-1888.* San Francisco, 1886, 1888. 2 vols.

———. *History of the Northwest Coast.* San Francisco, 1884. 2 vols.

———. *History of Washington, Idaho and Montana 1845-1889.* San Francisco, 1890.

Bancroft's Guide for Travelers by Railway, Stage, and Steam Navigation in the Pacific States, No. 6, December, 1869. San Francisco, 1869.

Barker, Burt Brown (ed.) *Letters of Dr. John McLoughlin Written at Fort Vancouver, 1829-1832.* Portland, Ore., 1948.

Barnett, Joel. *A Long Trip in a Prairie Schooner.* Glendale, Calif., 1928.

Barry, J. Neilson. "Early Oregon Country Forts: A Chronological List," *Oregon Historical Quarterly,* 46 (June, 1945), 101-11.

Barton, C.M. "Washington." *See* 51st Cong., 2nd sess.

Beardsley, Arthur S. "Later Attempts to Relocate the Capital of Washington," *Pacific Northwest Quarterly,* 32 (October, 1941), 401-47.

Beidleman, Richard G. "Nathaniel Wyeth's Fort Hall," *Oregon Historical Quarterly,* 58 (September, 1957), 197-250.

Bennett, Guy Vernon. "Eastward Expansion of Population from the Pacific Slope," *Washington Historical Quarterly,* 3 (April, 1912), 115-23.

Blodget, Lorin. *Climatology of the United States*. Philadelphia, 1857.

Bolton, Frederick E., and Thomas W. Bibb. *History of Education in Washington*. (Office of Education Bulletin No. 9.) Washington, D.C.: U.S. Dept. of the Interior, 1935.

Booth, Margaret (ed.). "Overland from Indiana to Oregon: The Dinwiddie Journal, 1853," *Sources of Northwest History, No. 2*. Missoula, Mont., n.d.

Boyce, Todd Vernon. "A History of the Beef Cattle Industry in the Inland Empire." Unpublished Master's thesis, State College of Washington, 1937.

Brackett, W. S. "An Exploring Expedition in Northern Idaho," *The Northwest*, 19 (January, 1901), 7-10.

Bretz, J. Harlen. "The Channeled Scablands of the Columbia Plateau," *Journal of Geology*, 31 (November-December, 1923), 617-49.

Briggs, Harold E. *Frontiers of the Northwest: A History of the Upper Missouri Valley*. New York, 1950.

Briggs, Lyman J., and J. O. Belz. *Dry Farming in Relation to Rainfall and Evaporation*. (Bureau of Plant Industry Bulletin No. 188.) Washington, D.C.: U.S. Dept. of Agriculture, 1910.

Brode, H. S. (ed.). "Diary of Dr. Augustus J. Thibodo of the Northwest Exploring Expedition, 1859," *Pacific Northwest Quarterly*, 31 (July, 1940), 287-347.

Brown, Ralph H. *Historical Geography of the United States*. New York, 1948.

Brown, William C. "Old Fort Okanogan and the Okanogan Trail," *Oregon Historical Quarterly*, 15 (March, 1914), 1-38.

Buechner, Helmut K. "Some Biotic Changes in the State of Washington, Particularly During the Century 1853-1953," *Research Studies of the State College of Washington*, 21 (June, 1953), 154-92.

Burpee, Lawrence J. *The Search for the Western Sea: The Story of the Exploration of Northwestern America*. London, 1908.

Burroughs, Raymond Darwin. *The Natural History of the Lewis and Clark Expedition*. East Lansing, Mich., 1961.

Calkins, Frank C. *Geology and Water Resources of a Portion of East-Central Washington*. (Water-Supply and Irrigation Paper No. 118.) Washington, D.C.: U.S. Geological Survey, 1905.

Campbell, C. D. "Washington Geology and Resources," *Research Studies of the State College of Washington*, 21 (June, 1953), 114-53.

Campbell, John V. "The Sinclair Party—An Emigration Overland Along the Old Hudson Bay Company Route from Manitoba to the Spokane Country in 1854," *Washington Historical Quarterly*, 7 (July, 1916), 187-201.

"A Canadian in Eastern Washington" (Correspondence from the Milton [Ontario] *Champion*), *The Northwest*, 2 (August, 1884), 13.

Carman, J. Neale. *Foreign Language Units of Kansas.* Vol. I: *Historical Atlas and Statistics.* Lawrence, Kan., 1962.

Carrere, John F. *Spokane Falls, Washington Territory, and Its Tributary Country, Comprising All of Eastern Washington and the Idaho Panhandle.* Spokane Falls, 1889.

Castle, Gwen. "Belshaw Journey, Oregon Trail, 1853," *Oregon Historical Quarterly,* 32 (September, 1931), 217-39.

Chadwick, S. J. "Whitman County Washington," *The Coast,* 14 (December, 1907), 365-441.

"Cheney and Medical Lake," *The Northwest,* 2 (September, 1884), 4-6.

Chittenden, Hiram M. *The American Fur Trade of the Far West.* New York, 1935. 2 vols.

Chittick, V. L. O. (ed.). *Northwest Harvest: A Regional Stock-Taking.* New York, 1948.

Chohlis, G. John. "Range Conditions in Eastern Washington Fifty Years Ago and Now," *Journal of Range Management,* 5 (May, 1952), 129-34.

Church, Phil E. "Climates of the Pacific Northwest." In Freeman and Martin (ed.), *The Pacific Northwest,* pp. 95-117.

Clark, J. Allen, John H. Martin, and Carleton R. Ball. *Classifications of American Wheat Varieties.* (U.S. Dept. of Agriculture Bulletin No. 1074.) November 8, 1922.

Clark, Pal (ed.). *Sources of Northwest History, No. 18.* Missoula, Mont., n.d.

Clark, Robert Carlton. "Military History of Oregon, 1849-59," *Pacific Northwest Quarterly,* 36 (March, 1945), 14-59.

"Climates of the United States," in *Climate and Man.* Washington, D.C.: Yearbook of Agriculture. U.S. Dept. of Agriculture, 1941. Pp. 701-1228.

Coan, C. F. "The Adoption of the Reservation Policy in the Pacific Northwest, 1853-55," *Oregon Historical Quarterly,* 23 (March, 1922), 1-38.

Coke, Henry J. *A Ride Over the Rocky Mountains to Oregon and California.* London, 1852.

Collier, Donald, Alfred E. Hudson, and Arlo Ford. "Archeology of the Upper Columbia River Region," *University of Washington Publications in Anthropology,* 9 (September, 1942), 1-178.

Cook, S. F. "The Epidemic of 1830-33 in California and Oregon," *University of California Publications in American Archaeology and Ethnology,* 43, No. 3 (1955), 303-26.

Cosgrove, S. G. "Valuable Opinions on Farming Our Lands," *East Washingtonian Pioneer Edition* (Pomeroy), June 6, 1914.

Cotton, J. S. *Range Management in the State of Washington.* (Bureau of Plant Industry Bulletin No. 75.) Washington, D.C.: U.S. Dept. of Agriculture, May 23, 1905.

Coues, Elliott (ed.). *New Light on the Early History of the Greater*

Northwest: The Manuscript Journals of Alexander Henry and David Thompson, 1799-1814. New York, 1897. 3 vols.

Cox, Ross. *The Columbia River; or, Scenes and Adventures During a Residence of Six Years in the Western Side of the Rocky Mountains among Various Tribes of Indians Hitherto Unknown; Together with a Journey Across the American Continent*. [1st ed., 1831.] 3rd ed.; London, 1832. 2 vols.

Crawford, P. V. "Journal of a Trip Across the Plains, 1851," *Oregon Historical Quarterly*, 25 (June, 1924), 136-39.

Crofutt, George A. *Crofutt's Overland Tours*. Chicago and Philadelphia, 1889.

Crop Tests. (Idaho Agricultural Experiment Station Bulletin No. 24.) May, 1900.

Crosthwait, G. A. *Indian Corn, Its Production and Improvement*. (Idaho Agricultural Experiment Station Bulletin No. 57.) April, 1907.

———. *A Soil Fertility Test*. (Idaho Agricultural Experiment Station Bulletin No. 59.) May, 1907.

Dana, Edmund. *Geographical Sketches on the Western Country: Designed for Emigrants and Settlers*. . . . Cincinnati, 1819.

Danhof, Clarence H. "The Fencing Problem in the Eighteen-fifties," *Agricultural History*, 18 (October, 1944), 168-86.

Darby, William. *View of the United States, Historical, Geographical, and Statistical*. Philadelphia, 1828.

Daubenmire, R. F. "An Ecological Study of the Vegetation of Southeastern Washington and Adjacent Idaho," *Ecological Monographs*, 12 (1942), 53-79.

Davenport, Bishop. *A new Gazetteer, or Geographical Dictionary, of North America and the West Indies*. Baltimore, 1833.

Davidson, Gordon Charles. *The North West Company*. (University of California Publications in History, Vol. 7.) Berkeley, 1918.

Davis, Ellis A. *New Commercial Encyclopedia, Washington, Oregon and Idaho; The Pacific Northwest*. Berkeley, Calif., 1909.

DeSmet, P. J. *Letters and Sketches with a Narrative of a Year's Residence Among the Indian Tribes of the Rocky Mountains*. Philadelphia, 1843. Reprinted in Reuben Gold Thwaites (ed.). *Early Western Travels*. Cleveland, 1906. Vol. XXVII.

Deutsch, Herman J. "The Evolution of Territorial and State Boundaries in the Inland Empire of the Pacific Northwest," *Pacific Northwest Quarterly*, 51 (July, 1960), 115-31.

———. "Geographic Setting for the Recent History of the Inland Empire," *Pacific Northwest Quarterly*, 49 (October, 1958), 150-61; 50 (January, 1959), 14-25.

———. "Indian and White in the Inland Empire: The Contest for the Land, 1880-1912," *Pacific Northwest Quarterly*, 47 (April, 1956), 44-51.

"Documents Relating to the Oregon Emigration Movement, 1842-43," *Oregon Historical Quarterly*, 4 (June, 1903), 170-77.

Douglas, David. *Journal Kept by David Douglas During His Travels in North America, 1823-27. . . .* London, 1914.

———. "Sketch of a Journey to Northwestern Parts of the Continent of North America During the Years 1824-'25-'26-'27." Reprinted from *Companion to the Botanical Magazine* (London, 1836), Vol. 2, in *Oregon Historical Quarterly*, 5 (1904), 230-71, 325-69; 6 (1905), 76-97, 206-27.

Douglas, Jesse S. "Origins of the Population of Oregon in 1850," *Pacific Northwest Quarterly*, 41 (April, 1950), 95-108.

Drumheller, Daniel M. *Uncle Dan Drumheller Tells Thrills of Western Trails in 1852.* Spokane, Wash., 1925.

Drury, Clifford M. (ed.). *The Diaries and Letters of Henry H. Spalding and Asa Bowen Smith Relating to the Nez Perces Mission 1838-1842.* Glendale, Calif., 1958.

———. *Elkanah and Mary Walker, Pioneers Among the Spokanes.* Caldwell, Ida., 1940.

———. *Henry Harmon Spaulding.* Caldwell, Ida., 1936.

———. *Marcus Whitman, M.D., Pioneer and Martyr.* Caldwell, Ida., 1937.

The Dry Farming Congress Bulletin, Vol. 3, No. 23 (Dec. 1, 1910). (Report of the Fifth Dry Farming Congress, Spokane, October 3-6, 1910.)

Dufur, A. J. *Statistics of the State of Oregon.* Salem, Ore., 1869.

Dunn, John. *The Oregon Territory, and the British North American Fur Trade.* Philadelphia, 1845.

Dyar, Richard E. *News for an Empire: The Story of the Spokesman-Review of Spokane, Washington and of the Field It Serves.* Caldwell, Ida., 1952.

Eastern Washington. (Pamphlet.) Walla Walla, *ca.* 1885.

Eastern Washington Territory and Oregon. Farmington, W.T., 1888.

Edwards, Jonathan. *An Illustrated History of Spokane County, State of Washington.* 1900.

Eells, Myron. *Marcus Whitman, Pathfinder and Patriot.* Seattle, Wash., 1909.

Elkins, Stanley, and Eric McKitrick, "Turner Thesis: Predictive Model." In Edward N. Saveth (ed.), *American History and the Social Sciences.* Glencoe, Ill., and London, 1964.

"Ellensburg, in Central Washington," *The Northwest*, 7 (April, 1889), 14-24.

Elliot, E. E. *Growing Alfalfa Without Irrigation.* (Washington Agricultural Experiment Station Bulletin No. 80.) 1907.

Elliott, T. C. "British Values in Oregon, 1847," *Oregon Historical Quarterly*, 32 (March, 1931), 27-45.

————. "The Coming of the White Women, 1836," *Oregon Historical Quarterly,* Part 2, 37 (September, 1936), 171-91; Part 3, 37 (December, 1936), 275-90.

————. "The Dalles-Celilo Portage: Its History and Influence," *Oregon Historical Quarterly,* 16 (June, 1915), 133-74.

————. "David Thompson and Beginnings in Idaho," *Oregon Historical Society Quarterly,* 21 (June, 1920), 49-61.

———— (ed.). "David Thompson's Journeys in Idaho," *Washington Historical Quarterly,* 11 (April and July, 1920), 97-103, 163-73.

———— (ed.). "David Thompson's Journeys in the Pend Oreille Country," *Washington Historical Quarterly,* 23 (January, April, July, 1932), 18-24, 88-93, 173-76.

———— (ed.). "David Thompson's Journeys in the Spokane Country," *Washington Historical Quarterly,* 8 (July and October, 1917), 183-87, 261-64; 9 (January, April, July, October, 1918), 11-16, 103-6, 169-73, 284-87; 10 (January, 1919), 17-20.

————. "The Discovery of the Source of the Columbia River," *Oregon Historical Society Quarterly,* 26 (March, 1925), 23-49.

———— (ed.). "Journal of Alexander Ross–Snake Country Expedition, 1824," *Oregon Historical Quarterly,* 14 (December, 1913), 366-88.

———— (ed.). "Journal of David Thompson, *Oregon Historical Quarterly,* 15 (March and June, 1914), 39-63, 104-25.

———— (ed.). "Journal of John Work, Covering Snake Country Expedition of 1830-31," *Oregon Historical Quarterly,* 13 (December, 1912), 363-71; 14 (September, 1913), 280-314.

———— (ed.). "Journal of John Work, June-October, 1825," *Washington Historical Quarterly,* 5 (April, July, October, 1914), 83-115, 163-91, 258-87; 6 (January, 1915), 26-49.

————. "Letter of Donald Mackenzie to Wilson Price Hunt, July 30, 1822," *Oregon Historical Quarterly,* 43 (September, 1942), 194-97.

Elsensohn, Sister M. Alfreda. *Pioneer Days in Idaho County.* Caldwell, Ida., 1947. 2 vols.

"Eureka Flat," *The Northwest,* 7 (October, 1889), 20.

Evans, Elwood. *Washington Territory: Her Past, Present and the Elements of Wealth Which Insure Her Future.* Olympia, Wash., 1877.

Fahey, John. *Inland Empire: D. C. Corbin and Spokane.* Seattle, Wash., 1965.

Farnham, Thomas J. "Products of the Oregon Territory," *American Agriculturist,* 2 (November, 1843), 273-74.

————. *Travels in the Great Western Prairies, The Anahuac and Rocky Mountains, and in the Oregon Territory.* New York, 1843. Reprinted in Reuben Gold Thwaites (ed.). *Early Western Travels.* Cleveland, 1906. Vol. XXVIII.

"The Far Northwest," *Chicago Times,* Sept. 30, 1881.

Feichter, Nancy Koehler. "The Chinese in the Inland Empire During the Nineteenth Century." Unpublished Master's thesis, Washington State University, 1959.

Fenneman, Nevin M. *Physiography of Western United States.* New York and London, 1931.

Fifty Years on Tracks. Peoria, Ill., 1954.

Fleming, R. Harvey (ed.). *Minutes of Council Northern Department of Rupert Land, 1821-31.* London, 1940.

Flint, Timothy. *The History and Geography of the Mississippi Valley. To which is appended a condensed Physical Geography of the Atlantic United States and the whole American Continent.* 3rd. ed.; Cincinnati and Boston, 1833. 2 vols.

Forness, Norman Olaf. "The Up-to-the-Times Magazine, 1906-1911: A Promoter of Enterprise and Reflection of Culture in Walla Walla." Unpublished Master's thesis, Washington State University, 1960.

"Fort Boise: From Imperial Outpost to Historic Site," *Idaho Yesterdays,* 6 (Spring, 1962), 15-16, 33-39.

Franchère, Gabriel. *Narrative of a Voyage to the Northwest Coast of America in the Years 1811, 1812, 1813, and 1814 or the First American Settlement on the Pacific.* Trans. and ed. by J. V. Huntington. New York, 1854. In Reuben Gold Thwaites (ed.). *Early Western Travels.* Cleveland, 1904, Vol. VI.

Freeman, Otis W., and Howard H. Martin (ed.). *The Pacific Northwest: An Overall Appreciation.* 2nd ed.; New York, 1954.

Freeman, O. W., J. D Forrester, and R. L. Lupher, "Physiographic Divisions of the Columbia Intermontane Province," *Annals of the Association of American Geographers,* 35 (June, 1945), 53-75.

Fremont, John C. *Report of the Exploring Expedition to the Rocky Mountains in the Year 1842, and to Oregon and North California in the Years 1843-44.* Washington, D.C., 1845.

French, Giles. *The Golden Land: A History of Sherman County, Oregon.* Portland, Ore., 1958.

"From Eastern Oregon," *The Northwest,* 2 (February, 1884), 6.

Fulmer, Elton, and C. C. Fletcher. *Washington Soils.* (Washington Agricultural Experiment Station Bulletin No. 13.) 1894.

"Fur Trade Returns—Columbia District & New Caledonia, 1825-1857." MS of the unpublished record book in the Archives of British Columbia, Victoria.

Galbraith, John S. *The Hudson's Bay Company as an Imperial Factor, 1821-1869.* Berkeley and Los Angeles, 1957.

Garfielde, Selucius. *Climates of the Northwest.* Philadelphia, 1871.

Garth, Thomas R., Jr. "Waiilatpu After the Massacre," *Pacific Northwest Quarterly,* 38 (October, 1947), 315-18.

Gilbert, Frank T. *Historic Sketches of Walla Walla, Whitman, Columbia and Garfield Counties, Washington Territory.* Portland, Ore., 1882.

Gill, Frank B. "Oregon's First Railway," *Oregon Historical Society Quarterly,* 25 (September, 1924), 171-235.

Glisan, Rodney, *Journal of Army Life.* San Francisco, 1874.

Goddard, Frederick B. *Where to Emigrate and Why.* New York, 1869.

Gouldin, Helen W. "Here's Our Little Electric Brother," *Union Pacific Magazine,* 7 (June, 1928), 9.

Gray, R. G. *Development of the Agricultural Tractor in the United States. Part I: Up to 1919 Inclusive.* (U.S. Dept. of Agriculture, Agriculture Research Service, Agric. Engineering Research Branch, Farm Machinery Section, Information Series No. 107.) Beltsville, Md., June, 1954.

Great Facts About a Great Region. (Pamphlet issued by Lewiston Commercial Club.) Lewiston, Ida., *ca.* 1909.

Great Northern Railway Company. *Annual Report.* 1890-91, 1902, 1910, 1913-14.

————. *Time Table.* Sept. 20, 1894; October, 1910.

Greely, A. W. *Rainfall. See* 50th Cong., 1st sess.

Greenhow, Robert. *The History of Oregon and California, and the Other Territories on the North-West Coast of North America.* Boston, 1844.

Gregory, Homer. "A Study of the Cost of Wheat Production in Eastern Washington," *Washington Agriculturist,* 8 (April, 1914), 28.

Griffith, David. *Forage Conditions and Problems in Eastern Washington, Eastern Oregon, Northeastern California, and Northwestern Nevada.* (Bureau of Plant Industry Bulletin No. 38.) Washington, D.C.: U.S. Dept. of Agriculture, 1903.

Guie, H. Dean. *Bugles in the Valley: The Story of Garnett's Fort Simcoe.* Yakima, Wash., 1956.

Gwinn, C. A. *The Sugar Beet.* (Washington Agricultural Experiment Station Bulletin No. 3) February, 1892.

Hafenrichter, A. L. "The Natural Grasslands of the Northwest: Their Importance and Management." In Freeman and Martin (ed.), *The Pacific Northwest,* pp. 149-59.

Haines, Francis D. "Mackenzie's Winter Camp, 1812-13," *Oregon Historical Quarterly,* 37 (December, 1936), 329-33.

————. "The Northward Spread of Horses Among the Plains Indians," *American Anthropologist,* 40 (July, 1938), 429-37.

————. "The Western Limits of the Buffalo Range," *Pacific Northwest Quarterly,* 31 (October, 1940), 389-98.

Hargreaves, Mary Wilma M. *Dry Farming in the Northern Great Plains, 1900-1925.* Cambridge, Mass., 1957.

Haring, H. A. *Warehousing.* New York, 1925.

Harmon, Daniel Williams. *A Journal of Voyages and Travels in the Interior of North America*. Toronto, 1904.

Haskell, Daniel C. (ed.). *On Reconnaissance for the Great Northern: Letters of C. F. B. Haskell, 1889-1891*. New York, 1948.

Hastings, Lansford W. *The Emigrants' Guide to Oregon and California*. Cincinnati, 1845.

Hayter, Earl W. "Barbed Wire Fencing—A Prairie Invention," *Agricultural History*, 13 (October, 1939), 189-207.

Hedges, James Blaine. *Henry Villard and the Railways of the Northwest*. New Haven, Conn., 1930.

Henry, Robert S. "The Railroad Land Grant Legend in American History Texts," *Mississippi Valley Historical Review*, 32 (September, 1945), 171-94.

Hewitt, Randall H. *Across the Plains and Over the Divide: A Mule Train Journey from East to West in 1862, and Incidents Connected Therewith*. New York, 1964.

Hidy, Ralph W., Frank Ernest Hill, Allan Nevins. *Timber and Men: The Weyerhaeuser Story*. New York, 1963.

Higgins, F. Dale. "John M. Horner and the Development of the Combined Harvester," *Agricultural History*, 32 (January, 1958), 14-24.

Hilgard, E. W. "The Big Bend Region," *The Northwest*, 2 (April, 1884), 1-4.

————. "Report of E. W. Hilgard to Professor R. Pumpelly, Director." June 4, 1883, MS in the Land Department, Northern Pacific Railroad, St. Paul, Minn.

————. *A Report on the Relations of Soil to Climate*. (Weather Bureau Bulletin No. 3.) Washington, D.C.: U.S. Dept. of Agriculture, 1892. Pp. 26-30.

————. *Soils, Their Formation, Properties, Composition, and Relations to Climate and Plant Growth in the Humid and Arid Regions*. New York and London, 1906.

————. "The Yakima and Klickitat Regions," *The Northwest*, 2 (March, 1884), 1-2.

————, T. C. Jones, and R. W. Furnas. *Report on the Climatic and Agricultural Features and the Agricultural Practices and Needs of the Arid Regions of the Pacific Slope, with notes on Arizona and New Mexico*. (U.S. Dept. of Agriculture Report No. 20.) Washington, D.C., 1882.

Hillgen, Marcella M. "The Wascopam Mission," *Oregon Historical Quarterly*, 39 (September, 1938), 222-34.

Hines, Gustavus. *Oregon: Its History, Condition and Prospects*. Buffalo, N.Y., 1851.

Historical and Descriptive Review of the Industries of Walla Walla, 1891. Walla Walla, Wash., 1891.

History of North Idaho. See An Illustrated History of North Idaho.

Holmes, J. Garnett. "Soil Survey of the Walla Walla Area, Washington." In *Field Operations of the Bureau of Soils 1902.* Washington, D.C.: U.S. Dept. of Agriculture, 1902. Pp. 711-28.

"Horse Heaven," *The Northwest,* 3 (October, 1885), 17.

Howard, Helen A. (ed.). "Diary of Charles Rumley from St. Louis to Portland, 1862," *Frontier and Midland,* 19 (Spring, 1939), 190-200; also in *Sources of Northwest History, No. 28* (Missoula, Mont., 1939).

Howay, F. W., W. N. Sage, and W. F. Angus. *British Columbia and the United States.* Toronto, 1942.

Hussey, John A. *The History of Fort Vancouver and Its Physical Structure.* Portland, Ore., 1957.

Hulbert, Archer Butler. *The Call of the Columbia: Iron Men and Saints Take the Oregon Trail, 1830-35.* Colorado Springs and Denver, 1934.

———. *Where Rolls the Oregon: Prophet and Pessimist Look Northwest, 1825-30.* Colorado Springs and Denver, 1933.

———, and Dorothy Printup Hulbert. *Marcus Whitman, Crusader: 1802-1839; 1839-1843; 1843-1847.* Colorado Springs and Denver, 1936, 1938, 1941. 3 vols.

Hull, Lindley M. *A History of Central Washington, Including the Famous Wenatchee, Entiat, Chelan and the Columbia Valleys....* Spokane, Wash., 1929.

Hunter, Byron. *Farm Practices in the Columbia Basin Uplands.* (Farmers' Bulletin No. 294.) Washington, D.C.: U.S. Dept. of Agriculture, 1907.

Idaho Yesterdays (contemporary reports on Clearwater and Salmon mining rushes, various titles), 3 (Winter, 1959-60), 19-29; 4 (Spring, 1960), 12-26; 4 (Winter, 1960-61), 14-22; 5 (Summer, 1961), 8-20; 6 (Spring, 1962), 40-48.

An Illustrated History of Klickitat, Yakima, and Kittitas Counties. Spokane, Wash., 1904.

An Illustrated History of North Idaho. Spokane, Wash., 1903.

An Illustrated History of Southeastern Washington including Walla Walla, Columbia, Garfield and Asotin Counties, Washington. Spokane, Wash., 1906.

"Information Concerning Fort Colville, Washington." MSS of typewritten letters, largely extracts from original sources, compiled by various offices of the Hudson's Bay Company, dated Feb. 16, 1923, in the Archives, Washington State University Library, Pullman.

Ingersoll, Ernest. "Wheat Fields of the Columbia," *Harper's Monthly,* 69 (September, 1884), 500-515.

Innis, Harold A. *The Fur Trade in Canada: An Introduction to Canadian Economic History.* New Haven and London, 1930.

Irving, Washington. *The Adventures of Captain Bonneville*. New York, 1843.

————. *Astoria or, Anecdotes of an Enterprise Beyond the Rocky Mountains*. Rev. ed.; New York, 1850.

Jackson, W. Turrentine. *Wagon Roads West: A Study of Federal Road Surveys and Construction in the Trans-Mississippi West, 1846-1869*. Berkeley and Los Angeles, 1952.

Jacobs, Melville. "Historic Perspective in Indian Languages of Oregon and Washington," *Pacific Northwest Quarterly*, 28 (January, 1937), 55-74.

Jenny, Hans. *E. W. Hilgard and the Birth of Modern Soil Science*. Pisa, 1961.

Jensen, C. A., and B. A. Olshausen. "Soil Survey of the Yakima Area, Washington." In *Field Operations of the Bureau of Soils, 1901*. Washington, D.C.: U.S. Dept. of Agriculture, 1902. Pp. 392-419.

Johnson, F. H. *Brief Record of the Development of the Milwaukee Road*. Chicago, 1935.

————. "Fur-Trading Days at Kamloops," *British Columbia Historical Quarterly*, 1 (July, 1937), 171-85.

Johnson, Hildegard Binder. "The Location of German Immigrants in the Middle West," *Annals of the Association of American Geographers*, 41 (March, 1951), 1-41.

Johnson, Overton, and William H. Winter. *Route Across the Rocky Mountains, with a Description of Oregon and California. Their Geographical Features, Their Resources, Soil, Climate, Productions, etc., etc.* Lafayette, Ind., 1846. Reprinted in the *Oregon Historical Quarterly*, 7 (March, June, September, 1906), 62-104, 163-210, 291-327.

Jones, J. S., H. P. Fishburn, and C. W. Colver. *A Report on the Milling Properties of Idaho Wheat*. (Idaho Agricultural Experiment Station Bulletin No. 72.) December, 1911.

Josephy, Alvin M., Jr. *The Nez Perce Indians and the Opening of the Northwest*. New Haven and London, 1965.

Julian, R. C. "Wallula, Washington," *Pasco Express Souvenir Illustrated Edition*, July 19, 1906.

Kane, Paul. *Wanderings of a Artist Among the Indians of North America from Canada to Vancouver's Island and Oregon Through the Hudson's Bay Company's Territory and Back Again*. Toronto, 1925.

Killinger, J. P. (comp.). *Dalles City Directory, 1884-85*. The Dalles, Ore., 1885.

Kincaid, Garret D., and A. H. Harris. "Palouse in the Making." (Unpublished pamphlet.)

Kingston, C. S. "Territorial Road," *Spokesman-Review* (Spokane), Aug. 26, 1951.

———. "The Walla Walla Separation Movement," *Washington Historical Quarterly*, 24 (April, 1933), 91-109.

Kip, Lawrence, *Army Life on the Pacific; A Journal of the Expedition Against the Northern Indians, the Tribes of the Coeur d'Alenes, Spokans, and Pelouzes, in the Summer of 1858*. New York, 1859.

Klickitat, Yakima, and Kittitas. See An Illustrated History of Klickitat, Yakima, and Kittitas Counties.

Klose, Nelson. *A Concise Study Guide to the American Frontier*. Lincoln, Neb., 1964.

Laing, F. W. "Pioneers of the Cattle Industry," *British Columbia Historical Quarterly*, 7 (October, 1942), 257-75.

Lang, T. S. "Oregon." *See* 51st Cong., 2nd sess.

Langley, Henry G. *The Pacific Coast Business Directory for 1867*. San Francisco, 1867.

Lawton, Viola (ed.). "History of Grazing in the State of Washington." MS in the Washington State University Library, Pullman.

Lent, D. Geneva. *West of the Mountains: James Sinclair and the Hudson's Bay Company*. Seattle, Wash., 1963.

"Letters of Rev. H. H. Spaulding and Mrs. Spaulding, Written Shortly After Completing Their Trip Across the Continent," *Oregon Historical Quarterly*, 13 (December, 1912), 371-79.

Lever, W. H. *An Illustrated History of Whitman County*. N.p., 1901.

Lewis, Meriwether, and William Clark. *Travels to the Source of the Missouri River and Across the American Continent to Pacific Ocean*. London, 1815. 3 vols.

———. *Original Journals of the Lewis and Clark Expedition, 1804-1806*, ed. by Reuben Gold Thwaites. New York, 1905. 7 vols. and atlas.

Lewis, William S. *The Story of Early Days in the Big Bend Country*. Spokane, Wash., 1926.

———, and Paul C. Phillips (ed.). *The Journal of John Work, A Chief-Trader of the Hudson's Bay Company During His Expedition from Vancouver to the Flatheads and Blackfeet of the Pacific Northwest*. Cleveland, 1923.

Libby, E. H. "Lewiston Valley and the Buffalo Hump District," *The Northwest*, 17 (March, 1899), 11.

Lomax, Alfred L. *Pioneer Woolen Mills in Oregon: History of Wool and the Woolen Textile Industry in Oregon, 1811-1875*. Portland, Ore., 1941.

Long, J. O. "Review of Stock Industry of Garfield County," *East Washingtonian Pioneer Edition* (Pomeroy), June 6, 1914.

Longmire, David. "First Immigrants to Cross the Cascades," *Washington Historical Quarterly*, 8 (January, 1917), 22-28.

Lyman, W. D. *The Columbia River: Its History, Its Myths, Its Scenery, Its Commerce*. New York and London, 1909.

————. *History of the Yakima Valley, Washington, comprising Yakima, Kittitas and Benton Counties.* 1919.

————. *An Illustrated History of Walla Walla County, State of Washington.* 1901.

————. "Through Central Oregon on Horseback," *The West Shore,* 6 (December, 1880), 316-17.

Lyons, Sister Letitia Mary. *Francis Norbert Blanchet and the Founding of the Oregon Missions (1838-1848).* Washington, D.C., 1940.

McCormick, S. J. *McCormick's Almanac for the Year 1873.* Portland, Ore., 1873.

Mackenzie, Alexander. *Voyages from Montreal, on the River St. Lawrence, Through the Continent of North America, to the Frozen and Pacific Oceans; in the Years 1789 and 1793.* London, 1801.

Malin, James C. *The Grassland of North America: Prolegomena to Its History.* Lawrence, Kan., 1948.

Martig, Ralph Richard. "Hudson's Bay Company Claims, 1846-69," *Oregon Historical Quarterly,* 36 (March, 1935), 60-70.

Meier, W. F. "Will There Be a New State—Lincoln?" *World Today,* 12 (April, 1907), 400-403.

Meinig, Donald W. "Isaac Stevens: Practical Geographer of the Early Northwest," *Geographical Review,* 45 (October, 1955), 542-58.

————. *On the Margins of the Good Earth: The South Australian Wheat Frontier, 1869-1884.* Chicago, 1962; London, 1963.

Melish, John. *A Geographical Description of the United States.* Philadelphia, 1822.

Merk, Frederick (ed.). *Fur Trade and Empire: George Simpson's Journal, 1824-1825.* Cambridge, Mass., 1931.

Mesmer, Louis. "Soil Survey of the Lewiston Area, Idaho." In *Field Operations of the Bureau of Soils, 1902.* Washington, D.C.: U.S. Dept. of Agriculture, pp. 889-909.

Mickelesen, John. "Notebooks." MSS in the Northern Pacific General Offices, St. Paul, Minn. 8 vols. containing research notes, articles, maps, photographs, correspondence on the railroads of the Northwest.

Miller, Elmer. "The European Background and Assimilation of a Russian-German Group." Unpublished Master's thesis, State College of Washington, 1929.

Mills, Randall V. *Stern-wheelers Up Columbia: A Century of Steamboating in the Oregon Country.* Palo Alto, Calif., 1947.

Minto, John. "Sheep Husbandry in Oregon," *Oregon Historical Quarterly,* 3 (September, 1902), 219-47.

The Missionary Herald, Containing the Proceedings at Large of the American Board of Commissioners for Foreign Missions (Boston). Various issues, 1830's and 1840's.

Mitchell, John H. "Oregon, Its History, Geography, and Resources," *National Geographic Magazine,* 6 (April, 1895), 239-84.

Moore, Albert C. "The Grain Bag Problem," *Up-to-the-Times Magazine,* 1 (May, 1907), 357.

Moore, Miles C. "A Pioneer Railroad Builder," *Oregon Historical Quarterly,* 4 (September, 1903), 195-201.

Morris, Thomas B. *Report of the Chief Engineer of the Seattle and Walla Walla Railroad and Transportation Company to the Trustees and Stockholders, November, 1874.* Seattle, Wash., 1874.

Mullan, John. "From Walla Walla to San Francisco," *Washington Statesman* (Walla Walla), November 29, December 6, 1862. Reprinted in *Oregon Historical Quarterly,* 4 (1903), 202-26.

———. "Journal from Fort Dalles O.T. to Fort Wallah Wallah W.T. July, 1858." In Clark (ed.), *Sources of Northwest History.*

Nash, Wallis. *The Settler's Handbook to Oregon.* Portland, Ore., 1904.

Nesmith, James W. "Diary of the Emigration of 1843," *Oregon Historical Quarterly,* 7 (December, 1906), 329-59.

"New Regions for Farmers," *The Northwest,* 6 (August, 1888), 1-15.

Nicolay, C. G. *The Oregon Territory: A Geographical and Physical Account of That Country and Its Inhabitants with Outlines of Its History and Discovery.* London, 1846.

Nielsen, Jean C. "Donald McKenzie in the Snake Country Fur Trade, 1816-1821," *Pacific Northwest Quarterly,* 31 (April, 1940), 161-79.

Northern Pacific Railway Company. *Annual Report.* 1876-1915.

———. *Branch Line Data, Western District.* May, 1922. Contains exact construction history and current traffic status of each line.

———. *The Palouse Country, Washington.* (Folder with map and text.) Chicago, *ca.* 1890.

———. *Time Schedules—Employees.* Oct. 28, 1883; May 5, 1901; June 11, 1916.

———. *Time Table.* August, 1884; Spring, 1890; Oct. 25, 1899; June, 1908; June, 1910.

———. "Townsite Plat Books." MSS in the Northern Pacific Archives, St. Paul, Minn. 4 vols. covering every town and town addition filed by the Northern Pacific.

"North Yakima and the Cascade Branch," *The Northwest,* 2 (September, 1885), 7-8.

Notices and Voyages of the Famed Quebec Mission to the Pacific Northwest. Portland, Ore., 1956.

Nunis, Doyce B., Jr. (ed.). *The Golden Frontier: The Recollections of Herman Francis Reinhart, 1851-1869.* Austin, Tex., 1962.

Oates, James Wyatt. "Washington Territory," *Californian,* 1 (February 1, 1880), 113-18.

Oliphant, J. Orin. "The Benjamin P. Cheney Academy," *Washington Historical Quarterly*, 15 (April, 1924), 106-16.

———. "The Cattle Herds and Ranches of the Oregon Country, 1860-1890," *Agricultural History*, 21 (October, 1947), 217-38.

———. "The Cattle Trade from the Far Northwest to Montana," *Agricultural History*, 6 (April, 1932), 69-83.

———. "The Cattle Trade on Puget Sound, 1858-1890," *Agricultural History*, 7 (July, 1933), 129-49.

———. "The Eastward Movement of Cattle from the Oregon Country," *Agricultural History*, 20 (January, 1946), 19-43.

———. "Legislative Reapportionment in Washington," *Washington Historical Quarterly*, 22 (January, 1931), 3-25.

———. "Notes on Early Settlements and on Geographic Names of Eastern Washington," *Washington Historical Quarterly*, 22 (July, 1931), 172-202.

———. "Winter Losses of Cattle in the Oregon Country, 1847-1890," *Washington Historical Quarterly*, 23 (January, 1932), 3-17.

Orcott, E. A. "Washington Territory Correspondence" (datelined Walla Walla, W. T., December 4, 1868), *Dodge County Republican* (no date or town), Minnesota. Newspaper clipping, Eastern Washington State College Library, Cheney.

The Oregon Farmer. What he has accomplished in every part of the state. A preliminary agricultural survey. Portland, 1913.

The Oregonian's Handbook of the Pacific Northwest. Portland, Ore., 1894.

Oregon Improvement Company. *Annual Report.* 1882-88.

Oregon Railway and Navigation Company. *Annual Report.* 1880-88; 1898-99.

———. *Local Freight Tariff.* March 20, 1881.

———. *Time Table.* Nov. 16, 1890; June 2, 1897.

"The Oregon Territory," *Monthly Chronicle* (Boston), 7 (August, 1842), 337-50.

Oregon-Washington Railroad and Navigation Company. *Report to the Interstate Commerce Commission Corporate History, as Required by Valuation Order No. 20, June 30, 1916.* Compiled by F. B. Gill. 159 pp., mimeo. On file in the Legal Department, Union Pacific Railway, Salt Lake City, Utah.

———. *Time Table.* July 10, 1914; June 24, 1916.

Osborne, Douglas. "Archaeological Occurrences of Pronghorn Antelope, Bison, and Horse in the Columbia Plateau," *Scientific Monthly*, 77 (November, 1953), 260-69.

Osgood, Ernest Staples. *The Day of the Cattleman.* Chicago, 1929.

"Our New Era in Transportation," *Up-to-the-Times Magazine*, 1 (December, 1906), 11-13.

Oviatt, Alton B. "Pacific Coast Competition for the Gold Camp Trade of Montana," *Pacific Northwest Quarterly,* 56 (October, 1965), 168-76.

The Pacific Northwest: Facts Relating to the History, Topography, Climate, Soil, Agriculture, Forests, Fisheries, Mineral Resources, Commerce, Industry, Lands, Means of Communication, etc., etc., etc., of Oregon and Washington Territory. (Pamphlet "Issued for the Information and Guidance of Settlers and Others" by the Bureau of Immigration, Portland, Ore.) New York, 1882. 88pp.

Palmer, Joel. *Journal of Travels over the Rocky Mountains to the Mouth of the Columbia River; Made During the Years 1845 and 1846.* Reprinted in Reuben Gold Thwaites (ed.). *Early Western Travels.* Cleveland, 1906. Vol. XXX.

Pambrun, Andrew D. "Andrew D. Pambrun: The Story of His Life as He Tells It." MS in the Eastern Washington State College Library, Cheney.

Parker, Frank J. *Washington Territory* (collection of articles published in the *Daily and Weekly Statesman,* Walla Walla, W.T.). *Ca.* 1882.

Parker, Samuel. *An Exploring Tour Beyond the Rocky Mountains in North America under the Direction of the American Board of Commissioners for Foreign Missions. Performed in the Years 1835, 1836, and 1837.* Dublin, 1840.

Parsons, William, and W. S. Shiach. *An Illustrated History of Umatilla County and of Morrow County.* 1902.

Partoll, Albert J. "Frank L. Worden, Pioneer Merchant, 1830-1887," *Pacific Northwest Quarterly,* 40 (July, 1949), 189-202.

Peffer, E. Louise. *The Closing of the Public Domain: Disposal and Reservation Policies, 1900-50.* Stanford, Calif., 1951.

Phillips, Paul C. *The Fur Trade.* Norman, Okla., 1961. 2 vols.

————, and W. S. Lewis (ed.). "The Oregon Missions as Shown in the Walker Letters, 1839-51," in *Sources of Northwest History, No. 13.* Missoula, Mont., 1930.

Pine, George W. *Beyond the West.* 2nd ed.; Utica, N.Y., 1871.

Piper, Charles V. *Flora of the State of Washington.* Washington, D.C., 1906.

————. *The Present Status of the Russian Thistle in Washington.* (Washington Agricultural Experiment Station Bulletin No. 37.) October, 1898.

Polk, R. L., and Company. *Idaho State Gazetteer and Business Directory 1910-1911.* St. Paul, Minn., 1910.

————. *Oregon and Washington Gazetteer and Business Directory, 1909-1910.* Seattle, Wash., 1909.

————. *Oregon, Washington and Idaho Gazetteer and Business Directory, 1889-90.* Portland, Ore., 1889.

Pollard, Lancaster. "The Pacific Northwest." In Merrill Jensen (ed.), *Regionalism in America.* Madison, Wis., 1952.

Powell, Fred Wilbur. *Hall J. Kelley on Oregon.* Princeton, N.J., 1932.

"The Practical Value of the Farming Demonstration Train especially the Northern Pacific, 1910, *Dry Farming Special.*" MS in the Washington State University Library, Pullman.

"The Present and Future of Sprague," *The West Shore,* 13 (September, 1887), 657-66.

Proceedings of a Railroad Meeting Held at the Court House, on the evening of January 27th, 1868, on the subject of the Columbia Branch. Umatilla, Ore., 1868.

Proceedings of the Convention of Producers, Shippers and Millers, otherwise known as the Wheat Convention. Pullman, Wash., Jan. 11, 12, 1906.

Pubols, Ben H., and Carl P. Heisig. *Historical and Geographic Aspects of Wheat Yields in Washington.* (Washington Agricultural Experiment Station Bulletin No. 355.) December, 1937.

Pumpelly, Raphael. *Northern Transcontinental Survey: First Annual Report of Raphael Pumpelly, Director of the Survey, September, 1882.* New York, 1882.

"The Railroad Situation in Washington and Oregon," *The Northwest,* 3 (December, 1885), 11.

Ray, Verne F. "Cultural Relations in the Plateau of Northwestern America," *Publications of the Frederick Webb Hodge Anniversary Publication Fund.* Los Angeles: Southwest Museum, 1939. Vol. III.

———. "Native Villages and Groupings of the Columbia Basin," *Pacific Northwest Quarterly,* 27 (April, 1936), 99-152.

———, and Nancy Oestreich Lurie. "The Contributions of Lewis and Clark to Ethnology," *Journal of the Washington Academy of Sciences,* 44 (November, 1954), 358-70.

———, *et al.* "Tribal Distribution in Eastern Oregon and Adjacent Regions," *American Anthropologist,* 40 (July-September, 1938), 384-415.

"Records of the Washington Superintendency of Indian Affairs, Letters Received (Nez Perces)." MSS in the National Archives, Washington, D.C.

Redington, J. W. "Heppner and Morrow County," *The West Shore,* 13 (November, 1887), 773-74.

Report of Committee on New State, submitted to Spokane Chamber of Commerce. (Pamphlet.) Spokane, Wash., *ca.* 1909.

Report of Washington State Grain Inspector, 1898-1900. Olympia, 1900.

Rich, E. E. *The History of the Hudson Bay Company, 1670-1870.* London, 1959. 2 vols.

—— (ed.). *The Letters of John McLoughlin: First Series, 1825-38; Second Series, 1839-44; Third Series, 1844-46.* London, 1941, 1943, 1944. 3 vols.

—— (ed.). *Part of Dispatch from George Simpson Esqr., Governor of Ruperts Land, to the Governor & Committee of the Hudson's Bay Company, London, March 1, 1829. Continued and Completed March 24 and June 5, 1829.* Intro. by W. Stewart Wallace. London, 1947.

—— (ed.). *Peter Skene Ogden's Snake Country Journals, 1824-25 and 1825-26.* London, 1950.

Ritz, Philip. "Settlement of the Great Northwest Interior." MS in the Bancroft Library, Berkeley, Calif.

Robbins, Roy M. *Our Landed Heritage: The Public Domain, 1776-1936.* Princeton, N.J., 1942.

Robinson H. P. "Spokane Falls," *The Northwest,* 2 (July, 1884), 11-16.

Robinson, Samuel E. "The Improvement of the Wheats of Eastern Washington by Selection." Unpublished thesis, State College of Washington, 1905.

Rockie, W. A. "Soils and Their Conservation." In Freeman and Martin (ed.), *The Pacific Northwest,* pp. 121-48.

Rockwell, Cleveland. "The Columbia River," *Harper's Monthly,* 66 (December, 1882), 3-14.

Rollins, Philip Ashton (ed.). "Journey of Mr. Hunt and His Companions from Saint Louis to the Mouth of the Columbia by a New Route Across the Rocky Mountains." In Rollins (ed.), *The Discovery of the Oregon Trail.* New York and London, 1935. Pp. 281-328.

Rollinson, John K. *Wyoming Cattle Trails: History of the Migration of Oregon-raised Herds to Mid-Western Markets.* Caldwell, Ida., 1948.

Ross, Alexander. *Adventures of the First Settlers on the Oregon or Columbia River.* London, 1849. Reprinted in Reuben Gold Thwaites (ed.). *Early Western Travels.* Cleveland, 1904. Vol. VII.

Roush, J. F. "Legislative Reapportionment in Washington State," *Pacific Northwest Quarterly,* 28 (July, 1937), 263-300.

Ruffner, W. H. *A Report on Washington Territory.* New York, 1889.

Russell, Israel Cook. *A Geological Reconnaissance in Central Washington.* (Bulletin of the U.S. Geological Survey No. 108.) Washington, D.C., 1893.

——. *A Reconnaissance in Southeastern Washington.* (Water Supply and Irrigation Paper No. 4.) U.S. Geological Survey, Washington, D.C., 1897.

Russell, Osborne. *Journal of a Trapper.* Portland, Ore., 1955.

Samuels, L. *The Traveler's Guide and Oregon Railroad Gazetteer, August, 1872.* Portland, Ore., 1872.

Schafer, Joseph (ed.). "Documents Relative to Warre and Vavasour's Military Reconnaissance in Oregon 1845-46," *Oregon Historical Quarterly,* 10 (March, 1909), 1-99.

Schneider, Edward A. "An Analysis of a Soil from Washington Territory and Some Remarks on the Utility of Soil-Analysis," *American Journal of Science,* 3rd series, 36 (October, 1888), 236-47.

Schroeder, Carlton Raymond. "The Physical Geography of the Palouse Region, Washington and Idaho, and Its Relation to the Agricultural Economy." Unpublished Ph.D. thesis, University of California (Los Angeles), 1958.

Scobey, J. O. "Dairy Farming in Washington." In *Report of Farmers' Institute Held at Colton, Washington, January 30, 1892.* (Washington Agricultural Experiment Station Bulletin No. 2.) January, 1892.

———. "Farm Resources." In *Report of Farmers' Institute Held at Pomeroy, Washington, May 15, 1892.* (Washington Agricultural Experiment Station Bulletin No. 5.) May, 1892.

Shaver, F. A., Arthur P. Rose, R. F. Steele, and A. E. Adams. *An Illustrated History of Central Oregon Embracing Wasco, Sherman, Gilliam, Wheeler, Crook, Lake and Klamath Counties.* Spokane, Wash., 1905.

Shaver, Henry C. "In the Famous Palouse Country, Idaho," *The Northwest,* 19 (June, 1901), 30-31.

Shaw, Thomas. *A Farmers Paradise: The Columbia River Valley as a Land of Grain and Fruit.* St. Paul, Minn., 1898.

Sheller, Roscoe. *Courage and Water: A Story of Yakima Valley's Sunnyside.* Portland, Ore., 1952.

Simpson, George. *Narrative of a Journey Round the World.* London, 1847. 2 vols.

Simpson Dispatch, 1829. See Rich, E. E. (ed.). *Part of Dispatch from George Simpson....*

Smalley, E. V. "In the Big Bend Country," *The Northwest,* 8 (May, 1890), 15.

Smith, Rollin E. *Wheat Fields and Markets of the World.* St. Louis, Mo., 1908.

Soule, S. H. *The Rand-McNally Guide to the Great Northwest.* Chicago and New York, 1903.

Spalding, H. H. "Letters and Papers of Reverend Henry Harmon Spalding, 1833-1874." MSS in Archives of the Washington State University Library, Pullman.

Spaulding, Kenneth A. (ed.). *On the Oregon Trail: Robert Stuart's Journey of Discovery, 1812-1813.* Norman, Okla., 1953.

Spence, Clark C. "A Brief History of Pluviculture," *Pacific Northwest Quarterly,* 52 (October, 1961), 129-38.

Spencer, Robert F., Jesse D. Jennings *et al. The Native Americans.* New York, Evanston, and London, 1965.

Spier, Leslie, and Edward Sapir. "Wishram Ethnography," *University of Washington Publications in Anthropology*, 3, No. 3 (1930), 151-300.

Spillman, W. J. *The Hybrid Wheats*. (Washington Agricultural Experiment Station Bulletin No. 89.) 1909.

Splawn, A. J. *Ka-mi-akin, Last Hero of the Yakimas*. 2nd ed.; Portland, Ore., 1944.

"Sprague and the Big Bend Country," *The Northwest*, 2 (September, 1884), 6-7.

Starmont, Leon. "50 Years of the Good Roads Fight," *Spokesman-Review* (Spokane), Oct. 10, 1948.

Stearns, D. H. *The Official Gazette, and Travelers' and Immigrants' Guide to Oregon and Washington Territory*. Portland, Ore., 1876.

Steele, Richard F., and Arthur P. Rose. *An Illustrated History of the Big Bend Country Embracing Lincoln, Douglas, Adams and Franklin Counties, State of Washington*. Spokane, Wash., 1904.

Stephenson, James, Jr. *Irrigation in Idaho*. (Office of Experiment Stations Bulletin No. 216.) Washington, D.C.: U.S. Dept. of Agriculture, 1909.

Stevens, Hazard. *Life of Isaac Ingalls Stevens*. Boston, 1900. 2 vols.

Stevens, Isaac I. *Message of the Governor of Washington Territory, also the Correspondence with the Secretary of War, Major Gen. Wool, the Officers of the Regular Army, and of the Volunteer Service of Washington Territory*, Olympia, Wash., 1857.

Stevens Report. See 36th Cong., 1st sess.

Stewart, Earle K. "Transporting Livestock by Boat Up the Columbia, 1861-1868," *Oregon Historical Quarterly*, 50 (December, 1949), 251-59.

Strahorn, Carrie Adell. *Fifteen Thousand Miles by Stage*. New York, 1911.

Sugar Beet Investigation in 1898. (Idaho Agricultural Experiment Station Bulletin No. 18). 1899.

Sugar Beets in Idaho. (Idaho Agricultural Experiment Station Bulletin No. 12.) 1898.

Swanson, Robert Wayne. "A History of Logging and Lumbering on the Palouse River, 1870-1905." Unpublished Master's thesis, State College of Washington, 1958.

Sweetser, M. F. *King's Handbook of the United States*. Buffalo, N.Y., 1891.

Swift, Lon L. "Land Tenure in Oregon," *Oregon Historical Quarterly*, 10 (June, 1909), 31-135.

Thatcher, R. W. "The Fertility of the Palouse Soils," *Pacific Farmers Union*, 34 (Sept. 3, 1909), 8.

———. "Some Recent Results of Dry Farming Investigations in Washington," *Dry Farming Congress Bulletin*, 3 (Feb. 1, 1910), 240-46.

———. *Washington Soils*. (Washington Agricultural Experiment Station Bulletin No. 85.) 1908.

Thorn, C. C. "Moisture Conditions and Climatic Regions of the Inland Empire," *Washington Agriculturist,* 5 (November, 1911), 5-8. Reprinted in *Pacific Farmers Union,* 3 (Dec. 8, 1911).

Thornbury, William D. *Regional Geomorphology of the United States.* New York, 1965.

Thornton, J. Quinn. *Oregon and California in 1848.* New York, 1849. 2 vols.

Thwaites, Reuben Gold (ed.). *Journals of Lewis and Clark.* See Lewis, Meriwether.

The Touchet Valley, Dayton and Waitsburg, Washington. Waitsburg, *ca.* 1909.

Townsend, John K. *Narrative of a Journey Across the Rocky Mountains, to the Columbia River, and a Visit to the Sandwich Islands, Chili, &c., with a Scientific Appendix.* Philadelphia, 1839. Reprinted in Reuben Gold Thwaites (ed.). *Early Western Travels.* Cleveland, 1905. XXI, 107-369.

Traill, Katherine Parr. *The Oregon Territory, Consisting of a Brief Description of the Country and Its Productions; and of the Habits and Manners of the Native Indian Tribes.* London, 1846.

Trimble, W. J. *Mining Advance into the Inland Empire.* (University of Wisconsin Studies, History Series, Vol. III, No. 2.) Madison, 1914.

True, Alfred Charles. *A History of Agricultural Experimentation and Research in the United States, 1607-1925.* (U. S. Dept. of Agriculture Miscellaneous Publications No. 251.) Washington, D.C., June, 1937.

Turner, Frederick Jackson. "The Significance of the Frontier in American History." *American Historical Association Annual Report for 1893.* Washington, D.C., pp. 199-227.

Twelve of Idaho's Worst Weeds. (Idaho Agricultural Experiment Station Bulletin No. 14.) 1898.

Tyrrell, J. B. (ed.). *David Thompson's Narrative of His Explorations in Western America, 1784-1812.* Toronto, 1914.

Union Pacific Railway Company. *Historical Catalogue.* Comp. Raul Rigdon. 8 vols., plus 2 vols. index, 1961. Available in Union Pacific Historical Museum, Omaha. Encyclopedic compilation on Union Pacific and related western railroads.

————. *Letters Received.* Vol. 83. W. H. Holcomb, March 5-Nov. 20, 1888. Union Pacific Archives, Omaha.

Victor, Frances Fuller. *All Over Oregon and Washington: Observations on the Country, Its Scenery, Soil, Climate, Resources, and Improvements.* San Francisco, 1872.

Victor, W. G. "Pioneers of the Mayview Country," *East Washingtonian Pioneer Edition* (Pomeroy), June 6, 1914.

Wade, Richard C. *The Urban Frontier: The Rise of Western Cities, 1790-1830.* Cambridge, Mass., 1959.

"Walker Letters." Elkanah Walker Collection. MSS in the Archives of the Washington State University Library, Pullman.

Walla Walla and Columbia River Railroad. *Time Table No. 1.* April 1. 1880.

"Walla Walla and the Palouse Country [1879]" in "Two Railroad Reports on Northwest Resources," *Pacific Northwest Quarterly*, 37 (July 1946), 176-85.

Walla Walla Valley, Washington. Walla Walla, 1910.

Waller, O. L. *Irrigation in the State of Washington.* (Office of Experiment Stations Bulletin No. 214.) Washington, D.C.: U. S. Dept. of Agriculture, June 22, 1909.

Warre, Henry J. *Sketches in North America and the Oregon Territory.* London, n.d.

Watkins, John B. *Wheat Exporting from the Pacific Northwest.* (Washington Agricultural Experiment Station Bulletin No. 201.) May, 1926.

The Wealth and Resources of Oregon and Washington, The Pacific Northwest. Portland, Ore., 1889.

Webb, Walter Prescott. *The Great Plains.* Boston, 1931.

Wells, Merle W. "The Creation of the Territory of Idaho," *Pacific Northwest Quarterly*, 40 (April, 1949), 106-23.

————. "Politics in the Panhandle: Opposition to the Admission of Washington and North Idaho, 1886-1888," *Pacific Northwest Quarterly*, 46 (July, 1955), 79-89.

————. "Territorial Government in the Inland Empire: The Movement to Create Columbia Territory, 1864-69," *Pacific Northwest Quarterly*, 44 (April, 1953), 80-87.

Wheat Supply and Distribution in the Pacific Northwest. (Oregon Wheat Commission Statistical Bulletin No. 1.) Pendleton, December, 1956.

White, Elijah. *A Concise View of Oregon Territory.* Washington, D.C., 1846.

White, M. Catherine (ed.). *David Thompson's Journals Relating to Montana and Adjacent Regions, 1808-1812.* Missoula, Mont., 1950.

————. "Saleesh House: The First Trading Post Among the Flathead," *Pacific Northwest Quarterly*, 33 (July, 1942), 251-63.

"Whitman National Monument." (Illustrated pamphlet.) Washington, D.C.: National Park Service, 1948.

Wik, Reynold M. *Steam Power on the American Farm.* Philadelphia, 1953.

Wilkes, Charles. *Narrative of the United States Exploring Expedition, During the Years 1838, 1839, 1840, 1841, 1842.* Philadelphia, 1845. 5 vols.

————. *Western America, Including California and Oregon with Maps of those Regions, and of the Sacramento Valley.* Philadelphia, 1849.

Williams, Joseph. *Narrative of a Tour from the State of Indiana to the Oregon Territory in the Years 1841-2*. Cincinnati, 1843.

Winans, W. P. "Fort Colville 1859 to 1869," *Washington Historical Quarterly*, 3 (October, 1908), 78-82.

Winther, Oscar O. *The Old Oregon Country: A History of Frontier Trade, Transportation, and Travel*. (Indiana University Publications, Social Science Series No. 7.) Bloomington, 1950.

Winthrop, Theodore. *The Canoe and the Saddle or Klalam and Klickatat, to which are now first added his Western Letters and Journals*. Edited, with an introduction and notes, by John H. Williams. Tacoma, Wash., 1913.

Wright, E. W. (ed.). *Lewis and Drydens Marine History of the Pacific Northwest*. Portland, Ore., 1895.

"The Yakima Country," *The Northwest*, 2 (February, 1884), 14.

Yeager, Walter M. "The Pioneer's Problems of Land Acquisition Under the Public Land Laws in Southeastern Washington, 1850-1883." Unpublished Master's thesis, Washington State University, 1961.

Yoder, Fred R. "Pioneer Social Adaptations in Lincoln County, Washington, 1875-90," *Research Studies of the State College of Washington*, 10 (September, 1942), 179-97.

————. "Pioneer Social Adaptation in the Palouse Country of Eastern Washington, 1870-90," *Research Studies of the State College of Washton*, 6 (December, 1938), 131-59.

————. "Stories of Early Pioneers in Whitman County, Washington" (collected by personal interviews in the summers of 1936-37). MSS in the Washington State University Library, Pullman. Summarized in Yoder, "Pioneer Social Adaptation in the Palouse Country."

Young, F. G. (ed.). "The Correspondence and Journal of Captain Nathaniel J. Wyeth 1831-6," *Sources of the History of Oregon* (Eugene, 1899). Vol. I, Parts 3-6.

Zapoleon, L. B. *Geography of Wheat Prices*. (U. S. Dept. of Agriculture Bulletin No. 594.) Feb. 21, 1918.

II. CONGRESSIONAL RECORD
(arranged chronologically by Congress and session)

Annals of Congress, 16th Cong., 2nd sess. (1820-21).

Report of the Committee ... to Inquire into the Situation of the Settlements upon the Pacific Ocean, and the Expediency of Occupying the Columbia River, January 25, 1821. (16th Cong., 2nd sess. H. Rept. 45.) Washington, D.C., 1821.

Annals of Congress, 17th Cong., 2nd sess. (1822-23).

Message from the President of the United States Communicating the Letter of Mr. Prevost, and Other Documents, Relating to an Establishment Made at the Mouth of Columbia River, January 27, 1823. (17th Cong., 2nd sess., H. Ex. Doc. 45.) Washington, D.C., 1823.

Report of Mr. Benton, from the Committee on Indian Affairs, March 18, 1824. (18th Cong., 1st sess., S. Ex. Doc. 56.) Washington, D.C., 1829.

Exploration of the Northwest Coast. (19th Cong., 1st sess., H. Rept. 35.) Washington, D.C., 1826.

Northwest Coast of America (Second Report). (19th Cong., 1st sess., H. Rept. 213.) Washington, D.C., 1826.

Register of Debates in Congress. (20th Cong., 2nd sess.) Washington, D.C., 1830.

Report of the Committee on Indian Affairs. (20th Cong., 2nd sess., S. Rept. 67.) Washington, D.C., 1829.

Report of the Secretary of War in Compliance with a Resolution of the Senate Concerning the Fur Trade, and Inland Trade to Mexico, February 8, 1832. (22nd Cong., 1st sess., S. Ex. Doc. 90.) Washington, D.C., 1832.

Wyeth, Nathaniel J. *Mr. Wyeth's Memoir.* (25th Cong., 3rd sess., H. Rept. 101, Appendix 1 of Supplemental Report, dated Feb. 16, 1839.)

Report of the Committee on Military Affairs on the Establishment of a Chain of Military Posts from Council Bluffs to the Pacific Ocean. (27th Cong., 3rd sess., H. Rept. 31.) Washington, D.C., 1843.

Report to the Secretary of War Communicating Information ... relative to Oregon. (31st Cong., 1st sess., S. Rept. 47.) Washington, D.C., 1849-50.

Report of the Secretary of the Interior. (33rd Cong., 1st sess., S. Ex. Doc. 1.) Washington, D.C., 1854.

Correspondence of General Wool with the Government. (33rd Cong., 2nd sess., S. Ex. Doc. 16.) Washington, D.C., 1855.

Report of the Secretary of the Interior. (33rd Cong., 2nd sess., S. Ex. Doc. 1.) Washington, D.C., 1854.

Stevens, Isaac I. *Report of Explorations for a Route for the Pacific Railroad, near the Forty-seventh and Forty-ninth Parallels of North Latitude from St. Paul to Puget Sound* (Pacific Railroad Surveys, Vol. I). (33rd Cong., 2nd sess., S. Ex. Doc. 78.) Washington, D.C., 1860.

Indian Hostilities in Oregon and Washington. (34th Cong., 1st sess., H. Ex. Doc. 93.) Washington, D.C., 1856.

Indian Hostilities in Oregon and Washington Territories. (34th Cong., 1st sess., H. Ex. Doc. 118.) Washington, D.C., 1856.

Report of the Secretary of War. (34th Cong., 1st sess., H. Ex. Doc. 1, Pt. 2.) Washington, D.C., 1856.

Correspondence Relative to the Indian Disturbances in California. (34th Cong., 2nd sess., S. Ex. Doc. 26.) Washington, D.C., 1856.

Indian Affairs on the Pacific. (34th Cong., 3rd sess., H. Ex. Doc. 76.) Washington, D.C., 1856.

Letters from the Commissioner of Indian Affairs, the Commissioner of the General Land Office, and the Secretary of the Interior, Recommending that the land laws be extended east of the Cascade Mountains, in Oregon and Washington Territories. (34th Cong., 3rd sess., S. Misc. Doc. 28.) Washington, D.C., 1857.

Report of the Secretary of War. (34th Cong., 3rd sess., H. Ex. Doc. 1.) . Washington, D.C., 1856.

Browne, J. Ross. *Indian Reservation Survey in Oregon and Washington Territory.* (35th Cong., 1st sess., H. Ex. Doc. 39.) Washington, D.C., 1858.

————. *Indian War in Oregon and Washington Territories.* (35th Cong., 1st sess., H. Ex. Doc. 38.) Washington, D.C., 1857-58.

Report of the Secretary of War. (35th Cong., 1st sess., H. Ex. Doc. 11.) Washington, D.C., 1857.

————. "Speech of Hon. Isaac I. Stevens, of Washington Territory, in the House of Representatives, May 25, 1858," *Appendix to the Congressional Globe.* (35th Cong., 1st sess., 1858.)

Cram, T. J. *Topographical Memoir of the Department of the Pacific.* (35th Cong., 2nd sess., H. Ex. Doc. 114.) Washington, D.C., 1859.

Mullan, John. *Topographical Memoir and Map of Colonel Wright's Late Campaign Against the Indians in Oregon and Washington Territories.* (35th Cong., 2nd sess., S. Ex. Doc. 32.) Washington, D.C., 1859.

The Dalles-Great Salt Lake Wagon Road. (36th Cong., 1st sess., S. Ex. Doc. 34.) Washington, D.C., 1859-60.

Report of the Secretary of the Interior. (36th Cong., 1st sess., S. Ex. Doc. 1, Vol. I.) Washington, D.C., 1859-60.

Report of the Secretary of War. (36th Cong., 1st sess., S. Ex. Doc. 2.) Washington, D.C., 1859-60.

Stevens, Isaac I. *Narrative and Final Report of Explorations* . . . (Pacific Railroad Surveys Vol. XII) . (36th Cong., 1st sess., S. Ex. Doc. 78.) Washington, D.C., 1860.

————. "Speech in House of Representatives, May 29, 1860." *Congressional Globe.* (36th Cong., 1st sess.)

Mullan, John. *Report of Lieutenant Mullan, in charge of the Construction of the Military Road from Fort Benton to Fort Walla-Walla.* (36th Cong., 2nd sess., H. Ex. Doc. 44.) Washington, D.C., 1860.

Report of the Secretary of the Interior. (36th Cong., 2nd sess., S. Ex. Doc. 1.) Washington, D.C., 1860.

Memorial of the Legislature of the Washington Territory for Aid in Constructing a Railroad from Wallula to Fort Walla-Walla, in that Territory. (38th Cong., 1st sess., H. Misc. Doc. 55.) Washington, D.C., 1864.

Memorial Relating to Washington Territory. (39th Cong., 1st sess., S. Misc. Doc. 83.) Washington, D.C., 1866.

Military Posts. (39th Cong., 2nd sess., H. Ex. Doc. 20.) Washington, D.C., 1867.

Report of the Secretary of War. (40th Cong., 2nd sess., H. Ex. Doc. 1.) Washington, D.C., 1867.

Report of the Secretary of War. (40th Cong., 2nd sess., H. Ex. Doc. 1, Pt. 2.) Washington, D.C., 1867-68.

Eastern Boundary of Oregon. (41st Cong., 3rd sess., H. Misc. Doc. 23.) Washington, D.C., 1870.

Report of the Secretary of War. (41st Cong., 3rd sess., H. Ex. Doc. 1.) Washington, D.C., 1870.

Young, Edward. *Special Report on Immigration.* (42nd Cong., 1st sess., H. Ex. Doc. 1.) Washington, D.C., 1871.

McMicken, W. "Report of the Surveyor-General of Washington Territory." In *Report of the Secretary of the Interior.* (43rd Cong., 1st sess., Ex. Doc. 1, Pt. 5.) Washington, D.C., 1873.

Report of the Select Committee on Transportation—Routes to the Seaboard, April 24, 1874. (43rd Cong., 1st sess., S. Rept. 307, Pt. 1.) Washington, D.C., 1874.

Seattle Walla-Walla Railroad and Transportation Company. (43rd Cong., 1st sess., S. Rept. 420.) Washington, D.C., 1874.

Memorial of the Legislative Assembly of Washington for the Improvement of the Navigation of the Columbia River. (44th Cong., 1st sess., H. Misc. Doc. 17.) Washington, D.C., 1875.

Nimmo, Joseph, Jr. *Report on the Internal Commerce of the United States, December, 1879.* (45th Cong., 3rd sess., Ex. Doc. 32, Pt. 3.) Washington, D.C., 1879.

Report of the Governor of Washington Territory made to the Secretary of the Interior for the Year 1878. (45th Cong., 3rd sess., Ex. Doc. 1.) Washington, D.C., 1878.

McMicken, W. "Report of the Surveyor-General of Washington Territory." In *Report of the Secretary of the Interior.* (46th Cong., 2nd sess., H. Ex. Doc. 1, Pt. 5, pp. 898-907.) Washington, D.C., 1879.

Laws of the United States of a Local or Temporary Character and exhibiting the entire legislation of Congress upon which the Public Land Titles in each State and Territory have depended, December 1, 1880. (46th Cong., 3rd sess., H. Ex. Doc. 47, Pt. 2, 3.) Washington, D.C., Dec. 1, 1880.

McMicken, W. "Report of the Surveyor-General of Washington Territory." In *Report of the Secretary of the Interior.* (47th Cong., 1st sess., H. Ex. Doc. 1, Pt. 5, pp. 915-31.) Washington, D.C., 1881.

Powell, Charles F. *Survey of the Columbia River at the Dalles in Oregon.* (47th Cong., 1st sess., S. Ex. Doc. 184.) Washington, D.C., 1882.

Symons, Thomas W. *The Upper Columbia River and the Great Plain of the Columbia.* (47th Cong., 1st sess., S. Ex. Doc. 186.) Washington, D.C., 1882.

Nimmo, Joseph, Jr. "The Commercial, Industrial and Transportation Interests of the Pacific Slope" and "The Range and Ranch Cattle Business of the United States." Parts 1 and 3 of *Report on the Internal Commerce of the United States, May 6, 1885.* (48th Cong., 2nd sess., H. Ex. Doc. 7, Pt. 1, 3.) Washington, D.C., 1885.

Congressional Record, Feb. 23, 1886. (49th Cong., 1st sess.)

Jones, William A. *Annual Report on River Improvements in Oregon and Washington Territory, for year ended June 30, 1885.* (49th Cong., 1st sess., S. Ex. Doc. 114.) Washington, D.C., 1886.

Greely, A. W. *The Climate of Oregon and Washington Territory.* (50th Cong., 1st sess., S. Ex. Doc. 282.) Washington, D.C., 1888.

———. *Rainfall of the Pacific Slope and the Western States and Territories.* (50th Cong., 1st sess., S. Ex. Doc. 91.) Washington, D.C., 1888.

Greene, Frank. *Report on the Interior Wheat Lands of Oregon and Washington Territory.* (50th Cong., 1st sess., S. Ex. Doc. 229.) Washington, D.C., 1888.

Mitchell, John H. *Report, from the Committee on Transportation Routes to the Seaboard, on the Dalles of the Columbia River.* (50th Cong., 1st sess., S. Rept. 859.) Washington, D.C., 1888.

Mendell, G. H. *Obstructions to Navigation in Columbia River.* (50th Cong., 2nd sess., H. Ex. Doc. 73.) Washington, D.C., 1889.

Memorial of the Legislature of the State of Washington Praying for an Appropriation for Clearing Palouse River. (51st Cong., 1st sess., S. Misc. Doc. 68.) Washington, D.C., 1890.

Moore, Miles C. *Report of the Governor of Washington Territory to the Secretary of the Interior.* Washington, D.C., 1889. Reprinted from *Report of the Secretary of the Interior.* (51st Cong., 1st sess., Ex. Doc. 1, Pt. 5., pp. 503-60.) Washington, D.C., 1889.

Report on the Special Committee on the Irrigation and Reclamation of Arid Land. (51st Cong., 1st sess., S. Rept. 928, Pt. 1.) Washington, D.C., 1889-90.

Barton, Clarence M. "Washington." In S. G. Brock, *Report on the Internal Commerce of the United States for the Year 1890.* (51st Cong., 2nd sess., H. Ex. Doc. 6, Pt. 2, pp. 955-1045.) Washington, D.C., 1891.

Lang, T. S. "Oregon." In S. G. Brock, *Report on the Internal Commerce of the United States for the Year 1890.* (51st Cong., 2nd sess., H. Ex. Doc. 6, Pt. 2, pp. 705-840.) Washington, D.C., 1891.

Smith, Alanson. "Idaho." In S. G. Brock, *Report on the Internal Commerce of the United States for the Year 1890.* (51st Cong., 2nd sess., H. Ex. Doc. 6, pp. 501-81.) Washington, D.C., 1891.

Kappler, D. J. *Indian-Affairs, Laws and Treaties.* (57th Cong., 1st sess., S. Ex. Doc. 452, Vol. II.) Washington, D.C., 1901-2.

III. MISCELLANEOUS OFFICIAL DOCUMENTS

Andrews, Frank. "Freight Costs and Market Values," *Yearbook of the U. S. Dept. of Agriculture.* Washington, D.C., 1906, pp. 371-86.

Brewer, William H. "Report on the Cereal Production of the United States." Special report, *Tenth Census of the United States, 1880.* Vol. III.

Gordon, Clarence. "Report on Cattle, Sheep and Swine." Special report, *Tenth Census of the United States, 1880.* Vol. III.

Census of the United States. Volumes pertaining to Population, Agriculture, and Manufactures, Eighth (1860) through Fourteenth (1920) Censuses.

"Investigations of American Cereals and Their Products." In *Report of the Commissioner of Agriculture for the Year 1884.* Washington, D.C., 1884, pp. 70-122.

Moore, Willis L. *A Report on the Influence of Forests on Climates and Floods.* Committee on Agriculture, House of Representatives. Washington, D.C., 1910.

Newell, F. H. *Report on Agriculture by Irrigation in the Western Part of the United States at the Eleventh Census, 1890.* Washington, D.C., 1894.

Report on Indians Taxed and Indians Not Taxed in the United States at the Eleventh Census, 1890. Washington, D.C., 1894.

Report of the Commissioner of Agriculture. Washington, D.C., various years.

Report of Washington State Grain Inspector. Olympia, Wash., No. 1, 1895-98; No. 5, 1908.

A Review of the Resources and Industries of Washington. Olympia, Wash.: State Bureau of Statistics, Agriculture and Immigration, 1901, 1903, 1905, 1907, 1909.

Squire, Watson C. "Resources and Development of Washington Territory." *Message and Report of the Governor of Washington Territory to the Legislative Assembly, Session 1885-6.* Seattle, Wash., 1886.

State of Idaho. *Fifth Biennial Report, Commissioner of Immigration, Labor and Statistics.* Boise, 1907-8.

———. *Sixth Biennial Report, Commissioner of Immigration, Labor and Statistics.* Boise, 1909-10.

Sullivan, Richard H. "The So-called Change of Climate in the Semiarid West." *Yearbook of the United States Department of Agriculture, 1908.* Washington, D.C., 1909. Pp. 289-300.

U. S. Dept. of Agriculture, Weather Bureau. *Climatic Summary of the United States.* Washington, D.C., 1936.

IV. Maps

Approximate Map of the Nez Perce Reservation in Washington Territory. 1862. Copy in the University of Washington Library, Seattle.

Land Sales, 1870, 1887, 1910. Maps for various areas compiled by the author from Federal Land Office records, Bureau of Land Management, Spokane (for eastern Washington) and Portland (for Oregon).

Land Sales to Pioneers. Maps for Whitman and Latah counties compiled by the author from plat books of the Whitman Title Company, Colfax, and the Latah Title Company, Moscow.

Map of Lewis and Clark's Track Across the Western Portion of North America from the Mississippi to the Pacific Ocean. Prepared by order of the Executive of the U. S. in 1804, 1805, and 1806. London: Longman, Hurst, Rees, Orme, and Brown, 1814.

Map of Military Reconnaissance from Fort Dalles, Oregon via Fort Wallah-Wallah, to Fort Taylor, W. T. Compiled by John Mullan, 1858. Scale: 1:300,000. Copy in the University of Washington Library, Seattle.

Map of the North West Territory of the Province of Canada from actual survey during the years 1792 to 1814 ... by David Thompson, Astronomer and Surveyor.

Map of Parts of Oregon, Washington & Idaho showing the various operated and projected lines of the Oregon Railway & Navigation Co., also the Oregon Improvement Co.'s Property.... Compiled by John R. Hanson. Portland, Ore. May, 1881. Scale: 8 miles to 1 inch.

Map of the Oregon Territory. Prepared by the U.S. Exploring Expedition, Charles Wilkes, Commander. 1841. Copy in the University of Washington Library, Seattle.

Map Showing Land Grant of the Northern Pacific Railroad Co. in Eastern Washington and Northern Idaho. Corrected to Aug. 1, 1884. Scale: 6 miles to 1 inch. Copy in the Bancroft Library, Berkeley, Calif.

————. Corrected to April 1, 1887. Copy in the Bancroft Library, Berkeley, Calif.

————. Corrected to July 1, 1891. Copy in the Department of Agricultural Development, Northern Pacific Railway, St. Paul, Minn.

Metsker County Maps. Compiled by Charles F. Metsker. Tacoma, Seattle, and Portland. Twenty-six counties; various scales. Undated.

Oregon and Upper California. S. Augustus Mitchell, Philadelphia. 1846. Copy in the University of Idaho Library, Moscow.

Raisz, Erwin. *Landforms of the Northwestern States.* 1941. Scale: 20 miles to 1 inch. Included in back pocket of Freeman and Martin (ed.), *The Pacific Northwest*; also available separately.

U. S. Army, Corps of Engineers. *Map of the Department of the Columbia....* Compiled by Thomas W. Symons. Jan. 1, 1881. Scale: 16 miles to 1 inch.

U. S. Coast and Geodetic Survey. *World Aeronautical Chart.* 2 sheets: Bitterroot Range (268), Columbia River (269). June, 1946. Scale: 1:1,000,000.

U. S. Dept. of Agriculture, Bureau of Soils. *Soil Map, Idaho. Nez Perce and Lewis Counties Sheet.* In J. H. Agee and P. P. Peterson, *Soil Surveys of Nez Perce and Lewis Counties, Idaho.* 1917. Scale: 1 mile to 1 inch.

U. S. Dept. of Agriculture, Bureau of Soils. *Soil Map, State of Idaho. Latah County Sheet.* In J. H. Agee *et al., Soil Survey of Latah County, Idaho.* 1915. Scale: 1 mile to 1 inch.

U. S. Dept. of Agriculture, Forest Service. *Forest Type Map, State of Washington.* 1936. Scale: 4 miles to 1 inch.

U. S. Dept. of the Interior, General Land Office. *State of Oregon.* 1884. Scale: 15 miles to 1 inch.

———. 1889. Scale: 12 miles to 1 inch.

U. S. Dept. of the Interior, General Land Office. *Washington Territory.* 1883. Scale: 15 miles to 1 inch.

———. 1887.

U. S. Dept. of the Interior, Office of Indian Affairs. *Map of Former Nez Perce Indian Reservation, Idaho.* 1911. Scale: 2½ miles to 1 inch.

U. S. Dept. of War. *Map No. 3. Rocky Mountains to Puget Sound.* Prepared by Isaac I. Stevens. 1853-54. Scale: 1:1,200,000.

U. S. Dept. of War, Bureau of Topographical Engineers. *Map of the State of Oregon and Washington Territory.* Compiled by order of John B. Floyd. 1859. Scale: 1:1,500,000.

U. S. Dept. of War, Bureau of Topographical Engineers. *Map of the United States Territory of Oregon West of the Rocky Mountains.* (Exhibiting trading depots and forts of the Hudson's Bay Company.) Compiled under the direction of J. J. Abert, 1838.

U. S. Geological Survey, *Professional Paper No. 4,* Plate I. *Map of the State of Oregon Showing the Classification of Lands and Forests.* Drawn by Gilbert Thompson from information supplied by A. J. Johnson. 1900. Scale: 12 miles to 1 inch.

U. S. Geological Survey, *Professional Paper No. 5,* Plate 1. *Map of Washington Showing Classification of Lands.* Prepared by George H. Plummer, F. G. Plummer, and J. H. Rankine. 1902. Scale: 6 miles to 1 inch.

U. S. Geological Survey. *State of Oregon.* 1914; revised, 1923. Scale: 1:500,000.

U. S. Geological Survey. *State of Washington.* 1914. Scale: 1:500,000.

U. S. Geological Survey. *Topographical Quadrangles.* 61 sheets covering in total the area of the Great Columbia Plain. Scales: 1:24,000; 1:62,500; 1:125,000. Various dates.

U. S. Geological Survey. *Topographical Quadrangles.* Sheets depicting status of settlement *ca.* 1910: Beverly, 1912; Blalock, 1908; Moses Lake, 1912; Oakesdale, 1905; Pullman, 1910; Umatilla, 1908; Winchester, 1910; Zillah, 1910.

U. S. Geological Survey. *Western United States.* 10 sheets. Scale: 1:250,000. Various dates.

Washington State Highway Commission. *Road Map of Washington, 1912, Showing Main Travelled Roads.* Compiled by William J. Roberts. (Showing "Roads open to Automobile Travel.")

V. NEWSPAPERS AND NEWS MAGAZINES

Arlington, *Arlington Record*

Asotin, *The Sentinel*

Cheney, *North-West Tribune*

Colfax, *North-West Tribune*
      Palouse Gazette
      Weekly Commoner

Condon, *Condon Globe*

Davenport, *Davenport Tribune*

Goldendale, *Klickitat County Agriculturist*

Grass Valley, *Grass Valley Journal*

Heppner, *Heppner Gazette*

Lewiston, *Lewiston Morning Tribune,* "Lewiston Centennial Edition,"
        July 16, 1961
      Lewiston Teller

Moro, *Moro Bulletin*

Moscow, *Daily Idahonian,* "50th Anniversary Historical Edition," September 29, 1961

New Tacoma, *North Pacific Coast* (semimonthly)

North Yakima, *Yakima Herald*

Palouse City, *Palouse Republican*

Pasco, *Columbia Journal of Commerce* (monthly)
      Pasco Express
      The Pasconian (monthly)
      Tri-City Herald, Special historical edition, December 12, 1958

Pendleton, *Pendleton Tribune*
      East Oregonian

Pomeroy, *East Washingtonian,* "First Garfield County Pioneer Edition," June 6, 1914

Portland, *Commercial Review*
    The West Shore (monthly)
Pullman, *Pacific Farmers Union*
    Washington Agriculturist (monthly)
Ritzville, *Ritzville Journal-Times,* "Adams County Pioneer Edition,"
    September 15, 1949
    Ritzville Times
St. Paul, *The Northwest* (monthly)
Spokane Falls or Spokane, *Inland Herald*
    Morning Review
    Spokan Times
    Spokane Falls Review
    Spokane Review
    The Spokesman
    Spokesman-Review
Sprague, *Weekly Advertiser*
The Dalles, *Weekly Mountaineer*
Umatilla, *Columbia Press*
Walla Walla, *Spirit of the West*
    Daily Statesman
    Inland Empire (monthly)
    Walla Walla Statesman
    Washington Statesman
    Up-to-the-Times Magazine
Waterville, *Big Bend Empire*
Wenatchee, *Wenatchee Daily World*
Wilson Creek, *Big Bend Chief*

Index